Environmental Economics and Policy

SIXTH EDITION

THE ADDISON-WESLEY SERIES IN ECONOMICS

Abel/Bernanke/Croushore
*Macroeconomics**

Bade/Parkin
*Foundations of Economics**

Bierman/Fernandez
*Game Theory with Economic
Applications*

Binger/Hoffman
Microeconomics with Calculus

Boyer
*Principles of Transportation
Economics*

Branson
Macroeconomic Theory and Policy

Bruce
*Public Finance and the American
Economy*

Byrns/Stone
Economics

Carlton/Perloff
Modern Industrial Organization

Caves/Frankel/Jones
*World Trade and Payments:
An Introduction*

Chapman
*Environmental Economics:
Theory, Application, and Policy*

Cooter/Ulen
Law and Economics

Downs
An Economic Theory of Democracy

Ehrenberg/Smith
Modern Labor Economics

Ekelund/Ressler/Tollison
*Economics**

Fusfeld
The Age of the Economist

Gerber
International Economics

Ghiara
Learning Economics

Gordon
Macroeconomics

Gregory
Essentials of Economics

Gregory/Stuart
*Russian and Soviet Economic
Performance and Structure*

Hartwick/Olewiler
*The Economics of Natural
Resource Use*

Hoffman/Averett
*Women and the Economy:
Family, Work, and Pay*

Holt
*Markets, Games and Strategic
Behavior*

Hubbard
*Money, the Financial System,
and the Economy*

Hughes/Cain
American Economic History

Husted/Melvin
International Economics

Jehle/Reny
Advanced Microeconomic Theory

Johnson-Lans
A Health Economics Primer

Klein
Mathematical Methods for Economics

Krugman/Obstfeld
*International Economics:
Theory & Policy**

Laidler
The Demand for Money

Leeds/von Allmen
The Economics of Sports

Leeds/von Allmen/Schiming
*Economics**

Lipsey/Ragan/Storer
*Economics**

Melvin
International Money and Finance

Miller
*Economics Today**

Miller
*Understanding Modern
Economics*

Miller/Benjamin
The Economics of Macro Issues

Miller/Benjamin/North
The Economics of Public Issues

Mills/Hamilton
Urban Economics

Mishkin
*The Economics of Money,
Banking, and Financial Markets**

Mishkin
*The Economics of Money, Banking,
and Financial Markets, Business
School Edition**

Murray
*Econometrics:
A Modern Introduction*

Parkin
*Economics**

Perloff
*Microeconomics**

Perloff
*Microeconomics: Theory and
Applications with Calculus*

Perman/Common/McGilvray/Ma
*Natural Resources and
Environmental Economics*

Phelps
Health Economics

**Riddell/Shackelford/Stamos/
Schneider**
*Economics: A Tool for Critically
Understanding Society*

Ritter/Silber/Udell
*Principles of Money, Banking,
and Financial Markets**

Rohlf
Introduction to Economic Reasoning

Ruffin/Gregory
Principles of Economics

Sargent
Rational Expectations and Inflation

Scherer
*Industry Structure, Strategy,
and Public Policy*

Sherman
Market Regulation

Stock/Watson
Introduction to Econometrics

Stock/Watson
*Introduction to Econometrics,
Brief Edition*

Studenmund
*Using Econometrics:
A Practical Guide*

Tietenberg/Lewis
*Environmental Economics
and Policy*

Tietenberg/Lewis
*Environmental and Natural
Resource Economics*

Todaro/Smith
Economic Development

Waldman
Microeconomics

Waldman/Jensen
*Industrial Organization:
Theory and Practice*

Weil
Economic Growth

Williamson
Macroeconomics

*denotes (X) myeconlab titles   Log onto www.myeconlab.com to learn more.

Environmental Economics and Policy

SIXTH EDITION

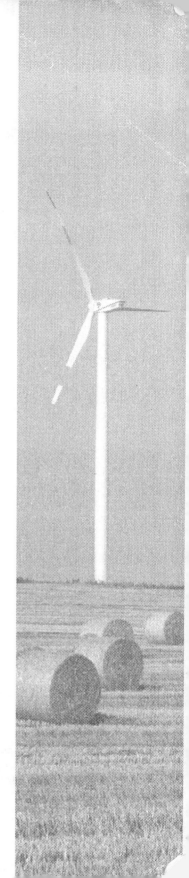

Tom Tietenberg
Colby College, Emeritus

Lynne Lewis
Bates College

Addison-Wesley

Boston Columbus Indianapolis New York San Francisco Upper Saddle River
Amsterdam Cape Town Dubai London Madrid Milan Munich Paris Montreal Toronto
Delhi Mexico City Sao Paulo Sydney Hong Kong Seoul Singapore Taipei Tokyo

Publisher: Denise Clinton
Editor in Chief: Donna Battista
Acquisitions Editor: Noel Kamm Seibert
Project Manager: Gavin Broady
Managing Editor: Nancy Fenton
Senior Design Supervisor/Cover Designer: Andrea Nix
Design Coordinator: Christina Gleason
Supplements Editor: Alison Eusden
Marketing Manager: Elizabeth Averbeck
Permissions Project Manager: Shannon Barbe
Senior Manufacturing Buyer: Carol Melville
Production Coordination, Composition,
    Text Design, and Illustrations: Gillian Hall, The Aardvark Group
Copy Editor: Kathleen Cantwell, C4 Technologies
Proofreader: Holly McLean-Aldis
Indexer: Jack Lewis
Cover photo: Art Clausen/Shutterstock

Library of Congress Cataloging-in-Publication Data

Tietenberg, Thomas H.
  Environmental economics and policy / Tom Tietenberg, Lynne Lewis. -- 6th ed.
    p. cm.
  Includes bibliographical references and index.
  ISBN-13: 978-0-321-59949-0 (alk. paper)
  ISBN-10: 0-321-59949-7 (alk. paper)
  1. Environmental economics. I. Lewis, Lynne. II. Title.
  HD75.6.T54 2009
  333.7--dc22   2009024118

Addison-Wesley
is an imprint of

ISBN-10: 0-321-59949-7
ISBN-13: 978-0-321-59949-0

www.pearsonhighered.com

Brief Contents

Detailed Contents

3 Valuing the Environment: Methods   34

4 Property Rights, Externalities, and Environmental Problems   64

8 Energy   140

13 Common-Pool Resources: Fisheries and Other Commercially Valuable Species   273

14 Environmental Economics: An Overview   301

15 Stationary-Source Local and Regional Air Pollution   326

16 Climate Change   350

17 Transportation   366

18 Water Pollution   393

19 Managing Waste   424

Preface to the Sixth Edition

About two decades ago, while on a plane heading for a conference, Tom struck up a conversation with the passenger next to him. During the course of that conversation, the passenger asked Tom what he did for a living. After mulling over Tom's response that he was an environmental economist, the passenger asked, "Isn't that a contradiction in terms?" Much more recently, Lynne had a very similar conversation, with the response, "Environmental economist?! Isn't that an oxymoron?"

They both had a point. The economy has been a major source of environmental degradation. Developers pave over wetlands. Timber companies denude forests. Fishermen deplete oceans. Industries pollute waters. And on and on.

Recently, however, those same powerful forces that have historically been associated with environmental degradation have been enlisted in the struggle to protect the environment. Buying and selling quotas have helped restore New Zealand fisheries. Pharmaceutical companies are investing in biodiversity preservation. Peak-load and congestion pricing have encouraged the better use of existing power plants and roads rather than the building of new ones. By-the-bag charging for solid waste has stimulated recycling and reduced the volume of waste. "Green fees" are raising revenues for environmental improvement while discouraging environmentally destructive behavior. Cap-and-trade policies are being used to control climate change. The list goes on.

The success of these approaches in providing a politically feasible and effective means of changing environmentally destructive behavior has attracted much wider interest in the field of environmental economics. Environmental groups, states, local governments, national governments, and even international organizations are beginning to incorporate the principles and techniques of environmental economics in their efforts to preserve and protect the environment. With its strong emphasis on public policy, this book shows how economics can be used to understand the behavioral sources of environmental problems and to provide the foundation for innovative solutions.

New to This Edition

* Completely new chapter (10) on land use that includes coverage of: community land trusts, conservation easements, conservation land trusts, development impact fees, eco-tourism, eminent domain, GIS systems and land use control, grazing rights, leapfrogging, the public infrastructure problem, regulatory takings, safe harbor agreements, sprawl, transferable development rights, wetland and conservation banking.
* Climate change now has its own chapter (16) with expanded and updated coverage.
* GIS analysis is now treated throughout the text, in such areas as environmental valuation, water management, water pollution control, and land use.

⁂ New Example Boxes cover such topics as experimental economics, passive use and contingent valuation, the strategic petroleum reserve, the impacts of growing corn for ethanol instead of food, the use of conservation banking to save wildlife and conservation land trusts to save farmland, tax strategies to reduce inefficient land conversion, Debt-for-Nature swaps, controlling water pollution in Colombia, Maine's Energy and Carbon Savings Trust, and trading water for bees in Bolivia.

⁂ New Debate Boxes cover such topics as the difference between willingness to pay and willingness to accept estimates, whether landowners should be compensated for regulatory takings, controversies concerning the legal definition of "public purpose," linkages between ecotourism and sustainability, the merits of industrial-scale organic farming, the role of aquaculture, and the economic efficiency of bottle bills.

The *Environmental Economics and Policy* Approach

Environmental economics is not a naturally hospitable field. Most of the economic principles that underlie these approaches flow from some intimidating mathematical models, making them inaccessible to all but those who are willing to invest the time and effort to learn the underlying mathematics. This lack of accessible textbooks has created a void. *Environmental Economics and Policy* is designed specifically to fill that void. It was written to communicate the powerful insights of the field to those taking economics courses designed for nonmajors or, more generally, to an audience with little or no training in economics.

Chapters 1 through 5 describe the basic economic approach to the environment, laying out the underlying values, as well as the procedures used to translate those values into policy-relevant principles. Chapters 6 through 19 deal with natural resource economics (analyzing the flow of materials and energy from the environment into the economy) and environmental economics (analyzing the flow of waste products into the environment). Chapters 20 through 22 focus on sustainable development, reflecting the demonstrated, current global interest in finding new, environmentally compatible means of lifting the world's poor out of poverty. Throughout, the manner in which the principles can be applied is illustrated by a host of specific international examples. Considerable attention has been paid to environmental problems and policies in Eastern and Western Europe, Japan, China and the developing nations, as well as in the United States.

This Sixth Edition of *Environmental Economics and Policy* is an economics book, but it transcends economics. Insights from the natural and physical sciences, literature, and political science, as well as other disciplines, are scattered liberally throughout the text. In some cases, these references raise unresolved issues that economic analysis can help resolve, whereas in others they affect the structure of the economic analysis or provide a contrasting point of view.

Additional Resources

Students looking for additional sources of information on this subject don't have to look very far. A number of journals are now devoted either exclusively or mostly to the topics covered in this book. One, *Ecological Economics*, is dedicated to bringing economists and ecologists closer together in a common search for appropriate solutions for environmental challenges. The *Review of Environmental Economics and Policy* provides state of the art essays that are designed to be accessible to a broad audience. Interested readers can also find advanced work in the field in *Land Economics, Journal of Environmental Economics and Management, Environmental and Resource Economics, Resource and Energy Economics*, and *Natural Resources Journal*, among others.

New resources for student research projects have been made available in response to the growing popularity of the field. Original research on topics related to international environmental and natural resource issues was formerly very difficult for students to conduct because of the paucity of data. A number of good sources now exist; among these are Earth Trends, published by the World Resources institute in Washington DC, *World Development Indicators*, published by the World Bank, and *OECD Environmental Data* (Paris: Organization for Economic Co-operation and Development, published periodically).

Further sources on the field and the profession of environmental economics can be found on the book's Companion Website, www.aw-bc.com/tietenberg, which features "Web Sites of Interest" and new chapter-specific quizzes complementing the text material. An updated *Instructor's Manual*, reflective of changes to the Sixth Edition, is available online for instructors' reference. This edition retains a strong policy orientation. Though a great deal of theory and empirical evidence is discussed, their inclusion is motivated by the desire to increase understanding of intriguing policy problems, and these aspects are discussed in the context of those problems.

This explicit integration of research and policy within each chapter avoids the problem frequently encountered in applied economics textbooks—that is, in such texts the theory developed in earlier chapters is often only loosely connected to the rest of the book. The many insights gleaned from other disciplines have an important role to play in overcoming the typical textbook's tendency to accept the material uncritically at a superficial level; instead, this text highlights those characteristics that make the economics approach unique.

Acknowledgments

Perhaps the most rewarding part of writing this book is that it has put us in touch with many thoughtful people we had not previously met. We very much appreciate the faculty and students who pointed out areas of particular strength or areas where coverage could be expanded in this edition. The support this book has received from faculty and students has been gratifying and energizing. One can begin to understand the magnitude of our debt to our colleagues by glancing at the several hundred names in the lists of references that appear at the end of each chapter. Because their research contributions make this an exciting field, full of insights worthy of being shared, our task was easier and a lot more fun than it might otherwise have been.

We would like to acknowledge the valuable assistance we received during various stages of the writing of this text from the following individuals:

John Adrian · *Auburn University*

Dan S. Alexio · *U.S. Military Academy at West Point*

Gregory S. Amacher · *Virginia Polytechnic Institute and State University*

Michael Balch · *University of Iowa*

Maurice Ballabon · *Baruch College*

Edward Barbier · *University of Wyoming*

A. Paul Baroutsis · *Slippery Rock University of Pennsylvania*

Kathleen P. Bell · *University of Maine*

Fikret Berkes · *Brock University*

Trond Björndahl · *Norwegian School of Economics and Business Administration*

Sidney M. Blumner · *California State Polytechnic University—Pomona*

Vic Brajer · *California State University—Fullerton*

Stacy Brook · *University of Sioux Falls*

Richard Bryant · *University of Missouri—Rolla*

David Burgess · *University of Western Ontario*

Mary A. Burke · *Florida State University*

Richard V. Butler · *Trinity University*

Trudy Ann Cameron · *UCLA*

Gary Campbell · *Michigan Technological University*

Duane Chapman · *Cornell University*

Charles J. Chicchetti · *University of Wisconsin—Madison*

Gregory B. Christiansen · *California State University—Hayward*

Hal Cochrane · *Colorado State University*

Maria Concetta Chiuri · *Università di Bari*

Jon Conrad · *Cornell University*

William Corcoran · *University of Nebraska at Omaha*

Maureen L. Cropper · *University of Maryland*

John H. Cumberland · *University of Maryland*

Alessio D'Amato · *University of Rome "Tor Vergata"*

Herman E. Daly · *University of Maryland*

Patrick Dolenc · *Keene State College*

Diane P. Dupont · *University of Guelph*

Randall K. Filer · *Hunter College*

Ann Fisher · *Pennsylvania State University*

Anthony C. Fisher · *University of California—Berkeley*

Marvin Frankel · *University of Illinois—Urbana-Champaign*

A. Myrick Freeman III · *Bowdoin College*

James Gale · *Michigan Technological University*

David E. Gallo · *California State University—Chico*

Haynes Goddard · *University of Cincinnati*

Nicholas Gotsch · *Institute of Agricultural Economics (Zurich)*

Doug Greer · *San Jose State University*

Ronald Griffin · *Texas A&M University*

W. Eric Gustafson · *University of California—Davis*

A. R. Gutowsky · *California State University—Sacramento*

Jon D. Harford · *Cleveland State University*

Gloria E. Helfand · *University of Michigan*

Ann Helwege · *Tufts University*

Joseph A. Herriges · *Iowa State University*

John J. Hovis · *University of Maryland*

Paul Huszar · *Colorado State University*

Craig Infanger · *University of Kentucky*

Allan Jenkins · *University of Nebraska at Kearney*

Donn Johnson · *Quinnipiac College*

James R. Kahn · *Washington and Lee University*

Chris Kavalec · *Sacramento State*

Derek Kellenberg · *University of Colorado—Boulder*

John O. S. Kennedy · *LaTrobe University*

Thomas Kinnaman · *Bucknell University*

Andrew Kliet · *Louisiana State University*

Richard F. Kosobud · *University of Illinois at Chicago*

Douglas M. Larson · *University of California—Davis*

Dwight Lee · *University of Georgia*

Joseph N. Lekakis · *University of Crete*

Ingemar Leksell · *University of Goteberg*

Randolph M. Lyon · *Executive Office of the President (U.S.)*

Richard S. Main · *Butler University*

Giadomenico Majone · *Harvard University*

David Martin · *Davidson College*

Charles Mason · *University of Wyoming*

Ross McKitrick · *University of Guelph*

Frederic C. Menz · *Clarkson University*

Nicholas Mercuro · *University of New Orleans*

David E. Merrifield · *Western Washington University*

Michael J. Mueller · *Clarkson University*

Kankana Mukherjee · *Clarkson University*

Noelwah Netusil · *Reed College*

Thomas C. Noser · *University of Alabama*

Lloyd Orr · *Indiana University*

Peter J. Parks · *Rutgers University*

Alexander Pfaff · *Columbia University*

Raymond Prince · *University of Colorado—Boulder*

H. David Robison · *La Salle University*

Duane Rosa · *West Texas A&M University*

J. Barkley Rosser, Jr. · *James Madison University*

Jonathan Rubin · *University of Tennessee—Knoxville*

Milton Russell · *University of Tennessee*

Frederick O. Sargent · *University of Vermont*

Salah El Serafy · *World Bank*

Aharon Shapiro · *St. John's University*

W. Douglas Shaw · *University of Nevada—Reno*

James S. Shortle · *Pennsylvania State University*

Leah J. Smith · *Swarthmore College*
V. Kerry Smith · *Duke University*
Rob Stavins · *Harvard University*
Joe B. Stevens · *Oregon State University*
Gert Svendsen · *The Aarhus School of Business*
Kenneth N. Townsend · *Hampden-Sydney College*
Robert W. Turner · *Colgate University*
Wallace E. Tyner · *Purdue University*

Nora Underwood · *University of California––Davis*
Myles Wallace · *Clemson University*
Frank Ward · *New Mexico State University*
Patrick Welle · *Bemidji State University*
John Whitehead · *Appalachian State University*
Richard T. Woodward · *Texas A&M University*
Anthony Yezer · *George Washington University*

In preparing this edition, we are especially indebted to Okmyung Bin (East Carolina University), Jacqueline Geoghegan (Clark University), Katherine Kiel (College of the Holy Cross), Stephan Kroll (Colorado State University), Sharon Levick (L.A. Pierce College), Jennie Popp (University of Arkansas), and Aaron Swoboda (Carleton College) for detailed, helpful suggestions. Lynne would like to thank Zach Ross and Jessie Govindasamy for valuable assistance during the editing process.

Finally, Tom would like to express publicly his deep appreciation to his wife Gretchen, his daughter Heidi, and his son Eric for their love and support. Lynne would like to express her gratitude to John for unwavering support, patience and generosity. Thank you.

Tom Tietenberg
Sand Cove
Prospect Harbor, Maine

Lynne Lewis
Portland, Maine

Visions of
the Future

From the arch of the bridge to which his guide has carried him, Dante now sees the Diviners ... coming slowly along the bottom of the fourth Chasm. By help of their incantations and evil agents, they had endeavored to pry into the future which belongs to the almighty alone, and now their faces are painfully twisted the contrary way; and being unable to look before them, they are forced to walk backwards.

—DANTE ALIGHIERI, *Divine Comedy: The Inferno,*
translated by Carlyle (1867)

Introduction

The Self-Extinction Premise

About the time the American colonies became independent, Edward Gibbon completed his monumental work, *The History of the Decline and Fall of the Roman Empire.* In a particularly poignant passage that opens the last chapter of his opus, he re-creates a scene in which the learned Poggius, a friend, and two servants ascend the Capitoline Hill after the fall of Rome. They are awed by the contrast between what Rome once was and what Rome had become:

> In the time of the poet it was crowned with the golden roofs of a temple; the temple is overthrown, the gold has been pillaged, the wheel of fortune has accomplished her revolution, and the sacred ground is again disfigured with thorns and brambles. ... The forum of the Roman people, where they assembled to enact their laws and elect their magistrates is now enclosed for the cultivation of potherbs, or thrown open for the reception of swine and buffaloes. The public and private edifices, that were founded for eternity lie prostrate, naked, and broken, like the limbs of a mighty giant; and the ruin is the more visible, from the stupendous relics that have survived the injuries of time and fortune. [Vol. 6, pp. 650–651]

What could cause the demise of such a grand and powerful society? Gibbon weaves a complex thesis to answer this question, ultimately suggesting that the seeds for Rome's destruction were sown by the empire itself. Although Rome finally succumbed to such external forces as fires and invasions, its vulnerability was based upon internal weakness.

1

The premise that societies can germinate the seeds of their own destruction has long fascinated scholars. In 1798 Thomas Malthus published his classic "An Essay on the Principle of Population" in which he foresaw a time when the urge to reproduce would cause population growth to exceed the land's potential to supply sufficient food, resulting in starvation and death. In his view, the adjustment mechanism would involve rising death rates caused by environmental constraints, rather than a recognition of impending scarcity followed either by innovation or self-restraint.

Actual historical examples suggest that Malthus's vision may have merit. Example 1.1 examines two specific cases: the Mayan civilization and Easter Island.

● Future Environmental Challenges

Future societies, like those just discussed, will be confronted by both resource scarcity and accumulating pollutants. Many specific examples of these broad categories of problems are discussed in detail in the following chapters. This section provides a flavor of what is to come by illustrating the challenges posed by one pollution problem (climate change) and one resource scarcity problem (water accessibility).

Climate Change

Energy from the sun drives the earth's weather and climate. Incoming rays heat the earth's surface, radiating energy back into space. Atmospheric "greenhouse" gases (water vapor, carbon dioxide, and other gases) trap some of the outgoing energy.

Without this natural *greenhouse effect*, temperatures on Earth would be much lower than they are now, and life as we know it today would not be possible. It is possible, however, to have too much of a good thing. Problems arise when the concentration of greenhouse gases increases beyond normal levels, retaining excessive heat, somewhat like a car with its windows closed in the summer.

Since the industrial revolution, greenhouse gas emissions have increased considerably. These increases have enhanced the heat-trapping capability of the earth's atmosphere. According to the Intergovernmental Panel on Climate Change (2007), "Warming of the climate system is unequivocal ...". That study concludes that most of the warming over the last 50 years is attributable to human activities.

As the earth warms, extreme heat conditions are expected to affect both humans and ecosystems. Some damage to humans is caused directly by the more extreme heat, as illustrated by the heat waves that caused thousands of deaths in Europe in the summer of 2003. Human health can also be affected by pollutants such as smog, which are exacerbated by warmer temperatures. Rising sea levels (as warmer water expands and glaciers melt), coupled with an increase in storm intensity, are expected to flood coastal communities. Ecosystems will be subjected to unaccustomed temperatures; some will adapt by migrating to new areas, but others may not be able to adapt in time.

Climate change also has an important moral dimension. Many developing countries, which have contributed relatively small amounts of greenhouse gases, are expected to be the hardest hit as the climate changes, due to their more limited adaptation capabilities.

EXAMPLE

1.1

Historical Examples of Self-Extinction

The Mayan civilization, a vibrant and highly cultured society that occupied parts of Central America, did not survive. One of the major settlements, Copán, has been studied in sufficient detail to learn reasons for its collapse (Webster et al., 2000).

The Webster et al. study reports that after A.D. 400 the population growth began to bump into environmental constraints, specifically the agricultural carrying capacity of the land. The growing population depended heavily on a single, locally grown crop (maize) for food. By early in the sixth century however, the carrying capacity of the most productive local lands was exceeded, and farmers began to depend upon more fragile parts of the ecosystem. The economic result was diminishing returns to agricultural labor and the production of food failed to keep pace with the increasing population.

By the mid-eighth century, when the population was reaching its historic apex, widespread deforestation and erosion had set in, thereby intensifying the declining productivity problems associated with moving onto marginal lands. By the eighth and ninth centuries, the evidence reveals not only high levels of infant and adolescent mortality, but also widespread malnutrition. The royal dynasty, an important source of leadership in this society, collapsed rather abruptly sometime about A.D. 820–822.

The second case study, Easter Island, shares some remarkable similarities with the Mayan case and the Malthusian vision. Easter Island lies some 2,000 miles off the coast of Chile. Current visitors note that it is distinguished by two features: (1) its enormous statues carved from volcanic rock and (2) a surprisingly sparse vegetation, given the island's favorable climate and conditions, which typically support fertile soil. Both the existence of the imposing statues and the fact that they were erected at a considerable distance from the quarry suggests the presence of an advanced civilization, but to current observers it is nowhere in evidence. What happened to that society?

The short answer is that a rising population, coupled with a heavy reliance on wood for housing, canoe building, and statue transportation, decimated the forest (Brander and Taylor, 1998). The loss of the forest contributed to soil erosion, declining soil productivity, and ultimately, diminished food production. How did the community react to the impending scarcity? Apparently the social response was war, and ultimately, cannibalism.

We would like to believe not only that in the face of impending scarcity societies would react by changing behavior to adapt to the diminishing resource supplies, but also that this benign response would follow automatically from a recognition of the problem. We even have a cliché to capture this sentiment: "necessity is the mother of invention." While these stories do *not* imply that the cliché is always wrong (it isn't), they do point out that nothing is automatic about a problem-solving response. Sometimes societal reactions not only fail to solve the problem, but also they actually make it worse.

Source: Webster, David, Anncorinne Freter, and Nancy Golin. *Copán: The Rise and Fall of an Ancient Maya Kingdom.* (Fort Worth: Harcourt Brace Publishers, 2000); Brander, J. A. and M. S. Taylor (1998). "The Simple Economics of Easter Island: A Ricardo-Malthus Model of Renewable Resource Use," *The American Economic Review* 88(1): 119–138.

Dealing with climate change will require a coordinated international response. That is a significant challenge to a world system where the nation state reigns supreme and international organizations are relatively weak.

Water Accessibility

Another class of threats is posed by the interaction of a rising demand for resources in the face of a finite supply. Water provides a particularly interesting example because it is fundamental to life.

According to the United Nations—about 40 percent of the world's population lives in areas with moderate-to-high water stress. (Moderate stress is defined in the UN Assessment of Freshwater Resources as "human consumption of more than 20 percent of all accessible renewable freshwater resources, whereas severe stress denotes consumption greater than 40 percent.") By 2025 it is estimated that about two-thirds of the world's population—about 5.5 billion people—will live in areas facing either moderate or severe water stress.

This stress is not uniformly distributed around the globe. In areas such as the United States, China, and India, groundwater is being consumed faster than it is being replenished, resulting in steadily falling water levels. Some rivers, such as the Colorado in the United States and the Yellow in China, often run dry before they reach the sea.

According to United Nations data, Africa and Asia suffer the most from the lack of water supply and sanitation in urban areas. Up to 50 percent of Africa's urban residents and some 75 percent of Asians lack adequate access to a water supply.

The availability of potable water is being further limited by human activities that contaminate the finite supplies. According to the UN, 90 percent of sewage and 70 percent of industrial waste in developing countries are discharged without treatment.

Some arid areas have responded to their lack of water by transporting it via aqueducts from more richly endowed regions. In addition to promoting political conflict (regions from which the water is obtained may resist the transfer), the aqueducts may be vulnerable. In California, for example, many of the aqueducts cross or lie on known earthquake-prone fault lines (Reisner, 2003).

Meeting the Challenges

Had we known long ago that human activities could seriously impact environmental life support systems and could deny future generations the quality of life to which our generation has become accustomed, we might have chosen a different, more sustainable path for improving human welfare. The fact that we did not have that knowledge and therefore could not make that choice years ago means that current generations are faced with making more difficult choices with fewer options. These choices will test the creativity of our solutions and the resilience of our social institutions.

As the scale of economic activity has proceeded steadily upward, the scope of environmental problems triggered by that activity has transcended both geographic and generational boundaries. The nation state used to be a sufficient form of political organization for resolving environmental problems, but that may no longer be the case. Whereas each generation used to have the luxury of being able to satisfy its own needs without worrying about the needs of gener come, that no longer is the case either. Solving problems such as poverty, climate change depletion, and the loss of biodiversity requires international cooperation. Because future tions cannot speak for themselves, current generations must speak for them. Current p must incorporate our obligation to future generations, however difficult or imperfect that poration might prove to be.

International cooperation is by no means a foregone conclusion. Global environmental problems can trigger very different effects on the countries that will sit around the negotiating table. While low-lying countries could be completely submerged by the sea level rise predicted by some climate change models or arid nations could see their marginal agricultural lands succumb to desertification, other nations may see agricultural productivity rise as warmer climates support longer growing seasons in traditionally intemperate climates.

Countries that unilaterally set out to improve the global environmental situation run the risk of making their businesses vulnerable to competition from less conscientious nations. Industrialized countries that undertake stringent environmental policies may not suffer greatly at the national level (due to offsetting employment and income increases in the industries producing renewable, cleaner energy and pollution control equipment), but some individual industries facing stringent regulations will face higher costs than their competitors, and can be expected to suffer accordingly. Declining market share and employment in industries confronted by especially stringent regulations are powerful political weapons that can be used to derail efforts to implement an aggressive environmental policy. The search for solutions must accommodate these concerns.

Currently, many individuals and institutions have a large stake in maintaining the status quo, even when it involves environmental destruction. Fishermen harvesting their catch from an overexploited fishery are loathe to undertake any reduction in harvests, even if the reduction is necessary to conserve the stock and to return the population to a healthy level. Farmers who have come to depend on fertilizer and pesticide subsidies will be reluctant to give them up. The principle of inertia applies to politics as fully as it does to physical bodies; a body at rest will tend to stay at rest unless a significant outside force is introduced.

How Will Societies Respond?

The fundamental question is how societies will respond to these challenges. One way to think systematically about this question involves feedback loops.

Positive feedback loops are those in which secondary effects tend to reinforce the basic trend. The process of capital accumulation illustrates one positive feedback loop. New investment generates greater output, which when sold, generates profits. These profits can be used to fund additional new investments. Notice that with positive feedback loops the process is self-reinforcing. Positive feedback loops are also involved in climate change. Scientists believe, for example, that the relationship between emissions of methane and climate change may be described as a positive feedback loop. Since methane is a greenhouse gas, increases in methane emissions contribute to warmer temperatures. As the planetary temperature rises, however, it could trigger the release of extremely large quantities of additional methane that are currently trapped in the permafrost; the larger quantities of methane would further increase temperature, which could release more methane, and so on.

Human responses can also intensify environmental problems by contributing to positive feedback loops. For example, when shortages of a commodity are imminent, consumers typically begin to hoard the commodity. Hoarding intensifies the shortage. Similarly, people faced with food shortages may eat the seed that is the key to more plentiful food in the future. Situations giving rise to this kind of downward spiral are particularly troublesome.

In contrast, *negative feedback loops* are self-limiting rather than self-reinforcing. Perhaps the best-known planetary-scale example of negative feedback is provided in a theory advanced by James Lovelock, an English scientist. Called the *Gaia hypothesis* after the Greek concept for Mother Earth, this view of the world suggests that the earth is a living organism with a complex feedback system that seeks an optimal physical and chemical environment. Deviations from this optimal environment trigger natural, nonhuman response mechanisms that restore the balance. In essence, according to the Gaia hypothesis, the planetary environment is, within limits, a self-regulating process.

Negative feedback loops are not inevitable, however. As Jared Diamond's best-selling book *Catastrophe* points out, the self-extinction case examined in Example 1.1 is not an isolated example. History reveals many examples of societies that succumbed to the environmental challenges they faced; societal success in overcoming these challenges is certainly not inevitable. As we proceed with our investigation, the degree to which our economic and political institutions serve to intensify or to limit emerging environmental problems will be a key concern.

● The Role of Economics

How societies respond to challenges will depend largely on the behavior of humans acting individually or collectively. Economic analysis provides an incredibly useful set of tools for anyone interested in understanding and/or modifying human behavior, particularly in the face of scarcity. As shown in Debate 1.1, both ecological economics and environmental economics provide a basis not only for helping to identify the circumstances that degrade the environment, but also for clarifying how and why that set of circumstances supports degradation. This understanding can then be used as the basis for designing new incentives that harmonize the relationship between the economy and the environment. Harnessing the power of market forces allows them to be used in the service of sustainable environmental outcomes. Ignoring them means having to live with consequences that not only can be much more expensive to correct after the fact, but also may even be irreversible.

The Use of Models

All of the topics covered in this book will be examined as a part of the general focus on economic development in the presence of limited environmental and natural resources. Because this subject is complex, it is better understood when broken into manageable portions. Once we master the components, we will reassemble them to form a more complete picture. In economics, as in most other disciplines, we use models to investigate complex subjects, such as relationships between the economy and the environment.

DEBATE 1.1

Ecological Economics Versus Environmental Economics

Over the last decade or so, the community of scholars dealing with the interaction of the economy and the environment has settled into two camps: *ecological economics* (http://www .ecoeco.org/) and *environmental economics* (http://www.aere.org/). Although they share many similarities, ecological economics is consciously more methodologically pluralist. While environmental economics is based solidly on the standard paradigm of *neoclassical economics*, ecological economics uses a variety of methodologies, including neoclassical economics, depending upon the purpose.

While some see the two approaches as competitive (presenting an "either-or" choice), others, including the authors of this text, see them as complementary. Complementarity, of course, does not mean universal acceptance. Significant differences exist not only between these two fields, but also within them over such topics as the valuation of environmental resources, the impact of trade on the environment, and the appropriate means for evaluating policy strategies for long-duration problems such as climate change. These differences arise not only over methodologies, but also over the values that are brought to bear on the analysis.

Since the senior author of this book has published in both fields and has been on the editorial boards of leading journals in both fields, it probably will not be surprising that this book draws from both fields. Although the basic foundation for the analysis is environmental economics, the chapters draw heavily from ecological economics to both critique that view when it is controversial and to complement it with useful insights drawn from outside the neoclassical paradigm when appropriate. Pragmatism is the reigning criterion. If a particular approach or study helps us understand environmental problems and their resolutions, it has been included in the text.

Models are simplified characterizations of reality. For example, although a road map, by design, leaves out much detail, it is a useful guide to reality. The map shows how various locations relate to each other and gives an overall perspective. It cannot, however, capture the unique details that characterize any particular location. The map highlights only those characteristics that are crucial for the purpose at hand. The models in this text are similar. Through simplification, less detail is shown so that the retained concepts become clear.

Models allow us to study issues that are interrelated and global in scale rigorously, but, through their selectivity, models may yield conclusions that are dead wrong. Details that are omitted may turn out, in retrospect, to be crucial in understanding a particular dimension. Therefore, models are useful abstractions that should always be viewed with some skepticism. Most people's views of the world are based on models; although frequently, the assumptions and relationships involved may be hidden, perhaps even subconscious. In economics the models are typically explicit; objectives, relationships, and assumptions are clearly specified so that the reader understands exactly how the conclusions were derived.

The validity and reliability of economic models are tested by examining the degree to which they can explain actual behavior in markets or other settings. The empirical field of econometrics uses statistical techniques, primarily regression analysis, to derive key economic functions. These data-derived functions, such as cost curves or demand functions, can then be used for such diverse purposes as testing hypotheses about the effects of policies or forecasting future oil prices.

Examining human behavior in a non-laboratory setting, however, poses special challenges because it is nearly impossible to control completely for all the various factors that influence an outcome beyond those of primary interest. The search for more control over the circumstances that provide the data we use to understand human behavior has given rise to the use of another analytical approach—*experimental economics*, as discussed in Example 1.2. Together econometrics and experimental economics can provide different lenses to help us understand human behavior and its impact on the world around us.

**EXAMPLE
1.2**

Experimental Economics: Studying Human Behavior in a Laboratory

The appeal of experimental economics is based upon its ability to study human behavior in a more controlled setting. During the mid-twentieth century economists began to design controlled laboratory experiments with human subjects. The experimental designs mimic decision situations in a variety of settings. Paid participants are informed of the rules of the experiment and asked to make choices. Perhaps, for example, in an experiment to mimic the current carbon trading market the participants are told how much it costs to control each unit of their carbon emissions and they are asked to place bids to buy carbon allowances. The team running the experiment would then calculate how many allowances each successful participant would acquire, based on all the bids, as well as the cost consequences of that outcome.

To the extent that the results of these experiments have proved to be replicable, they have created a deeper understanding about the effectiveness of markets, policies, and institutions. The large and growing literature on experimental economics has already shed light on such widely divergent topics as the effectiveness of alternative policies for controlling pollution and allocating scarce water, how uncertainty affects choices, and how the nature of cooperative agreements affects the sustainability of shared natural resources.

While experiments have the advantage of being able to control the decision-making environment, the artificiality of the laboratory setting raises questions about the degree to which the results from laboratories can shed light on actual human behavior outside the lab. While the degree of artificiality can be controlled by careful research design, it cannot be completely eliminated. Over the years, however, this approach has provided valuable information that can complement what we have learned from observed behavior using econometrics.

Sources: Ronald G. Cummings and Laura O. Taylor, "Experimental Economics in Natural Resource and Environmental Management" The International Yearbook of Environmental and Natural Resource Economics 2001/2002, Henk Former and Tom Tietenberg, eds. (Cheltenham, UK: Edward Elgar, 2001): 123–149 and Vernon L. Smith, "Experimental Methods in Economics" The New Palgrave Dictionary of Economics: Volume 2, John Eatwell, Murray Milgate, and Peter Newman, eds. (London, UK: The Macmillan Press Limited): 241–249.

The Road Ahead

Does the existing situation justify pessimism or optimism about the future?

Debate 1.2 examines the controversial question of whether or not societies are on a self-destructive path. In part, the differences between these two very different views depend on how human behavior is perceived. If increasing scarcity results in a behavioral response that involves positive feedback loops (intensifies the pressure on the environment), pessimism is justified. If, on the other hand, the human responses are either currently reducing those pressures or could be reformed so as to reduce those pressures, then optimism may be justified.

The field of environmental and natural resource economics has become an important source of ideas for coping with these problems. Not only does the field provide a firm basis for understanding the human sources of environmental problems, but also it provides a firm foundation for crafting specific solutions to them. In subsequent chapters, for example, you will be

---

DEBATE 1.2

What Does the Future Hold?

Is the economy on a collision course with the environment? Or has the process of reconciliation begun? One group, led most notably by Bjørn Lomborg (2001), concludes that societies have resourcefully confronted environmental problems in the past and environmentalist concerns to the contrary are excessively alarmist. In his book *The Skeptical Environmentalist*, he states:

> The fact is, as we have seen, that this civilization over the last 400 years has brought us fantastic and continued progress. ... And we ought to face the facts—that on the whole we have no reason to expect that this progress will not continue.

On the other end of the spectrum is the Worldwatch Institute, which believes that current development paths and the attendant strain they place on the environment are unsustainable. As reported in *State of the World 2004*:

> This rising consumption in the U.S., other rich nations, and many developing ones is more than the planet can bear. Forests, wetlands, and other natural places are shrinking to make way for people and their homes, farms, malls, and factories. Despite the existence of alternative sources, more than 90 percent of paper still comes from trees—eating up about one fifth of the total wood harvest worldwide. An estimated 75 percent of global fish stocks are now fished at or beyond their sustainable limit. And even though technology allows for greater fuel efficiency than ever before, cars and other forms of transportation account for nearly 30 percent of world energy use and 95 percent of global oil consumption.

These views not only interpret the available historical evidence differently, but also they imply very different strategies for the future.

Sources: Bjørn Lomborg. *The Skeptical Environmentalist: Measuring the Real State of the World* (Cambridge, UK: Cambridge University Press. The Worldwatch Institute. *The State of the World 2004* (New York: W.W. Norton & Co., 2004).

exposed to how economic analysis can be (and has been) used to forge solutions to climate change (Chapter 16), biodiversity loss (Chapters 12 and 13), population growth (Chapter 6), and water scarcity (Chapter 9). Many of the solutions are quite innovative.

The search for solutions must recognize that market forces are extremely powerful. Attempts to solve environmental problems that ignore these forces run a high risk of failure. It is both possible and desirable to harness these forces and channel them into directions that protect the environmental base on which the economy ultimately depends. Environmental and natural resource economics provides a specific set of directions for how that can be accomplished.

The Issues

Obviously, the two opposing visions of the future identified in Debate 1.2 present us with rather different conceptions of what the future holds, as well as different views of what policy choices should be made. They also suggest that to act as if one vision is correct, when it is not, could prove to be a costly error. Thus, it is important to determine whether one of these two views or, alternatively, some third view, is correct.

In order to assess any model or view, it is necessary to address the basic issues:

- ✺ Is the problem correctly conceptualized as exponential growth with fixed, immutable resource limits? Does the earth have a finite carrying capacity? If so, how can the carrying-capacity concept be operationalized? Do current levels of economic activity exceed the earth's carrying capacity?

- ✺ How does the economic system respond to scarcities? Is the process mainly characterized by positive or negative feedback loops? Would the responses intensify or ameliorate any initial scarcities?

- ✺ What is the role of the political system in controlling these problems? In what circumstances is government intervention necessary? What forms of intervention work best? Is government intervention uniformly benign, or can it make the situation worse? What roles are appropriate for the executive, legislative, and judicial branches?

- ✺ Many environmental problems involve a considerable degree of uncertainty about the severity of the problem and the effectiveness of possible solutions. Can our economic and political institutions respond to this uncertainty in reasonable ways or does uncertainty become a paralyzing force?

- ✺ Can the economic and political systems work together to eradicate poverty and social injustice while respecting our obligations to future generations? Or do our obligations to future generations inevitably conflict with the desire to raise the living standards of those currently in absolute poverty or the desire to treat all people, especially the most vulnerable, with fairness? Can short-term and long-term goals be harmonized? Is sustainable development feasible? How can it be achieved? What does the need to preserve the environment imply about the future of economic activity in the industrialized nations? In the less industrialized nations?

The rest of the book uses economic analysis to suggest answers to these complex questions.

An Overview of the Book

In the following chapters you will study the rich and rewarding field of environmental and natural resource economics. The menu of topics is broad and varied. Economics provides a powerful analytical framework for examining the relationships between the environment on the one hand and economic and political systems on the other. The study of economics can assist in identifying circumstances that give rise to environmental problems, in discovering causes of these problems, and in searching for solutions. Each chapter provides an introduction to a unique topic in environmental and natural resource economics, and our overarching focus on growth in a finite environment weaves these topics into a single theme.

We begin by comparing perspectives being brought to bear on these problems by economists and noneconomists. The manner in which scholars in various disciplines view problems and potential solutions depends on how they organize the available facts, how they interpret those facts, and what kinds of values they apply in translating these interpretations into policy. Before taking a detailed look at environmental problems, we will compare the ideology of conventional economics to other prevailing ideologies in both the natural and social sciences. This comparison explains why reasonable people may, upon examining the same set of facts, reach different conclusions. It also conveys some sense of the strengths and weaknesses of economic analysis as it is applied to environmental problems. Specific evaluation criteria are defined and examples demonstrate how economic criteria can be applied to specific environmental problems.

After examining the major perspectives shaping environmental policy, we will turn to specific examples of resource scarcities and to the manner in which the economic and political institutions have dealt with the resulting problems. We begin our examination with an inquiry into the nature, causes, and consequences of population growth—a major factor in determining how rapidly scarcity could develop.

The next section of the book deals with several topics that traditionally fall within natural resource economics. Energy is discussed as an example of a depletable, nonrecyclable resource. The degree to which the current situation approximates an efficient, sustainable ideal is assessed, with particular attention paid to policy choices facing the current generation.

The chapters on renewable or replenishable resources (e.g., water, land, food, forestry, fisheries) show that the effectiveness with which current institutions manage renewable resources depends on whether the resources are living or inanimate and whether they are treated as private or as free-access common property.

Then we move on to an area of public policy—pollution control—that is coming to rely much more heavily on the use of economic incentives to produce the desired response. The overview chapter emphasizes not only the nature of the problems but also the differences among policy approaches taken to resolve them. The unique aspects of local and regional air pollution, climate change, automobile air pollution, water pollution, and the control of both toxic and nontoxic waste are explored in subsequent chapters.

Following this examination of the individual environmental and natural resource problems and the policies that can be, and have been used to ameliorate these problems, the book turns to the growth process itself. Certain questions must be asked: What are the causes and consequences of economic growth? What roles do natural resources and environmental control play in the sustainable development process? What is the likely future for sustainable development? Is an immediate transition to a zero-economic-growth path necessary? Or, if unnecessary, is it desirable?

The book closes by assembling the bits and pieces of evidence accumulated in each of the preceding chapters and fusing them into an overall response to the questions posed in this chapter. The last chapter also suggests some of the major unresolved issues in environmental policy that are likely to be among those commanding center stage over the next several years or decades.

Summary

Is our society so myopic that it has chosen a path that can only lead to the destruction of society as we now know it? We have examined briefly two views that provide two different answers to that question. The Worldwatch Institute responds in the affirmative, whereas Bjørn Lomborg responds negatively. The pessimistic view is based upon the inevitability of exceeding the carrying capacity of the planet as the population and the level of economic activity grow. The optimistic view sees initial scarcity triggering sufficiently powerful reductions in population growth and increases in technological progress such that the future brings further abundance, not deepening scarcity.

Our examination of these rather different visions has revealed a number of questions that must be answered if we are to assess what the future holds. Seeking answers to these questions requires that we accumulate a much better understanding about how choices are made in economic and political systems and how those choices affect, and are affected by, the natural environment. We will begin that process in Chapter 2, where the economic approach is developed in broad terms and is contrasted with other conventional approaches.

Key Concepts

ecological economics, *p. 7*

environmental economics, *p. 7*

experimental economics, *p. 9*

Gaia hypothesis, *p. 6*

greenhouse effect, *p. 2*

negative feedback loops, *p. 6*

neoclassical economics, *p. 7*

positive feedback loops, *p. 5*

Further Reading

Lovins, A., L. H. Lovins, and P. Hawken. "A Road Map for Natural Capitalism," *Harvard Business Review* (1999): 145–158. A vision suggesting that business strategies built on a more productive use of natural resources can solve many environmental problems at a profit.

Meadows, Donella, Jorgen Randers, and Dennis Meadows. *The Limits to Growth: The 30-Year Global Update* (White River Junction, VT: Chelsea Green Publishing, 2004). In 1972 four young scientists at MIT wrote a book called *The Limits to Growth*, based upon a computer model that attempted to simulate the future. Incorporating the types of positive and negative feedback effects described in this chapter, they concluded that the current path of human activity would inevitably lead the economy to overshoot the carrying capacity of the earth, leading in turn to a collapse of society as we now know it. This sequel brings data on overshoot and global ecological collapse to the present moment.

Oates, W. E., ed. *The RFF Reader in Environmental and Resource Policy*, 2nd ed. (Washington, DC: Resources for the Future, Inc., 2005). A collection of short, highly readable commentaries on subjects ranging from biodiversity and climate change to environmental justice.

Stavins, R., ed. *Economics of the Environment: Selected Readings*, 5th ed. (New York: W. W. Norton & Co., 2005). An excellent set of complementary readings that captures both the power of the discipline and the controversy it provokes.

Additional References

Ascher, William. *Why Governments Waste Natural Resources: Policy Failures in Developing Countries* (Baltimore, MD: Johns Hopkins University Press, 1999).

Brander, James A. and M. Scott Taylor. "The Simple Economics of Easter Island: A Ricardo-Malthus Model of Renewable Resource Use," *American Economic Review* 88 (March 1998) (1): 119–138.

Diamond, Jared. *Collapse: How Societies Choose to Fail or Succeed*, (New York: Viking, 2005).

Intergovernmental Panel on Climate Change, *Climate Change 2007: The Physical Basis. Contribution of Working Group I to the Fourth Assessment Report of the Intergovernmental Panel on Climate Change* (Cambridge, UK: Cambridge University Press).

Lomborg, Bjørn. *The Skeptical Environmentalist: Measuring the Real State of the World* (Cambridge, UK: Cambridge University Press, 2001).

Portney, P. R. "The Growing Role of Economics in Environmental Decisionmaking," *Environment* 40 (1998) (2): 14.

Reisner, Mark. *A Dangerous Place: California's Unsettling Fate* (New York: Penguin Books, 2003).

Webster, David, Anncorinne Freter, and Nancy Golin. *Copán: The Rise and Fall of an Ancient Maya Kingdom* (Fort Worth, TX: Harcourt Brace Publishers, 2000).

Worldwatch Institute. *The State of the World 2004* (New York: W. W. Norton & Co., 2004).

Historically Important References

Krutilla, John. "Conservation Reconsidered," *The American Economic Review* 57 (September 1968): 777–786.

World Commission on Environment and Development. *Our Common Future* (Oxford: Oxford University Press, 1987).

Discussion Questions

1. In *The Ultimate Resource*, Julian Simon makes the point that calling the resource base "finite" is misleading. To illustrate this point he uses a yardstick, with its one-inch markings, as an analogy. The distance between two markings is finite—one inch—but an infinite number of points is contained within that finite space. Therefore, in one sense, what lies

between the markings is finite, but in another, equally meaningful sense, it is infinite. Is the concept of a finite resource base useful or not? Why?

2. This chapter contains two rather different views of the future. Because the validity of these views cannot be completely tested until the time period covered by the forecast has passed (so that predictions can be matched against actual events), how can we ever hope to establish whether one is a better view than the other? What criteria might be proposed for evaluating predictions?

3. Positive and negative feedback loops lie at the core of systematic thinking about the future. As you examine the key forces shaping the future, what examples of positive and negative feedback loops can you uncover?

Valuing the Environment: Concepts

When you have eliminated the impossible, whatever remains, however improbable, must be the truth.

—SHERLOCK HOLMES, from Sir Arthur Conan Doyle's
The Sign of Four (1890)

Introduction

Before examining specific environmental problems and the policy responses to them, it is important that we develop and clarify the economics approach, so that we will have some sense of the forest before examining each of the trees. By having a feel for the conceptual framework, it becomes easier not only to deal with individual cases, but also, perhaps more importantly, to see how they fit into a comprehensive approach.

In this chapter we develop the general conceptual framework used in economics to approach environmental problems. We begin by examining the relationship between human actions, as manifested through the economic system, and the environmental consequences of those actions. We can then establish criteria for judging the desirability of the outcomes of this relationship. These criteria provide a basis for identifying the nature and severity of environmental problems, and a foundation for designing effective policies to deal with them.

Throughout this chapter the economic point of view is contrasted with alternative points of view. These contrasts bring the economic approach into sharper focus and stimulate deeper and more critical thinking about all possible approaches.

The Human Environment Relationship

The Environment as an Asset

In economics the environment is viewed as a composite asset that provides a variety of services. It is a very special asset, to be sure, because it provides the life support systems that sustain our very existence, but it is an asset nonetheless. As with other assets, we wish to prevent undue

15

lue of this asset so that it may continue to provide aesthetic and life-

provides the economy with raw materials, which are transformed into the production process, and energy, which fuels this transformation. naterials and energy return to the environment as waste products (see

also provides services directly to consumers. The air we breathe, the nourishment we receive from food and drink, and the protection we derive from shelter and clothing are all benefits we receive either directly or indirectly from the environment. In addition, anyone who has experienced the exhilaration of white-water canoeing, the total serenity of a wilderness trek, or the breathtaking beauty of a sunset will readily recognize that the environment provides us with a variety of amenities for which no substitute exists.

If the environment is defined broadly enough, the relationship between the environment and the economic system can be considered a *closed system*. For our purposes, a closed system is one in which no inputs (energy, matter, and so on) are received from outside the system and no outputs are transferred outside the system. An *open system*, by contrast, is one in which the system imports or exports matter or energy.

If we restrict our conception of the relationship in Figure 2.1 to our planet and the atmosphere around it, then clearly we do not have a closed system. We derive most of our energy

FIGURE 2.1   The Economic System and the Environment

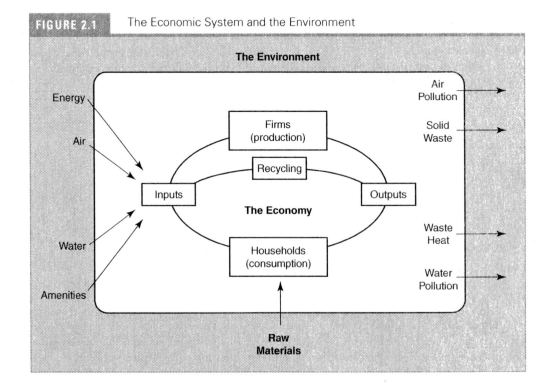

from the sun, either directly or indirectly. We have also sent spaceships well beyond the boundaries of our atmosphere. Nonetheless, historically speaking, for material inputs and outputs (not including energy), this system can be treated as a closed system because the amount of exports (such as abandoned space vehicles) and imports (e.g., moon rocks) are negligible. Whether the system remains closed depends on the degree to which space exploration opens up the rest of our solar system as a source of raw materials.

The treatment of our planet and its immediate environs as a closed system has an important implication which is summed up in the *first law of thermodynamics*—energy and matter cannot be created or destroyed.[1] The law implies that the mass of materials flowing into the economic system from the environment has either to accumulate in the economic system or return to the environment as waste. When accumulation stops, the mass of materials flowing into the economic system is equal in magnitude to the mass of waste flowing into the environment.

Excessive wastes can, of course, depreciate the asset; when they exceed the absorptive capacity of nature, wastes reduce the services that the asset provides. Examples are easy to find—air pollution can cause respiratory problems, polluted drinking water can cause cancer, and smog obliterates scenic vistas.

The relationship of people to the environment is also conditioned by another physical law, the *second law of thermodynamics*. Known popularly as the *entropy law*, this law states that entropy increases. *Entropy* is the amount of energy not available for work. Applied to energy processes, this law implies that no conversion from one form of energy to another is completely efficient and that the consumption of energy is an irreversible process. Some energy is always lost during conversion, and the rest, once used, is no longer available for further work. The second law also implies that in the absence of new energy inputs, any closed system must eventually use up its energy. Since energy is necessary for life, life ceases when energy ceases.

We should remember that our planet is not even approximately a closed system with respect to energy; we gain energy from the sun. The entropy law does suggest, however, that this flow of solar energy establishes an upper limit on the flow of energy that can be sustained. Once the stocks of stored energy (such as fossil fuels and nuclear energy) are gone, the amount of energy available for useful work will be determined solely by this flow and by the amount that can be stored (dams, trees, and so on). Thus, over the very long run, the growth process will be limited by the availability of renewable energy and our ability to put it to work.

The Economic Approach

Two different types of economic analysis can be applied to increase our understanding of the relationship between the economic system and the environment: *Positive economics* attempts to describe *what is, what was,* or *what will be. Normative economics,* by contrast, deals with what *ought to be.* Disagreements within positive economics can usually be resolved by an appeal to the facts. Normative disagreements, however, involve value judgments.

Both branches are useful. Suppose, for example, we want to investigate the relationship between trade and the environment. Positive economics could be used to describe the kinds of

---

[1]We know, however, from Einstein's famous equation ($E = mc^2$) that matter can be transformed into energy. This transformation is the source of energy in nuclear power.

impacts trade would have on the economy and the environment. It could not, however, provide any guidance on the question of whether trade was desirable. That judgment would have to come from normative economics.

Normative analysis can arise in several different contexts. It might be used, for example, to evaluate the desirability of a proposed new pollution control regulation or a proposal to preserve an area currently scheduled for development. In these cases the analysis helps to provide guidance on the desirability of a program before that program is put into place. In other contexts it might be used to evaluate how an already-implemented program has worked out. Both of these types of situations share the characteristic that the alternatives being evaluated are well defined in advance. Here the relevant question is: Should we do it or shouldn't we?

A rather different context for normative economics can arise when the possibilities are more open-ended. For example, we might ask how much should we control emissions of greenhouse gases (which contribute to global warming) and how should we achieve that degree of control? Or we might ask how much forest of various types should be preserved? Answering these questions requires us to consider the entire range of possible outcomes and to select the best or optimal one. Although that is a much more difficult question to answer than one that asks us only to compare two predefined alternatives, the basic normative analysis framework is the same in both cases.

● Normative Criteria for Decision Making

Evaluating Predefined Options

If you were asked to evaluate the desirability of some proposed action, you would probably begin by attempting to identify the gains and losses from that action. If the gains exceed the losses, then it seems natural to support the action.

That simple *benefit/cost analysis* framework provides the starting point for the economic approach. Economists suggest that actions have both benefits and costs. If the benefits exceed the costs, then the action is desirable. On the other hand, if the costs exceed the benefits, then the action is not desirable.

We can formalize this in the following way. Let B be the benefits from a proposed action and C be the costs. Our decision rule would then be:

If $B > C$, then support the action.
Otherwise, oppose the action.[2]

As long as B and C are positive, an equivalent formulation would be:

If $B/C > 1$, then support the action.
Otherwise, oppose the action.

So far so good, but how do we measure benefits and costs? In economics the system of measurement is anthropocentric, which simply means human-centered. All benefits and costs are valued in terms of their effects (broadly defined) on humanity. As will be pointed out later, that does *not* imply (as it might first appear) that ecosystem effects are ignored unless they *directly* affect humans. The fact that large numbers of humans contribute voluntarily to organizations that are

---

[2]Actually, if $B = C$, it wouldn't make any difference if the action occurs or not; the benefits and costs are a wash.

dedicated to environmental protection provides ample evidence that humans place a value on environmental preservation that goes well beyond any direct use they might make of it. Nonetheless, the notion that humans are doing the valuing is a controversial point (see Debate 2.1).

Benefits can be derived from the demand curve for the good or service provided by the action. Demand curves measure the amount of a particular good people would be willing to purchase at various prices. In a typical situation, a person will purchase less of a commodity (or environmental service) the higher is its price. In Figure 2.2, when the price is P_0, Q_0 will be purchased, but if the price rises to P_1, purchases will fall to Q_1.

DEBATE 2.1

Should Humans Place an Economic Value on the Environment?

Arne Naess, the late Norwegian philosopher, used the term "deep ecology" to refer to the view that the nonhuman environment has "intrinsic" value, a value that is independent of human interests. Intrinsic value is contrasted with "instrumental" value in which the value of the environment is derived from its usefulness in satisfying human wants.

Two issues are raised by the Naess critique: (1) What is the basis for valuing the environment? and (2) How is the valuation accomplished? The belief that the environment may have a value that goes beyond its direct usefulness to humans is in fact quite consistent with modern economic valuation techniques. As we show in Chapter 3, economic valuation techniques now include the ability to quantify a wide range of nonuse values as well as the more traditional use values.

Controversies over how the values are derived are less easily resolved. As described in this chapter, economic valuation is based firmly upon human preferences. Deep ecology, on the other hand, would argue that allowing humans to determine the value of other species would have no more moral basis than allowing other species to determine the value of humans. Rather, deep ecologists argue, humans should only use environmental resources when necessary for survival; otherwise nature should be left alone. And, because economic valuation is not helpful in determining survival necessity, deep ecologists argue that it contributes little to environmental management.

Those who oppose all economic valuation, however, face a dilemma: When humans fail to value the environment it may be assigned a default value of zero in calculations designed to guide policy. A value of zero, however derived, will tend to justify a great deal of environmental degradation that could not be justified with proper economic valuation. As a 1998 issue of "Ecological Economics" demonstrated, a number of environmental professionals now support economic valuation as a way to demonstrate just how valuable the environment is to modern society. At the very least, support seems to be growing for the proposition that economic valuation can be a very useful means of demonstrating when environmental degradation is senseless, even when judged from a limited anthropomorphic perspective (see Example 2.1).

Sources: Costanza, R. et al., "The value of ecosystem services: putting the issues in perspective" *Ecological Economics* 25 (1998) (1): 67–72 and the other articles on valuation in that issue. Daily, Gretchen and Katherine Ellison, *The New Economy of Nature: The Quest to Make Conservation Profitable* (Washington: Island Press, 2003).

FIGURE 2.2   The Individual Demand Curve

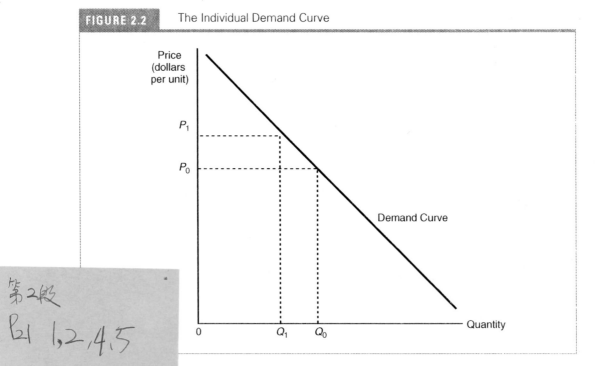

of these demand curves can be illustrated with the following hypothetical
se you were asked: At a price of X dollars, how much commodity Y would you
could be recorded as a point on a diagram, as shown in Figure 2.2. By repeat-
any times for different prices, we could trace out a locus of points. Connecting
these points would yield an individual *demand curve*. Adding up all of the individual amounts
demanded by all individuals at some stipulated price yields one point on the market demand
curve. Connecting the points for various prices reveals the market demand curve.

For each quantity purchased, the corresponding point on the market demand curve represents the amount of money some person is willing to pay for the last unit of the good. The *total
willingness to pay* for some quantity of this good—say, three units—is the sum of the willingness
to pay for each of the three units. Thus, the total willingness to pay for three units would be measured by the sum of the willingness to pay for the first, second, and third units, respectively. It is
now a simple extension to determine that the total willingness to pay is the area under the continuous market demand curve to the left of the allocation in question. For example, in Figure 2.3
the total willingness to pay for five units of the commodity is the shaded area.[3] Total willingness
to pay is the concept we will use to define *total benefits*, specifically total benefits is equal to total
willingness to pay.

---

[3]From simple geometry it can be noticed that for linear demand curves this area is the sum of the areas of the triangle on
top plus the rectangle on the bottom. The area of a right triangle is $1/2 \times$ base $\times$ height. Therefore, in our example this area
is $1/2 \times \$5 \times 5 + \$5 \times 5 = \$37.50$.

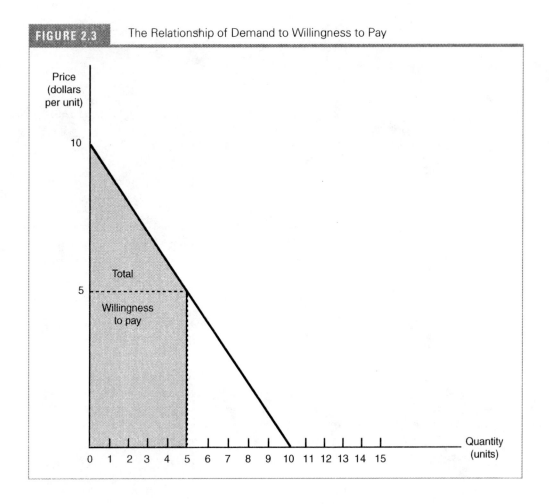

FIGURE 2.3   The Relationship of Demand to Willingness to Pay

Measuring total costs on the same set of axes involves logic similar to measuring total benefits. It is important to stress that environmental services have costs even though they are produced without any human input. All costs should be measured as opportunity costs.

As illustrated in Example 2.1, the *opportunity cost* for using resources is the net benefit lost when specific environmental services are foregone in the conversion to the new use. The notion that it is costless to convert a forest to a new use is obviously wrong if valuable ecological services are lost in the process.

To firm up this notion of opportunity cost, consider another example. Suppose a particular stretch of river can be used for white-water canoeing or to generate electric power. Since the dam that generates the power would flood the rapids, the two uses are incompatible. The opportunity cost of producing power is the forgone net benefit that would have resulted from the white-water canoeing.

In graphing costs, we will use the marginal opportunity cost curve to correspond to the *marginal willingness to pay* function used above to graph benefits. The *marginal opportunity cost*

EXAMPLE
2.1

Valuing Ecological Services from Preserved Tropical Forests

As Chapter 11 explains, one of the main threats to tropical forests comes when the forested land is converted to some other use (agriculture, residences, and so on). Whether economic incentives favor conversion of the land depends upon the magnitude of the value that would be lost through conversion. How large is that value? Is it large enough to support preservation?

A group of ecologists decided to tackle this question for a specific set of tropical forest fragments in Costa Rica. They chose to value one specific ecological service provided by the local forest: wild bees using the nearby tropical forest as a habitat provided pollination services to aid coffee production. While this coffee (*C. Arabica*) can self-pollinate, pollination from wild bees has been shown to increase coffee productivity 15–50 percent.

When the ecologists placed an economic value on this particular ecological service, they found that the pollination services from two specific preserved forest fragments (46 and 111 hectares, respectively) were worth approximately $60,000 per year for one large, nearby Costa Rican coffee farm. As the authors conclude:

> The value of forest in providing crop pollination service alone is ... of at least the same order [of magnitude] as major competing land uses, and infinitely greater than that recognized by most governments (i.e., zero).

These estimates only partially capture the value of this forest because they consider only a single farm and a single type of ecological service. (This forest also provides carbon storage and water purification services, for example, and these were not included in the calculation.) Despite their partial nature, however, these calculations begin to demonstrate the considerable economic value of preserving the forest, even when considering only specific instrumental values.

Source: Ricketts, Taylor H. et al., "Economic Value of Tropical Forest to Coffee Production" *PNAS (Proceedings of the National Academy of Science)* 101 August 24, 2002 (34): 12579–12582.

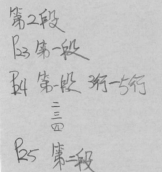

第2段
P3 第一段
P4 第一段 新一5行
三
四

P5 第三段

...ional cost of producing the last unit. In purely competitive markets, the ...cost curve is identical to the supply curve.

...the sum of the *marginal costs*.[4] The total cost of producing three units is ...oducing the first unit plus the cost of producing the second unit plus the ...hird unit. As with total willingness to pay, the geometric representation of ...ual elements of a continuous marginal cost curve is the area under the ...illustrated in Figure 2.4 by the shaded area *FGIJK*.[5]

the marginal costs is equal to total variable cost. In the short run, this is smaller than total ...d cost. For our purposes this distinction is not important.

[5]Notice again that this area is the sum of a right triangle and a rectangle. In Figure 2.4 the total variable cost of producing five units is $18.75. Why?

FIGURE 2.4   The Relationship of Marginal Cost and Total Cost

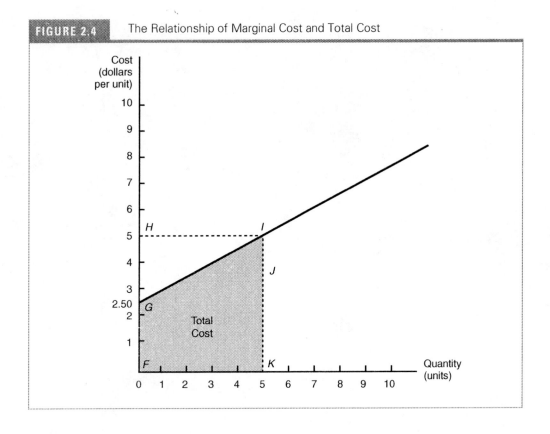

Since net benefit is defined as the excess of benefits over costs, it follows that net benefit is equal to that portion of the area under the demand curve that lies above the supply curve. Consider Figure 2.5, which combines the information in Figures 2.3 and 2.4

Let's now use this apparatus to illustrate the use of the decision rules introduced earlier. Let's suppose for example that we are considering preserving a four-mile stretch of river and that the benefits and costs of that action are reflected in Figure 2.5. Should that stretch be preserved?

The answer is clearly yes. The total benefits (the area under the marginal willingness to pay curve) are clearly larger than the total costs (the area under the marginal cost curve). Since *net benefits* are positive, it makes sense to preserve four miles of the river.

Incorporating the Timing of Benefits and Costs: The Present Value Criterion

The analysis we have covered so far is very useful for thinking about actions where time is not an important factor. Yet many of the decisions made now have consequences that persist well into the future. Time is a factor. Exhaustible energy resources, once used, are gone. Biological renewable resources (such as fisheries or forests) can be overharvested, leaving smaller and possibly weaker populations for future generations. Persistent pollutants can accumulate over time. How can we make choices when the benefits and costs occur at different times?

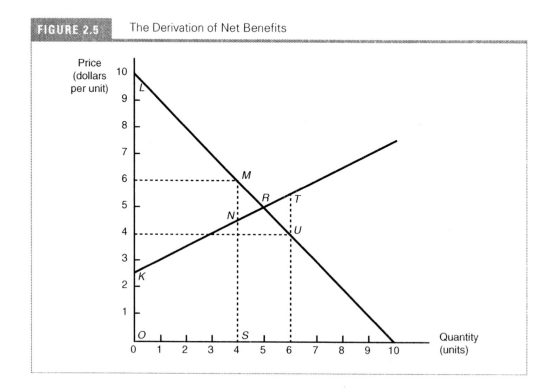

FIGURE 2.5   The Derivation of Net Benefits

Incorporating time into the analysis requires an extension of the concepts we have already developed. This extension provides a way of thinking not only about the magnitude of benefits and costs, but also about timing. In order to incorporate timing, the decision rule must provide a way to compare the net benefit received in one period with the net benefit received in another. The concept that allows this comparison is called *present value*. Therefore, before introducing this expanded decision rule, we must clarify present value.

Present value explicitly incorporates the time value of money. A dollar today invested at 10 percent interest yields $1.10 a year from now (the return of the $1 principal plus $0.10 interest). The present value of $1.10 received one year from now is therefore, $1, because given $1 now, you can turn it into $1.10 a year from now by investing it at 10 percent interest. We can find the present value of any amount of money (X) received one year from now by computing $X/(1 + r)$, where r is the appropriate interest rate (10 percent in our example above).

What could your dollar earn in two years at r percent interest? Because of compound interest, the amount would be $\$1(1 + r)(1 + r) = \$1(1 + r)^2$. It follows then that the present value of X received two years from now is $X/(1 + r)^2$.

By now the pattern should be clear. The net present value of a *one-time* net benefit received n years from now is

$$NPV[B_n] = \frac{B_n}{(1+r)^n}$$

The net present value of a stream of net benefits $\{B_0, \ldots, B_n\}$ received over a period of n years is computed as

$$NPV[B_0, \ldots, B_n] = \sum_{i=0}^{n} \frac{B_i}{(1+r)^i}$$

where r is the appropriate interest rate and B_0 is the amount of net benefits received immediately. The process of calculating the present value is called *discounting*, and the rate r is referred to as the *discount rate*.[6]

The number resulting from a present-value calculation has a straightforward interpretation. Suppose you were investigating an allocation that would yield the following pattern of net benefits on the last day of each of the next five years: $3,000, $5,000, $6,000, $10,000, and $12,000. If you use an interest rate of 6 percent ($r = 0.06$) and the above formula, you will discover that this stream has a present value of $29,205.92 (see Table 2.1).

What does that number mean? If you put $29,205.92 in a savings account earning 6 percent interest and wrote yourself checks, respectively, for $3,000, $5,000, $6,000, $10,000, and $12,000 on the last day of each of the next five years, your last check would just restore the account to a zero balance (see Table 2.2). Thus, you should be indifferent about receiving $29,205.92 now or in the specific five-year stream of benefits totaling $36,000; given one, you can get the other. Hence, the method is called present value because it translates everything back to its current worth.

TABLE 2.1   Demonstrating Present Value Calculations

Year	1	2	3	4	5	Sum
Annual Amounts	3,000	5,000	6,000	10,000	12,000	36,000
Present Value ($r = .06$)	$2,830.19	$4,449.98	$5,037.72	$7,920.94	$8,967.10	$29,205.92

TABLE 2.2   Interpreting Present Value Calculations

Year	1	2	3	4	5	6
Balance at Beginning of Year	$29,205.92	$27,958.28	$24,635.77	$20,113.92	$11,320.75	$0.00
Year-end Fund Balance before Payment ($r = .06$)	$30,958.28	$29,635.77	$26,113.92	$21,320.75	$12,000.00	
Payment	3,000	5,000	6,000	10,000	12,000	

---

[6]The discount rate should equal the social opportunity cost of capital. In Chapter 4 we examine the questions of whether private firms can be expected to use the socially correct discount rate. In Chapter 3 we discuss how the discount rate is chosen by the government.

It is now possible to show how this analysis can be used to evaluate actions. First, calculate the present value of net benefits from the action. If the present value is greater than zero, the action should be supported. Otherwise it should be rejected.

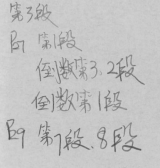

...e Optimal Outcome

...ection we examined how benefit/cost analysis can be used to evaluate the desir-
...redefined actions. In this section we examine how this approach can be used to
... best approaches.

...t chapters that address individual environmental problems, the normative
...ed in three steps: (1) We will identify an optimal outcome; (2) we will attempt
...ent to which our institutions produce optimal outcomes, and where diver-
...een actual and optimal outcomes, to uncover the behavioral sources of the
... we can use both our knowledge of the nature of the problems and their under-
lying behavioral causes as a basis for designing appropriate policy solutions. How these three steps are applied to each of the environmental problems will reflect the uniqueness of each situation, but the overarching framework used to shape that analysis will be the same.

To provide some concreteness of this approach, consider two examples: one drawn from natural resource economics and another from environmental economics. These are meant to be illustrative and to convey a flavor of the argument; the details are left to upcoming chapters.

Consider the rising number of depleted ocean fisheries. Depleted fisheries, which involve fish populations that have fallen so low as to threaten their viability as commercial fisheries, not only jeopardize oceanic biodiversity, but also pose a threat to the individuals who make their living from the sea and the communities that depend on fishing to support their local economies.

How would an economist attempt to understand and resolve this problem? The first step would involve defining the optimal stock or the optimal rate of harvest of the fishery. The second step would compare this level with the actual stock and harvest levels. Once this economic framework was actually applied, not only did it reveal that stocks are much lower than optimal for many fisheries, but it also identified the reason for excessive exploitation. Understanding the nature of the problem has led quite naturally to some solutions. Once implemented, these policies have allowed some fisheries to begin the process of renewal. The details of this analysis and the policy implications that flow from it are covered in Chapter 13.

Another problem involves solid waste. As local communities run out of room for landfills in the face of an increasing generation of waste, what can be done?

Economists start by thinking about how one would define the optimal amount of waste. The definition necessarily incorporates waste reduction and recycling as aspects of the optimal outcome. The actual analysis not only revealed that current waste levels are excessive, but also suggested some specific behavioral sources of the problem. Based upon this understanding, targeted economic solutions have been identified and implemented. Communities that have adopted these measures have generally experienced lower levels of waste and higher levels of recycling.

In the rest of the book, similar analysis is applied to population, energy, minerals, agriculture, air and water pollution, and a host of other topics. In each case the economic analysis helps to point the way toward solutions. To initiate that process we must begin by defining what is meant by optimal.

Static Efficiency

The chief normative economic criterion for choosing among various allocations occurring at the same point in time is called *static efficiency*, or merely *efficiency*. An allocation of resources is said to satisfy the static efficiency criterion if the net benefit from the use of those resources is maximized by that allocation.

Let's show how this concept can be applied by returning to Figure 2.5. Previously we asked whether an action that preserved four miles of river was worth doing. The answer was yes because the net benefits from that action were positive.

Static efficiency, however, requires us to ask a rather different question: What is the efficient number of miles to be preserved? We know from the definition that the efficient amount of preservation would maximize net benefits. Do four units maximize net benefits?

We can answer that question by establishing whether it is possible to increase the net benefit by preserving more or less of the river. If the net benefit can be increased by preserving more miles, clearly preserving four miles could not have maximized the net benefit and, therefore, could not have been efficient.

Consider what would happen if society were to choose to preserve five miles instead of four. What happens to the net benefit? It increases by area MNR. Since we can find another allocation with greater net benefit, four miles of preservation could not have been efficient. Are five? Yes. Let's see why.

We know that five miles of preservation convey more net benefits than four. If this allocation is efficient, then it must also be true that the net benefit is smaller for levels of preservation higher than five. Notice that the additional cost of preserving the sixth unit (the area under the marginal cost curve) is larger than the additional benefit received from preserving it (the corresponding area under the demand curve). Therefore, the triangle RTU represents the reduction in net benefit that occurs if six miles are preserved rather than five.

Since the net benefit is reduced, both by preserving less than five and by preserving more than five, we conclude that five units is the preservation level that maximizes net benefit. Therefore, from our definition, preserving five miles constitutes an efficient allocation.[7]

One implication of this example, which will be very useful in succeeding chapters, is what we will call the *first equimarginal principle*:

First Equimarginal Principle (the Efficiency Equimarginal Principle): Net benefits are maximized when the marginal benefits from an allocation equal the marginal costs.

This criterion helps to minimize wasted resources, but is it fair? The ethical basis for this criterion is derived from a concept called *Pareto optimality*, named after the Italian-born Swiss economist Vilfredo Pareto, who first proposed it around the turn of the twentieth century.

Allocations are said to be Pareto optimal if no other feasible allocation could benefit some people without any deleterious effects on at least one other person.

Allocations that do not satisfy this definition are suboptimal. Suboptimal allocations can always be rearranged so that some people are better off and no one is hurt by the rearrangement. Therefore, the gainers could use a portion of their gains to compensate the losers sufficiently to ensure they were at least as well off as they were prior to the reallocation. Efficient allocations are

---

[7]The monetary worth of the net benefit is the sum of two right triangles, and it equals $(\frac{1}{2})(\$5)(5) + (\frac{1}{2})(\$2.50)(5)$ or $\$18.75$. Can you see why?

Pareto optimal. Since net benefits are maximized by an efficient allocation, it is not possible to increase the net benefit by rearranging the allocation. Without an increase in the net benefit, there is no way the gainers could sufficiently compensate the losers; the gains to the gainers would necessarily be smaller than the losses to the losers.

Inefficient allocations are judged inferior because they do not maximize the net benefit. By failing to maximize net benefit, they are forgoing an opportunity to make some people better off without harming others.

For a different lens on determining efficiency consider the following numerical example:

Suppose the demand (marginal willingness to pay) for some environmental service can be expressed as $MWP = \$80 - 2q$ and the marginal cost curve as $MC = \$10$.

What level of q would represent the static efficient allocation of that environmental service and how large are the net benefits? We know from the first equimarginal principle that in an efficient allocation, where net benefits are maximized, $MWP = MC$.

So $MWP = \$80 - 2q = MC = \$10$.

Solving this for q yields $q = 35$, the static efficient level of q. The associated marginal willingness to pay and marginal cost are both $10.

We can now draw the diagram that shows the net benefits (see Figure 2.6).

To calculate the net benefits we need to subtract the total cost (the area under the marginal cost curve) from the total benefits (the area under the marginal willingness to pay curve). Geometrically speaking, the total benefits are the sum of the triangle bounded by the MWP curve, the vertical axis and the MC curve from $q = 0$ to $q = 35$ plus the rectangle formed by the horizontal axis from $q = 0$ to $q = 35$ and $MC = \$10$ over that same interval.

The area of the benefit triangle is

$$\frac{1}{2}(base)(height) = \frac{1}{2}(\$35)(\$70) = \$1,225.$$

FIGURE 2.6   Finding the Efficient Outcome

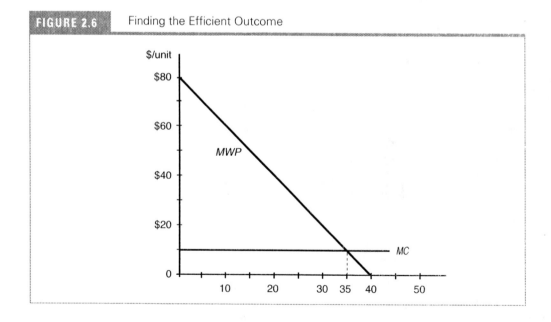

Do you see where the $70 comes from? It is the vertical distance from the value of the *MWP* when $q = 0$ (in other words the place where it crosses the vertical axis) minus the height of the *MC* ($10).

The area of the benefit rectangle is $(base)(height) = (\$35)(\$10) = \$350$.

Hence, total benefits are the sum or $1,575. Total costs are the rectangle under $MC = \$10$ from $q = 0$ to $q = 3\ 5$ or $(base)(height) = (\$35)(\$10) = \$350$.

Net benefits are total benefits minus total cost or $1,225. Notice that in this case the net benefits are simply equal to the benefit triangle. In general, that will be true when the marginal cost is constant as it is in this example.

If you want more practice, find the efficient level of q and both the *MWP* and the *MC* if the marginal cost function were $MC = \$2q$ instead of $MC = \$10$. If you obtained $q = 20$ and $MC = MWP = \$40$, you nailed it!

Dynamic Efficiency

The static efficiency criterion is very useful for comparing resource allocations when time is not an important factor. How can we make choices when the benefits and costs may occur at different times?

The traditional criterion used to find an optimal allocation when time is involved is called *dynamic efficiency*, a generalization of the static efficiency concept already developed. In this generalization, the present-value criterion provides a way for comparing the net benefits received in one period with the net benefits received in another.

An allocation of resources across n time periods satisfies the dynamic efficiency criterion if it maximizes the present value of net benefits that could be received from all the possible ways of allocating those resources over the n periods.

Applying the Concepts

Having now spent some time developing the concepts we need, let's take a moment to examine some actual studies in which they have been used.

Pollution Control

Benefit/cost analysis has been used to assess the desirability of efforts to control pollution. Pollution control certainly confers many benefits, but it also has costs. Do the benefits justify the costs? That was a question the U.S. Congress wanted answered. So, in Section 812 of the Clean Air Act Amendments of 1990 it required the Environmental Protection Agency (EPA) to evaluate the benefits and costs of the United States air pollution control policy over the 1970–1990 period (see Example 2.2).

In responding to this congressional mandate, the EPA set out to quantify and monetize the benefits and costs of achieving the emissions reductions required by United States policy. Benefits quantified by this study included reduced death rates and lower incidences of chronic bronchitis, lead poisoning, stroke, respiratory disease, and heart disease as well as the benefits of better visibility, reduced damage to structures, and improved agricultural productivity. They were unable to quantify many suspected ecosystem effects.

EXAMPLE
2.2

Does Reducing Pollution Make Economic Sense?

In its 1997 report to Congress, the EPA presented the results of its attempt to discover whether the Clean Air Act had produced positive net benefits between 1970–1990. The results suggested that the present value of benefits (using a discount rate of 5 percent) was $22.2 trillion, while the costs were $0.523 trillion. Performing the necessary subtraction reveals that the net benefits were therefore equal to $21.7 trillion. According to this study, the United States air pollution control policy during this period made very good economic sense.

Monetized Benefits and Costs of the U.S. Clean Air Act, 1970–1990
(billions of 1990 dollars)

	1975	1980	1985	1990	Present Value[c]
Benefits[a]	355	930	1,155	1,248	22,200
Costs[b]	14	21	25	26	523
Net Benefits	341	909	1,130	1,220	21,677

[a]These are the mean (average) benefits. Due to the uncertainties involved, EPA also calculated low and high estimates.
[b]These are the annualized costs. (Many investments in pollution control involve the purchase of durable equipment that lasts many years.) Rather than put all of the expense in the year of purchase, EPA distributed the costs over the useful lives of this equipment.
[c]Represents the present value of all years from 1971 to 1990 using a 5 percent discount rate.

Source: Created by the author from information presented in U.S. Environmental Protection Agency report, *The Benefits and Costs of the Clean Air Act, 1970 to 1990* (Washington, DC: Environmental Protection Agency, 1997): Table 18 on p. 56.

Two categories of costs were also quantified. The first category included the higher costs of goods and services as the costs of installing, operating, and maintaining pollution control equipment were passed on to the consumers in the form of higher prices. The second category included the costs associated with designing and implementing the regulations as well as monitoring and enforcing compliance with them.

We will return to this study later in the book for a deeper look at how these estimates were derived, but a couple of comments are relevant now. First, despite the fact that this study did not attempt to value the pollution damage to ecosystems that was avoided by this policy, the net benefits are strongly positive. While presumably the case for controlling pollution would have been even stronger had they been included, the case is strong enough even when they are omitted. An inability to monetize everything does not necessarily jeopardize the ability to reach sound policy conclusions.

Although these results justify the conclusion that pollution control made economic sense, they do not justify the stronger conclusion that the policy was efficient. To justify that conclusion, the study would have had to show that the present value of net benefits was maximized, not merely positive. In fact, this study did not attempt to calculate the maximum net benefits outcome and if it had, it would have discovered that the policy during this period was not completely efficient. With an optimal policy mix, the net benefits would have been even higher.

Preservation Versus Development

One of the most basic conflicts faced by environmental policy occurs when a currently underdeveloped but ecologically significant piece of land becomes a candidate for development. If developed, the land may provide jobs for workers, wealth for owners, and goods for consumers, but it may also degrade the ecosystem, possibly irreversibly. Wildlife habitat may be eliminated, wetlands may be paved over, and recreational opportunities may be gone forever. On the other hand, if the land is preserved, the ecosystem benefits will be retained, but the opportunity for increased income and employment will be lost. These conflicts become intensified if unemployment rates in the area are high and the local ecology is rather unique.

One such conflict arose in Australia from a proposal to mine a piece of land that was in an area known as the Kakadu Conservation Zone (KCZ). Should it be mined? Or should it be preserved? One way to examine this question is to use the techniques above to examine the net benefits of the two alternatives (see Example 2.3).

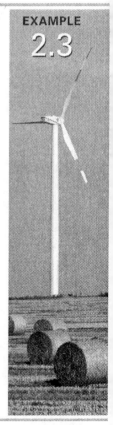

Choosing Between Preservation and Development in Australia

EXAMPLE 2.3

The Kakadu Conservation Zone (KCZ), a 50-square-kilometer area lying entirely within the Kakadu National Park (KNP), was initially set aside as part of a government grazing lease. The current issue was whether it should be mined (it was believed to contain significant deposits of gold, platinum, and palladium) or added to the KNP, one of Australia's major parks. In recognition of its unique ecosystem and extensive wildlife as well as its aboriginal archeological sites, much of the park has been placed on the United Nation's World Heritage List. Mining would produce income and employment, but it could also cause the ecosystems in both the KCZ and KNP to experience irreversible damage. What value was to be placed on those risks? Would they outweigh the employment and income effects from mining?

To provide answers to these crucial questions, economists conducted a benefit/cost analysis using a technique known as contingent valuation. (We will go into some detail about how this technique works in Chapter 3, but for now it can suffice to note that this is a technique for eliciting "willingness to pay" information.) The value of preserving the site was estimated to be A\$435 million, while the present value of mining the site was estimated to be A\$102million.

According to this analysis, preservation was the preferred option and it was the option chosen by the government.

Source: Richard T. Carson, Leanne Wilks, and David Imber, "Valuing the Preservation of Australia's Kakadu Conservation Zone," *Oxford Economic Papers* 46 Supplement (1994): 727–749.

Summary

The relationship between humanity and the environment requires many choices. Some basis for making rational choices is absolutely necessary. If not made by design, decisions will be made by default.

The economics approach views the environment as a composite asset, supplying a variety of services to humanity. The intensity and composition of those services depend on the actions of humans as constrained by physical laws, such as the first and second laws of thermodynamics.

Economics has two rather different means of enhancing the understanding of environmental and natural resource economics. Positive economics is useful in describing the actions of people and the impact of those actions on the environmental asset. Normative economics can provide guidance on how optimal service flows can be defined and achieved.

Normative economics invokes benefit/cost analysis for judging the desirability of the level and composition of provided services. A static efficient allocation is one that maximizes the net benefit over all possible uses of those resources. The dynamic efficiency criterion, which is appropriate when time is an important consideration, is satisfied when the outcome maximizes the present value of net benefits from all possible uses of the resources. Later chapters examine the degree to which our social institutions yield allocations that conform to these criteria.

Key Concepts

benefit/cost analysis, *p.* 18

closed system, *p.* 16

demand curve, *p.* 20

discount rate, *p.* 25

discounting, *p.* 25

dynamic efficiency, *p.* 29

efficiency, *p.* 27

entropy, *p.* 17

entropy law, *p.* 17

first equimarginal principle, *p.* 27

first law of thermodynamics, *p.* 17

marginal cost, *p.* 22

marginal opportunity cost curve, *p.* 21

marginal willingness to pay, *p.* 21

net benefits, *p.* 23

normative economics, *p.* 17

open system, *p.* 16

opportunity cost, *p.* 21

Pareto optimality, *p.* 27

positive economics, *p.* 17

present value, *p.* 24

second law of thermodynamics, *p.* 17

static efficiency, *p.* 27

total benefits, *p.* 20

total cost, *p.* 22

total willingness to pay, *p.* 20

Further Reading

Freeman, A. Myrick III. *The Measurement of Environmental and Resource Values,* 2nd ed. (Washington, DC: Resources for the Future, Inc., 2003). A comprehensive and analytically rigorous survey of the concepts and methods for environmental valuation.

Hanley, Nick and Clive L. Spash. *Cost-Benefit Analysis and the Environment* (Brookfield, VT: Edward Elgar Publishing Company, 1994). An account of the theory and practice of this form of analysis applied to environmental problems. Contains numerous specific case studies.

Norton, Bryan and Ben A. Minteer. "From Environmental Ethics to Environmental Public Philosophy: Ethicists and Economists: 1973–Future," *The International Yearbook of Environmental and Resource Economics: 2002/2003,* Tietenberg, T. and H. Folmer eds. (Cheltenham, UK: Edward Elgar, 2002): 373–407. A review of the interaction between environmental ethics and economic valuation.

Scheraga, Joel D. and Frances G. Sussman. "Discounting and Environmental Management," *The International Yearbook of Environmental and Resource Economics 1998–1999,* Tietenberg, T. and H. Folmer, eds. (Cheltenham, UK: Edward Elgar, 1998): 1–32. A summary of the "state of the art" for the use of discounting in environmental management.

Discussion Question

1. It has been suggested that we should use the "net energy" criterion to make choices among various types of energy. Net energy is defined as the total energy content in the energy source minus the energy required to extract, process, and deliver it to consumers. According to this criterion, we should use those sources with the highest net energy content first. Would the dynamic efficiency criterion and the net energy criterion be expected to yield the same choice? Why or why not?

3 Valuing the Environment: Methods

For it so falls out, That what we have, we prize not to the worth, Whiles we enjoy it, but being lack'd and lost, Why, then we rack the value, then we find The virtue that possession would not show us, Whiles it was ours.

—WILLIAM SHAKESPEARE, *Much Ado about Nothing*

Introduction

In Chapter 2 we explored the concepts that lie behind economic valuation of the environment. These concepts can provide the basis for *ex ante valuation*, which is used to assess the desirability of proposed actions, or *ex post analysis*, which is used to judge either the desirability of implemented policy actions or the damage done by environmentally injurious acts such as oil spills. In this chapter we explore some of the issues and methods associated with making these concepts operational.

Historically, the process for controlling environmental risks has been broken into two components: *risk assessment* and *risk management*. Risk assessment is designed to identify the magnitude of the risk and risk management examines the desirability of various options to control it.

Risk Assessment[1]

The process of risk assessment determines if, and to what degree, exposure to a substance is harmful to the health of a given population. A distinction is made between toxicity (relative ability of any agent to cause adverse health environmental effects), hazard (an agent in a dosage harmful to a population), and risk (determination of what duration and exposure to an agent will cause detrimental effects). The risk assessment process is used in regulations dealing with water and ambient discharge, occupational and consumer product safety, and soil contamination.

---

[1]This section relies heavily on Paustenbach (2002).

(Risk assessment is typically a four-step process, although fewer steps may be involved if a substance is determined to be not harmful or if immediate action is called for.

* **Hazard identification** determines whether human or ecological exposure to an agent results in harm to that population, considering the nature and strength of the evidence of the effects.

* **Dose-response assessment** characterizes the relationship between the strength and duration of exposure to the agent and the occurrence of adverse health effects. This step considers such factors as age, pattern of exposure, sex, and lifestyle of those exposed, and relates data from animal exposure to that of humans as well as extrapolating a range of high and low exposures to the agent.

* **Exposure assessment** estimates the intensity at which populations are exposed to an agent, considering the duration and frequency of the exposure. This step must examine the size and nature of the population exposed, as well as the various pathways for exposure.

* **Risk characterization** involves the estimation of the overall effect of an agent on a given population based on the dose-response and exposure assessments.)

One of the intriguing findings that emerges from recent assessment research is that children are affected differently by environmental factors than are adults, and, therefore, a policy that does not take these differences into account may provide inadequate protection for children. The evidence reveals that children are often adversely affected by levels of toxicants deemed acceptable for adults. Risk for children may be higher because they have higher respiratory rates, higher skin-surface-to-body-mass ratios, higher metabolic rates, and kidneys that are less effective at excreting harmful substances.

Government organizations and other groups are working to evaluate old laws and regulations, particulary in regard to determining acceptable toxicant levels, creating new laws, and educating the public. In 1996 the EPA set forth its "Environmental Threats to Children" plan that included such measures as ensuring that the standards reflect elevated risks to children.

Valuing Benefits for Risk Management

While the valuation techniques we will cover can be applied to both valuing the damage caused by pollution and valuing the services provided by the environment, each context offers its unique problems. We begin our investigation of valuation techniques by exposing some of the difficulties associated with one of those contexts: pollution control.

In the United States, damage estimates are not only used in the design of policies, but they have also become important in the courts. In thinking about how much should be spent reducing risks, one component of that analysis involves calculating how large the benefits would be. Additionally, under the Comprehensive Environmental Response, Compensation, and Liability Act, local, state, or federal governments can seek monetary compensation from responsible parties for natural resources that are injured or destroyed by spills and releases of hazardous wastes. Some basis for deciding the magnitude of the award is necessary.

Types of Values

(Economists have decomposed the total economic value conferred by resources into three main components: (1) *use value*, (2) *option value*, and (3) *nonuse value*. Use value reflects the direct use of the environmental resource. Examples include fish harvested from the sea, timber harvested from the forest, water extracted from a stream for irrigation, even the scenic beauty conferred by a natural vista. If you used one of your senses—sight, sound, touch, taste or smell—to experience the resource, then you have *used* the resource. Some of these uses are called *passive use values* or *nonconsumptive use values* if the resource is not actually used up (consumed) in the process of experiencing it.) Pollution can cause a loss of use value such as when air pollution increases the vulnerability to illness, an oil spill adversely affects a fishery, or when smog enshrouds a scenic vista.

(Option value reflects the willingness to pay to preserve an option to use the environment in the future even if one is not currently using it.) Whereas use value reflects the value derived from current use, option value reflects the desire to preserve a potential for possible future use. Are you planning to go to Yellowstone National Park next summer? Would you like to pay to preserve the option to go?

(Nonuse value reflects the common observation that people are more than willing to pay for improving or preserving resources that they will never use. A pure nonuse value is also called *existence value*. Another type of nonuse value is a *bequest* value; the willingness to pay to preserve the resource for future generations.) When the Bureau of Reclamation began looking at sites for dams near the Grand Canyon, groups such as the Sierra Club protested the potential loss of this unique resource. With Glen Canyon already flooded by Lake Powell, even those who never intended to visit the area recognized the potential loss. Because this value does not derive either from direct use or potential use, it represents a very different category of value.

(These categories of value can be combined to produce the total willingness to pay (*TWP*):

$$TWP = \text{Use Value} + \text{Option Value} + \text{Nonuse Value.})$$

Since nonuse values are derived from motivations other than personal use, they are obviously less tangible than use values. Estimated nonuse values can be quite large. Therefore, it is not surprising that they are controversial. Indeed when the Department of Interior drew up its regulations on the appropriate procedures for performing natural resource damage assessment, it prohibited the inclusion of nonuse values unless use values for the incident under consideration were zero. A subsequent 1989 decision by the District of Columbia Court of Appeals (880 F. 2nd 432) overruled this decision and allowed nonuse values to be included as long as they could be measured.

Classifying Valuation Methods

Typically, the researcher's goal is to estimate the total willingness to pay for the good or service in question. This is the area under the demand curve up to the quantity consumed (recall the discussion from Chapter 2). For a market good, this calculation is relatively straightforward. However, as we examine in this chapter, nonmarket goods and services require the estimation of willingness to pay either through examining 1) behavior; 2) responses to surveys; or 3) extracting the willingness to pay from markets for related goods.

Several methods are available to estimate these values. This section will provide a brief overview to convey some sense of the range of possibilities and how they are related. Subsequent sections will provide more specific information about how they are actually used.

The possibilities are presented in Table 3.1. Direct revealed preference methods are those that are based on actual observable choices and from which actual resource values can be directly inferred. For example, in calculating the economic damage to local fishermen from an oil spill, the *revealed preference method* might calculate how much the catch declined and the resulting lost value of the lower catch. In this case, prices are directly observable, and their use allows the direct calculation of the loss in value.

Compare this with the direct stated preference case that might be used when the value is not directly observable. For example, the nonuse value of a panda bear, a right whale, or another endangered species is not directly observable. Hence, a survey might be used to derive this value by attempting to elicit the respondents' willingness to pay (their *stated preference*) for the preservation of the species.

This approach, called *contingent valuation*, provides a means of deriving values that cannot be obtained more traditionally. The simplest version of this approach merely asks respondents what value they would place on an environmental change (such as the loss of a wetlands or increased exposure to pollution) or on preserving the resource in its current state. Another version asks whether the respondent would pay $X to prevent the change or to preserve the species. The answers reveal either an upper bound (in the case of a "no" answer) or a lower bound (in the case of a "yes" answer). This version, however, presents the respondent with a more familiar question: a good with an associated price.

The major concern with the use of the contingent valuation method has been the potential for survey respondents to give biased answers. Five types of potential bias have been the focus of a large amount of research: (1) strategic bias, (2) information bias, (3) starting-point bias, (4) hypothetical bias, and (5) the observed discrepancy between willingness to pay (*WTP*) and willingness to accept (*WTA*).

Strategic bias arises when the respondent provides a biased answer in order to influence a particular outcome. For example, if a decision to preserve a stretch of river for fishing depends on whether or not the survey produces a sufficiently large value for fishing, the respondents who enjoy fishing may be tempted to provide an answer that ensures a high value rather than a lower value that reflects their true valuation.

Information bias may arise whenever respondents are forced to value attributes with which they have little or no experience. For example, the valuation by a recreationist of a loss in water quality in one body of water may be based on the ease of substituting recreation on another body

TABLE 3.1   Economic Methods for Measuring Environmental and Resource Values

Methods	Revealed Preferences	Stated Preferences
Direct	Market price	Contingent valuation
	Simulated markets	
Indirect	Travel cost	Attribute-based models
	Hedonic property values	Conjoint analysis
	Hedonic wage values	Choice experiments
	Avoidance expenditures	Contingent ranking

of water. If the respondent has no experience using the second body of water, the valuation will be based on an entirely false perception.

Starting-point bias may arise in those survey instruments in which a respondent is asked to check off his or her answers from a predefined range of possibilities. How that range is defined by the designer of the survey may affect the resulting answers. A range of $0 to $100 may produce a valuation by respondents different from, for example, a range of $10 to $100, even if no bids are in the $0 to $10 range. In a study of willingness to pay to protect nature areas in Denmark from new highway development, Ladenburg and Olsen (2008) found a gender-specific starting point bias attributed to female respondents.

Hypothetical bias can enter the picture because the respondent is being confronted by a contrived, rather than an actual, set of choices. Since he or she will not actually have to pay the estimated value, the respondent may treat the survey casually, providing ill-considered answers. One way to get a handle on the magnitude of this bias is to compare willingness to pay estimates derived from surveys directly with actual expenditures. In one survey of 10 studies, Hannemann (1994) found that although some of the studies concluded that the willingness to pay estimates derived from surveys exceeded actual expenditures, the majority found that the differences were not statistically significant. More recently, Ehmke, Lusk, and List (2008) tested whether hypothetical bias depends on national culture. In a study based on student experiments in China, France, Indiana, Kansas, and Niger, they find significant differences in bias across nations. Given that policymakers frequently rely on existing benefits estimates when making decisions on other locations, this finding should not be taken lightly, a subject we treat in more depth in a subsequent section of this chapter.

Increasingly, environmental economists are using these types of experiments to try to determine the severity of some of these biases as well as to learn how to reduce bias. Some of these experiments are conducted in a lab, such as a computer lab or a classroom.

The biases may be quite subtle. In one such experiment on voluntary provision of public goods (donations), Landry et al. (2006) found that for door-to-door interviews, an increase in physical attractiveness of the interviewer led to sizable increases in giving. When isolated by gender, they find the effect to be even stronger with solely female interviewers, partially by inducing more households to contribute (e.g., increased participation rates when males answered the door!). Their findings suggest that personal attractiveness "elicits contributions from agents who would not otherwise elect to contribute" (p. 770).

The final source of bias addresses observed gaps between willingness to pay and willingness to accept compensation. Respondents to contingent valuation surveys tend to report much higher values when asked for their willingness to accept compensation for a specified loss than if asked for their willingness to pay for a specified improvement in quantity or quality. Economic theory suggests the two should be equal. Debate 3.1 explores some possible reasons offered for the difference.

Much experimental work has been done on contingent valuation to determine how serious a problem these biases may present. One survey (Carson et al., 1994) uncovered 1,672 contingent valuation studies. Are the results from these surveys reliable enough for the policy process?

Faced with the need to answer this question in order to compute damages from oil spills, the National Oceanic and Atmospheric Administration (NOAA) convened a panel of independent economic experts (including two Nobel Prize laureates) to evaluate the use of contingent valuation methods for determining lost passive use or nonuse values. Their report, issued on January 15, 1993 (58 FR 4602), was cautiously supportive.

DEBATE 3.1

Willingness to Pay Versus Willingness to Accept: Why So Different?

Many contingent valuation studies have found that respondents tend to report much higher values for questions that ask what compensation the respondent would be willing to accept (WTA) to give something up than for questions that ask for the willingness to pay (WTP) for an incremental improvement he or she would receive. Economic theory suggests that differences between WTP and WTA should be small, but experimental findings both in environmental economics and in other microeconomic studies have found large differences. Why?

Some economists have attributed the discrepancy to a psychological endowment effect; the value of something you own is greater than something you do not. Psychologists attribute this to a form of loss aversion; their research sugests that humans tend to value losses more highly than comparable gains (Kahneman, Knetsch, and Thaler, 1990).

Others have suggested that the difference is explainable in terms of the market context. In the absence of good substitutes, large differences between WTA and WTP would be the expected outcome. In the presence of close substitutes, WTP and WTA should not be that different, but the divergence between the two measures should increase as the degree of substitution decreases (Hanemann, 1991 and Shogren et al., 1994).

The characteristics of the good may matter as well. In their review of the evidence provided by experimental studies, Horowitz and McConnell (2002) find that for "ordinary goods" the difference between WTA and WTP is smaller than for public and nonmarket goods. Their results support the notion that property rights are not neutral.

The moral context of the valuation may matter as well. Croson et al. (draft) show that WTA increases with culpability as long as the party causing the damage is also paying for the repairs. If, however, a third party is paying, WTA is insensitive to culpability. This difference suggests that the valuation includes an amount levied in punishment for the party who caused the damage (the WTA becomes the lost value plus a sanction).

Ultimately, the choice of which concept to use in environmental valuation comes down to how the associated property right is allocated. If someone owns the right to the resource, using WTA is the appropriate approach. If the respondent does not have the right, using WTP is the right approach. However, as Horowitz and McConnell point out, since the holders and nonholders of "rights" value them differently, the initial allocation of property rights will have strong influence on valuation decisions for environmental amenities.

Sources: Croson, R., J. J. Rachlinski, and J. Johnston, "Culpability as an Explanation of the WTA-WTP Discrepancy in Contingent Valuation." (Draft 2005). Hanemann, W. M., "Willingness to Pay and Willingness to Accept: How Much Can They Differ?" *American Economic Review*, 81, 635–647, 1991. Horowitz, J. K. and K. E. McConnell, "A Review of WTA/WTP Studies," *Journal of Environmental Economics and Management*, 44, 426–447, 2002. Kahneman, D., J. Knetsch, and R. Thaler, "Experimental Tests of the Endowment Effect and the Coase Theorem," *Journal of Political Economy*, 98, 1325–1348, 1990. Shogren, J. F., Senung Y. Shin, D. J. Hayes, and J. B. Kliebenstein, "Resolving Differences in Willingness to Pay and Willingness to Accept." *American Economic Review* 84 (1), 1994: 255–270.

The committee reported that it had several concerns with the technique, including the following: (1) the tendency for contingent valuation willingness to pay estimates to seem unreasonably large, (2) the difficulty in assuring the respondents have understood and absorbed the issues in the survey, and (3) the difficulty in assuring that respondents are responding to the specific issues in the survey rather than reflecting general warm feelings about public-spiritedness or the "warm glow" of giving.[2]

But the panel also made clear its conclusion that suitably designed surveys could eliminate or reduce these biases to acceptable levels and in an appendix it provided specific guidelines for determining whether a particular study was suitably designed. The panel suggested that when practitioners follow these guidelines they

> can produce estimates reliable enough to be the starting point of a judicial process of damage assessment, including lost passive-use values. ... [A well-constructed contingent valuation study] contains information that judges and juries will wish to use, in combination with other estimates, including the testimony of expert witnesses.

These guidelines have been influential in shaping more recent studies. For example, Example 3.1 shares the results of a large contingent valuation survey designed to estimate the value of preventing future oil spills. The NOAA panel report created an interesting dilemma. Although it legitimized the use of contingent valuation for estimating passive-use (nonconsumptive use) and nonuse values, the panel also set some rather rigid guidelines that reliable studies should follow. The cost of completing an "acceptable" contingent valuation study will be sufficiently high that they will only be useful for incidents in which the damages are high enough to justify their use. Yet due

---

EXAMPLE
3.1

Leave No Behavioral Trace: Using the Contingent Valuation Method to Measure Passive Use Values

Soon after the Exxon Valdez oil tanker ran aground on the Bligh Reef in Prince William Sound off the coast of Alaska on March 24, 1989, spilling approximately 11 million gallons of crude oil, the Exxon Corporation (now Exxon Mobil) accepted the liability for the damage caused by the leaking oil. This liability consisted of two parts: (1) the cost of cleaning up the spilled oil and restoring the site insofar as possible and (2) compensation for the damage caused to the local ecology. Approximately $2.1 billion was spent in cleanup efforts and Exxon also spent approximately $303 million to compensate fishermen whose livelihoods were dramatically damaged for the five years following the spill.[3] Litigation on environmental damages settled with Exxon agreeing to pay $900 million over 10 years. The punitive damages phase of this case began in May 1994. In January 2004, after many rounds of appeals, the U.S. District Court for the State of Alaska awarded punitive damages to the plaintiffs in the amount of $4.5 billion.[4] This amount was later cut almost in

---

[2] A more detailed description of the methodological issues and concerns with contingent valuation with respect to the actual Exxon Valdez contingent valuation survey can be found in Mitchell (2002).

[3] U.S. District Court for the State of Alaska, Case Number A89-0095CV, January 28, 2004.

[4] Ibid.

half to $2.5 billion—still believed to be the largest punitive damage judgment ever awarded in U.S. courts. In June 2008 the Supreme Court cut the punitive award from $2.5 billion to $507 million.

Until the Exxon Valdez tanker spilled 11 million gallons of crude oil into Prince William Sound in Alaska, the calculation of nonuse (or passive use) values was not a widely researched topic. However, following the 1989 court ruling in *Ohio v. U.S. Department of the Interior* that said lost passive use values could now be compensated within natural resources damages assessments and the passage of The Oil Pollution Act of 1990, the estimation of nonuse and passive use values became not only a topic of great debate, but also a rapidly growing research area within the economics community.

One study (Carson et al., 2003) discusses the design, implementation, and results of a large survey designed to estimate the passive use values related to large oil spills. In particular, the survey asked respondents their willingness to pay to prevent a similar disaster in the future by funding an escort ship program that would help prevent and/or contain a future spill. The survey was conducted for the State of Alaska in preparation for litigation in the case against Exxon Valdez.

The survey followed the recommendations made by the NOAA panel for conducting contingent valuation surveys and for ensuring reliable estimates. It relied upon face-to-face interviews and the sample was drawn from the national population. The study used a binary discrete choice (yes or no) question where the respondent was asked whether he or she would be willing to pay a specific amount with the amount varying across four versions of the survey. Of possible payment vehicles, the researchers chose a one-time increase in taxes as the method of payment. They also avoided any difficulty respondents may have had valuing multiple goods by using a survey that valued a single good. The survey also contained numerous pictures, maps, and background information to make sure the respondent was familiar with the good they were being asked to value.

Using the survey data, the researchers were able to estimate a valuation function by using a statistical technique known as regression analysis, which related the respondent's willingness to pay (*WTP*) to respondent characteristics. After multiplying the estimate of the median respondent's willingness to pay by the population sampled, they reported aggregate lost passive use values at $2.8 billion (in 1990 dollars). They point out that this number is a lower bound since willingness to accept (*WTA*) compensation would be a more appropriate measure of actual lost passive use from the spill (see Debate 3.1) and because median willingness to pay is less than the mean.

The Exxon Valdez spill sparked a debate about the measurement of nonuse and passive use values. Laws put into place after the spill have ensured that passive use values will be included in natural resource damage assessments. Should other parts of the world follow suit?

Source: Richard T. Carson, Robert C. Mitchell, Michael Hanemann, Raymond J. Kopp, Stanley Presser, and Paul A. Ruud, "Contingent Valuation and Lost Passive Use: Damages from the Exxon Valdez Oil Spill," *Environmental and Resource Economics* 25 (2003): 257–286.

to the paucity of other techniques, the failure to use contingent valuation may, by default, result in passive-use values of zero. Since values of zero are unlikely, a reliable method is important.

Another possible solution to the cost of new surveys is to use *benefits transfer*. Since original studies are time consuming and expensive, benefits transfer involves the application of estimates from other studies to the site being evaluated. Benefits transfer methods have been widely used in situations for which financial, time, or data constraints preclude original analysis. Policymakers frequently look to previously published studies for information that could inform a current decision. It has the advantage of being quick and inexpensive, but the accuracy of the estimates deteriorates the further the new context deviates temporally or spatially from the context used to derive the estimates.[5] Additionally, for contingent valuation estimates, as noted above, Ehmke, Lusk, and List (2008) find that hypothetical bias varies considerably across countries, possibly making benefits transfer unreliable.[6]

One key to resolving this dilemma may be provided by a technique called meta-analysis. Meta-analysis, sometimes called the "analysis of analyses," takes empirical estimates from a sample of studies, statistically relates them to the characteristics of the studies, and asks whether the reported differences can be attributed to quantifiable differences in location, subject matter, or methodology. Meta-analysis would use this cross section of contingent valuation studies as a basis for isolating the determinants of nonuse value. Once these determinants have been isolated and related to specific policy contexts, it may be possible to transfer estimates reliably from one context to another without incurring the time and expense of conducting new surveys each time.

A third category of benefit estimation involves indirect revealed preference methods. These are "observable" because they involve actual behavior and "indirect" because they infer a value rather than estimate it directly. Suppose, for example, a particular sport fishery is being threatened by pollution, and one of the damages caused by that pollution is a reduction in sportfishing. How is this loss to be valued when access to the fishery is free?

One way is through travel-cost methods. Travel-cost methods infer the value of a recreational resource (such as a sport fishery, a park, or a wildlife preserve where visitors hunt with a camera) by constructing a demand curve for willingness to pay for a "visitor day" from information on how much the visitors spent in getting to the site.

Freeman (2003) identifies two variants of this approach. In the first, analysts examine the number of trips visitors make to a site. In the second, the analysts examine whether people decide to visit a site and, if so, which site.

The first variant allows the construction of a travel-cost demand function. The value of the *flow* of services from that site is the area under the estimated demand curve for those services or for access to the site, aggregated over all who visit the site.

The second variant allows the analysis of how specific site characteristics influence choice and, therefore, indirectly how valuable those characteristics are. Knowledge of how the value of each site varies with respect to its characteristics allows the analyst to value how degradation of those characteristics (e.g., from pollution) would lower the value of the site.

---

[5]Whittington (2002) examines the reasons why so many contingent valuation studies in developing countries are unhelpful. Poorly designed or rapidly implemented surveys could result in costly policy mistakes on topics that are very important in the developing world. The current push for cheaper, quicker studies is risky and researchers need to be very cautious.

[6]Several examples of the use of meta-analysis and benefits transfer are given in (Florax et al., 2002). A critique and alternative to benefits transfer is offered in (Smith et al., 2002).

Travel-cost models have been used to value beach closures during oil spills, fish consumption advisories, the cost of development that has eliminated a recreation area, and even activities such as rock climbing. The methodology for both variants is detailed in Parsons (2003). In an approach known as the random utility model, a person choosing a particular site takes into consideration site characteristics and its price (trip cost). Characteristics affecting the site choice include ease of access and environmental quality. Each site results in a unique level of utility and a person is assumed to choose the site giving the highest level of utility. Welfare losses from an event such as an oil spill can then be measured by the resulting change in utility should the person have to choose an alternate site.

Two other indirect observable methods are known as the *hedonic property value method* and the *hedonic wage method*. They share the characteristic that they use multiple regression analysis to isolate and identify the environmental component of value in a related market. For example, it is possible to discover that, all other things being equal, property values are lower in polluted neighborhoods than in clean neighborhoods. (Property values fall in polluted neighborhoods because they are less desirable places to live.) Freeman (2003) examines the hedonic approach in detail.

Hedonic property value models decompose market data (house prices) by breaking down the house sales price into its components, including the house characteristics (e.g., number of bedrooms, lot size, and features); the neighborhood characteristics (e.g., crime rates and school quality); and environmental characteristics (e.g., air quality, percentage of open space nearby, and distance to a local landfill). Hedonic models allow for the measurement of the marginal willingness to pay for discrete changes in an attribute.

Numerous studies have utilized this approach to examine the effect on property value of things such as distance to a hazardous waste site (Michaels and Smith, 1990); large farm operations (Palmquist et al., 1997); and open space and land use patterns (Bockstael, 1996; Geoghegan et al., 1997; and Acharya and Bennett, 2001). Quite a few studies incorporate air quality variables. (For a meta-analysis on air pollution and housing prices see Smith and Huang (1993).)

Hedonic wage approaches are similar except that they attempt to isolate the component of wages that serve to compensate workers in risky occupations for taking on the risk. It is well known that workers in high-risk occupations demand higher wages in order to be induced to undertake the risks. When an environmental risk (such as exposure to a toxic substance) is known to those exposed, the results of the multiple regression analysis can be used to construct a willingness to pay to avoid this kind of environmental risk. Additionally, the compensating wage differential can be used to calculate the value of a statistical life (Taylor, 2003), a topic discussed in a later section of this chapter.

A final example of an indirect observable method involves examining "averting or defensive expenditures." Averting expenditures are those designed to reduce the damage caused by pollution by taking some kind of averting or defensive action. An example would be to install indoor air purifiers in response to an influx of polluted air or to rely on bottled water as a response to the pollution of local drinking water supplies (see Example 3.2). Since people would not normally spend more to prevent a problem than would be caused by the problem itself, averting expenditures can provide a lower-bound estimate of the damage caused by pollution.

The final category, indirect hypothetical methods, includes several *attribute-based methods*. Attribute-based methods such as *contingent ranking* and choice-based, conjoint models are useful when project options have multiple levels of different attributes. Like contingent valuation, *conjoint analysis* is also a survey-based technique, but instead of stating a willingness to pay,

EXAMPLE
3.2

Valuing Damage from Groundwater Contamination Using Averting Expenditures

How many resources should be allocated to the prevention of groundwater contamination? In part that depends on how serious a risk is posed by the contamination. One way to obtain a lower-bound estimate on the damage caused by contamination is to discover how much people are willing to spend to defend themselves against the threat.

In late 1987 trichloroethylene (TCE) was detected in one of the town wells in Perkasie, a town in southeastern Pennsylvania. Concentrations of the chemical were seven times the EPA's safety standard. Since no temporary solution was available to reduce concentrations to safe levels, the county required the town to notify customers of the contamination.

Once notified, consumers took one or more of the following actions: (1) they purchased more bottled water; (2) they started using bottled water; (3) they installed home water treatment systems; (4) they hauled water from alternative sources; and (5) they boiled water. Through a survey, analysts were able to discover the extent of each of these actions and combine that information with their associated costs.

The results indicated that residents spent between $61,313.29 and $131,334.06 over the 88-week period of the contamination to protect themselves from the effects. They further indicated that families with young children were more likely to take averting actions and, among those families who took averting actions, to spend more on those actions than childless families.

Source: Charles W. Abdalla et al., "Valuing Environmental Quality Changes Using Averting Expenditures: An Application to Groundwater Contamination," *Land Economics* 68(2), 1992: 163–169.

respondents choose between alternate states of the world. Each state of the world has a set of attributes and a price.

Consider an example (Boyle et al., 2001) that surveyed Maine residents on their preferences for alternative forest harvesting practices. The State of Maine was considering purchasing a 23,000-acre tract of forest land to manage. Attributes used in the survey included the number of live trees, management practice for dead trees, percent of land set aside, and a tax payment. Three levels of each management attribute and 13 different tax prices were considered. Table 3.2 reproduces the specific attributes used in the study.

Respondents were given a choice set of four different alternative management plans and the status quo (no purchase). Table 3.3 demonstrates a sample survey question. This type of survey has evolved from both contingent valuation and marketing studies. This approach allows the respondent to make a familiar choice (choose a price-attribute bundle) and allows the researcher to derive marginal willingness to pay for an attribute from that choice.

(Contingent ranking, another survey method, also falls within this final category. Respondents are given a set of hypothetical situations that differ in terms of the environmental amenity available (instead of a bundle of attributes) and are asked to rank order them. These rankings

TABLE 3.2   Attributes in the Maine Forest Harvesting Conjoint Analysis

Attribute	Level
Live trees after harvesting	No trees (clear cut)
	153 trees/acre
	459 trees/acre
Dead trees after harvesting	Remove all
	5 trees/acre
	10 trees/acre
Percent of forest set aside from harvest	20%
	50%
	80%

Source: Boyle et al. (2001) and Holmes and Adamovicz (2003).

TABLE 3.3   A Sample Conjoint Analysis Survey Question

Attribute	Alternatives				
	A	B	C	D	E
Remaining live trees	No trees	459/acre	No trees	153/acre	No change
Removing dead trees	Remove all	Remove all	5/acre	10/acre	No change
Percent set aside	80%	20%	50%	20%	No change
Tax	$40	$200	$10	$80	No change
I would vote for (please check off)	☐	☐	☐	☐	☐

Source: Holmes, Thomas P. and Wiktor L. Adamowicz, "Attribute-Based Methods," *A Primer on Nonmarket Valuation*, Bateman, Ian, ed. (The Netherlands: Kluwer Academic Publishers, 2003): Chapter 6.

can then be compared to see the implicit trade-offs between more of the environmental amenity and less of the other characteristics. When one or more of these characteristics can be expressed in terms of a monetary value, it is possible to use this information and the rankings to impute a value to the environmental amenity.)

Sometimes a valuation exercise may use more than one of these techniques simultaneously. In some cases multiple techniques are necessary to capture the total economic value; in other cases they are used to provide independent estimates of the value being sought.

Using Geographic Information Systems for Economic Valuation

Geographic Information Systems (GIS) are computerized mapping models and analysis tools. A GIS map is made up of layers such that many variables can be visualized simultaneously using overlays. Use of Geographic Information Systems (GIS) to inform economic analysis is a relatively recent addition to the economist's tool kit. GIS offers a powerful collection of tools for depicting and examining spatial relationships. Most simply, GIS can be used to produce compelling graphics that convey the spatial structure of data and communicate analytic results with a force and clarity otherwise impossible. But the technology's real value lies in the potential it brings to ask novel questions and enrich our understanding of social and economic processes by explicitly considering their spatial structure. Models that address environmental externalities have, almost by definition, a strong spatial component. GIS can contribute, for example, to incorporating spatial dimensions into such areas as benefit/cost analysis (Bateman et al., 2002) and urban and real estate economics (Clapp et al., 1997).

Hedonic property valuation models have also recently been refined using GIS technology. Since hedonic property models are fundamentally spatial in nature, their use of GIS is a natural fit. Housing prices vary systematically and predictably from neighborhood to neighborhood. Spatial characteristics, from air quality to the availability of open space, can influence property values of entire neighborhoods; if one house enjoys abundant open space or especially good air quality, it is highly likely that its neighbors do as well.

Lewis, Bohlen, and Wilson (2008) use GIS and statistical analysis to evaluate the impacts of dams and dam removal on local property values. In a unique "experiment" they collected data on property sales for 10 years (before and after) the removal of the Edwards Dam on the Kennebec River in Maine, the first federally licensed hydropower dam to be removed primarily for the purpose of river restoration. They also collected data on property sales approximately 20 miles upstream where two other dams remained in place. GIS technology enhanced this study by facilitating the calculation of the distance from each home to both the river and the nearby dams. Lewis et al. found that living close to a dam extracted a penalty relative to living further away.[7] In other words, willingness to pay for identical housing was higher, the further away from the dam the house was located. They also found that the penalty near the Edwards Dam site dropped to nearly zero after the dam was removed. Interestingly, the penalty associated with the upstream dams remained, but its magnitude also fell after the removal of the downstream dam. Can you think of reasons why?[8] Example 3.3 shows how the use of GIS can enable hedonic property value models to investigate how the view from a particular piece of property might affect its value.

Valuing Human Life

One fascinating public policy area where these various approaches have been applied is in the valuation of human life. Many government programs, from those controlling hazardous pollutants in the workplace or in drinking water, to those improving nuclear power plant safety, are designed to save human lives as well as to reduce illness. How resources should be allocated among these programs depends crucially on the value of human life. How is life to be valued?

The simple answer, of course, is that life is priceless, but that observation turns out to be not very helpful. Because the resources used to prevent loss of life are scarce, choices must be made. The economic approach to valuing lifesaving reductions in environmental risk is to calculate the

---

[7]And relative to other waterfront housing.

[8]Lewis, Lynne Y., Curtis Bohlen, and Sarah Wilson. 2008. "Dams, Dam Removal and River Restoration: A Hedonic Analysis," *Contemporary Economic Policy*, 26(2):175–186. Interestingly, after this study was complete, one of the two upstream dams, the Fort Halifax Dam, was removed in July 2008 after years of litigation about its removal.

EXAMPLE

3.3

Using GIS to Inform Hedonic Property Values: Visualizing the Data

For nonmarket valuation, GIS has proven to be especially helpful in enhancing hedonic property value models by incorporating both the proximity of environmental characteristics and their size or amount. GIS studies have also allowed for the incorporation of variables that reflect nearby types and diversity of land use.

Geo-coding housing transactions assigns a latitude and longitude coordinate to each sale. GIS allows other spatial data such as land use, watercourses, and census data to be "layered" on top of the map. By drawing a circle around each house of the desired circumference, GIS can help analysts calculate the amount of each amenity that is in that circle as well as the density and types of people who live there. Numerous census data are available on variables such as income, age, education, crime rates, commuting time, and so on. GIS also makes it relatively easy to calculate straight-line distances to desired (or undesired) locations such as parks, lakes, schools, or landfills.

In their paper entitled "Out of Sight, Out of Mind? Using GIS to Incorporate Visibility in Hedonic Property Value Models," Paterson and Boyle (2002) use GIS to measure the extent to which visibility measures affect house prices in Connecticut. In their study visibility is measured as the percentage of land visible within one kilometer of the property, both in total and broken out for various land use categories. Finally, they added variables that measured the percentage of area within one kilometer of each house transaction that is developed, in agriculture, forested, or covered by water.

They find that visibility is indeed an important environmental variable in explaining property values, but the nature of the viewshed matters. While simply having a view is not a significant determinant of property values, viewing certain types of land use is. For example, proximity to development reduces property values, but only if the development is visible, suggesting that out of sight, really does mean out of mind! They conclude that any analysis that omits variables that reflect nearby environmental conditions can lead to misleading or incorrect conclusions about the impacts of land use on property values. GIS is a powerful tool for helping researchers include these important variables.

Source: Robert Paterson and Kevin Boyle, "Out of Sight, Out of Mind? Using GIS to Incorporate Visibility in Hedonic Property Value Models" *Land Economics*, 2002.

change in the probability of death resulting from the reduction in environmental risk and to place a value on the probability change. Thus, it is not life itself that is being valued, but rather a reduction in the probability that some segment of the population could be expected to die earlier than otherwise. Debate 3.2 examines this controversy.

Although it is the increased probability of death that is being evaluated, it is possible to translate the value derived from this procedure into an "implied value of human life." This is accomplished by dividing the amount each individual is willing to pay for a specific reduction in the probability of death by the probability reduction. Suppose, for example, that a particular environmental policy could be expected to reduce the average concentration of a toxic substance

DEBATE 3.2

Is Valuing Human Life Immoral?

In 2004 economist Frank Ackerman and lawyer Lisa Heinzerling teamed up to write a book that questions the morality of using benefit/cost analysis to evaluate regulations designed to protect human life. In *Priceless: On Knowing the Price of Everything and the Value of Nothing* (2004), they argue that benefit/cost analysis is immoral because it represents a retreat from the traditional standard that all citizens have an absolute right to be free from harm caused by pollution. When it justifies a regulation that will allow some pollution-induced deaths, benefits/cost analysis violates this absolute right.

Economist Maureen Cropper responds that to the contrary it would be immoral not to consider the effectiveness of lifesaving measures. Resources are scarce and they must be allocated so as to produce the greatest good. If all pollution were reduced to zero, even if that were possible, the cost would be extremely high and the resources to cover that cost would have to be diverted from other beneficial uses. Professor Cropper also suggests that it would be immoral to impose costs on people about which they have no say—for example, the costs of additional pollution controls—without at least trying to consider what choices people would make themselves. Like it or not, hard choices must be made.

Cropper also points out that people are always making decisions that recognize a trade-off between the cost of more protection and the health consequences of not taking the protection. Thinking in terms of trade-offs is a familiar concept. She points out that people drive faster to save time, thereby increasing their risk of dying. They also decide how much money to spend on medicines to lower their risk of disease or they may take jobs that pose morbidity or even mortality risks if the wages are high enough.

In her response to Ackerman and Heinzerling, Cropper acknowledges that benefit/cost analysis has its flaws and that it should never be the only decision-making guide. Nonetheless, she argues that it does add useful information to the process and throwing that information away could prove to be detrimental to the very people that Ackerman and Heinzerling seek to protect.

Sources: Frank Ackerman and Lisa Heinzerling, *Priceless: On Knowing the Price of Everything and the Value of Nothing* (New York: The New Press, 2004); Frank Ackerman, "Morality, Cost-Benefit and the Price of Life," *Environmental Forum* (21)5, 2004: 46–47; and Maureen Cropper, "Immoral Not to Weigh Benefits Against Costs," *Environmental Forum* (21)5, 2004: 47–48.

to which one million people are exposed. Suppose further that this reduction in exposure could be expected to reduce the risk of death from 1 out of 100,000 to 1 out of 150,000. This implies that the number of expected deaths would fall from 10 to 6.67 in the exposed population as a result of this policy. If each of the one million people exposed is willing to pay $15 for this risk reduction (for a total of $15 million), then the implied value of a life is approximately $4.5 million ($15 million divided by 3.33).

What actual values have been derived from these methods? A survey (Viscusi, 1996) of a large number of studies examining reductions in a number of life-threatening risks found that most implied values for human life (in 1984 dollars) were between $3 million and $7 million. This same survey went on to suggest that the most appropriate estimates were probably closer to the $5 million estimate. In other words, all government programs resulting in risk reductions costing less than $5 million would be justified in benefit/cost terms. Those costing more might or might not be justified, depending on the appropriate value of a life saved in the particular risk context being examined. In 2008 the Bush administration's EPA used $6.9 million in current dollars as the value of a human life. Interestingly this value represents a drop of nearly $1 million from just five years earlier. The controversial rationale for the drop was based on some newer studies that produced lower estimates, a rationale that was not even universally accepted within EPA. The agency's water division, for example, never adopted the change and as of 2006 was using $8.7 million in current dollars.

How have health, safety, and environmental regulations lived up to this recommendation? As Table 3.4 suggests, not very well. A very large number of regulations listed in that table could be justified only if the value of a life saved were much higher than the upper value of $7 million.

TABLE 3.4   The Cost of Risk-Reducing Regulations

	Agency, Year, and Status	Initial Annual Risk[a]	Annual Lives Saved	Cost Per Life Saved (millions of 1984 $)
Unvented space heaters	CPSC 1980 F	2.7 in 10^5	63.000	$ .10
Cabin fire protection	FAA 1985 F	6.5 in 10^8	15.000	.20
Passive restraints/belts	NHTSA 1984 F	9.1 in 10^5	1,850.000	.30
Seat cushion flammability	FAA 1984 F	1.6 in 10^7	37.000	.60
Floor emergency lighting	FAA 1984 F	2.2 in 10^8	5.000	.70
Concrete & masonry construction	OSHA 1988 F	1.4 in 10^5	6.500	1.40
Hazard communication	OSHA 1983 F	4.0 in 10^5	200.000	1.80
Benzene/fugitive emissions	EPA 1984 F	2.1 in 10^4	0.310	2.80
Radionuclides/uranium mines	EPA 1984 F	1.4 in 10^4	1.100	6.90
Benzene	OSHA 1987 F	8.8 in 10^4	3.800	17.10
Asbestos	EPA 1989 F	2.9 in 10^5	10.000	104.20
Benzene/storage	EPA 1984 R	6.0 in 10^7	0.043	202.00
Radionuclides/DOE facilities	EPA 1984 R	4.3 in 10^6	0.001	210.00
Radionuclides/elemental phosphorous	EPA 1984 R	1.4 in 10^5	0.046	270.00
Benzene/ethylbenzenol styrene	EPA 1984 R	2.0 in 10^6	0.006	483.00
Arsenic/low-arsenic copper	EPA 1986 R	2.6 in 10^4	0.090	764.00
Benzene/maleic anhydride	EPA 1984 R	1.1 in 10^6	0.029	820.00
Land disposal	EPA 1988 F	2.3 in 10^8	2.520	3,500.00
Formaldehyde	OSHA 1987 F	6.8 in 10^4	0.010	72,000.00

[a] "Initial Annual Risk" indicates annual deaths per exposed population; an exposed population of 10^3 is 1,000, 10^4 is 10,000, and so on. In the "Agency Year and Status" column, R and F represent Rejected and Final rule, respectively.

Sources: Adapted from Viscusi, W. Kip, "Economic Foundations of the Current Regulatory Reform Efforts," *The Journal of Economic Perspectives* 10 (1996): Tables 1 and 2, 124–125.

Issues in Benefit Estimation

The analyst charged with the responsibility for performing a benefit/cost analysis encounters many decision points requiring judgment. If we are to understand benefit/cost analysis, the nature of these judgments must be clear in our minds.

Primary Versus Secondary Effects. Environmental projects usually trigger both primary and secondary consequences. For example, a primary effect of cleaning up an urban park will be an increase in recreational uses of the park. This primary effect will cause a further ripple effect on services provided to the increased number of users of the park by providers outside the park (such as restaurants or souvenir shops). Are these secondary benefits to be counted?

The answer depends upon the employment conditions in the surrounding area. If this increase in demand results in employment of previously unused resources, such as labor, the value of the increased employment should be counted. If, on the other hand, the increase in demand is met by a shift in previously employed resources from one use to another, it is a different story. In general, secondary employment benefits should be counted in high unemployment areas or when the particular skills demanded are underemployed at the time the project is commenced. This should not be counted when the project simply results in a rearrangement of productively employed resources.

Accounting Stance. The accounting stance refers to the geographic scale at which the benefits are measured. Who benefits? If a proposed project is funded by a national government, but benefits a local or regional area, a cost-benefit analysis will look quite different depending on whether the analysis is done at the regional or national scale.

Tangible Versus Intangible Benefits. *Tangible benefits* are those that can reasonably be assigned a monetary value. *Intangible benefits* are those that cannot be assigned a monetary value, either because data are not available or reliable enough or because it is not clear how to measure the value even with data.[9]

How are intangible benefits to be handled? One answer is perfectly clear: They should not be ignored. To ignore intangible benefits is to bias the results. That benefits are intangible does not mean they are unimportant.

Intangible benefits should be quantified to the fullest extent possible. One frequently used technique is to conduct a sensitivity analysis of the estimated benefit values derived from less than perfectly reliable data. We can determine, for example, whether or not the outcome is sensitive, within wide ranges, to the value of this benefit. If not, then very little time has to be spent on the problem. If the outcome is sensitive, the person or persons making the decision bear the ultimate responsibility for weighing the importance of that benefit.

Approaches to Cost Estimation

Estimating costs is generally easier than estimating benefits, but that does not mean it is easy. One major problem for both derives from the fact that benefit/cost analysis is forward-looking and thus requires an estimate of what a particular strategy *will* cost, which is much more difficult than tracking down what an existing strategy *does* cost.

---

[9]The division between tangible and intangible benefits changes as our techniques improve. Recreation benefits were, until the advent of the travel-cost model, treated as intangible.

(Another frequent problem is posed by collecting cost information when availability of that information is controlled by a firm having an interest in the outcome.) Pollution control is an obvious example. Two approaches have been used to deal with this problem.

The Survey Approach.   One way to discover the costs associated with a policy is to ask those who bear the costs, and presumably know the most about them, to reveal the magnitude of the costs to policymakers. Polluters, for example, could be asked to provide control-cost estimates to regulatory bodies. The problem with this approach is the strong incentive not to be truthful. An overestimate of the costs can trigger less stringent regulation; therefore, it is financially advantageous to provide overinflated estimates.

The Engineering Approach. The engineering approach bypasses the source being regulated by using general engineering information to catalog the possible technologies that could be used to meet the objective and to estimate the costs of purchasing and using those technologies. The final step in the engineering approach is to assume that the sources would use technologies that minimize cost. This produces a cost estimate for a "typical," well-informed firm.

The engineering approach has its own problems. These estimates may not approximate the actual cost of any particular firm. Unique circumstances may cause the costs of that firm to be higher, or lower, than estimated; the firm, in short, may not be typical.

The Combined Approach. To circumvent these problems, analysts frequently use a combination of survey and engineering approaches. The survey approach collects information on possible technologies, as well as special circumstances facing the firm. Engineering approaches are used to derive the actual costs of those technologies, given the special circumstances. This combined approach attempts to balance information best supplied by the source with that best derived independently.

In the cases described so far, the costs are relatively easy to quantify and the problem is simply finding a way to acquire the best information. This is not always the case, however. Some costs are not easy to quantify, although economists have developed some ingenious ways to secure monetary estimates even for those costs.

Take, for example, a policy designed to conserve energy by forcing more people to carpool. If the effect of this is simply to increase the average time of travel, how is this cost to be measured?

For some time, transportation analysts have recognized that people value their time, and much literature has evolved to provide estimates of this valuation. The basis for this valuation is opportunity cost—how the time might be used if it weren't being consumed in travel. Although the results of these studies depend on the amount of time involved, individuals seem to value their time typically at a rate not more than half their wage rates.

The Treatment of Risk

For many environmental problems, it is not possible to state with certainty what consequences a particular policy will have, because scientific estimates themselves often are imprecise. Determining the efficient exposure to potentially toxic substances requires obtaining results at high doses and extrapolating to low doses, as well as extrapolating from animal studies to humans. It also requires relying upon epidemiological studies that infer a pollution-induced adverse human health impact from correlations between indicators of health in human populations and recorded pollution levels.

For example, consider the potential damages from climate change. While most scientists now agree on the potential impacts of climate change such as sea level rise and species losses, the timing and extent of those losses is uncertain.

As noted in the opening of this chapter, the treatment of risk in the policy process involves two major dimensions: (1) identifying and quantifying the risks and (2) deciding how much risk is acceptable. The former is primarily scientific and descriptive, while the latter is more evaluative and normative.

Benefit/cost analysis grapples with the evaluation of risk in several ways. Suppose, for example, that we have a range of policy options *A, B, C, D* and a range of possible outcomes *E, F, G* for each of these policies depending on how the economy evolves over the future. These outcomes, for example, might depend on whether the demand growth for the resource is low, medium, or high. Thus, if we choose policy *A*, we might end up with outcomes *AE, AF,* or *AG*. Each of the other policies has three possible outcomes as well, yielding a total of 12 possible outcomes.

We could conduct a separate benefit/cost analysis for each of the 12 possible outcomes. Unfortunately, the policy that maximizes net benefits for *E* may be different from that which maximizes net benefits for *F* or *G*. Thus, if we only knew which outcome would prevail, we could select the policy that maximized net benefits; the problem is that we do not. Furthermore, choosing the policy that is best if outcome *E* prevails may be disastrous if *G* results instead.

When a dominant policy emerges, this problem is avoided. A *dominant policy* is one that confers higher net benefits for every outcome. In this case, the existence of risk concerning the future is not relevant for the policy choice. This fortuitous circumstance is exceptional rather than common, but it can occur.

Other options exist even when dominant solutions do not emerge. Suppose, for example, that we were able to assess the likelihood that each of the three possible outcomes would occur. Thus, we might expect outcome *E* to occur with probability 0.5, *F* with probability 0.3, and *G* with probability 0.2. Armed with this information, we can estimate the expected present value of net benefits. The *expected present value of net benefits* for a particular policy is defined as the sum over outcomes of the present value of net benefits for that policy where each outcome is weighted by its probability of occurrence. Symbolically this is expressed as

$$EPVNB_j = \sum_{i=0}^{I} P_i PVNB_{ij}, \qquad j = 1, \ldots, J,$$

where

$EPVNB_j$ = expected present value of net benefits for policy *j*
P_i = probability of the *i*th outcome occurring
$PVNB_{ij}$ = present value of net benefits for policy *j* if outcome *i* prevails
J = number of policies being considered
I = number of outcomes being considered

The final step is to select the policy with the highest expected present value of net benefits.

This approach has the substantial virtue that it weighs higher probability outcomes more heavily. It also, however, makes a specific assumption about society's preference for risk. This approach is appropriate if society is risk-neutral. *Risk-neutrality* can be defined most easily by the use of an example. Suppose you were allowed to choose between being given a definite $50 or entering a lottery in which you had a 50 percent chance of winning $100 and a 50 percent chance of winning nothing. (Notice that the expected value of this lottery is $50 = 0.5($100) + 0.5($0).) You would be said to be risk-neutral if you would be indifferent between these two choices. If you view the lottery as more attractive, you would be exhibiting *risk-loving* behavior, while a preference for the definite $50 would suggest *risk-averse* behavior. Using the expected present value of net benefits approach implies that society is risk-neutral.

Is that a valid assumption? The evidence is mixed. The existence of gambling suggests that at least some members of society are risk-loving while the existence of insurance suggests that at least for some risks, others are risk-averse. Since the same people may gamble and own insurance policies, it is likely that the type of risk may be important.

Even if individuals were demonstrably risk-averse, this would not be a sufficient condition for the government to forsake risk-neutrality in evaluating public investments. One famous article (Arrow and Lind, 1970) argues that risk-neutrality is appropriate since "when the risks of a public investment are publicly borne, the total cost of risk-bearing is insignificant and, therefore, the government should ignore uncertainty in evaluating public investments." The logic behind this result suggests that as the number of risk bearers (and the degree of diversification of risks) increases, the amount of risk borne by any individual diminishes to zero.

When the decision is irreversible, as demonstrated by Arrow and Fisher (1974), considerably more caution is appropriate. Irreversible decisions may subsequently be regretted, but the option to change course will be lost forever. Extra caution also affords an opportunity to learn more about alternatives to this decision and its consequences before acting. Isn't it comforting to know that occasionally procrastination can be optimal?

National policy in both the courts and the legislature has demonstrated some tendency to search for imaginative ways to define acceptable risk. In general, the policy approaches reflect a case-by-case approach. We will see that current policy reflects a high degree of risk aversion toward a number of environmental problems.

Choosing the Discount Rate

In Chapter 2 we discussed how the discount rate could be defined conceptually as the social opportunity cost of capital. This cost of capital can be divided further into two components: (1) the riskless cost of capital and (2) the risk premium. The choice of the discount rate can influence policy decisions. Recall that discounting allows us to compare all costs and benefits in current dollars, regardless of when the benefits accrue or costs are charged. Suppose, for example, that a project will cost $4,000,000 up front (today's dollars). Revenue or benefits will not be earned until five years out and will equal $5,500,000. Is this project a good idea? On the surface it might seem like it is, but recall that $5,500,000 in five years is not the same as $5,500,000 today. At a discount rate of 5%, the present value of benefits minus the present value of costs is positive. However, at a 10 percent discount rate, this same calculation yields a negative value! The present value of costs exceeds the benefits. Can you see why?

As Example 3.4 indicates, this has been, and continues to be, an important issue. When the public sector uses a discount rate lower than that in the private sector, the public sector will find more projects with longer payoff periods worthy of authorization. And, as we have already seen, the discount rate is a major determinant of the allocation of resources among generations as well.

EXAMPLE

3.4

The Historical Importance of the Discount Rate

For years the United States and Canada had been discussing the possibility of constructing a tidal power project in the Passamaquoddy Bay between Maine and New Brunswick. This project would have heavy initial capital costs, but low operating costs that presumably would hold for a long time into the future. As part of their analysis of the situation, a complete inventory of costs and benefits was completed in 1959.

Using the same benefit and cost figures, Canada concluded that the project should not be built, while the United States concluded that it should. Because these conclusions were based on the same benefit/cost data, the differences can be attributed solely to the use of different discount rates. The United States used 2.5 percent while Canada used 4.125 percent. The higher discount rate makes the initial cost weigh much more heavily in the calculation, leading to the Canadian conclusion that the project would yield a negative net benefit. Since the lower discount rate weights the lower future operating costs relatively more heavily, Americans saw the net benefit as positive.

Other examples are not hard to find. In 1962 Congress authorized a number of water projects that had been justified by benefit/cost analysis using a discount rate of 2.63 percent. Upon examining these projects, economists (Fox and Herfindahl, 1964, p. 202) found that, at a discount rate considered more reasonable at the time (8 percent), only 20 percent of the projects would have had favorable benefit/cost ratios.

The choice of the discount rate played a major role following a highly publicized dispute between President Jimmy Carter and Congress. President Carter wanted to rescind authorization from many previously approved water projects that he viewed as wasteful, but Congress did not. The President based his conclusions on a 6.38 percent discount rate while Congress was using a lower one.

Far from being an esoteric subject, the choice of the discount rate is fundamentally important in defining the role of the public sector, the types of projects undertaken, and the allocation of resources across generations.

Sources: Edith Stokey and Richard Zeckhauser, *A Primer for Policy Analysis* (New York: W. W. Norton, 1978): 164–165; Raymond Mikesell, *The Rate of Discount for Evaluating Public Projects* (Washington, DC: The American Enterprise Institute for Public Policy Research, 1977): 3–5; Irving K. Fox and Orris C. Herfindahl, "Attainment of Efficiency in Satisfying Demands for Water Resources," *American Economic Review* 54 (May 1964): 202.

Traditionally, economists have used long-term interest rates on government bonds as one measure of the cost of capital, adjusted by a risk premium that would depend on the riskiness of the project considered. Unfortunately, the choice of how large an adjustment to make has been left to the discretion of the analysts. This ability to affect the desirability of a particular project or policy by the choice of discount rate led to a situation in which government agencies were using a variety of discount rates to justify programs or projects they supported. One set of hearings conducted by Congress during the 1960s discovered that, at one time, agencies were using discount rates ranging from 0 to 20 percent.

During the early 1970s the Office of Management and Budget published a circular that required, with some exceptions, all government agencies to use a 10 percent discount rate in their benefit/cost analysis. A revision issued in 1992 reduced the required discount rate to 7 percent. This circular also includes guidelines for benefit/cost analysis and specifies that certain rates will change annually.[11] This standardization reduces biases by eliminating the agency's ability to choose a discount rate that justifies a predetermined conclusion. It also allows a project to be considered independently of fluctuations in the true social cost of capital due to cycles in the behavior of the economy. On the other hand, when the social opportunity cost of capital differs from this administratively determined level, the benefit/cost analysis will not, in general, define the efficient allocation.

A Critical Appraisal

We have seen that it is sometimes, but not always, difficult to estimate benefits and costs. When this estimation is difficult or unreliable, it limits the value of a benefit/cost analysis. This problem would be particularly disturbing if biases tended to increase or decrease net benefits systematically. Do such biases exist?

In the early 1970s Robert Haveman (1972) conducted a major study that sheds some light on this question. Focusing on Army Corps of Engineers water projects, such as flood control, navigation, and hydroelectric power generation, Haveman compared the *ex ante* (before the fact) estimate of benefits and costs with their *ex post* (after the fact) counterparts. Thus, he was able to address the issues of accuracy and bias. He concluded the following:

> *In the empirical case studies presented,* ex post *estimates often showed little relationship to their* ex ante *counterparts. On the basis of the few cases and the* a priori *analysis presented here, one could conclude that there is a serious bias incorporated into agency* ex ante *evaluation procedures, resulting in persistent overstatement of expected benefits. Similarly in the analysis of project construction costs, enormous variance was found among projects in the relationship between estimated and realized costs. Although no persistent bias in estimation was apparent, nearly 50 percent of the projects displayed realized costs that deviated by more than plus or minus 20 percent from* ex ante *projected costs.*[12]

In the cases examined by Haveman, at least, the notion that benefit/cost analysis is purely a scientific exercise was clearly not consistent with the evidence; the biases of the analysts were merely translated into numbers.

Does their analysis mean that benefit/cost analysis is fatally flawed? Absolutely not! It does, however, highlight the importance of calculating an accurate value and of including all of the potential benefits and costs (for example, nonmarket values). It also serves to remind us, however, that benefit/cost analysis is not a stand-alone technique. It should be used in conjunction with other available information. Economic analysis, including benefit/cost analysis, can provide useful information, but it should not be the only determinant for all decisions.

Another shortcoming of benefit/cost analysis is that it does not really address the question of who reaps the benefits and who pays the cost. It is quite possible for a particular course of action to yield high net benefits, but to have the benefits borne by one group of society and the

---

[11]Annual rates can be found at http://www.whitehouse.gov/omb/.

[12]A more recent assessment of costs (Harrington et al., 1999) found evidence of both overestimation and underestimation, although overestimation was more common. The authors attributed the overestimation mainly to a failure to anticipate technical innovation.

costs borne by another. This admittedly extreme case does serve to illustrate a basic principle—ensuring that a particular policy is efficient provides an important, but not always the sole, basis for public policy. Other aspects, such as who reaps the benefit or bears the burden, are also important.

In summary, on the positive side, benefit/cost analysis is frequently a very useful part of the policy process. Even when the underlying data are not strictly reliable, the outcomes may not be sensitive to that unreliability. In other circumstances, the data may be reliable enough to give indications of the consequences of broad policy directions, even when they are not reliable enough to fine-tune those policies. Benefit/cost analysis, when done correctly, can provide a useful complement to the other influences on the political process by providing a constructive collection of information to decision makers.

On the negative side, benefit/cost analysis has been attacked as seeming to promise more than can actually be delivered, particularly in the absence of solid benefit information. This concern has triggered two responses. First, regulatory processes have been developed that can be implemented with very little information and yet have desirable economic properties. The recent reforms in air pollution control, which we will cover in Chapter 16, provide one powerful example.

The second response involves techniques that supply useful information to the policy process without relying on controversial techniques to monetize environmental services that are difficult to value. The rest of this chapter deals with the two most prominent of these—*cost-effectiveness analysis* and *impact analysis*.

Even when benefits are difficult or impossible to quantify, economic analysis has much to offer. Policy-makers should know, for example, how much various policy actions will cost and what their impacts on society will be, even if the efficient policy choice cannot be identified with any certainty. Cost-effectiveness analysis and impact analysis both respond to this need, albeit in different ways.

⬤ Cost-Effectiveness Analysis

What can be done to guide policy when the requisite valuation for benefit/cost analysis is either unavailable or not sufficiently reliable? Without a good measure of benefits, making an efficient choice is no longer possible.

In such cases, frequently it is possible, however, to set a policy target on some basis other than a strict comparison of benefits and costs. One example is pollution control. What level of pollution should be established as the maximum acceptable level? In many countries, studies of the effects of a particular pollutant on human health have been used as the basis for establishing that pollutant's maximum acceptable concentration. Researchers attempt to find a threshold level below which no damage seems to occur. That calculated threshold can then be further lowered to provide a margin of safety and the adjusted threshold becomes the pollution target.

Approaches could also be based upon expert opinion. Ecologists, for example, could be enlisted to define the critical numbers of certain species or the specific critical wetlands resources that should be preserved.

Once the policy target is specified, however, economic analysis can have a great deal to say about the cost consequences of choosing a means of achieving that objective. The cost consequences are important not only because eliminating wasteful expenditures is an appropriate goal in its own right, but also to assure that choices do not trigger a political backlash.

Typically, several means of achieving the specified objective are available; some will be relatively inexpensive, while others turn out to be very expensive. The problems are frequently complicated enough that identifying the cheapest manner of achieving an objective cannot be accomplished without a rather detailed analysis of the choices.

Cost-effectiveness analysis frequently involves an *optimization procedure*. An optimization procedure, in this context, is merely a systematic method for finding the lowest-cost means of accomplishing the objective. This procedure does not, in general, produce an efficient allocation because the predetermined objective may not be efficient. All efficient policies are cost-effective, but not all cost-effective policies are efficient.

In Chapter 2 we introduced the efficiency equimarginal principle. According to that principle, net benefits are maximized when the marginal benefit is equal to the marginal cost.

A similar, and equally important, equimarginal principle exists for cost effectiveness:

Second equimarginal principle (the cost-effectiveness equimarginal principle): The least-cost means of achieving an environmental target will have been achieved when the marginal costs of all possible means of achievement are equal.

Suppose, for example, that we want to achieve a specific emission reduction across a region, and several possible techniques exist for reducing emissions. How much of the control responsibility should each technique bear? The cost-effectiveness equimarginal principle suggests that the techniques should be used such that the desired reduction is achieved and the cost of achieving the last unit of emission reduction (in other words, the marginal control cost) should be the same for all sources.

To demonstrate why this principle is valid, suppose that we have an allocation of control responsibility where marginal control costs are much higher for one set of techniques than for another. This cannot be the least-cost allocation since we could lower cost while retaining the same amount of emission reduction. Costs could be lowered by allocating more control to the lower marginal cost sources and less to the high marginal cost sources. Since it is possible to find a way to lower cost, then clearly the initial allocation could not have minimized cost. Once marginal costs are equalized, it becomes impossible to find any lower-cost way of achieving the same degree of emissions reduction; therefore, that allocation must be the allocation that minimizes costs.

In our pollution control example, cost-effectiveness can be used to find the least-cost means of meeting a particular standard and its associated cost. Using this cost as a benchmark case, we can estimate how much costs could be expected to increase from this minimum level if policies that are not cost-effective are implemented. Cost-effectiveness analysis can also be used to determine how much compliance costs can be expected to change if the EPA chooses a more stringent or less stringent standard. The case study presented in Example 3.5 not only illustrates the use of cost-effectiveness analysis, but also shows that costs can be very sensitive to the regulatory approach chosen by the EPA.

Impact Analysis

What can be done when the information needed to perform a benefit/cost analysis or a cost-effectiveness analysis is not available? The analytical technique designed to deal with this problem is called *impact analysis*. An impact analysis, regardless of whether it focuses on economic impact or environmental impact or both, attempts to quantify the consequences of various actions.

EXAMPLE

3.5

NO$_2$ Control in Chicago: An Example of Cost-Effectiveness Analysis

In order to compare compliance costs of meeting a predetermined ambient air quality standard in Chicago, (Seskin, Anderson, and Reid, 1983) gathered information on the cost of control for each of 797 stationary sources of nitrogen oxide emissions in Chicago, along with measured air quality at 100 different locations within the city. The relationship between ambient air quality at those receptors and emissions from the 797 sources was then modeled using mathematical equations. Once these equations were estimated, the model was calibrated to ensure that it was capable of re-creating the actual situation in Chicago. Following successful calibration, this model was used to simulate what would happen if EPA were to take various regulatory actions.

The results indicated that a cost-effective strategy would cost less than one-tenth as much as the traditional approach to control and less than one-seventh as much as a more sophisticated version of the traditional approach. In absolute terms, moving to a more cost-effective policy was estimated to save more than $100 million annually in the Chicago area alone. In Chapters 15 and 16 we will examine in detail the current movement toward cost-effective policies, a movement triggered in part by studies such as this one.

In contrast to benefit/cost analysis, a pure impact analysis makes no attempt to convert all these consequences into a one-dimensional measure, such as dollars, to ensure comparability. In contrast to cost-effectiveness analysis, impact analysis does not necessarily attempt to optimize. Impact analysis places a large amount of relatively undigested information at the disposal of the policy-maker. It is up to the policymaker to assess the importance of the various consequences and act accordingly.

On January 1, 1970, President Nixon signed the National Environmental Policy Act of 1969. This Act, among other things, directed all agencies of the federal government to

> *include in every recommendation or report on proposals for legislation and other major Federal actions significantly affecting the quality of the human environment, a detailed statement by the responsible official on—*
>
>   i. *the environmental impact of the proposed action,*
>   ii. *any adverse environmental effects which cannot be avoided should the proposal be implemented,*
>   iii. *alternatives to the proposed action,*
>   iv. *the relationships between local short-term uses of man's environment and the maintenance and enhancement of long-term productivity, and*
>   v. *any irreversible and irretrievable commitments of resources which would be involved in the proposed action should it be implemented.*[13]

This was the beginning of the environmental impact statement, which is now a familiar, if controversial, part of environmental policymaking.

---

[13]83 Stat. 853.

Current environmental impact statements are more sophisticated than their early predecessors and may contain a benefit/cost analysis or a cost-effectiveness analysis in addition to other more traditional impact measurements. Historically, however, the tendency had been to issue huge environmental impact statements that are virtually impossible to comprehend in their entirety.

In response, the Council on Environmental Quality, which, by law, administers the environmental impact statement process, has set content standards that are now resulting in shorter, more concise statements. To the extent that they merely quantify consequences, statements can avoid the problem of "hidden value judgments" that sometimes plague benefit/cost analysis, but they do so only by bombarding the policy-makers with masses of noncomparable information. All three of the techniques discussed in this chapter are useful, but none of them can stake a claim as being universally the "best" approach. The nature of the information that is available and its reliability make a difference.

Summary

In this chapter we have examined the most prominent but certainly not the only techniques available to supply policy-makers with the information needed to implement efficient policy. Finding the total economic value of the service flows requires estimating three components of value: (1) use value, (2) option value, and (3) nonuse or passive-use value.

Our review of these various techniques available to estimate these values included direct observation, contingent valuation, contingent ranking, conjoint analysis, *travel cost*, hedonic property and wage studies, and averting or defensive expenditures.

Because benefit/cost analysis is both very powerful and very controversial, in 1996 a group of economists of quite different political persuasions got together to attempt to reach some consensus on its proper role in environmental decision-making. Their conclusion is worth reproducing in its entirety:

> *Benefit-cost analysis can play an important role in legislative and regulatory policy debates on protecting and improving health, safety, and the natural environment. Although formal benefit-cost analysis should not be viewed as either necessary or sufficient for designing sensible policy, it can provide an exceptionally useful framework for consistently organizing disparate information, and in this way, it can greatly improve the process and, hence, the outcome of policy analysis. If properly done, benefit-cost analysis can be of great help to agencies participating in the development of environmental, health and safety regulations, and it can likewise be useful in evaluating agency decision-making and in shaping statutes.*[14]

Even when benefits are difficult to calculate, however, economic analysis in the form of cost effectiveness can be valuable. This technique can establish the least expensive ways to accomplish predetermined policy goals and to assess the extra costs involved when policies other than the least-cost policy are chosen. What it cannot do is answer the question of whether those predetermined policy goals are efficient.

At the end of the spectrum is impact analysis, which merely identifies and quantifies the impacts of particular policies without any pretense of optimality or even comparability of the information generated. Impact analysis does not guarantee an efficient outcome.

---

[14]From Kenneth Arrow et al. "Is There a Role for Benefit-Cost Analysis in Environmental, Health and Safety Regulation?" *Science* 272 (April 12, 1996): 221–222. Reprinted with permission from AAAS.

Key Concepts

Further Reading

Barde, Jean-Philippe and David W. Pearce. *Valuing the Environment: Six Case Studies* (London: Earthscan Publications, 1991). A series of essays describing the use of economic valuation of environmental resources to inform public policy. Includes case studies from Germany, Italy, the Netherlands, Norway, the United Kingdom, and the United States.

Boardman, Anthony E., David H. Greemberg, Aiden R. Vining, and David L. Weimer. *Cost-Benefit Analysis: Concepts and Practice* (Upper Saddle River, NJ: Prentice-Hall, 1996). An excellent basic text on the use of benefit/cost analysis.

Costanza, R. et al. "The Value of the World's Ecosystem Services and Natural Capital" (Reprinted from *Nature* 387 (1997) 253, *Ecological Economics* 25 (1998) (1): 3–15. An ambitious but ultimately flawed attempt to place an economic value on ecosystem services. This issue of *Ecological Economics* also contains a number of articles that demonstrate some of the flaws.

Cummings, Ronald G., David S. Brookshire, and William D. Schulze. *Valuing Environmental Goods: An Assessment of the Contingent Valuation Method* (Totowa, NJ: Rowman and Littlefield, 1986). A critical evaluation of the contingent valuation method by both practitioners and impartial reviewers.

Diamond, Peter A. and Jerry A. Hausman. "Contingent Valuation. Is Some Number Better Than No Number?" *Journal of Economic Perspectives* 8 (Fall 1994) (4): 45–64. The critics of contingent valuation weigh in.

Dixon, John A. and Maynard M. Hufschmidt. *Economic Valuation Techniques for the Environment* (Baltimore: The Johns Hopkins University Press, 1986). Several case studies on the application of valuation techniques to environmental problems in less developed countries.

Hausman, Jerry A., ed. *Contingent Valuation: A Critical Assessment* (Amsterdam: North-Holland, 1993). The critics of contingent valuation weigh in.

Kneese, Allen V. *Measuring the Benefits of Clean Air and Water* (Washington, DC: Resources for the Future, 1984). An accessible introduction to a large number of studies attempting to quantify the benefits of cleaner air and water.

Kopp, Raymond J. and V. Kerry Smith, eds. *Valuing Natural Assets: The Economics of Natural Resource Damage Assessment* (Washington, DC: Resources for the Future, Inc., 1993). A comprehensive set of essays by some of the chief practitioners in the field evaluating both the legal framework for damage assessment and the validity and reliability of the methods currently being used.

Mitchell, Robert Cameron and Richard T. Carson. *Using Surveys to Value Public Goods: The Contingent Valuation Method* (Washington: Resources for the Future, 1989). A comprehensive examination of contingent valuation research with brief summaries of representative studies.

Additional References

Acharya, Gayatri and Lynne Lewis Bennett. "Valuing Open Space and Land Use Patterns in Urban Watersheds," *Journal of Real Estate Finance and Economics* 22 (2001) (2/3): 221–237.

Ackerman, Frank, Lisa Heinzerling, and Rachel Massey. "Applying Cost-Benefit to a Past Decision: Was Environmental Protection *Ever* a Good Idea?," Center for Progressive Regulation White Paper (July 2004) (http://www.progressiveregulation.org/).

Arrow, K. J. and A. C. Fisher. "Preservation, Uncertainty, and Irreversibility," *Quarterly Journal of Economics* 87 (1974): 312–319.

Arrow, Kenneth J. and Robert C. Lind. "Uncertainty and the Evaluation of Public Investment Decisions," *American Economic Review* 60 (June 1970) (3): 364–378.

Bateman, I. J., A. P. Jones, A. A. Lovett, I. R. Lake and B. H. Day. "Applying GIS to Environmental and Resource Economics," *Environmental and Resource Economics* 22 (2002): 219–269..

Bockstael, N. E. "Economics and Ecological Modeling: The Importance of a Spatial Perspective," *American Journal of Agricultural Economics* (December 1996): 1168–1180.

Boyle, Kevin J., Thomas P. Holmes, Mario F. Teisl, and Brian Roe. "A Comparison of Conjoint Analysis Response Formats," *American Journal of Agricultural Economics* 83 (2001) (2): 441–454.

Brookshire, D. S. and M. McKee. "Is the Glass Half Empty, Is the Glass Half Full?—Compensable Damages and the Contingent Valuation Method," *Natural Resources Journal* 34 (1994) (1): 51–72.

Carson, R. T. et al. "Contingent Valuation and Revealed Preference Methodologies: Comparing the Estimates for Quasi-Public Goods," *Land Economics* 72 (1996) (1): 80–99.

Carson, Richard T. et al. *A Bibliography of Contingent Valuation Studies* (La Jolla, CA: Natural Resource Damage Assessment, Inc., 1994).

Clapp, J. M., M. Rodriguez and G. Thrall. "How GIS can Put Urban Economic Modeling on the Map," *Journal of Housing Economics* (1997) (6): 368–386.

Cummings, Ronald G. and Glenn W. Harrison. "The Measurement and Decomposition of Nonuse Values: A Critical Review," *Environmental and Resource Economics* 5 (1995) (3): 225–247.

Dixon, John. *Economics of Protected Areas: A New Look at Benefits and Costs* (Washington, DC: Island Press, 1990).

Ehmke, M. D., J. L. Lusk, and J.A. List. 2008. "Is Hypothetical Bias a Universal Phenomenon? A Multinational Investigation," *Land Economics* 84(3): 489–500.

Florax, R.J.G.M. "Methodological Pitfalls in Meta-Analysis: Publication Bias." In R.J.G.M. Florax, P. Nijkamp and K. G. Willis (eds.), *Comparative Environmental Economic Assessment* (Cheltenham, UK: Edward Elgar, 2002).

Freeman, A. Myrick, III. *The Measurement of Environmental and Resource Values: Theory and Methods* (Washington, DC: Resources of the Future, Inc., 2003).

Geoghegan, J., L. A. Wainger, and N. E. Bockstael. "Spatial Landscape Indices in a Hedonic Framework: An Ecological Economics Analysis Using GIS," *Ecological Economics* 23 (1997): 251–264.

Griffin, Ronald C. "The Fundamental Principles of Cost-Benefit Analysis," *Water Resources Research* 34 (1998) (8): 2063–2071.

Hanemann, W. Michael, "Valuing the Environment through Contingent Valuation," *Journal of Economic Perspectives* 8 (Fall 1994) (4): 19–43.

Harrington, W., R. D. Morgenstern, and P. Nelson. "Predicting the Costs of Environmental Regulations: How Accurate Are Regulators' Estimates?," *Environment* 41 (1999) (7): 10–14, 40–44.

Haveman, R. H. *The Economic Performance of Public Investments: An Ex Post Evaluation of Water Resources Investments* (Baltimore, Johns Hopkins University Press for Resources for the Future, 1972).

Holmes, Thomas P. and Wiktor L. Adamowicz. "Attribute-Based Methods," *A Prime on Non-Market Valuation,* Bateman, Ian, ed. (The Netherlands: Kluwer Academic Publishers, 2003).

Kosz, M. "Valuing Riverside Wetlands: The Case of the 'Donau-Auen' National Park," *Ecological Economics* 16 (1996) (2): 109–127.

Ladenburg, J. and S. B. Olsen. 2008. "Gender-Specific Starting Point Bias in Choice Experiments: Evidence from an Empirical Study," *Journal of Environmental Economics and Management* 56: 275–285.

Landry, C. A. Lange, J. A. List, M. K. Price, and N. G. Rupp. 2006. "Toward an Understanding of the Economics of Charity: Evidence from a Field Experiment." *Quarterly Journal of Economics* May: 747–782.

Loomis, J. B. "Measuring the Economic Benefits of Removing Dams and Restoring the Elwha River: Results of a Contingent Valuation Survey," *Water Resources Research* 32 (1996) (2): 441–447.

Michaels, R. G. and V. K. Smith. "Market Segmentation and Valuing Amenities with Hedonic Models: The Case of Hazardous Waste Sites," *Journal of Urban Economics* 28 (1990): 223–242.

Mitchell, Robert Cameron. "On Designing Constructed Markets in Valuation Surveys," *Environmental and Resource Economics* 22 (2002): 297–321.

Mitchell, Robert C. and Richard T. Carson. *Using Surveys to Value Public Goods: The Contingent Valuation Method* (Washington, DC: *Resources for the Future,* 1989).

Palmquist, R. B., F. M. Roka, and T. Vukina. "Hog Operations, Environmental Effects, and Residential Values," *Land Economics* 73 (1997) (11): 114–124.

Parsons, George. "The Travel Cost Model," *A Primer on NonMarket Valuation,* Bateman, Ian, ed. (The Netherlands: Kluwer Academic Publishers, 2003).

Paustenbach, Dennis J. (2002). "Primer on Human and Ecological Risk Assessment," *Human and Ecological Risk Assessment: Theory and Practice,* Paustenbach, Dennis J., ed. (New York: John Wiley & Sons, Inc.): 3–83.

Smith, V. K., G. van Houtven and S. K. Pattanayak. "Benefit Transfer Via Preference Calibration: 'Prudential Algebra' for Policy," *Land Economics* 78 (2002) (1): 132–152.

Smith, V. Kerry and Ju Chin Huang. "Hedonic Models and Air Pollution: Twenty-Five Years and Counting," *Environmental & Resource Economics* 3 (August 1993) (4): 381–394.

Taylor, Laura O., "The Hedonic Method," in *A Primer on NonMarket Valuation,* Bateman, Ian, ed. (The Netherlands: Kluwer Academic Publishers, 2003).

Van Houten, George and Maureen L. Cropper. "When Is a Life Too Costly to Save? The Evidence from U.S. Environmental Regulations," *Journal of Environmental Economics and Management* 30 (1996) (3): 348–368.

Viscusi, W. Kip. "Economic Foundations of the Current Regulatory Reform Efforts," *Journal of Economic Perspectives* 10 (Summer 1996) (3): 119–134.

Whittington, Dale, "Improving the Performance of Contingent Valuation Studies in Developing Countries," *Environment and Resource Economics* 22 (2002): 323–367.

Discussion Questions

1. Is risk neutrality an appropriate assumption for benefit/cost analysis? Why or why not? Does it seem more appropriate for some environmental problems than others? If so, which ones? If you were evaluating the desirability of locating a hazardous waste incinerator in a particular town, would the Arrow-Lind rationale for risk neutrality be appropriate? Why or why not?

2. Was President George W. Bush's order mandating a heavier use of benefit/cost analysis in regulatory rule making a step toward establishing a more rational regulatory structure, or was it a subversion of the environmental policy process? Why?

3. Certain environmental laws prohibit EPA from considering the costs of meeting various standards when the levels of the standards are set. Is this a good example of "putting first things first" or simply an unjustifiable waste of resources? Why?

4

Property Rights, Externalities, and Environmental Problems

The charming landscape which I saw this morning, is indubitably made up of some twenty or thirty farms. Miller owns this field, Locke that, and Manning the woodland beyond. But none of them owns the landscape. There is a property in the horizon which no man has but he whose eye can integrate all the parts, that is, the poet. This is the best part of these men's farms, yet to this their land deeds give them no title.

—Ralph Waldo Emerson, *Nature* (1836)

Introduction

In Chapter 2 we developed specific normative criteria for making rational choices about the relationship between the economic system and the environment. According to those criteria, an environmental problem exists when resource allocations are inefficient.

When would breaches of efficiency occur? Why would individual or group interests diverge from those of society at large? What circumstances give rise to this division of interests, and what can be done about it? One useful way to examine this question is based on the concept known as a *property right*. In this chapter we explore this concept and how it can be used to understand why the environmental asset can be undervalued by both the market and governmental policy. We also discuss how the government and the market can, on occasion, use knowledge of property rights and their effects on incentives to orchestrate a coordinated approach to resolving these difficulties.

Property Rights

Property Rights and Efficient Market Allocations

The manner in which producers and consumers use environmental resources depends on the property rights governing those resources. In economics, property right refers to a bundle of entitlements defining the owner's rights, privileges, and limitations for use of the resource. By examining such entitlements and how they affect human behavior, we will better understand how environmental problems arise from government and market allocations.

These property rights can be vested either with individuals, as in a capitalist economy, or with the state, as in a centrally planned economy. According to one view the source of environmental problems in a capitalist economy is the market system itself or, more specifically, the pursuit of profits. You may have heard this point of view expressed as "Corporations are more interested in profits than in the needs of people." Those who espouse this view look longingly at centrally planned economies as a means of avoiding environmental excess.

Simple answers rarely suffice for complex problems; environmental and natural resource problems are not an exception. Centrally planned economies, such as the former Soviet Union, have not historically avoided pollution excesses (see Example 4.1). On the other hand, the pursuit of profits is not inevitably inconsistent with fulfilling the needs of the people. Although the pursuit of profits may sometimes be inconsistent with fulfilling these needs, it is not always inconsistent. In fact, this pursuit is often the essential ingredient in meeting people's needs. How can we tell when the pursuit of profits is consistent with societal objectives, such as efficiency, and when it is not?

Efficient Property Right Structures

Let's begin by describing the structure of property rights that could produce efficient allocations in a well-functioning market economy. An *efficient property right structure* has three main characteristics:

1. *Exclusivity*—All benefits and costs accrued as a result of owning and using the resources should accrue to the owner, and only to the owner, either directly or indirectly by sale to others.

2. *Transferability*—All property rights should be transferable from one owner to another in a voluntary exchange.

3. *Enforceability*—Property rights should be secure from involuntary seizure or encroachment by others.

An owner of a resource with a well-defined property right (one exhibiting these three characteristics) has a powerful incentive to use that resource efficiently because a decline in the value of that resource represents a personal loss. Farmers who own the land they cultivate have an incentive to fertilize and irrigate it because the resulting increased production raises income. Similarly, they have an incentive to rotate crops when that raises the productivity of their land.

EXAMPLE 4.1

Pollution in Transition Economies

Since environmental problems are thought to be caused by a divergence between individual incentives and collective incentives, the belief that centrally planned economies avoid environmental problems seems plausible. Centralizing power in the state, as occurred in the centrally planned economies of Eastern Europe and the former Soviet Union, could potentially allow collective decisions to be made at the outset.

Studies of air and water pollution in the former Soviet Union and other Eastern European countries, however, suggest that the problems found in market economies occur with equal intensity in the Eastern Bloc. Copsa Mica, Romania, for example, is called Europe's most polluted urban area. Weakened by acid rain, monuments in Krakow, Poland, are crumbling. Women with newborn babies in Czechoslovakia have priority access to bottled water because tap water is considered injurious to infant health.

How can this be? Goldman suggests that the centralized planning system creates different, but no less potent, divergences between individual and collective incentives. According to the State of the Environment in Russia report, two-thirds of Russia's population lives in territories where the air pollution level is unhealthy. By the year 2000 more than two billion tons of toxic waste had accumulated in Russia. Preventing this pollution was a low priority because the managers of the polluting factories were rewarded for output, not pollution control. The central plans, which established national priorities, emphasized growth over environmental protection.

In his summary Goldman states the following:

> … *not private enterprise but industrialization is the primary cause of environmental disruption. This suggests that state ownership of all the productive resources is no cure-all.*

As these formerly centrally planned economies transition to market-oriented economies, what has changed? Cornillie and Fankhauser (2004) point to differences in energy intensities (energy use per GDP) as one cause of high levels of pollution in transition economies. Energy intensities of transition economies have traditionally been much higher than other industrialized economies. These have come down significantly since the beginning of the transition away from central planning. The amount of the decrease varies significantly, but what is clear is that declines in energy intensity have brought about both economic and environmental benefits including a 70 to 90 percent change in air pollution and greenhouse gas emission between 1992–1998 (European Bank for Reconstruction and Development (2001)).

Sources: Marshall I. Goldman, "Economics of Environmental and Renewable Resources in Socialist Systems," in Allen V. Kneese and James L. Sweeney, eds. *Handbook of Natural Resource and Energy Economics*, Vol. II (Amsterdam: North Holland, 1985): 725–745; State of the Environment in Russia (http://eco.priroda.ru/); Louis Berney, "Black Town of Transylvania Is Called Europe's Most Polluted," *The Boston Globe* (March 28, 1990): 2; Hilary F. French, "Industrial Wasteland," *Worldwatch* (November/December 1988): 21–30; Vladimir Kotov and Elena Nikitina, "Russia in Transition: Obstacles to Environmental Protection," *Environment* 35 (December 1993): 10–19. Jan Cornillie and Samuel Fankhauser, "The Energy Intensity of Transition Countries," *Energy Economics* 26 (2004).

When well-defined property rights are exchanged, as in a market economy, this exchange facilitates efficiency. We can illustrate this point by examining the incentives consumers and producers face when a well-defined system of property rights is in place. Because the seller has the right to prevent the consumer from consuming the product in the absence of payment, the consumer must pay to receive the product. Given a market price, the consumer decides how much to purchase by choosing the amount that maximizes his or her individual net benefit (see Figure 4.1).

The consumer's net benefit is the area under the demand curve minus the area representing cost. The cost to the consumer is the area under the price line up to the quantity purchased, since that area represents the expenditure on the commodity. Obviously, for a given price P^*, consumer net benefit is maximized by choosing to purchase Q_d units. Area A is then the geometric representation of the net benefit received, known as *consumer surplus*. It is the area under the demand curve that lies above the price, bounded from the left by the vertical axis and from the right by the quantity of the good being considered.

Meanwhile, sellers face a similar choice (see Figure 4.2). Given price P^*, the seller maximizes his or her own net benefits by choosing to sell Q_s units. The net benefit received (Area B) by the seller is called *producer surplus*. It is the area under the price line that lies over the supply curve, bounded from the left by the vertical axis and the right by the quantity of the good being considered.

FIGURE 4.1   The Consumer's Choice

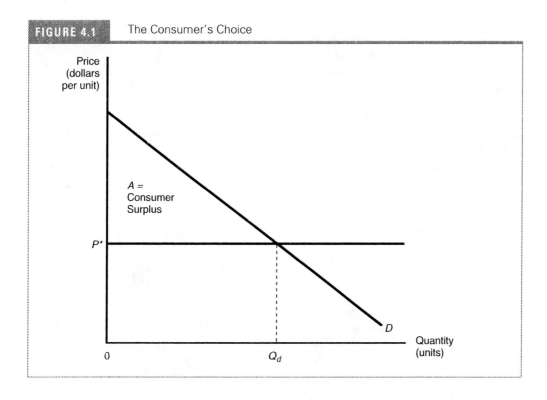

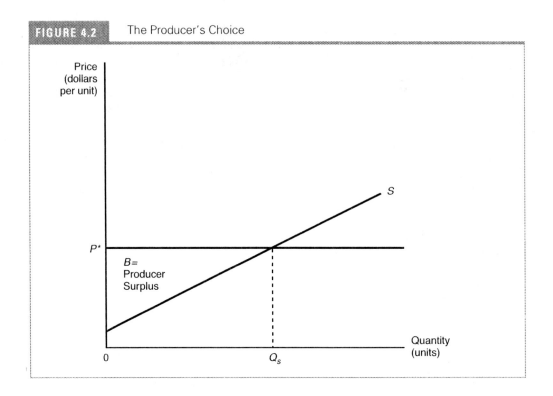

FIGURE 4.2   The Producer's Choice

The price level that producers and consumers face will adjust until supply equals demand, as shown in Figure 4.3. Given that price, consumers maximize their surplus, producers maximize their surplus, and the market clears.

Is this allocation efficient? According to our definition of static efficiency from Chapter 2, it is clear the answer is yes. The net benefit is maximized by the market allocation and, as seen in Figure 4.3, it is equal to the sum of consumer and producer surpluses. Thus, we have established a procedure for measuring net benefits, and a means of describing how the net benefits are distributed between consumers and producers.

This distinction is crucially significant. Efficiency is *not* achieved because consumers and producers are seeking efficiency. They aren't! In a system with well-defined property rights and competitive markets in which to sell those rights, producers try to maximize their surplus and consumers try to maximize their surplus. The price system, then, induces those self-interested parties to make choices that are efficient from the point of view of society as a whole. It channels the energy motivated by self-interest into socially productive paths.

Familiarity may have dulled our appreciation, but it is noteworthy that a system designed to produce a harmonious and congenial outcome could function effectively while allowing consumers and producers so much individual freedom in making choices. This is truly a remarkable accomplishment.

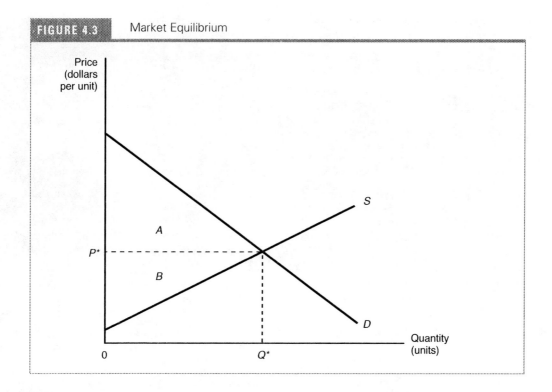

FIGURE 4.3   Market Equilibrium

Producer's Surplus, Scarcity Rent, and Long-Run Competitive Equilibrium

Since the area under the price line is total revenue, and the area under the marginal-cost curve (supply curve) is total variable cost, producer's surplus is related to profits. In the short run when some costs are fixed, producer's surplus is equal to profits plus fixed cost. In the long run when all costs are variable, producer's surplus is equal to profits plus rent, the return to scarce inputs owned by the producer. As long as new firms can enter into profitable industries without raising the prices of purchased inputs, long-run profits and rent will equal zero.

Scarcity Rent. Most natural resource industries, however, do give rise to rent and, therefore, producer's surplus is not eliminated by competition, even with free entry. This producer's surplus, which persists in long-run competitive equilibrium, is called *scarcity rent.*

David Ricardo was the first economist to recognize the existence of scarcity rent. Ricardo suggested that the price of land was determined by the least fertile marginal unit of land. Since the price had to be sufficiently high to allow the poorer land to be brought into production, other, more fertile land could be farmed at an economic profit. Competition could not erode that profit because the amount of land was limited and lower prices would serve only to reduce the supply of land below demand. The only way to expand production would be to bring additional, less fertile land (more costly to farm) into production; consequently, additional production does not lower price, as it does in a constant-cost industry. As we shall see, other circumstances also give rise to scarcity rent for natural resources.

Externalities as a Source of Market Failure

The Concept Introduced

Exclusivity is one of the chief characteristics of an efficient property rights structure. This characteristic is frequently violated in practice. One broad class of violations occurs when an agent making a decision does not bear all of the consequences of his or her action.

Suppose two firms are located by a river. The first produces steel, while the second, somewhat downstream, operates a resort hotel. Both use the river, although in different ways. The steel firm uses it as a receptacle for its waste, while the hotel uses it to attract customers seeking water recreation. If these two facilities have different owners, an efficient use of the water is not likely to result. Because the steel plant does not bear the cost of reduced business at the resort resulting from waste being dumped into the river, it is not likely to be very sensitive to that cost in its decision making. As a result, it could be expected to dump too much waste into the river, and an efficient allocation of the river would not be attained.

This situation is called an externality. (An *externality* exists whenever the welfare of some agent, either a firm or household, depends not only on his or her activities, but also on activities under the control of some other agent.) In the example, the increased waste in the river imposes an external cost on the resort, a cost the steel firm could not be counted upon to consider appropriately in deciding the amount of waste to dump.

The effect of this external cost on the steel industry is illustrated in Figure 4.4, which shows the market for steel. Steel production inevitably involves producing pollution as well as steel. The demand for steel is shown by the demand curve D, and the private marginal cost of producing the steel (exclusive of pollution control and damage) is depicted as MC_p. Because society considers both the cost of pollution and the cost of producing the steel, the social marginal-cost function (MC_s) includes both of these costs as well.

If the steel industry faced no outside control on its emission levels, it would seek to produce Q_m. That choice, in a competitive setting, would maximize its private producer surplus. But that is clearly not efficient, since the net benefit is maximized at Q^* not Q_m.

With the assistance of Figure 4.4, we can draw a number of conclusions about market allocations of commodities causing pollution externalities:

- ◈ The output of the commodity is too large.
- ◈ Too much pollution is produced.
- ◈ The prices of products responsible for pollution are too low.
- ◈ As long as the costs are external, no incentives to search for ways to yield less pollution per unit of output are introduced by the market.
- ◈ Recycling and reuse of the polluting substances are discouraged because release into the environment is so inefficiently cheap.

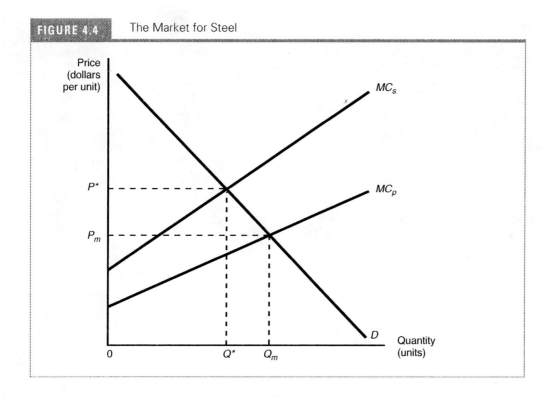

FIGURE 4.4   The Market for Steel

The effects of a market imperfection for one commodity end up affecting the demands for raw materials, labor, and so on. The ultimate effects are felt through the entire economy.

Types of Externalities

External effects can be positive or negative. Historically, (the terms *external diseconomy* and *external economy* have been used to refer, respectively, to circumstances in which the affected party is damaged by or benefits from the externality. Clearly, the water pollution example represents an external diseconomy. External economies are not hard to find, however. Private individuals who purchase a particularly scenic area that is visible to the public provide an external economy to all who pass. Generally, when external economies are present, the market will undersupply the resources.

One other distinction is important. One class of externalities, known as *pecuniary externalities*, does not present the same kinds of problems as pollution does. Pecuniary externalities arise when the external effect is transmitted through altered prices. Suppose that a new firm moves into an area and drives up the rental price of land. That increase creates a negative effect on all those paying rent and, therefore, is an external diseconomy.

This pecuniary diseconomy, however, does not cause a market failure because the resulting higher rents are reflecting the scarcity of land. The land market provides a mechanism by which the parties can bid for land; the prices that result reflect the value of the land in its various uses. Without pecuniary externalities, the price signals would fail to sustain an efficient allocation.

The pollution example is *not* a pecuniary externality because the effect is not transmitted through prices. In this example, prices do not adjust to reflect the increasing waste load. The scarcity of the water resource is not signaled to the steel firm. An essential feedback mechanism that is present for pecuniary externalities is not present for the pollution case.

The externalities concept is a broad one covering a multitude of sources of market failure (Example 4.2 illustrates one). The next step is to investigate some specific circumstances that can give rise to externalities.

**EXAMPLE
4.2**

Shrimp Farming Externalities in Thailand

In the Tha Po village on the coast of Surat Thani Province in Thailand more than half of the 1,100 hectares of mangrove swamps have been cleared for commercial shrimp farms. Although harvesting shrimp is a lucrative undertaking, mangroves serve as nurseries for fish and as barriers for storms and soil erosion. Following the destruction of the local mangroves, Tha Po villagers experienced a decline in fish catch and suffered storm damage and water pollution. Can market forces be trusted to strike the efficient balance between preservation and development for the remaining mangroves?

Calculations by economists Sathirathai and Barbier (2001), demonstrated that the value of the ecological services that would be lost from further destruction of the mangrove swamps exceeded the value of the shrimp farms that would take their place. Preservation of the remaining mangrove swamps would be the efficient choice.

Would a potential shrimp-farming entrepreneur make the efficient choice? Unfortunately the answer is no. This study estimated the economic value of mangroves in terms of local use of forest resources, off-shore fishery linkages, and coastal protection to be in the range of $27,264 to $35,921 per hectare. In contrast, the economic returns to shrimp farming, once they are corrected for input subsidies and for the costs of water pollution, are only $194 to $209 per hectare. However, as shrimp farmers are heavily subsidized and do not have to take into account the external costs of pollution, their financial returns are typically $7,706.95 to $8,336.47 per hectare. In the absence of some sort of external control imposed by collective action, development would be the normal, if inefficient, result. The externalities associated with the ecological services provided by the mangroves support a biased decision that results in fewer social net benefits, but greater private net benefits.

Source: Suthawan Sathirathai and Edward B. Barbier, "Valuing Mangrove Conservation in Southern Thailand," Contemporary Economic Policy (19)2, April 2001: 109–122.

Improperly Designed Property Rights Systems

Other Property Rights Regimes[1]

Private property is, of course, not the only possible way of defining entitlements to resource use. Other possibilities include state-property regimes (where the government owns and controls the property), common-property regimes (where the property is jointly owned and managed by a specified group of co-owners), and *res nullius* or open-access regimes (in which no one owns or exercises control over the resources). All of these create rather different incentives for resource use.

State-property regimes exist not only in former communist countries (as discussed in Example 4.1), but also to varying degrees in virtually all countries of the world. Parks and forests, for example, are frequently owned and managed by the government. As Example 4.1 indicates, problems with both efficiency and sustainability can arise in state-property regimes when the incentives of bureaucrats who implement and/or make the rules for resource use diverge from collective interests.

Common-property resources are those that are jointly managed in common rather than privately. Entitlements to use common-property resources may be formal, protected by specific legal rules, or they may be informal, protected by tradition or custom. Common-property regimes exhibit varying degrees of efficiency and sustainability, depending on the rules that emerge from collective decision-making. While some very successful examples of common-property regimes exist, unsuccessful examples are even more common.[2]

One successful example of a common-property regime involves the system of allocating grazing rights in Switzerland. Although agricultural land is normally treated as private property in Switzerland, grazing rights on the Alpine meadows have been treated as common property for centuries. Overgrazing is protected by specific rules, enacted by an association of users, which limit the amount of livestock permitted on the meadow. The families included on the membership list of the association have been stable over time as rights and responsibilities have passed from generation to generation. This stability has apparently facilitated reciprocity and trust, thereby providing a foundation for continued compliance with the rules.

Unfortunately, that kind of stability may be the exception rather than the rule, particularly in the face of heavy population pressure. The more common situation can be illustrated by the experience of Mawelle, a small fishing village in Sri Lanka. Initially, a complicated but effective rotating system of fishing rights was devised by villagers to assure equitable access to the best spots and best times while protecting the fish stocks. Over time, population pressure and the infusion of outsiders raised demand and undermined the collective cohesion sufficiently that the traditional rules became unenforceable, producing overexploitation of the resource and lower incomes for all the participants.

---

[1]This section relies on the classification system presented in Bromley (1991).

[2]The two cases that follow, and many others, are discussed in Ostrom (1992).

Res nullius property resources, the main focus of this section, can be exploited on a first-come, first-served basis because no individual or group has the legal power to restrict access. *Open-access resources*, as we shall henceforth call them, have given rise to what has become known popularly as the "tragedy of the commons."

The problems created by open-access resources can be illustrated by recalling the fate of the American bison. Bison are an example of "common-pool" resources. *Common-pool resources* are characterized by *nonexclusivity* and *divisibility*. Nonexclusivity implies that resources can be exploited by anyone while divisibility means that the capture of part of the resource by one group subtracts it from the amount available to the other groups. (Note the contrast between common-pool resources and public goods in the next section.) In the early history of the United States, bison were plentiful; unrestricted hunting access was not a problem. Frontier people who needed hides or meat could easily get whatever they needed; the aggressiveness of any one hunter did not affect the time and effort expended by other hunters. In the absence of scarcity, efficiency was not threatened by open access.

As the years slipped by, however, the demand for bison increased and scarcity became a factor. As the number of hunters increased, eventually every additional unit of hunting activity increased the amount of time and effort required to produce a given yield of bison. Figure 4.5 shows the social benefits and costs of bison hunting. Total benefits are calculated by multiplying, for each level of hunting activity, the (assumed constant) price of bison by the amount harvested. The marginal benefit curve is downward sloping because as the amount of hunting effort expended increases, the resulting population size decreases. Smaller populations support smaller harvests per unit of effort expended.

The efficient level of hunting activity in this model (E_1) is the level where the marginal benefit curve crosses the marginal-cost curve. At this level of harvest the marginal benefits would equal the (assumed constant) marginal cost implying that net benefits would be maximized.

With all hunters having completely unrestricted access to the bison, the resulting allocation would not be efficient. No individual hunter would have an incentive to protect scarcity rent by restricting hunting effort. Individual hunters, without exclusive rights, would exploit the resource until their total benefit equaled total cost, implying a level of effort equal to (E_2). Excessive exploitation of the herd occurs because individual hunters cannot appropriate the scarcity rent; therefore, they ignore it. One of the losses from further exploitation that could be avoided by exclusive owners—the opportunity cost of overexploitation—is not part of the decision-making process of open-access hunters.

Two characteristics of this formulation of the open-access allocation are worth noting: (1) in the presence of sufficient demand, unrestricted access will cause resources to be overexploited and (2) the scarcity rent is dissipated; no one appropriates the rent, so it is lost.

Why does this happen? Unlimited access destroys the incentive to conserve. A hunter who can preclude others from hunting his stock has an incentive to keep the herd at an efficient level. This restraint results in lower costs in the form of less time and effort expended to produce a given yield of bison. On the other hand, a hunter exploiting an open-access resource would not have an incentive to conserve because the benefits derived from restraint would, to some extent, be captured by other hunters. Thus, unrestricted access to resources promotes an inefficient allocation. As a result of excessive harvest and the loss of habitat as land was converted to farm and pasture, the Great Plains bison herds nearly became extinct (Lueck, 2002).

FIGURE 4.5   Bison Harvesting

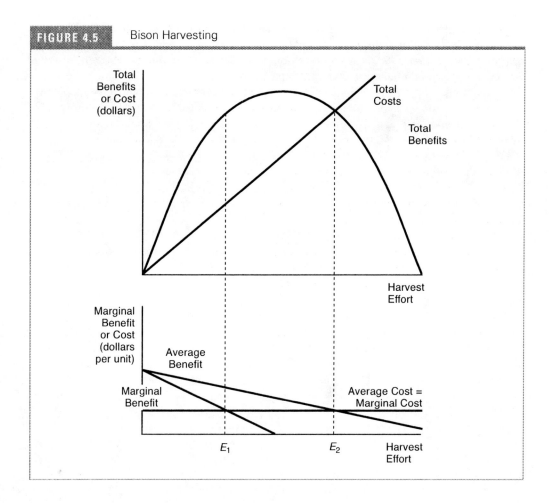

Public Goods

Public goods, defined as those that exhibit both consumption indivisibilities and nonexcludability, present a particularly complex category of environmental resources. *Nonexcludability* refers to a circumstance where, once the resource is provided, even those who fail to pay for it cannot be excluded from enjoying the benefits it confers. *Indivisible consumption* occurs when one person's consumption of a good does not diminish the amount available for others. Several common environmental resources are public goods, including not only the "charming landscape" referred to by Emerson in the opening quote, but also clean air, clean water, and biological diversity.[3]

---

[3]Notice that public "bads," such as dirty air and dirty water, are also possible.

Biological diversity includes two related concepts: (1) the amount of genetic variability among individuals within a single species and (2) the number of species within a community of organisms. *Genetic diversity*, critical to species survival in the natural world, has also proved to be important in the development of new crops and livestock. It enhances the opportunities for crossbreeding and, thus, the development of superior strains. The availability of different strains was the key, for example, in developing new, disease-resistant barley.

Because of the interdependence of species within ecological communities, any particular species may have a value to the community far beyond its intrinsic value. Certain species contribute balance and stability to their ecological communities by providing food sources or holding the population of the species in check.

The richness of diversity within and among species has provided new sources of food, energy, industrial chemicals, raw materials, and medicines. Yet there is considerable evidence that biological diversity is decreasing.

Can we rely on the private sector to produce the efficient amount of a public good such as biological diversity? Unfortunately, the answer is no! Suppose that in response to diminishing biological diversity we decide to take up a collection to provide some means of preserving endangered species. Would you expect the collection to yield sufficient revenue to pay for an efficient level of ecological diversity? The general answer is no. Let's see why.

In Figure 4.6 individual-demand curves for preserving biodiversity have been presented for two consumers A and B. The market demand curve is represented by the vertical summation of the two individual-demand curves. A vertical summation is necessary because everyone can simultaneously consume the same amount of biological diversity. Therefore, we are able to determine the market demand by finding the sum of the amounts of money they would be willing to pay for that level of diversity.

What is the efficient level of diversity? It can be determined by a direct application of our definition of efficiency. The efficient allocation maximizes net benefits. Net benefits, in turn, are represented geometrically by the portion of the area under the market demand curve that lies above the marginal-cost curve. The allocation that maximizes net benefits is Q^*, the allocation where the demand curve crosses the marginal-cost curve.

Both consumers consume this amount. At this level of availability, the marginal net benefit to person B is OB whereas the marginal net benefit to person A is OA. Adding these together produces $OA + OB$, society's marginal net benefit, which equates to marginal cost.

Would a private market supply this amount? In general, the answer is that it would not. The typical market will undersupply diversity.

One further insight can be gained from Figure 4.6, and it is this insight that led to characterizing public-good problems as "complex" in the opening sentence of this section. The efficient market equilibrium for a public good requires different prices for each consumer. In Figure 4.6 if consumer A is charged price P_a (=OA), and consumer B is charged price P_b (=OB), then both consumers will be satisfied with the efficient allocation (the efficient allocation would have maximized their net benefits given the prices).

Furthermore, the revenue collected will be sufficient to finance the supply of the public good (because $P_b \times Q^* + P_a \times Q^* = MC \times Q^*$). Thus, although an efficient pricing system exists, it is very difficult to implement. The efficient pricing system requires charging a different price to each consumer; in the absence of excludability, consumers may not choose to reveal the strength

FIGURE 4.6   Efficient Provision of Public Goods

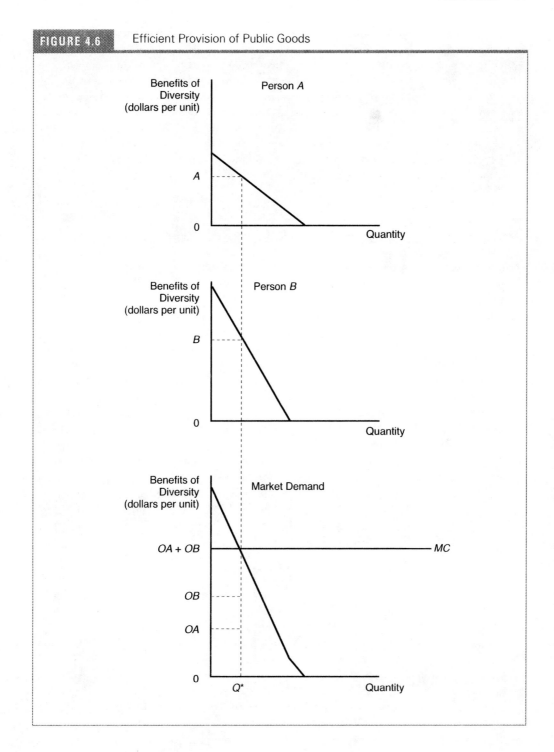

of their preference for this commodity. Therefore, the producer could not possibly know what prices to charge.

Inefficiency results because each person is able to become a free rider on the other's contribution. A *free rider* is someone who derives the benefits from a commodity without contributing to its supply. Because of the consumption indivisibility and nonexcludability properties of the public good, consumers receive the benefits of any diversity purchased by other people. When this happens it tends to diminish incentives to contribute, and the contributions are not sufficiently large to finance the efficient amount of the public good; it would be undersupplied.

The privately supplied amount may not be zero. Some diversity would be privately supplied. Indeed, as suggested by Example 4.3, the privately supplied amount may be considerable.

EXAMPLE 4.3

Public Goods Privately Provided: The Nature Conservancy

Can the demand for a public good such as biological diversity be observed in practice? Would the market respond to that demand? Apparently so, according to the existence of an organization called The Nature Conservancy.

The Nature Conservancy was born of an older organization called the Ecologist Union on September 11, 1950, for the purpose of establishing natural area reserves to aid in the preservation of areas, objects, and fauna and flora that have scientific, educational, or aesthetic significance. This organization purchases, or accepts as donations, land that has some unique ecological or aesthetic significance, to keep it from being used for other purposes. In so doing it preserves many species by preserving the habitat.

From humble beginnings, The Nature Conservancy has, as of 2008, been responsible for the preservation of 119 million acres of forests, marshes, prairies, mounds, and islands around the world. Additionally, The Nature Conservancy has protected 5,000 miles of rivers and operates 100 marine conservation projects. These areas serve as home to rare and endangered species of wildlife and plants. The Conservancy owns and manages the largest privately owned nature preserve system in the world.

This approach has considerable merit. A private organization can move more rapidly than the public sector. Because it has a limited budget, The Nature Conservancy sets priorities and concentrates on acquiring the most ecologically unique areas. Yet the theory of public goods reminds us that if this were to be the sole approach to the preservation of biological diversity, it would preserve a smaller-than-efficient amount.

Source: The Nature Conservancy, http://nature.org/aboutus/.

● Imperfect Market Structures

Environmental problems also occur when one of the participants in an exchange of property rights is able to exercise an inordinate amount of power over the outcome. This can occur, for example, when a product is sold by a single seller, or *monopoly*.

It is easy to show that monopolies violate our definition of *efficiency* in the goods market (see Figure 4.7). According to our definition of *static efficiency* (see Chapter 2), the efficient allocation would result when *OB* is supplied. This would yield net benefits represented by triangle *HIC*. The monopoly, however, would produce and sell *OA*, where marginal revenue equals marginal cost, and would charge price *OF*. At this point, the producer's surplus, albeit maximized, is clearly inefficient, because this choice causes society to lose net benefits equal to triangle *EDC*.[4] Monopolies supply an inefficiently small amount of the good.

Imperfect markets clearly play some role in environmental problems. For example, the major oil-exporting countries have formed a cartel, resulting in higher-than-normal prices and

FIGURE 4.7   Monopoly and Inefficiency

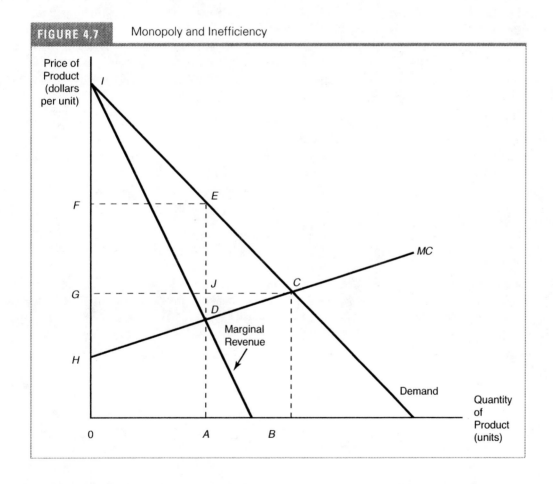

[4]Producers would lose area *JDC* compared to the efficient allocation, but they would gain area *FEJG,* which is much larger. Meanwhile, consumers would be worse off, because they lose area *FECJG.* Of these, *FEJG* is merely a transfer to the monopoly, whereas *EJC* is a pure loss to society. The total pure loss (*EDC*) is called a *deadweight loss.*

lower-than-normal production. A *cartel* is a collusive agreement among producers to restrict production and raise prices. This collusive agreement allows the group to act as a monopolist. The inefficiency in the goods market would normally be offset to some degree by the reduction in social costs caused by the lower levels of pollution resulting from the reduction in the combustion of oil.

Divergence of Social and Private Discount Rates

Earlier we concluded that producers, in their attempt to maximize producer surplus, also maximize the present value of net benefits under the "right" conditions, such as the absence of externalities, the presence of properly defined property rights, and the presence of competitive markets within which the property rights can be exchanged.

Now let's consider one more condition. If resources are to be allocated efficiently, firms must use the same rate to discount future net benefits as is appropriate for society at large. If firms were to use a higher rate, they would extract and sell resources faster than would be efficient. Conversely, if firms were to use a lower-than-appropriate discount rate, they would be excessively conservative.

Why might private and social rates differ? The social discount rate is equal to the social opportunity cost of capital. This cost of capital can be separated into two components: the risk-free cost of capital and the risk premium. The *risk-free cost of capital* is the rate of return earned when there is absolutely no risk of earning more or less than the expected return. The *risk premium* is an additional cost of capital required to compensate the owners of this capital when the expected and actual returns may differ. Therefore, because of the risk premium, the cost of capital is higher in risky industries than in no-risk industries.

One difference between private and social discount rates may stem from a difference in social and private risk premiums. If the risk of certain private decisions is different from the risks faced by society as a whole, then the social and private risk premiums may differ. One obvious example is the risk *caused* by the government. If the firm is afraid its assets will be taken over by the government, it may choose a higher discount rate to make its profits before nationalization occurs. From the point of view of society—as represented by government—this is not a risk and, therefore, a lower discount rate is appropriate. When private rates exceed social rates, current production is higher than is desirable to maximize the net benefits to society. Both energy production and forestry have been subject to this source of inefficiency.

Although private and social discount rates do not always diverge, they may. When those circumstances arise, market decisions are not efficient.

Government Failure

Market processes are not the only sources of inefficiency. Political processes are fully as culpable. As will become clear in the chapters that follow, some environmental problems have arisen from a failure of political rather than economic institutions. To complete our study of the ability of institutions to allocate environmental resources, we must understand this source of inefficiency as well.

Government failure shares with market failure the characteristic that improper incentives are the root of the problem. Special interest groups use the political process to engage in what has become known as *rent seeking*. Rent seeking is the use of resources in lobbying and other activities directed at securing protective legislation. Successful rent-seeking activity will increase the net benefits going to the special interest group, but it will also frequently lower net benefits to society as a whole. In these instances it is a classic case of the aggressive pursuit of a larger slice of the pie leading to a smaller pie.

Why don't the losers rise up to protect their interests? One main reason is voter ignorance. It is economically rational for voters to remain ignorant on many issues simply because of the high cost of keeping informed and the low probability that any single vote will be decisive. In addition, it is difficult for diffuse groups of individuals, each of whom is affected only to a small degree, to organize a coherent, unified opposition. Successful opposition is, in a sense, a public good, with its attendant tendency for free riding on the opposition of others. Opposition to special interests would normally be underfunded.

Rent seeking can take many forms. Producers can seek protection from competitive pressures brought by imports or can seek price floors to hold prices above their efficient levels. Consumer groups can seek price ceilings or special subsidies to transfer part of their costs to the general body of taxpayers. Rent seeking is not the only source of inefficient government policy. Sometimes governments act without full information and establish policies that are ultimately very inefficient. For example, as we will discuss in Chapter 17, one technological strategy chosen by the government to control motor vehicle pollution involved adding the chemical substance MTBE to gasoline. Designed to promote cleaner combustion, this additive turned out to create a substantial water pollution problem.

Governments may also pursue social policy objectives that have the side effect of causing an environmental inefficiency. For example, looking back at Figure 4.4, suppose that the government, for reasons of national security, decides to subsidize the production of steel. Figure 4.8 illustrates the outcome. The private marginal cost curve shifts down and to the right causing a further increase in production, lower prices, and even more pollution produced. Thus, the subsidy moves us even further away from where net benefits are maximized at Q^*. The shaded triangle *A* shows the deadweight loss (inefficiency) without the subsidy. With the subsidy, the deadweight loss grows to areas $A + B + C$. This social policy has the side effect of increasing an environmental inefficiency. In another example, in Chapter 8 we will see how the desire to hold down natural gas prices for consumers led to massive shortages. These examples provide a direct challenge to the presumption that more direct intervention by the government automatically leads to either greater efficiency or greater sustainability.

These cases illustrate the general economic premise that environmental problems arise because of a divergence between individual and collective objectives. This is a powerful explanatory device because not only does it suggest why these problems arise, but also it suggests how they might be resolved—by realigning individual incentives to make them compatible with collective objectives. As self-evident as this approach may be, it is controversial. The controversy involves discerning whether the problem is our improper values or the improper translation of our quite proper values into action.

Economists have always been reluctant to argue that values of consumers are warped, because that would necessitate dictating the "correct" set of values. Both capitalism and

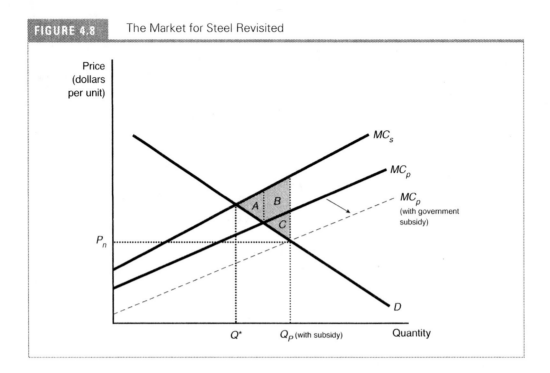

FIGURE 4.8   The Market for Steel Revisited

democracy are based on the presumption that the majority knows what it is doing, whether it is casting ballots for representatives or dollar votes for goods and services.

The Pursuit of Efficiency

We have seen that environmental problems arise when property rights are ill defined, when these rights are exchanged under something other than competitive conditions, and when social and private discount rates diverge. We can now use our definition of efficiency to explore possible remedies, such as private negotiation, judicial remedies, and regulation by the legislative and executive branches of government.

Private Resolution through Negotiation

The simplest means to restore efficiency occurs when the number of affected parties is small, making negotiation feasible. Suppose, for example, we return to the case used earlier in this chapter to illustrate an externality—the conflict between the polluting steel company and the downstream resort.

Because the steel company does not exclusively bear all the costs of its actions, inefficiency occurs and the firm produces too much output and too much pollution. Without considering the resort's welfare, the steel company chooses an output level of Q_m, a choice dictated solely by the firm's maximization of its private net benefits (see Figure 4.9).

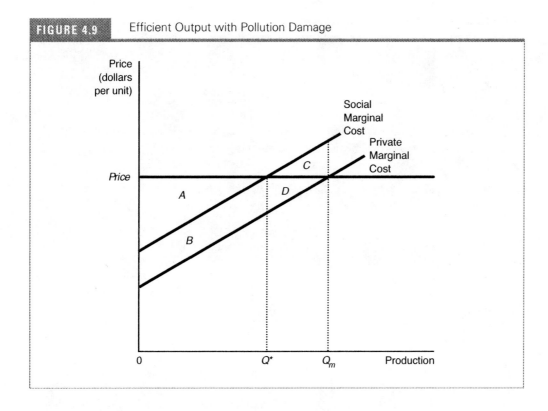

FIGURE 4.9 Efficient Output with Pollution Damage

Meanwhile, the efficient level of output Q^* is the level that maximizes the net benefit for society as a whole because it takes into account all costs, not merely the subset borne by the steel company. How can efficiency be restored in this nonmarket relationship? The first possibility is individual negotiation. The resort could bribe the steel company. Suppose, for example, the resort offered to pay an amount equal to the damages it would otherwise incur for every level of output the steel company would reduce. What level of output would the steel company choose?

Figure 4.9 reveals the answer. Suppose the resort offers a bribe up to $C + D$, the damage reduction they would experience from the reduction in production from Q_m to Q^*. Let's assume for the moment that the bribe is equal to this amount. Would the steel company be willing to reduce production to the desired level? If they refused the bribe, their producer surplus would be $A + B + D$. If they accepted the bribe, their producer surplus would be $A + B$, but they would also get the bribe so their total return would be $A + B + C + D$. Clearly they are better off by C if they accept the bribe. Society as a whole is better off by amount C as well since net benefits from Q_m are $A - C$ and net benefits for Q^* are A.

Would the resort bribe the firm to cut back more than that? It would not. The bribe that the resort would offer for further reductions (which would certainly be no larger than the damage caused if the production were to occur) would necessarily be smaller than the firm's loss of net benefits from further production cutbacks. Can you see why?

Bribes are, of course, not the only means victims have at their disposal for lowering pollution. They can attempt to inflict costs on the polluter as well. When the victims also consume the products produced by the polluters, for example, consumer boycotts are possible. When the victims are employed by the producer, strikes or other forms of labor resistance are possible. We will examine these approaches later in the book.

Our discussion of individual negotiations raises two questions: (1) Should the property right always belong to the party who gained or seized it first (in this case the steel company)? and (2) How can environmental risks be handled when prior negotiation is clearly impractical? These questions are routinely answered by the court system.

The Courts: Property Rules and Liability Rules

The court system can respond to environmental conflicts by imposing either *judicial property rules* or *judicial liability rules*. Property rules specify the initial allocation of the entitlement. The entitlements at conflict in our example are, on the one hand, the right to add waste products to the river and, on the other, the right to an attractive river. In applying property rules, the court merely decides which right is preeminent and places an injunction against violating that right. The injunction is removed only upon obtaining the consent of the party whose right was violated. Consent is usually obtained in return for an out-of-court monetary settlement.

Notice that in the absence of a court decision the entitlement is naturally allocated to the party that can most easily seize it. In our example the natural allocation would give the entitlement to the steel company. The courts must decide whether to overturn this natural allocation.

How would they decide? And what difference would their decision make? The answer may surprise you.

In a classic article, economist Ronald Coase (1960) held that as long as negotiation costs are negligible and affected consumers can negotiate freely with each other (when the number of affected parties is small), the court could allocate the entitlement to *either* party, and an efficient allocation would result. The only effect of the court's decision would be to change the distribution of costs and benefits among the affected parties. This remarkable conclusion is known as the *Coase theorem*.

Why is this so? In Figure 4.9 we have shown that if the steel company has the property right, it is in the resort's interest to offer a bribe that results in the desired level of output. Now suppose that the resort has the property right instead. To pollute in this case, the steel company must bribe the resort. Suppose it could pollute only if it compensated the resort for all damages. (In other words, it would agree to pay the difference between the two marginal cost curves up to the level of output actually chosen.) As long as this compensation was required, the steel producer would choose to produce Q^* since that is the level at which its private net benefits are maximized. (Notice that, due to the compensation, the curve the steel company uses to calculate private net benefits is the MC_s curve.)

The difference between these two ways of allocating property rights lies in how the cost of obtaining the efficient level of output is shared between the parties. When the property right is assigned to the steel company, the cost is borne by the resort (part of the cost is the damage and part is the bribe to reduce the level of damage). When the property right is assigned to the resort, the cost is borne by the steel company (it now must compensate for all damage). In either case the efficient level of production results. The Coase theorem shows that the very existence of an inefficiency triggers pressures for improvements. Furthermore, the existence of this pressure does not depend on the assignment of property rights.

This is an important point. As we will see in succeeding chapters, private efforts triggered by inefficiency can frequently prevent the worst excesses of environmental degradation. Yet the importance of this theorem should not be overstated. Both theoretical and practical objections can be raised. The chief theoretical qualification concerns the implicit assumption that wealth effects do not matter. The decision to confer the property right on a particular party results in a transfer of wealth to that party. This transfer might shift out the demand curve for either steel or resorts, as long as higher incomes result in greater demand. Whenever wealth effects are significant, the type of property rule issued by the court affects the outcome by shifting the level of the marginal benefit curve.

Wealth effects normally are small, so the zero-wealth-effect assumption is probably not a fatal flaw. Some serious practical flaws, however, do mar the usefulness of the Coase theorem. The first involves the incentives for polluting that result when the property right is assigned to the polluter. Since pollution would become a profitable activity with this assignment, other polluters might be encouraged to increase production and pollution in order to earn the bribes. That certainly would not be efficient.

Negotiation is also difficult to apply when the number of people affected by the pollution is large. You may have already noticed that in the presence of several affected parties, pollution reduction is a public good. The free-rider problem would make it difficult for the group to act cohesively and effectively for the restoration of efficiency.

When individual negotiation is not practical for one reason or another, the courts can turn to liability rules. These are rules that award monetary damages, after the fact, to the injured party. The amount of the award is designed to correspond to the amount of damage inflicted. Thus, returning to Figure 4.9, a liability rule would force the steel company to compensate the resort for all damages incurred. In this case it could choose any production level it wanted, but it would have to pay the resort an amount of money equal to the area between the two marginal cost curves from the origin to the chosen level of output. In this case the steel plant would maximize its net benefits by choosing Q^*. (Why wouldn't the steel plant choose to produce more than that? Why wouldn't the steel plant choose to produce less than that?)

The moral of this story is that appropriately designed liability rules can also correct inefficiencies by forcing those who cause damage to bear the cost of that damage. Internalizing previously external costs reestablishes the compatibility between profit maximization and efficiency.

Liability rules are interesting from an economics point of view because early decisions create precedents for later ones. Imagine, for example, how the incentives to prevent oil spills facing an oil company are transformed once it has a legal obligation to clean up after an oil spill and to compensate fishermen for reduced catches. It quickly becomes evident that accident prevention is cheaper than retrospectively dealing with the damage once it has occurred.

This approach, however, also has its limitations. It relies on a case-by-case determination based on the unique circumstances for each case. Administratively, such a determination is very expensive. Expenses, such as court time, and lawyers' fees fall into a category called *transaction costs* by economists. In the present context, these are the administrative costs incurred in attempting to correct the inefficiency. When the number of parties involved in a dispute is large and the circumstances are common, we are tempted to correct the inefficiency by statutes or regulations rather than court decisions.

Legislative and Executive Regulation

Legislative remedies can take several forms. The legislature could dictate that no one produce more steel or pollution than Q^*. This dictum might then be backed up with sufficiently large jail sentences or fines to deter potential violators. Alternatively, the legislature could impose a tax on steel or on pollution. A per unit tax equal to the vertical distance between the two curves, for example, would induce the steel company to reduce the output to Q^*.

Legislatures could also establish rules to permit greater flexibility and yet reduce damage. For example, zoning laws might establish separate areas for steel plants and resorts. This approach assumes that the damage is substantially smaller if nonconforming uses are kept apart.

They could also require the installation of particular pollution control equipment (as when catalytic converters were required on cars), or deny the use of a particular production ingredient (as when lead was removed from gasoline). In other words, they can regulate outputs, inputs, production processes, emissions, and even the location of production in their attempt to produce an efficient outcome. In subsequent chapters we will examine the various options policymakers have not only to modify environmentally destructive behavior, but also to establish the degree to which they can promote efficiency.

Bribes are, of course, not the only means victims have at their disposal for lowering pollution. Victims can lead consumer boycotts. When the victims are employed by the producer, strikes or other forms of labor resistance are possible. In later chapters we will examine how likely these approaches are to restore efficiency.

◉ An Efficient Role for Government

While the economic approach suggests that government action could well be used to restore efficiency, it also suggests that inefficiency is not a sufficient condition to justify government intervention. Any corrective mechanism involves transaction costs. If these transaction costs are high enough, and the benefit to be derived from correcting the inefficiency is small enough, then it is best simply to live with the inefficiency.

Consider, for example, the pollution problem. Wood-burning stoves, which were widely used for cooking and heating in the late 1800s in the United States, were sources of pollution, but because of the enormous capacity of the air to absorb the emissions, no regulation resulted. In 2008, however, the resurgence of demand for wood-burning stoves precipitated in part by high oil prices resulted in strict regulations for wood-burning stove emissions.

As society has evolved, the scale of economic activity (and emissions) has expanded. In dealing with many air and water pollutants, cities are experiencing severe problems because of the clustering of activities. Both the expansion and the clustering have increased the amount of emissions per unit volume of air or water. As a result, pollutant concentrations have caused perceptible problems with human health, vegetation growth, and aesthetics.

Historically, as incomes have risen, the demand for leisure activities has also risen. Many of these leisure activities, such as canoeing and backpacking, take place in unique, pristine environmental areas. With the number of these areas declining as a result of conversion to other uses, the value of remaining areas has increased. Thus, the benefits from protecting some areas have risen over time until they have exceeded the transaction costs of protecting them from pollution and/or development.

The level and concentration of economic activity, having increased pollution problems and driven up the demand for clean air and pristine areas, have created the preconditions for government action. Can government respond or will rent seeking prevent efficient political solutions? We devote much of this book to searching for the answer.

Summary

How producers and consumers use the resources that make the environmental asset depends on the nature of the property rights governing resource use. When property right systems are exclusive, transferable, and enforceable, the owner of a resource has a powerful incentive to use that resource efficiently, since the failure to do so results in a personal loss.

The economic system will not always sustain efficient allocations, however. Specific circumstances that could lead to inefficient allocations include externalities, improperly defined property-right systems (such as free-access resources and public goods), imperfect markets for trading the property rights to the resources (monopoly), and the divergence of social and private discount rates (such as under the threat of nationalization). When these circumstances arise, market allocations do not maximize the present value of the net benefit.

Due to rent-seeking behavior by special interest groups or the less than perfect implementation of efficient plans, the political system can produce inefficiencies as well. Voter ignorance on many issues coupled with the public-good nature of any results of political activity tend to create a situation in which private, but not social, net benefits are maximized.

The efficiency criterion can be used to assist in the identification of circumstances in which our political and economic institutions lead us astray. It can also assist in the search for remedies by facilitating the design of regulatory, judicial, or legislative solutions.

Key Concepts

biological diversity, *p. 76*

cartel, *p. 79*

Coase theorem, *p. 84*

common-pool resources, *p. 74*

common-property resources, *p. 73*

consumer surplus, *p. 67*

deadweight loss, *p. 79*

divisibility, *p. 74*

efficiency, *p. 79*

efficient property right structure, *p. 65*

external diseconomy, *p. 71*

external economy, *p. 71*

externality, *p. 70*

genetic diversity, *p. 76*

indivisible consumption, *p. 75*

judicial liability rules, *p. 84*

judicial property rules, *p. 84*

monopoly, *p. 78*

nonexcludability, *p. 75*

nonexclusivity, *p. 74*

open-access resources, *p. 74*

pecuniary externalities, *p. 71*

producer surplus, *p. 67*

property right, *p. 64*

public goods, *p. 75*

rent seeking, *p. 81*

res nullius, p. 73

risk premium, *p. 80*

risk-free cost of capital, *p. 80*

scarcity rent, *p. 69*

static efficiency, *p. 79*

transaction costs, *p. 85*

Further Reading

Bromley, Daniel W. *Environment and Economy: Property Rights and Public Policy* (Oxford: Basil Blackwell, Inc., 1991). A detailed exploration of the property rights approach to environmental problems.

Bromley, Daniel W., ed. *Making the Commons Work: Theory, Practice and Policy* (San Francisco: ICS Press, 1992). An excellent collection of 13 essays exploring various formal and informal approaches to controlling the use of common-property resources.

Lueck, Dean. "The Extermination and Conservation of the American Bison," *Journal of Legal Studies* (2002). A fascinating look at the role property rights played in the fate of the American bison.

Ostrom, Elinor, Thomas Dietz, Nives Dolsak, Paul Stern, Susan Stonich, and Elke U. Weber (eds). *The Drama of the Commons* National Academy Press, 2002. A compilation of articles and papers on common-pool resources.

Ostrom, Elinor. *Crafting Institutions for Self-Governing Irrigation Systems* (San Francisco: ICS Press, 1992). Argues that common-pool problems are sometimes solved by voluntary organizations rather than by a coercive state; among the cases considered are communal tenure in meadows and forests, irrigation communities, and fisheries.

Sandler, Todd. *Collective Action: Theory and Applications* (Ann Arbor: University of Michigan, 1992). A formal examination of the forces behind collective action's failures and successes.

Stavins, Robert N. "Harnessing Market Forces to Protect the Environment," *Environment* 31 (1989): 4–7, 28–35. An excellent, nontechnical review of the many ways in which the creative use of economic policies can produce superior environmental outcomes.

Several books of readings provide a wealth of additional material to interested readers. They include the following:

Bromley, Daniel W. *The Handbook of Environmental Economics* (Cambridge, MA: Blackwell, 1995).

Krishnan, Rajaram, Jonathan M. Harris, and Neva Goodwin, eds. *A Survey of Ecological Economics* (Washington, DC: Island Press, 1995).

Markandya, Anil and Julie Richardson, eds. *Environmental Economics: A Reader* (New York: St. Martin's Press, 1992).

Oates, Wallace E., ed. *The Economics of the Environment* (Brookfield, VT: Edward Elgar, 1992).

Stavins, Robert, *The Economics of the Environment: Selected Readings*, 5th ed. W. W. Norton and Company, 2005.

van den Berg, Jeroen C.J.M., ed. *Handbook of Environmental and Resource Economics* (Cheltenham, UK: Edward Elgar, 1999).

Discussion Questions

1. In a well-known legal case, *Miller* v. *Schoene* (287 U.S. 272), a classic conflict of property rights was featured. Red cedar trees, used only for ornamental purposes, carried a disease that could destroy apple orchards within a radius of two miles. There was no known way of curing the disease except by destroying the cedar trees or by ensuring that apple orchards were at least two miles away from the cedar trees. Apply the Coase theorem to this situation. Does it make any difference to the outcome whether the cedar tree owners are entitled to retain their trees or the apple growers are entitled to be free of them? Why or why not?

2. In primitive societies the entitlements to use land were frequently possessory rights rather than ownership rights. Those on the land could use it as they wished, but they could not transfer it to anyone else. One could acquire a new plot by simply occupying and using it, leaving the old plot available for someone else. Would this type of entitlement system cause more or less incentive to conserve the land than an ownership entitlement? Why? Would a possessory entitlement system be more efficient in a modern society or a primitive society? Why?

5 Sustainable Development: Defining the Concept

We usually see only the things we are looking for—so much so that we sometimes see them where they are not.

—ERIC HOFFER, *The Passionate State of Mind* (1993)

Introduction

In previous chapters we have developed two specific means for identifying environmental problems. The first, static efficiency, allows us to evaluate those circumstances where time is not a crucial aspect of the allocation problem. Typical examples might include allocating resources such as water or solar energy where next year's flow is independent of this year's choices. The second, more complicated criterion, dynamic efficiency, is suitable for those circumstances where time is a crucial aspect. One typical example might include the allocation of depletable resources, since resources used now are unavailable for use by future generations.

After defining these criteria and showing how they can be operationally invoked, we demonstrated how helpful they can be. They contribute not only by identifying environmental problems and ferreting out their behavioral sources, but also by providing a basis for identifying types of remedies and even for designing the various policy instruments that might restore some sense of balance.

But the fact that these are powerful and useful tools in the quest for a sense of harmony between the economy and the environment does not imply that they are the only criteria in which we should be interested. In a general sense the efficiency criteria are designed to prevent wasting environmental and natural resources. That is a desirable attribute, but it is not the only possible desirable attribute. We might care, for example, not only about the value of the environment (the size of the pie), but also how this value is shared (the size of each piece to all users). In other words, fairness or justice concerns should accompany efficiency considerations.

90

In this chapter we investigate one particular fairness concern—the treatment of future generations. We begin by considering a specific, ethically challenging situation—the allocation of a depletable resource over time. Using a numerical example, we will trace out the temporal allocation of a depletable resource and show how this allocation is affected by changes in the discount rate. To lay the groundwork for our evaluation of whether this is a fair allocation, we then turn to the task of defining what we mean by a fair intertemporal allocation. Finally, we take this theoretical definition and consider how it can be made operationally measurable.

A Two-Period Model

Dynamic efficiency balances present and future uses of a depletable resource by maximizing the present value of the net benefits derived from its use. This implies a particular allocation of the resource across time. We can investigate the properties of this allocation and the influence of such key parameters as the discount rate with the aid of a simple numerical example. We begin with the simplest of models (the *two-period model*)—deriving the dynamic efficient allocation across two time periods. In subsequent chapters we show how these conclusions generalize to longer time periods and to more complicated situations.

Assume that we have a fixed supply of a depletable resource to allocate between two periods. Assume further that demand is constant in the two periods, the marginal willingness to pay is given by the formula $P = 8 - 0.4Q$, and marginal cost is constant at \$2 per unit (see Figure 5.1). Notice that if the total supply was 30 or greater, and we were concerned only with these

FIGURE 5.1   The Allocation of an Abundant Depletable Resource (a) Period 1 (b) Period 2

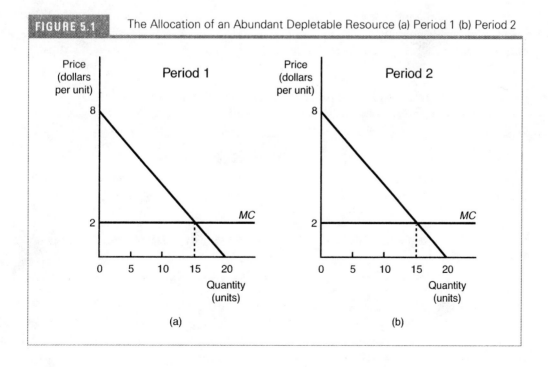

two periods, an efficient allocation would produce 15 units in each period, *regardless of the discount rate*. The supply is sufficient to cover the demand in both periods; the production in Period 1 does not reduce the production in Period 2. In this case the static efficiency criterion is sufficient, since the allocations are not interdependent.

Examine, however, what happens when the available supply is less than 30. Suppose it is equal to 20. How do we determine the efficient allocation? According to the dynamic efficiency criterion, the efficient allocation is the one that maximizes the present value of the net benefit. The present value of the net benefit for both years is simply the sum of the present values in each of the two years. To take a concrete example, consider the present value of a particular allocation: 15 units in the first period and 5 in the second. How would we compute the present value of that allocation?

The present value in the first period would be that portion of the geometric area under the demand curve that is over the supply curve—$45.[1] The present value in the second period is that portion of the area under the demand curve that is over the supply curve from the origin to the 5 units produced multiplied by $1/(1 + r)$. If we use $r = 0.10$, then the present value of the net benefit received in the second period is $22.73,[2] and the present value of the net benefits for the two years is $67.73.

We now know how to find the present value of net benefits for any specified allocation. How does one find the allocation that maximizes present value? One way, with the aid of a computer, is to try all possible combinations of Q_1 and Q_2, which sum to 20. The one yielding the maximum present value of net benefits can then be selected. That is tedious and, for those who have the requisite mathematics, unnecessary.

The dynamically efficient allocation of this resource has to satisfy the condition that the present value of the marginal net benefit from the last unit in Period 1 equals the present value of the marginal net benefit in Period 2. Even without mathematics, this principle is easy to understand, as can be demonstrated with the use of a simple graphical representation of the two-period allocation problem.

Figure 5.2 depicts the present value of the marginal net benefit for each of the two periods. The net benefit curve for Period 1 is to be read from left to right. The net benefit curve intersects the vertical axis at $6; demand would be zero at $8, and the marginal cost is $2, so the difference (marginal net benefit) is $6. The marginal net benefit for the first period goes to zero at 15 units because, at that quantity, the willingness to pay for that unit exactly equals its cost.

The only tricky aspect of drawing the graph involves constructing the curve for the present value of net benefits in Period 2. Two aspects are worth noting. First, the zero axis for the Period 2 net benefits is on the right, rather than the left, side. Therefore, increases in Period 2 are recorded from right to left. This way, all points along the horizontal axis yield a total of 20 units allocated between the two periods. Any specific point on that axis picks a unique allocation between the two periods.[3]

Second, the present value of the marginal benefit curve for Period 2 intersects the vertical axis at a different point than does the comparable curve in Period 1. (Why?) This intersection is lower

---

[1]The height of the triangle is $6 [$8 − $2] and the base is 15 units. The area is therefore $1/2($6) \times (15) = 45.

[2]The undiscounted net benefit is $25. (Why?) The discounted net benefit is therefore $25/1.10 = 22.73$.

[3]Note that the sum of the two allocations in Figure 5.2 is always 20. The left-hand axis represents an allocation of all 20 units to Period 2, and the right-hand axis represents an allocation entirely to Period 1.

FIGURE 5.2   The Dynamically Efficient Allocation

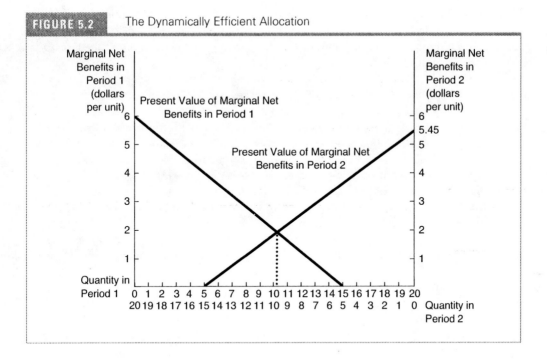

because the marginal benefits in the second period are discounted. Thus, with the 10 percent discount rate we are using, the marginal net benefit is $6 and the present value is $6/1.10 = $5.45. Notice that larger discount rates rotate the Period 2 marginal-benefit curve around the point of zero marginal net benefit ($Q_1 = 5$, $Q_2 = 15$) toward the right-hand axis. We will use this fact in a moment.

The efficient allocation is now readily identifiable as the point where the two curves representing present value of marginal net benefits cross.

We can solve for this point by setting the present value of marginal net benefits in Period 1 to the present value of marginal net benefits in Period 2 and solving for the values of Q_1 and Q_2 that sum to 20.

$$PVMNB_1 = PVMNB_2$$

$$8 - 0.4Q_1 - 2 = \frac{8 - 0.4Q_2 - 2}{1.10} \text{ and } Q_1 + Q_2 = 20.$$

Solving these equations to the third decimal place yields $Q_1 - 10.238$ and $Q_2 = 9.762$.

The total present value of net benefits is then the area under the marginal net-benefit curve for Period 1 up to the efficient allocation, plus the area under the present value of marginal net-benefit curve for Period 2 from the right-hand axis up to its efficient allocation. Because we have an efficient allocation, the sum of these two areas is maximized.[4]

---

[4]Demonstrate by first allocating slightly more to Period 2 (and therefore less to Period 1) and showing that the total area decreases. Conclude by allocating slightly less to Period 2 and showing that, in this case as well, total area declines.

Since we have developed our efficiency criteria independent of an institutional context, these criteria are equally appropriate for evaluating resource allocations generated by markets, government rationing, or even the whims of a dictator. *Any* efficient allocation method must take scarcity into account.

Intertemporal scarcity imposes an opportunity cost that we henceforth refer to as the *marginal user cost*. When resources are scarce, greater current use diminishes future opportunities. The marginal user cost is the present value of these forgone opportunities at the margin. To be more specific, uses of those resources that would have been appropriate in the absence of scarcity may no longer be appropriate once scarcity is present. Using large quantities of water to keep lawns lush and green may be wholly appropriate for an area with sufficiently large replenishable water supplies, but quite inappropriate when it denies drinking water to future generations. Failure to take the higher scarcity value of water into account in the present would lead to inefficiency or an additional cost to society due to the additional scarcity imposed on the future. This additional marginal value that scarcity creates is the marginal user cost.

We can illustrate how this concept is used by returning to our numerical example. With 30 or more units, each period would be allocated 15 and the resource would not be scarce. With 30 or more units, therefore, the marginal user cost would be zero.

With 20 units, however, scarcity does exist. No longer can 15 units be allocated to each period; each period will have to be allocated less than would be the case without scarcity. The marginal user cost for this case is not zero. As can be seen from Figure 5.2, the present value of the marginal user cost, the additional value created by scarcity, is graphically represented by the vertical distance between the quantity axis and the intersection of the two present-value curves. It is identical to the present value of the marginal net benefit in each of the periods. This value can be determined from the underlying equations by substituting the solution for Q into either *PVMNB* equation.

For example, $PVMNB_1 = 8 - 0.4Q_1 - 2$.

Using the fact that $Q_1 = 10.238$ we have $PVMNB_1 = 8 - 0.4(10.238) - 2 = 6 - 4.095 = 1.905$.

The present value of the marginal user cost in this example is 1.905.

We can make this concept even more concrete by considering its use in a market context. An efficient market would have to consider not only the marginal cost of extraction for this resource, but also the marginal user cost. Whereas in the absence of scarcity, the price would equal the marginal cost of extraction, with scarcity, the price would equal the sum of marginal extraction cost and marginal user cost.

To see this, solve for the prices that would prevail in an efficient market facing scarcity over time. Inserting the efficient quantities (10.238 and 9.762, respectively) into the willingness to pay function ($P = 8 - 0.4Q$) yields $P_1 = 3.905$ and $P_2 = 4.095$. The corresponding supply and demand diagrams are given in Figure 5.3.

In an efficient market the marginal user cost for each period is the difference between the price and the marginal cost of extraction. Notice that it takes the value \$1.905 in the first period and \$2.095 in the second. In both years the present value of the marginal user cost is \$1.905. In the second year the actual marginal user cost is $\$1.905(1 + r)$. Since in this example $r = 0.10$, the marginal user cost for the second period is \$2.095.[5] Thus, while the present value of marginal user cost is equal in both periods, the actual marginal user cost rises over time.

---

[5]You can verify this by taking the present value of \$2.095 and showing it to be equal to \$1.905.

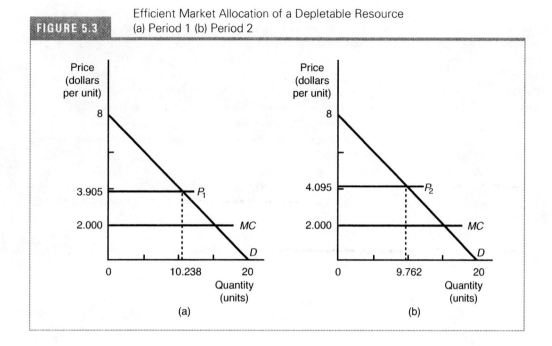

FIGURE 5.3   Efficient Market Allocation of a Depletable Resource
(a) Period 1 (b) Period 2

Both the size of the marginal user cost and the allocation of the resource between the two periods are affected by the discount rate. In Figure 5.3, because of discounting, the efficient allocation allocates somewhat more to Period 1 than to Period 2. A discount rate larger than 0.10 would be incorporated in this diagram by rotating the Period 2 curve an appropriate amount toward the right-hand axis, holding the point at which it intersects the horizontal axis fixed. (Can you see why?)

Notice that larger discount rates produce larger rotations. In Figure 5.2 a discount rate larger than 0.10 would move the intersection point between the two *PVMNB* curves to the right. This implies that the amount allocated to the second period would be necessarily smaller with larger discount rates. The general conclusion, which holds for all models we consider, is that higher discount rates tend to skew resource extraction toward the present because they give the future less weight in balancing the relative value of present and future resource use.

Defining Intertemporal Fairness

While no generally accepted standards of fairness or justice exist, some have more prominent support than others. One such standard concerns the treatment of future generations. What legacy should earlier generations leave to later ones? This is a particularly difficult issue because, in contrast to other groups for which we may want to ensure fair treatment, future generations cannot articulate their wishes, much less negotiate with current generations ("We'll take your radioactive wastes, if you leave us plentiful supplies of titanium.").

One starting point for intergenerational equity is provided by philosopher John Rawls (1971) in his monumental work *A Theory of Justice*. Rawls suggests one way to derive general principles of justice is to place, hypothetically, every person in an original position behind a "veil of ignorance." This veil of ignorance would prevent them from knowing their eventual position in society. Once behind this veil, people would decide on rules to govern the society that they would, after the decision, be forced to inhabit.

In our context this approach would suggest a hypothetical meeting of all members of present and future generations to decide on rules for allocating resources among generations. Because these members are prevented by the veil of ignorance from knowing the generation to which they will belong, they will not be excessively conservationist (lest they turn out to be a member of an earlier generation) or excessively exploitative (lest they become a member of a later generation).

What kind of rule would emerge from such a meeting? One possibility is the sustainability criterion. The *sustainability criterion* suggests that, at a minimum, future generations should be left no worse off than current generations. Allocations that impoverish future generations, in order to enrich current generations, are, according to this criterion, patently unfair.

In essence, the sustainability criterion suggests that earlier generations are at liberty to use resources that would thereby be denied to future generations as long as the well-being of future generations remains just as high as that of all previous generations. On the other hand, diverting resources from future use would violate the sustainability criterion if it reduced the well-being of future generations below the level enjoyed by preceding generations.

One of the implications of this definition of sustainability is that it is possible to use resources (even depletable resources) as long as the interests of future generations could be protected. Do our institutions provide adequate protection for future generations? We begin with examining the conditions under which efficient allocations satisfy the sustainability criterion. Are all efficient allocations sustainable?

Are Efficient Allocations Fair?

In the numerical example we have constructed, it certainly does not appear that the efficient allocation satisfies the sustainable criterion. In the two-period example, more resources are allocated to the first period than to the second. Therefore, net benefits in the second period are lower than in the first. Since sustainability does not allow earlier generations to profit at the expense of later generations, this example certainly appears to violate the sustainability criterion.

Yet what matters is who receives the benefits of these resources, not merely when they are extracted. Choosing this particular extraction path does not prevent those in the first period from saving some of the net benefits for those in the second period. If the allocation is dynamically efficient, it will always be possible to set aside sufficient net benefits accrued in the first period for those in the second period so that those in the second period will be at least as well off as they would have been with any other extraction profile.

We can illustrate this point with a numerical example that compares a dynamic efficient allocation with sharing to an allocation where resources are committed equally to each generation. Suppose, for example, you believe that setting aside half (10 units) of the available resources for each period would be a better allocation than the dynamic efficient allocation. The net benefits to each period from this alternative scheme would be $40. (Can you see why?)

Now let's compare this to an allocation of net benefits that could be achieved with the dynamic efficient allocation. If the dynamic efficient allocation is to satisfy the sustainability criterion, we must be able to show that it can produce an outcome such that each generation would be at least as well off as it would be with the equal allocation. Can that be demonstrated?

In the dynamic efficient allocation the net benefits to the first period were 40.466, while those for the second period were 39.512.[6] Clearly, if no sharing between the periods took place, this example would violate the sustainability criterion; the second generation is worse off than it would be with equal sharing.

But suppose benefits are shared across periods. If the first generation keeps net benefits of $40 (thereby making it just as well off as if equal amounts were extracted in each period) and invests the extra $0.466 (the $40.466 net benefits earned during the first period in the dynamic efficient allocation minus the $40 reserved for itself) at 10 percent interest for those in the next period, this investment would grow to $0.513 by the second period [0.466(1.10)]. Add this to the net benefits received directly from the dynamic efficient allocation ($39.512), and the second generation would receive $40.025. Those in the second period would be better off by accepting the dynamic efficient allocation with sharing than they would if they demanded that resources be allocated equally between the two periods.

This example demonstrates that although dynamic efficient allocations do not automatically satisfy *sustainability criteria*, they are not automatically inconsistent with sustainability either, even in an economy relying heavily on depletable resources. The possibility that the second period can be better off is not a guarantee; the required degree of sharing must take place. As Example 5.1 points out, some sharing does sometimes take place. In subsequent chapters we will examine both the conditions under which we could expect the appropriate degree of sharing to take place and the conditions under which it would not.

The Alaskan Permanent Fund

One example of an intergenerational sharing mechanism that fits this sustainability model currently exists in Alaska. Extraction from Alaska's oil fields generates significant income, but depreciates one of the state's main environmental assets. As the Alaska pipeline construction neared completion in 1976, Alaska voters approved a constitutional amendment to protect the interests of future generations by authorizing the establishment of a dedicated fund: the Alaska Permanent Fund. This fund was designed to capture a portion of the rents received from the sale of the state's oil to share with future generations. The amendment requires the following:

> At least 25 percent of all mineral lease rentals, royalties, royalty sales proceeds, federal mineral revenue-sharing payments, and bonuses received by the state be placed in a permanent fund, the principal of which may only be used for income-producing investments.

Since the principal of this fund can only be invested in income-producing assets, it cannot be used to cover current expenses without a majority vote of Alaskans.

The fund is fully invested in capital markets and diversified among various asset classes. It generates income from interest on bonds, stock dividends, real estate rents, and capital gains from the sale of assets. To date, the legislature has used some of these annual

---

[6]The supporting calculations are (1.905)(10.238) + 0.5(4.095)(10.238) for the first period and (2.095)(9.762) + 0.5(3.905)(9.762) for the second period.

earnings to provide dividends to every eligible Alaska resident, while using the rest to increase the size of the principal, thereby assuring that it is not eroded by inflation.

Though this fund does preserve some of the revenue for future generations, two characteristics are worth noting. First, the principal could be used for current expenditures if a majority of current voters agreed. To date that has not happened, but it has been discussed. Second, only 25 percent of the oil revenue is placed in the fund; full sustainability would require dedicating all 100 percent. The current generation gets 75 percent of the proceeds from oil as well as some portion of the income from the permanent fund.

_____

Source: The Alaska Permanent Fund Web site: http://www.apfc.org/homeobjects/tabpermfund.cfm.

⬤ Applying the Sustainability Criterion

One of the difficulties in assessing the fairness of intertemporal allocations using this version of the sustainability criterion is that it is so difficult to apply. Discovering whether the well-being of future generations is lower than that of current generations requires us to know not only something about the allocation of resources over time, but also something about the preferences of future generations (in order to establish how valuable various resource streams are to them). That is a tall (impossible?) order!

Is it possible to develop a version of the sustainability criterion that is more operational? Fortunately it is, thanks to what has become known as the *Hartwick Rule*. In an early article, John Hartwick (1977) demonstrated that a constant level of consumption could be maintained perpetually if all the scarcity rent were invested in capital. Furthermore, that level of investment would be sufficient to assure that the value of the total capital stock would not decline.

How do we apply this to the environment? In general, the Hartwick Rule suggests that the current generation has been given an endowment. The endowment contains both environmental and natural resources (known as "natural capital") and physical capital (such as buildings, equipment, schools, roads, and so on). Sustainable use of this endowment implies that we should keep the principal (the value of the endowment or total capital stock) intact and live off only the flow of services provided. We should not, in other words, chop down all the trees and use up all the oil, leaving future generations to fend for themselves. Rather, we need to ensure that the value of the total capital stock is maintained, not depleted.

Two important insights flow from this reinterpretation of the sustainability criterion. First, with this version it is possible to judge the sustainability of an allocation by examining whether or not the value of the total capital stock is nondeclining. That test can be performed each year without knowing anything about future allocations or preferences. Second, this analysis suggests the specific degree of sharing that would be necessary to produce a sustainable outcome, namely all scarcity rent must be invested.

Let's pause to make sure we understand what is being said here and why it is being said. Although we will return to this subject later in the book, it is important now to have at least an intuitive understanding of the implications of this analysis. Consider an analogy. Suppose a grandparent left you an inheritance of $10,000, and you put it in a bank where it earns 10 percent interest.

What are the choices for allocating that money over time and what are the implications of those choices? If you spent exactly $1,000 per year, the amount in the bank would remain

$10,000 and the income would last forever; you are spending only the interest, leaving the principal intact. If you spend more than $1,000 per year, the principal would necessarily decline over time and eventually the balance in the account would go to zero. In the language of this chapter, spending $1,000 per year or less would satisfy the sustainability criterion while spending more would violate the sustainability criterion.

What does the Hartwick Rule mean in this context? It suggests that one way to tell whether an allocation (spending pattern) is sustainable or not is to examine what is happening to the principal over time. If the principal is declining, the allocation (spending pattern) is not sustainable. If the principal is increasing or remaining constant, the allocation (spending pattern) is sustainable.

The desirability of this version of the sustainability criterion depends crucially on how substitutable the two forms of capital (natural and physical) are. If physical capital can readily substitute for natural capital, then maintaining the value of the sum of the two is sufficient. If, however, physical capital cannot completely substitute for natural capital, investments in physical capital may not be enough to offset the threat posed to sustainability by using up natural capital.

How strong is the assumption of complete substitutability between physical and natural capital? Clearly it is untenable for certain categories of environmental resources. Though we can contemplate the replacement of natural breathable air with universal air-conditioning in domed cities, both the expense and the artificiality of this approach make it an absurd compensation device. Obviously intergenerational compensation must be approached carefully (see Example 5.2).

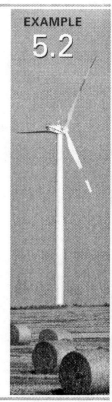

Nauru: Weak Sustainability in the Extreme

EXAMPLE
5.2

The weak sustainability criterion is used to judge whether the depletion of natural capital is offset by sufficiently large increases in physical or financial capital as to prevent total capital from declining. It seems quite natural to suppose that a violation of that criterion does demonstrate *unsustainable* behavior. But does fulfillment of the weak sustainability criterion provide an adequate test of *sustainable* behavior? Consider the case of Nauru.

Nauru is a small Pacific island that lies some 3,000 kilometers northeast of Australia. It contains one of the highest grades of phosphate rock ever discovered. Phosphate is a prime ingredient in fertilizers.

Over the course of a century, first colonizers and then, after independence, the Nauruans decided to extract massive amounts of this rock. This decision has simultaneously enriched the remaining inhabitants (including the creation of a trust fund believed to contain over $1 billion) and destroyed most of the local ecosystems. Local needs are now mainly met by imports financed from the revenues created by the sales of the phosphate.

However wise or unwise the choices made by the people of Nauru were, they could not be replicated globally. Everyone cannot subsist solely on imports financed with trust funds; every import must be exported by someone! The story of Nauru demonstrates the value of complementing the weak sustainability criterion with other, more demanding criteria. Satisfying the weak sustainability criterion may be a necessary condition for sustainability, but it is not always sufficient.

Source: Gowdy, J. W. and C. N. McDaniel, "The Physical Destruction of Nauru: An Example of Weak Sustainability," *Land Economics* 75(2) 1999: 333–338.

Recognizing the weakness of the constant total capital definition in the face of limited substitution possibilities has led some economists to propose a more restrictive definition—a sustainable allocation is one that maintains the value of the stock of *natural* capital. This definition assumes that it is natural capital that drives future well being, and further assumes that little or no substitution between physical and natural capital is possible. To differentiate these two definitions the maintenance of total capital is now known as the *weak sustainability* definition, while maintaining natural capital is known as the *strong sustainability* definition.

Recognizing that even the strong sustainability criterion may not be sufficient to maintain intergenerational fairness has led to a third definition of sustainability. This final definition, known as *environmental sustainability*, requires that certain physical flows of specified individual resources should be maintained. This definition suggests that for these resources it is not sufficient to maintain the value of an aggregate. For a fishery, for example, this definition would emphasize assuring that catch levels did not exceed the growth of the biomass for the fishery, thereby preserving the size of the stock for succeeding generations. For wetlands, it would involve the preservation of the specific ecological functions so the actual functions remain available to future generations.

Implications for Environmental Policy

In order to be useful guides to policy, our sustainability and efficiency criteria must be neither synonymous nor incompatible. Do these criteria meet that test?

They do. As we will see later in the book, not all efficient allocations are sustainable and not all sustainable allocations are efficient. Yet some sustainable allocations are efficient and some efficient allocations are sustainable. Furthermore, market allocations may be either efficient or inefficient and either sustainable or unsustainable.

Do these differences have any policy implications? Indeed they do. In particular they suggest a specific strategy for policy. Among the possible uses for resources that fulfill the sustainability criterion, choose the one that maximizes either dynamic or static efficiency as appropriate. In this formulation the sustainability criterion acts as an overriding constraint on social decisions. Yet by itself, the sustainability criterion is insufficient because it fails to provide any guidance on which of the infinite number of sustainable allocations should be chosen. That is where efficiency comes in. It provides a means for maximizing the wealth derived from all the possible sustainable allocations.

This combination of efficiency with sustainability turns out to be very helpful in guiding policy. Many unsustainable allocations are the result of inefficient behavior. Correcting the inefficiency can either restore sustainability or move the economy a long way in that direction. Furthermore, and this is important, correcting inefficiencies can frequently produce win-win situations. In win-win changes, the various parties affected by the change are all either better off or at least no worse off after the change than before. This contrasts sharply with changes in which gains to the gainers are more than offset by losses to the losers.

Win-win situations are possible because removing inefficiency increases net benefits. The increase in net benefits provides a means for compensating those who might otherwise lose from the change. Compensating losers reduces the opposition to change, thereby making change more likely. Do our economic and political institutions normally produce outcomes that are both efficient and sustainable? In future chapters we will provide explicit answers to this important question.

Summary

Both efficiency and ethical considerations can guide the desirability of private and social choices involving the environment. Whereas the former is concerned mainly with eliminating waste in the use of resources, the latter is concerned with ensuring the fair treatment of all parties.

Previous chapters have focused on the static and dynamic efficiency criteria. This chapter examines one possible characterization of the obligation previous generations owe to generations that follow and the policy implications that flow from acceptance of that obligation.

The specific obligation examined in this chapter—sustainable development—is based upon the notion that earlier generations should be free to pursue their own well-being as long as in so doing they do not diminish the welfare of future generations. This notion gives rise to three alternative definitions of sustainable allocations:

⊛ **Weak Sustainability.** Resource use by previous generations should not exceed a level that would prevent subsequent generations from achieving a level of well-being at least as great. One of the implications of this definition is that the value of the capital stock (natural plus physical capital) should not decline. Individual components of the aggregate could decline in value as long as other components were increased in value (normally through investment) sufficiently to leave the aggregate value unchanged.

⊛ **Strong Sustainability.** According to this interpretation, the value of the remaining stock of natural capital should not decrease. This definition places special emphasis on preserving natural (as opposed to total) capital under the assumption that natural and physical capital offer limited substitution possibilities. This definition retains the focus of the previous definition on preserving value (rather than a specific level of physical flow) and on preserving an aggregate of natural capital (rather than any specific component).

⊛ **Environmental Sustainability.** Under this definition the physical flows of individual resources should be maintained, not merely the value of the aggregate. For a fishery, for example, this definition would emphasize maintaining a constant fish catch over time that is no greater than the growth of the fishery (referred to as a sustainable yield), rather than a constant value of the fishery. For a wetlands it would involve preserving specific ecological functions, not merely its value.

It is possible to examine and compare the theoretical conditions that characterize various allocations (including market allocations and efficient allocations) to the necessary conditions for an allocation to be sustainable under these definitions. According to the theorem, which is now known as the Hartwick Rule, if all of the scarcity rent from the use of scarce resources is invested in capital, the resulting allocation will satisfy the first definition.

In general, not all efficient allocations are sustainable and not all sustainable allocations are efficient. Furthermore, market allocations can be: (1) efficient, but not sustainable, (2) sustainable, but not efficient, (3) inefficient and unsustainable, and (4) efficient and sustainable. One class of situations, known as "win-win" situations, provides an opportunity to increase the welfare of both current and future generations simultaneously.

We will explore these themes much more intensively as we proceed through the book. In particular we will inquire into when market allocations can be expected to produce allocations that satisfy the sustainability definitions and when they cannot. We will also see how the skillful use of economic incentives can allow policymakers to exploit win-win situations to promote a transition onto a sustainable path for the future.

Key Concepts

environmental sustainability, *p.* 100

Hartwick Rule, *p.* 98

marginal user cost, *p.* 94

strong sustainability, *p.* 100

sustainability criteria, *p.* 97

two-period model, *p.* 91

weak sustainability, *p.* 100

win-win situations, *p.* 100

Further Reading

Atkinson, G. et al. *Measuring Sustainable Development: Macroeconomics and the Environment.* (Cheltenham, UK: Edward Elgar, 1997). This book tackles the tricky question of how one can tell whether development is sustainable or not.

Desimone, L. D. *Eco-Efficiency: The Business Link to Sustainable Development.* (Cambridge, MA: MIT Press, 1997). What is the role for the private sector in sustainable development? Is concern over the bottom line consistent with the desire to promote sustainable development?

May, P. and R.S.D. Motta, eds. *Pricing the Planet: Economic Analysis for Sustainable Development.* (New York: Columbia University Press, 1996). Ten essays dealing with how sustainable development might be implemented.

Perrings, C. *Sustainable Development and Poverty Alleviation in Sub-Saharan Africa: The Case of Botswana.* (New York, Macmillan, 1996). One of the leading practitioners in the field examines the problems and prospects for sustainable development in Botswana.

Pezzey, J.C.V. and Michael A. Toman, "Progress and Problems in the Economics of Sustainability" in Tietenberg, T. and H. Folmer, eds. *The International Yearbook of Environmental and Resource Economics: A Survey of Current Issues.* (Cheltenham, UK: Edward Elgar, 2002). An excellent survey of the economics literature on sustainable development.

Scheraga, J. and F. Sussman. "Discounting and Environmental Management," in *The International Yearbook of Environmental and Resource Economics 1998/1999*, T. Tietenberg and H. Folmer, eds. (Cheltenham, UK: Edward Elgar): 1–31. A review of the state of the art on the role of discounting in environmental management.

Additional References

Abdalla, K. (2008). "Special issue on sustainable development in Africa." *Natural Resources Forum* 32(2): 89.

Clark, G.E. (2008). "War and sustainability: The economic and environmental costs." *Environment* 50(1): 3–4.

Howarth, R. B. "Discount Rates and Sustainable Development," *Ecological Modeling* 92 (1996) (2–3): 263–270.

Hull, Z. (2008). "Sustainable development: Premises, understanding and prospects." *Sustainable Development* 16(2): 73–80.

Jordan, A. (2008). "The governance of sustainable development: taking stock and looking forward." *Environment and Planning C-Government and Policy* 26(1): 17–33.

Maler, K.G. (2008). "Sustainable development and resilience in ecosystems." *Environmental & Resource Economics* 39(1): 17–24.

Martinez-Alier, J. (2008). "Inequality, cooperation, and environmental sustainability." *Ecological Economics* 64(4): 912–913.

Neumayer, Eric. *Weak versus Strong Sustainability: Exploring the Limits of Two Opposing Paradigms* (Cheltenham, UK: Edward Elgar, 1999).

Pawlowski, A. (2008). "How many dimensions does sustainable development have?" *Sustainable Development* 16(2): 81–90.

Skowronski, A. (2008). "A civilization based on sustainable development: Its limits and prospects." *Sustainable Development* 16(2): 117–125.

Zidansek, A. (2007). "Sustainable development and happiness in nations." *Energy* 32(6): 891–897.

Historically Significant References

Hartwick, J.M. "Intergenerational Equity and the Investing of Rents from Exhaustible Resources," *American Economic Review* 67 (1977): 972–974. The classic article that formulated the Hartwick Rule.

Rawls, John. *A Theory of Justice.* (Cambridge, MA: Harvard University Press, 1971).

Solow, R. "On the Intergenerational Allocation of Natural Resources," *Scandinavian Journal of Natural Resources,* 88 (1986) (1): 141–149.

Discussion Questions

1. The notion of sustainability is not the same in the natural sciences as in economics. In the natural sciences sustainability frequently means maintaining a constant physical flow of each and every resource (e.g., fish from the sea or wood from the forest), while in economics it means maintaining the *value* of those service flows. When might the two criteria lead to different choices? Why?

2. To maintain the same state of well-being per person, a rapidly growing population creates the need for the current generation to set aside more resources than if the population were stable. Should the obligation of the current generation be limited to assuring that well-being will not decline for future generations as long as populations are comparable, or should the obligation take into account population growth and assure resources enough for larger populations? Why?

6 The Population Problem

We will not achieve the Millennium Development Goals (MDGs) to eradicate extreme poverty and hunger, advance gender equality, improve maternal health, reduce child mortality, ensure universal education, combat HIV/AIDS, and protect the environment unless more attention and resources are devoted to population and reproductive health. This is particularly true in the poorest nations, where there are high rates of fertility and mortality, rapid population growth, and high unmet need for family planning.

—Thoraya Ahmed Obaid, Executive Director, UNFPA,
Demographics and Socio-Economic Development, 2006

Introduction

In 2005 the world population stood at 6.45 billion people, projected to grow to 8.13 billion by 2030. In Chapter 1 we examined two strikingly different views of what the future holds for the world economic system. At the heart of those differences lie divergent views of the world population problem. One view sees population growth as continuing relentlessly, putting enormous pressure on food and environmental resources. The other view foresees human ingenuity erasing those limits as it has in the past.

These views are symptomatic of a debate that has deep historical roots. Thomas Malthus, a late-eighteenth century and early-nineteenth century classical economist, concluded that population growth posed a trap for nations seeking to develop. Temporary increases in income were seen as triggering increases in population until the land could no longer supply adequate food. Cornell University Professor David Pimentel (1994) has brought this argument into the twentieth century by suggesting that the *optimum global population*, defined as the largest population that could be supported sustainably in relative prosperity, is about 2 billion people. Since this is approximately one-third of the current population, his analysis suggests the need for considerable reductions in current population *levels,* not merely reductions in growth.

Contrasting views are held by representatives of Third World countries and some prominent population economists. The late Julian Simon maintained that not only have the pessimists overstated the seriousness of the problem, but also they have failed to recognize that population growth in many of the developing countries is desirable. Clearly, no consensus exists.

In this chapter we examine the manner in which population affects and is affected by the development process, as well as the microeconomic issues dealing with economic determinants of fertility. This economic perspective provides one basis for understanding the causes and consequences of population growth and provides an approach for controlling population.

Historical Perspective

World Population Growth

It has been estimated that at the beginning of the Common Era, world population stood at about 250,000,000 people and was growing at 0.04 percent per year (not 4 percent!). When the world's population passed 6 billion, it was growing at an annual rate around 1.5 percent per year. Since the beginning of time, the population has grown to over 6 billion people; at a 1.5 percent growth rate, the next 6 billion could take only 50 years.

In recent years the average rate of population growth has declined (see Table 6.1). This slowdown has been experienced in developed and less-developed countries, although rates remain higher in the less-developed countries. The World Fertility Survey, a multinational survey of some 400,000 women in 61 countries, found several apparent causes, including increased use of contraception, a growing preference for fewer children, and later marriages.

Although the trend toward falling birthrates is pervasive, the fact remains that most developing countries still have, and are expected to have in the future, substantial increases in their populations. Some 98 percent of the population growth between 1998 and 2025 is expected to occur in the poorer countries. For example, in early 2009 Niger had a growth rate of 3.68%, while Italy, had a negative growth rate.

Population Growth in the United States

Population growth in the United States has followed the general declining pattern of most of the developed world, although in most periods American growth rates have exceeded the average for Europe by a substantial margin. The reductions in American population growth rates have been due primarily to declines in the birthrate, which fell from a high of 55.2 live births per thousand in 1820 to a record low of 13.9 live births per thousand in 2002. The 2005 U.S. birthrate was 14.0 live births per thousand (see Figure 6.1).

Birthrates, however, provide a rather crude measure of the underlying population trends, primarily because they do not account for age structure. To understand the effect of age structure, let's separate the birthrate experience into two components: (1) the number of persons in the childbearing years and (2) the number of children those persons are bearing.

To quantify the second of these components, the Census Bureau uses a concept known as the *total fertility rate*, which is the number of live births an average woman has in her lifetime if, at each year of age, she experiences the average birthrates occurring in the general population of similarly aged women. Between 2000 and 2005, world fertility rates averaged 2.7 live births per woman. In Sub-Saharan Africa, the average is 5.4 live births per woman with a range as high as

TABLE 6.1   Rate of Population Growth by Region and Development Category: 1950 to 2050 (in percent)

Region	1950–60	1960–70	1970–80	1980–90	1990–00	2000–10	2010–25	2025–50
World	1.7	2.0	1.8	1.7	1.4	1.1	0.9	0.6
Less-Developed Countries	2.0	2.4	2.2	2.0	1.7	1.3	1.1	0.7
More-Developed Countries	1.2	1.0	0.7	0.6	0.4	0.3	0.1	(Z)
Africa	2.2	2.4	2.7	2.8	2.5	2.0	1.6	1.4
Sub-Saharan Africa	2.1	2.5	2.7	2.8	2.6	2.0	1.7	1.6
North Africa	2.4	2.4	2.5	2.7	2.1	1.7	1.3	0.8
Near East	2.7	2.6	3.0	2.9	2.3	2.2	1.9	1.4
Asia	1.7	2.2	2.0	1.8	1.4	1.1	0.9	0.4
Latin America and the Caribbean	2.7	2.7	2.4	2.0	1.7	1.3	1.0	0.5
Europe and the New Independent States	1.1	0.9	0.7	0.5	0.2	0.1	(Z)	−0.2
Western Europe	0.7	0.8	0.4	0.3	0.3	0.2	(Z)	−0.3
Eastern Europe	1.2	0.8	0.8	0.4	−0.1	−0.1	−0.2	−0.5
New Independent States	1.7	1.3	0.9	0.8	0.1	0.1	0.2	(Z)
North America	1.8	1.3	1.1	1.0	1.2	0.9	0.8	0.7
Oceania	2.3	2.1	1.6	1.6	1.5	1.2	0.9	0.5
Excluding China:								
World	1.8	1.9	1.8	1.8	1.5	1.3	1.0	0.7
Less-Developed Countries	2.2	2.4	2.4	2.3	1.9	1.6	1.3	0.9
Asia	1.9	2.2	2.2	2.0	1.7	1.4	1.1	0.6
Less-Developed Countries	2.0	2.3	2.2	2.1	1.8	1.5	1.1	0.7

(Z) Between −0.05 percent and +0.05 percent.

Note: Reference to China encompasses China, Hong Kong S.A.R., Macau S.A.R., and Taiwan. Direct access to this table and the International Data Base is available at www.census.gov/ipc/www.

Source: U.S. Census Bureau, International Programs Center, International Data Base. Internet Release Date: March 22, 2004.

8.0 in Angola and 7.3 in Somalia to as low as 2.6 in South Africa. Europe averaged a fertility rate of 1.4 during the same time period and the United States averaged 2.0 live births per woman.

Total fertility rates can be used to determine what level of fertility would, if continued, lead to a stationary population. A *stationary population* is one in which age- and sex-specific fertility

U.S. Birthrates: 1909–2005

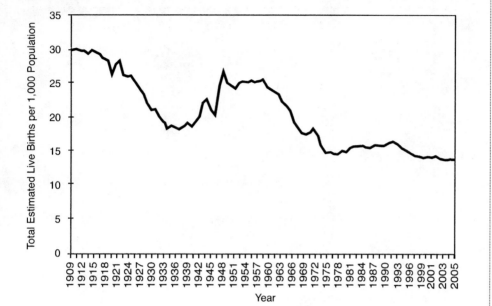

Note: Birthrates before 1960 are adjusted for underregistration.

Sources: *Vital Statistics of the United States* Vol. 1 (2001); and National Vital Statistics System, available on the Web at http://www.cdc.gov/nchs/datawh/vitalstats/vitalstatsbirths.htm.

rates yield a birthrate that is constant and equal to the death rate, so the growth rate is zero. The level of the total fertility rate that is compatible with a stationary population is called the *replacement rate*. Rates higher than the replacement rate would lead to population growth, while rates lower would lead to population declines. Once the replacement fertility rate is reached, the World Bank estimates that it takes approximately 25 years before the population stabilizes, due to the large numbers of families in the childbearing years. As the age structure reaches its older equilibrium, the growth rate declines until a stationary population is attained.

In the United States the replacement rate is 2.11. The two children replace the mother and her mate, while the extra 0.11 is to compensate for those women who do not survive the child-bearing years and because slightly more than 50 percent of births are males. The U.S. total fertility rate dropped below the replacement rate in 1972 and has remained below it ever since (see Figure 6.2). In 2006 (the latest year for which data were available) the rate stood at 2.10, almost equal to the replacement rate.

Two questions arise when we think about how population growth affects sustainability: (1) What is the relationship between population growth and economic development? and (2) How can the rate of population growth be altered when alteration is appropriate? The first question lays the groundwork for considering the effect of population growth on quality of life, including the effects of a stationary population. The second allows us to consider public policies geared toward manipulating the rate of population growth when desirable.

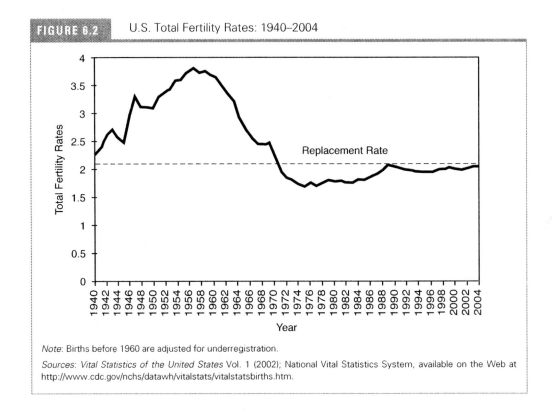

FIGURE 6.2   U.S. Total Fertility Rates: 1940–2004

Note: Births before 1960 are adjusted for underregistration.

Sources: *Vital Statistics of the United States* Vol. 1 (2002); National Vital Statistics System, available on the Web at http://www.cdc.gov/nchs/datawh/vitalstats/vitalstatsbirths.htm.

Effects of Population Growth on Economic Development

A number of questions guide our inquiry. Does population growth enhance or inhibit the opportunities of a country's citizens? Does the answer depend on the stage of development? Given that several countries are now entering a period of declining population growth, what are the possible effects of this decline on economic growth?

Population growth affects economic growth and, as long as each person contributes something, those effects generally are positively correlated. As long as their marginal product is positive, additional people mean additional output. Since a positive marginal product is not a very restrictive condition, it should usually hold true.

However, the existence of a positive marginal product is not a very appropriate test of the desirability of population growth! Perhaps a better one is to ask whether population growth positively affects the average citizen. Whenever the marginal product of an additional person is lower than the average product, adding more persons simply reduces the welfare of the average citizen. Why?

In the range of marginal productivities between zero and the average product, economic growth measured in aggregate terms would increase, but measured in per capita terms, would decrease. Similarly, there is a range of marginal productivities—those greater than the average product—where economic growth increases regardless of whether it is measured in aggregate or per capita terms. Whether or not the material status of the average citizen is improved by population growth becomes a question of whether the marginal product of additional people is higher or lower than the average product.

To facilitate our examination of the population-related determinants of economic development, let's examine a rather simple definition of output:

$$O = L \cdot X$$

where O is the output level, X is the output per worker, and L is the number of workers. This equation can be expressed in per capita terms by dividing both sides by population, denoted as P:

$$\frac{O}{P} = \frac{L}{P} \cdot X$$

This equation now states that output per capita is determined by the product of two factors: the share of the population that is in the labor force and the output per worker. Each of these two factors provides a channel through which population growth affects economic growth.

The most direct effect of population growth on the percentage of the population employed, the *age structure effect*, results from induced changes in the age distribution. Suppose that we were to compare two populations, one rapidly growing and one slowly growing. The one with the rapid growth would contain a much larger percentage of younger persons (see Figure 6.3).

Due to its slow growth, the U.S. population is in general older than the Mexican population. Approximately 45.1 percent of Mexico's population is 14 years of age or younger; the comparable figure for the United States is 21.4 percent. This is reinforced at the other end of the age structure, where some 12.4 percent of the U.S. population is 65 or older, compared with only 3.8 percent in Mexico.

These differences in the age structure have mixed effects on the percentage of the labor force available to be employed. The abundance of youth in a rapidly growing population creates a large supply of people too young to work, a situation referred to as the *youth effect*. On the other

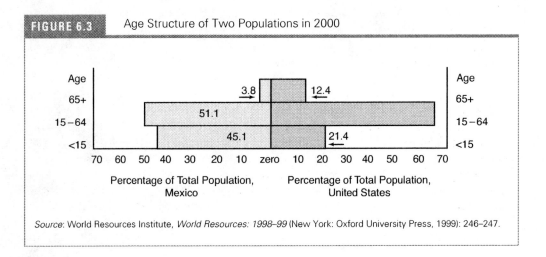

FIGURE 6.3   Age Structure of Two Populations in 2000

Percentage of Total Population, Mexico

Percentage of Total Population, United States

Source: World Resources Institute, *World Resources: 1998–99* (New York: Oxford University Press, 1999): 246–247.

hand, a country characterized by slow population growth has a rather larger percentage of persons who have reached, or are past, the traditional retirement age of 65, a situation referred to as the *retirement effect*. Some developing countries are experiencing both effects simultaneously as better public health policies reduce death rates while birthrates remain high. How do the youth and retirement effects interact to determine the percentage of the population in the labor force? Does the youth effect dominate the retirement effect?

Examine the percentage of population in the prime working ages, 15 through 64. As Figure 6.3 shows, this percentage is much higher for the United States. A larger percentage of the population is in the labor force in the United States than in Mexico. For Mexico, the youth effect dominates.

This dominance of the youth effect generalizes to other countries. For example, in 2000 African countries had an average of 53.8 percent of the population in the prime working age while European countries averaged 65.5 percent. High population growth retards per capita economic growth by decreasing the percentage of the population in the labor force.

Rapid growth also affects the percentage available to be employed through the *female availability effect*. With a slower growth rate and fewer children to care for, more women are available to join the labor force. Both the dominance of the youth effect (over the retirement effect) and the female availability effect suggest that rapid population growth reduces the percentage of the population in the labor force, which, in turn, has a depressing effect on economic growth per capita.

How about possible relationships between population growth and the second factor, the amount of output produced by the average worker? The most common way to enhance productivity is through the accumulation of capital. As the capital stock is augmented (for example, through the introduction of assembly lines or production machinery), workers become more productive. Are population growth and capital accumulation connected?

One main connection involves the link between savings and capital accumulation. Limits on the availability of savings constrain the level of additions to the capital stock. Availability of savings, in turn, is affected in part by the age structure of the population. Older populations are presumed to save more because less is spent directly on the care and nurturing of children. Therefore, all other things being equal, societies with rapidly growing populations could be expected to save proportionately less. This lowered availability of savings would lead to lower amounts of capital stock augmentation and lower productivity per worker.

Apparently the magnitude of the effect of demographic change on savings in the 1960s and 1970s was small, but that has changed. A large study by Kelley and Schmidt (1994) found that population growth and demographic dependency exerted a sizable negative impact on savings in the 1980s.

A final model suggesting a negative effect of population growth on economic growth involves the presence of some fixed essential factor for which limited substitution possibilities exist (land or raw materials, for example). In this case the *law of diminishing marginal productivity* applies. This law states that in the presence of a fixed factor (land), successively larger additions of a variable factor (labor) will eventually lead to a decline in the marginal productivity of the variable factor. It suggests that in the presence of fixed factors, successive increases in labor will drive the marginal product down. When it falls below the average product, per capita income will decline with further increases in the population.

Not all arguments suggest that growth in output per capita will be restrained by population growth. Perhaps the most compelling arguments for the view that population growth enhances per capita growth are those involving technological progress and *economies of scale* (see Figure 6.4).

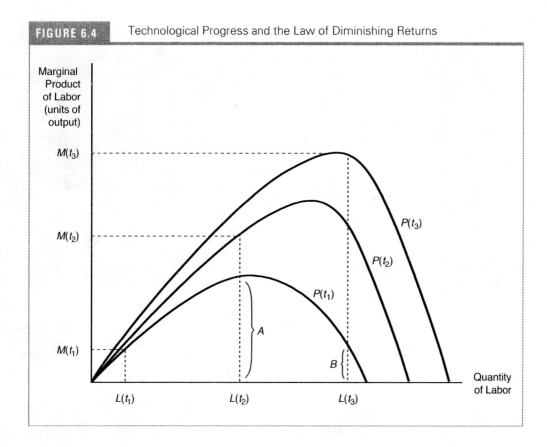

FIGURE 6.4   Technological Progress and the Law of Diminishing Returns

The vertical axis shows marginal productivity measured in units of output. The horizontal axis describes various levels of labor employed on a fixed amount of land. Population growth implies an increase in the labor force, which is recorded on the graph as a movement to the right on the horizontal axis.

The curve labeled $P(t_1)$ shows the functional relationship between the marginal product of labor and the amount of labor employed on a fixed plot of land at a particular point in time (t_1). Different curves represent different points in time because in each period of time there exists a unique state of the art in the knowledge of how to use the labor most effectively. Thus, as time passes, technological progress occurs, advancing the state of the art and shifting the productivity curves outward, as demonstrated by $P(t_2)$ and $P(t_3)$.

Three situations are demonstrated in Figure 6.4. At time t_1, an application of $L(t_1)$ yields a marginal product of $M(t_1)$. At times t_2 and t_3, the application of $L(t_2)$ and $L(t_3)$ units of labor respectively yield $M(t_2)$ and $M(t_3)$ marginal units of output. Marginal products have increased as larger amounts of labor were added.

Consider what would have happened, however, if the state of technical knowledge had not increased. The increase in labor from $L(t_2)$ to $L(t_3)$ would have been governed by the $P(t_1)$ curve, and the marginal product would have declined from A to B. This is precisely the result anticipated by the law of diminishing marginal productivity. Technological progress provides one means of escaping the law of diminishing marginal productivity.

The second source of increase in output per worker is economies of scale. Economies of scale occur when increases in inputs lead to a more-than-proportionate increase in output. Population growth, by increasing demand for output, allows these economies of scale to be exploited. In the United States, at least, historically this has been a potent source of growth. While it seems clear that the population level in the United States is already sufficient to exploit economies of scale, the same is not necessarily true for all developing countries.

In the absence of trade restrictions, however, the relevant market now is the global market, not the domestic market. The level of domestic population has little to do with the ability to exploit economies of scale in the modern global economy unless tariffs, quotas, or other trade barriers prevent the exploitation of foreign markets. If trade restrictions are a significant barrier, the appropriate remedy would be reducing trade restrictions, not boosting the local population.

Because these *a priori* arguments suggest that population growth could either enhance or retard economic growth, it is necessary to rely on empirical studies to sort out the relative importance of these effects. Several researchers have attempted to validate the premise that population growth inhibits per capita economic growth. Their attempts were based on the notion that if the premise were true, one should be able to observe lower growth in per capita income in countries with higher population growth rates, all other things being equal.

A study for the National Research Council (1986) conducted an intensive review of the evidence. Did the evidence support the expectations? In general they did not find a strong correlation between population growth and the growth in per capita income. However, they did determine the following:

1. Slower population growth is associated with an increase in the amount of capital per worker and, hence, the productivity per worker.
2. Slower population growth is unlikely to result in a net reduction in agricultural productivity and might well raise it.
3. National population density and economies of scale are not significantly related.
4. Rapid population growth puts more pressure on both depletable and renewable resources.

A subsequent study by Kelley and Schmidt (1994) found that "A statistically significant and quantitatively important negative impact of population growth on the rate of per capita output growth appears to have emerged in the 1980s." This result is consistent with the belief that population growth may initially be advantageous but ultimately, as capacity constraints become binding, becomes an inhibiting factor. Kelley and Schmidt also found that the net negative impact of demographic change diminishes with the level of economic development; the impact is larger in the relatively impoverished less developed countries. According to this analysis, those most in need of increased living standards are the most adversely affected by population growth.

Rapid population growth may also increase the inequality of income. High population growth can increase the degree of inequality for a variety of reasons, but the most important reason is that the high growth has a depressing effect on the earning capacity of children and on wages.

The ability to provide for the education and training of children, given fixed budgets of time and money, is a function of the number of children in the family—the fewer the children, the higher the proportion of income (and wealth, such as land) available to develop each child's earning capacity. Since low-income families tend to have larger families than high-income families do, the offspring from low-income families are usually more disadvantaged. The result is a growing gap between the rich and the poor.

What happens to the marginal cost of an additional child as the number of children increases? According to Table 6.2, the existing estimates suggest that child-rearing expenses rise from approximately a quarter of household expenditures for one-child families to approximately one-half for three-child families. These estimates also find that the total dollar amount spent on children increases with net income, but as a percentage of net income, it declines.

Another link between population growth and income inequality results from the effect of population growth on the labor supply. High population growth could increase the supply of labor faster than otherwise, depressing wage rates vis à vis profit rates. Since low-income groups have a higher relative reliance on wages for their income than do the rich, this effect would also increase the degree of inequality.

After an extensive review of the historical record for the United States, historian Peter Lindert concludes the following:

> There seems to be good reason for believing that extra fertility affects the size and "quality" of the labor force in ways that raise income inequalities. Fertility, like immigration, tends to reduce the average "quality" of the labor force, by reducing the amounts of family and public school resources devoted to each child. The retardation in the historic improvement in labor force quality has in turn held back the rise in the incomes of the unskilled relative to those enjoyed by skilled labor and wealth-holders. [p. 258]

Lindert's interpretation of the American historical record seems to be valid for developing countries as well. The National Research Council study found that slower population growth would decrease income inequality, and it would raise the education and health levels of the children. This link between rapid population growth and income inequality provides an additional powerful motivation for controlling population. Slower population growth reduces income inequality.

TABLE 6.2   Estimates of Child-Rearing Expenditures[a]

Economist and Year of Study	Data Years[a]	Average Child-Rearing Expenditures as a Percent of Total Family Expenditure		
		One Child	Two Children	Three Children
Espenshade (1984)	1972–1973	24%	41%	51%
Betson (1990)	1980–1986	25%	37%	44%
Lino (2000)	1990–1992	26%	42%	48%
Betson[b] (2001)	1996–1998	25%	35%	41%
Betson[b] (2001)	1996–1998	30%	44%	52%

Notes:
[a] All estimates were developed using data from the Federal Bureau of Labor Statistics Consumer Expenditure Survey.
[b] Betson (2001) developed two separate sets of estimates based on two somewhat different methodologies.

Source: Policy Studies, Inc. "Report on Improving Michigan's Child Support Formula" submitted to the Michigan State Court Administrative Office on April 12, 2002. Available on the Web at http://www.courts.mi.gov/scao/services/focb/formula/psireport.htm/.

The Population/Environment Connection

Historically, population growth has also been identified as a major source of environmental degradation. If supported by the evidence, this could provide another powerful reason to control population. What is the evidence?

On an individual country level, some powerful evidence has emerged on the negative effects of population density, especially when it is coupled with poverty. In some parts of the world, forestlands are declining as trees are harvested to provide fuel for an expanding population or to make way for the greater need for agricultural land to supply food. Lands that historically were allowed to recover their nutrients by letting them lay fallow for periods of seven years or longer are now, of necessity, brought into cultivation before nutrient recovery is complete.

As the population expands and the land does not, new generations must either intensify production on existing lands or bring marginal lands into production. Inheritance systems frequently subdivide the existing family land among the children, commonly only male children. After a few generations the resulting parcels are so small and so intensively farmed as to be incapable of supplying adequate food for a family.

Migration to marginal lands can be problematic as well. Generally those lands are available for a reason. Many of them are highly erodible, which means that they degrade over time as the topsoil and the nutrients it contains are swept away. Migration to coastal river deltas may initially be rewarded by high productivity of this fertile soil, but due to their location, those areas may be vulnerable to storm surges resulting from cyclones. This danger is, as we shall see, exacerbated by climate change.

In thinking about the long run, it is necessary to incorporate some knowledge of feedback effects. Would initial pollution pressure on the land result in positive (self-reinforcing) or negative (self-limiting) feedback effects? (See Debate 6.1.)

The traditional means of poverty reduction is economic development. What feedback effects on population growth is development expected to have? Are development and the reduction of population pressure on the environment compatible or conflicting objectives? The next section takes up these issues.

Effects of Economic Development on Population Growth

Up to this point we have considered the effect of population growth on economic development. We now have to examine the converse relationship. Does economic development affect population growth? Table 6.1 suggests that it may, since the higher-income countries are characterized by lower population growth rates.

This suspicion is reinforced by some further evidence. Most of the industrialized countries have passed through three stages of population growth. The conceptual framework that organizes this evidence is called the *theory of demographic transition*. This theory suggests that as nations develop, they eventually reach a point where birthrates fall (see Figure 6.5).

DEBATE 6.1

Does Population Growth Inevitably Degrade the Environment?

Research in this area has traditionally been focused on two competing hypotheses.

Ester Boserup, a Danish economist, posited a negative feedback mechanism that has become known as the *induced innovation hypothesis*. In her view increasing populations trigger an increasing demand for agricultural products. As land becomes scarce relative to labor, incentives emerge for agricultural innovation. This innovation results in the development of more intensive, yet sustainable land-management practices in order to meet the food needs. In this case the environmental degradation is self-limiting because human ingenuity is able to find ways to farm the land more intensively without triggering degradation.

The opposite view, called the "*downward spiral hypothesis*," envisions a positive feedback mechanism in which the degradation triggers a reinforcing response that only intensifies the problem.

Clearly these very different visions have very different implications for the role of population in environmental degradation. Does the evidence suggest which is right?

Although quite a few studies have been conducted, neither hypothesis always dominates the other. Apparently the nature of the feedback mechanism is very context specific. Grepperud (1996) found that as population pressure rose and exceeded a carrying capacity threshold, land degradation took place in Ethiopia. Tiffen and Mortimore (2002) found that as family farms became smaller under conditions of population growth, some people migrated to new areas or took up new occupations, while others attempted to raise the value of output (crops or livestock) per hectare. They also found that investments in improving land and productivity are constrained by poverty.

Kabubo-Mariara (2007) points to the importance of secure property rights in triggering the Boserup hypothesis in an examination of land conversion and tenure security in Kenya. Using survey data from a cross-section of 1,600 farmers in 1999 and 2000 (73 percent of whom held land under private property), she examined the correlation between population density, land conservation, and property rights. She found that population density was highest for farmers who had adopted land conservation practices. She also found that tenure security was correlated with high population density and farmers with secure land rights were more likely to adopt soil improvements and plant drought-resistant vegetation, while common-property owners were less likely to invest in any land improvement. It appears, at least for this case, that the externalities associated with common property are exacerbated with increased population densities.

Sources: Grepperud, Sverre, "Population Pressure and Land Degradation: The Case of Ethiopia," *Journal of Environmental Economics and Management*. 30 (1996); 18–33; Tiffen, M. and M. Mortimore, "Questioning Desertification in Dryland Sub-Saharan Africa," *Natural Resources Forum* 26 (2002): 218–233; Kabubo-Mariara, Jane, "Land Conversion and Tenure Security in Kenya: Boserup's Hypothesis Revisited," *Ecological Economics* 64 (2007); 25–35.

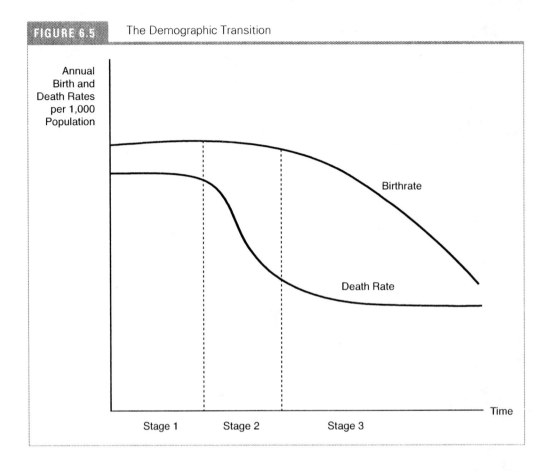

FIGURE 6.5   The Demographic Transition

According to this theory, during Stage 1 the period immediately prior to industrialization, birthrates are stable and slightly higher than death rates, ensuring population growth. During Stage 2, the period immediately following the onset of industrialization, death rates fall dramatically with no accompanying change in birthrates. This decline in mortality results in a marked increase in life expectancy and a rise in the population growth rate. In Western Europe Stage 2 is estimated to have lasted somewhere around 50 years.

Stage 3, the period of demographic transition, involves large declines in the birthrate that exceed the continued declines in the death rate. Thus, the period of demographic transition involves further increases in life expectancy, but rather smaller population growth rates than characterized during the second stage. The Chilean experience with demographic transition is illustrated in Figure 6.6. Can you identify the stages?

One substantial weakness of the theory of demographic transition as a guide to the future lies in the effect of HIV/AIDS on death rates. Demographic transition theory presumes that with development comes falling death rates and increasing life expectancy, producing an increase in population growth until the subsequent fall in birthrates. Over 33 million people worldwide are infected with HIV/AIDS. The AIDS pandemic is so pervasive in some Sub-Saharan African

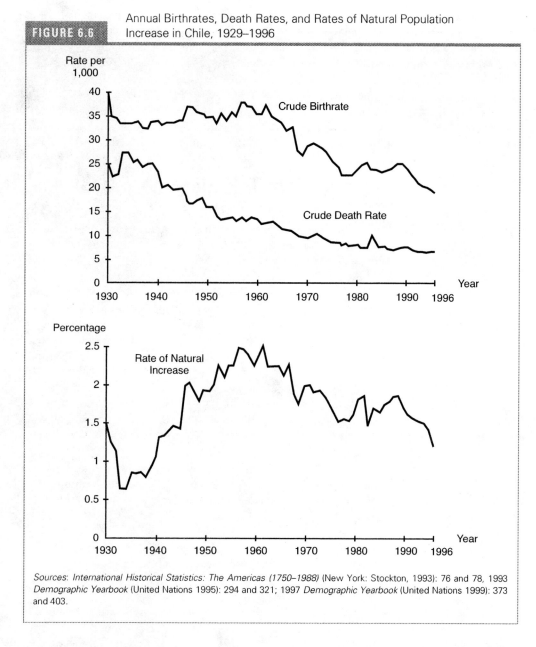

FIGURE 6.6   Annual Birthrates, Death Rates, and Rates of Natural Population Increase in Chile, 1929–1996

Sources: International Historical Statistics: The Americas (1750–1988) (New York: Stockton, 1993): 76 and 78, 1993 *Demographic Yearbook* (United Nations 1995): 294 and 321; 1997 *Demographic Yearbook* (United Nations 1999): 373 and 403.

nations that the resulting large increase in death rates and decrease in life expectancy is causing population to decline, not increase. According to the U.S. Census Bureau, Botswana, South Africa, and Zimbabwe are in that position. The average adult life span in these countries has decreased by 21 years. In 2005 13.2 million adult women (58.9 percent of total adults living with HIV) in Sub-Saharan Africa were infected.

The demographic transition is beneficial in countries where death rates have fallen because it suggests that reductions in population growth might accompany rising standards of living, at least in the long run. However, it also leaves many questions unanswered: Why does the fall in birthrates occur? Can the process be hastened? Will lower-income countries automatically experience demographic transition as living standards improve? Are industrialization or agricultural reform possible solutions to "the population problem"?

To answer these questions it is necessary to begin to look more deeply into the sources of change behind the demographic transition. Once these sources are identified and understood, they can be manipulated in such a way as to produce the maximum social benefit.

The Economic Approach to Population Control

Is the current rate of population growth efficient? Is it sustainable? The issue of sustainability is most easily dealt with in specific natural resource settings (such as the ability to produce sufficient food), so intensive consideration of that question will be deferred until succeeding chapters.

The demonstration that population growth reduces per capita income, however, is not sufficient to prove that inefficiency exists. If the reduced output is borne entirely by the families of the children, this reduction may represent a conscious choice by parents to sacrifice production in order to have more children. The net benefit gained from having more children would exceed the net benefit lost as output per person declined.

To establish whether or not population control is efficient, we must discover any potential behavioral biases toward overpopulation. Will parents always make efficient childbearing decisions?

A negative response seems appropriate for three specific reasons. First, childbearing decisions impose external costs outside the family. Second, the prices of key commodities or services related to childbearing and/or rearing may be inefficiently low, thereby sending the wrong signals. And finally, parents may not be fully informed about, or may not have reasonable access to, adequate means for controlling births.

Some sources of market failure can be identified immediately. Adding more people to a limited space gives rise to "*congestion externalities,*" higher costs resulting from the attempt to use resources at a higher-than-optimal capacity. Examples include too many people attempting to farm too little land and too many travelers attempting to use a specific roadway. These costs are intensified when all users of the resource are allowed free-access to it. And, as noted above, high population growth may exacerbate income inequality. Income equality is a public good. The population as a whole cannot be excluded from the existing degree of income equality. Furthermore, it is indivisible because, in a given society, the prevailing income distribution is the same for all the citizens of that country.

Why should individuals care about inequality *per se* as opposed to simply caring about their own income? Aside from a purely humane concern for others, particularly the poor, people care about inequality because it can create social tensions. When these social tensions exist, society is a less pleasant, perhaps even dangerous, place to live.

The demand to reduce income inequality clearly exists in modern society, as evidenced by the large number of private charitable organizations created to transfer income or services to the poor. Because the reduction of income inequality is a public good, we also know that these organizations cannot be relied on to reduce inequality as much as would be socially justified. Similarly, parents are not likely to take into account either the effect of more children on income inequality or congestion externalities when they make their family-size decisions. Decisions that may well be optimal for individual families could well result in inefficiently large populations.

Excessively low prices on key commodities can create a bias toward inefficiently high populations as well. Two particularly important ones are: (1) the cost of food and (2) the cost of education. It is common for developing countries to subsidize food by holding prices below market levels. Lower-than-normal food prices artificially lower the cost of children as long as the quantities of food available are maintained by government subsidy.

The second area in which the costs of children are not fully borne by the parents is education. Primary education is usually state financed, with the funds collected by taxes. The point is *not* that parents do not pay these costs; in part they do. The point is rather that their level of contribution is not usually sensitive to the number of children they have. The school taxes parents pay are generally the same whether parents have two children, ten children, or even no children. Thus, the marginal educational expenditure for a parent—the additional cost of education due to the birth of a child—is certainly lower than the true social cost of educating that child.

Unfortunately, very little has been accomplished on assessing the empirical significance of these externalities. Despite this lack of evidence, the interest in controlling population is clear in many, if not most, countries.

Controlling population is difficult. In many cultures the right to bear children is considered an inalienable right immune to influences outside the family. Indira Gandhi, the Prime Minister of India, lost an election in the late 1970s due principally to her aggressive and direct approach to population control. Though she subsequently regained her position, political figures in other democratic countries are not likely to miss the message. Dictating that no family can have more than two children is not politically palatable at this time in most countries. Such a dictum is seen as an unethical infringement on the rights of those who are mentally, physically, and monetarily equipped to care for larger families.

Yet the failure to control population growth can prove devastating to the quality of life, particularly in high-population-growth, low-income countries. Partha Dasgupta (1993) describes the pernicious, self-perpetuating process that can result:

> Children are borne in poverty, and they are raised in poverty. A large proportion suffer from undernourishment. They remain illiterate, and are often both stunted and wasted. Undernourishment retards their cognitive (and often motor) development...

What, then, is a democratic country to do? How can it gain control over population growth while allowing individual families considerable flexibility in choosing their family size? Successful population control involves two components: (1) lowering the desired family size and (2) providing sufficient access to contraceptive methods and family planning information to allow that size family to be realized.

The economic approach to population control *indirectly* controls population by lowering the desired family size. This is accomplished by identifying those factors that affect desired family size and changing those factors. To use the economic approach, we need to know how fertility decision-making is affected by the economic environment experienced by the family.

The major model attempting to assess the determinants of childbirth decision-making from an economic viewpoint is called the *microeconomic theory of fertility*. The point of departure for this theory is viewing children as consumer durables. The key insight is that the demand for children will be, as with more conventional commodities, downward sloping. All other things being equal, the more expensive children become, the fewer will be demanded.

With this point of departure, childbearing decisions can be modeled within a traditional demand-and-supply framework (see Figure 6.7). We shall designate the initial situation, before the imposition of any controls, as the point where marginal benefit, designated by MB_1, and marginal cost, designated by MC_1, are equal. The desired number of children at this point is Q_1. Note that, according to the analysis, the desired number of children can be reduced either by an inward shift of the marginal benefit curve to MB_2, or an upward shift in the marginal cost of children to MC_2, or both. What would cause these curves to shift?

FIGURE 6.7   The Marginal Benefits and Marginal Costs of Children

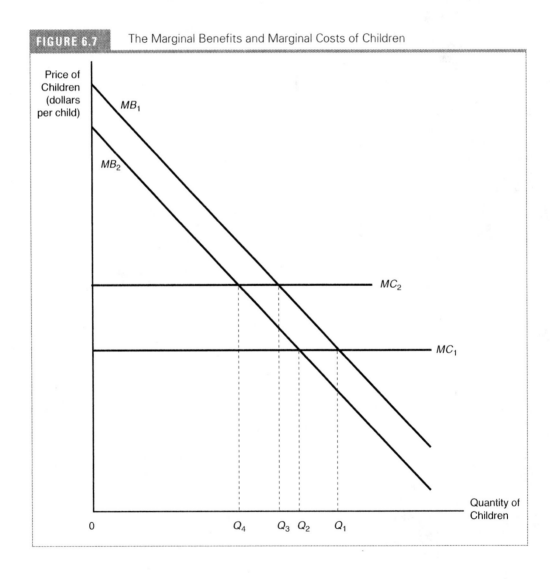

Let's consider the demand curve. Why might it have shifted inward during the demographic transition? Several sources of this shift have emerged.

1. The transition from an agricultural to an industrial economy reduces the productivity of children. In an agricultural economy, extra hands are useful, but in an industrial economy, child labor laws result in children contributing substantially less to the family. Therefore, the investment demand for children is reduced.

2. In countries with primitive savings systems one of the very few ways a person can provide for old-age security is to have plenty of children to provide for him or her in the twilight years. One would not, at first glance, think of children as social security systems, but, in many societies, they are precisely that. When alternative means of providing for old-age security are developed, the marginal benefit from additional children decreases.

3. In some countries a woman's status is almost exclusively defined in terms of the number of children she bears. If personal status is positively correlated with desired family size, this will increase the marginal benefit from an additional child. If status is no longer defined by the number of children, the marginal benefit may decrease.

4. A decrease in infant mortality can also cause the marginal benefit curve to shift inward. When infant mortality is high, it takes more births to produce the desired number of adult offspring.

5. Some evidence also suggests that the amount the marginal benefit curve shifts inward as a result of economic growth depends on the manner in which the increased employment associated with development is shared among the members of society. Those countries that have typically entered into a phase of sustained fertility decline in spite of low levels of average per capita income levels are usually characterized by a relatively equal distribution of income and a relatively widespread participation in the benefits of growth. The rather dramatic fertility decline in Korea from 1960 to 1974 provides an historical illustration of this point.

Desired family size is also affected by changes in the cost of children. The costs of raising children can be changed as a means of controlling population.

1. One of the main components of the cost of children is the opportunity cost of the mother's time. By increasing the educational and labor market opportunities for women, the opportunity cost of raising children is increased. This can affect the observed fertility rate both by deferring the time of marriage and by causing a reduction in the desired number of children, once married.

2. As societies urbanize and industrialize, housing space becomes more expensive due to the concentrated demands in specific locations. Thus, while the cost of extra space for children may be low in rural settings, it is much higher in urban settings.

3. The cost of children to parents may also be affected to a large extent by the cost of education. As nations struggle to improve their literacy rates by universal compulsory education, simultaneously they may raise the cost of children. These costs rise not only because of direct additional parental expenditures on education but also because of the earnings that are forgone when the children are in school rather than working.

4. As development occurs, generally parents demand more education and a higher-quality education for their children. Depending on the system for financing education, providing this higher-quality education may raise the cost of every child even if the cost of a given quality of education is not rising.

All of this provides a menu of opportunities for population control. The reasons listed above represent potent forces for change. Yet these methods should be used with care. Inducing a family to have fewer children without assisting the family in satisfying the basic needs the children were fulfilling (such as old-age security) would be inequitable.

In China policies illustrate just how far economic incentives can be carried. In announced regulations, one-child parents received subsidized health expenditures; priority in education, health care, and housing; and additional subsidized food. Meanwhile, parents with more than two children received a reduction of 5 percent in the total income for the third child (6 percent for the fourth, and so on). Also, families were denied access to further subsidized grain beyond that which they would already receive for their first two children. As a result, the total fertility rate, which was 5.97 in 1968, fell to 1.8 by 2000 and has stayed at that level.

Countries seeking to reduce fertility do not have to resort to such extreme measures. Policies such as enhancing the status of women, providing alternative sources of old-age security, and supplying employment opportunities that equalize the income distributions are both humane and effective. And, it is important to note that these policies can make headway even in very-low-income areas (see Example 6.1).

Studies that have evaluated the effects of this type of approach find that: (a) greater family wealth sustains higher education levels and better health; (b) a rise in the value of the mother's time has a positive effect on the demand for contraceptive services and a negative effect on fertility; (c) a rise in the value of the father's earnings has a positive effect on completed family size, child health, and child education; and (d) an increase in the mother's schooling has a negative effect on fertility and infant mortality and a positive effect on nutrition and children's schooling.

One way to empower women is to increase their income-earning potential. The typical way to increase income-earning potential is through investment in either human capital (education and training) or physical capital (looms, agricultural equipment, and so on). Funds for investment are normally obtained from banks. In order to minimize their risk, banks usually require *collateral*— property that can be sold to cover the proceeds of the loan in a case of failure to repay. In many developing countries women are not allowed to own property so they have no collateral. As a result, traditional credit facilities are closed to them and good investment opportunities are forgone.

One innovative solution to this problem was developed by the Grameen Bank in Bangladesh. This bank uses peer pressure rather than collateral to lower the risk of nonpayment. Small loans are made to individual women who belong to a group of five or so members. Upon complete repayment of all individual loans within the group, the members of the group become eligible for additional loans. If any member of the group fails to repay, all members remain ineligible until the full loan is repaid. Not only have repayment rates reportedly been very high, but also the increasing income-earning capacity generated by these loans has enhanced the effect of family planning programs (see Example 6.2).

In terms of population growth, child nutrition, and health these studies indicate a large payoff to making women fuller partners in the quest for improved living standards in the Third

EXAMPLE

6.1

Achieving Fertility Declines in Low-Income Countries: the Case of Kerala

Conventional wisdom suggests that achieving fertility declines in low-income countries is very difficult. Stories about countries that overcome the income barrier can therefore be very revealing.

One such case is Kerala, one of the poorer states in India. Despite ranking near the bottom of India in terms of per capita income, the state achieved the below replacement level of fertility two decades ahead of the all-India target year of 2011. The total fertility rate (TFR) declined from a high of 5.6 children per woman in the period 1951–1961 to about 1.7 in 1993.

Kerala apparently achieved this reduction in fertility because state and local governments focused on delivering reproductive and community health care, education (especially for females), and sanitation services to their citizens. The other key factor in this transition is the much higher social status accorded women in Kerala.

The advances in the field of social development have failed, however, to spur economic development. Kerala's per capita income and average annual growth rate during the 1980s were not only low; they were below the Indian average. The great potential for investments in human and social capital to spur sustainable development was not realized. Persistent problems included agricultural stagnation; massive "educated" unemployment; persistent poverty, especially among tribal populations, elderly women, and widows; a high and still-rising suicide rate among young people; and continued environmental degradation.

Recognizing these deficiencies, the Indian government is now pursuing a more ambitious approach to improve the economic condition of its inhabitants and the environment on which they depend. The new Kerala model relies on a community-based approach to sustainable development that draws upon the knowledge and aspirations of the various local populations.

Although it is too early to form a judgment on the success of this new approach, the early signs are encouraging. One project, for example, has been able to break the deadlock between decreasing land-use intensity and declining labor productivity. Two years after its implementation in 1998, the project has led to agricultural intensification and employment creation, and to a reversal of the environmentally unsound conversion of wetlands. This institutional innovation has apparently been economically beneficial for both participating laborers and farmers.

This experiment is one worth keeping an eye on.

Source: S. Irudaya Rajan and K. C. Zachariah, "Long-Term Implications of Low Fertility in Kerala, India," *Asia-Pacific Population Journal* (13)3, 1998: 41–66; and René Véron, "The 'New' Kerala Model: Lessons for Sustainable Development," *World Development* (29)4, April 2001: 601–617.

EXAMPLE

6.2

Income-Generating Activities as Fertility Control: Bangladesh

In Bangladesh the Grameen Bank and other organizations have begun to combine family planning programs with projects designed to generate income for women. Relying on peer pressure to encourage repayment of small loans, such programs have been successful, as loan recovery rates range between 96 percent and 100 percent. Results show that credit provision has been associated with productive self-employment, increase in income, accumulation of capital, and meeting basic needs of the poor borrowers.

A variety of income-generating activities is undertaken by participating women in order to pay back the loans. Such activities include: paddy husking, poultry raising, weaving, goat raising, and horticulture. In addition, other complementary government-financed social development activities such as sanitation, health care, nutrition, functional education, and population education are emphasized by all three programs. Family planning is actively and routinely promoted in group meetings, loan workshops, and training sessions that are financed by the agencies.

Results from this case study show that knowledge of contraceptive methods (through the population education component and group meetings with staff members) and the desire for no more children were higher among the beneficiaries of income-generating projects compared to the control group. About 60 percent of the beneficiaries were current users of contraceptives, compared to about 38 percent use by the control group. Also, about 80 percent of the beneficiaries desired no more children, while only 63 percent of the control group shared the same desire.

The income-generating projects led to an increase in contraceptive use regardless of their population education components. Over 50 percent who did not participate in their population education components were current users of contraceptives, compared to 38.4 percent of the control group. This suggests that the income-generating projects have an independent effect on the demand for fertility regulation and contraception.

Source: J. Chowdhury, Ruhul Amin, and A. U. Amhed, "Poor Women's Participation in Income Generating Projects and Their Fertility Regulation in Rural Bangladesh: Evidence from a Recent Survey," *World Development* April 1994: 555–564; and the Web site: http://www.colby.edu/personal/thtieten/pop-ban.html.

World. According to Lawrence Summers (1992), who at the time held the post of Chief Economist at the World Bank, the rate of return on investments in power plants in developing countries (a common investment) averaged less than 4 percent, while investments in education for girls produced returns of 20 percent or more.

In the words of Dr. Nafis Sadik (1989), then Executive Director of the U.N. Population Fund:

The extent to which women are free to make decisions affecting their lives may be the key to the future, not only of the poor countries, but the rich ones too. As mothers; producers or suppliers of food, fuel and water; traders and manufacturers; political and community leaders, women are at the center of the process of change. [p. 3]

The desire to reduce family size, however, is not sufficient if access to birth control information and contraceptives is inadequate. The adequacy of family planning programs varies markedly among countries even within the same continent. Yet where access is very good, fertility has declined, particularly when access is coupled with better education and opportunities for women.

Urbanization

In 2008 more than one-half of the world's population (3.3 billion people) lived in urban areas. The United Nations Population Fund estimates that this number will rise to almost 5 billion by 2030. The 2007 report on the State of the World's Population notes the following:

> *The United Nations Millennium Declaration drew attention to the growing significance of urban poverty, specifying, in Target 11, the modest ambition of achieving by 2020 "a significant improvement in the lives of at least 100 million slum dwellers."*

UN-Habitat's Third World Urban Forum, as well as its State of the World's Cities 2006/7, successfully focused world interest on the deteriorating social and environmental conditions of urban localities. The process of globalization has also drawn attention to the productive potential of cities as well as to their human cost. Yet the enormous scale and impact of future urbanization have not penetrated public consciousness.

So far, attention has centered mostly on immediate concerns, problems such as how to accommodate the poor and improve living conditions; how to generate employment; how to reduce cities' ecological footprint; how to improve governance; and how to administer increasingly complex urban systems.

These are all obviously important questions, but they shrink in comparison with the problems raised by the impending future growth of the urban population. Up to now, policymakers and civil society organizations have reacted to challenges as they arise. This is no longer enough. A preemptive approach is needed if urbanization in developing countries is to help solve social and environmental problems, rather than make them catastrophically worse.[1]

In the following chapters many of the topics are affected by increasing urbanization: land use, water pollution, air pollution, trash disposal, poverty, and so on. The distribution of costs and benefits of policy responses will depend to a large extent on how we respond to increased urbanization.

Using GIS to Map Population Data

Geographic information systems provide powerful mapping tools with which to visualize many of the concepts discussed in this chapter. The United Nations Environment Program has a GEO Data Portal through which numerous data can be accessed as files readable by GIS mapping software. Population density, population distribution, and dynamics are all accessible at various geographic scales. These can be displayed as maps or data tables or downloaded.

---

[1]UNFPA, *State of the World Population, 2007: Unleashing the Potential of Urban Growth,* http://www.unfpa.org/swp /swpmain.htm.

Summary

World population growth has slowed considerably in recent years. Population declines are already occurring in Germany and are expected in the near future in a number of northern European countries. The U.S. total fertility rate is below the replacement level. If maintained for a number of years, this fertility behavior would usher in an era of zero or negative population growth for the United States as well.

Those countries experiencing declines in their population growth will also experience a rise in the average age of their population. This transition to an older population should boost income per capita growth by increasing the share of the population in the labor force and by allowing more family wealth to be concentrated on the nutrition, health, and education of the children.

All other things being equal, lower population growth should also help to reduce income inequality. On average this effect will be felt most strongly in lower-income families, since they typically are larger. This tendency for incomes of lower-income families to increase faster than those of higher-income families should be reinforced by the effects on labor supply. By preventing an excess supply of labor, which holds wages down, slower population growth benefits wage earners. Wages are a particularly important source of income for lower-income families.

Finally, while population growth is not the sole or perhaps even the most important source of nonsustainability, it definitely plays a significant role. If, as seems reasonable, there exists a maximum level of economic activity that can be sustained without undermining the resource base upon which it depends, population growth determines how the fruits of that activity are shared. While a smaller global population could experience relatively high individual standards of living, a larger population would have to settle for less.

Key Concepts

age structure effect, *p.* 109
collateral, *p.* 122
congestion externalities, *p.* 118
downward spiral hypothesis, *p.* 115
economies of scale, *p.* 110
female availability effect, *p.* 110
induced innovation hypothesis, *p.* 115
law of diminishing marginal
   productivity, *p.* 110

microeconomic theory of fertility, *p.* 119
optimum global population, *p.* 104
replacement rate, *p.* 107
retirement effect, *p.* 110
stationary population, *p.* 106
theory of demographic transition, *p.* 114
total fertility rate, *p.* 105
youth effect, *p.* 109

Further Reading

Dasgupta, Partha. *An Inquiry into Well-Being and Destitution* (Oxford: Oxford University Press, 1993). A seminal work that deals comprehensively with the forces that create and accentuate poverty, including population growth.

Kelley, Allen C. "Economic Consequences of Population Change in the Third World," *Journal of Economic Literature* Vol. 26 (December 1988): 1685–1728. An excellent review of a complex literature with a detailed bibliography.

Kelley, Allen C. and Robert M. Schmidt. *Population and Income Change: Recent Evidence* (Washington, DC: The World Bank, 1994). An excellent review of the theory and evidence underlying the relationship between population growth and economic development; the review is complemented by some original empirical studies that reveal distinct new patterns.

Sharif, M. (2007). *Poverty Reduction—An Effective Means of Population Control: Theory, Evidence and Policy.* Aldershot, UK, Ashgate Publishing Limited. Uses econometrics to analyze the links between poverty and fertility behavior among the poor. It concludes that poverty reduction is the key link in reducing fertility.

Simon, Julian L. *Population and Development in Poor Countries: Selected Essays* (Princeton, NJ: Princeton University Press, 1992). A collection of essays from the primary proponent of the idea that moderate population growth (as opposed to zero or high) may be helpful to developing countries.

Historically Significant References

Boserup, E. *The Conditions of Agricultural Growth: The Economics of Agrarian Change Under Population Pressure.* Chicago: Aldine, 1965.

Cleaver, K. M. and G. A. Schreiber. *Reversing the Spiral: The Population, Agriculture and Environment Nexus in Sub-Saharan Africa.* Washington, DC: The World Bank, 1994.

Lindert, Peter. *Fertility and Scarcity in America.* Princeton: Princeton University Press, 1978.

Discussion Questions

1. Fertility rates vary widely among various ethnic groups in the United States. Black and Spanish-speaking Americans have above-average rates, for example, while Jews have below-average fertility rates. This may be due to different ethnic beliefs, but it may also be due to economic factors. How could you use economics to explain these fertility rate differences? What tests could you devise to see whether this explanation has validity?

2. The microeconomic theory of fertility provides an opportunity to determine how public policies that were designed for quite different purposes could affect fertility rates. Identify some public policies (for example, subsidies to people who own their own home, or subsidized day care) that could have an effect on fertility rates, and describe the relationship.

7 Natural Resource Economics: An Overview

The whole machinery of our intelligence, our general ideas and laws, fixed and external objects, principles, persons, and gods, are so many symbolic, algebraic expressions. They stand for experience; experience which we are incapable of retaining and surveying in its multitudinous immediacy. We should flounder hopelessly, like the animals, did we not keep ourselves afloat and direct our course by these intellectual devices. Theory helps us to bear our ignorance of fact.

—SANTAYANA, *The Sense of Beauty* (1896)

Introduction

How do societies react when finite stocks of depletable resources become scarce? Is it reasonable to expect that self-limiting feedback mechanisms would facilitate the transition to a sustainable steady state? Or is it more reasonable to expect that self-reinforcing feedback mechanisms would cause the system to overshoot the resource base, ultimately precipitating a societal collapse?

We begin to seek answers to these questions by studying the implications of both efficient and profit-maximizing decision making. What kinds of feedback mechanisms are implied by decisions motivated by efficiency and by profit maximization? Are they compatible with a smooth transition or are they more likely to produce *overshoot and collapse*?

We begin with the simple but useful *resource taxonomy* (classification system) that is used to distinguish various categories (measures) of resource availability. Confusing these categories and thereby using published information incorrectly can cause, and has caused, considerable mischief.

We then turn to the question of how markets allocate these resources over time. Whether or not the market is capable of yielding a dynamically efficient allocation in the presence or absence of a renewable substitute provides a focal point for the analysis. Succeeding chapters will use these principles to examine the allocation of energy, food, and water resources and as a basis for developing more elaborate models of renewable biological populations such as fisheries and forests.

A ResourceTaxonomy

Three separate concepts are used to classify the stock of depletable resources: (1) *current reserves*, (2) *potential reserves*, and (3) *resource endowment*. In the United States the U.S. Geological Survey (USGS) has the official responsibility for keeping records of the U.S. resource base, and it has developed the classification system described in Figure 7.1.

FIGURE 7.1   A Categorization of Resources

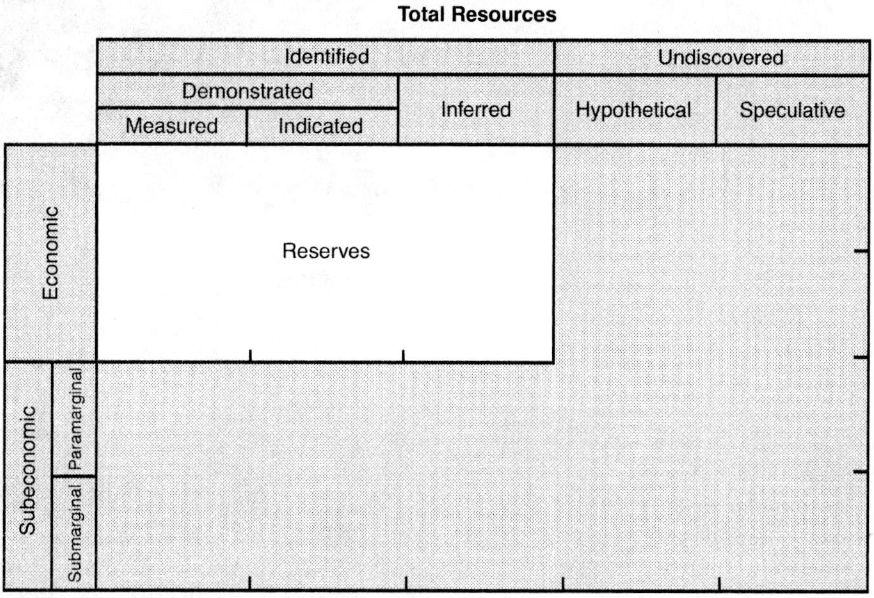

Terms

Identified resources Specific bodies of mineral-bearing material whose location, quality, and quantity are known from geological evidence, supported by engineering measurements

Measured resources Material for which quantity and quality estimates are within a margin of error of less than 20 percent, from geologically well-known sample sites

Indicated resources Material for which quantity and quality have been estimated, partly from sample analyses and partly from reasonable geological projections

Inferred resources Material in unexplored extensions of demonstrated resources based on geological projections

Undiscovered resources Unspecified bodies of mineral-bearing material surmised to exist, on the basis of broad geological knowledge and theory

Hypothetical resources Undiscovered materials reasonably expected to exist in a known mining district under known geological conditions

Speculative resources Undiscovered materials that may occur either in known types of deposits in favorable geological settings where no discoveries have been made, or in yet unknown types of deposits that remain to be recognized

Source: U.S. Bureau of Mines and the U.S. Geological Survey, "Principle of the Mineral Resource Classification System of the U.S. Bureau of Mines and the U.S. Geological Survey," *Geological Survey Bulletin* 1450-A, 1976.

Notice the two dimensions—one economic and one geological. A movement from top to bottom represents movement from cheaply extractable resources to those extracted at substantially higher prices. A movement from left to right represents increasing geological uncertainty about the size of the resource base.

Current reserves (white area in Figure 7.1) are defined as known resources that can profitably be extracted at current prices. The magnitude of these current reserves can be expressed as a number. *Potential reserves,* on the other hand, are most accurately defined as a function rather than a number. The amount of reserves potentially available depends upon the price people are willing to pay for those resources—the higher the price, the larger the potential reserves. For example, studies examining the amount of additional oil that could be recovered from existing oil fields using enhanced recovery techniques such as injecting solvents or steam into the well to lower the density of the oil, find that as the price per barrel increases, the amount of oil that can be economically recovered also increases.

The *resource endowment* represents the natural occurrence of resources in the earth's crust. Because prices have nothing to do with the size of the resource endowment, the latter is a geological rather than an economic concept. This concept is important because it represents an upper limit on the availability of terrestrial resources.

The distinctions among these concepts are significant. One common mistake in failing to respect these distinctions is that of using data on current reserves as if it represented the maximum potential reserves. This fundamental error can cause a huge understatement of the time until exhaustion.

A second common mistake is to assume that the entire resource endowment can be made available as potential reserves at some price people would be willing to pay. Clearly, if an infinite price were possible, then the entire resource endowment could be exploited. However, an infinite price is not likely.

Certain mineral resources are so costly to extract that it is inconceivable that any current or future society would be willing to pay the price necessary to extract them. Thus, it seems likely that the maximum feasible size of the potential reserves is smaller than the resource endowment. Exactly how much smaller cannot yet be determined with any degree of certainty.

Other distinctions among resource categories are also useful. The first such category includes all depletable, recyclable resources, such as copper. A *depletable resource* is one for which the natural-replenishment feedback loop can safely be ignored. The rate of natural replenishment for these resources is so low that it does not offer a potential for augmenting the stock in any reasonable time frame.

A *recyclable resource* is one that, although currently being used for some particular purpose, exists in a form allowing its mass to be recovered once that purpose is no longer necessary or desirable. For example, copper wiring from an automobile can be recovered after the car has been shipped to the junkyard. The degree to which a resource is recycled is determined by economic conditions, a subject covered in Chapter 19.

The current reserves of a depletable, recyclable resource can be augmented by economic replenishment as well as by recycling. Economic replenishment takes many forms, all sharing the characteristic that they turn previously unrecoverable resources into recoverable ones. One obvious stimulant for this replenishment is price. As price rises, producers find it profitable to explore more widely, dig more deeply, and use lower-concentration ores.

Higher prices also stimulate technological progress. *Technological progress* simply means advancement in the state of knowledge that allows us to do things we were not able to do before. One profound, if controversial, example can be found in the successful harnessing of nuclear power.

The other side of the coin for depletable, recyclable resources is that their potential reserves can be exhausted. The depletion rate is affected by the demand for and durability of the products built with the resource and by the ability to reuse the products. Except where demand is totally *price inelastic* (i.e., insensitive to price), higher prices tend to reduce the quantity demanded. Durable products last longer, reducing the need for newer ones. Reusable products provide a substitute for new products. As new products become more expensive, the demand for used products rises, which is demonstrated by the proliferation of consignment shops and flea markets.

For some resources, the size of the potential reserves depends explicitly on our ability to store the resource. For example, helium is found commingled with natural gas in common fields. Unless the helium is simultaneously captured and stored as the natural gas is extracted, it diffuses into the atmosphere. This results in such low concentrations that extraction of helium from the air is not economical at current or even likely future prices. Thus, the useful stock of helium depends crucially on how much we decide to store.

Not all depletable resources permit recycling or reuse. Some combustible resources such as coal, oil, and gas cannot be recycled or reused. Once they are combusted and turned into heat energy, the heat dissipates into the atmosphere and becomes nonrecoverable.

Since the endowment of depletable resources is of finite size, current use of depletable, non-recyclable resources precludes future use. Thus, the issue of how they should be shared across generations is raised in its starkest, least-forgiving form.

Depletable, recyclable resources raise this same issue, though somewhat less starkly. Recycling and reuse make the useful stock last longer, all other things being equal. It is tempting to suggest that depletable recyclable resources could last forever with 100 percent recycling, but unfortunately the physical theoretical upper limit on recycling is less than 100 percent—one implication of the entropy law defined in Chapter 2. Since some of the mass is always lost during recycling, the cumulative useful stock is finite, and current consumption patterns still have an effect on future generations.

For example, pennies can be melted down to recover the copper, but the amount rubbed off during circulation would never be recovered. As long as less than 100 percent of the mass is recycled, the useful stock must eventually decline to zero.

Renewable resources are distinguished from depletable resources primarily by the fact that natural replenishment augments their flow at a nonnegligible rate. Solar energy, water, cereal grains, fish, forests, and animals are all examples of renewable resources. Thus, it is possible, though not inevitable, that a flow of these resources could be maintained perpetually.[1]

For some renewable resources, the continuation and volume of their flow depend crucially on humans. Soil erosion and nutrient depletion reduce the capability of the soil to produce food. Excessive fishing reduces the stock of fish, which in turn reduces the growth of the fish

---

[1]Even renewable resources are ultimately finite, because their renewability is dependent on energy from the sun, and the sun is expected to serve as an energy source for only the next five or six billion years. That fact does not eliminate the need to manage resources effectively until that time. Furthermore, the finiteness of renewable resources is sufficiently far into the future to make the distinction useful.

population. Other examples abound. For other renewable resources, such as solar energy, the flow is independent of humans. The amount consumed by one generation does not reduce the amount that can be consumed by subsequent generations.

Some renewable resources can be stored; others cannot. For those that can, storage provides a valuable way to manage the allocation of the resource over time. We are not left simply at the mercy of natural ebbs and flows of the source. Without proper care, food perishes rapidly, but with appropriate storage, it can be used to feed the hungry in times of famine. Unstored solar energy radiates off the earth's surface and dissipates into the atmosphere. Although solar energy can be stored in many forms, the most common natural form of storage occurs when it is converted to biomass by photosynthesis.

Storage of renewable resources usually performs a different service than does storage of depletable resources. Storing depletable resources extends their economic life; storing renewable resources, on the other hand, can serve as a means of "smoothing out" the cyclical imbalances of supply and demand. Surpluses are stored for later times when deficits may occur. Food stockpiles and the use of dams to store hydropower are two familiar examples.

Managing renewable resources presents a different challenge than managing depletable resources, although an equally significant one. The challenge for depletable resources involves allocating dwindling stocks among generations while meeting the ultimate transition to renewable resources. In contrast, the challenge for managing renewable resources involves the maintenance of an efficient, sustainable flow. Chapters 8 through 13 deal with how the economic and political sectors have responded to these challenges for particularly significant types of resources.

Efficient Intertemporal Allocations

If we are to judge the adequacy of market allocations, we must define what is meant by efficiency in relation to the management of depletable and renewable resource allocations. Because allocation over time is the crucial issue, dynamic efficiency becomes the core concept. As we noted earlier, the dynamic-efficiency criterion assumes that society's objective is to maximize the present value of net benefits coming from the resource. For a depletable, nonrecyclable resource, this maximization requires a balancing of the current and subsequent uses of the resource. In order to review how the dynamic-efficiency criterion defines this balance, we will elaborate on the very simple two-period model developed in Chapter 5.

The Two-Period Model Revisited

In Chapter 5 we defined a situation involving the allocation, over two periods, of a finite resource that could be extracted at a constant marginal cost. With a stable demand curve for the resource, an efficient allocation meant that more than half of the resource was allocated to the first period and less than half to the second period. This allocation was affected both by the marginal cost of extraction and by the marginal user cost. Because of the fixed and finite supplies of depletable resources, production of a unit today precludes production of that unit tomorrow. Therefore, production decisions today must take forgone future net benefits into account. Marginal user cost is the opportunity cost measure that allows balancing to take place.

The marginal cost of extraction is assumed to be constant, but the current value of the marginal user cost rises over time. In fact, as was demonstrated in Chapter 5, when the demand curve is stable over time and the marginal cost of extraction is constant, the rate of increase in the current value of the marginal user cost is equal to r, the discount rate. Thus, in Period 2, the marginal user cost would be $1 + r$ times as large as it was in Period 1.[2] In an efficient allocation, marginal user cost rises at rate r in order to preserve the balance between present and future production.

In summary, our two-period example suggests that an efficient allocation of a finite resource with a constant marginal cost of extraction involves rising marginal-user cost and falling quantities consumed.

If we were to think about longer time periods and not limit ourselves to two periods, in this case (as in the two-period case), the efficient marginal user cost rises steadily. This rise in the efficient marginal user cost reflects increasing scarcity and the accompanying rise in the opportunity cost of current consumption imposed by this increasing scarcity. In response to the rising costs over time, the quantity extracted falls over time until the remaining stock finally reaches zero. At this point, *total marginal cost* is equal to the highest price anyone is willing to pay, so that demand and supply simultaneously equal zero. Thus, even in this difficult case involving no increase in the marginal cost of extraction, an efficient allocation envisions a smooth transition to the exhaustion of a resource. The resource does not "suddenly" run out—although in this case it does eventually run out.

Transition to a Renewable Substitute

So far we have discussed the allocation of a depletable resource when no substitute is available to take its place. However, suppose we consider the nature of an efficient allocation when a substitute renewable resource, a *backstop resource*, is available at a constant marginal cost. This resource is considered sufficiently abundant that its total marginal cost is equal to the marginal cost of extraction, implying that the marginal user cost of the substitute is zero. This scenario could describe the efficient allocation of oil or natural gas with a solar substitute, for example, or the efficient allocation of exhaustible groundwater with a surface-water substitute. How could we define an efficient allocation in this circumstance?

Because this problem is very similar to the one already discussed, we can use what we have already learned as a foundation for mastering this new situation. The depletable resource would be exhausted in this case, just as it was in the previous case. However, that will be less of a problem in this case because we will merely switch to the renewable resource at the appropriate time.

The total marginal cost for the depletable resource would never exceed the marginal cost of the substitute because society could always use the renewable resource instead, whenever it was cheaper to do so. Thus, although the maximum willingness to pay (the *choke price*) sets the upper limit on total marginal cost when no substitute is available, the marginal cost of extraction of the substitute sets the upper limit when an alternative resource is available at a marginal cost that is lower than the choke price.

In this efficient allocation, the transition with an abundant substitute is once again smooth. Quantity extracted is gradually reduced as the marginal use cost rises until the switch is made to the substitute. No abrupt change is evident in either the marginal-cost or quantity profile.

---

[2]The condition that marginal user cost rises at rate r is true only when the marginal cost of extraction is constant. For the more complicated case see Tietenberg and Lewis (2009).

Because the renewable substitute is available, more of the depletable resource would be extracted in the earlier periods than would be the case without the substitute (due to the lower marginal user cost). As a result, the depletable resource would be exhausted sooner than it would have been without the renewable-resource substitute.

At the transition point, called the *switch point*, consumption of the renewable resource begins. Prior to the switch point, only the depletable resource is consumed, whereas after the switch point, only the renewable resource is consumed. This sequencing of consumption patterns results from the cost patterns. Prior to the switch point, the depletable resource is cheaper. At the switch point, the marginal cost of the depletable resource (including the marginal user cost) rises to meet the marginal cost of the substitute, and the transition occurs.

Exploration and Technological Progress

The search for new resources is expensive. As the more easily discovered resources are exhausted, the search for new sources must progress to more challenging environments, such as the bottom of the ocean or locations deep within the earth. This suggests that the *marginal cost of exploration*, which is the marginal cost of finding additional units of the resource, should be expected to rise over time, just as the marginal cost of extraction does.

As the total marginal cost for a resource rises over time, society has new incentives to actively explore possible new sources of that resource. The higher the expected rise in the total marginal cost for known sources, the larger is the potential increase in net benefits from exploration.

Some of this exploration would be successful—new sources of the resource would be discovered. As a result, relative to a case with no successful exploration, the new finds would tend to encourage more consumption of the depletable resource. Successful exploration would cause a smaller and slower decline in consumption by dampening the rise in total marginal cost.

Our concept of efficient resource allocations can also be expanded to include consideration of technological progress. In the present context, technological progress would be manifested as reductions in the cost of extraction. For a resource that can be extracted at constant marginal cost, a one-time breakthrough lowering the future marginal cost of extraction, but not the present marginal cost, would raise the marginal user cost (can you see why?), shifting more of the extraction into the future (when the marginal extraction cost would be lower).[3]

The most pervasive effects of technological progress involve continuous downward shifts in the cost of extraction over some extended time period. The total marginal cost of the resource could actually fall over time if the cost-reducing nature of technological progress became so potent that, in spite of increasing reliance on inferior ore, the marginal cost of extraction decreased (Example 7.1). With a finite amount of this resource, the fall in total marginal cost would necessarily be transitory, because ultimately it would have to rise. This period of transition could last quite a long time, however.

---

[3]To see what happens to the marginal user cost, go back to Figure 5.2. A lower marginal extraction cost in the second period would be reflected in Figure 5.2 as an upward shift in the PVMNB curve for the second period. This shift would result in a higher marginal user cost, resulting in less of the resource extracted in Period 1 and more of the resource extracted in Period 2.

Technological Progress in the Iron Ore Industry

EXAMPLE

7.1

The term technological progress plays an important role in the economic analysis of mineral resources. Yet, at times, it can appear abstract, even mystical. It shouldn't! Far from being a "blind faith" assertion detached from reality, technological progress refers to a host of ingenious ways in which people have reacted to impending shortages with sufficient imagination that the available supply of resources has been greatly expanded at reasonable cost. To illustrate how concrete a notion technological progress is, let's discuss one historically important example.

In 1947 the president of Republic Steel, C. M. White, calculated the expected life of the Mesabi range of northern Minnesota (the source of some 60 percent of iron ore consumed during World War II) as being about five to seven years. By 1955, only eight years later, *U.S. News and World Report* was able to conclude that worry over the scarcity of iron ore could be dismissed. The source of this remarkable transformation of scarcity into abundance was the discovery of a new technique, called *pelletization,* for preparing iron ore.

Prior to pelletization, the standard ores from which iron was derived contained from 50 to more than 65 percent iron in crude form. Although a significant percentage of taconite ore was known to be available, it contained less than 30 percent iron in crude form, and no one knew how to use such low concentrations at reasonable cost. That changed when pelletization allowed the profitable use of the taconite ores. Pelletization is a process by which these ores are processed and concentrated at the mine site prior to shipment to the blast furnaces.

While expanding the supply of iron ore, pelletization reduced its cost—in spite of the use of an inferior ore grade. This cost reduction had several sources. First, substantially *less* energy was used: The shift in ore technology toward pelletization produced net energy savings of 17 percent even though the pelletization process itself required additional energy. The reduction came from the discovery that the blast furnaces could be operated much more efficiently using pelletization inputs. The process also reduced labor requirements per ton by some 8.2 percent while increasing the output of the blast furnaces. By 1960 a blast furnace owned by Armco Steel in Middletown, Ohio, which had a rated capacity of approximately 1,500 tons of molten iron per day, was able to achieve production levels of 2,700 and 2,800 tons per day when fired with 90 percent pellets. Pellets nearly doubled the blast furnace's productivity!

Sources: Kakela, Peter J., "Iron Ore: Energy Labor and Capital Changes with Technology," *Science* 202 (December 15, 1978): 1151–1157; "Iron Ore: From Depletion to Abundance," *Science* 212 (April 10, 1981): 132–136.

Market Allocations

In the preceding sections we have examined in detail how the efficient allocation of substitutable depletable and renewable resources over time would be defined in a variety of circumstances. We must now address the question of whether actual markets can be expected to produce an efficient allocation. Can the private market—a market involving millions of consumers and producers each reacting to his or her own unique preferences—*ever* result in a dynamically efficient allocation? Is profit maximization compatible with dynamic efficiency?

Appropriate Property-Right Structures

The most common misconception of those who believe that even a perfect market could never achieve an efficient allocation is a belief that producers want to extract and sell the resources as fast as possible because that is how they derive the most value from the resource. This misconception makes people see markets as myopic and unconcerned about the future.

As long as the property-rights structures governing natural resources have the characteristics of exclusivity, universality, transferability, and enforceability (Chapter 4), the markets in which those resources are bought and sold will not necessarily lead to myopic choices; myopic choices result in lower profits. When bearing the marginal user cost, the producer acts efficiently. A resource in the ground has two potential sources of value to its owner: (1) a use value when it is sold (the only source considered by those diagnosing inevitable myopia) and (2) an asset value when it remains in the ground (a source any profit-maximizing owner must also consider). As long as the price of a resource continues to rise over time, the resource in the ground is becoming more valuable. However, the owner of this resource accrues this capital gain only if the resource is conserved. A producer who sells all resources in the earlier periods loses the chance to take advantage of higher prices in the future and loses the additional profits that would accrue from those higher prices.

A prescient, profit-maximizing producer attempts to balance present and future production in order to maximize the value of the resource and hence, the present value of profits. Because higher prices in the future provide an incentive to conserve, a producer who ignores this incentive would not be maximizing the value of the resource. We would expect the resource to be bought by someone willing to conserve it and prepared to maximize its value. As long as social and private discount rates coincide, property-right structures are well-defined, and reliable information about future prices is available, a producer who selfishly pursues maximum profits simultaneously provides the maximum present value of net benefits for society.

The implication of this analysis is that, in prescient, competitive resource markets with fully specified property rights, the price of the resource would equal the total marginal cost and the market ccould achieve an efficient outcome.

Environmental Costs

Not all actual market situations satisfy these conditions, of course. One of the most important situations in which property-right structures may not be well defined occurs when the extraction of a natural resource imposes an *environmental cost* on society that is not internalized by the producers. The aesthetic costs of strip mining, the health risks associated with uranium tailings, and the acids leached into streams from mine operations are all examples of associated environmental costs. Not only is the presence of environmental costs empirically important, it is also conceptually important. It forms one of the bridges between the traditionally separate fields of environmental economics and natural resource economics.

Suppose, for example, that the extraction of the depletable resource caused some damage to the environment not adequately reflected in the costs faced by the extracting firms. This would be an external cost. The cost of getting the resource out of the ground, as well as processing and shipping it, is borne by the resource owner and considered in the calculation of how much of the resource to extract. The environmental damage, however, is not borne by the owner and, in the absence of any outside attempt to internalize that cost, it will not be part of the extraction decision. How would the market allocation, based on only the former cost, differ from the efficient allocation, which is based on both?

The inclusion of environmental costs results in higher prices, which tend to dampen demand. This lowers the rate of consumption of the resource, which, all other things being equal, would make it last longer.

What can we learn about the allocation of depletable resources over time when environmental side effects are not borne by the agent determining the extraction rate? The price of the depletable resource would be inefficiently low and the resource would be extracted too rapidly, demonstrating once again the interdependencies of the various decisions we have to make about the future. Environmental and natural resource decisions are intimately and inextricably linked.

Summary

The efficient allocation of substitutable depletable and renewable resources depends on the circumstances. When the resource can be extracted at a constant marginal cost, the efficient quantity of the depletable resource extracted declines over time. If no substitute is available, the quantity declines smoothly to zero. If a renewable, constant-cost substitute is available, the quantity of the depletable resource extracted will decline smoothly to the quantity available from the renewable resource. In both cases, all of the available depletable resource would be eventually used up and marginal user cost would rise over time, reaching a maximum when the last unit of depletable resource was extracted.

As Example 7.1 demonstrates introducing technological progress and exploration activity can expand the size of current reserves. This expansion keeps marginal user cost from rising as fast as it otherwise would. If these effects are sufficiently potent, marginal extraction cost could actually decline for some period of time, causing the quantity extracted to rise.

When property-right structures are properly defined, market allocations of depletable resources can be efficient. Self-interest and efficiency are not necessarily incompatible.

When the extraction of resources imposes an external environmental cost, however, market allocations will not generally be efficient. The market price of the depletable resource would be too low, and too much of the resource would be extracted too rapidly.

In an efficient market allocation, the transition from depletable to renewable resources is smooth and exhibits no overshoot and collapse characteristics. Whether the actual market allocations of these various types of resources are efficient is explored in subsequent chapters. To the extent that they are efficient, a laissez-faire policy would represent an appropriate response by the government. On the other hand, if the market is not capable of yielding an efficient allocation, some form of government intervention may be necessary. In the next few chapters we will examine these questions for a number of different types of depletable and renewable resources.

Key Concepts

backstop resource, *p.* 133
choke price, *p.* 133
current reserves, *p.* 130
depletable resource, *p.* 130
environmental cost, *p.* 136
marginal cost of exploration, *p.* 134
potential reserves, *p.* 130
price inelastic, *p.* 131

recyclable resource, *p.* 130
renewable resources, *p.* 131
resource endowment, *p.* 130
resource taxonomy, *p.* 128
switch point, *p.* 134
technological progress, *p.* 131
total marginal cost, *p.* 133

Further Reading

Bohi, Douglas R. and Michael A. Toman. *Analyzing Nonrenewable Resource Supply* (Washington, DC: Resources for the Future, 1984). A reinterpretation and evaluation of existing research that attempts to weave theoretical, empirical, and practical insights concerning the management of depletable resources.

Chapman, Duane. "Computation Techniques for Intertemporal Allocation of Natural Resources," *American Journal of Agricultural Economics* 69 (February 1987) (1): 134–142. Shows how to find numerical solutions for the types of depletable resource problems considered in this chapter.

Conrad, Jon M. and Colin W. Clark. *Natural Resource Economics: Notes and Problems* (Cambridge, UK: Cambridge University Press, 1987). Reviews techniques of dynamic optimization and shows how they can be applied to the management of various resource systems.

Toman, Michael A. "'Depletion Effects' and Nonrenewable Resource Supply," *Land Economics* 62 (November 1986): 341–353. An excellent, nontechnical discussion of the increasing-cost case with and without exploration and additions to reserves.

Additional References

Dasgupta, P. (2008). "Nature in Economics." *Environmental & Resource Economics*, 39(1): 1-7.

Kolstad, C. D. "Energy and Depletable Resources: Economics and Policy, 1973–1998," *Journal of Environmental Economics and Management*, 39 (2000) (3): 282–305.

Tietenberg, T. H. and Lynne Lewis. *Environmental and Natural Resource Economics* (Reading, MA: Addison-Wesley, 2009): Chapter 7.

Historically Significant References

Dasgupta, P. S. and G. M. Heal. *Economic Theory and Exhaustible Resources.* (Cambridge, UK: Cambridge University Press, 1979).

Hotelling, H. "The Economics of Exhaustible Resources," *Journal of Political Economy* 39 (1931) (2): 137–175.

Discussion Questions

1. Identify any external costs that might be associated with the following activities: (1) extracting timber from public lands, (2) extracting timber from one's own land, (3) harvesting fish from the ocean, and (4) taking water from a shared groundwater source. How would these external costs affect the extraction of these resources over time?

2. What causes technological progress? Can the rate of technological progress be influenced by the government? Why or why not?

3. Suppose a depletable resource is controlled by a monopoly. Compared to a situation where the same resource was allocated by a competitive market, would the marginal user cost be higher or lower for the monopoly case? Would you expect the monopoly resource to be extracted more rapidly or more slowly? Why?

8 Energy

If it ain't broke, don't fix it!

—OLD MAINE PROVERB

Introduction

Energy is one of our most critical resources; without it, life would cease. We derive energy from the food we eat. Through photosynthesis, the plant life we consume—both directly and indirectly (when we eat meat)—depends on energy from the sun. The materials we use to build our houses and produce the goods we consume are extracted from the earth's crust, and then transformed into finished products through expenditures of energy.

Currently, most industrialized countries depend on oil and natural gas for most of their energy needs. Worldwide these resources together supply 62 percent of all energy consumed. Both are depletable, nonrecyclable sources of energy. Proven crude oil reserves peaked during the 1970s and natural gas peaked in the 1980s in the United States and Europe. Since then, the amount extracted has exceeded additions to reserves. Kenneth Deffeyes (2001) and Campbell and Laherrere (1998) estimate that global oil production will peak in the first decade of the twenty-first century. As Example 8.1 points out, however, due to the methodology used, the predictions of the timing of the peak are controversial.

Even if we cannot precisely determine when the fuels on which we currently depend so heavily will run out, we still need to think about the process of transition to new energy sources.

According to depletable resource models, oil and natural gas would be transition fuels in an efficient allocation. They would be used until the marginal cost of further use exceeded the marginal cost of substitute resources—either more abundant depletable resources, such as coal, or renewable sources, such as solar energy.[1] In an efficient market path, the transition to these alternative sources would be smooth and harmonious. Have the allocations of the last several decades been efficient or not?

---

[1]When used for other purposes, oil can be recycled. Waste lubricating oil is now routinely recycled.

EXAMPLE

8.1

Hubbert's Peak

When can we expect to run out of oil? It's a simple question with a complex answer. In 1956 geophysicist M. King Hubbert, then working at the Shell Research Lab in Houston, predicted that U.S. oil production would reach its peak in the early 1970s. Though *Hubbert's Peak* failed to win much acceptance from experts in the oil industry or among academics, his prediction came true in the early 1970s. With some modifications, Hubbert's methodology has since been used to predict the timing of a downturn in the global annual oil production as well as to forecast when we could run out of oil.

These forecasts and the methods that underlie them are controversial, in part because they ignore such obvious economic factors as prices. The Hubbert model assumes that the annual rate of production follows a bell-shaped curve, regardless of what is happening in oil markets; the model ignores the impact of oil prices. It seems reasonable to believe, however, that by affecting the incentive to explore new oil sources and to bring them into production, prices should affect the shape of the production curve.

What is the impact of incorporating prices into the model? Pesaran and Samiei (1995) found, as expected, that modifying the model to include price effects causes the estimated ultimate resource recovery to be larger than implied by the basic Hubbert model. A separate study by Kaufman and Cleveland (2001) concludes that forecasting with a Hubbert-type model is fraught with peril:

> ...production in the lower 48 states stabilizes in the late 1970s and early 1980s, which contradicts the steady decline forecast by the Hubbert model. Our results indicate that Hubbert was able to predict the peak in U.S. production accurately because real oil prices average real cost of production, and [government decisions] co-evolved in a way that traced what appears to be a symmetric bell-shaped curve for production over time. A different evolutionary path for any of these variables could have produced a pattern of production that is significantly different from a bell-shaped curve and production may not have peaked in 1970. In effect, Hubbert got lucky.

Does this mean we are not running out of oil? No. It simply means we have to be cautious when interpreting forecasts that attempt to assign a specific date to the transition to other sources of energy.

In 2005 the Administrator of the U.S. Energy Information Agency presented a compendium of 36 studies of global oil production and all but one forecasted a production peak. The EIA's own estimates on the timing of the peak range from 2031 to 2068 (Caruso, 2005). The issue, it seems, is no longer whether oil production will peak, but when.

Sources: Pesaran, M. and H. Samiei, "Forecasting Ultimate Resource Recovery," *International Journal of Forecasting* 11(4), 1995: 543–555; Kaufman, R. and C. Cleveland, "Oil Production in the Lower 48 States: Economic, Geological, and Institutional Determinants," *Energy Journal,* 22(1), 2001: 27–49; Caruso, G., "When Will World Oil Production Peak? A presentation at the 10th Annual Asia Oil and Gas Conference in Kuala Lumpur, Malaysia, June 13, 2005.

Is the market mechanism flawed in its allocation of depletable recyclable resources? If so, is it a fatal flaw? If not, what caused the inefficient allocations? Is the problem correctable?

In this chapter we will examine some of the major issues associated with the allocation of energy resources over time and we will see how economic analysis can clarify our understanding of both the sources of the problems and their solutions. However, because energy is too complex a subject to treat comprehensively in one chapter, additional references are provided.

Natural Gas: Price Controls

In the United States during the winter of late 1974 and early 1975, serious shortages of natural gas developed. Customers who had contracted and were willing to pay for natural gas were unable to get as much as they wanted. The shortage (or *curtailment* as the Federal Energy Regulatory Commission calls it) amounted to 2 trillion cubic feet of natural gas in 1974–1975, which represented roughly 10 percent of the marketed production in 1975. In an efficient allocation, shortages of that magnitude would never have happened. Why did they?

The source of the problem can be traced directly to government *price controls* on natural gas. This story begins, oddly enough, with the rise of the automobile, which traditionally has not used natural gas as a fuel. The increasing importance of the automobile for transportation created a rising demand for gasoline, which in turn stimulated a search for new sources of crude oil. This exploration activity uncovered large quantities of natural gas (known as *associated gas*), in addition to large quantities of crude oil, which was the object of the search.

As natural gas was discovered, it replaced manufactured gas—and some coal—as an energy source in the geographic areas where it was found. Then, as a geographically dispersed demand developed for this increasingly available gas, a long-distance system of gas pipelines was designed and constructed. In the period following World War II, natural gas became an important source of energy for the United States.

The regulation of natural gas began in 1938 with the passage of the *Natural Gas Act*. This Act transformed the Federal Power Commission (FPC) into a federal regulatory agency charged with maintaining "just" prices. In 1954 a Supreme Court decision in *Phillips Petroleum Co.* v. *Wisconsin* forced the FPC to extend its price control regulations to the producers. Previously, it had merely limited its regulation to pipeline companies.

Because the process of setting price ceilings proved cumbersome, the hastily conceived initial ("interim") ceilings remained in effect for almost a decade before the commission was able to impose more carefully considered ceilings. What was the effect of this regulation?

The ceilings prevented prices from reaching their normal levels. Because price increases are the source of the incentive to conserve, the lower prices caused more of the resource to be used in earlier years. Consumption levels in those years were higher with price controls than without them. Attracted by artificially low prices, consumers would invest in equipment to use natural gas, only to discover—after the transition—that natural gas was no longer available.

Price controls may cause other problems as well. Up to this point we have discussed permanent controls. Not all price controls are permanent; they can change at the whim of the political process, unpredictably. The fact that prices can suddenly rise when the ceiling is lifted also creates unfortunate incentives. If producers expect a large price increase in the near future, they have an incentive to stop production and wait for the higher prices. Needless to say, this circumstance could cause severe problems for consumers.

For legal reasons the price controls on natural gas were placed solely on gas shipped across state lines. Gas consumed within the states where it was produced could be priced at what the market would bear. As a result, gas produced and sold within a given state received a higher price than that sold in other states. Consequently, the share of gas in the interstate market fell over time, as producers found it more profitable to commit reserve additions to the *intrastate,* rather than the *interstate,* market. During 1964–1969 about 33 percent of the average annual reserve additions were committed to the interstate market. By 1970–1974 this commitment had fallen to a little less than 5 percent.

The practical effect of forcing lower prices for gas destined for the interstate market was to cause the shortages to be concentrated in states served by pipeline and dependent on the interstate shipment of gas. As a result, the ensuing damage caused was greater than it would have been if all consuming areas had shared somewhat more equitably in the shortfall. Governmental control of prices not only precipitated the damage, it intensified it!

It seems fair to conclude that, by sapping the economic system of its ability to respond to changing conditions, price controls on natural gas created a significant amount of turmoil. If this kind of political control is likely to recur with some regularity, perhaps the overshoot and collapse scenario might have some validity. In this case it would be caused by government interference rather than by any pure market behavior. If so, the proverb that opens this chapter becomes particularly relevant!

Why did Congress embark on such a counterproductive policy? The answer is found in rent-seeking behavior that can be explained through the use of our consumer- and producer-surplus model. Let's examine the political incentives in a simple model.

Consider Figure 8.1. An efficient market allocation would result in quantity Q^* supplied at price P^*. The net benefits received by the country would be represented by the total geometric

FIGURE 8.1   The Effect of Price Controls

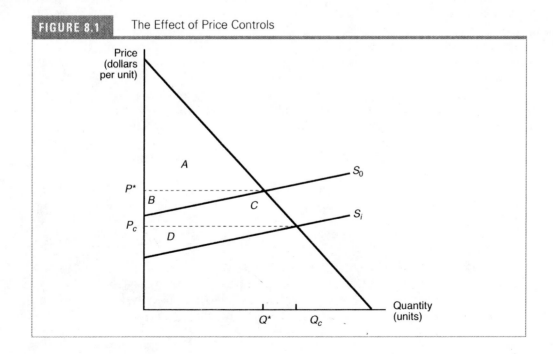

area encompassed by areas *A* and *B*. Of these net benefits, area *A* would be received by consumers as consumer surplus and *B* would be received by producers as producer surplus.

Now suppose that a price ceiling were established. From the preceding discussion we know that this ceiling would reduce the marginal user cost because higher future prices would no longer be possible. In Figure 8.1 this has the effect for current producers of lowering the perceived-supply curve because of the lower marginal user cost. As a result of this shift in the perceived-supply curve, current production would expand to quantity Q_c and price would fall to P_c. Current consumers would unambiguously be better off, because consumer surplus would be area $A + B + C$ instead of area *A*. They would have gained a net benefit equal to $B + C$.

It may appear that producers could also gain if $D > B$, but that is not correct. Because producers would be overproducing, they would be giving up the scarcity rent they could have gotten without price controls. Area *D* measures current profits only, without considering scarcity rent. When the loss in scarcity rent is considered, producers unambiguously lose net benefits.

Future consumers are also unambiguously worse off. In terms of Figure 8.1, which represents the allocation in a given year, as the resource was depleted the supply curve for each subsequent year would shift up, thereby reflecting the higher marginal extraction costs for the remaining endowment of the resource. When the marginal extraction cost ultimately reached the level of the price control, the amount supplied would drop to zero. Extracting more would make no sense to suppliers because their cost would exceed the controlled price. Since the demand would not be zero at that price, a shortage would develop. Although consumers would be willing to pay higher prices and suppliers would be happy to supply more of the resource at those higher prices (if they were not prevented from doing so by the price control), the price ceiling would keep those resources in the ground.

Congress may view scarcity rent as a possible source of revenue to transfer from producers to consumers. As we have seen, however, scarcity rent is an opportunity cost that serves a distinct purpose—the protection of future consumers. When government attempts to reduce this scarcity rent through price controls, the result is an over allocation to current consumers and an under allocation to future consumers. Thus, what appears to be a transfer from producers to consumers is, in large part, also a transfer from future consumers to present consumers. Because current consumers mean current votes and future consumers may not know whom to blame by the time shortages appear, price controls are politically attractive. Unfortunately, they are also inefficient: The losses to future consumers and producers are greater than the gains to current consumers. Because they distort the allocation toward the present, controls are also unfair. Thus, markets in the presence of price controls are indeed myopic, but the problem lies with the controls, not with the market.

Over the long run, price controls end up harming consumers rather than helping them. Scarcity rent plays an important role in the allocation process, and attempts to eliminate it can create more problems than solutions. After long debating the price control issue, Congress passed the *Natural Gas Policy Act* on November 9, 1978. This Act initiated the eventual phased decontrol of natural gas prices. Included among its other provisions was a movement away from the average cost pricing of substitute gas for industrial customers and the imposition of price controls for the first time on intrastate gas, until such time as all prices should be decontrolled. On July 27, 1989, President George Bush signed a bill removing in stages all remaining controls on natural gas. By January 1993, no sources of natural gas were subject to price controls.

Since that time the demand for natural gas has been increasing (due in part to the fact that its combustion products cause fewer adverse air quality impacts than either oil or coal) and domestic production in many industrialized nations (including the United States) has not kept pace. This has put an upward pressure on prices. For example, in the United States the residential price of natural gas rose from $5.54 per thousand cubic feet in December 1992 to $12.53 per thousand cubic feet in December 2006.

Necessarily, imports have risen. While some imports come through pipelines from contiguous countries, the bulk of increasing imports has come in the form of liquefied natural gas (LNG). Liquefied natural gas is created when natural gas is cooled to minus 259 degrees Fahrenheit (minus 161 degrees Celsius). In this state it becomes a clear, colorless, odorless liquid. The super-chilled LNG is transported over water in specially built carriers that are up to 1,000 feet long, and require a minimum water depth of 40 feet when fully loaded.

Although using LNG as a fuel is relatively attractive from an air quality point of view, its transport and storage poses some significant potential hazards. According to the U.S. Congressional Research Service, if LNG were to spill near an ignition source, the resulting combustible gas-air concentration would burn much hotter and faster than oil or gasoline fires. These LNG fires cannot be extinguished except by the combustion of all the material. Because LNG fires are so hot, the heat from the fireball could injure people and damage property a considerable distance from the fire itself.

Historically, the safety record of LNG has been quite good, but the enhanced potential for terrorism has raised security concerns. Since experts believe that LNG facilities would pose tempting targets for terrorists, those facilities have been identified as high security risks. In light of these dangers attempts to locate new LNG terminals in coastal communities have typically aroused considerable local opposition. These political considerations are having, and presumably will continue to have, as much impact on the future supply of LNG available to importing nations as the size of the worldwide reserves.

Oil: The Cartel Problem

Inasmuch as we have considered similar effects on natural gas, we will merely note that historically price controls have been responsible for much mischief in the oil market as well. A second source of misallocation in the oil market, however, deserves consideration. Most of the world's oil is produced by a cartel called the *Organization of Petroleum Exporting Countries (OPEC)*. The members of this organization collude to exercise power over oil production and prices. Seller power over resources due to a lack of effective competition leads to an inefficient allocation. Sellers with market power can restrict supply and thus force prices higher than they would be otherwise.

A monopolist can extract more scarcity rent from a depletable resource base than competitive suppliers can, simply by restricting supply. The monopolistic transition results in slower production and higher prices. Therefore, the monopolistic transition to a substitute occurs later than a competitive transition. It also reduces the net present value society receives from these resources.

The cartelization of the oil suppliers has apparently been very effective (Smith, 2005). Why? Were the conditions that made it profitable unique to oil, or could oil cartelization be the harbinger of a wave of natural resource cartels? To answer these questions, we must isolate the factors that make cartelization possible. Many factors are involved, but four stand out: (1) the price elasticity of demand for OPEC oil in both the long run and the short run, (2) the income elasticity of demand for oil, (3) the supply responsiveness of the oil producers who are not OPEC members, and (4) the compatibility of interests among members of OPEC.

Price Elasticity of Oil Demand

The price elasticity of oil demand is an important ingredient because it determines how responsive demand is to price. When demand elasticities are between 0 and –1.0 (i.e., when the percent quantity response is smaller than the percent price change), price increases lead to increased revenue. Exactly how much the revenue would increase when prices increase depends on the *price elasticity of demand*. Generally, the smaller the absolute value of the price elasticity of demand (the closer to 0.0), the larger the gains to be derived from forming a cartel.

The price elasticity of demand for oil depends on the opportunities for conservation as well as on the availability of substitutes. As storm windows cut heat losses, the same temperature can be maintained with less heating oil. Smaller, more fuel efficient automobiles reduce the amount of gasoline needed to travel a given distance. The larger the set of these opportunities and the smaller the cash outlays required to exploit them, the more price elastic the demand. This suggests that demand will be more price elastic in the long run (when sufficient time has passed to allow adjustments) than in the short run.

The availability of substitutes is important because it limits the degree to which prices can be raised by a producer cartel. Abundant quantities of substitutes available at prices not far above competitive oil prices can set an upper limit on the cartel price. Unless OPEC controls those sources as well—and it doesn't—any attempts to raise prices above those limits would cause the consuming nations to simply switch to these alternative sources; OPEC would price itself out of the market.

As detailed below alternative sources clearly exist, although they are expensive and the time of transition is long.

Income Elasticity of Oil Demand

The *income elasticity of oil demand* is important because it indicates how sensitive oil demand is to growth in the world economy. At constant prices, as income grows, oil demand should grow. This continual increase in demand fortifies the ability of OPEC to raise its prices. High income elasticities of demand support the cartelization of oil. All other things being equal, the higher the income elasticity of demand, the higher the price would have to rise to bring demand to zero (in the absence of substitutes) or the more rapidly it would have to rise to the level of substitute resource, when one is available.

The income elasticity of demand is also important because it registers how sensitive demand is to the business cycle. The higher the income elasticity of demand, the more sensitive demand is to periods of rapid economic growth or to recessions. This sensitivity was a major source of the 1983 weakening of the cartel and the significant fall in oil prices starting in 2008. A recession caused a large reduction in the demand for oil, putting new pressure on the cartel to absorb this demand reduction. Conversely, when the global economy recovers the cartel benefits disproportionately.

Non-OPEC Suppliers

Another key factor in the ability of producer nations to exercise power over a natural resource market is their ability to prevent new suppliers (i.e., those not part of the cartel) from entering the market and undercutting the price. Currently, OPEC produces about two-thirds of the world's oil. If the remaining producers were able, in the face of higher prices, to expand their supply dramatically, they would cause the prices to fall, which would decrease OPEC's market share. If this response were large enough, the allocation of oil would approach the competitive allocation.

Currently, only Mexico appears to have large enough reserves to make an individual difference in the world oil market. However, because both the size of its reserves and its production profile are uncertain, it is difficult to assess Mexico's ultimate impact on the future world market.

This does not mean that non-OPEC members collectively do not have an impact on price. They do. The cartel must take the nonmembers into account when setting *optimal cartel prices*. The impact of this competitive fringe on OPEC behavior was dramatically illustrated by events during 1985–1986. In 1979 OPEC accounted for approximately 50 percent of world oil production, but by 1986 this had fallen to approximately 30 percent. Total world oil production during this period was down more than 10 percent for all producers, so the pressures on the cartel mounted, and ultimately prices fell. The real cost of crude oil imports in the United States fell from $34.95 per barrel in 1981 to $11.41 in 1986 (see Figure 8.2). OPEC simply was not able to hold the line on prices. The necessary reductions in production were too large for the cartel members to sustain.

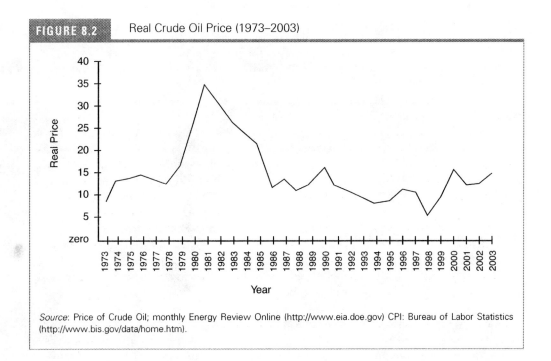

FIGURE 8.2   Real Crude Oil Price (1973–2003)

Source: Price of Crude Oil; monthly Energy Review Online (http://www.eia.doe.gov) CPI: Bureau of Labor Statistics (http://www.bis.gov/data/home.htm).

In 2004 the price of crude oil exceeded $50 a barrel (more than $27 a barrel in real prices), eventually soaring to more than $100 a barrel in January 2008. The price increase was due to strong worldwide demand coupled with restricted supply from Iraq because of the war. However, these high prices also underscored the major oil companies' difficulty finding new sources outside of OPEC countries. High oil prices in the 1970s drove Western multinational oil companies away from low-cost Middle-Eastern oil to high-cost new oil in places such as the North Sea and Alaska. Most of these oil companies are now running out of big non-OPEC opportunities, which diminishes their ability to moderate price.

Compatibility of Member Interests

The final factor we will consider in determining the potential for cartelization of natural resource markets is the internal cohesion of the cartel. With only one seller, the objective of that seller can be pursued without worrying about alienating others who could undermine the profitability of the enterprise. In a cartel composed of many sellers, that freedom is no longer as wide ranging. The incentives of each member and the incentives of the group as a whole may diverge.

Cartel members have a strong incentive to cheat. A cheater, if undetected by the other members, could surreptitiously lower its oil price and steal part of the market away from the others. Formally, the price elasticity of demand facing an individual member is substantially higher than that for the group as a whole, because some of the increase in individual sales at a lower price represents sales reductions for other members. With higher price elasticity, lower prices maximize profits. Thus, successful cartelization presupposes a means for detecting cheating and enforcing the collusive agreement.

In addition to cheating, however, the stability of cartels face another threat—the degree to which members fail to agree on pricing and output decisions. Oil provides an excellent example of how these dissensions can arise. Since the 1974 rise of OPEC as a world power, Saudi Arabia has exercised a moderating influence on the pricing decisions of OPEC. Why?

One highly significant reason is the size of Saudi Arabia's oil reserves (see Table 8.1). Saudi Arabia holds approximately 33 percent of the OPEC proven reserves; its reserves are larger than those of any other member. Because of this, Saudi Arabia has an incentive to preserve the value of those resources. It is worried about setting prices so high as to undercut the future demand for its oil. As previously stated, the demand for oil in the long run is more price elastic than in the short run. Meanwhile, the countries with smaller reserves, such as Nigeria, know that in the long run their reserves will be gone, and they are more concerned about the near future. Because alternative sources of supply are not much of a threat in the near future because of long development times, other countries with small reserves want to extract as much rent as possible now.

The size of Saudi Arabia's production also gives it the potential to make its influence felt. Its capacity to produce is so large that it can unilaterally affect world prices.

Cartelization is not an easy path for producers to pursue. However, when it is possible it can be very profitable. When the resource is a strategic and pervasive raw material, cartelization can be very costly for consuming nations.

Strategic-material cartelization also confers on the member's political, as well as economic, power. Economic power can become political power when the revenue is used to purchase weapons or the capacity to produce weapons. The producer nations can also use an *embargo* of the material as a lever to cajole reluctant adversaries into foreign policy concessions.

TABLE 8.1   The World's Largest Oil Reserves

Country	Reserves (in billions of barrels)
Saudi Arabia	261.5
Iraq	112.5
United Arab Emirates	97.8
Kuwait	96.5
Iran	93.0
Venezuela	71.7
Russia	48.6
Mexico	40.0
Libya	29.5
China	24.0
United States	22.5
Nigeria	16.8

Source: Oil and Gas Journal. (http://www.eia.doe.gov/emeu/iea/table81.htm).

Fossil Fuels: National Security and Climate Considerations

The Climate Dimension

All fossil fuels contain carbon. When these fuels are burned, unless captured, this carbon is released into the atmosphere as carbon dioxide. As explained in more detail in Chapter 17, CO_2 is a greenhouse gas, which means that it is a contributor to what is popularly known as global warming, or more accurately (since the changes are more complex than simply universal warming) as climate change.

Climate considerations affect energy policy in two ways: (1) the level of energy consumption matters (as long as carbon emitting sources are part of the mix) and (2) the mix of energy sources matters (since some emit more carbon than others). As can be seen from Table 8.2, among the fossil fuels, coal contains the most carbon per unit of energy produced and natural gas contains the least.

From an economic point of view the problem with how the market makes energy choices is that emissions of carbon generally involve an externality to the energy user. Therefore, we would expect that market choices, which are based upon the relative private costs of using these fuels, would involve an inefficient bias toward fuels containing carbon, thereby jeopardizing the timing and smooth transition toward fuels that pose less of a climate change threat. Another implication of our models is that our consumption of energy is inefficiently high because energy users are not bearing the full costs of that energy; the energy appears to be cheaper than it actually is. In Chapter 17 we will cover a host of policies that can be used to internalize those costs, but in the absence of those policies it might be necessary to subsidize renewable sources of energy that have little or no carbon.

TABLE 8.2   Carbon Content of Fuels

Fuel Type	Metric Tons of Carbon per Billion BTUs (1994 value)
Coal	25.61
Coal (Electricity Generation)	25.71
Natural Gas	14.47
Residual Fuel Oil	21.49
Oil (Electricity Generation)	19.95
Liquid Petroleum Gas	17.02
Distillate Fuel Oil	19.95

Source: Energy Information Administration 1994.

The National Security Dimension

Vulnerable strategic imports also have an added cost that is not reflected in the marketplace. National security is a classic public good. No individual importer correctly represents our collective national security interests in making a decision on how much to import. Thus, leaving the determination of the appropriate balance between imports and domestic production to the market generally results in an excessive dependence on imports due to both climate change and national security considerations (see Figure 8.3).

In order to understand the interaction of these factors, five supply curves are relevant. Domestic supply is reflected by two options. The first, S_{d1}, is the long-run domestic supply curve without considering the climate change damages resulting from burning more oil, and the second, S_{d2}, is the domestic supply curve that includes these per unit damages. Their upward slopes reflect increasing availability of domestic oil at higher prices, given sufficient time to develop those resources. Imported foreign oil is reflected by three supply curves: P_{w1} reflects the observed world price, P_{w2} includes a *vulnerability premium* in addition to the world price and P_{w3} adds in the per unit climate change damages due to consuming more imported oil. The vulnerability premium reflects the additional *national security costs* caused by imports. All three curves are drawn horizontally to the axis to reflect the assumption that any importing country's action on imports is unlikely to affect the world price for oil.

As shown in Figure 8.4, in the absence of any correction for national security and climate change considerations the market would generally demand and receive *D* units of oil. Of this total amount, *A* would be domestically produced and *D-A* would be imported. (Why?)

In an efficient allocation incorporating the national security and climate change considerations, only *C* units would be consumed. Of these, *B* would be domestically produced and *C-B* would be imported. Notice that when national security and climate change are considered an issue, the market in general tends to consume too much oil and vulnerable imports exceed their efficient level.

What would happen during an embargo? Be careful! At first glance you would guess that we would consume where domestic supply equals domestic demand, but that is not right. Remember that S_{d1} is the domestic supply curve, *given enough time to develop the resources*. If an embargo hits, developing additional resources cannot happen immediately (six-year time lags are common). Therefore, in the short run, the supply curve becomes perfectly inelastic (vertical) at *A*.

FIGURE 8.3	The National Security Problem

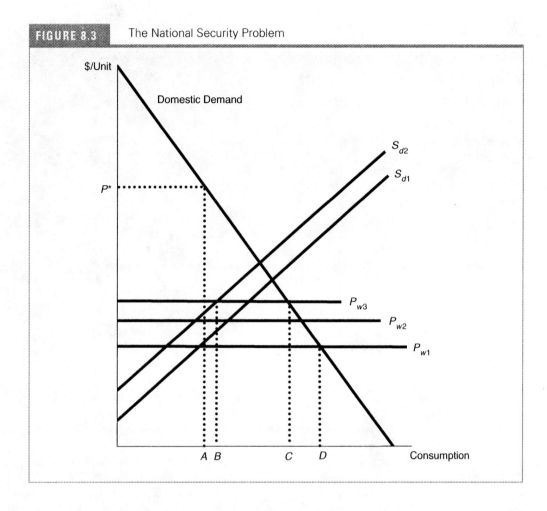

The price will rise to P^* to equate supply and demand. As the graph indicates, the loss in consumer surplus during an embargo can be very large indeed.

How can importing nations react to this inefficiency? As Debate 8.1 shows, several strategies are available. Should the importing country seek *energy self-sufficiency*? If the situation is adequately represented by Figure 8.3, then the answer is clearly no. The net benefit from self-sufficiency (the allocation where domestic supply S_{d1} crosses the demand curve) is clearly lower than the net benefits from the efficient allocation (C).

The explanation is that the vulnerability premium is lower than the cost of becoming self-sufficient, but that response merely begs the question. Why is the vulnerability premium lower? It is lower for three primary reasons: (1) embargoes are not certain events—they may never occur, (2) domestic steps can be taken to reduce vulnerability of the remaining imports, and (3) accelerating domestic production would incur a user cost by lowering the domestic amounts available to future users.

DEBATE 8.1

How Should the United States Deal with the Vulnerability of Its Imported Oil?

The United States currently imports most of its oil and its dependence on OPEC is growing. Since oil is such a strategic material, how can that vulnerability be addressed? The 2008 presidential campaign outlined two very different approaches.

Senator John McCain articulated a strategy of increasing domestic production, not only of oil, but also of natural gas and coal. His vision included opening up a portion of the Arctic National Wildlife Refuge for oil drilling. Tax incentives and subsidies were to be used to promote production.

Senator Barack Obama's vision, on the other hand, promoted a much larger role for energy efficiency and energy conservation. Pointing out that expanded domestic production could exacerbate environmental problems (including climate change), he supported such strategies as mandating standards for fuel economy in automobiles and energy efficiency standards in appliances.

Using economic analysis, figure out what the effects of the McCain and Obama strategies would be on the following: (1) oil prices in the short run and the long run? (2) emissions affecting climate change? and (3) U.S. imports in the short run and the long run? If you were in charge of OPEC, which strategy would you like to see chosen by Americans? Why?

The expected damage caused by one or more embargoes depends on the likelihood of occurrence, as well as the intensity and duration. This means that the P_{w2} curve will be lower for imports having a lower likelihood of being embargoed. Imports from countries less hostile to our interests are more secure and the vulnerability premium on those imports is smaller.[2]

For vulnerable imports, we can adopt specific contingency programs to reduce the damage an embargo would cause. The most obvious measure is to develop a domestic stockpile of oil to be used during an embargo. The United States has taken this route. The stockpile, called the *strategic petroleum reserve,* was originally designed to contain one billion barrels of oil (see Example 8.2). A one billion barrel stockpile would replace three million barrels a day for slightly less than one year or a larger number of barrels per day for a shorter period of time. This reserve would serve as an alternative source of supply, which, unlike other oil resources, could be rapidly deployed on short notice. It is, in short, a form of insurance protection. The less expensive this protection is, the lower P_{w2} is and the more attractive imports are.

To understand the third and final reason why paying the vulnerability premium would be less costly than self-sufficiency, we must consider vulnerability in a dynamic, rather than static, framework. Because oil is a depletable resource, a user cost is associated with its efficient use. To reorient the extraction of that resource toward the present, as a self-sufficiency strategy would require, reduces future net benefits. Thus, the self-sufficiency strategy tends to be myopic, in that it solves the short-term vulnerability problem by creating a more serious one in the future.

---

[2]This fact explains the tremendous U.S. interest in Mexican oil, in spite of the fact that, historically, it has not been cheaper.

Strategic Petroleum Reserve

EXAMPLE

8.2

The U.S. Strategic Petroleum Reserve (SPR) is the world's largest supply of emergency crude oil. The federally owned oil stocks are stored in huge underground salt caverns along the coastline of the Gulf of Mexico.

Decisions to withdraw crude oil from the SPR are made by the president under the authority of the Energy Policy and Conservation Act. In the event of an "energy emergency," SPR oil would be distributed by competitive sale. What constitutes an energy emergency goes well beyond embargoes. The SPR has been used only twice and neither drawdown involved an embargo:

- In 1991 during Operation Desert Storm, sales of 17.3 million barrels were used to stabilize the oil market in the face of supply disruptions arising from the war.

- In 2005 after Hurricane Katrina caused massive damage to the oil production facilities, terminals, pipelines, and refineries along the Gulf regions of Mississippi and Louisiana, sales of 11 million barrels were used to offset the domestic shortfall.

The SPR has never reached the original one billion barrel target, but the Energy Policy Act of 2005 directed the Secretary of Energy to bring the reserve to its authorized one billion barrel capacity. Acquiring the oil to build up the reserve is financed by the Royalty-in-Kind program. Under the royalty-in-kind program producers who operate leases on the federally owned Outer Continental Shelf are required to provide from 12.5 percent to 16.7 percent of the oil they produce to the U.S. government. This oil is either added directly to the stockpile or sold to provide the necessary revenue to purchase oil to add to the stockpile.

Sources: U.S. Department of Energy Strategic Petroleum Reserve Web site: http://www.fe.doe.gov/programs/reserves/index.html and http://www.spr.doe.gov/dir/dir.html (accessed June 20, 2007).

Paying the vulnerability premium creates a more efficient balance between the present and future, as well as between current imports and domestic production.

We have established the fact that government can reduce our vulnerability to imports, which tends to keep the risk premium as low as possible. Certainly for oil, however, even after the stockpile has been established, the risk premium is not zero; P_{w1} and P_{w2} will not coincide. Consequently, the government must also concern itself with achieving both the efficient level of consumption and the efficient share of that consumption borne by imports. Let's examine some of the policy choices.

Energy conservation is one popular approach to the problem. One way to accomplish additional conservation is by means of a tax on fossil fuel consumption. Graphically, this approach would be reflected as a shift inward of the after-tax demand curve. Such a tax would reduce energy consumption and emissions of greenhouse gases (an efficient result) but would not achieve the efficient share of imports (an inefficient result). An energy tax falls on *all* energy consumption, whereas the security problem involves imports only. While energy conservation may increase the net benefit, it can never be the sole policy instrument used or an efficient allocation will not be attained.

Another possible strategy employs the subsidization of domestic supply. Diagrammatically, this would be portrayed in Figure 8.3 as a shift of the domestic supply curve to the right. Notice that the effect would be to reduce the share of imports in total consumption (an efficient result) but neither consumption nor climate change emissions would be reduced (an inefficient result). This strategy also tends to drain domestic reserves faster, which makes the nation more vulnerable in the long run (another inefficient result). While subsidies of domestic fossil fuels can reduce imports, they will tend to intensify the climate change problem and increase long run vulnerability.

A third approach would tailor the response more closely to the national security problem. One could use either a tariff on imports equal to the vertical distance between P_{w1} *and* P_{w2} or a quota on imports equal to $Q_4 - Q_2$. With either of these approaches, the price to consumers would rise to P_1, total consumption would fall to Q_4, and imports would be $C - B$. This achieves the appropriate balance between imports and domestic production (an efficient result), but it does not internalize the climate change cost from using domestic production (an inefficient result). The use of tariffs or quotas has some redistributive consequences. Suppose a tariff were imposed on imports equal to the difference between P_{w1} and P_{w2}. The rectangle represented by that price differential times the quantity of imports would then represent tariff revenue collected by the government.

If a quota system were used instead of a tariff and the import quotas were simply given to importers, that revenue would go to the importers rather than the government. This explains why importers prefer quotas to a tariff system.

The effect of either system on domestic producer surplus should also be noticed. Producers of domestic oil would be better off with a tariff or quota on imported oil than without it. Each raises the cost or reduces the availability of the foreign substitute, which results in higher domestic prices. The higher domestic prices induce producers to produce more, but they also result in higher profits on the oil that would have been produced anyway, echoing the premise that public policies may restore efficiency, but also tend to redistribute wealth.

The Other Depletable Sources: Unconventional Oil, Coal, and Nuclear

While the industrialized world currently depends on conventional sources of oil and gas for most of our energy, in terms of both climate change and national security issues over the long run the obvious solution involves a transition to domestic renewable sources of energy that do not emit greenhouse gases. What role does that leave for the other depletable resources, namely unconventional oil, coal, and uranium?

Although some observers believe the transition to renewable sources will proceed so rapidly that using these fuels will be unnecessary, many believe that depletable transition fuels will probably play a significant role. Although other contenders, such as natural gas from deep wells do exist, the fuels receiving the most attention (and controversy) as transition fuels are unconventional sources of oil, coal, and uranium. Coal, in particular, is abundantly available, both globally and domestically, and its use frees nations with coal from dependencies on foreign sources.

The role of technology is an important part of the picture. Resource availability is a problem with uranium as long as we depend on conventional reactors. However, if countries move to a new generation of breeder reactors, which can use a wider range of fuel, availability would cease to be an important issue. In the United States, for example, on a heat-equivalent basis, domestic uranium resources are 4.2 times as great as domestic oil and gas resources if they are used in conventional reactors. With breeder reactors, the U.S. uranium base is 252 times the size of its oil and gas base.

Unconventional Oil Sources

The term "unconventional oil" refers to sources that are typically more difficult and expensive to extract than conventional oil. While many unconventional oil resources may still be economically out of reach now, two unconventional oil sources are currently being tapped—extra-heavy oil from Venezuela's Orinoco oil belt region and bitumen—a tar-like hydrocarbon that is abundant in Canada's tar sands. The Canadian source is particularly important from the U.S. national security perspective, coming as it does, from a friendly neighbor to the North.

The main concern about these sources is their environmental impact. It not only takes much more energy to extract these unconventional resources (making the net energy gain smaller), but also in the case of Canadian tar sands, large amounts of water are necessary either to separate bitumen from the sand and other solids, or to produce steam, depending on the oil-recovery method. Emissions of air pollutants, including CO_2, are greater for unconventional than for conventional sources.

Coal

Coal's main drawback is its contribution to air pollution. Its high sulfur content makes it a potentially large source of sulfur dioxide emissions, one of the chief culprits in the acid-rain problem. It is also a major source of particulate emissions, mercury, and carbon dioxide, one of the greenhouse gases.

Coal is heavily used in electricity generation and the rate of increase in coal use for this purpose is especially high in China. With respect to climate change the biggest issue for coal is whether it could be used without adding considerably to greenhouse gas emissions. As the fossil fuel with the highest carbon emissions per unit of energy supplied that is a tall order.

Capturing CO_2 emissions from coal-fired plants before they are released into the environment and sequestering the CO_2 in underground geologic formations is now technologically feasible. Energy companies have extensive experience in injecting captured CO_2 into oil fields as one means to increase the pressure and, hence, increase the recovery rate from those fields. Whether this practice can be extended to saline aquifers and other geologic formations without leakage at reasonable cost is the subject of considerable current research.

Implementing these carbon capture and storage systems requires modifications to existing power plant technologies, which are quite expensive. In the absence of any policy controls on carbon emissions, the cost of these sequestration approaches would rule them out simply because the economic damages imposed by failing to control the gases are externalities. The existence of suitable technologies is not sufficient if the underlying economic forces prevent them from being adopted.

Uranium

Uranium, another potential transition fuel used in nuclear electrical generation stations, has its own limitations, principally safety. Two sources of concern stand out: (1) nuclear accidents and (2) the storage of radioactive waste. Is the market able to make efficient decisions on the role of nuclear power in the energy mix? In both cases the answer is no, given the current decision-making environment. Let's consider these issues one by one.

The production of electricity by nuclear reactors involves radioactive elements. If these elements escape into the atmosphere (say, during a nuclear accident) and come in contact with humans in sufficient concentrations, they can induce birth defects, cancer, and death. Although some radioactive elements may also escape during the normal operation of a plant, the greatest risk of nuclear power is posed by the threat of nuclear accidents.

Nuclear accidents may inject large doses of radioactivity into the environment. There are many possible ways in which this might happen. The most dangerous of these possibilities is the core meltdown. Unlike other types of electrical generation, nuclear processes continue to generate heat even after the reactor is turned off. This means that the nuclear fuel must be continuously cooled or the heat levels will escalate beyond the design capacity of the reactor shield. If, in this case, the reactor vessel should fracture, clouds of radioactive gases and particulates would be released into the atmosphere.

For some time, conventional wisdom had held that nuclear accidents involving a core meltdown were only a remote possibility. On April 25, 1986, however, a serious core meltdown occurred at the Chernobyl nuclear plant in the Ukraine. Although safety standards are generally conceded to be much higher in the Western industrialized world than in the countries of the former Soviet Union, this incident has added yet another burden to bear for an already troubled industry.

Nuclear power has been beset by economic as well as political forces. New nuclear power plant construction has become much more expensive, partly because of the increasing regulatory requirements designed to provide a safer system. Its economic advantage over coal has dissipated, and the demand for new nuclear plants has been eliminated. For example, in 1973 in the United States 219 nuclear power plants were either planned or in operation. By the end of 1998 that number had fallen to 104, the difference due to cancellations. After a period with no new applications, high oil prices and concerns about climate change have caused some resurgence of interest.

Not all nations are making the same choice with respect to the nuclear option. Sweden has pledged not to build any new nuclear plants. Additionally, it plans to shut down those currently in operation by early in the twenty-first century. In France and Japan, however, standardized plant design and regulatory stability have resulted in electricity generating costs for nuclear power that are lower than those for coal-generated power. Both countries rely heavily on nuclear power.

An additional concern relates to storing nuclear wastes. The waste storage issue relates to both ends of the nuclear fuel cycle—the disposal of uranium tailings from the mining process and of spent fuel from the reactors, although the latter receives most of the publicity. Uranium tailings contain several elements, the most prominent being thorium-230, which decays with a half-life of 78,000 years to a radioactive, chemically inert gas, radon-222. Once formed, this gas has a very short half-life (38 days).

The spent fuel from nuclear reactors contains a variety of radioactive elements with quite different half-lives. In the first few centuries, the dominant contributors to radioactivity are fission products, principally strontium-90 and cesium-137. After approximately 1,000 years, most of these elements will have decayed, leaving the transuranic elements having substantially longer half-lives. These remaining elements would remain a risk for up to 240,000 years. Thus, decisions made today affect not only the level of risk borne by the current generation—in the form of nuclear accidents—but also that borne by a host of succeeding generations (because of the longevity of radioactive risk from the disposal of spent fuel).

Can we expect the market to make the correct choice with respect to nuclear power and accident possibilities? Because this seems to be a clear case of externalities, we might expect the answer to be no. Third parties, those living near the reactor, would receive the brunt of the damage from a nuclear accident. Would the utility have an incentive to choose the efficient level of precaution?

If the utility had to compensate fully for all the damages caused, then the answer would be yes. In the United States full compensation is not paid by the individual utilities for two reasons: (1) the role of the government in sharing the risk and (2) the role of insurance in underwriting the risk.

When the government first allowed private industry to use atomic power to generate electricity, there were no takers. No utility could afford the damages if an accident occurred. No insurance company would underwrite the risk. Then, in 1957, with the passage of the *Price-Anderson Act*, the government underwrote the liability. That Act provided for a *liability ceiling* of $560 million (i.e., once that amount had been paid, no more claims would be honored), of which the government would bear $500 million. The industry would pick up the remaining $60 million. The Act was originally designed to expire in 10 years, at which time the industry would assume full responsibility for the liability.

The Act didn't expire, although over time a steady diminution of the government's share of the liability has occurred. Currently, the liability ceiling still exists, albeit at a higher level; the amount of private insurance has increased; and a system has been set up to assess all utilities a retrospective premium in the event an accident occurs.

The effect of the Price-Anderson Act is to reduce the expected cost of nuclear power to the utility choosing to use it. Both the liability ceiling and the portion of the liability borne by government reduce the potential compensation the utility would have to pay. As the industry assumes an increasing portion of the liability burden, the risk sharing embodied in the retrospective premium system (the means by which it assumes that burden) breaks the link between *precautionary behavior* by the individual utility and the compensation it might have to pay. Under this system, increased safety by the utility does not reduce its premiums.

The individual utilities pay into a fund that compensates victims. The important point is that the actual cost of an accident to the utility is not sensitive to the level of precautions it takes. The cost to all utilities, whether they have accidents or not, is the premium paid both before and after any accident. These premiums are not reduced by the amount of precautionary measures taken by an individual plant; therefore, individual utilities have little incentive to provide an efficient amount of safety. In recognition of the utilities' lower-than-efficient concern for safety, the U.S. government has established the *Nuclear Regulatory Commission (NRC)*, which is empowered to oversee the safety of nuclear reactors, among its other responsibilities.

To further complicate the problem, the private sector is not the only source of excessive nuclear waste. The U.S. Department of Energy, for example, presides over a nuclear weapons complex containing 15 major facilities and a dozen or so smaller ones.

Both the operating safety issue and the nuclear waste storage issue can be viewed as a problem of determining appropriate compensation. Those who gain from nuclear power should be forced to compensate those who lose. If they can't, in the absence of externalities, the net benefits from adopting nuclear power are not positive. If nuclear power is efficient, by definition, the gains to the gainers will exceed the losses to the losers. Nonetheless, it is important that this compensation actually be paid, because without compensation, the losers can block the efficient allocation.

A compensation approach is already being taken in those countries still expanding the role of nuclear power. The French government, for example, announced a policy of reducing electricity rates by roughly 15 percent for those living near nuclear stations. And in Japan during 1980, the Tohoku Electric Power Company paid the equivalent of $4.3 million to residents of Ojika, in northern Japan, to get them to withdraw their opposition to a nuclear power plant being built there.

This approach could also help resolve the current political controversy over the location of nuclear waste disposal sites. Under a *compensation scheme*, those consuming nuclear power would be taxed in order to compensate those who live in the areas of the disposal site. If the compensation is adequate to induce them to accept the site, then nuclear power is a viable option and the costs of disposal are ultimately borne by the consumers. Some towns, such as Naurita, Colorado, have actively sought to become disposal sites. If taxes to obtain a sufficient number of disposal sites are so high that nuclear energy becomes noncompetitive, then nuclear energy is not an efficient source.

Are future generations adequately represented in the transaction? The quick answer is no, but that answer is not correct. Those living around the sites will experience declines in the market value of land, reflecting the increased risk of living or working there. The payment system is designed to compensate those who experience the reduction, the current generation. Future generations, should they decide to live near a disposal site, would be compensated by lower land values. If the land values were not cheap enough to compensate them, they would not have to live there. As long as full information on the risks posed is available, those who do bear the cost of locating near the sites do so only if they are willing to accept the risk in return for lower land values. For further discussion of possible compensation schemes, see Mitchell and Carson (1986), and Kunreuther and Kleindorfer (1986).

Electricity

For a number of electric utilities, conservation has assumed an increasingly significant role. To a major extent, conservation has already been stimulated by market forces. High oil and natural gas prices, coupled with the rapidly increasing cost of both nuclear and coal-fired generating stations, have reduced electrical demand significantly. Yet many regulatory authorities are coming to the conclusion that more conservation is needed.

Perhaps the most significant role for conservation is its ability to defer capacity expansion. Each new electrical generating plant tends to cost more than the last, and frequently the cost increase is substantial. When the new plants come on line, rate increases to finance the new plant are necessary. By reducing the demand for electricity, conservation delays the date when the new capacity is needed to satisfy the higher demand. Delays in the need to construct new plants translate into delays in rate increases as well.

The dominant electricity pricing system is ill-designed to stimulate the efficient amount of conservation. Average cost pricing is common. This pricing system implies that the new, higher-cost sources are averaged in with the lower-cost sources, yielding a rate that is substantially lower than the true marginal cost of the power being generated. Thus, the consumer considering investing in conservation would save less money with average cost pricing than would be the case if the energy saved were priced at its true marginal cost. Less than an efficient amount of conservation would be the expected outcome.

Governments are reacting to this situation in a number of ways. One is to promote investments in conservation, rather than in new plants, when conservation is the cheaper alternative. Typical programs have established systems of rebates for residential customers who install conservation measures in their homes, have provided free home weatherization to qualified low-income homeowners, have offered owners of multifamily residential buildings incentives for installing solar water-heating systems, and have provided subsidized energy audits to inform customers about money-saving conservation opportunities. Similar incentives have been provided to the commercial, agricultural, and industrial sectors.

The total amount of electrical energy demanded in a given year is not the only concern. How that energy demand is spread out over the year is also a concern. The capacity of the system must be high enough to satisfy the demand during the periods when the energy demand is highest (called the peak period). During other periods, much of the capacity remains underutilized.

Demand during the peak period imposes two rather special costs on utilities. First, the peaking units, those generating facilities fired up only during the peak periods, produce electricity at a much higher marginal cost than do base-load plants, those fired up virtually all the time. Peaking units are typically cheaper to build than base-load plants, but they have higher operating costs. Second, it is the growth in peak demand that frequently triggers the need for capacity expansion. Slowing down the growth in peak demand may delay the need for new, expensive capacity expansion so that a higher proportion of the power needs can be met by the most efficient generating plants.

Utilities are responding to this problem by adopting *load management* techniques to produce a more balanced use of this capacity over the year. One economic load management technique is called *peak-load pricing*. Peak-load pricing attempts to impose the full (higher) marginal cost of supplying peak power on those consuming peak power by charging higher prices during the peak period.

Although many utilities have now begun to use simple versions of this approach, some are experimenting with very innovative ways of implementing rather refined versions of this system. One system, for example, transmits electricity prices every five minutes over regular power lines. In a customer's household, the lines attached to one or more appliances can be controlled by switches that turn the power off any time the prevailing price exceeds a limit established by the customer. Other, less sophisticated pricing systems simply inform consumers in advance what prices will prevail in predetermined peak periods.

Studies by economists indicate that even the rudimentary versions of peak-load pricing work. The greatest shifts are typically registered by the largest residential customers and those with several electrical appliances.

Also affecting energy choices is the movement to deregulate electricity production. Historically, electricity was generated by regulated monopolies. In return for accepting both government control of prices and an obligation to service all customers, utilities were given the exclusive rights to service specific geographic areas.

Recently, it has been recognized that while electricity distribution has elements of natural monopoly, generation does not. Therefore, several states and a number of national governments have deregulated the generation of electricity, while keeping the distribution under the exclusive control of a monopoly. In the Unites States *electricity deregulation* officially began in 1992 when Congress allowed independent energy companies to sell power on the wholesale electricity market. Forcing generators to compete for customers, it was believed, would produce lower electricity bills for customers. Experience reveals that lower prices have not always been the result (see Example 8.3).

EXAMPLE

8.3

Electricity Deregulation in California: What Happened?

In 1995 the state legislature in California reacted to electricity rates that were 50 percent higher than the U.S. average by unanimously passing a bill to deregulate electricity generation within the state. The bill had three important features: (1) all utilities would have to divest themselves of their generation assets, (2) retail prices of electricity would be capped until the assets were divested, and (3) the utilities were forced to buy power in a huge open-auction market for electricity, known as a spot market, where supply and demand were matched every day and hour.

The system was seriously strained by a series of events that restricted supplies and raised prices. Despite the fact that demand had been growing rapidly, no new generating facility had been built in over a decade and much of the existing capacity was shut down for maintenance. An unusually dry summer reduced generating capacity at hydroelectric dams and electricity generators in Oregon and Washington, traditional sources of imported electricity. In addition, prices rose for existing supplies of natural gas, a fuel that supplied almost one-third of the state's electricity.

This combination of events gave rise to higher wholesale prices, as would be expected, but the price cap prevented them from being passed on to consumers. Since prices could not equilibrate the retail market, blackouts (involving a complete loss of electricity to certain areas at certain times) resulted. To make matters worse, the evidence suggests that wholesale suppliers were able to take advantage of the short-term inflexibility of supply and demand to withhold some power from the market, thereby raising prices more and creating some monopoly profits. On April 6, 2001, Pacific Gas and Electric, a utility that served a bit more than one-third of all Californians declared bankruptcy.

Why had a rather simple quest for lower prices resulted in such a tragic outcome? Are the deregulation plans in other states headed for a similarly dismal future? Time will tell, of course, but that outcome seems unlikely. A reduction of supplies could affect other areas, although the magnitude of the confluence of events in California seems unusually harsh. Furthermore, the design of the California deregulation plan was clearly flawed. The price cap coupled with the total dependence on the spot market created a circumstance in which the market could not respond to the shortage and in some ways made it worse. Since neither of those features is an essential ingredient of a deregulation plan, other areas can choose more prudent designs.

Sources: Borenstein, Severin, Jim Bushnell, and Frank Wolak, "Measuring Market Inefficiencies in California's Restructured Wholesale Electricity Market," a paper presented at the American Association meetings in Atlanta, January 2001; and Joskow, P. L., "California's Electricity Market Meltdown," *Economies et Sociétés* 35(1–2), January–February 2001: 281–296.

Electricity deregulation has also raised some environmental concerns (Palmer and Burtraw, 1997). Since electricity costs typically do not include all the costs of environmental damage, the sources offering the lowest prices could well be highly polluting sources. In this case, environmentally benign generation sources would not face a level playing field; polluting sources would have an inefficient advantage.

One policy approach for dealing with these concerns involves a system of *renewable energy credits* (RECs). *Renewable energy* sources, such as wind or solar power, are frequently characterized by relatively large capital costs, relatively low variable costs (since the fuel is costless), and low pollution emissions. Energy markets may ignore the advantages of low pollution emissions (since pollution imposes an external cost) and are likely to emphasize investments with low capital costs and short payback periods. Under these circumstances, investments in capital-intensive, renewable energy technologies are unlikely to be sufficient to reach an efficient outcome.

Renewable energy credits are designed to facilitate the transition to renewable power by overcoming these obstacles. Under this system, certified production of qualified renewable power is recorded via certificates that are granted to producers in proportion to the amounts of qualified power produced. The certificates are transferable and can be sold separately from the power. Companies may demonstrate compliance with energy initiatives by either producing renewable power or purchasing certificates from other producers. Since the electricity from renewable energy and conventional energy are physically indistinguishable, both forms of electricity are sold in the same market at the same price. Producers of renewable power can seek to recover their additional costs through the sale of credits (since the renewable energy producer will receive the revenue from the sale of both the physical energy and the certificates). Whether or not the revenue is sufficient to cover the extra cost obviously depends on the credit price, which, in turn, depends on the strength of demand.

Demand for these credits is usually driven by government directives. For example, in September 2001 the European Union Council of Ministers and the European Parliament adopted a directive designed to promote electricity from renewable energy sources in their internal electricity market. The EU target specifies that 22 percent of electricity should be produced from qualified renewable sources by 2010. These EU-wide requirements result in quotas being assigned to individual countries and, ultimately, even to individual companies.

The transferability of these credits reduces the cost of the mandate by increasing the flexibility of how the directive can be met; requiring each company to meet the 22 percent target on its own would typically be much more expensive. Some companies, due to their location, have many more available options (such as more sunny days or access to stronger, more frequent winds) and can more easily (and more cheaply) fulfill their quotas.

RECs are no panacea. Experience in several U.S. states shows that a poorly designed system does little to increase renewable generation (Rader, 2000). On the other hand, appropriate designed systems can provide a significant boost to renewable energy (see Example 8.4). The details matter.

Another approach, adopted by some jurisdictions, involves consumer *right-to-know laws*. These laws require power generators to disclose not only the types of fuels they use, but also the emissions that result from their energy production. Emissions are generally compared to regional benchmarks to provide some reasonable basis for comparison. The hope is that this information will allow environmentally conscious consumers to base their electricity purchase choices on environmental considerations as well as on costs. In many states it is now possible for consumers to choose to have their electricity supplied from sources that emit fewer (or even no) pollutants, usually by paying a price premium.

EXAMPLE
8.4

Renewable Energy Credits: The Texas Experience

Texas has rapidly emerged as one of the leading wind power markets in the United States, in no small part due to a well-designed and carefully implemented government directive known as a *renewable portfolio standard* (RPS) coupled with renewable energy credits. The RPS specifies targets and deadlines for producing specific proportions of electricity from renewable resources (wind, in this case) while the credits lower compliance cost by increasing the options available to any party required to comply.

The early results have been impressive. Initial RPS targets in Texas were easily exceeded by the end of 2001, with 915 megawatts of wind capacity installed in that year alone. The response has been sufficiently strong that it has become evident that the RPS capacity targets for the next few years will also be met early. RPS compliance costs are reportedly very low, in part due to a complementary production tax credit (a subsidy to the producer). Additionally, especially favorable wind conditions in Texas and an RPS target that was ambitious enough to allow economies of scale to be exploited have contributed to the program's success. The fact that the cost of administering the program is also low, due to an efficient, Web-based reporting and accounting system, also helps.

Finally, and significantly, retail suppliers have been willing to enter into long-term contracts with renewable generators, reducing exposure of both producers and consumers to potential volatility of prices and sales. Long-term contracts ensure developers a stable revenue stream and, as a result, access to low-cost financing, while offering customers a reliable, steady supply of electricity.

Source: Langniss, O. and R. Wiser, "The Renewables Portfolio Standard in Texas: An Early Assessment," *Energy Policy* 31, 2003: 527–535.

Another quite different approach is promoting the use of renewable resource in the generation of electric power. Used in Germany this approach, known as a *feed-in tariff*, focuses on establishing a stable price guarantee rather than a subsidy or a government mandate (see Example 8.5).

● Energy Efficiency

As the world grapples with creating the right energy portfolio for the future, energy efficiency policy is playing an increasingly prominent role. In recent years the amount of both private and public money being dedicated to promoting energy efficiency has increased a great deal.

The role for energy efficiency in the broader mix of energy policies depends of course on how large the opportunity is. Estimating the remaining potential is not a precise science, but the conclusion that significant opportunities remain seems inescapable.

The existence of these opportunities can be thought of as a necessary, but not sufficient condition for government intervention. Depending upon the level of energy prices and the discount rate, the economic return on these investments may be too low to justify intervention.

EXAMPLE

8.5

Feed-in Tariffs

Promoting the use of renewable resources in the generation of electricity is both important and difficult. Germany provides a very useful example of a country that seems to be especially adept at overcoming these barriers. According to one benchmark, at the end of 2007, renewable energies were supplying more than 14 percent of the electricity used in Germany, exceeding the original 2010 goal of 12.5 percent.

What prompted this increase? The responsible economic mechanism is called a "feed-in tariff." This mechanism determines the prices received by anyone who installs qualified renewable capacity that feeds electricity into the grid. In general, a fixed incentive payment per kilowatt-hour is guaranteed for that installation. The level of this payment (determined in advance by the rules of the program) is based upon the costs of supplying the power and is set at a sufficiently high level so as to assure installers that they will receive a reasonable rate of return over the life of their investment. While this incentive payment is guaranteed for 20 years for each installed facility, each year the level of that guaranteed 20-year payment is reduced (typically in the neighborhood of 1–2 percent per year) for new facilities to reflect expected technological improvements and economies of scale.

This approach has a number of interesting characteristics:

- It seems to work.
- No subsidy from the government is involved; the costs are borne by the consumers of the electricity.
- The cost of the electricity from feed-in tariff sources is typically higher in the earlier years than for conventional sources, but lower in subsequent years (as fossil fuels become more expensive). In Germany the year in which electricity becomes cheaper due to the feed-in tariff is estimated to be 2025.
- This approach actually offers two different incentives: (1) it provides a price high enough to promote the desired investment and (2) it guarantees the stability of that price rather than forcing investors to face the market uncertainties associated with fluctuating fossil fuel prices or subsidies that come and go.

Source: Jeffrey H. Michel (2007), "The Case for Renewable Feed-In Tariffs" Online Journal of the EUEC, Volume 1, Paper 1, available at http://www.euec.com/journal/Journal.htm.

Additionally, policy intervention could be so administratively costly as to outweigh any gains that would result.

The strongest case for government intervention flows from the existence of externalities. Markets are not likely to internalize these external costs on their own. The natural security and climate change externalities mentioned above, as well as other external co-benefits such as pollution-induced community health effects, certainly imply that the market undervalues investments in energy efficiency.

The analysis provided by economic research in this area, however, makes it clear that the case for policy intervention extends well beyond externalities.[3] Internalizing externalities is a very important, but insufficient policy response.

Consider just a few of the other foundations for policy intervention. Inadequately informed consumers can impede rational choice as can a limited availability of capital (preventing paying more up front for the more energy efficient choice even when the resulting energy savings would justify the additional expense in present value terms). Perverse incentives can also play a role as anyone who has lived in a room (think dorm) or apartment where the amount of energy used is not billed directly, resulting in a marginal cost of additional energy use that is zero.

A rather large suite of policy options has been implemented to counteract these other sources of deficient levels of investment in energy efficiency. Some illustrations include the following:

⊛ Certification programs such as Energy Star for appliances or LEED (Leadership in Energy and Environmental Design) for buildings attempt to provide credible information for consumers to make informed choices on energy efficiency options.

⊛ Minimum efficiency standards (e.g., for appliances) prohibit the manufacture, sale, or importation of clearly inefficient appliances.

⊛ An increased flow of public funds into the market for energy efficiency has led to an increase in the use of targeted investment subsidies. The most common historic source of funding in the electricity sector involved the use of a small mandatory per kilowatt-hour charge (typically called a "system benefit charge" or "public benefit charge") attached to the distribution service bill. The newest source of funding comes from the revenue accrued from the sale of carbon allowances in several state or regional carbon cap-and-trade programs (described in detail in Chapter 16). The services funded by these sources include supplementing private funds for diverse projects such as weatherization of residences for low-income customers to more efficient lighting for commercial and industrial enterprises.

The evidence suggests that none of these policies either by themselves or in concert are completely efficient, but that they have collectively represented a move toward a more efficient use of energy. Not only does the evidence seem to suggest that they have been effective in reducing wasteful energy demand, but also that the programs have been quite cost effective, with program costs well below the cost of the alternative, namely generating the energy to satisfy that demand.

⊛ Transitioning to Renewables

Ultimately, our energy needs will have to be fulfilled from renewable energy sources, either because the depletable energy sources have been exhausted or, more likely, because the environmental costs of using the depletable sources have become so high that renewable sources are cheaper.

One compelling case for the transition is being made by the mounting evidence that the global climate is being jeopardized by current and prospective energy-consumption patterns. To the extent that rapidly developing countries such as China and India were to follow the energy-intensive, fossil-fuel-based path to development pioneered by the industrialized nations, the

---

[3]For a review of this literature see Tietenberg, T. H. (2009). "Reflections on Energy Efficiency" Review of Environmental Economics and Policy (forthcoming).

amount of CO_2 emissions injected into the air would be unprecedented. A transition away from fossil fuels to other energy forms in both industrialized and developing nations would be an important ingredient in any strategy to reduce CO_2 emissions. Can our institutions manage that transition in a timely and effective manner?

It is unlikely that any one source will provide the long run solution in part because both the timing (peak demands) and form (gases, liquids, or electricity) of energy matter. Different sources will have different comparative advantages; so, ultimately a mix of sources will be necessary. Consider some of the options. The extent to which these sources will penetrate the market will depend upon their relative cost and consumer acceptance.

Hydroelectric Power

Hydroelectric power passed that economic test a long time ago and is already an important source of power. Hydroelectric power is generated when turbines convert the kinetic energy from a flowing body of water into electricity. This source of power is clean from an emissions point of view and domestic hydropower can help with national security concerns as well. On the other hand, hydroelectric dams can be a significant impediment to fish migrations, the impounded water can flood ecosystems, and the buildup of silt behind the dams not only can lower the life of the facility, but also alter the upstream and downstream ecosystems.

According to the U.S. Department of Energy (DOE)[4] hydropower in the United States rose from 15 percent of electricity generation in 1907 to 40 percent in 1940, but it had fallen back to only 10 percent by 2003. DOE currently estimates that some 80,000 megawatts of hydropower are currently operating in the United States and their resource assessment identified 5,677 sites in the United States with an undeveloped capacity of about 30,000 megawatts.

While hydroelectric power has been cost-effective for some time, other renewable resources have not been. Some like wind have become cost-effective, while the cost-effectiveness of others awaits further technological developments or additional increases in the costs of fossil fuels.

Wind

Wind power is also beginning to penetrate the market on a rather large scale. New designs for the turbines that convert the wind energy to electricity have reduced the cost and increased the reliability of wind-generated electricity to the point that it now can compete with conventional sources in favorable sites even when environmental costs have not been internalized. (Favorable sites are those with sufficiently steady, strong winds.) Although many unexploited favorable sites still exist around the world, the share of wind power in the total energy mix will ultimately be limited by the diminishing availability of unexploited sites. Wind also has environmental effects that have triggered strong local controversies (see Debate 8.2).

Photovoltaics

Technological change can lower the relative cost of renewable resources. Perhaps the best example of how research can lower costs is provided by the experience with photovoltaics. *Photovoltaics* involves the direct conversion of solar energy to electricity (as opposed to indirect

---

[4]U.S. Department of Energy Web site: http://www1.eere.energy.gov/windandhydro/hydro_history.html.

Dueling Externalities: Should the U.S. Promote Wind Power?

On the surface it seems like a no-brainer, since wind power is a renewable energy source that emits no greenhouse gases, unlike all the fossil fuels it would be likely to replace. Yet some highly visible, committed environmentalists including Robert F. Kennedy, Jr. have strongly opposed wind projects. Why has this become such a public, contentious issue?

Opposition to wind power within the environmental community arises for a variety of reasons. Some point out that the turbines can be noisy for those who live, camp, or hike close to them. Others note that these very large turbines can be quite destructive to bats and birds, particularly if they are constructed in migratory pathways. And a number of opponents object to the way the view would be altered by a large collection of turbines on otherwise pristine mountaintops or off the coast.

Notice that both the benefits from wind power (reduced impact on the climate) and the costs (effects on aesthetics, birds, and noise) are typically externalities. This implies that the developers and consumers of wind power will neither reap all of the environmental benefits from reduced impact on the climate, nor will they typically bear all of the environmental costs. Making matters even more difficult, some of the environmental costs will be concentrated on a relatively few people (e.g., those living nearby), while the benefits will be conferred on all global inhabitants, most of whom will bear absolutely no costs whatsoever. The concentrated local costs may be an effective motivator to attend the hearings, which are likely to be held near the proposed site, but the diffuse benefits will likely not be.

Since the presence of externalities typically undermines the ability of a market to produce an efficient outcome, it is not surprising that the permitting process for new wind power facilities is highly regulated. Regulatory processes generally encourage public participation by holding hearings. With environmental externalities lying on both sides of the equation and with many of the environmental costs concentrated on a relatively small number of people, it is neither surprising that the hearings have become so contentious, nor that the opposition to wind power is so well represented.

Sources: Robert F. Kennedy, Jr., "An Ill Wind Off Cape Cod," *The New York Times* Op Ed, December 16, 2005; Felicity Barringer, "Debate over Wind Power Creates Environmental Rift," *The New York Times*, June 6, 2006.

conversions such as when steam energy is used to drive a turbine). Anticipating a huge potential market, private industry has been very interested in photovoltaics and has poured a lot of research dollars into improving its commercial viability. The research has paid off. In 1976 the average market price for a photovoltaic module was $44 per peak watt installed, and 0.5 megawatts were sold. By 2002 this had fallen to $3.75.[5] Rural electrification projects using photovoltaics are slowly spreading into the third world.

---

[5]http://www.eia.doe.gov/cneaf/solar.renewables/pubs.html/.

Active and Passive Solar Energy

The sun's energy can also be used for heating in either an active or passive mode. The difference between the two is that while the passive mode uses no external energy sources, the active mode may use nonsolar energy to power pumps or fans. Solar energy can be used to provide space heating or to provide hot water.

Since the input energy comes from the sun's rays, it is costless, but the system to collect those rays, to transform them into useful heat and to distribute the heat requires capital investment. When storage or backup systems are required, they add to the cost.

Ocean Tidal Power[6]

One energy source that relies on the natural cycles of the earth is tidal power. It capitalizes on the fact that coastal areas experience two high and two low tides in a period of time somewhat longer than 24 hours. The energy in the water as it rushes in or out of an inlet or cove is transformed into electricity by a conversion device, commonly a turbine. According to the U.S. Department of Energy, for the tidal differences to be harnessed into electricity, the difference between high and low tides must be at least five meters, or more than 16 feet. Only about 40 sites on the earth have tidal ranges of this magnitude. Although no tidal power plants currently are operating in the United States, conditions are good for tidal power generation in both the Pacific Northwest and the Atlantic Northeast regions of the country.

Tidal power plants are not without their environmental impacts in that some designs can impede sea life migration, and silt build-ups behind such facilities can impact local ecosystems.

Like many other renewable sources, the input energy is free, but construction costs are high. As a result, the U.S. Department of Energy estimates that the cost per kilowatt-hour of tidal power is currently not competitive with conventional fossil fuel power, but internalizing all the external costs of fossil fuel power could affect that outlook.

Biofuels

Currently, biofuels, fuels made from plant material, are receiving a lot of attention in policy circles because they can potentially reduce greenhouse gases and imports of oil simultaneously. These include two alcohols—ethanol and methanol—and biodiesel, an oxygenated fuel produced from a range of biomass-derived feedstocks including oilseeds, waste vegetable oils, cooking oil, and even animal fats. How cost effective are they? Hill et al. (2006) examine this issue in some detail and provide some useful insights:

- Ethanol yields 25 percent more energy than the energy invested in its production, whereas biodiesel yields 93 percent more.
- Compared with ethanol, biodiesel releases just 1 percent, 8.3 percent, and 13 percent of the agricultural nitrogen, phosphorus, and pesticide pollutants, respectively, per net energy gain.

---

[6]The information in this section was derived from http://www.eere.energy.gov/consumer/renewable_energy/ocean/index.cfm/mytopic=50008.

◦ Relative to the fossil fuels they displace, greenhouse gas emissions are reduced 12 percent by the production and combustion of ethanol and 41 percent by biodiesel. The advantages of biodiesel over ethanol come from lower agricultural inputs and more efficient conversion of feedstocks to fuel.

How about economic impacts? The authors also point out that neither biofuel can replace much petroleum without impacting food supplies and costs, and those impacts could be serious. Their estimates suggest that even dedicating all U.S. corn and soybean production to biofuels would meet only 12 percent of gasoline demand and 6 percent of diesel demand.

The bottom line is that both the type of fuel produced and the type of biomass used to produce it matter. Biodiesel has significant energy and environmental benefits over ethanol. Furthermore, biofuels produced from low-input biomass grown on agriculturally marginal land or from waste biomass, would, they believe, provide much greater supplies and stronger environmental benefits than food-based biofuels. This analysis certainly raises serious questions about the wisdom of the current U.S. approach that relies heavily on subsidizing ethanol from corn.

Geothermal Energy

A rather different source, geothermal energy, is derived from the earth's heat. Geothermal reservoirs of steam or hot water occur where hot magma comes close enough to the surface to heat groundwater. How geothermal is used depends upon the temperature of the geothermal source. When the temperature of a geothermal source is around 50 degrees Fahrenheit and up, it can be used in combination with heat pumps to provide both for space heating in the winter and for cooling (air conditioning) in the summer. (Heat pumps are electric devices that use compression and decompression of gas to heat and/or cool a house. Geothermal heat pumps are similar to ordinary heat pumps, but they use the geothermal resource instead of outside air as the input source for the pump.) When the temperature reaches 220 degrees Fahrenheit or higher, geothermal energy can be used to generate electricity.

Generally, geothermal systems have a higher initial (capital) cost than alternative heating and cooling systems. Based on the estimated yearly energy and maintenance cost savings, the payback period (the number of years it takes for an investor to recover the capital cost from annual cost savings) for a geothermal heat pump system can range from 2 to 10 years.

Hydrogen

One fuel that is currently receiving intense interest for the long run is hydrogen. (Iceland, for example, has announced its intention to become a *hydrogen-fueled economy*.) Although hydrogen is the most plentiful element in the universe, it is normally combined with other elements. Water, for example, combines two atoms of hydrogen with one of oxygen (H_2O). Hydrogen is also found in the hydrocarbons that make up many of the fossil fuels, such as gasoline, natural gas, methanol, and propane.

Reformed hydrogen can be made by separating it from hydrocarbons by using heat. Currently, most hydrogen is made this way from natural gas. Alternatively, it can be produced by separating the hydrogen and oxygen molecules in water. If an electric current (e.g., produced by photovoltaics) is conducted through a reservoir of water, the liquid splits into its constituent elements, hydrogen and oxygen. NASA has used liquid hydrogen since the 1970s to propel the space shuttle and other rockets into orbit.

In addition to being directly combusted, hydrogen can be used in fuel cells. Fuel cells offer a promising technology for use as a source of heat and electricity for buildings and as an electrical power source for electric vehicles. Hydrogen fuel cells power the NASA space shuttle's electrical systems, producing a clean byproduct—pure water, which the crew drinks.

Although fuel cells would ideally run off pure hydrogen, in the near term they may be fueled by hydrogen that comes from natural gas, methanol, or even gasoline. Although using these fossil fuels as feedstocks results in more pollution than pure hydrogen fuel cells, reforming these fuels to create hydrogen would allow the use of much of our current energy infrastructure—gas stations, natural gas pipelines, and so on—while fuel cells are phased in.

Several barriers must be overcome if the hydrogen-based economy is to become a reality. The technologies that use hydrogen as a fuel are currently very expensive and the infrastructure needed to deliver hydrogen to consumers is undeveloped.

It is unlikely that hydrogen will be able to be fully competitive with more conventional fuels in the absence of a specific government role. One potentially substantial cost saving from using hydrogen—the reduction in air pollution damage—is an externality. Since consumers are likely to ignore, or at least value less, external costs in their choice of fuels, demand will be biased away from hydrogen and potential suppliers will be discouraged from entering the market unless corrective government policies are established (such as a tax on more polluting fuels).

Consumer acceptance is an important ingredient in the transition to any alternative source of energy. New systems are usually less reliable and more expensive than old systems. Once they become heavily used, their reliability normally increases and cost declines; experience is a good teacher. Because the early consumers—the pioneers—experience both lower reliability and higher costs, procrastination can be an optimal individual strategy. If every consumer procrastinates about switching, however, the industry will not be able to operate at a sufficient scale and will not be able to gain enough experience to produce the reliability and lower cost that will assure a large, stable market. How can this initial consumer reluctance be overcome?

One strategy involves using tax dollars to subsidize purchases by the pioneers. Once the market is sufficiently large that it can begin to take advantage of economies of scale and can eliminate the initial sources of unreliability, the subsidies can be eliminated. The available empirical historical evidence suggests that the tax-credit approach significantly increased the degree of market penetration of solar equipment in the United States (Fry, 1986; Durham, Colby, and Longstreth, 1988).

An alternative approach would involve removing inefficient subsidies in order to create a level playing field for sustainable energy sources. Typical *energy subsidies* take many forms. Currently, governments subsidize the production of some fuels through tax breaks or, in the case of nuclear energy, they absorb a significant portion of the cost of liability for accidents (thereby significantly lowering insurance premiums). Governments also subsidize the research and development costs associated with the future use of these fuels.

How significant are these subsidies? Would their removal make a difference? One study (Myers and Kent, 2001) concludes that the worldwide subsidies to fossil fuels and nuclear energy are on the order of $131 billion per year and that uninternalized externalities for the same energy sources run about $200 billion per year. An over $300 billion annual subsidy is a substantial barrier that less favored energy sources, such as renewable resources, have to overcome.

Removing subsidies has a certain political appeal. Removal can lower government expenditures (or raise tax revenue in the case of eliminating tax breaks)—welcome news during periods of tight budgets. The fact that renewal could improve efficiency does not, however, mean that this step is easily taken. The producers of favored energy sources clearly benefit from those subsidies and would fight their removal.

The penetration by renewable energy resources would have been even greater if the cartel had been able to sustain the very high oil prices that were in effect at the beginning of the 1980s. As oil prices fell in real terms, both residential and commercial enthusiasm for transitioning to solar energy was undermined. Because saving money is a primary motivation for making the switch and low oil prices translate into relatively low or even negative savings, uncertainty associated with the path of future oil and natural gas prices could continue to be a barrier to the transition.

Summary

We have seen that the relationship between government and the market is not always harmonious and efficient. In the past, price controls have tended to reduce energy conservation, to discourage exploration and supply, to cause biases in the substitution among fuel types that penalize future consumers, and to create the potential for abrupt, discontinuous transitions to renewable sources. This important example makes a clear case for less, not more, regulation.

This conclusion is not universally valid, however. Other dimensions of the energy problem such as climate change and national security issues suggest the need for some government role. Insecure foreign sources require policies such as tariffs and strategic reserves to reduce vulnerability and to balance the true costs of imported and domestic sources. Additionally, government must ensure that the costs of energy fully reflect not only the potentially large environmental costs, including climate change, but also the national security costs associated with our dependence on foreign sources of energy. Government action must also assure that inefficient subsidies do not undermine the transition to sustainable energy resources.

Economic analysis reveals that no single strategy is sufficient to solve the national security and climate change problems simultaneously. Subsidizing domestic supply, for example, would reduce the share of imports in total consumption (an efficient result), but it would reduce neither consumption nor climate change emissions (inefficient results). The expansion of domestic production also tends to drain domestic reserves faster, which makes the nation more vulnerable in the long run (another inefficient result). On the other hand, energy conservation (promoted by a tax on energy, for example) would reduce energy consumption and emissions of greenhouse gases (efficient outcomes) but would not achieve the efficient share of imports (an inefficient result) since an energy tax falls on all energy consumption, whereas the national security problem involves only imports.

Given the inefficient biases against public safety in the Price-Anderson Act, government should also continue to oversee nuclear reactor safety and should ensure that communities accepting nuclear waste disposal sites are fully compensated. Given the environmental difficulties with all three of the depletable transition fuels (unconventional oil, coal, and uranium), energy efficiency, energy conservation, and electric load-management techniques are now playing (and will continue to play) a larger role.

The menu of energy options as the economy transitions to renewable sources offers a large number of choices, including photovoltaics, active and passive solar energy, wind, ocean tidal power, biomass fuels, geothermal energy, and hydrogen. It is far from clear what the ultimate mix will turn out to be, but it is very clear that government policy is a necessary ingredient in any smooth transition to a sustainable energy future. Since many of the most important costs of energy use are externalities, an efficient transition to these renewable sources will not occur unless the playing field is leveled. The potential for an efficient and sustainable allocation of energy resources by our economic and political institutions clearly exists, even if historically it has not always occurred.

Key Concepts

associated gas, *p.* 142

compensation scheme, *p.* 158

electricity deregulation, *p.* 159

embargo, *p.* 148

energy self-sufficiency, *p.* 151

energy subsidies, *p.* 169

feed-in tariff, *p.* 162

Hubbert's Peak, *p.* 141

hydrogen-fueled economy, *p.* 168

income elasticity of demand (for energy),
    p. 146

liability ceiling, *p.* 157

load management, *p.* 159

national security costs (caused by imports),
    p. 150

Natural Gas Act, *p.* 142

Natural Gas Policy Act, *p.* 144

Nuclear Regulatory Commission (NRC),
    p. 157

optimal cartel prices, *p.* 147

Organization of Petroleum Exporting
    Countries (OPEC), *p.* 145

peak-load pricing, *p.* 159

photovoltaics, *p.* 165

precautionary behavior, *p.* 157

price controls (in allocating depletable
    resources), *p.* 142

price elasticity of demand (for energy), *p.* 147

Price-Anderson Act, *p.* 157

renewable energy, *p.* 161

renewable energy credits (RECs), *p.* 161

renewable portfolio standard (RPS), *p.* 162

right-to-know laws, *p.* 161

strategic petroleum reserve, *p.* 152

vulnerability premium, *p.* 150

Further Reading

Goldemberg, J. "Solving the Energy Problems in Developing Countries," *Energy Journal* 11 (1990) (1): 19–24. The energy-development connection from a developing-country perspective.

International Energy Agency. *Taxing Energy: Why and How?* (Paris: OECD, 1993). Examines energy taxation in five OECD countries.

Additional References

Dubin, Jeffrey A. and Geoffrey S. Rothwell. "Subsidy to Nuclear Power through Price Anderson Liability Limit," *Contemporary Policy Issues* 8 (July 1990): 73–79.

Durham, Catherine A., Bonnie G. Colby, and Molly Longstreth. "The Impact of State Tax Credits and Energy Prices on Adoption of Solar Energy Systems," *Land Economics* 64 (November 1988): 347–355.

Fry, Gene R. "The Economics of Home Solar Water Heating and the Role of Solar Tax Credits," *Land Economics* 62 (May 1986): 134–144.

Griffin, James M. "OPEC Behavior: A Test of Alternative Hypotheses," *American Economic Review* 75 (December 1985): 954–963.

Hall, Darwin C., ed. "Social and Private Costs of Alternative Energy Technologies," a special issue of *Contemporary Policy Issues* (July 1990).

Hill, J. E. Nelson, E. D. Tilman, S. Polasky, and D. Tiffany. "Environmental, Economic, and Energetic Costs and Benefits of Biodiesel and Ethanol Biofuels," PNAS Vol.103, No. 30; 11206-11210 (2006). Available at: http://www.pnas.org/cgi/doi/10.1073/pnas.0604600103.

Joskow, Paul L. and Donald B. Matron. "What Does Utility-Subsidized Energy Efficiency Really Cost?" *Science* 260 (April 16, 1993): 281, 370.

Kunreuther, Howard and Paul R. Kleindorfer. "A Sealed-Bid Auction Mechanism for Siting Noxious Facilities," *American Economic Review* 76 (May 1986): 295–299.

Lind, Robert C. et al. *Discounting for Time and Risk in Energy Policy* (Washington, DC: Resources for the Future, 1982).

Mason, C. F. and S. Polasky. "What Motivates Membership in Non-Renewable Resource Cartels? The Case of OPEC," *Resource and Energy Economics* 27 (2005) (4): 321–342.

Mitchell, Robert Cameron and Richard T. Carson. "Property Rights, Protest, and the Siting of Hazardous Waste Facilities," *American Economic Review* 76 (May 1986) (2): 285–290.

Moreira, J. R. and J. Goldemberg. "The Alcohol Program," *Energy Policy* 27 (1999) (4): 229–245.

Myers, N. and J. Kent, *Perverse Subsidies: How Tax Dollars Can Undercut the Environment and the Economy* (Washington, DC: Island Press, 2001).

Nielsen, L. and T. Jeppesen, "Tradable Green Certificates in Selected European Countries—Overview and Assessment," *Energy Policy* 31, 2003: 3–14.

Oliver, M. and T. Jackson. "The Market for Solar Photovoltaics," *Energy Policy* 27 (1999) (7): 371–385.

Palmer, K. and D. Burtraw. "Electricity Restructuring and Regional Air Pollution," *Resource and Energy Economics* 19 (1997) (1–2): 139–174.

Rader, N., "The Hazards of Implementing Renewables Portfolio Standards," *Energy and Environment* 11(4), 2000: 391–405.

Reynolds, D. B. "Modeling OPEC Behavior: Theories of Risk Aversion for Oil Producer Decisions," *Energy Policy* 27 (1999) (15): 901–912.

Smith, J. L. "Inscrutable OPEC? Behavioral Tests of the Cartel Hypothesis," *The Energy Journal* 26 (2005) (1): 51–82.

Spilimbergo, A. "Testing the Hypothesis of Collusive Behavior Among OPEC Members," *Energy Economics* 23 (2001) (3): 339–353.

Unger, T. and E. O. Ahgren (2005). "Impacts of a Common Green Certificate Market on Electricity and CO_2-Emission Markets in the Nordic Countries," *Energy Policy* 33(16): 2152–2163.

U.S. Agency for International Development (AID), *Decentralized Hydropower in AID's Development Assistance Program* (Washington, DC: AID, 1986).

Historically Significant References

Lee, Dwight R. "Price Controls, Binding Constraints, and Intertemporal Economic Decision Making," *Journal of Political Economy* 86 (1978): 293–301.

Salant, S. W. "Exhaustible Resources and Industrial Structure: A Nash-Cournot Approach to the World Oil Market," *Journal of Political Economy* 84 (1976): 1079–1093.

The President's Commission on the Accident at Three Mile Island, *The Need for Change: The Legacy of TMI* (New York: Pergamon Press, 1979).

Discussion Questions

1. Should benefit/cost analysis play the dominant role in deciding the proportion of U.S. electrical energy to be supplied by nuclear power? Why or why not?

2. Economist Abba Lerner once proposed that the United States impose a tariff on oil imports equal to 100 percent of the import price. This tariff is designed to reduce dependence on foreign sources as well as to discourage OPEC from raising prices (because, as a result of the tariff, the delivered price would rise twice as much as the OPEC increase, causing a large subsequent reduction in consumption). Should this become public policy? Why or why not?

3. Does the fact that the Strategic Petroleum Reserve has never been used to offset shortfalls caused by an embargo mean that the money spent in creating the reserve has been wasted? Why or why not?

9 Water

When the Well's Dry, We Know the Worth of Water.

—Benjamin Franklin, *Poor Richard's Almanack, 1746*

Introduction

To the red country and part of the gray country of Oklahoma, the last rains came gently, and they did not cut the scarred earth. … The sun flared down on the growing corn day after day until a line of brown spread along the edge of each green bayonet. The clouds appeared and went away, and in a while they did not try anymore.

With these words John Steinbeck sets the scene for his powerful novel *The Grapes of Wrath.* Drought and poor soil-conservation practices combined to destroy the agriculture institutions that had provided nourishment and livelihood to Oklahoma residents since settlement in that area had begun. In desperation, many of those who had worked that land were forced to abandon not only their possessions, but also their past. Moving to California to seek employment, they were uprooted, only to be caught up in a web of exploitation and hopelessness.

Based on an actual situation, the novel demonstrates how the social fabric can tear when subject to tremendous stress, such as an inadequate availability of water, and how painful those tears can be.[1] Recent evidence suggests that water scarcity, precipitated by drought, may have triggered the demise of the Maya civilization (Haug et al., 2003). Clearly, problems such as these should be anticipated and prevented as much as possible.

Water is one of the essential elements of life. Humans depend not only on an intake of water to replace the continual loss of body fluids but also on food sources that need water to survive. This resource deserves special attention.

In this chapter we will examine how our economic and political institutions have allocated this important resource in the past and how they might improve on its allocation in the future. We

---

[1]Popular films such as *The Milagro Beanfield War* and *Chinatown* have played on similar themes.

initiate our inquiry by examining the likelihood and severity of water scarcity. Turning to the management of our water resources, we will define the efficient allocation of groundwater and surface water over time and compare these allocations to current practice, particularly in the United States. Finally, we will examine the menu of opportunities for meaningful institutional reform.

The Potential for Water Scarcity

The earth's renewable supply of water is governed by the hydrologic cycle, a system of continuous water circulation (see Figure 9.1). Enormous quantities of water are cycled each year through this system, though only a fraction of circulated water is available each year for human use.

Of the estimated total volume of water on Earth, only 2.5 percent (1.4 billion km^3) of the total volume is fresh water. Of this amount, only 200,000 km^3, or less than 1 percent of all fresh water resources (and only .01 percent of all the water on Earth), is available for human consumption and for ecosystems (Gleick, 1993).

FIGURE 9.1   The Hydrologic Cycle

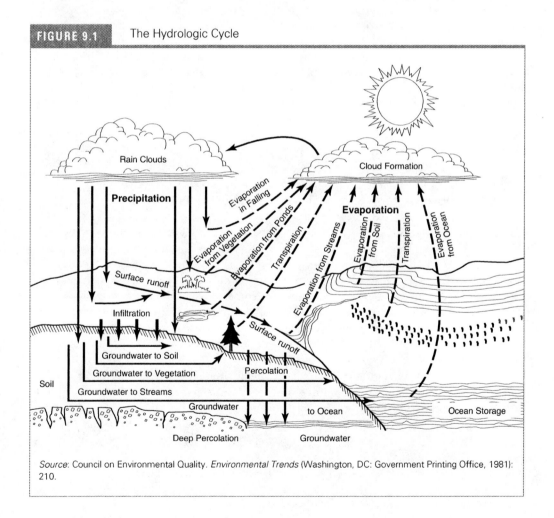

Source: Council on Environmental Quality. *Environmental Trends* (Washington, DC: Government Printing Office, 1981): 210.

If we were simply to add the available supply of fresh water (total runoff) on a global scale and compare it with current consumption, we would discover that the supply is currently about 10 times larger than consumption. Though comforting, that statistic is also misleading because it masks the impact of growing demand and the rather severe scarcity situation that already exists in certain parts of the world. Together, these insights suggest that in many parts of the world water scarcity is already evident, and other areas, including several parts of the United States, can be expected to experience water scarcity in the next few decades.

Available supplies are derived from two rather different sources—surface water and groundwater. As the name implies, *surface water* collects and flows on the earth's surface. Surface water sources include rivers, lakes, and reservoirs. By contrast, *groundwater* collects in porous layers of underground rock known as *aquifers*. Although some groundwater is renewed by percolation of rain or melted snow, most was accumulated over geologic time and, because of its location, cannot be recharged once it is depleted.

According to the UN Environment Program (2002), 90 percent of the world's readily available freshwater resource is groundwater. And only 2.5 percent of this is available on a renewable basis. The rest is a finite, depletable resource.

In 2000 water withdrawals in the United States amounted to 262 billion gallons per day. Of this, approximately 83 billion gallons per day came from groundwater. Water withdrawals, both surface and groundwater, vary considerably geographically. Figure 9.2 shows how surface and groundwater withdrawals for the United States vary by state. California, Texas, Nebraska, Arkansas, and Florida are the states with the largest groundwater withdrawals.

While surface water withdrawals in the United States have been relatively constant since 1985, groundwater withdrawals are up 14 percent (Hutson et al., 2004). Globally, annual water withdrawal is expected to grow by 10 to 12 percent every 10 years. Most of this growth is expected to occur in South America and Africa (UNESCO, 1999).

Approximately 1.5 billion people depend on groundwater for their drinking supplies (UNEP, 2002). However, agriculture is still the largest consumer of water. In the United States irrigation accounts for approximately 65 percent of total water withdrawals and over 80 percent of water consumed (Hutson et al., 2004). This number is much higher in the Southwest. Worldwide in 2000, agriculture accounted for 67 percent of world freshwater withdrawal and 86 percent of its use (UNESCO, 2000).[2]

Tucson, Arizona, demonstrates how some western communities cope. Tucson, which averages about 11 inches of rain annually, was (until the completion of the Central Arizona Project, which diverts water from the Colorado River) the largest city in the United States to rely entirely on groundwater. The water levels in some wells in the Tucson area dropped 100 feet in 10 years. Tucson annually pumped five times as much water out of the ground as nature put back in. At current consumption rates, the aquifers supplying Tucson would have been exhausted in less than 100 years. Despite the rate at which its water supplies were being depleted, Tucson continued to grow at a rapid rate. To head off this looming gap between increasing water consumption and declining supply, a giant network of dams, pipelines, tunnels, and canals known as the Central Arizona Project was constructed to transfer water from the Colorado River to Tucson. Some

---

[2]"Use" is measured as the amount of water withdrawn that does not return to the system in the form of return or unused flow.

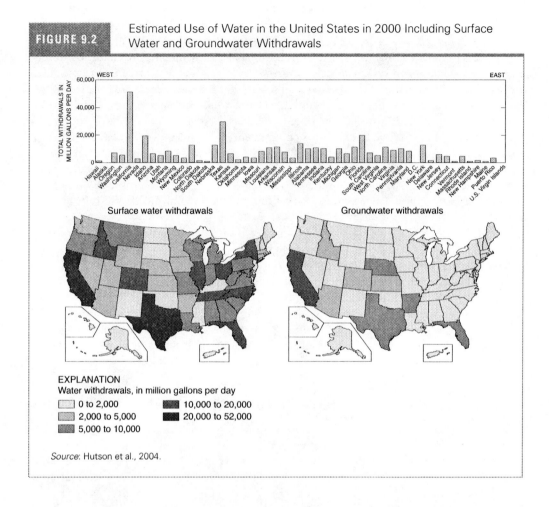

FIGURE 9.2   Estimated Use of Water in the United States in 2000 Including Surface Water and Groundwater Withdrawals

EXPLANATION
Water withdrawals, in million gallons per day

- 0 to 2,000
- 2,000 to 5,000
- 5,000 to 10,000
- 10,000 to 20,000
- 20,000 to 52,000

Source: Hutson et al., 2004.

of this water is being pumped underground in an attempt to recharge the aquifer. While this project has a capacity to deliver Arizona's 2.8 million acre-foot share of the Colorado River (negotiated by Federal Interstate Compact), it is still turning out not to be enough water for Phoenix and Tucson.[3, 4] Water diversions have been common, but are increasingly unavailable as a policy response to water scarcity.

Although the discussion thus far has focused on the quantity of water, quality is also a problem. Much of the available water is polluted with chemicals, radioactive materials, salt, or bacteria. We will reserve a detailed look at the water pollution problem for Chapter 19, but it is important to keep in mind that water scarcity has an important qualitative dimension that further limits the supply of potable water.

---

[3] One acre-foot of water is the amount of water that could cover one acre of land, one foot deep.

[4] An Interstate Compact is an agreement negotiated among states along an interstate river. Once ratified by Congress, it becomes a federal law and is one mechanism for allocating water.

Globally, access to clean water is a growing problem. More than 600 million people lack access to clean drinking water and 58 percent of those people are in Asia (UNDP 2006).[5] Relocation of rivers to rapidly growing urban areas is creating local water shortages. China, for example, built a huge diversion project to help ensure water supply at the 2008 summer Olympics. The depletion and contamination of water supplies are not the only problems. Excessive withdrawal from aquifers is a major cause of land subsidence. (Land subsidence is a gradual settling or sudden sinking of the earth's surface owing to subsurface movement of the earth's materials, in this case water.) In 1997 the USGS estimated subsidence amounts of 6 feet in Las Vegas, 9 feet in Houston, and approximately 18 feet near Phoenix. More than 80 percent of land subsidence in the United States has been caused by human impacts on groundwater (USGS, 2000).[6]

In Mexico City, land has been subsiding at a rate of 1–3 inches per year. The city has sunk 30 feet over the last century! The Monumento a la Independencia, built in 1910 to celebrate the 100th anniversary of Mexico's War of Independence, now needs 23 additional steps to reach its base. Mexico City, with its population of approximately 20 million, is facing large water problems. Not only is the city sinking, but also, with an average population growth of 350,000 per year, the city is running out of water (Rudolph, 2001).

What this brief survey of the evidence suggests is that in certain parts of the world, groundwater supplies are being depleted to the potential detriment of future users. Supplies that for all practical purposes will never be replenished are being "mined" to satisfy current needs. Once used, they are gone. Is this allocation efficient, or are there demonstrable sources of inefficiency? Answering this question requires us to be quite clear about what is meant by an efficient allocation of surface water and groundwater.

The Efficient Allocation of Scarce Water

What efficiency means for *water allocation* depends crucially on whether surface water or groundwater is being tapped. In the absence of storage, the problem with surface water is to allocate a renewable supply among competing users. Intergenerational effects are less important, as future supplies depend on natural phenomena (e.g., precipitation) rather than on current withdrawal practices. For groundwater, on the other hand, withdrawing water now does affect the resources available to future generations. In this case, the allocation over time is a crucial aspect of the analysis. Because it represents a somewhat simpler analytical case, we will start by considering the efficient allocation of surface water.

Surface Water

An efficient allocation of surface water must (1) strike a balance among a host of competing users and (2) supply an acceptable means of handling the year-to-year variability in surface water flow. The former issue is acute, because many different potential users have legitimate competing claims: Some (e.g., municipal drinking water suppliers and farmers) withdraw the water for consumption; others (e.g., swimmers and boaters) use but do not consume the water. The latter challenge arises because surface water supplies are not constant from year to year or month to month.

---

[5]http://www.un.org/apps/news/story.asp?NewsID=17891&Cr=water&Cr1.

[6]http://water.usgs.gov/ogw/pubs/fs00165/.

Because precipitation, runoff, and evaporation change from year to year, less water will be available to be allocated in some years than in others. Not only must a system for allocating the average amount of water be in place, but also above-average and below-average flows must be anticipated and allocated.

With respect to the first problem, the dictates of efficiency are quite clear—the water should be allocated so that the marginal net benefit is equalized for all uses. (Remember that the marginal net benefit is the vertical distance between the demand curve for water and the marginal cost of extracting and distributing that water for the last unit of water consumed.) To demonstrate why efficiency requires equal marginal net benefits, consider a situation in which the marginal net benefits are *not* equal. Suppose for example, that at the current allocations, the marginal net benefit to a municipal user is $2,000 per acre-foot while the marginal net benefit to an agricultural user is $500 per acre-foot. If an acre-foot of water were transferred from the farm to the city, we would lose marginal net benefits of $500 to the farm, but gain $2,000 in marginal net benefits to the city. Total net benefits rise by $1,500. Since marginal benefits fall with use, the new marginal net benefit to the city at the new allocation will be less than $2,000 per acre foot and the marginal net benefit to the farmer will be greater than $500 (a smaller allocation means moving up the marginal benefits curve), but until these two are equalized, we can still reallocate water to increase net benefits. Because net benefits could be increased by this reallocation, the initial allocation could not have maximized net benefits. Inasmuch as an efficient allocation maximizes net benefits, the allocation through which net benefits are not equalized cannot be efficient. Additionally, if the farmer sells the water to the city for something more than $500 and the city buys for something less than $2,000, net benefits are still increased.

If marginal net benefits have not been equalized, it is always possible to increase net benefits by transferring water from those uses with low net marginal benefits to those with higher net marginal benefits. By transferring water to the users who value the marginal water more, the net benefits of the water use are increased; those losing water are giving up less than those receiving the additional water are gaining. When the marginal net benefits are equalized, no such transfer is possible without lowering net benefits.

Groundwater

When withdrawals exceed recharge from a particular aquifer, the resource will be mined over time until supplies are exhausted or until the marginal cost of pumping additional water becomes prohibitive. The marginal extraction cost (the cost of pumping the last unit to the surface) would rise over time as the water table fell. Pumping would stop either (1) when the water table ran dry or (2) when the marginal cost of pumping was either greater than the marginal benefit of the water or greater than the marginal cost of acquiring water from some other source.

Abundant surface water in proximity to the location of the groundwater could serve as a substitute for groundwater, effectively setting an upper bound on the marginal cost of extraction. The user would not pay more to extract a unit of groundwater than it would cost to acquire surface water. Unfortunately, in many parts of the country where groundwater overdrafts are particularly severe, the competition for surface water is already keen; a cheap source of surface water doesn't exist.

In efficient groundwater markets, the water price would rise over time. The rise would continue until the point of exhaustion, the point at which the marginal pumping cost becomes prohibitive or the marginal cost of pumping becomes equal to the next-least-expensive source of water. At that point the marginal pumping cost and the price would be equal.

In some regions groundwater and surface water supplies are not physically separate. For example, due to the porous soils in the Arkansas River Valley, groundwater withdrawals in the region affect surface water flows near the Colorado–Kansas border (Bennett, 2000). Lack of conjunctive use management led the state of Kansas to sue the state of Colorado for depleted surface water flows at the border. (*Conjunctive use* refers to the combined management of surface and groundwater resources to optimize their joint use and to minimize adverse effects of excessive reliance on a single source.) The hydrologic nature of the water source must be taken into consideration when designing a water allocation scheme if problems like this are to be avoided.

The Current Allocation System

Riparian and Prior-Appropriation Doctrines

Within the United States the means of allocating water differ from one geographic area to the next, particularly with respect to the legal doctrines that govern conflicts. In this section we will focus on the allocation systems that prevail in the arid Southwest, which must cope with the most potentially serious and imminent scarcity of water.

In the earliest days of European settlement in the U.S. Southwest and West, the government had a minimal presence. Residents were pretty much on their own in creating a sense of order. Property rights played a very important role in reducing conflicts in this potentially volatile situation.

As water was always a significant factor in the development of an area, the first settlements were usually oriented near bodies of water. The property rights that evolved, called *riparian rights*, allocated the right to use the water to the owner of the land adjacent to the water. This was a practical solution because, by virtue of their location, these owners had easy access to water. Furthermore, enough sites had access to water that virtually all who sought water could be accommodated.

With population growth and the consequent rise in the demand for land, this allocation system became less appropriate. As demand increased, the amount of land adjacent to water became scarce, forcing some spillover onto land that was not adjacent to water. The owners of this land began to seek means of acquiring water to make their land more productive.

About this time, with the discovery of gold in California, mining became an important source of employment. With the advent of mining came a need to divert water away from streams to other sites. Unfortunately, riparian property rights made no provision for water to be diverted to other locations. The rights to the water were tied to the land and could not be separately transferred.

This situation created a demand for a change in the property-right structure from riparian rights to one that was more concordant with the need for transferability. The waste resulting from the lack of transferability became so great that it outweighed any transition costs of changing the system of property rights. The evolution that took place in the mining camps became the forerunner of what has become known as the *prior-appropriation doctrine.*

The miners established the custom that the first person to arrive had the superior claim on the water. In practice, this severed the relationship that had existed under the riparian doctrine between the rights to the land and the rights to the water. As this new doctrine became adopted in legislation, court rulings, and seven state constitutions, widespread diversion of water based on prior appropriation became possible. Stimulated by the profits that could be made in shifting water to more valuable uses, private companies were formed to construct irrigation systems and to transport water from surplus to deficit areas. Agriculture flourished.

Although prior to 1860 the role of the government was rather minimal, after 1860 that began to change—slowly at first, but picking up momentum as the twentieth century began. The earliest incursion involved establishing the principle that the ownership of water properly belonged to the state. Claimants were accorded a right to use, known as a *usufruct right*, rather than an ownership right. The establishment of this principle of public ownership was followed in short order by the establishment of state control over the rates charged by the private irrigation companies, the imposition of restrictions on the ability to transfer water out of the district, and the creation of a centralized bureaucracy to administer the process.

This was only the beginning. The demand for land in the arid West and Southwest was still growing, creating a complementary demand for water to make the desert bloom. The tremendous profits to be made from large-scale water diversion created the political climate necessary for the federal government to get involved.

The federal role in water resources originated in the early 1800s, largely out of concern for the nation's regional development and economic growth. Toward these ends, the federal government built a network of inland waterways to provide transportation. Since the *Reclamation Act of 1902*, the federal government has built almost 700 dams to provide water and power to help settle the West.

To promote growth and regional development, the federal government has paid an average of 70 percent of the combined construction and operating costs of such projects, leaving states, localities, and private users to carry the remaining 30 percent. Such subsidies have even been extended to cover some of the costs of providing marketable water services.

For example, according to a 1996 General Accounting Office report, irrigators repay only approximately $0.47 for every $1 of construction costs. Interest-free loans and cheap water are additional subsidies. Farmers using Central Valley Project Water in California, pay approximately $17 per acre foot of water while urban users pay up to 10 times that amount. While the size of these subsidies may on the surface seem enormous, regional benefits have made some projects pass a benefit/cost test (recall the accounting stance from Chapter 3). This, in a nutshell, is the current situation for water in the southwestern United States. Both the state and federal governments play a large role. State laws may vary considerably, especially with respect to sales of water and with respect to groundwater withdrawal. Though the prior-appropriation doctrine stands as the foundation of this allocation system, it is heavily circumscribed by government regulations and direct government appropriation of a substantial amount of water.

Sources of Inefficiency

The current system is not efficient. The prime source of inefficiency involves restrictions that have been placed on water transfers, preventing their gravitation to the highest valued use, though other sources, such as charging inefficiently low prices, must bear some of the responsibility.

Restrictions on Transfers. To achieve an efficient allocation of water, the marginal net benefits would have to be equalized across all uses (including nonconsumptive instream uses) of the water. With a well-structured system of water property rights, efficiency can be a direct result of the transferability of the rights (Griffin and Hsu, 1993). Users receiving low marginal net benefits from their current allocation would trade their rights to those who would receive higher net benefits. Both parties would be better off. The payment received by the seller would exceed the net benefits forgone, while the payment made by the buyer would be less than the value of the water acquired.

Unfortunately, the existing mixed system of prior appropriation rights coupled with quite restrictive federal and state laws have diminished the degree of transferability that can take place. Diminished transferability in turn reduces the market pressures toward equalization of the marginal net benefits. By itself this indictment is not sufficient to demonstrate the inefficiency of the existing system. If it could be shown that this regulatory system were able to substitute some bureaucratic process for finding and maintaining this equalization, efficiency would still be possible. Unfortunately, that has not been the case, as can be seen by examining in more detail the specific nature of these restrictions. The allocation is inefficient.

One of the earliest restrictions required users to fully exercise their water rights or else they would lose them. The principle of *beneficial use* was typically applied to offstream consumptive uses. It is not difficult to see what this "use it or lose it" principle does to the incentive to conserve. Particularly careful users who, at their own expense, find ways to use less water would find their allocations reduced accordingly. The regulations strongly discourage conservation.

A second restriction, known as *preferential use* attempts to establish bureaucratically a value hierarchy of uses. With this doctrine, the government attempts to establish allocation priorities across categories of water. Within categories (e.g., irrigation for agriculture), the priority is determined by prior appropriation ("first in time—first in right"), but among categories the preferential-use doctrine governs.

The preferential-use doctrine supports three rather different kinds of inefficiencies. First, it substitutes a bureaucratically determined set of priorities for market priorities, resulting in a lower likelihood that marginal net benefits will be equalized. Second, it reduces the incentive to make investments that complement water use in lower preference categories for the simple reason that their water could be involuntarily withdrawn as the needs in higher-level categories grow. Finally, it allocates the risk of shortfalls in an inefficient way.

Although the first two inefficiencies are rather self-evident, the third merits further explanation. Because water supplies fluctuate over time, unusual scarcities can occur in any particular year. With a well-specified system of property rights, damage caused by this risk would be minimized by allowing those most damaged by a shortfall to purchase a larger share of the diminished amount of water available during a drought from those suffering the increased shortfall with smaller consequences.

By diminishing, and in some cases eliminating, the ability to transfer rights from so-called "high preferential use" categories to "lower preferential use" categories during times of acute need, the damage caused by shortfalls is higher than necessary. In essence, the preferential-use doctrine fails to adequately consider the marginal damage caused by temporary shortfalls, something a well-structured system of property rights would do automatically.

Another factor that makes water difficult to transfer is the fact that only a portion of the water withdrawn from a stream is typically consumed. As long as the withdrawal gets put to a use in the same river basin, a portion of that water returns to the stream eventually in the form of *return flow*. Crops grown with irrigated water, for example, use only a portion of water put on the field; called the *consumptive use* portion. The remainder either evaporates or flows through the soil, eventually finding its way back to the original source. Typically, a farmer (or another user) downstream owns the right to this return flow. Since transfers of water cannot as a matter of law affect a downstream owner of that water, water courts in the Southwest are very busy and cases can take several years before a ruling is issued.

Inhibiting transfers has very practical implications. Due to low energy costs and federal subsidies, agricultural irrigation became the dominant use of water in the West. Yet, the marginal net benefits from agricultural uses are lower, sometimes substantially lower, than the marginal net benefits of water use by municipalities and industry. A transfer of water from irrigated agriculture to these other uses would raise net benefits. It is therefore not surprising that transfers from agriculture to municipalities are becoming more common.

Federal Reclamation Projects and Agricultural Water Pricing. By providing subsidies to approved projects, federal reclamation projects have diverted water to these projects even when the net benefits were negative. Why was this done? What motivated the construction of inefficient projects?

Some work by Howe (1986) provides a possible explanation. He examined the benefits and costs of constructing the Colorado-Big Thompson Project in Northeastern Colorado. With this project the water is pumped to an elevation that allows it to flow through a tunnel from the western to the eastern side of the Rocky Mountains. On that side, electric power is produced at several points. At lower elevations, the water is channeled into natural streams and feeder canals for distribution to irrigation districts and front-range cities.

Howe calculated that the national net benefits for this project, which includes all benefits and costs, were either –$341.4 million or –$237 million, depending on the number of years included in the calculations. The project cost substantially more to construct than it returned in benefits. However, regional net benefits for the geographic region served by the facility were strongly positive ($766.9 million or $1,187 million, respectively). This facility was an extraordinary boon for the local area because a very large proportion of the total cost had been passed on to national taxpayers. The local political pressure was able to secure project approval despite its inherent inefficiency.

While the very existence of these facilities underwritten by the federal government is a source of inefficiency, the manner in which the water is priced is another. The subsidies have been substantial. Frederick (1989) reported on some work done by the Natural Resources Defense Council to calculate the subsidies to irrigated agriculture in the Westlands Water District, one of the world's richest agricultural areas located on the west side of California's San Joaquin Valley. The Westlands Water District paid $10 to $12 per acre-foot, less than 10 percent of the unsubsidized cost of delivering water to the district. The resulting subsidy was estimated to be $217 per irrigated acre or $500,000 per year for the average-sized farm.

Municipal and Industrial Water Pricing. Restrictions on transfer are not the only source of inefficiency in the current allocation system. The prices charged by water distribution utilities do not promote efficiency of use either.

Both the level of prices and the rate structure are at fault. In general, the price level is too low and the rate structure does not adequately reflect the costs of providing service to different types of customers. Water utilities apply a variety of fees and charges to water. Some are better at reflecting cost than others. Water fees and charges reflect the costs of storage, treatment, and distribution of the water to customers. Rarely, however, does the rate reflect the actual value of water.

In part, perhaps because water is considered an essential commodity, the prices charged by public water companies are too low. For surface water the rates are too low for two rather distinct reasons: (1) historic average costs are used to determine rates and (2) marginal scarcity rent is rarely included.

Efficient pricing requires the use of marginal, not average, cost. In order to adequately balance conservation with use, the customer should be paying the marginal cost of supplying the last unit of water. Yet regulated utilities are typically allowed to charge prices just high enough to cover the costs of running the operation as revealed by figures from the recent past. Water utilities are capital intensive with very large fixed costs in the short run. This means that short-run average costs will be falling, implying a marginal cost that falls below average cost. In this circumstance, marginal-cost pricing would cause the utility to fail to generate enough revenue to cover costs. (Can you see why?)

Circumstances may be changing, however. Now long-run costs may be rising since new supplies are typically much more expensive to develop and the old supplies are limited by their fixed capacity (Hanneman, 1998).

The second source of the problem is the failure of regulators overseeing the operations of water distribution companies to allow a scarcity rent to be incorporated in the calculation of the appropriate price, a problem that is even more severe when groundwater is involved. One study found that due to a failure to include a user cost, rates in Tucson, Arizona, were about 58 percent too low, despite increases (Martin et al., 1984). Debate 9.1 illustrates the inconsistencies in both agricultural and municipal pricing.

Both low pricing and ignoring the marginal scarcity rent promote an excessive demand for water. Simple actions, such as fixing leaky faucets or planting native lawn grasses, are easy to overlook when water is excessively cheap. Yet in a city such as New York, leaky faucets can account for a significant amount of wasted water.

Instream Flows. Conflicts between offstream and instream uses of water are not uncommon. Since instream flows are *nonconsumptive uses*, instream flows are not covered by traditional prior apppropriation rights. In 2001 the federal government cut off water to farmers in the Klamath River Basin to protect threatened Coho salmon, which are protected under the Federal Endangered Species Act. Farmers responded by forcing open irrigation gates and forming a bucket brigade to dump water on their fields. Secretary of the Interior Gale Norton subsequently decided to resume the traditional diversion of water to the more than 1,400 farmers using Klamath River water. Six months later, a huge fish kill (estimated to be at least 35,000 salmon) was blamed on the low flows in the river. This ongoing dispute provides an illustration of the problem with the legal and institutional structures governing water resources. Without formal recognition of instream flow rights, the value of species, including salmon, cannot be properly incorporated into the allocation decision. A study on the Rio Grande River in New Mexico found that diverting water from upstream agriculture in order to provide minimum instream flows for an endangered minnow species, *increased* net benefits by making water available for high valued downstream uses (Ward and Booker, 2003). Other studies have found the recreational value of water to be higher than that for irrigation water.

Common Property Problems. The allocation of groundwater must confront one additional problem. When many users tap the same aquifer, that aquifer can become an open-access

DEBATE 9.1

What Is the Value of Water?

As mentioned earlier in this chapter, the Colorado-Big Thompson (C-BT) project moves water from the Colorado River to the eastern slope of Colorado. The Northern Colorado Conservancy District distributes the approximately 270,000 acre-feet of water per year to irrigators, towns, cities, and industries in northeastern Colorado. Irrigators with original rights currently pay approximately $3.50 per share. (A share is, on average, .7 acre-feet per year.) Cities pay approximately $7 per share if they hold original rights.

Shares of C-BT water are transferable and are actively traded in the district. Market prices have been at a minimum of $1,800 per share, which translates to approximately $2,600 per acre-foot for perpetual supply or about $208 per year using an 8 percent discount rate. Additionally, prices in the rental market (for users who want to sell or buy water on a yearly basis) range from $7.50 to $25 per acre-foot.

The cities using the water charge their customers a variety of prices. Boulder uses an *increasing block rate pricing* structure with an initial block at $1.65 per thousand gallons for the first 5,000 gallons, $3.30 per thousand gallons for the next 16,000 gallons, and $5.50 per thousand gallons over 21,000 gallons per month. Ft. Collins has some unmetered customers, who pay a fixed monthly fee, but no marginal cost for additional use. Its metered customers pay a fixed charge of $12.72 plus water charges determined by an increasing block rate. In the first block the charge is $1.72 per thousand gallons for the first 7,000 gallons. The highest block rate in Ft. Collins is $3.07 for users consuming more than 20,000 gallons per month. Longmont has both metered and unmetered customers and uses an *increasing* block rate for its residential customers and a *decreasing* block rate for its small commercial customers.

Economic theory makes clear not only that the marginal net benefits for all uses and users of a given water project should be equal, but also that the common marginal net benefit metric provides a useful indication of the value of the marginal water unit to all users of this resource.

What do we make of the huge variation in these prices? The only difference in observed prices should be a difference in the marginal cost of delivering water to those customers (since marginal net benefit should be the same for all users). The prices from the C-BT project exhibit much more variation than can be explained by marginal conveyance cost, so they clearly are not only inefficient, but also they are sending very mixed signals about the value of this water.

Source: Howe, Charles, "Forms and Functions of Water Pricing: An Overview," *Urban Water Demand Management and Planning*, Baumann, Boland, and Hanemann, eds. (New York: McGraw-Hill, Inc. 1998). With rate updates from the Cities of Boulder, Longmont, and Ft. Collins, Colorado, and the Northern Colorado Conservancy District (2004).

resource. Tapping an open-access resource will tend to deplete it too rapidly; users lose the incentive to conserve. The marginal scarcity rent will be ignored.

The incentive to conserve a groundwater resource in an efficient market is created by the desire to prevent pumping costs from rising too rapidly and the desire to capitalize on the higher prices that could reasonably be expected in the future. With open-access resources, neither of these desires translates into conservation for the simple reason that water conserved by one party may simply be used by someone else because the conserver has no exclusive right to the water that is saved. Water saved by one party to take advantage of higher prices can easily be pumped out by another user before the higher prices ever materialize.

For open-access resources, economic theory suggests several direct consequences. Pumping costs would rise too rapidly, initial prices would be too low, and too much water would be consumed by the earliest users. The burden of this waste would not be shared uniformly. Because the typical aquifer is bowl-shaped, users on the periphery of the aquifer would be particularly hard hit. When the water level declines, the edges go dry first, while the center can continue to supply water for substantially longer periods. Future users would also be hard hit relative to current users.[7] For coastal aquifers, salt water intrusion is an additional potential cost.

Potential Remedies

Economic analysis points the way to a number of possible means of remedying the current water situation in the southwestern United States. These reforms would promote efficiency of water use while affording more protection to the interests of future generations of water users.

The first reform would reduce the number of restrictions on water transfers. The "use it or lose it" component that often accompanies the prior appropriation doctrine can promote the extravagant use of water and discourage conservation. Typically, water saved by conservation is forfeited. Allowing users to capture the value of water saved by permitting them to sell it would stimulate water conservation and allow the water to flow to higher valued uses (see Example 9.1).

Water markets and water banks are being increasingly utilized to transfer water seasonally via short-term leases or on a long-term basis, either by multiple-year leases or permanent transfers. While most markets and banks are restricted to certain geographic areas, water is allowed to move to its higher valued uses to some extent. Buyers and sellers are brought together through bulletin boards, water brokers, and electronic computer networks. For example, the Westland Water Irrigation District in California uses an electronic network to match buyers and sellers (Howitt, 1998). Drought-year banks have been successful in California (Howitt, 1994; Israel and Lund, 1995). One unique water market in Colorado is explored in Example 9.2. The transfer of water, however, can incur high transaction costs, both in the time necessary for approval (up to two years in some cases) and in potential downstream impacts (Saliba, 1987).

Achieving a balance between instream and consumptive uses is not easy. As the competition for water increases, the pressure to allocate larger amounts of the stream for consumptive uses increases as well. Eventually, the water level becomes too low to support aquatic life and recreation activities.

Although they do exist (see Example 9.3), water rights for instream flow maintenance are few in number relative to rights for consumptive purposes. Those few instream rights that typically exist have a low priority relative to the more senior consumptive rights. As a practical matter this means that in periods of low water flow, the instream rights lose out and the water is withdrawn for consumptive uses. As long as the definition of "beneficial use" requires diversion, as it does in many states, water left for fish habitat or recreation is undervalued.

---

[7]In *Salt River User's Association* v. *Kavocovich* [411 P. 2d 201(1966)], the Arizona Court of Appeals ruled that irrigators who lined their ditches could not apply "saved" water to adjacent land.

Using Economic Principles to Conserve Water in California

EXAMPLE

9.1

In 1977 when then-California governor Jerry Brown negotiated a deal to settle one of the state's perennial water fights by building a new water diversion project, environmental groups were opposed. The opposition was expected. What was not expected was the form it took. Rather than simply block every imaginable aspect of the plan, the Environmental Defense Fund (EDF) set out to show project supporters how the water needs could be better supplied by ways that put no additional pressure on the environment.

According to this strategy, if the owners of the agricultural lands to the west of the water district seeking the water could be convinced to reduce their water use by adopting new, water-saving irrigation techniques, the conserved water could be transferred to the district in lieu of the project. But the growers had no incentive to conserve because conserving the water required the installation of costly new equipment and as soon as the water was saved it would be forfeited under the "use it or lose it" regulations. What could be done?

On January 17, 1989, largely through the efforts of EDF, an historic agreement was negotiated between the growers association, a major user of irrigation water, and the Metropolitan Water District (MWD) of California, a public agency that supplies water to the Los Angeles area. Under that agreement the MWD bears the capital and operating costs, as well as the indirect costs (such as reduced hydropower), of a huge program to reduce seepage losses as the water is transported to the growers and to install new water-conserving irrigation techniques in the fields. In return the MWD will get all of the conserved water. Everyone gains. The district gets the water it needs at a reasonable price; the growers retain virtually the same amount of irrigation benefits without being forced to bear large additional expenditures.

Because the existing regulatory system created a very large inefficiency, moving to a more efficient allocation of water necessarily increased the net benefits. By using those additional net benefits in creative ways, it was possible to eliminate a serious environmental threat.

The success of this agreement has spawned others. For example, two water transfer agreements, finalized in October 2003, provide an additional 200,000 acre-feet of water annually to the San Diego region as a result of conservation measures taken in the Imperial Valley and financed by the municipal payments for the water.

Sources: Robert E. Taylor, *Ahead of the Curve: Shaping New Solutions to Environmental Problems* (New York: Environmental Defense Fund, 1990); San Diego County Water Authority http://www.sdcwo.org/manage/pdf/QSA_2004.pdf.

This undervaluation of instream uses is not inevitable, however, as some enterprising fishermen have discovered.[8] In the Yellowstone River Valley in Montana, several spring creeks are wholly contained within the boundaries of property owned by a single landowner. Since these

---

[8]These examples were drawn from Anderson (1983).

EXAMPLE

9.2

Water Transfers in Colorado: What Makes a Market for Water Work?

The Colorado-Big Thompson (C-BT) Project, highlighted in Debate 9.1, pumps water from the Colorado River on the west side of the Rocky Mountains up hill and through a tunnel under the Continental Divide where it finds its way into the South Platte River. With a capacity of 310,000 acre-feet, an average of 270,000 acre-feet of water is transferred annually through an extensive system of canals and reservoirs. Shares in the project are transferable and The Northern Colorado Water Conservancy District (NCWCD) facilitates the transfer of these C-BT shares among agricultural, industrial, and municipal users. An original share of C-BT water in 1937 cost $1.50. Permanent transfers of C-BT water for municipal uses have traded for $2,000–$2,500 (Howe and Goemans, 2003). Prices rose as high as $10,000 per share in 2006 (www.waterstrategist.com).

This market is unique because shares are homogeneous and easily traded; the infrastructure needed to move the water around exists and the property rights are well-defined (return flows do not need to be accounted for in transfers since the water comes from a different basin). Thus, unlike most markets for water, transactions costs are low. This market has been extremely active and is the most organized water market in the West. When the project started almost all shares were used in agriculture. By 2000 over half of C-BT shares were used by municipalities. Howe and Goemans (2003/2003) compare the NCWCD market to two other markets in Colorado to show how different institutional arrangements affect the size and types of water transfers. They examine water transfers in the South Platte River Basin and the Arkansas River Basin. For most markets in the West, traditional water rights fall under the appropriation doctrine and as such are difficult to transfer and water does not easily move to its highest valued use. They find that the higher transactions costs in the Arkansas River Basin result in fewer, but larger transactions than for the South Platte and NCWCD. They also find that the negative impacts from the transfers are larger in the Arkansas River Basin given the externalities associated with water transfers (primarily out of basin transfers) and the long court times for approval. Water markets can help achieve economic efficiency, but only if the institutional arrangements allow for relative ease of transfer of the rights. They suggest that the set of criteria used to evaluate the transfers be expanded to include secondary economic and social costs imposed on the area of origin.

Sources: http://www.ncwcd.org/project_features/cbt_main.asp; *The Water Strategist 2006*, available at www.waterstrategist.com; Howe, Charles W. and Christopher Goemans. "Water Transfers and Their Impacts: Lessons from Three Colorado Water Markets," *Journal of the American Water Resources Association* (2003): 1055–1065.

creeks are not subject to the same legal restrictions as waterways crossing property boundaries, landowners can sell the daily fishing rights. The revenues from these sales provide owners with an incentive to develop spawning beds, protect the fish habitat, and in general, make the fishing

Protecting Instream Uses Through Acquiring Water Rights

EXAMPLE
9.3

Attempts by environmental groups to protect instream water uses must confront two problems. First, any acquired rights are usually public goods, implying that others can free ride on their provision without contributing to the cause. Consequently the demand for instream rights will be inefficiently low. The private acquisition of instream rights is not a sufficient remedy. Second, once the rights have been acquired, their use to protect instream flows may not be considered "beneficial use" (and therefore could be confiscated and granted to others for consumptive use) or they could be so junior as to be completely ineffective in times of low flow, the times when they would most be needed.

Some movement toward protecting instream rights has occurred, however. In 1979 in what was then a precedent setting action, The Nature Conservancy, an environmental, public-interest organization, applied to Arizona's Department of Water Resources for a permit for "instream flow" at the Ramsey Canyon Preserve, asking essentially for both the right to a certain amount of water and for the right simply to leave it in the stream. When the permit was approved in 1983, this was the first legal recognition in Arizona of the right to appropriate water for wildlife and recreational uses without diverting water from a streambed. Protected by these water rights and other conservation measures, the preserve has become a haven for one of the largest arrays of plant and animal species of any preserve in the United States. Some 210 species of birds (including 14 species of hummingbirds), 420 species of plants, 45 species of mammals, and 20 species of reptiles and amphibians can be found in the canyon. Modest supplemental financial support is now derived from the access fees paid by the many visitors.

What worked at Ramsey Canyon was simple and straightforward, but it is not an adequate protection device in many places. Under the prior appropriation doctrine, any rights that predate the 1983-granted instream flow right would have entitled the holder to priority for the water.

Another approach has been followed in Colorado. Several years ago a subsidiary of the Chevron Corporation gave The Nature Conservancy a gift entitling it to a 300 cubic-feet-per-second flow rate of water in the Black Canyon of Colorado's Gunnison River. Although Chevron held consumptive rights to the water, The Nature Conservancy was interested in instream rights. Because Colorado law stipulates that instream flow rights can be held only by the state, The Conservancy was faced with the "use it or lose it" rule under the prior appropriation doctrine. Taking the only step available, a transfer of the instream flow rights to the state was negotiated.

Sources: Ken Wiley, "Untying the Western Water Knot," *The Nature Conservancy* 40 (March/April 1990): 5–13; and Bonnie Colby Saliba and David B. Bush, *Water Markets in Theory and Practice: Market Transfers and Public Policy* (Boulder, CO: Westview Press, 1987): 74–77.

experience as desirable as possible. By limiting the number of fishermen, the owners prevent overexploitation of the resource.

In England and Scotland, markets are relied upon to protect instream uses more than they are in the United States. Private angling associations have been formed to purchase fishing rights from landowners. Once these rights have been acquired, the associations charge for fishing, using some of the revenues to preserve and to improve the fish habitat. Since fishing rights in England sell for as much as $220,000, the holders of these rights have a substantial incentive to protect their investments. One of the forms this protection takes is illustrated by the Anglers Cooperative Association, which has taken on the responsibility of monitoring the streams for pollution and alerting the authorities to any potential problems.

Getting the prices right is another avenue for reform. Recognizing the inefficiencies associated with subsidizing the consumption of a scarce resource, the U.S. Congress passed the *Central Valley Project Improvement Act* in 1992. The Act raises prices that the federal government charges for irrigation water, though the full-cost rate is imposed only on the final 20 percent of water received. Collected revenues will be placed in a fund to mitigate environmental damage in the Central Valley. The Act also allows water transfers to new uses.

Tsur et al. (2004) reviewed and evaluated actual pricing practices for irrigation water in developing countries. Table 9.1 summarizes their findings with respect to both the types and properties of pricing systems they discovered. As the table reveals, they found some clear trade-offs between what efficiency would dictate and what was possible given the limited information available to water administrators.

Two-part charges and volumetric pricing, while quite efficient, require information on the amount of water used by each farmer and are rarely used in developing countries. (The two-part charge combines volume pricing with a monthly fee that doesn't vary with the amount of water consumed. The monthly fee is designed to help recover fixed costs.) Individual-user water meters can provide information on the volume of water used, but they are relatively expensive. *Output pricing* (where the charge for water is linked to agricultural output, not water use), on the

TABLE 9.1   Pricing Methods and Their Properties

Pricing Scheme	Implementation	Efficiency Achieved	Time Horizon of Efficiency	Ability to Control Demand
Volumetric	Complicated	First-best	Short-run	Easy
Output	Relatively easy	Second-best	Short-run	Relatively easy
Input	Easy	Second-best	Short-run	Relatively easy
Per-area	Easiest	None	n.a.	Hard
Block-rate (tiered)	Relatively complicated	First-best	Short-run	Relatively easy
Two-part	Relatively complicated	First-best	Long-run	Relatively easy
Water market	Difficult without preestablished institutions	First-best	Short-run	n.a.

n.a. not applicable.

Source: Tsur, Yacov, Terry Roe, Rachid Doukkall, and Ariel Dinar, *Pricing Irrigation Water Principles and Cases from Developing Countries* (Washington, DC: Resources for the Future, 2004).

other hand, is less efficient, but only requires data on each water user's production. Input-based pricing is even easier because it doesn't require monitoring either water use or output. Block-rate or *tiered pricing* is most common when demand has seasonal peaks. Tiered pricing examples can be found in Israel and California. Under *input pricing*, irrigators are assessed taxes on water-related inputs, such as a per-unit charge on fertilizer. *Area pricing* is probably the easiest to implement since the only information necessary is the amount of irrigated land and the type of crop produced on that land. Although this method is the most common, it is not efficient since the marginal cost of extra water use is zero.

Tsur et al. proposed a set of water reforms for developing countries, including pricing at marginal cost where possible and using block-rate prices to transfer wealth between water suppliers and farmers. This particular rate structure puts the burden of fixed costs on the relatively wealthier urban populations, who would, in turn, benefit from less expensive food.

For water distribution utilities, the traditional practice of recovering only the costs of distributing water and treating the water itself as a free good should be abandoned. Instead, utilities should adopt a pricing system that reflects increasing marginal cost and that includes a scarcity value for groundwater. Since scarce water is not in any meaningful sense a free good, the user cost of that water must be imposed on current users. Only in this way will the proper incentive for conservation be created and the interests of future generations of water users be preserved.

Including this user cost in water prices is rather more difficult than it may first appear. Water utilities are typically regulated because they have a monopoly in the local area. One typical requirement for the rate structure of a regulated monopoly is that it earns only a "fair" rate of return. Excess profits are not permitted. Charging a uniform price for water to all users where the price includes a user cost would generate profits for the seller. (Recall the discussion of scarcity rent in Chapter 4.) The scarcity rent accruing to the seller as a result of incorporating the user cost would represent revenue in excess of operating and capital costs.

Water utilities have a variety of options to choose from when charging their customers for water. Figure 9.3 illustrates the most common volume-based price structures. A surprisingly large number of U.S. utilities are using a flat fee, which from a scarcity point of view is the worst possible form of pricing. Since a flat fee is not based on volume, the marginal cost of additional water consumption is zero. ZERO! Water use by individual customers is not even metered.

While more complicated versions of a flat-fee system are certainly possible, they do not solve the incentive-to-conserve problem. At least up until the late 1970s, Denver, Colorado, used eight different factors (including number of rooms, number of persons, number of bathrooms, and so on) to calculate the monthly bill. Despite the complexity of this billing system, because the amount of the bill was unrelated to actual volume used (water use was not metered), the marginal cost of additional water consumed was still zero.

Declining block pricing, another inefficient pricing system, has historically been much more prevalent than increasing block pricing. By charging customers a higher marginal cost for low levels of water consumption and a lower marginal cost for higher levels, regulators are placing an undue financial burden on low-income people who consume little water, and confronting high-income people with a marginal cost that is too low to provide adequate incentives to conserve. Declining block rates were popular in cities with excess capacities, especially in the eastern United States, because they encouraged higher consumption as a means of spreading the fixed costs more widely. Additionally, municipalities attempting to attract business may find this rate appealing.

| FIGURE 9.3 | Overview of the Various Variable Charge Rate Structures |

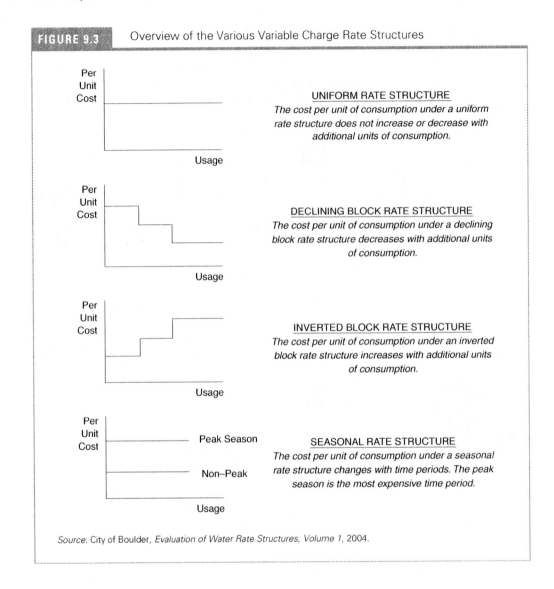

Source: City of Boulder, *Evaluation of Water Rate Structures, Volume 1*, 2004.

One way that water utilities are attempting to respect the rate of return requirement while promoting water conservation is through the use of an *inverted (increasing) block rate*. Under this system, the price per unit of water consumed rises as the amount consumed rises.

This type of structure encourages conservation by ensuring that the marginal cost of consuming additional water is high. At the margin, where the consumer makes the decision of how much extra water to be used, quite a bit of money can be saved by being frugal with water use. However, it also holds revenue down by charging a lower price for the first units consumed. This has the added virtue that those who need some water, but cannot afford the marginal price paid by more extravagant users, can have access to water without placing their budget in as much jeopardy as would be the case with a uniform price. For example, in Durban, South Africa, the first block is actually free (Loftus, 2005). Many utilities base the first block on average winter (indoor) use.

How many U.S. utilities are using increasing block pricing? As Table 9.2 indicates, the number of water utilities using increasing block rates is increasing, but remains small relative to other types of rates. In Canada the practice is not common either. In fact, in 1999 only 56 percent of the population was metered. Without a water meter, volume charges are impossible (see Example 9.4).

Other aspects of the rate structure are important as well. Efficiency dictates that prices equal the marginal cost of provision (including marginal user cost when appropriate). Several practical corollaries follow from this theorem. First, prices during peak demand periods should exceed prices during off-peak periods. For water, peak demand is usually during the summer. It is peak use that strains the capacity of the system and triggers the needs for expansion. Therefore, seasonal users should pay the extra costs associated with system expansion by being charged higher rates. Few current water pricing systems satisfy this condition in practice though quite a few cities in the Southwest are beginning to use seasonal rates. For example, Tucson, Arizona, has a seasonal rate for the months of May–September. Also, for municipalities using increasing block rates with the first block equal to average winter consumption, one could argue that this is essentially a seasonal rate for the average user. The average user is unlikely to be in the second or third blocks, except during summer months. The last graph in Figure 9.3 illustrates a seasonal uniform rate.

In times of drought, seasonal pricing makes sense, but is rarely politically feasible. Under extreme circumstances, such as severe drought, however, cities are more likely to be successful in passing large rate changes that are specifically designed to facilitate coping with that drought. During 1987 to 1992, Santa Barbara, California, experienced one of the most severe droughts of the century. To deal with the crisis of excess demand, the city of Santa Barbara changed both its rates and rate structure 10 times between 1987 and 1995 (Loaiciga and Renehan, 1997). Between March and October of 1990 an increasing block rate rose to $29.43 per Ccf (748 gallons) in the highest block! Rates were subsequently lowered, but the higher rates were successful in causing water use to drop almost 50 percent. It seems that when a community is faced with severe drought and community support for using pricing to cope is apparent, major changes in price are indeed possible.[9]

TABLE 9.2   Pricing Structures for Public Water Systems in the United States (1982–1997)

	1982 %	1987 %	1991 %	1997 %
Flat Fee	1	—	3	2
Uniform Volume Charge	35	32	35	33
Decreasing Block	60	51	45	34
Increasing Block	4	17	17	31
Total	100	100	100	100

Source: Household Water Pricing in OECD Countries. Copyright OECD 1999 and 2002 Water and Wastewater Rate Survey, Raftelis Financial Consulting, 2002.

---

[9]Hugo A. Loaiciga and Stephen Renehan. "Municipal Water Use and Water Rates Driven by Severe Drought: A Case Study," *Journal of the American Water Resources Association* Vol. 33, No. 6 (1997): 1313–1326.

EXAMPLE
9.4

Water Pricing in Canada

Water meters allow water pricing to be tied to actual use. The various pricing mechanisms suggested in this chapter require volume to be measured. Households with water meters typically consume less water than households without meters. A number of Canadian municipalities are adopting *full cost pricing* mechanisms. Full cost pricing seeks to recover not only the total cost of providing water and sewer services, but also the costs of replacing older systems. However, in order to price water efficiently, user volume must be measured. A 1999 study by Environment Canada found that only 56 percent of Canada's urban population was metered; some 44 percent of the urban population received water for which the perceived marginal cost of additional use was zero.

About 45 percent of the metered population was found to be under a rate structure that provided an incentive to conserve water. The study found that water use was 70 percent higher under the flat rate than the volume based rates!

According to Environment Canada, "Introducing conservation-oriented pricing or raising the price has reduced water use in some jurisdictions, but it must be accompanied by a well articulated public education program that informs the consumer what to expect."

As metering becomes more extensive, some municipalities are also beginning to meter return flows to the sewer system. Separate charges for water and sewer better reflects actual use. Several studies have shown that including sewage treatment in rate calculations generates greater water savings.

Source: http://www.ec.gc.ca/water/en/manage/effic/e_rates.htm.

Another corollary of the marginal cost pricing theorem is that when it costs a water utility more to serve one class of customers than another, each class of customers should bear the costs associated with its respective service. Typically, this implies that those farther away from the source or at higher elevations (requiring more pumping) should pay higher rates. In practice, utility water rates make fewer distinctions among customer classes than would be efficient. As a result, higher-cost water users are in effect subsidized; they receive too little incentive to conserve and too little incentive to locate in parts of the city that can be served at lower cost.

Regardless of the choice of price structure, do consumers respond to higher water prices by consuming less? The examples from Canada in Example 9.4 suggest they do. A useful piece of information for utilities, however, is *how much* their customers respond to given price increases. Recall from microeconomics that the price elasticity of demand measures consumer responsiveness to price increases. Municipal water use is expected to be price inelastic, meaning that for a 1 percent increase in price, consumers reduce consumption, but by less than 1 percent. A meta-analysis of 24 water demand studies in the United States (Espey, Espey, and Shaw, 1997) found a range of price elasticities with a mean of –0.51. Omstead and Stavins (2007) find similar results in their summary paper. These results suggest that municipal water demand is indeed price inelastic, but not unresponsive to price. It also turns out that climate also influences the price elasticity of demand. Residential demand for water is more price elastic in arid climates than in wet ones. Why do you think this is true?

Until recently, desalinized seawater has been prohibitively expensive and thus not a viable option outside of the Middle East. However, technological advances in reverse osmosis, nanofiltration, and ultrafiltration methods have reduced the price of desalinized water, making it a potential new source for water-scarce regions. Reverse osmosis works by pumping seawater at high pressure through permeable membranes. As of 2005 more than 10,000 desalting plants had been installed or contracted worldwide. Since 2000 desalination capacity has been growing at approximately 7 percent per year. Over 130 countries utilize some form of desalting technology (Gleick, 2006). According to the World Bank, the cost of desalinized water has dropped from $1 per cubic meter to an average of $0.50 per cubic meter in a period of five years (World Bank, 2004). Costs are expected to continue to fall, though not as rapidly. In the United States, Florida, California, Arizona, and Texas have the largest installed capacity. However, actual production has been mixed. In Tampa Bay, for example, a large desalination project was contracted in 1999 to provide drinking water. This project, while meant to be a low cost ($0.45/m^3) state-of-the-art project, was hampered by difficulties. Although the plant became fully operational at the end of 2007, projected costs were $0.67/m^3 (Gleick, 2006). In 1991 Santa Barbara, California, commissioned a desalination plant in response to the drought previously described. The cost of the water was estimated to be $1.22/m^3. Shortly after construction was completed, however, the drought ended and the plant was never operated. In 2000 the city sold the plant to a company in Saudi Arabia. It has been decommissioned, but remains available should current supplies run out. 2007 was the driest year in over 100 years, but the city projects that the plant will not be needed in the near future. (While desalination holds some appeal as an option, it is only currently economically feasible for coastal cities, and concerns about the environmental impacts such as energy usage and brine disposal remain to be addressed.[10])

In general, any solution should involve more widespread adoption of the principles of marginal-cost pricing. More-expensive-to-serve users should pay higher prices for their water than their cheaper-to-serve counterparts. Similarly, when new, much-higher-cost sources of water are introduced into a water system to serve the needs of a particular category of user, those users should pay the marginal cost of that water, rather than the lower average cost of all water supplied. Finally, when a rise in the peak demand triggers a need for expanding the water supplies or the distribution system, the peak demanders should pay the higher costs associated with the expansion.

These principles suggest a much more complicated rate structure for water than merely charging everyone the same price. However, the political consequences of introducing these changes may be rather drastic.

One strategy that has received more attention in the last couple of decades is the *privatization of water supplies.* The controversies that have arisen around this strategy are intense (see Debate 9.2).

However, it is important to distinguish between the different types of privatization since they can have quite different consequences. Privatization of water supplies creates the possibility of monopoly power and excessive rates, but privatization of access rights (as discussed in Example 9.1 and Debate 9.1) does not.

Whereas privatization of water supplies turns the entire system over to the private sector, privatization of access rights only establishes specific quantified rights to use the publicly supplied water.

---

[10]California Coastal Commission, http://www.coastal.ca.gov/.

DEBATE 9.2

Should Water Systems Be Privatized?

Faced with crumbling water supply systems and the financial burden from water subsidies, many urban areas in both industrialized and developing countries have privatized their water systems. Generally this is accomplished by selling the publicly owned water supply and distribution assets to a private company. The impetus behind this movement is the belief that private companies can operate more efficiently (thereby lowering costs and, hence, prices) and do a better job of improving both water quality and access by infusing these systems with new investment.

The problem with this approach is that water suppliers in many areas can act as a monopoly, using their power to raise rates beyond competitive levels, even if those rates are, in principle, subject to regulation. What happened in Cochabamba, Bolivia, illustrates just how serious a problem this can be.

After privatization in Cochabamba, water rates increased immediately, in some cases by 100 to 200 percent. The poor were especially hard hit. In January 2000, a four-day general strike in response to the water privatization brought the city to a total standstill. In February the Bolivian government declared the protests illegal and imposed a military takeover on the city. Despite over 100 injuries and one death, the protests continued until April when the government agreed to terminate the contract.

Is Cochabamba typical? It certainly isn't the only example of privatization failure. Failure (in terms of a prematurely terminated privatization contract) also occurred in Atlanta, Georgia. The evidence is still out on its overall impact in other settings and whether we can begin to extract preconditions for its successful introduction. The moral seems to be that statements such as "privatization is a failure" or "privatization is a panacea" are too simplistic. Context matters.

As discussed earlier in this chapter, privatization of access rights is one way to solve the excesses that follow from the free-access problem, since the amount of water allocated by these rights would be designed to correspond to the amount available for sustainable use. And if these access rights are allocated fairly (a big if!) and if they are enforced consistently (another big if!), the security that enforceability provides can protect users, including poor or indigenous users, from encroachment. The question then becomes "Are these rights allocated fairly and enforced consistently?" When they are, privatization of access rights can become beneficial for all users, not merely the rich.

● GIS and Water Resources

Allocation of water resources is complicated by the fact that water moves! Water resources do not pay attention to jurisdictional boundaries. Geographic information systems (GIS) help researchers use watersheds and water courses as organizing tools. For example, Hascic and Wu

(2006) use GIS to help examine the impacts of land use changes in the United States on watershed health, while Lewis, Bohlen, and Wilson (2008) use GIS to analyze the impacts of dams and rivers on property values in Maine. This enormously powerful tool is making economic analysis easier and the visualizing of economic and watershed data in map form helps in the communication of economic analysis to noneconomists. Check out the EPA's *Surf Your Watershed* site at http://cfpub.epa.gov/surf/locate/index.cfm for GIS maps of your watershed including stream flow, water use, and pollution discharges.

Summary

On a global scale the amount of available water exceeds the demand, but at particular times and in particular locations, water scarcity is already a serious problem. In a number of locations, the current use of water exceeds replenishable supplies, implying that aquifers are being irreversibly drained.

Efficiency dictates that replenishable water be allocated so as to equalize the marginal net benefits of water use even when supplies are higher or lower than normal. The efficient allocation of groundwater requires that the user cost of that depletable resource be considered. When marginal cost pricing (including marginal user cost) is used, water consumption patterns strike an efficient balance between present and future uses. Typically, the marginal pumping cost would rise over time until either it exceeded the marginal benefit received from that water or the reservoir runs dry.

In earlier times in the United States, markets played the major role in allocating water. But more recently governments have begun to play a much larger role in allocating this crucial resource.

Several sources of inefficiency are evident in the current system of water allocation in the southwestern United States. Transfers of water among various users are restricted so that the water remains in low-valued uses while high-valued uses are denied. Instream uses of water are actively discouraged in many western states. Prices charged for water by public suppliers typically do not cover costs, and the rate structures are not designed to promote efficient use of the resource. For groundwater, user cost is rarely included, and for all sources of water, the rate structure does not usually reflect the cost of service. These deficiencies combine to produce a situation in which we are not getting the most out of the water we are using and we are not conserving sufficient amounts for the future.

Reforms are possible. Allowing conservers to capture the value of water saved by selling it would stimulate conservation. Creating separate fishing rights that can be sold or allowing environmental groups to acquire and retain instream water rights would provide some incentive to protect streams as fish habitats. More utilities could adopt increasing block pricing as a means of forcing users to realize and to consider all of the costs of supplying the water.

Water scarcity is not merely a problem to be faced at some time in the distant future. In many parts of the world it is already a serious problem and unless preventive measures are taken, it will get worse. The problem is not insoluble, though to date the steps necessary to solve it have not yet been taken.

Key Concepts

acre-foot, *p.* 183

aquifers, *p.* 176

area pricing, *p.* 191

beneficial use, *p.* 182

Central Valley Project Improvement Act, *p.* 190

conjunctive use, *p.* 180

consumptive use, *p.* 182

declining block pricing, *p.* 191

full cost pricing, *p.* 194

groundwater, *p.* 176

increasing block rate pricing, *p.* 185

input pricing, *p.* 191

inverted block rate pricing, *p.* 192

nonconsumptive use, *p.* 184

output pricing, *p.* 190

preferential use, *p.* 182

prior-appropriation doctrine, *p.* 180

privatization of water supplies, *p.* 195

Reclamation Act of 1902, *p.* 181

return flow, *p.* 182

riparian rights, *p.* 180

surface water, *p.* 176

tiered pricing, *p.* 191

two-part charges, *p.* 190

usufruct right, *p.* 181

water allocation, *p.* 178

Further Reading

Anderson, Terry L. *Water Crisis: Ending the Policy Drought* (Washington, DC: Cato Institute, 1983). A provocative survey of the political economy of water, concluding that we have to rely more on the market to solve the crisis.

Dinar, Ariel and David Zilberman, eds. *The Economics and Management of Water and Drainage in Agriculture* (Norwell, MA: Kluwer Academic Publishers, 1991). Examines the special issues associated with water use in agriculture.

Easter, K. William, M. W. Rosegrant, and Ariel Dinar, (eds.). *Markets for Water: Potential and Performance* (Dordrecht: Kluwer Academic Publishers, 1998). This book not only develops the necessary conditions for water markets and illustrates how they can improve water management and economic efficiency, but also it provides an up-to-date picture of what we have learned about water markets in a wide range of countries, from the United States to Chile and India.

Gibbons, Diana. *The Economic Value of Water* (Washington, DC: Resources for the Future, 1986). A detailed survey and synthesis of existing studies on the economic value of water in various uses.

Harrington, Paul. *Pricing of Water Services* (Organization for Economic Co-operation and Development, 1987). An excellent survey of the water-pricing practices in OECD countries.

MacDonnell, L. J. and D. J. Guy, "Approaches to Groundwater Protection in the Western United States," *Water Resources Research* 27 (1991): 259–265. Discusses groundwater protection in practice.

Martin, William E., Helen M. Ingram, Nancy K. Laney, and Adrian H. Griffin. *Saving Water in a Desert City* (Washington, DC: Resources for the Future, 1984). A detailed look at the political and economic ramifications of an attempt by Tucson, Arizona, to improve the pricing of its diminishing supply of water.

Saliba, Bonnie Colby and David B. Bush. *Water Markets in Theory and Practice: Market Transfers and Public Policy* (Boulder, CO: Westview Press, 1987): 74–77. A highly recommended, accessible study of the way western water markets work in practice in the United States.

Spulber, Nicholas and Asghar Sabbaghi, *Economics of Water Resources: From Regulation to Privatization* (Hingham, MA: Kluwer Academic Publishers, 1993). Detailed analysis of the incentives structures created by alternative-water-management régimes.

Additional References

Anderson, Terry L., ed. *Water Rights: Scarce Resource Allocation, Bureaucracy, and the Environment* (Cambridge, MA: Ballinger, 1983).

Bennett, Lynne Lewis. "The Integration of Water Quality into Transboundary Allocation Agreements: Lessons from the Southwestern United States," *Agricultural Economics* 24(2000): 113–125.

California Coastal Commission. *Seawater Desalination in California* (October 1993).

Custodio, E. and A. Gurgui, eds. *Groundwater Economics: Selected Papers from a United Nations Symposium Held in Barcelona, Spain* (New York: Elsevier, 1989).

Espey, M., J. Espey, and W.D. Shaw, "Price Elasticity of Residential Demand for Water: A Meta-Analysis," *Water Resources Research* 33 (1997) (6): 1369–1374.

Frederick, K. D. "Water Supplies," in *Current Issues in Natural Resource Policy*, Paul R. Portney, ed. (Washington, DC: Resources for the Future, 1982): 216–252.

Frederick, K. D. *Scarce Water and Institutional Change* (Washington, DC: Resources for the Future, 1986).

Frederick, Kenneth. "Water Resource Management and the Environment: The Role of Economic Incentives," *Renewable Natural Resources: Economic Incentives for Improved Management* (Paris: Organization for Economic Co-operation and Development, 1989).

Gleick, Peter, ed. *Water in Crisis: A Guide to the World's Freshwater Resources* (Oxford, UK: Oxford University Press, 1993).

Gleick, Peter. *The World's Water 2006-2007: The Biennial Report on Freshwater Resources.* Island Press, 2006.

Griffin, Ronald C. and Shih-Hsun Hsu. "The Potential for Water Market Efficiency When Instream Flows Have Value," *American Journal of Agricultural Economics* 75 (May 1993): 292–303.

Hanneman, W. Michael. "Price and Rate Structures," *Urban Water Demand Management and Planning*, Baumann, Boland, and Hanneman, eds. (New York: McGraw-Hill, Inc. 1998).

Harrington, Paul. *Household Water Pricing in OECD Countries* (Paris: Organization for Economic Co-operation and Development, 1999): 21.

Hascic, Ivan and JunJie Wu, "Land Use and Watershed Health in the United States," *Land Economics* 82, (2006): 214–239.

Haug, Gerald H. et al. "Climate and the Collapse of Maya Civilization," *Science* 299 (March 14, 2003) (5613): 1731–1735.

Howe, Charles W. "Project Benefits and Costs from National and Regional Viewpoints: Methodological Issues and Case Study of the Colorado–Big Thompson Project," *Natural Resources Journal* 26 (Winter 1986).

Howitt, Richard E. "Empirical Analysis of Water Market Institutions: The 1991 California Water Market," *Resource and Energy Economics* 16 (1994) (4): 357–371.

Howitt, Richard E. "Spot Prices, Option Prices and Water Markets: An Analysis of Emerging Markets in California," In *Markets for Water: Potential and Performance* (Easter, Rosegrant and Dinar, Editors) Kluwer Academic Publishers, 1998.

Hutson, Susan, Nancy Barber, Joan Kenney, Kristin Linsey, Deborah Lumia, and Molly Maupin. *Estimated Use of Water in the United States in 2000.* U.S. Geological Survey Circular 1268, U.S. Department of the Interior, 2004.

Israel, Morris and Jay R. Lund. "Recent California Water Transfers: Implications for Water Management," *Natural Resources Journal* 35 (1995) (1): 1–32.

Kanazawa, M. "Pricing Subsidies and Economic Efficiency: The Bureau of Reclamation," *Journal of Law and Economics* 36 (1993): 205–234.

LaVeen, Phillip E. and Laura B. King. *Turning Off the Tap of Federal Water Subsidies: Volume 1, The Central Valley Project* (San Francisco: Natural Resources Defense Council, 1985).

Lewis, Lynne Y., Curtis Bohlen and Sarah Wilson, "Dams, Dam Removal and River Restoration," *Contemporary Economic Policy* 26 (April 2008) (2): 175–186.

Livingston, Marie L. and Thomas A. Miller. "The Impact of Instream Water Rights on Choice Domains," *Land Economics* 62 (August 1986): 269–277.

Loaiciga, Hugo A. and Stephen Renehan. "Municipal Water Use and Water Rates Driven by Severe Drought: A Case Study," *Journal of the American Water Resources Association* 33(1997)(6): 1313–1326.

Loftus, A "Free Water as Commodity: The Paradoxes of Durban's Water Service Transformation in the Age of Commodity" in *Water Privatization in Southern Africa*, (D. A. McDonald and G. Ruiters, Editors). Earthscan (2005): 189–203.

Olmstead, Sheila M. and Robert Stavins. *Managing Water Demand: Price vs. Non-Price Conservation Programs.* Pioneer Institute White Paper No. 39 (2007).

Organization for Economic Co-operation and Development. *Renewable Natural Resources: Economic Incentives for Improved Management* (Paris: OECD, 1987).

Pantell, Susan E. *Seawater Desalination in California.* San Francisco: California Coastal Commission, 1993.

Postel, Sandra. "Saving Water for Agriculture," in *State of the World: 1990,* Lester Brown et al. (New York: W. W. Norton, 1990).

Raftelis Financial Consulting, *2002 Water and Wastewater Rate Survey,* (Boca Raton, FL: CRC Press, 2003).

Rubin, Kenneth. *Efficient Investments in Water Resources: Issues and Options* (Washington, DC: Congressional Budget Office, 1983).

Rudolph, Meg. "Sinking of a Titanic City," American Geological Institute *GeoTimes* (July 2001).

Saliba, Bonnie. "Do Water Markets 'Work'? Market Transfers and Trade-offs in the Southwestern States," *Water Resources Research* 23 (July 1987).

Steinbeck, John. *The Grapes of Wrath* (New York: Viking Press, 1939).

Torell, L. Allen, James D. Libbin, and Michael D. Miller. "The Market Value of Water in the Ogallala Aquifer," *Land Economics* 66 (May 1990): 163–175.

Tsur, Yacov, Terry Roe, Rachid Doukkali, and Ariel Dinar. *Pricing Irrigation Water Principles and Cases from Developing Countries* (RFF Press, 2004).

UNEP, *An Overview of the State of the World's Fresh and Marine Waters.* (United Nations Environment Program, 2002).

UNESCO, *World Water Resources at the Beginning of the 21st Century* (Paris: United Nations Educational, Scientific and Cultural Organization, 1999).

UNESCO. *Water Use in the World: Present Situation/Future Needs* (Paris: United Nations Educational, Scientific and Cultural Organization, 2000).

Wahl, Richard W. *Markets for Federal Water: Subsidies, Property Rights, and the Bureau of Reclamation* (Washington, DC: Resources for the Future, 1989).

World Bank. *Regional Desalination Study for the Middle East, North Africa and Central Asia: Summary Note.* (Washington, DC: World Bank, 2004).

Discussion Questions

1. What pricing system identified in Table 9.1 best describes the pricing system used to price the water you use at your college or university? Does this pricing system affect your behavior about water use (e.g., length of showers)? How? Could you recommend a better pricing system in this circumstance? What would it be?

2. What system is used in your home town to price the publicly supplied water? Why was that pricing system chosen? Would you recommend an alternative?

3. Suppose you come from a part of the world that is blessed with abundant water. Demand never comes close to the available amount. Should you be careful about the amount you use, or should you simply use whatever you want whenever you want it? Why?

10 Land

Buy land, they're not making it anymore.

—MARK TWAIN (*American Humorist*)

A land ethic ... reflects the existence of an ecological conscience, and this is turn reflects a conviction of individual responsibility for the health of the land. Health is the capacity of the land for self-renewal. Conservation is our effort to understand and preserve this capacity.

—ALDO LEOPOLD (*Sand County Almanac*)

Introduction

Land occupies a special niche, not only in the marketplace, but also deep in the human soul. In its role as a resource, land has special characteristics that affect its allocation. Topography matters, of course, but so does location, especially because in contrast to many other resources, land's location is fixed. It matters not only *absolutely* in the sense that the land's location directly affects its value, but also *relatively* in the sense that the value of any particular piece of land is also affected by the uses of the land around it. Additionally, land supplies many ecological services, including providing habitat for all terrestrial creatures.

Some contiguous uses of land are compatible with each other, but others are not. In the case of incompatibility conflicts must be resolved. Whenever the prevailing legal system treats land as private property, as in the United States, the market is one arena within which those conflicts are resolved.

How well does the market do? Are the land use outcomes and transactions efficient and sustainable? Do they reflect the deeper values people hold for land? Why or why not?

In this chapter we shall begin to investigate these questions. How does the market allocate land? How well do market allocations fulfill our social criteria? Where divergences between market and socially desirable outcomes occur, what policy instruments are available to address the problems? How effective are they? Can they restore conformance between goals and outcomes?

The Economics of Land Allocation

Land Use

In general, as with other resources, markets tend to allocate land to its highest valued use. Consider Figure 10.1, which graphs three hypothetical land uses—residential development, agriculture, and wilderness.[1] The left-hand side of the horizontal axis represents the location of the marketplace where agricultural produce is sold. Moving to the right on that axis reflects an increasing distance away from the market.

The vertical axis represents net benefits per acre. Each of the three functions, known in the literature as *bid rent functions*, records the relationship between distance to the center of the town or urban area and the net benefits per acre received from each type of land use. A bid rent function expresses the maximum net benefit per acre that could be achieved by that land use as a function of the distance from the center. All three functions are downward sloping because the cost of transporting both goods and people lowers net benefits per acre more for distant locations.

| FIGURE 10.1 | The Allocation of Land |

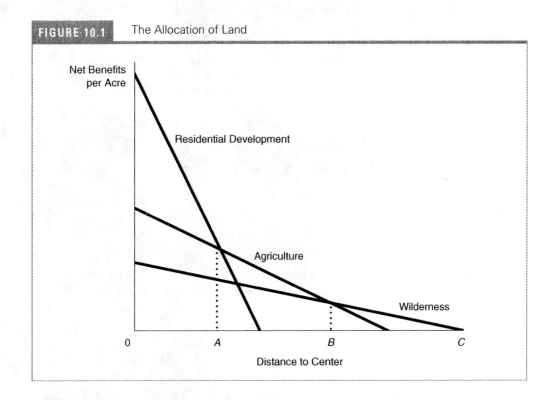

<hr />

[1]For our purposes wilderness is a large, uncultivated tract of land that has been left in its natural state.

In general, as with other resources, markets tend to allocate land to its highest valued use. According to Figure 10.1, a market process that allocates land to its highest valued use would allocate the land closest to the center to residential development (a distance of *A*), agriculture would claim the land with the next best access (*A* to *B*), and the land farthest away from the market would remain wilderness (from *B* to *C*). This allocation maximizes the net benefits society receives from the land.

Although very simple, this model also helps to clarify both the processes by which land uses change over time and the extent to which market processes are efficient, subjects we explore in the next two sections.

Land Use Conversion

Conversion from one land use to another can occur whenever the underlying bid rent functions shift. Conversion of agricultural land to residential development could occur when the bid rent function for residential development shifts up, the bid rent function for agriculture shifts down, or any combination of the two.

As demonstrated in Chapter 11 more than 50 percent of the agricultural cropland in the United States has been converted to nonagricultural purposes since 1920. Two sources of this conversion stand out: (1) increasing urbanization and industrialization rapidly shifted upward the bid rent functions for nonagricultural land, including residential development; (2) rising productivity of the remaining agricultural land allowed the smaller amount of land to produce a lot more food. Less agricultural land was needed to meet the rising food demand.

Many developing countries are witnessing the conversion of wilderness areas into agriculture.[2] Our simple model also suggests some reasons why that may be occurring.

Relative increases (shifts up) in the bid rent function for agriculture could result from the following:

* Domestic population growth that increases the domestic demand for food

* Opening of export markets for agriculture that increase the foreign demand for local crops

* Shifting from subsistence crops to cash crops (such as coffee or cocoa) for exports, thereby increasing the profit per acre

* New planting or harvesting technologies that lower the cost and increase the profitability of farming

* Lower agricultural transport costs due, for example, to the building of new roads into forested land

Some offsetting increases in the bid rent function for wilderness could result from an increasing demand for wilderness-based recreation or increases in preferences for wilderness due to increases in public knowledge about the many functions wilderness performs.

Although only three land uses are drawn in Figure 10.1 for simplicity, in actual land markets, of course, all other uses, including commercial and industrial, must be added to the mix. Changes in the bid rent functions for any of these uses could trigger conversions.

---

[2]Wilderness is also being lost in many of the more remote parts of industrialized countries in part due to the proliferation of second homes in particularly scenic areas.

Sources of Inefficient Use and Conversion

In the absence of any government regulation are market allocations of land efficient? In some circumstances they are, but certainly not in all, or even in most, circumstances.

We shall consider several sets of problems associated with land use inefficiencies that commonly arise in the industrialized countries: sprawl and leapfrogging, the effects of taxes on land use conversion, incompatible land uses, undervaluation of environmental amenities, and market power. While some of these may also plague developing countries, we follow with a section that looks specifically at some special problems developing countries face.

Sprawl and Leapfrogging

Two problems associated with land use that are receiving a lot of current attention are *sprawl* and *leapfrogging*. From an economic point of view, sprawl occurs when land uses in a particular area are inefficiently dispersed, rather than efficiently concentrated. The related problem of leapfrogging refers to a situation in which new development continues not on the very edge of the current development, but farther out. Thus, developers "leapfrog" over contiguous, perhaps even vacant, land in favor of land that is farther from the center of economic activity.

Several environmental problems are intensified with dispersed development. Trips to town to work, shop, or play become longer. Longer trips not only mean more energy consumed, but also frequently they imply a change from the least polluting modes of travel (such as biking or walking) to automobiles, a much more heavily polluting source. Assuming the cars used for commuting are fueled by gasoline internal combustion engines, dispersal drives up the demand for oil (including imported oil), results in higher air pollutant emissions levels (including greenhouse gases), and increases the need for more steel, glass, and other raw materials to supply the increase in the number of vehicles demanded.

The Public Infrastructure Problem.   To understand why inefficient levels of sprawl and leapfrogging might be occurring we must examine the incentives faced by developers and how those incentives affect location choices.

One set of inefficient incentives can be found in the pricing of public services. New development beyond the reach of current public sewer and water systems may necessitate extending those facilities if the new development is to be served. The question is "who pays for this extension?"

If the developer pays for the extension to internalize the cost, she or he will automatically consider this as part of the cost of locating farther out. When those costs are passed on to the buyers of the newly developed properties, they will also consider the marginal cost of living farther out.

Suppose, however, as is commonly the case, that the extensions of these services are financed by metropolitan-wide taxes. When the development costs are being subsidized by all taxpayers in the metropolitan area, both the developers and potential buyers of the newly developed property find living farther out to be artificially cheap. This bias, known as the *public infrastructure problem*, prevents developers from efficiently considering the trade-off between developing the land more densely within the currently served areas and developing the land outside those areas, thereby promoting inefficient levels of sprawl. By lowering the cost of developing farther out it also increases the likelihood of leapfrogging.

The desirability of development farther from the center of economic activity can also be promoted either by transportation subsidies or negative externalities. As potential residential buyers choose where to live, transportation costs matter. Living farther out may mean a longer commute or longer shopping trips. Implicitly, when living farther out means more and/or longer trips, these transport costs should figure into the decision of where to live; higher transportation costs promote the relative net benefits of living closer to the center.

The implication is that if transportation costs are inefficiently low due to subsidies or any uninternalized negative externalities from travel, a bias will be created that inefficiently favors more distant locations. Finding examples of inefficiently low transportation costs is not difficult. While we reserve a full discussion of this topic for Chapter 17, for our current purpose, consider just two examples: pollution externalities and parking subsidies.

- When the social cost associated with pollution from car exhaust is not fully internalized, the marginal cost of driving an extra mile is inefficiently low. This implies not only that an excessive number of miles will be driven, but also that dispersed development has become inefficiently attractive.

- Many employers provide free employee parking even though providing that parking is certainly not free to the employer. Free parking represents a subsidy to the user and lowers the cost of driving to work. Since commuting costs (including parking) are typically an important portion of total local transportation costs, free parking creates a bias toward more remote residential developments and encourages sprawl.

While these factors can promote sprawl and make leapfrogging more likely, they don't completely explain why developers skip over land that is closer in. Economic analysis explains some specific sources of leapfrogging (Burchfield et al., 2006). The first explanation notes that when residential dwellers place a sufficiently large amenity value on public open space, they may be willing to incur the additional commuting costs associated with leapfrogging in order to take advantage of the larger amount of open space that is available farther out. Developers can supply more public open space in these outer areas since land is cheaper.

Another explanation for leapfrogging suggests that by locating outside of the municipal boundaries (and skipping over land that is at the edge of, but still within those boundaries), developers may be able to avoid the costs associated with extending municipal services altogether. New development in these remote areas can be accommodated simply by drilling on-site wells for drinking water and by installing septic systems on each building lot.

GIS and Land Use Control. Since the spatial dimension of land use control is so important, GIS analysis can be very helpful. In one case it has been used to try to understand how big a problem sprawl represents. (See Example 10.1).

Incompatible Land Uses

As mentioned earlier in this chapter, the value of a parcel of land will be affected not only by its location, but also by how the nearby land is used. This interdependence can be another source of inefficiency.

We know from previous discussions in this book that even in the presence of fully defined property rights, private and social incentives can diverge in the presence of externalities. When any decision confers external costs on another party, the allocation that maximizes net benefits for the decision-maker may not be the allocation that maximizes net benefits for society as a whole.

Using GIS to Analyze Sprawl

EXAMPLE

10.1

As outlined in Chapter 3 geographic information systems (GIS) offer economists and others powerful tools for analyzing spatial data and spatial relationships. Land use is an obvious candidate for this form of analysis.

In a 2006 article entitled "Causes of Sprawl: A Portrait from Space," Burchfield et al. used GIS technology to examine urban development in the United States. While determining the extent of sprawl in U.S. cities, they also investigated why some cities are more sprawling than others.

To examine these questions they created a data set that compares high altitude photographs from 1976 with satellite images from 1992, using digital land cover and land use data from the same time periods. In order to calculate sprawl, first they calculated the percentage of open space within a square kilometer of the development. Then they calculated an index of sprawl by averaging across all the residential development in each of the metropolitan areas in the study. Atlanta, for example, has a 1992 sprawl index of 55.57 while San Francisco's is 30.48. According to these data San Francisco was a more compact city than Atlanta.

They found that two-thirds of the land area in the United States developed by 1992 had already been developed in 1976. Only 0.3 percent of the 1992 residential development was found to be more than 1 kilometer away from other development, but 43 percent of the square kilometers surrounding this average development was undeveloped. They concluded that while overall development had increased, they did not find that development to be any more sprawling than before. In fact, the extent of sprawl seemed very stable over the time periods they analyzed.

Not surprisingly, the amount of sprawl varies by city. Geography, access to natural resources like water and access to infrastructure all proved to be determinants of the degree of sprawl. Rates of population growth and reliance on an automobile are also positively associated with sprawl. Interestingly, they found that 25 percent of the variation in sprawl across the studied cities can be explained by physical geography alone. The presence of groundwater aquifers, for example, allows housing to be more scattered since homeowners can drill inexpensive wells without the additional cost of municipal water lines. Mountains tend to contain development, but small hills encourage expansion. A temperate climate was also found to increase sprawl. Think about these results in the context of your hometown. Does the geography and climate in your hometown encourage or discourage sprawl?

Their results offer interesting policy prescriptions as well. Controlling access to groundwater, for example, is one way to control the spread of development. Holding local taxpayers accountable for infrastructure costs can also control sprawl since taxpayers will likely respond by demanding less costly infrastructure.

GIS technology allows us to combine all the features of the landscape including the human dimension into our analysis and allows us to ask more probing questions about complex subjects such as sprawl.

Source: Marcy Burchfield, Henry Burchfield, Diego Puga, and Matthew Turner, "Causes of Sprawl: A Portrait from Space," *Quarterly Journal of Economics*, May 2006.

Negative externalities are rather common in land transactions. Many of the costs associated with a particular land use may not accrue exclusively to the landowner, but will fall on the owner of nearby parcels. For example, houses near the airport are affected by the noise and neighborhoods near a toxic waste facility may face higher health risks.

One current controversial example involves an ongoing battle over the location of large industrial farms where hogs are raised for slaughter. Some of the costs of these farms (e.g., odors and water pollution from animal waste) fall on the neighbors. Since these costs are externalized, they tend to be ignored or undervalued by hog farm owners in decisions about the land, creating a bias. In terms of Figure 10.1 the private net benefit curve for agriculture would lie above the social net benefit curve, resulting in an inefficiently high allocation of land to agriculture (hog farms in this example).[3]

One traditional remedy for the problem of incompatible land uses involves a legal approach known as zoning. Zoning involves land use restrictions enacted via an ordinance to create districts or zones that establish permitted and special land uses within those zones. Land uses in each district are commonly regulated according to such characteristics as type of use (such as residential, commercial, and industrial), density, structure height, lot size, and structure placement among others. One aspect of the theory behind zoning is that by locating similar land uses together, negative externalities can be limited or at least reduced.

One major limitation of zoning is that it can actually promote urban sprawl. By setting stringent standards for all property (such as requiring a large lot for each residence and prohibiting multifamily dwellings), zoning mandates a lower density. By reducing the allowed residential density, it can actually contribute to urban sprawl by forcing more land to be used to accommodate a given number of people.[4]

Undervaluing Environmental Amenities

Positive externalities represent the mirror image of the negative externalities situation described above. Many of the beneficial services associated with a particular land use may also not accrue exclusively to the landowner. Hence, that particular use may be undervalued by the landowner.

Consider, for example, a large farm that provides both beautiful vistas of open space for neighbors (or even for travelers on an adjoining road) and provides habitat for wildlife in its forests, streams, and rangelands. The owner would be unlikely to reap all the benefits from providing the vistas because travelers could not always be excluded from enjoying them, despite the fact that they contribute nothing to their preservation.[5] In the absence of exclusion, the owners receive only a small proportion of the total benefits. If the owner of the large farm is approached by someone wanting to buy it for, say, residential development, the farmer will not consider the external benefits of the open space to wildlife and to travelers when setting a price. As a result, these benefits are likely to be ignored or undervalued by the landowner, thereby creating a bias in land use decisions. Specifically, in this case, uses that involve more of the undervalued activities will lose out to activities that convey more benefits to the landowner even when, from society's perspective, that choice is clearly inefficient.

---

[3]For an economic analysis of the magnitude of this impact see Herriges et al. (2005).

[4]For evidence on the empirical relevance of this point see McConnell et al. (2006b).

[5]Note that the aesthetic value from open space is a public good. In many, if not most cases, exclusion is either impossible or impractical (perhaps simply too expensive) and the benefits from the view are indivisible.

Consider the implication of these insights in terms of Figure 10.1. In the presence of externalities, a farmer's decision whether to preserve agricultural land that provides a number of external benefits or sell it to a developer is biased toward development. The owner's private net benefit curve for agriculture would be lower than the social net benefit curve. The implication of this bias is that the allocation of land to agriculture would inefficiently contract and the allocation to residential development would expand.

One remedy for environmental amenities that are subject to inefficient conversion due to the presence of positive externalities involves direct protection of those assets by regulation or statute. Take wetlands, for example. Wetlands help protect water quality in lakes, rivers, streams, and wells by filtering pollutants, nutrients, and sediments, and they reduce flood damage by storing runoff from heavy rains and snow melts. They also provide essential habitat for wildlife. Regulations help to preserve those functions by restricting activities that are likely to damage these ecological services. For example, draining, dredging, filling, and flooding are frequently prohibited in shoreland wetlands. As Debate 10.1 points out, however, the fact that these regulations diminish the value of the landowner's property in order to protect social values has created some controversy about their use.

DEBATE 10.1

Should Landowners Be Compensated for "Regulatory Takings"?

When environmental regulations, such as those protecting wetlands, are imposed, they tend to restrict the ability of the landowner to develop the land subject to the regulation. This loss of development potential frequently diminishes the value of the property and is known in the common law as a "*regulatory taking.*" Should the landowner be compensated for that loss in value?

Proponents say that compensation would make the government more likely to regulate only when it was efficient to do so. According to this argument, forcing governments to pay the costs of the regulation would force them to balance those costs against the societal benefits, making them more likely to implement the regulation only where the benefits exceeded the costs. Proponents also argue that it is unfair to ask private landowners to bear the costs of producing benefits for the whole society; the cost should be borne via taxes on the members of society.

Opponents argue that forcing the government to pay compensation in the face of the severe budget constraints, which most of them face, would result in many (if not most) of these regulations not being implemented despite their efficiency. They also argue that fairness does not dictate compensation when the loss of property value is due to simply preventing a landowner from causing societal damage (such as destroying a wetland); landowners are not understood to have an unlimited right to inflict social damage.

Current judicial decisions tend to award compensation only when the decline of value is so severe as to represent a virtual confiscation of the property (100 percent loss in value). Lesser declines are not compensated.

Disagreeing with this set of rulings, voters in Oregon in 2004 approved Measure 37, which allows individual landowners to claim compensation from the local community for any decrease in property value due to planning, environmental, or other government regulations. Which approach do you find most compelling?

The Influence of Taxes on Land Use Conversion

Many governments use taxes on land (and facilities on that land) as a significant source of revenue. For example, state and federal governments tax estates (including the value of land) at the time of death and local governments depend heavily on property taxes to fund such municipal services as education. In addition to raising revenue, however, taxes also can affect incentives to convert land from one use to another, even when such conversions would not be efficient.

The Property Tax Problem. In the United States the *property tax*, a tax imposed on land and facilities on that land, is the primary source of funding for local governments. A property tax has two components: the tax rate and the tax base. The tax base (the value of the land) is usually determined either by the market value, as reflected in a recent sale, or as estimated by a professional estimator called an assessor.

For our purposes the interesting aspect of this system is that the assessment is normally based upon perceived market value, not current use. This distinction implies that when a land-intensive activity such as farming is located in an area under significant development pressure, the tax assessment may reflect the development potential of the land, not its value in farming. Since the value of developable land is typically higher, potentially much higher, the tax payments required by this system may raise farming cost (and lower net income) sufficiently as to promote an inefficient conversion of farmland to development. When this tax does not actually reflect the current activity's use of the government services funded by the tax revenue, this choice of a funding mechanism can create a bias against land-intensive activities.

The Inheritance Tax Problem. The death of someone who has been engaging in land-intensive activities (such as farming) poses a specific tax problem to those who inherit the estate. Depending on the size of the estate the heirs may owe a considerable *estate tax*, a type of tax levied on the value of the assets held by the deceased at the time of death. Since the inherited land may not produce a sufficient cash flow to pay the taxes, part or all of the land might have to be sold to raise the necessary funds. In this case the conversion of the land would be dictated by tax-driven liquidity considerations, not efficiency considerations.

The inheritance tax can apparently be an empirically significant factor in land conversion. For example, Motohiro and Patel (1999) find among older landowners in Japan a rather large effect of the inheritance tax in motivating the conversion of agricultural land to development.

Market Power

For all practical purposes the total supply of land is fixed. Furthermore, since the location of each parcel is unique, an absence of good substitutes can sometimes give rise to market power problems. Because market power allows the seller to charge inefficiently high prices, market power can frustrate the ability of the market to achieve efficiency by preventing transfers that would increase social value. One example of this problem is when market power inhibits government acquisitions to advance some public purpose.

The "Frustration of Public Purpose" Problem. One of the functions of government is to provide certain services, such as parks, potable drinking water, sanitation services, public safety, and education. In the course of providing these services it may be necessary to convert land that is being used for a private purpose to a public use, say a new park.

Efficiency dictates that this conversion should take place only if the benefits from the conversion exceed its costs. The public sector could simply buy the land from its current owner of course, and that approach has much to recommend it. Not only would the owner be adequately compensated for giving up ownership, but also an outright purchase would make sure that the opportunity cost of this land (represented by the inability of the previous owner to continue its current use) would be reflected in the decision to convert the land to public purpose. If the benefits from the conversion were lower than the cost (including the loss of benefits to the previous owner as a result of the conversion), the conversion would not (and from an efficiency point of view should not) take place.

Suppose, however, the owner of the private land recognizes that his/her ownership of the specific parcel of land most suited for this public purpose creates an opportunity to become a monopolist seller. To capitalize on this opportunity she or he could hold out until such time as the public sector paid monopoly profits for the land. If and when this occurs, it could represent an inefficient frustration of the public purpose by raising its cost to an inefficiently high level.[6] Sellers with market power could inefficiently limit the amount of land acquired by the government to provide public access to such amenities as parks, bike paths, and nature trails.

The main traditional device for controlling the "frustration of public purpose" problem is the doctrine known as eminent domain. Under *eminent domain* the government can legally acquire private property for a "public purpose" by condemnation as long as the landowner is paid "just compensation."

Two characteristics differentiate an eminent domain condemnation from a market transaction. First, while the market transfer would be voluntary, the transfer under eminent domain is mandatory—the landowner cannot refuse. Second, the compensation to the landowner in an eminent domain proceeding is determined not by agreement of both the public and private parties, but by a legal determination of a fair price.

Notice that while this approach can effectively eliminate the "holdout" problem and force the public sector to pay for (and hence recognize in the choice) the opportunity cost of the land, it will only be efficient if the conversion is designed to fulfill a legitimate public purpose and the payment does in fact reflect the true opportunity cost of the land. Not surprisingly, both aspects have come under considerable legal scrutiny.

The eminent domain determination of just compensation typically involves one or more appraisals of the property provided by disinterested experts who specialize in valuing property. In the case of residential property, appraisals are commonly based on recent sales prices of comparable properties in the area, suitably adjusted to consider the unique characteristics of the parcel being transferred. Since in reasonable circumstances (e.g., a farm in the family for generations) this inferred value may not reflect a specific owner's true valuation,[7] it is not surprising that landowners frequently do not agree that the compensation that they are ultimately awarded by this process is "fair"; appeals are common.

---

[6]Although we are focusing here on a public sector action, the same logic would apply to a developer trying to buy several pieces of land to build a new large development. One of the potential sellers could hold out for an inflated price, recognizing that their parcel was necessary for the development to go forward.

[7]In this case "true valuation" means a price that would have been accepted in a voluntary transaction in the absence of monopoly considerations.

Controversy also is associated with the issue of determining what conversions satisfy the "public purpose" condition (see Debate 10.2).

Special Problems in Developing Countries

Insecure Property Rights. In many developing countries property rights to land are either informal or nonexistent. In these cases land uses may be determined on a first-come, first-served basis and the occupiers, called "squatters," do not actually hold title to the land. Rather, taking advantage of poorly defined or poorly enforced property rights, they acquire the land simply by occupying it, not by buying or leasing it. In this case the land is acquired for free, but the holders run the risk of eviction if someone else ultimately produces an enforceable claim for the land and mounts a successful action to enforce it.

The lack of clear property rights can introduce both efficiency and equity problems. The efficiency aspect is caused by the fact that a first-come, first-served system of allocating land affects both the nature of the land use and incentives to preserve its value. Early occupiers of the land determine the use and, since the land cost them nothing to acquire, the opportunity cost associated with other potentially more socially valuable uses is never considered. Hence, low-valued uses could dominate high-valued uses by default. This means, for example, extremely

---

DEBATE 10.2

What Is a "Public Purpose"?

The U.S. Constitution only allows the eminent domain power to be used to accomplish a "*public purpose.*" What exactly is a public purpose?

Although acquiring land for typical facilities such as parks and jails is settled terrain, recent decisions that justify the use of eminent domain to condemn private neighborhoods to facilitate urban renewal by private developers are much more controversial.

For example, in *Kelo* v. *City of New London, Conn. 125 S.Ct. 2655* (2005) the court upheld the city's development authority to use eminent domain to acquire parcels of land that it planned to lease to private developers in exchange for their agreement to develop the land according to the terms of a development plan. Can private development such as this fulfill the "public purpose" test?

Those who support this decision point out that large-scale private developments face many of the same market power obstacles (such as "holdouts") as faced by the public sector. Furthermore, since large-scale private developments of this type provide such societal benefits as jobs and increased taxes to the community, eminent domain is seen as justified to prevent inefficient barriers that inhibit development.

Opponents suggest that this is merely using governmental power to favor one set of private landowners (the developers) over others (the current owners of the land).

Should the scope of "public use" include large-scale private developments such as this? When it is allowed, should the developers be under any special requirements to assure that the public benefits are forthcoming?

valuable forests or biologically diverse land could be converted to housing or agriculture even when other locations might be much more efficient.

With respect to preservation incentives occupiers with firm property rights could sell the land to others. The ability to resell provides an incentive to preserve its value to achieve the best possible price. If, on the other hand, any movement off the land causes a loss of all rights to the land, those incentives can be diminished. The equity aspect points out that the absence of property rights gives occupiers no legal defense against competing claims. Suppose, for example, that some indigenous people have sustainably used a piece of land for a very long period of time, but any property rights they hold are simply unenforceable. If marketable natural resources are discovered on "their" land, enormous political pressure will be exerted to move the "squatters" somewhere else so that the resource can be exploited.

Efficiency mandates that land use conversion should take place only if the net benefits of the new use are larger than the net benefits of the old. The traditional means of determining when that test has been satisfied is to require that the current owners be sufficiently compensated that they would voluntarily give up their land. If their rights do not entitle them to compensation, or if those rights can simply be ignored, the land can be converted and they can be involuntarily displaced even when it is efficient to preserve the land in its current use. With formal enforceable property rights, current users could legally defend their interests. Informal rights having questionable enforceability would make current users much more vulnerable.

The Poverty Problem. In many developing countries poverty may constrain choices to the extent that degradation of the land can dominate sustainable use, simply as a matter of survival. Even when the present value of sustainable choices is higher, a lack of income or other assets may preclude taking advantage of the opportunity.

As Barbier (1997) points out, poor rural households in developing countries only have land and unskilled labor as their principal assets, and thus few human or physical capital assets. The unfortunate consequence of this situation is that poor households with limited asset holdings often face important labor, land, and cash constraints on their ability to invest in land improvements. Barbier relates the results of a study he conducted with Burgess in Malawi:

> In Malawi female-headed households make up a large percentage (42 percent) of the "core-poor" households. They typically cultivate very small plots of land (<0.5 ha) and are often marginalized onto the less fertile soils and steeper slopes.... They are often unable to finance agricultural inputs such as fertilizer, to rotate annual crops, to use "green manure" crops or to undertake soil and water conservation. As a result, poorer female headed households generally face declining soil fertility and crop yields, further exacerbating their poverty and increasing their dependence upon the land.

This degradation of land, due to inadequate investment in maintaining it, can cause farmers to migrate from that degraded land to other marginal land, only to have it suffer the same fate. For similar reasons poverty can exacerbate tropical deforestation, promote overgrazing and hasten the inefficient conversion of land to agriculture.

Government Failure. While both property rights and poverty can be sources of the inefficient allocation of land, government failure can be as well. Government failure occurs when the public policies have the effect of distorting land use allocations. A common example involves building roads into previously preserved land, rendering that land suitable (by increasing access and lowering transportation costs) for a number of new land uses. In this case, by lowering transportation costs the government makes the bid rent functions flatter, and coupled with the undervaluation of environmental amenities, this can lead to an inefficient conversion of land.

Innovative Market-Based Policy Remedies

The previous section has identified a number of sources of market failure in the allocation of land to its various uses. One way to deal with those failures is to establish some kind of complementary role between the economy and the government. If the policy remedies are to be efficient, however, they must be able to rectify the failures without introducing a new set of inefficiencies—no small task as we shall see.

Establishing Property Rights

Merely establishing enforceable property rights can rectify some market inefficiencies, but the circumstances must be right for the outcome to be efficient. In an early, highly influential article Harold Demsetz (1967) pointed out the nature of those circumstances. The establishment of property right systems can mitigate or avoid the problems of over exploitation that can occur when land is merely allocated on a first-come, first-served basis.

In cases where the land uses are relatively homogeneous and the land is abundant relative to the demand for it, any inefficiency associated with the absence of property rights could well be smaller than the significant cost associated with establishing a property rights system. As societies mature, however, a point will normally be reached when the inefficiencies associated with the absence of a property right system become so large that bearing the additional administrative costs of establishing it becomes justified. By establishing secure, enforceable, transferable claims, adequate property right systems can encourage both efficient transfer and efficient maintenance of the value of the property, since in both cases the seller would benefit directly. In the absence of the specific circumstances giving rise to the inefficiencies noted in this chapter, establishing secure property rights can cause private and social incentives to coincide.

Transferable Development Rights

Owners of land that efficiency suggests should be preserved are typically opposed to zoning ordinances designed to promote preservation because they bear all the costs of preservation while society as a whole reaps the benefits. One approach, *transferable development rights* (TDR), changes that dynamic.

TDR programs are a method for shifting residential development from one portion of a community to another. Local units of government identify *sending areas* (areas where development is prohibited or discouraged) and *receiving areas* (areas where development is encouraged).

Landowners in sending areas are allocated development rights based on criteria identified in adopted plans. Generally, the allocation depends upon the number of developable sites available on their property.

Landowners seeking to develop in a receiving area must first buy a certain amount of development rights from landowners in a sending area. In principle, the revenue from selling these rights compensates the sending area owners for their inability to develop their land and, hence, makes them more likely to support the restrictions.[8] It preserves land without burdening the public budget (see Example 10.2).

Wetlands Banking[9]

Recent administrations, both Republican and Democratic, have pledged that wetlands should experience "no net loss." Despite these bipartisan pledges to protect wetlands, as the pressure on coastal and shorefront properties has increased, the economic benefits from developing wetlands (and political pressures on obstacles to development) have significantly increased as well.

One policy instrument for attempting to preserve wetlands in the face of this pressure is known as *Wetlands Mitigation Banking* and involves providing incentives for creating off-site "equivalent" wetlands services when adverse impacts are unavoidable and when on-site compensation is either not practical or use of a mitigation bank is environmentally preferable to on-site compensation. According to the USEPA "The objective of a mitigation bank is to provide for the replacement of the chemical, physical, and biological functions of wetlands and other aquatic resources which are lost as a result of authorized impacts."

Controlling Land Development with TDRs

EXAMPLE
10.2

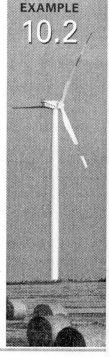

How transferable development rights (TDRs) work in practice can be illustrated with an example. The New Jersey Pinelands is a largely undeveloped, marshy area in the southeastern part of the state encompassing approximately 1 million acres. This area provides habitat for several endangered species. In an effort to direct development to the least environmentally sensitive areas, the Pinelands Development Commission created Pineland Development Credits (PDCs), a form of transferable development rights.

Landowners in environmentally sensitive areas receive 1 PDC in exchange for every 39 acres of existing preserved farmland, 1 PDC for every 39 acres of preserved upland, and 0.2 PDC for every 39 acres of wetlands. To create a demand for these credits, developers seeking to increase the standard density on land in the receiving area, which is specifically zoned for development, are required to acquire one PDC for every four units of increase. The price of credits is set by the market.

To assure that the market would be vigorous enough, the commission also established a Pinelands Development Credit Bank to act as a purchaser of last resort for PDCs at the statutory price of $10,000 per credit. In 1990 the bank auctioned its inventory at the price of $20,200 per PDC. By 1997 developers had used well over 100 PDCs.

Source: Robert C. Anderson, and Andrew Q. Lohof, *The United States Experience with Economic Incentives in Environmental Pollution Control Policy* (Washington, DC: Environmental Law Institute, 1997).

---

[8]For an analysis of how a program in Calvert County, MD, has worked, see McConnell et al. (2006a).

[9]The section benefited from Salzman, James, and Ruhl, J. B. (2006).

Mitigation banks involve wetlands, streams, or other aquatic resource areas that have been restored, established, enhanced, or (in certain circumstances) specifically preserved for the purpose of providing compensation for unavoidable impacts to aquatic resources. Mitigation banks involve a form of "third-party" compensatory mitigation, in which the responsibility for compensatory mitigation implementation and success is assumed by someone other than the party who, by causing an adverse impact to a wetland, is required by law to provide mitigation.

A mitigation bank may be created when a government agency, corporation, nonprofit organization, or other entity undertakes mitigation activities under a formal agreement with a regulatory agency. The value of those activities is defined in "compensatory mitigation credits." In principle, the number of credits available for sale is based upon the use of ecological assessment techniques to certify that the credited areas provide the specified ecological functions.

How has the program performed? As one recent review (Salzman and Ruhl, 2007) concludes:

> *Despite policies mandating that habitat trading ensure equivalent value and function, the experience is that most programs are not administered this way. In practice, most habitat trades to date in wetlands programs have been approved on the basis of acres, in many instances ensuring equivalence in neither value nor function.*

This experience is instructive. Merely assuring that the compensation involves a similar number of acres falls short of true equivalence unless the replacement ecological functions supplied by those acres are also the same.

Conservation Banking

Conservation banking transfers the concept of transferable credits used in wetland mitigation banking into endangered and threatened species conservation with a few slight differences. While in wetland mitigation banking the goal is to replace the exact function and values of the specific wetland habitats that would be adversely affected by a proposed project, in conservation banking the goal is to offset adverse impacts to a specific species.

A *conservation bank* is a parcel of land containing natural resource values that are conserved and managed in perpetuity, through a conservation easement (described below) held by an entity responsible for enforcing the terms of the easement. Banks are established for specified listed species (under the Endangered Species Act) and used to offset impacts to the species occurring on nonbank lands. The values of the natural resources are translated into quantified "credits." Project proponents are, therefore, able to complete their conservation needs through a one-time purchase of credits from the conservation bank (see Example 10.3).

Safe Harbor Agreements[10]

Safe harbor agreements are a new means of conserving endangered and threatened species on privately owned land. They overcome the disincentives that inhibit many landowners from implementing practices likely to benefit endangered species that flow from the Endangered Species Act. Under the approach taken by the Endangered Species Act the presence of an endangered species

---

[10]This section benefited from the information in Environmental Defense's Center for Conservation Incentives. For more information on safe harbor agreements see their Web site at http://www.environmentaldefense.org/article.cfm?ContentID=399.

Conservation Banking: The Gopher Tortoise Conservation Bank

EXAMPLE

10.3

In rapidly growing Mobile County, Alabama, the gopher tortoise faced survival problems due to the disappearance of its habitat. Since the tortoise is federally listed as a threatened species under the Endangered Species Act (ESA), small landowners were forced to observe some rather severe restrictions on their use of the land. Because these restrictions were quite burdensome for the landowners and the resulting fragmented, patchy habitat proved ineffective in protecting the tortoise, these restrictions created quite a conflict in the community.

A conservation bank established by the Mobile Area Water and Sewer System (MAWSS) in 2001 reduced the conflict, allowing development to continue on other areas while restoring and permanently protecting a much more suitable large tract of the long-leaf pine habitat that the tortoise prefers.

MAWSS owns a 7,000-acre forest that buffers and protects the county's water supply. Under the terms of its conservation bank, MAWSS has agreed to set aside 222 acres, forgo any development on that land, and manage it in perpetuity for the benefit of gopher tortoises. Landowners who want to build on tortoise habitat elsewhere in Mobile County can purchase "credits" from the bank, and thereby be relieved of their ESA responsibilities to set aside a small patch of their land. The tortoises benefit because the large tract of contiguous, suitable habitat is vastly superior to a network of small, unconnected patches of land, while the landowners can now develop their land by helping to fund (through the purchase of credits) this tortoise habitat.

Source: Environmental Defense Web site: Gopher Tortoise Conservation Bank. http://www.environmental defense.org/article.cfm?contented=2665 Accessed September14, 2007.

on a property may result in legally imposed restrictions on any activities deemed harmful to that species. Thus, if landowners were simply to restore wildlife habitats on their property, and those habitats attracted endangered animals, they might find themselves faced with many new restrictions on their use of the land. As a result, some landowners are not only unwilling to take such risks, but they may actually actively manage property to prevent endangered species from occupying their land.

Safe harbor agreements overcome these perverse incentive problems. Any landowner who agrees to carry out activities expected to benefit an endangered species is guaranteed that no added Endangered Species Act restrictions will be imposed as a result. A landowner's Endangered Species Act responsibilities are effectively frozen at their current levels for a particular species if he or she agrees to restore, enhance, or create a habitat for that species. Safe harbor agreements do not, however, confer a right to harm any endangered species already present when the agreement is entered into (established by the landowner's "baseline" responsibilities). Those responsibilities are unaffected by a safe harbor agreement.

Grazing Rights

Farmers have been allowed to graze their livestock on public lands since the early 1900s. The Taylor Grazing Act of 1934 attempted to prevent overgrazing by assuring that the amount of grazing was consistent with the carrying capacity of the land.

The law set up a system that involved the issuance of grazing permits to farmers. Each permit authorized a certain amount of livestock to be grazed on a specific piece of land for a specified period of time. The permits are denominated in animal unit months (AUM). An AUM is the amount of feed or forage required to maintain one animal unit (e.g., a 1,000 lb cow and calf) for one month. The number of issued permits is based upon the carrying capacity of the land (in terms of available forage). A grazing fee is charged for each AUM.

Conservation Easements

One approach to preserving land, which is increasingly being used around the world, is known as a conservation easement. A *conservation easement* is a legal agreement between a landowner and private or public agency that limits uses of the land (in many cases in perpetuity) in order to protect its conservation values.

Once created, conservation easements can be either sold or donated. If the donation benefits the public by permanently preserving important resources and meets other federal tax code requirements, it can qualify as a charitable tax deduction. The tax deductible amount is the difference between the land's value with and without the easement.

From an economic point of view, a conservation easement allows the bundle of rights associated with land ownership to be treated as separable transferable units. Separating the development rights and allowing them to flow to the highest valued use (conservation in this case) may allow the value of the entire bundle of rights the land to be increased, while simultaneously preserving the land. The value of the bundle of unseparated entitlements would only be maximized if the owner of the property happened to be the one who placed the highest value on each and every entitlement, an unlikely possibility.

Suppose, for example, a landowner wants to continue to harvest timber from her land, but not to convert it to housing. In the absence of a conservation easement, the owner is likely to face property taxes on the land that are based on highest valued use (development) rather than its current use (timber harvest). If, however, the owner executes an agreement with a public or private entity that can legally administer a conservation easement on the land, property taxes will fall (since the assessed value is now lower), and she will either get a substantial income tax break (in the case of a charitable donation of the easement) or the revenue (in the case of a sale of the easement). Meanwhile the land is protected in perpetuity from development, and the current owner can use the land for all purposes except those explicitly precluded by the easement agreement.

Conservation easements have much to recommend them. Since they are voluntary transactions, no one is forced to part with the development rights; consent is required for any transfer. This approach also allows land trusts to preserve land from development much more cheaply than would be possible if the only option were to purchase the land itself, rather than just the specific rights associated contained in the easement.

Easements, however, can have their own set of problems. Land uses affected by the conservation easement must be monitored to ensure that the terms of the agreement continue to be upheld and, if they are not, to bear the costs of a legal action to enforce compliance with the agreement. These legal actions are not cheap. In addition, the perpetual nature of conservation easements could become a problem if and when, in the far distant future, development became the universally preferred use.

Land Trusts

What kinds of entities can take on the monitoring and enforcement burdens associated with assuring compliance with the easement agreement, keeping in mind that these duties may last forever? In some cases government performs this role, but increasingly legal entities, known as conservation *Land Trusts*, have been created for this purpose. A *conservation land trust* is a nonprofit organization that, as all or part of its mission, actively works to conserve land using a variety of means. It can purchase land for permanent protection or accept donations or bequests of either land or easements. Because they are organized as charitable organizations under federal tax laws, donations of easements or land to a land trust can entitle the easement donor to a charitable deduction from his or her income tax.

A conservation land trust is actually only one of the two common forms of land trusts. The other, the *community land trust*, tends to focus on using land for housing and community service rather than land conservation. Community land trusts typically acquire and hold land, but sell off any residential or commercial buildings that are on the land. They then extend long-term leases to eligible tenants (see Example 10.4).

The land leases, in addition to being long term (typically 99 years) and renewable, are also assignable to the heirs of the leaseholder. Most, if not all, community land trusts have in place "limited equity" policies and formulas that restrict the resale price of the housing in order to maintain its long-term affordability. These features of the community land trust model provide homeownership opportunities to people who might otherwise be left out of the market and protect land in such land-intensive activities as farming that would otherwise be converted.

Ecotourism. Since one of the reasons that preserved land has difficulty competing with other land uses is the fact that many of the benefits of preserved land involve externalities, it stands to reason that one possible remedy involves trying to internalize those benefits. The most prominent example of this approach is *ecotourism*. According to the Nature Conservancy and the World Conservation Union ecotourism is defined as:

> *Environmentally responsible travel to natural areas, in order to enjoy and appreciate nature (and accompanying cultural features, both past and present) that promotes conservation, has a low visitor impact and provides for beneficially active socio-economic involvement of local peoples.*

The theory behind ecotourism is that it rectifies some of the bias against preserved land by providing an income stream from that land. In essence it shifts out the private preservation bid rent function, thereby bringing it closer to the social preservation bid rent function.

Not all ecotourism projects turn out to be consistent with this definition. Increasing the number of visitors to sensitive natural areas in the absence of appropriate oversight and control can threaten the integrity of both ecosystems and local cultures (see Debate 10.3). Additionally, the possible instabilities in this revenue source posed by climate fluctuations, volatile exchange rates, and political and social upheaval can make an excessive reliance upon tourism a risky business.

EXAMPLE

10.4

Using a Community Land Trust to Protect Farmland

A farm couple had run a community-supported agriculture program on leased land at Indian Line Farm in western Massachusetts for two years, growing organic vegetables to sell at the nearby Great Barrington Farmers' Market. During those two years they had built up a core group of shareholders who came each week to the farm for their share of the harvest.

When the farm came up for sale, the two could not afford to purchase both the high-priced Berkshire land and the buildings. If the farm were to stay in active vegetable production, something had to be done.

The owner agreed to sell the land for its $155,000 appraised value. In June 1999 the Community Land Trust in the Southern Berkshires purchased Indian Line Farm, simultaneously selling the buildings to the couple and the conservation restrictions to The Nature Conservancy.

As a result of the purchase, the Community Land Trust holds title to the land and leases it to the couple on a 99-year basis, providing security of tenure. The lease guarantees the lessees ownership of the house, barn, other outbuildings, and farm improvements, enabling the farmers to build equity as they continue to work the farm.

The lease not only requires that the buildings remain owner-occupied and not become rental property or vacation homes, but also it stipulates that the land be farmed, requiring minimum yearly commercial crop production over and above household self-sufficiency levels. The choice of crops is left to the farmers, based on their evaluation of local markets.

The lease also seeks to ensure that the buildings remain affordable at resale to the next farmer. The Community Land Trust retains an option to purchase the buildings and improvements at no more than their replacement cost and to resell them at the same price to another farmer. This provision is designed to ensure that the value of the land, purchased with community donations, is not included in any sale price for the buildings and improvements.

Source: E. F. Schumacher Society Web page at http://www.smallisbeautiful.org/publications/essay_group_effort. htm.

Development Impact Fees

Development impact fees are charges imposed on a developer to offset the additional public-service costs of new development. Normally applied at the time a developer receives a building permit, the revenues are dedicated to funding the additional services, such as water and sewer systems, roads, schools, libraries, and parks and recreation facilities, made necessary by the presence of new residents in the development. Since those fees are presumably passed on to those buying houses in the development, in principle they protect against the public infrastructure problem by internalizing the costs of extending services. Internalizing that externality restores the incentives associated with choosing the location of residential development and reduces one distortion that promotes inefficient leapfrogging and sprawl.

DEBATE 10.3

Does Ecotourism Provide a Pathway to Sustainability?

One of the ways ecotourism can promote conservation is by providing the necessary funds to implement an effective conservation program. Take the example of Bolivia's Eduardo Avaroa Reserve. This diverse landscape includes hot springs, and geysers surrounded by volcanoes and majestic mountains. Its freshwater and saltwater lakes provide habitat for year-round flocks of pink flamingos and other birds, while nearby 23 types of mammals and almost 200 species of plants flourish in the desert-like environment. With over 40,000 visitors per year, the park is Bolivia's most visited.

When a conservation planning initiative determined that tourism was a major threat to the reserve, The Nature Conservancy worked with the Bolivian National Park System to develop a visitor fee system. The program, which reportedly generated over half a million dollars in new funds, allows the reserve to fund efforts to mitigate these tourism-related threats. The visitor fee approach is now being extended across the Bolivian Park System. It is estimated that the national protected areas system could generate more than $3 million per year in new income for conservation.

Quite a different take on ecotourism is provided by a British academic, Rosaleen Duffy, about the former British colony of Belize—a popular ecotourist destination in Central America. Duffy relates stories of how scuba diving and snorkeling visitors have spoiled fragile corals and otherwise harassed marine wildlife.

In their pursuit of reefs, rainforests, and ruins, writes Duffy, they "did not reflect on the environmental impact of the construction of hotels, the use of airlines, the manufacture of diving equipment, the consumption of imported goods or even something as visible as taking a motorboat out to the reef, which polluted the water." As a *Time* article on her book notes: "To Duffy, it seems, the only good tourist is the one who stays home."

Sources: Rosaleen Duffy, A Trip Too Far—Ecotourism, Politics & Exploitation (Island Press, 2002), Mary Ann Bird. Ecotourism or Egotourism, *Time* online, 2002 at http://www.time.com/time/magazine/article/0,9171,338585,00.html (visited May 24, 2007); The Nature Conservancy, Ecotourism and Conservation Finance http://www.nature.org/aboutus/travel/ecotourism/about/art14824.html (visited May 24, 2007).

Property Tax Adjustments

Several states offer programs to discount property taxes as a means to protect a socially desired current use, particularly when undiscounted taxes are seen as an inefficient bias against that use. When property taxes are based upon market value rather than current use, the tax structure can put pressure on the owner to convert the land. This would be particularly true if the current activities are land-intensive (farming or a preserved forest, for example) and the land could be sold for a new residential development. This pressure can be inefficient to the extent that it ignores all the positive externalities of the current use.

Under schemes to try to counteract this tax bias, eligible property owners seen as conferring uncompensated external benefits on the community are offered specified reductions in their assessed value. Programs are typically available to the property owner through an application

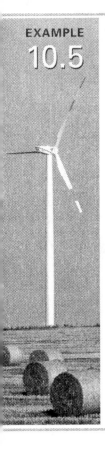

EXAMPLE
10.5

Tax Strategies to Reduce Inefficient Land Conversion: Maine's Open Space Program

Recognizing that property taxes can cause inefficient conversion away from desirable land-intensive activities, many states have adjusted their property tax systems to reduce or eliminate these biases. One such system is Maine's Open Space program.

To qualify for the program land must either be preserved or restricted in use so as to provide a public benefit. Benefits specifically recognized for eligibility include public recreation, scenic resources, game management, and wildlife habitat. The valuation (against which the tax is levied) placed on land qualifying for the open space designation is typically accomplished by first determining how many of the four categories of public benefits the land qualifies for. The percentage reductions associated with each of the applicable categories are then cumulated and the fair market value is reduced by this cumulative percentage. Those categories and their associated percentage reductions are as follows:

- Ordinary open space—20 percent reduction
- Permanently protected—30 percent reduction
- Forever wild—20 percent reduction
- Public access—25 percent reduction

The owner of any property satisfying all four of these benefit conditions (through selling or donating a conservation easement, for example) could therefore receive a cumulative reduction of up to 95 percent on the property taxes associated with the eligible land.

process run by the local municipality. Certain criteria must be met for each program in order for a parcel of land to be eligible and any future changes in the eligibility of the land enrolled in this tax relief program are subject to disqualification and a penalty[11] (see Example 10.5).

Summary

Land is an important environmental resource, not only in its own right, but also as a complement to many related ecosystems. By providing habitat for wildlife, recharge areas for aquifers, and the foundation for such land-intensive activities as forestry and agriculture, the allocation of land lies at the core of a harmonious relationship between humans and the environment.

In principle the market allocates land to its highest and best use. In practice several attributes of land and the allocation process can result in inefficient, unsustainable, and/or unjust outcomes. Sources of inefficiency include poorly specified property rights, market power and

---

[11]In the farmland program, for example, if the property no longer qualifies as a farmland tract, then the assessed penalty would be an amount equal to the taxes that would have been paid in the last five years if it had not been in the farmland, less the taxes that were originally assessed, plus any interest on that balance.

externalities, as well as inefficient tax and user fee structures. Furthermore, by constraining choices poverty can also lead to both inefficient and unfair allocations of land.

A number of policy instruments, some quite novel, are available to counteract some of these socially undesirable outcomes. They include the formalization of property rights to protect users from intrusion; ecotourism to provide a source of revenue for preserved land; transferable development rights; wetland and conservation banking to provide more flexibility in meeting environmental goals; conservation easements and land trusts to reduce the cost and increase the likelihood that efficient preservation can take place; and changes in property and inheritance tax structures as well as development impact fees to eliminate inefficient incentives and promote efficient land use decisions. While this collection of policy options can correct some of the imbalances in the land allocation system, most represent, at best, a movement in the right direction, not the full restoration of efficiency or sustainability.

Key Concepts

bid rent functions, *p.* 203
community land trust, *p.* 219
conservation easements, *p.* 218
conservation land trust, *p.* 219
development impact fees, *p.* 220
ecotourism, *p.* 219
eminent domain, *p.* 211
estate tax, *p.* 210
GIS and land use control, *p.* 206
grazing rights, *p.* 218
Land Trust, *p.* 219
leapfrogging, *p.* 205

property tax, *p.* 210
public infrastucture problem, *p.* 205
public purpose, *p.* 212
receiving areas, *p.* 214
regulatory takings, *p.* 209
safe harbor agreements, *p.* 216
sending areas, *p.* 214
sprawl, *p.* 205
transferable development rights, *p.* 214
wetlands mitigation banking, *p.* 215
conservation banking, *p.* 216

Further Reading

Barbier, E. B. "The Economic Determinants of Land Degradation in Developing Countries" (Philosophical Transactions of the Royal Society: Biological Sciences 1997) 352: 891–899. Investigates the economic determinants of land degradation in developing countries, focusing on rural households' decisions to degrade (as opposed to conserve) land resources, and the expansion of frontier agricultural activity that contributes to forest and marginal land conversion.

Bell, K. P., K. J. Boyle, and J. Rubin. *Economics of Rural Land-Use Change* (Aldershot, UK: Ashgate 2006). Presents an overview of the economics of rural land-use change; includes theoretical and empirical work on both the determinants and consequences of this change.

Johnston, R. J. and S. K. Swallow, eds. *Economics and Contemporary Land Use Policy* (Washington, DC: Resources for the Future, Inc. 2006) Explores the causes and consequences of rapidly accelerating land conversions in urban-fringe areas, as well as implications for effective policy responses.

Additional References

Burchfield, Marcy, Henry G. Overman, Diego Puga, and Matthew A. Turner (2006). "Causes of Sprawl: A Portrait from Space." *Quarterly Journal of Economics*, 121(2): 587–633.

Carrión-Flores, Carmen and Elena G. Irwin (2004). "Determinants of Residential Land-Use Conversion and Sprawl." *American Journal of Agricultural Economics* 86(4): 889–904.

Herriges, J. A., S. Secchi, and B. A. Babcock (2005). "Living with hogs in Iowa: The impact of livestock facilities on rural residential property values." *Land Economics*, 81(4): 530–545.

McConnell, V., E. Kopits, and M. Walls (2006a). "Using Markets for Land Preservation: Results of a TDR program." *Journal of Environmental Planning and Management*, 49(5): 631–651.

McConnell, V., M. Walls, and E. Kopits (2006b). "Zoning, TDRs and the density of development." *Journal of Urban Economics* 59(3): 440–457.

Motohiro Adachi and Kanak Patel (1999). "Agricultural Land Conversion and Inheritance Tax in Japan." *Review of Urban & Regional Development Studies*, 11(2), 127–140.

Salzman, James and J. B. Ruhl (2007). " 'No Net Loss' Instrument Choice in Wetland Protection" in Jody Freeman and Charles D. Kolstad, eds. *Moving to Markets in Environmental Regulation: Lessons from Twenty Years of Experience* (New York: Oxford University Press): 323–350.

Sundberg, J. O. (2006). "Private Provision of a Public Good: Land Trust Membership." *Land Economics*, 82(3): 353–366.

Historically Significant Reference

Demsetz, Harold (1967). "Toward a Theory of Property Rights." *American Economic Review*, 57: 347–359.

Discussion Questions

1. In the United States a principle responsibility for preserving endangered species (say a pair of endangered birds that chooses to nest on private land) and the costs of exercising that responsibility fall on private landowners, while in much of Europe the costs are borne by taxpayers. Which do you think is the better approach? Why?

2. Air pollution officials in California's Central Valley have opened a new front in the war against urban sprawl, and regulators and environmental advocates throughout the state are watching closely. Starting in March 2006 the San Joaquin Valley Air Pollution Control District in California became the first regulatory body in the country to impose fees on new residential and commercial development specifically focused on reducing air pollution. Critics argue that this is an ineffective way to control pollution and will mainly drive up housing prices, making housing less affordable for the poor. Is this policy a good idea or not?

Agriculture

We, the Heads of State and Government, Ministers and Representatives of 181 countries and the European Community, ... reaffirm the conclusions of the World Food Summit in 1996 ... and the objective ... of achieving food security for all through an ongoing effort to eradicate hunger in all countries, with an immediate view to reducing by half the number of undernourished people by no later than 2015, as well as our commitment to achieving the Millennium Development Goals (MDGs). ...

... We firmly resolve to use all means to alleviate the suffering caused by the current crisis, to stimulate food production and to increase investment in agriculture, to address obstacles to food access and to use the planet's resources sustainably, for present and future generations. We commit to eliminating hunger and to securing food for all today and tomorrow.

—World Food Summit (Rome, June 2008)

Introduction

In 1974 the World Food Conference set a goal for the eradication of hunger, food insecurity, and malnutrition within a decade. This goal was never met. The Food and Agriculture Organization of the United Nations (FAO) has estimated that without faster progress, 680 million people will still face hunger by the year 2010 and that more than 250 million of these people will be in Sub-Saharan Africa. Amidst growing concern about widespread malnutrition and about the capacity of agriculture to meet future food needs, a World Food Summit was called. The first World Food Summit was held at FAO headquarters in Rome in November 1996. 10,000 participants representing 185 countries and the European Community attended.

The Rome Declaration on World Food Security, which came out of the Food Summit, set a target of reducing by half the number of undernourished people by 2015. In 2008 delegates from 181 countries reaffirmed this pledge. How close are we to meeting these goals? The evidence is not encouraging.

According to the United Nations Hunger Project, the International Fund for Agricultural Development (2002), and FAO (2005):

◈ Of the more than 840 million people in the world who still suffer from chronic hunger and malnutrition, approximately 800 million live in developing countries. More than one-quarter of these, or 215 million, are children.

◈ From 1995–1997 to 1999–2001 the number of undernourished people actually increased by 18 million.

◈ About 24,000 people die each day from hunger or hunger-related causes. Malnutrition is a factor in more than half of the 10.8 million child deaths per year.

◈ One-third of all the children in the developing countries are malnourished. The problem is most severe in South Asia and Sub-Saharan Africa. In countries such as Haiti, Tajikistan, and Sierra Leone more than half the population is undernourished.[1]

In the United States approximately one in ten households (33.6 million people) experience hunger or the risk of hunger (U.S. Department of Agriculture, Economic Research Service, 2002).

According to the FAO, the total amount of available food is not the problem; the world produces plenty of food to feed everyone. World agriculture produces 17 percent more calories *per person* today than 30 years ago, despite the fact that population has increased by 70 percent over the same time period. If this is the case, why are so many people hungry? While the world produces enough food, currently, 54 nations do not produce enough food to feed their populations These same nations cannot afford to import enough food products to fill the gap. Most of these countries are in Sub-Saharan Africa.

Cereal grain, the world's chief supply of food, is a renewable private-property resource that, managed effectively, could be sustained as long as we receive energy from the sun. Are current agricultural practices sustainable? Are they efficient? Because land is typically not a common-property resource, farmers have an incentive to invest in irrigation and other means of increasing yield, because they can appropriate the additional revenues generated. On the surface, a flaw in the market process is not apparent. We must dig deeper to uncover the sources of the problem.

In this chapter we will explore the validity of three common hypotheses used to explain widespread malnourishment: (1) a persistent global scarcity of food, (2) a maldistribution of that food both among nations and within nations, and (3) temporary shortages caused by weather or other natural causes. These hypotheses are not mutually exclusive; they could all be valid sources of a portion of the problem. As we will see later in the chapter, it is important to distinguish among these sources and assess their relative importance, because each implies a different policy approach.

◉ Global Scarcity

To some, this onset of a food crisis suggests a need for dramatic changes in the relationship between the agricultural surplus nations and other nations. Garrett Hardin (1974), a human

---

[1]The FAO has created a world hunger map with accessible data. It can be found at http://www.fao.org/es/ess/faostat/foodsecurity/FSMap/flash_map.htm. Click the animation to see changes in hunger statistics over time.

ecologist, has suggested the situation is so desperate that our conventional ethics, which involve sharing the available resources, are not only insufficient, but also they are counterproductive. He argues that we must replace these dated notions of sharing with sterner *lifeboat ethics*.

The allegory he invokes envisions a lifeboat adrift in the sea that can safely hold 50 or, at most, 60 people. Hundreds of other people are swimming about, clamoring to get into the lifeboat, their only chance for survival. Hardin suggests that if passengers in the boat were to follow conventional ethics and allow swimmers into the boat, it would eventually sink, taking everyone to the bottom of the sea. In contrast, he argues, lifeboat ethics would suggest a better resolution of the dilemma; the 50 or 60 should row away, leaving the others to certain death, but saving those fortunate enough to get on the lifeboat. The implication is that food sharing is counterproductive. It encourages more population growth and ultimately would cause inevitable, and even more serious, shortages in the future.

The existence of a global scarcity of food is the premise that underlies this view; when famine is inevitable, sharing can become counterproductive. In the absence of global scarcity (i.e., when the lifeboat has a large enough capacity for all), a worldwide famine can be avoided by a sharing of resources. How accurate is the premise of global scarcity?

Examining Global Scarcity

Most authorities seem to agree that an adequate amount of food is currently being produced. Studies made by the Food and Agricultural Organization of the United Nations, which report that the available supplies of food are more than adequate to supply the nutritional needs of all the world, are typical.

Because this evidence is limited to a single point in time, however, it provides no sense of whether scarcity is decreasing or increasing. If we are to identify and evaluate trends, we must develop more precise, measurable notions of how the market allocates food.

As a renewable resource, cereal grains could be produced indefinitely, if managed correctly. However, two facets of the world hunger problem have to be taken into account. First, although population growth has slowed down, it has not stopped. Therefore, it is reasonable to expect the rising demand for food to continue. Second, the primary input for growing food is land, and land is ultimately fixed in supply. Thus, our analysis must explain how a market reacts in the presence of rising demand for a renewable resource that is produced using a fixed factor of production!

A substantial and dominant proportion of the Western world's arable land is privately owned. Access to this land is restricted; the owners have the right to exclude others and can reap what they sow. The typical owner of farmland has sufficient control over the resource to prevent undue depreciation, but not enough control over the market as a whole to raise the specter of monopoly profits.

What kind of outcome could we expect from this market in the face of rising demand and a fixed supply of land? What do we mean by *global scarcity* and how could we perceive its existence? The answer depends crucially on the nature and slope of the supply curve.

Suppose the market is initially in equilibrium. If demand shifts out over time, the resulting new equilibrium price and quantity will depend on the steepness of the supply curve. Can you draw a graph to illustrate why?

Scarcity is not the same thing as a shortage. Even under the relatively adverse supply circumstances (given a very steep supply curve) the amount of food supplied would equal the amount demanded. As prices rose, potential demand would be choked off and additional supplies would be called forth.

Some critics argue that the demand for food is not price sensitive. Because food is a necessary commodity for survival, they say, its demand is inflexible and doesn't respond to prices. Although it is a necessary commodity, not all food fits that category. We don't have to gaze very long at an average vending machine in a developed country to conclude that some food is far from a necessity.

Examples of food purchases being price responsive abound. During the 1960s, when the price of meat skyrocketed for what turned out to be a relatively short period, it wasn't long before hamburger substitute, made entirely out of soybean meal, appeared in supermarkets. The result was a striking reduction in meat consumption. This is a particularly important example because the raising of livestock for meat in Western countries consumes an enormous amount of grain and water. This evidence suggests that the balance between the direct consumption of cereal grains and the indirect consumption through meat is affected by prices.

But enough about the demand side; what do we know of the supply side? Although rising prices certainly stimulate a supply response, the question is, how much? As the demand for food rises, the supply can be increased either by expanding the amount of land under cultivation, by increasing the yields on the land already under cultivation, or by some combination of the two. Historically, both sources have been important.

Typically, the most fertile land is cultivated first. That land is then farmed more and more intensively until it is cheaper, at the margin, to bring additional, less-fertile land into production. Because it is less fertile, the additional land is brought into production only if prices rise high enough to make farming it profitable. Thus, the supply curve for arable land (and hence, for food, as long as land remains an important factor of production) can be expected to slope upward.

Two forms of the global scarcity hypothesis can be tested against the available evidence. The *strong form* posits that per capita food production is declining. The strong form of the hypothesis would imply a sufficiently steep slope of the supply curve that production fails to keep pace with increases in demand brought about by population growth. If the strong form is valid, we should observe declining per capita food production, a finding that would provide some support for lifeboat ethics.

The *weak form* of the global scarcity hypothesis can hold even if per capita production is increasing over time. This form posits that food prices increase more rapidly than other prices in general; the relative price of food would rise over time. If the weak form is valid, per capita welfare is declining, even if per capita production is rising. The problem is related more to the cost than the availability of food; in this case as supplies of food increase, the cost of food rises relative to the cost of other goods.

What about the evidence?

●   Globally the data show that between 1990 and 2005 global per capita agricultural production grew 13.5%. Apparently the strong form of the hypothesis is not yet upon us.

●   From 2000-2008, in the U.S. (the source of the most complete data for all consumer prices) all consumer prices rose 25%, while food prices rose 27.6%. This is too small a difference to confirm the weak hypothesis for the United States, but it certainly does not rule it out globally either. You might check to see how other countries have fared.

If anything, the dominant food problem in the United States involves obesity, not scarcity. According to the U.S. Department of Agriculture, the total per capita food consumption in the United States in 1970 was 1,675 pounds. By 2003 this number had risen to 1,950 pounds. Combined with changes in diet the resulting increase in per capita calorie consumption was 523 calories per day (an increase from 2,234 calories per person per day in 1970 to 2,757 calories in 2003).[2]

Outlook for the Future

What factors will influence the future relative costs of food? A continuation of past trends would suggest an increasing role for the developing nations as they expand production to meet their increasing shares of population while the developed nations continue their exports. The ability of developing nations to expand their role is considered in the next section as a part of the food-distribution problem. In this section, therefore, we will deal with forces affecting productivity in the industrialized nations to ascertain the sustainability of historic trends.

Rather dramatic historic increases in crop productivity were stimulated by improvement in machinery; increasing utilization of commercial fertilizers, pesticides, and herbicides; developments in plant and animal breeding; expanding use of irrigation water; and adjustments in location of crop production.

For example, in the United States, corn is produced on more acreage than any other crop. Yields per acre quadrupled between 1930 and 2000 from approximately 30 bushels per acre to about 130 bushels per acre. Milk and dairy production is another industry showing marked productivity improvements. In 1944 average production per cow was 4,572 pounds. By 1971 the average had risen to 10,000 pounds. By the end of the twentieth century the average had risen to 17,000 pounds per cow! Other areas of the livestock industry show similar trends.

Table 11.1 shows some of the trends in agriculture that occurred during the twentieth century. Among other aspects, the table points out the huge shift to mechanization that has occurred as farm equipment, which is dependent upon depletable fossil-fuels, replaces animal power fueled by renewable biological resources. This trend has provided the foundation for an increase in scale of the average farm and a reduction in the number of farms, but it also raises questions about sustainability.

Technological Progress. Technological progress provides the main source of support for optimism about continued productivity increases. Three techniques have received significant attention recently: (1) recombinant DNA, which permits genes from one species to be recombined with those of another; (2) tissue culture, which allows whole plants to be grown from single cells; and (3) cell fusion, which involves uniting the cells of species that would not normally cross in order to create new types of plants different from "parent" cells. Several applications for these genetic engineering techniques include the following:

- Making food crops more resistant to diseases and insect pests
- Creating hardy new crop plants capable of surviving in marginal soils
- Giving staple food crops such as corn, wheat, and rice the ability to make their own nitrogen-rich fertilizers by using solar energy to make ammonia from nitrogen in the air
- Increasing crop yields by improving the way plants use the sun's energy during photosynthesis

---

[2]http://www.ers.usda.gov/AmberWaves/November05/Findings/USFoodConsumption.htm.

TABLE 11.1   Trends in U.S. Agriculture: A Twentieth-Century Time Capsule

	Beginning of the Century (1900)	End of the Century (1997)
Number of Farms	5,739,657	1,911,859
Average Farm Acreage	147 acres	487 acres
Crops		
Percent of farms growing		
Corn	82%	23%
Hay	62%	46%
Vegetables	61%	3%
Irish potatoes	49%	1%
Orchards[a]	48%	6%
Oats	37%	5%
Soybeans	- 0 -	19%
Livestock		
Percent of farms raising		
Cattle	85%	55%
Milk cows	79%	6%
Hogs and pigs	76%	6%
Chickens[b]	97%	5%
Farm Mechanization		
Percent of farms with		
Wheel Tractors[c]	4%	89%
Horses	79%	20%
Mules	26%	2%
Government Payments	- 0 -	$5 billion
Percent Population Living on Farms[d]	39.2%	1.8% (1990)
Percent Labor Force on Farms[e]	38.8%	1.7% (1990)

Source: USDA. National Agricultural Statistics Service (http://www.nass.usda.gov/Publications/Trends_in_U.S._Agriculture/time_capsule.asp).

[a]1929 Census of Agriculture
[b]1910 Census of Agriculture
[c]1920 Census of Agriculture
[d]Bureau of the Census
[e]Bureau of Labor Statistics

Five concerns have arisen regarding the ability of the industrial nations to achieve further productivity gains: (1) the declining share of land allocated to agricultural use, (2) the rising cost of energy, (3) the rising environmental cost of traditional forms of agriculture, (4) the role of price distortions in agricultural policy, and (5) potential side effects from the new *genetically modified crops.* A close examination of these concerns reveals that current agricultural practices in the industrialized nations may be neither efficient nor sustainable and a transition to agriculture that satisfies both criteria could involve lower productivity levels.

Allocation of Agricultural Land. According to the 2002 Census of U.S. Agriculture, land in farms was estimated at 938 million acres, down from approximately 955 million acres in 1997. The corresponding acreage in 1974 was 1.1 billion acres. Total cropland in 2002 was approximately 434 million acres, 55 million of which was irrigated. The corresponding irrigated acreage in 1974 was approximately 41 million acres. While total land in farms has dropped considerably, irrigated acreage has risen.

More than 50 percent of the agricultural cropland has been converted to nonagricultural purposes. A simple extrapolation of this trend would certainly raise questions about our ability to increase productivity at historical rates. Is a simple extrapolation reasonable? What determines the allocation of land between agricultural and nonagricultural uses?

Agricultural land will be converted to nonagricultural land when its profitability in nonagricultural uses is higher. If we are to explain the historical experience, we must be able to explain the decline of the relative value of land in agriculture.

Two factors stand out. First, an increasing urbanization and industrialization of society rapidly raised the value of nonagricultural land. Second, rising productivity of the remaining land allowed the smaller amount of land to produce a lot more food. Less land was needed in agriculture to meet the demand for food.

It seems unlikely that simple extrapolation of the decline in agricultural land of the magnitude evidenced since 1920 would be accurate. Since the middle of the 1970s the urbanization process has diminished to the point that many urban areas are experiencing declining population. This shift is not entirely explained by suburbia spilling beyond the boundaries of what was formerly considered urban. For the first time in our history, significant numbers of the population have moved from urban to rural areas.

Furthermore, as increases in food demand are accompanied by increased prices of food, the value of agricultural land should increase. Higher food prices would tend to slow conversion of agricultural land to nonagricultural uses and possibly even reverse the trend. To make this impact even greater, several states have now allowed agricultural land either to escape the property tax (until it is sold for some nonagricultural purpose) or to be taxed at lower rates.

Worldwide, irrigated acreage is on the rise, though the rate of increase has been falling. In 1980 209,292 hectares were irrigated; 150,335 of these in developing countries. By 2003 these numbers had grown to 277,098 total irrigated hectares; 207,965 in developing countries (Gleick, 2006).[3]

What about agricultural land that is still used for agriculture, but not used for growing food? The recent trend in conversion of land to grow corn to be used solely in the production of ethanol has caused rising food prices and reduced food aid to developing countries. Example 11.1 explores this recent transition.

---

[3]One hectare is equivalent to 2.47 acres.

EXAMPLE

11.1

Growing Corn for Fuel, Not Food: The Expansion of Ethanol

The production of ethanol has risen dramatically in the last few years in a response to shifting world demand for more diverse sources of fuel and in the light of rising oil prices. (The market for biofuels was highlighted in Chapter 8.) In the United States, ethanol production rose from 1 billion gallons in 2005 to almost 5 billion gallons in 2006. Production capacity is expected to grow to 12 billion gallons by 2015 (USDA 2007 long-term projections). While some countries are making ethanol from sugar or from palm, the primary input to ethanol production in the United States is corn.

In a report from the Economic Research Service of the USDA entitled "Ethanol Expansion in the United States: How Will the Agricultural Sector Adjust?" these trends are analyzed, revealing that 14 percent of corn use went to ethanol production in the 2005–2006 crop year. USDA's 2007 long-term projections expect this amount to rise to more than 30 percent of the corn crop by 2009–2010. Even though ethanol represents a very small share of the overall gasoline market, its impacts on the agricultural sector are large.

As the use of corn for ethanol production continues to grow, corn prices have responded with rapid increases. Corn prices rose from about $1.80 per bushel in 2000–2001 to more than $3 per bushel in 2006–2007. Rising corn prices due to this expansion have caused the transition of land previously used to grow soybeans to corn production, and lands previously used to grow corn for feed grains are now being used to grow corn for ethanol. The resulting price increases for corn and soybeans, as well as for meats and other foods using corn or soybeans, has been dramatic. While higher prices bring higher farm incomes, it reduces affordability for consumers. Corn prices fell substantially in 2008, but volatility in food prices affects lower income consumers and developing country farmers dramatically.

Livestock feed is the largest use of U.S. corn. Higher corn prices require livestock producers to find alternative feed or absorb the higher prices or reduce production. While impacts can be partially offset by using ethanol distillers' grains as substitute feed, red meat production is expected to decline.

At the international level, rising corn prices have large impacts as well. Historically, 60–70 percent of world corn exports have come from the United States. Not only will the share of exports drop, but also world food prices will rise. Additionally, carryover corn stocks are also reduced, which in turn reduces the market's ability to absorb price shocks.

What does the future hold? *The New York Times* reported that food aid in 2007 has been half as effective as it was in 2000 because each dollar is buying less food. Attempts to reduce the U.S. dependence on foreign oil is having the largest impacts on the world's poorest, and likely hungriest, people. (Impacts on developing countries will be explored further in Chapter 20.)

In late 2007 Congress passed a new energy bill that requires, among other things, a mandate for renewable fuels, including 15 billion gallons of ethanol made from grains, primarily corn, by 2022. Corn ethanol production in 2006 was only 5 billion gallons. Ethanol currently carries a sizable subsidy inducing more farmers to grow corn for

ethanol. It remains to be seen what the future holds for food prices. One thing is for sure, however. The market's ability to absorb these price shocks has been dramatically reduced.

Sources: Paul C. Westcott, "Ethanol Expansion in the United States: How Will the Agricultural Sector Adjust? FDS-07D-01, Economic Research Service/USDA. 2007; Celia W. Dugger, "As Food Prices Soar, U.S. Food Aid Buys Less," *The New York Times*, September 29, 2007.

Energy Costs. Agricultural production in the industrialized nations is very energy intensive. Some major portion of the productivity gains resulted from energy generated by using mechanization and by the increased use of pesticides and fertilizers, which are derived from petroleum feedstocks and natural gas. The costs of petroleum and natural gas have risen substantially and probably can be expected to continue to rise in real terms over the long run as the available supplies of fossil fuels are exhausted or as global warming concerns diminish their use. To the extent that energy-intensive producers cannot develop cheaper substitutes, the supply curve must shift to the left to reflect the increasing costs of doing business.

As suggested by Table 11.1, energy and capital have become complements in agriculture. Because of this complementary relationship, energy price increases could be expected to trigger some reduction in capital, as well as some reduction in energy on the typical energy-intensive farm, thereby reducing the yield per acre.

Environmental Costs. Some of the past improvements in agricultural productivity have come from intensifying the environmental problems caused by agriculture. Not only has land use intensified in quality (with a resulting increase in the use of chemicals and fertilizers), but also its use has intensified in quantity, as grasslands and forests have been converted to farming.

Another source of environmental problems, soil erosion, has a different origin. Some soil erosion is natural, of course, and within certain tolerance limits does not harm productivity. The concern arises because some farm practices partially responsible for increasing productivity (e.g., continuous cropping rather than rotations with pasture or other soil-retaining crops) have tended to exacerbate soil erosion. The fears are further intensified by the belief that these losses are irreversible within one generation.

Given that increased soil erosion is taking place, why would a property owner allow this depletion? In the past, soil conservation simply did not pay. The techniques to avoid it were expensive, and the ready availability of cheap fertilizer to replace lost nutrients meant that the cost of soil depletion was low. Furthermore, the damage caused to rivers and streams by this eroding soil was not borne by the farmers, who could best control it.

The barriers that prevented erosion from being checked are now disappearing. As the level of topsoil reaches lower tolerance limits, the fertility of the land is affected. Rising cost is making fertilizers a less desirable substitute for soil erosion, and public policy has begun to subsidize soil erosion techniques. In 1985 the U.S. Congress authorized the Conservation Reserve Program, which was designed to reduce soil erosion and stimulate tree planting. Acreage enrolled in the program peaked at 36.4 million acres in 1996.

The Conservation Stewardship Program in the 2008 Farm Bill is one of the first attempts in the United States to integrate growing crops and livestock in a way that does not rely on leaving the land fallow after intensive farming. While voluntary, the Conservation Stewardship Program encourages the adoption of conservation activities and resource-conserving crop rotations. Farmers receive payments (up to $200,000) based on approved five-year contracts.

Some past agricultural practices have caused environmental damage, and continuing these would cause rising environmental costs. In recent years the frequency and quantity of agricultural chemicals used have increased dramatically. One effect of this has been rising levels of nitrates in drinking water. Additionally, some of the nutrients from fertilizers leak into lakes and stimulate the excessive algae growth. Aside from the aesthetic cost to a body of water choked with plant life, this nutrient excess can deprive other aquatic life forms of the oxygen they need to survive.

Pesticide use has been on the decline in many developed countries, but it is rising in developing countries (see Table 11.2). A great deal of pest control in the recent past has relied upon pesticides. Many of these substances persist in the environment, and there is an increasing recognition that some toxicity extends to species other than the target population. The herbicides and pesticides can contaminate water supplies, rendering them unfit for drinking and for supporting normal fish populations. These negative externalities have produced efforts to reduce toxicities and pursue new technologies such as *genetically modified organisms (GMOs)* that are resistant to pests. GMOs come with their own host of concerns which will be discussed later in this chapter. Throughout all OECD countries, *sustainable agriculture* is being increasingly associated with the reduced use of pesticides and mineral fertilizers, and policies have been established to facilitate the transition to low reliance on these substances. Denmark and Sweden are pursuing ambitious agricultural chemical reduction targets. In Austria, Finland, the Netherlands, and Sweden a variety of input taxes and input levies have recently been introduced. The charges provide an incentive to use smaller amounts of agricultural chemicals, and the revenue is used to ease the transition by funding research on alternative approaches and the dissemination of information. Many OECD countries expect little effect on crop yields.

Although most European countries are focusing on eliminating input subsidies (e.g., on pesticides and fertilizers), taxing inputs, or directly limiting input use, New Zealand has taken a more radical step by scrapping most of its agricultural supports. The initial results were impressive. According to Reynolds et al. (1993) in a study conducted for the New Zealand Ministry of Agriculture, the initial environmental consequences of this policy were rather profound. Fertilizer use declined, farms became more diversified, most marginal land was grazed less intensively, and the excessive conversion of land stopped. However, the longer term story for pesticide reduction proves unsustainable. A 2004 report to the Ministry of the Environment in New Zealand found that between 1999–2003 the volume of pesticide imports increased by 17 percent, herbicide imports by 42 percent, and fungicide imports by 10 percent. Only the imports of insecticides decreased—by 41 percent. The authors estimate that total pesticide use increased by 27

TABLE 11.2 Pesticide Consumption per Hectare of Agricultural Land (Kg/Ha)

	1989–1991	1994–1996	1998–2000
Developed Countries	.64	.54	.52
Developing Countries	.18	.25	.28
World	.40	.38	.39

Source: FAO Compendium of Agricultural-Environmental Indicators, 1989–2000 and Sexton et al., 2007.

percent. While changes in the fruit sector (in particular kiwis and apples) led to declines in the mid-1990s, total use has actually increased (Manktelow et al., 2005).

Irrigation can increase yields of most crops by 100 to 400 percent. The FAO estimates that over the next 30 years, 70 percent of gains in cereal production will come from irrigated land and by 2030, developing countries will have a 27 percent increase in irrigated land.

However, irrigation, a traditional source of productivity growth, is also running into limits, particularly in the western United States. Some traditionally important underground sources of water supplies are not being replenished at a rate sufficient to offset the withdrawals. Encouraged by enormous subsidies that transfer the cost to the taxpayers, these water supplies are being exhausted. Those that remain are subject to rising levels of salt. Irrigation of soils with naturally occurring salts causes a concentration of the salts near the surface. This salty soil is less productive and, in extreme cases, kills the crops.

One sign that a transition is underway is the rise of *organic farming*. The organic foods industry is the fastest growing U.S. food segment. Growth has been at about 20 percent annually since 1990 when the USDA National Organic Program was established. Acreage of certified organic cropland in the United States more than doubled between 1997 and 2001. Projections of organic product sales anticipate that they will triple over a four-year period.

Despite the large rise in annual sales, organic food sales still represent only approximately 2.8 percent of total U.S. food sales. Of this 2.8 percent, fresh fruits and vegetables make up 40 percent; breads and grains 10 percent; and dairy products 16 percent. The remainder comprises packaged and prepared foods, beverages, soy products, and meat and poultry. Although meat and poultry represents less than 3 percent of organic sales, it is the fastest-growing portion of this market at a rate of 55 percent in 2005 and 29 percent in 2006.[4]

A recent source of encouragement for organic farms has been the demonstrated willingness of consumers to pay a premium for organically grown fruits and vegetables. The average organic premium in 2004 was $0.35 above conventional produce. Carrots and lettuce carried the largest premium increases between 2001 and 2004. Tomatoes and apples also saw increases in organic price premiums of 52 percent and 72 percent.

Because it would be relatively easy for producers to claim their produce was organically grown, even if it were not, organic growers need a reliable certification process to assure consumers that they are indeed getting what they pay for. Additionally, fear of lost access to important foreign markets such as the European Union, led to an industry-wide push for mandatory labeling standards. Since the value of labeling depends largely on the credibility of the labeling service, a nationally uniform seal was sought. Voluntary U.S. certification programs varied greatly by state and thus had not ensured access to foreign markets such as the EU.

In response to these pressures the *Organic Foods Production Act (OFPA)* was enacted in the 1990 Farm Bill. Title 21 of that law states the following objectives: 1) to establish national standards governing the marketing of certain agricultural products as organically produced; 2) to assure consumers that organically produced products meet a consistent standard; and 3) to facilitate interstate commerce in fresh and processed food that is organically produced (Golan et al., 2000).

The *USDA National Organic Program*, established as part of this OFPA, is responsible for a mandatory certification program for organic production. The Act also established the

---

[4]USDA and Organic Trade Association's 2004, 2006, and 2007 Manufacturer Surveys.

National Organic Standards Board (NOSB) and charged it with defining the organic standards. The new rules, which took effect in October 2002, require *organic certification* by USDA for labeling. Foods labeled as "100 percent organic" must contain only organic ingredients. Foods labeled as "organic" must contain at least 95 percent organic agricultural ingredients, excluding water and salt. Products labeled as "made with organic ingredients" must contain at least 70 percent organic agricultural ingredients.

The European Union has followed a similar, but by no means identical policy. Table 11.3 compares the U.S. and EU programs. With the U.S. standards now in place, U.S. and EU officials are working on developing an equivalency agreement to expedite trade between the two regions.

How good a policy approach is labeling? Does it create efficient incentives? As Example 11.2 points out, labeling certainly represents a movement toward efficiency, but because it does not internalize all important externalities, it is unlikely to get us all the way there.

The rapid growth of the organic sector may also be shrinking the price premium that consumers have been willing to pay for organic foods. Debate 11.1 explores what happens when organic goes mainstream.

The Role of Agricultural Policies

Past gains in agricultural productivity have come at a large environmental cost. Why? Part of the answer, of course, can be found in an examination of the externalities associated with agriculture. Many of the costs of farming are shifted to others. They are borne not by the farmers, who bear the responsibility for making the decisions that determine the size of the environmental cost, but by others—those subjected to the contaminated groundwater and polluted streams. But that is not the whole story. Government policies must bear a considerable amount of the responsibility as well.

Government policies have completely subverted the normal functioning of the price system. Four types of agricultural policies are involved: (1) subsidies for specific farming inputs such as equipment, fertilizers, and pesticides; (2) guaranteed prices for outputs; (3) marketing loans based on crop prices, and (4) trade barriers to protect against competition from imports. The U.S. Farm Bill supports three types of these commodity production incentives. The *marketing loan program* pays the farmer the difference between the loan rate for a particular crop and the loan repayment rate which varies weekly with crop prices. *Counter cyclical program payments* are based on historical production of the crop. Payments equal the difference between target prices (guaranteed prices) and the national average market price for eligible acreage planted with the program crop. *Direct payments* are based on historical production, but land can be shifted to other uses. Between 2002 and 2006 marketing loans have been $2 billion to $11 billion; countercyclical program payments ranged from $1 billion to $4 billion; and direct payments were set at $5 billion. Corn received $9 billion in subsidies in 2006. Based on share of production, however, cotton and rice received the highest subsidies (see Figure 11.1) (Sumner and Buck, 2007).

Agricultural subsidies have helped to create a dependence on purchased inputs. Blackhurst and Anderson (1992) examined whether the size of the farm subsidy (as measured by its proportion to total income) across countries was correlated with fertilizer use in those countries. It was. Countries with the largest subsidies used considerably more fertilizer than those with few or no subsidies. The subsidies made it possible to use inefficient and unsustainable levels of fertilizer.

TABLE 11.3 Comparison of EU and U.S. Standards

I. Both systems share the following:

1. Third-Party Certification
2. Audit Trails
3. Annual Inspections
4. Accreditation
5. Materials List
6. Defined Conversion Periods
7. Sustainable Farm Plan

II. Agriculture Conversion Period

1. The U.S. requires a three-year conversion period with no exceptions.
2. The EU generally requires two years for annuals and three years for perennials, with some exceptions.

III. Manure Restrictions

1. The EU has load limits on manure applications for livestock and other organic cropping operations.
2. The U.S. requires minimum periods prior to harvest.

IV. Buffer Zones

1. The U.S. requires buffer zones.
2. The EU does not require buffer zones.

V. Milk Production

May be certified as organic in the U.S. after 12 months on 100 percent organic program, whereas EU rules allow for organic production at 6 months.

VI. Organic Feedstuffs

In-conversion allowances (30–60 percent) of transitional and conventional feedstuffs for organic livestock production in the EU are not found in the U.S. (requiring 100 percent).

VII. Health Care

1. No antibiotics or hormones are allowed in the United States.
2. The EU does include exemptions for synthetic veterinary medicines and allows for treatments up to three times per year.

VIII. Labeling Requirements

1. "Organic"—both agree that at least 95 percent of the ingredients must be organic.
2. "Made With"—both agree that 70 percent of the ingredients must be organic. In the EU the remaining 30 percent must be on published lists of "not commercially available ingredients." This list is subject to interpretation by the certifier or Member State.
3. "Below 70 percent"—the EU does not allow organic to appear anywhere on the label. The United States allows identification of organic ingredients on the information panel in products containing 50 percent or more organic ingredients.
4. Percent organic declarations in the U.S. are not mandatory, but in some EU situations declaration may be required.
5. Under EU regulations, "transition to organic" labeling is allowed. In the United States such labeling is not allowed.

Source: Organic Trade Association, 2003.

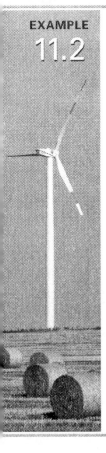

EXAMPLE 11.2

Do Mandatory Labels Correct Externalities?

Governments have a variety of policy tools available to address issues of asymmetric information and to control externalities, such as those associated with conventional farming. Policy options include taxes on externalities, bans, quotas, educational programs, disclosure strategies (such as organic labeling), and direct regulation of production or marketing. Economic theory suggests that labeling will be a sufficient policy tool only if all costs and benefits of consumption choices are borne by the consumer. However, if the consumption of a food creates an externality, then information-based policy will not result in efficient choices.

Are externalities involved? Clearly they are. Consider, for example, the potential effects of choosing to purchase organic foods based on the quality of drinking water. If conventional agriculture affects local drinking water by its application of fertilizers and pesticides, switching production to organically grown food will diminish the environmental damage. Do consumers of organic products reap all the benefits? Clearly not. All users of that drinking water benefit, whether or not they purchase organic foods. Consumers of organic food confer an external benefit on the others.

Mandatory food labeling does alleviate problems of asymmetric information (where the producer knows the production techniques, but in the absence of labeling, the consumer does not). In this case, consumers can use this information to make superior choices in terms of their own preferences. Labeling is, however, rarely effective in addressing problems related to environmental externalities or other spillover effects associated with food production or consumption.

Source: Golan, Elise et al., "The Economics of Food Labeling," *Journal of Consumer Policy*, 24(2), 2001: 117–184.

DEBATE 11.1

When Organic Goes Mainstream: Do You Get What You Pay For?

Organic foods typically cost more than conventionally grown foods. As the fastest growing agricultural sector, consumers have shown their willingness to pay a premium for organically grown food. Recognizing the potential for profits, however, larger agri-businesses and retail stores are jumping on the organic bandwagon.

The words organic, free-range, and antibiotic-free used to be associated with small farms and local foods. Not anymore says Michael Pollan, author of the *Omnivore's Dilemma*, and a frequent contributor to *The New York Times*. With plans to rollout organic food offerings in 4,000 stores, Wal-Mart says the prices will not be much higher than its other food products. How can this be? The price premium that organic products typically carry represents a willingness to pay not only for pesticide-free products for consumption, but also a willingness to pay to keep those same toxins out of the environment. Responsibly grown products cost more, right?

As larger and larger farms start producing organic foods, foods grown without chemical pesticides or herbicides, and as large-scale production of some foods is outsourced to other countries such as China and Mexico, the distinction between sustainable agriculture and cheaper industrial food gets blurred.

For example, is organic milk from cows that eat organic grain but are never allowed outside better for society? Does this industrial style of large-scale production get rid of the externalities of conventional farming or does it replace them with others (such as greenhouse gases from transporting commodities long distances) that are just as harmful? Pollan reminds us that the organic movement used to symbolize sustainability, but questions whether buying organic milk from New Zealand or organic asparagus from Argentina makes sense from a global perspective in an era of energy scarcity and climate change. Have we simply replaced drenching our food in pesticides with drenching it in petroleum?

Have you been snacking while reading this book? How far did your food travel?

For a continued debate on this matter, Whole Foods, the nation's largest natural foods supermarket posted an open letter to Michael Pollan on their Web site in response to his criticisms of the company's helping to support the industrialization, globalization, and dilution of organic agriculture. Michael Pollan's letter of response is also posted along with an ongoing exchange. You can find the debate at the following:

http://www.wholefoodsmarket.com/blogs/

Source: Michael Pollan, "The Way We Live Now" *The New York Times Magazine*, June 4, 2006.

FIGURE 11.1   Farm Program Payments as a Share of Production Value, 2002–2005 Crop Years

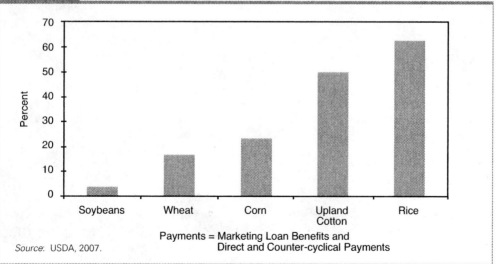

Payments = Marketing Loan Benefits and Direct and Counter-cyclical Payments

Source: USDA, 2007.

Guaranteed prices have the effect of increasing the profitability of agriculture, making it possible to convert formerly inappropriate land to agricultural purposes. As mentioned previously, New Zealand provides an interesting example. Frustrated with the high levels of subsidies that were being poured into the agricultural sector, the government in New Zealand eliminated most agricultural subsidies over a three-year period. Not only did fertilizer use fall 55 percent, but also it turned out that the resulting shakeout in the agricultural sector resulted in a much higher proportion of smaller farms, which have a less adverse impact on the environment. The subsidies had propped up the larger farms.[5]

Other countries have not been eager to follow New Zealand's lead. Subsidies have become an important component of farm income, making them politically difficult to eliminate. Agricultural subsidies in the United States and the European Union are responsible for about one-third and one-half of all farm income, respectively. In Japan farmers earn twice as much income from subsidies as from the practice of agriculture. In Switzerland the comparable figure is four times agricultural income.

Recently, however, governments have begun to encourage sustainable agriculture, not only by discouraging the harmful side effects of traditional agriculture, but also by learning more about sustainable practices and disseminating the information derived from this research. Additionally, both the United States and the European Union offer financial assistance for the transition to sustainable agriculture.

Farmers are not the only ones affected by subsidies, however. The demand side of the food market is also important to consider. Agricultural subsidies translate into cheaper calories for some foods. Consumers also receive subsidies. Food assistance programs such as school lunch programs and WIC are other forms of food subsidies. WIC provides aid to states for food and nutrition education for low-income pregnant women and women with infants and children up to age five who are at nutritional risk. Through WIC, a farmer's market nutrition program (FNMP) provides coupons for women and children to purchase fresh, local fruits and vegetables at local farmers' markets.

Summing Up

Agricultural productivity in the industrialized countries can be expected to rise in the future, but at lower rates. The large historic increases in agricultural productivity were partly based upon unsustainable, inefficient, and environmentally destructive agricultural practices, which were supported and encouraged by agricultural subsidies. In the future we can expect that as farmers become less insulated from the energy and environmental costs of agriculture (i.e., as subsidies are removed), some of the expected gains from technological progress will be offset.

In addition to future changes in the productivity of agriculture, we can also expect changes in agricultural practices. A transition to alternative techniques of agriculture appears to be underway.

While the growth of the organic foods industry provides one example, new technology in the form of genetically modified organisms (GMOs) is another. Genetically modified foods have

---

[5]It has been argued that these subsidies have been designed to help poor farmers, but this argument is not persuasive. Because they produced only one-tenth of the output, poor farmers received only $1 from every $10 of subsidies paid. "The Economist Agriculture Survey," *The Economist* (December 12, 1992): 7.

sparked considerable controversy (see Debate 11.2). Since the economic, social, and economic costs and benefits of GMOs are multifaceted and uncertain, it remains to be seen whether consumers will support or reject this new technology (see Example 11.3).

DEBATE 11.2

Should Genetically Modified Organisms Be Banned?

One controversy surrounding GMOs is whether the commercialization of these plants and animals should be banned or delayed because of its potentially damaging environmental impact. Because they contain genetic combinations that do not occur in nature through normal evolution, GMOs are exotic species. When introduced into open complex ecosystems, they raise the possibility of imposing significant social externalities. Since these modified plants and animals are new to the ecosystem, their effects on all the other elements of the ecosystem are simply unknown. Some of these effects could prove to be detrimental and irreversible (NRC, 2002). Even if these effects could in principle be managed (a controversial point), successful management would crucially depend upon what many see as an unrealistic degree of oversight and control by farmers.

Economic concerns have been raised as well. Some observers believe the new technologies could favor large farmers or multinational corporations to the detriment of smaller farmers (Nelson et al., 1999).

In contrast, supporters suggest that genetically modified plants and animals have the potential to considerably boost world food production at reasonable cost. Reducing the cost of food and fiber production would reduce the threat posed by the weak scarcity hypothesis. Using GMOs to reduce the rate of application of chemical pesticides could also lessen the chemical contamination of water supplies and reduce the exposure of farm workers to pest-control chemicals. Genetically modified food organisms offer the possibility of introducing more nutrients and reducing health-threatening substances (such as saturated fats) in traditional food sources as well as the possibility of creating plants that grow more productively in less hospitable climates or soil types.

Banning the use of GMOs could prevent the externalities and the possible associated irreversible damages, but it could also reduce food availability and increase cost.

One thing is clear. If GMOs offer increased opportunities to feed the world's poor, the private sector will under invest in these new technologies. Genetically modified varieties have appeared for many crops, but not for several staple crops consumed by the poor, such as wheat and cassava (Cooper, Lipper, and Zilberman, 2005).

Sources: Batie, Sandra S., "The Environmental Impacts of Genetically Modified Plants: Challenges to Decision-Making," *American Journal of Agricultural Economics* 85(5), 2003: 1107–1111; Huffman, Wallace E., "Consumers' Acceptance of (and Resistance to) Genetically Modified Foods in High-Income Countries: Effects of Labels and Information in an Uncertain Environment," *American Journal of Agricultural Economics* 85(5), 2003: 1112–1118; National Research Council (NRC). *Environmental Effects of Transgenic Plants: The Scope and Adequacy of Regulation* (Washington, DC: National Academy Press 2002); and Nelson, Gerald et al., *The Economics and Politics of Genetically Modified Organisms: Implications for WTO 2000* (University of Illinois, Bulletin 809, 1999).

EXAMPLE

11.3

Are Consumers Willing to Pay a Premium for GMO-Free Foods?

In the European Union, any food product containing an ingredient that consists of more than 1 percent genetically modified organisms (GMOs) must be labeled as "contains GMOs." Though biotechnology may help to increase crop yields, improve pest resistance, and enhance nutrition, the introduction of GMOs into food products has faced considerable hostility, particularly among European consumers. How widespread is this hostility? And does it suggest that consumers might be willing to pay a price premium for GMO-free food?

Economists Charles Noussair, Stéphane Robin, and Bernard Ruffieux (2004) reported that 79 percent of French survey respondents agreed with the statement "GMOs should be banned" and 89 percent were opposed to the presence of GMOs in food products. Wondering whether this apparent anti-GMO sentiment would be reflected in purchase behavior led them to design an experiment to find out.

Due to the lack of field data, they utilized an experimental method designed to elicit and compare the willingness to pay for GMO-free products with products containing GMOs. In particular, the laboratory experiment was designed to measure how the willingness to pay would change in response to new information about GMO content. Approximately 100 French consumers participated in the experiments.

Interestingly, in contrast to early studies, only 35 percent of the subjects completely refused to purchase a product containing GMOs. Some 42 percent turned out to be willing to purchase a product containing GMOs if it were sufficiently inexpensive. The remaining 23 percent were indifferent.

This study suggests the advantages of using labels to segment the market. The authors found that survey respondents were willing to pay 8 percent more for a product labeled GMO-free compared to a product with an unknown GMO status. However, respondents were willing to pay 46.7 percent more for a GMO-free product compared to a product that they knew to contain GMOs.

Source: Noussair, Charles, Stéphane Robin, and Bernard Ruffieux, "Do Consumers Really Refuse to Buy Genetically Modified Food?" *The Economic Journal,* 114 (January 2004) 102–120; and Huffman, W. E., M. Rousu, J. F. Shogrun, and A. Tegene, "The Public Good Value of Information from Agribusinesses on Genetically Modified Foods," *American Journal of Agricultural Economics* 85(5), 2003: 1309–1315.

● Distribution of Food Resources

Imperfections in food distribution, particularly those associated with inadequate purchasing power, provide a second source of the malnourishment problem. According to the *maldistribution hypothesis*, the basic problem is poverty. We would expect, therefore, that the poorest segments of society would be the most malnourished and that the poorest countries would contain the largest number of malnourished people.

If accurate, this representation suggests a very different policy orientation than that suggested by global scarcity. If the problem is maldistribution rather than shortage, the real issue is how to get the food to the poorest people. Eliminating poverty—thereby increasing the ability to pay for food—is a strategy that could alleviate the problem. If the problem were a lack of food, however, this strategy would be totally ineffective.

Defining the Problem

Considerable and persuasive evidence suggests that the problem is one of distribution, as shown in Table 11.4. Although the data are far from perfect, it is clear that the food is not uniformly distributed among the world's peoples. For the least-developed countries (LDCs), over one-third of the population is malnourished.

Equally revealing, however, is the trend. Though clear progress has been made in the world as a whole in increasing per capita food production, production in the LDCs has failed to keep pace with the population growth. For the poorest countries, the average diet is woefully inadequate. Furthermore, their dependency on food imports has grown.

Poverty, population growth, and the sufficiency of food production are related problems, as discussed in Chapter 6. High poverty levels are generally conducive to high population growth, and high population growth rates may increase the degree of income inequality. Furthermore, excessive population levels and poverty together increase the difficulty of achieving food sufficiency. Because we have already examined population control strategies in Chapter 6, we will now focus on strategies to increase the amount of food available to the poorest people. What can be done?

Domestic Production in LDCs

The first issue to be addressed concerns the relative merits of increasing domestic production in the less-developed countries as opposed to importing more from abroad. There are several reasons for believing that many developing countries can profitably increase the percentage of their consumption that is domestically produced. One of the most important is that food imports use up precious foreign exchange.

Most developing countries cannot pay for imports with their own currencies. They must pay in an internationally accepted currency, such as the U.S. dollar, earned through the sale of exports. As more foreign exchange is used for agricultural imports, less is available for imports such as capital goods, which could raise the productivity (and hence, incomes) of local workers.

The lack of foreign exchange has been exacerbated during periods of high oil prices. Many developing nations must spend large portions of export earnings merely to import energy. In

TABLE 11.4   Food Situation in Developing Countries

	Undernourished People (1990/1992) Percent of Total Population	Undernourished People (1999/2001) Percent of Total Population
All Developing Countries	21	17
Least-Developed Countries	35	37

Source: United Nations Development Program. Human Development Report: 2004 (New York: United Nations Development Program, 2004) (Table 7, p. 163).

1993 for example, fuel imports made up one-third of all imports for Kenya. That leaves little for capital goods or agricultural imports.

Although this pressure on foreign exchange supports a need for greater reliance on domestic agricultural production, it would be incorrect to carry that argument to its logical extreme by suggesting that all nations should become self-sufficient in food production. The reason why self-sufficiency is not always efficient is suggested by the *law of comparative advantage.*

Nations are better off specializing in those products for which they have a comparative advantage. If its comparative advantage is not in food but in textiles, for example, a given country would be better off producing and exporting textiles and using the earnings to purchase food (see Table 11.5). The opportunity costs of producing textiles and wheat (measured in hours of labor per unit of output) are given for a hypothetical less-developed country (LDC) and a developed country (DC).

Suppose we are considering an eight-hour day in each country. If the average worker in each country were to spend four hours of each day on each activity, then 8 units of textile (4 by the LDC and 4 by the DC) and $5\frac{1}{3}$ units of wheat ($1\frac{1}{3}$ by the LDC and 4 by the DC) would be produced by the two countries each day. (Be sure you can see how these numbers can be derived from the table.)

Suppose, however, that the LDC in this case were to specialize in textiles (by allocating all eight hours to textile production), whereas the DC specialized in wheat. It is easy to verify that the total world production would now be 8 units of textiles and 8 units of wheat. When countries specialize in those products in which they have a comparative advantage, total production can increase.

Why did this happen in our example? It happened because the opportunity cost of making textiles in the LDC (in terms of forgone wheat) was lower than in the DC, whereas the opportunity cost of growing wheat in the DC (in terms of forgone textile production) was lower than that in the LDC. By freeing labor in the DC from making textiles, the LDC would be able to reap some of the benefits of the increased wheat production.

Although this example is hypothetical, the principle it conveys is real. Total self-sufficiency in food for all nations is not an appropriate goal. Those nations with a comparative advantage in agriculture because of climate, soil type, available land, and so on (e.g., the United States) should be net exporters, whereas those nations (e.g., Japan) with comparative advantage in other commodities should remain net food importers. This balance should not be allowed to get out of line, however, by creating an excessive reliance on either domestic production or imports.

Because of price distortions and externalities in the agricultural sector, most developing countries have historically developed an excessive dependency on imports. What kind of progress has been made in reducing this dependency? According to the data shown in Table 11.4, dependency has increased, not fallen. And the lowest-income countries as a group are having trouble even keeping the level of dependency from increasing with population growth, much less making headway in reducing imports. Progress on this front is elusive, it seems.

TABLE 11.5 A Hypothetical Example of the Law of Comparative Advantage

	Hours to Produce One Unit of Textiles	Hours to Produce One Unit of Wheat
Less-Developed Country	1	3
Developed Country	1	1

The Undervaluation Bias

Why, for so many years has food production in the developing countries barely kept pace with population growth? Agriculture in the low-income countries has been undervalued, implying that the rate of return on investment in agriculture is well below what it would be if agricultural output were allowed to receive its full social value. As a result of this *undervaluation bias,* investments in agriculture have been lower than they would otherwise have been and productivity has suffered.

Governments have used many mechanisms that have the undesirable side effect of under-valuing agriculture and destroying incentives in the process. Two stand out—marketing boards and export taxes.

National *marketing boards* have been established in many developing countries to stabilize agricultural prices and hold food prices down in order to protect the poor from malnutrition. Typically, a marketing board sells food at subsidized prices. As the subsidy grows, the board looks around for ways to reduce the amount of the subsidy.

There are two strategies regularly employed by marketing boards: (1) wholesale importing of artificially cheap food from the United States (available under the food aid program originally designed to get rid of wheat surpluses) and (2) holding down prices paid to domestic farmers. Both, of course, have the long-term effect of disrupting local production.

Many developing countries depend on export taxes, levied on all goods shipped abroad, as a principal source of revenue. Some of these taxes fall on cash-crop food exports (bananas, cocoa beans, coffee, and so on). The impact of export taxes is to raise the cost to foreign purchasers, reducing the amount of demand. A reduction in demand generally means lower prices and lower incomes for the farmers. Thus, this strategy also impairs food production incentives.

Government policies in developing countries not only affect the level of agricultural production, but also the techniques employed. A 1987 study by the World Bank (1987) reported that in nine developing countries, pesticide subsidies ranged from 15 to 90 percent of full retail cost, with a median of 44 percent. Agricultural mechanization is another target for subsidies. As a result of this distortion of prices, farmers have been encouraged to rely heavily on pesticides and to embrace mechanization where possible. These strategies make little sense in the long run.

Having become dependent on the subsidies, it becomes difficult for these farmers to make the transition to sustainable agricultural practices. Nonetheless, some basis for optimism exists. Agricultural techniques that are both sustainable and profitable in a developing country can be identified. The World Resources Institute conducted a series of studies in India, the Philippines, and Chile to study the effects on farmer income of transitioning to a more sustainable form of agriculture (Faeth, 1993). Its conclusion was that sustainable agriculture could be profitable, but usually not without changing the current pricing structure to reflect the full environmental costs of production. Better means of diffusing information about sustainable agricultural techniques among farmers would also be needed.

Feeding the Poor

The undervaluation bias was caused by a misguided attempt to use price controls as the way to provide the poor with access to an adequate diet. It backfired because the price controls served to reduce the availability of food. Is there a way to reduce the nutritional gap among the poor while maintaining adequate food supplies?

Some countries (e.g., Sri Lanka, Colombia, and the United States) are using food stamp programs to subsidize food purchases by the poor. In Colombia this is accomplished by issuing food coupons to low-income women and children, who are particularly vulnerable to nutritional deficiency. The coupons can be used by recipients to purchase a number of high-nutrition, low-cost foods. By boosting the purchasing power of those with the greatest need, such programs provide access to food while protecting the incentives of farmers. In those countries that are lowering food prices to everyone, the government must make substantially higher payments in order to finance the programs. When governments seek ways to finance these subsidies, they are tempted to try to reduce the subsidies by paying below-market prices to farmers or by relying more heavily on artificially low-cost imported food aid. In the long run, either of these strategies can be self-defeating.

Targeting the assistance to those who need it is one strategy that works. Another approach to feeding the poor is to attempt to ensure that the income distribution effects of agricultural policies benefit the poor. One great hope associated with the green revolution was that new varieties of seeds produced by scientific research would expand the supply of food, holding down prices and making a better diet accessible to the poor. It was also hoped that this strategy would provide expanding employment opportunities for the poor to supply more grain. How did it work out?

The green revolution started with maize hybrids adapted in the 1950s from the United States and Rhodesia (now Zimbabwe) and later spread across large parts of Central America and East Africa. Since the mid-1960s, short-stalk, fertilizer-responsive varieties of rice have spread throughout East Asia and comparable varieties of wheat have spread throughout Mexico and the Indian and Pakistan Punjabs.

In many areas with access to these hybrids, productivity doubled or tripled over a 30-year period. Short-duration varieties have allowed many farmers to harvest two crops a year where only one was formerly possible. The transformation has been unprecedented.

The effects have been impressive, as shown in Lipton and Longhurst (1989). In most areas with access to these modern varieties, small farmers have adopted them no less widely, intensively, or productively than have others. Labor use per acre has increased, with a consequent increase in the wage bill received by the poor. Poor people's consumption and nutrition are better with the new varieties than without them.

However, the adoption of these varieties has had a darker side as well. Reliance on a few species of hybrid cereal grains increases the risk from diseases and pests. Every Wall Street portfolio manager knows that risk can be lowered by holding a diverse collection of stocks. The security offered by diversity of agricultural species has diminished as larger and larger areas are planted with these new varieties. Other areas, those without access to the new varieties, have probably lost out as large quantities of new grain enter the market, eliminating by competition some of the more traditional sources. Small farmers are not always the beneficiaries of these new agricultural hybrids.

We are now in a position to define the role for aid from the developed nations. Temporary food aid is helpful when traditional sources are completely inadequate (e.g., as the result of natural disasters) or when the food aid does not interfere with the earnings of domestic producers. In the long run, developed nations could provide both appropriate technologies (e.g., solar-powered irrigation systems) and the financial capital to get farmer-owned local cooperatives off the ground. These cooperatives would then provide some of the advantages of scale (e.g., risk sharing and distribution) while maintaining the existing structure of small-scale farms. Coupled with effective population-control efforts and a balanced development program designed to raise the general standard of living, this approach could provide a solution to the distributional portion of the world food problem.

Industrialized nations could also open their markets to agricultural products from the developing countries by eliminating subsidies and by removing trade barriers. These acts would level the agricultural playing field, remove some of the undervaluation bias that is due to external factors, and provide a source of income to some of the poorest farmers in developing countries.

Feast and Famine Cycles

The remaining dimension of the world food problem concerns the year-to-year fluctuations (*gluts and famines*) in food availability caused by vagaries of weather and planting decisions. Even if the average level of food availability were appropriate, the fact that the average consists of a sequence of overproduction and underproduction years means that society as a whole can benefit from smoothing out the fluctuations.

The point is vividly depicted by an analogy. If a person were standing in two buckets of water—the first containing boiling-hot water, the second, ice-cold water—his misery would not be assuaged in the least by a friend's telling him that, on average, the temperature was perfect. The average does not tell the whole story.

The fluctuations of supplies for food seem to be rather large, and the swings in prices even larger. Why? One characteristic of the farming sector suggests that farmers' production decisions may actually make the fluctuations worse, or at least prolong them. This tendency is explored via the cobweb model.

Suppose, because of a weather-induced shortage, the price of a crop product rises. For the next growing season, farmers have to plant well in advance of harvest time. Their decisions about how much to plant will depend on the price they expect to receive. Let us suppose they use this year's price as their guess of what next year's price will be.

They will plan to supply a larger amount. Because the market cannot absorb that much of the commodity, the price falls. If farmers use this new, lower price to plan the following year's crop, they will produce less. This will cause the price to rise again, and so on.

The fluctuations that occur normally produce a damped oscillation. In the absence of further supply shocks, the amplitude of price and quantity fluctuations decreases over time until the equilibrium price and quantity are obtained.[6]

The demand for many foods tends to be price inelastic. This has some important implications. The more price inelastic the demand curve, the higher the price has to go in order to bring the demand into line with supply when a weather-induced shortage occurs. One conclusion is immediately obvious—the more inelastic the demand curve, the more likely farmers as a group are to gain from the shortfall. As long as the demand curve is price inelastic in the relevant range (a condition commonly satisfied in the short run by food products), farmers as a group will be better off by supply shortfalls.[7] The recent expansion of ethanol production in the United States,

---

[6]Theoretically, undamped oscillations, which increase in amplitude over time, are possible under certain conditions, but this pattern does not seem to characterize existing food markets.

[7]This is not necessarily true for every farmer, of course. If the supply reduction is concentrated on a few, they will unambiguously be worse off, whereas the remaining farmers will be better off. The point is that the revenue gains received by the latter group will exceed the losses suffered by the former group.

covered in Example 11.1, highlights the point. Ethanol demand is very price inelastic, and more inelastic than demands for corn for other uses such as for feed or exports. As the share of corn grown used for ethanol grows, however, the overall price elasticity of demand for corn is expected to become more price inelastic. On the consumer side of this issue, a quite different picture emerges. Consumers are unambiguously hurt by shortfalls and helped by situations with excess supply. The more price inelastic the demand curve, the greater is the loss in consumer surplus from shortfalls and the greater is the gain in consumer surplus from excess supply.

This creates some interesting (and, from the policy point of view, difficult) incentives. Producers as a group do not have any particular interest in protecting against supply shortfalls, but they have a substantial interest in protecting against excess supply. Consumers, on the other hand, have no quarrel with excess supply but want to guard against supply shortfalls.

Although society as a whole would gain from the stabilization of prices and quantities, the different segments of society have rather different views of how that stabilization should come about. Farmers will be delighted with price stabilization as long as the average price is high; consumers will be delighted if the average price is kept low.

Commodity price supports complicate this situation further. Commodity support policies have the effect of lowering world prices if they stimulate production in the exporting country and if that country represents a large share of the world market. (In the United States for example, corn (currently subsidized) has a 40 percent share of world market production. Sumner and Buck (2007) estimate that U.S. corn subsidies would cause world prices to be suppressed by about 10 percent causing foreign production to drop by 5 percent. Increased demand for corn for ethanol production, however, has changed this story dramatically, as Example 11.1 showed.

The main means of attempting to stabilize prices and quantities is by creating stockpiles. These can be drawn upon during periods of scarcity and built up during periods of excess supply. Currently, two different types of food stockpiles exist. The first is a special internationally held emergency stockpile that would be used to alleviate the hunger caused by natural disasters (e.g., drought). Established in 1975 by the Seventh Special Session of the United Nations General Assembly, with an annual target of 500,000 tons, the World Emergency Stockpile has the potential to reduce suffering greatly without having any noticeable disruptive effect on the world grain market (involving some 70 million tons traded). Unfortunately, its full potential has not yet been reached. The bulk of accumulated reserves is distributed annually to needy nations, leaving little in reserve from year to year.

The second kind of stockpile represents those held individually by the various countries. Although it was hoped that these stockpiles would be internationally coordinated, that has proven difficult to achieve.

The process has started to increase food security on a worldwide basis but implementation of an effective system has proved difficult. Significant, difficult political decisions on stockpile management, such as timing purchases and sales, have yet to be agreed upon. Until that time, because the interests of producer and consumer nations are no different, it is unlikely that any uncoordinated system will be fully effective.

Summary

The world hunger problem is upon us, and it is real. Serious malnutrition is currently being experienced in many parts of the world. The root of the chronic problem is poverty—an inability to afford the rising costs of food, though solving the problem will become more difficult as past unsustainable agricultural practices are eliminated and food prices rise. The harm caused by poverty and rising food prices is intensified by fluctuations in the availability of food.

These problems are not insoluble. The FAO has concluded that developing countries *could* increase their food production well in excess of population growth. They conclude, however, that this will occur only if the developed nations share technology and provide the developing countries access to their markets and if the developing countries show a willingness to adopt pricing policies that do not restrict output. This can be accomplished without placing the poor in jeopardy by using direct food-purchase subsidies (e.g., a food-stamp program) rather than price controls.

Because a major part of the world hunger problem is poverty, it is not enough to simply produce more food. The ability of the poor to afford food also has to be improved. Reducing poverty can be accomplished by bolstering nonfarm employment opportunities as well as by enhancing the returns of smaller-scale farmers. Small-scale farmers can compete effectively, if given access to credit markets and new, improved technologies.

Food stockpiles—the key element in a program to provide food security—exist but are not yet fully effective. The emergency stockpile has not achieved its designed capacity and the system of national stockpiles is large but not effectively managed. The light is at the end of the tunnel and the train is moving, but the journey is distressingly slow.

GIS Data Availability on the World Food Problem

The Food and Agriculture Organization of the United Nations has a new software program called FAOSTAT. Accessible via their Web (www.faostat.fao.orgsite) and program are world and country statistics on food security, hunger, and land use. For GIS data related to agriculture by U.S. state, see the USDA Natural Resources Conservation Service Web site at http://www.nrcs .usda.gov/technical/.

Key Concepts

agricultural subsidies (economic and environmental effects of), *p.* 236

counter cyclical program payments, *p.* 236

direct payments, *p.* 236

genetically modified organisms (GMOs), *p.* 234

global scarcity, *p.* 227

   strong form, *p.* 228

   weak form, *p.* 228

gluts and famines, *p.* 247

law of comparative advantage, *p.* 244

lifeboat ethics, *p.* 227

maldistribution hypothesis, *p.* 242

marketing boards, *p.* 245

marketing loan program, *p.* 236

National Organic Standards Board (NOSB), *p.* 236

organic certification, *p.* 236

organic farming, *p.* 235

Organic Foods Production Act (OFPA), *p.* 235

sustainable agriculture, *p.* 234

undervaluation bias, *p.* 245

USDA National Organic Program, *p.* 235

Further Reading

Carlson, Gerald R., David Zilberman, and John A. Miranowski, eds. *Agricultural and Environmental Resource Economics* (New York: Oxford University Press, 1993). A textbook that provides considerably more detail about issues raised in this chapter.

Crosson, Pierre R. and Sterling Brubaker. *Resource and Environmental Effects of U.S. Agriculture* (Baltimore: Johns Hopkins University Press, for Resources for the Future, 1982). Identifies the environmental costs associated with future increases in production and suggests measures to deal with them.

Meier, Gerald M. *Leading Issues in Economic Development,* 5th ed. (New York: Oxford University Press, 1989). A highly regarded, extensive collection of integrated short articles on various aspects of the development process. Contains an excellent section on agricultural development, with an extensive bibliography.

Streeten, Paul. *What Price Food? Agricultural Policies in Developing Countries* (New York: St. Martin's Press, 1987). An excellent study of agricultural policies in developing countries.

Williams, Jeffrey C. and Brian D. Wright. *Storage and Commodity Markets* (Cambridge: Cambridge University Press, 1991). A primarily theoretical treatment of such issues as how large stockpiles should be, whether stockpiles are more useful in raw or in processed form, and how the existence of stockpiles affects commodity prices and production.

Additional References

Alexandros, Nikos, ed. *World Agriculture: Towards 2000* (New York: New York University Press, 1988).

Anderson, Kym and Richard Blackhurst, eds. *The Greening of World Trade Issues* (Ann Arbor: University of Michigan Press, 1992).

Blackhurst, Richard and Kym Anderson. "The Greening of World Trade as Cited in 'Agriculture Survey'," *The Economist* (December 12, 1992): 17.

Browder, John O., ed. *Fragile Lands of Latin America: Strategies for Sustainable Development* (Boulder, CO: Westview Press, 1988).

Brown, Lester R. "World Population Growth, Soil Erosion, and Food Security," *Science* 214 (November 27, 1981): 995–1002.

Collins, Robert A. and J. C. Headley. "Optimal Investment to Reduce the Decay of an Income Stream: The Case of Soil Conservation," *Journal of Environmental Economics and Management* 10 (March 1983): 60–71.

Crosson, Pierre R. *The Cropland Crisis: Myth or Reality?* (Washington, DC: Resources for the Future, 1982).

Crosson, Pierre R. *Productivity Effects of Cropland Erosion in the United States* (Washington, DC: Resources for the Future, 1983).

Faeth, P., ed. *Agricultural Policy and Sustainability: Case Studies from India, Chile, the Philippines and the United States* (Washington: World Resources Institute, 1993).

Food and Agriculture Organization of the United Nations. "The State of Food Insecurity," FAO Agricultural Series (2003).

Fulton, M. and K. Giannakas. "Inserting GM Products into the Food Chain: The Market and Welfare Effects of Different Labeling and Regulatory Regimes," *American Journal of Agricultural Economics* 86 (2004) (1): 42–60.

Gardner, B. L. "The Political Economy of Agricultural Pricing," *World Economy* 16 (1993): 611–619,

Gleick, Peter. *The World's Water 2006-2007: The Biennial Report on Freshwater Resources.* Island Press, 2006.

Golan, Elise, Fred Kuchler, Lorraine Mitchell, et al. "The Economics of Food Labeling," *Journal of Consumer Policy,* 24 (2001) (2): 117–184.

Hall, Darwin C. et al. "Organic Food and Sustainable Agriculture," *Contemporary Policy Issues* 7 (October 1989): 47–72.

Hardin, Garrett. "Living on a Lifeboat," *Bioscience* 24 (October 1974): 561–568.

Horowitz, J. K. and E. Lichtenberg. "Insurance, Moral Hazard, and Chemical Use in Agriculture," *American Journal of Agricultural Economics* 75 (1993): 926–935.

Huffman, W. E., M. Rousu, J. F. Shogrun, and A. Tegene. "The Public Good Value of Information from Agribusinesses on Genetically Modified Foods," *American Journal of Agricultural Economics* 85 (2003) (5): 1309–1315.

International Fund for Agricultural Development. *The State of Rural World Poverty* (New York: New York University Press, 1992).

Jensen, H. H. "Food Insecurity and the Food Stamp Program," *American Journal of Agricultural Economics* 84 (2002) (5): 1215–1228.

Lipton, Michael and Richard Longhurst. *New Seeds and Poor People* (Baltimore, MD: Johns Hopkins University Press, 1989).

Manktelow, D., P Stevens, J. Walker, S Gurnsey, N. Park, J. Zabkiewicz, D. Teulon, and A. Rahman. *Trends in Pesticide Use in New Zealand: 2004,* Horticulture and Food Research Institute of New Zealand (2005).

Nelson, Gerald et al. *The Economics and Politics of Genetically Modified Organisms: Implications for WTO 2000* (University of Illinois, Bulletin 809, 1999).

Noussair, Charles, Stéphane Robin, and Bernard Ruffieux. "Do Consumers Really Refuse to Buy Genetically Modified Food?" *The Economic Journal,* 114 (January 2004): 102–120.

Paarlberg, R. L. "The Real Threat to GM Crops in Poor Countries: Consumer and Policy Resistance to GM Foods in Rich Countries," *Food Politics* 27 (2002) (3): 247–250.

Pinstrup Andersen, P. "Food and Agricultural Policy for a Globalizing World: Preparing for the Future," *American Journal of Agricultural Economics* 84 (2002) (5): 1201–1214.

Reganold, John P. et al. "Soil Quality and Financial Performance of Biodynamic and Conventional Farms in New Zealand," *Science* 260 (April 16, 1993): 344–349.

Regev, Uri, Halm Shalit, and A. P. Gutteirrez. "On the Optimal Allocation of Pesticides with Increasing Resistance: The Case of Alfalfa Weevil," *Journal of Environmental Economics and Management* 10 (March 1983): 86–100.

Reynolds, Russ et al. "Impacts on the Environment of Reduced Agricultural Subsidies: A Case Study of New Zealand" (Ministry of Agriculture Technical Paper, December 1993).

Rosegrant, M. W. and X. M. Cai et al. "Will the World Run Dry? Global Water and Food Security," *Environment* 45 (2003) (7): 24–36.

Sexton, Steven E., Zhen Lei, and David Zilberman. *The Economics of Pesticides and Pest Control.* University of California, Berkeley, Department of Agricultural and Resource Economics Working Paper, 2007.

Sumner, Daniel A. and Frank H. Buck. *US Farm Bill Subsidies and World Commodity Markets,* IPC Policy Focus, Farm Bill Series No. 2. International Food and Agriculture Trade Policy Council (2007) April.

Thompson, G. D. and J. Kidwell. "Explaining the Choice of Organic Produce: Cosmetic Defects, Prices and Consumer Preferences," *American Journal of Agricultural Economics,* 80 (1998) (2): 277–287.

U.S. Department of Agriculture. *Census of Agriculture* (National Agricultural Statistics Service, 2002).

U.S. Department of Agriculture. *Statistical Highlights 2002/2003* (National Agricultural Statistics Service, 2004).

World Bank Development Committee. *Environment, Growth and Development* (Washington, DC: World Bank, 1987): 20.

Discussion Questions

1. "By applying modern technology to agriculture, the United States has become the most productive food-producing nation in the world. The secret to solving the world food problem lies in transferring this technology to developing countries." Discuss.

2. Under Public Law 480, the United States sells surplus grains to developing countries, which pay in local currencies. Because the United States rarely spends all of these currencies, much of this grain transfer is *de facto* an outright gift. Is this an equitable and efficient way for the United States to dispose of surplus grain? Why or why not?

Forests

There is nothing more difficult to carry out, nor more doubtful of success, nor more dangerous to handle, than to initiate a new order of things. For the reformer has enemies in all who profit by the old order, and only lukewarm defenders in all those who would profit from the new order. The lukewarmness arises partly from fear of their adversaries who have law in their favor; and partly from the incredulity of mankind, who do not truly believe in anything new until they have had actual experience of it.

—MACHIAVELLI, *The Prince* (1513)

Introduction

Forests provide a variety of products and services. The raw materials for housing and many products made out of wood are extracted from the forest. In many parts of the world wood is an important fuel. Paper products are derived from wood fiber. Trees cleanse the air by absorbing carbon dioxide and adding oxygen. Forests provide shelter and sanctuary for wildlife, and they play an important role in the ecology of watersheds that supply much of our drinking water.

Although the contributions that trees make to our everyday life are easy to overlook, even the most rudimentary calculations indicate their significance. Slightly less than one-third of the land in the United States is covered by forests, the largest category of land use with the exception of pasture and grazing land. In Maine, an example of a heavily forested state, 95 percent of the land area is covered by forest. In 1995 the comparable figure for the world was 31.7 percent (OECD, 1997).

A glance at some of the vital signs of the forest resource does not inspire confidence that it is being managed either efficiently or sustainably.[1] Deforestation is currently proceeding at an unprecedented rate. In 1998 the World Resources Institute reported that 185 million hectares of

---

[1]In this context, sustainability refers to harvesting no more than would be replaced by growth; sustainable harvest would preserve the interests of future generations by assuring that the volume of remaining timber was not declining over time. This is stronger than required by the criterion of weal sustainability, which only requires that future generations be as well off. It would conceivably be possible to make future generations better off even if the volume of wood were declining over time by providing a compensating amount of some commodity or service they value even more.

tropical forests, an area about the size of Mexico, were destroyed from 1980 through 1995, as trees were cut for timber and to clear land for agriculture and development (World Resource Institute, 1998).

Deforestation poses a significant threat to biodiversity because it destroys forest habitat. Pressures on forest habitat come from logging activities and from the conversion of forested land to other uses (such as residential development or agriculture). Logging activities not only remove trees that serve as habitat, but also the accompanying activities (such as road building) can degrade the surrounding habitat. The threat posed by conversion involves a different, but no less significant, set of economic forces.

The Food and Agricultural Organization of the United Nations reports in its *Global Forest Resources Assessment 2000* that during the 1990s the world lost 4.2 percent of its natural forests through deforestation, while it gained 1.8 percent through reforestation (with plantations), afforestation (replanting), and the natural expansion of forests, resulting in a net reduction of 2.4 percent over the 10-year period.

In the remainder of this chapter we show how economic forces can not only explain these high rates of deforestation, but also can provide some basis for protecting against this particular threat to biodiversity. We begin by characterizing what is meant by an "efficient allocation" of the forest resource when the value of the harvested timber is the only concern. Starting simply, we first consider the efficient decision to cut a single stand (or cluster of trees) with a common age by superimposing economic considerations on a biological model of tree growth. This model is then expanded to demonstrate not only how the multiple values of the forest resource *should* influence the harvesting decision, but also why they currently do not.

Characterizing Forest Harvesting Decisions

Special Attributes of the Forest

Although forests share many characteristics with other living resources, they also have some unique aspects. Trees provide a salable commodity when they are harvested. However, left standing, they are a capital asset, providing for increased growth the following year and a stream of environmental services such as watershed protection and wildlife habitat. Each year, the forest manager must decide whether or not to harvest a particular stand of trees. In contrast to many other living resources, however, the time period between initial investment (planting) and recovery of that investment (harvesting) is especially long. Intervals of 25 years or more are common in forestry, but not in many other industries.

The Biological Dimension

Tree growth is measured on a volume basis, typically cubic feet on a particular site. Trunks, exclusive of bark and limbs, between the stump and a four-inch top are included in the measurement. For larger trees, the stump is 24 inches from the ground. Only standing trees are measured; those toppled by wind or age are not included. In this sense the volume is measured in net rather than gross terms.

Based on this measurement of volume, the data reveal that even-aged tree stands go through distinct growth phases. Initially, when the trees are very young, growth is rather slow in volume terms, although the tree may experience a considerable increase in height. A period of sustained, rapid growth follows, with volume increasing considerably. Finally, slower growth sets in as the stand fully matures, until growth stops or even reverses.

The actual growth of a stand of trees depends on many factors, including the weather, the fertility of the soil, susceptibility to insects or disease, the type of tree, the amount of care devoted to the trees, and vulnerability to environmental factors or events, such as forest fire or air pollution. Thus, a tremendous amount of variability of tree growth can be observed from stand to stand. Some of these growth-enhancing or growth-retarding factors are under the influence of foresters; others are not.

Abstracting from these differences, it is possible to develop a hypothetical but realistic biological model of the growth of a stand of trees (see Figure 12.1). In this case, our model is based on the growth of a stand of Douglas Fir trees in the Pacific Northwest.[2]

Notice that the figure is consistent with the growth phases mentioned earlier. Following an early period of limited growth, the stand experiences rapid growth in its middle ages, with growth ceasing after 135 years.

FIGURE 12.1   Model of Tree Growth in a Stand of Douglas Fir

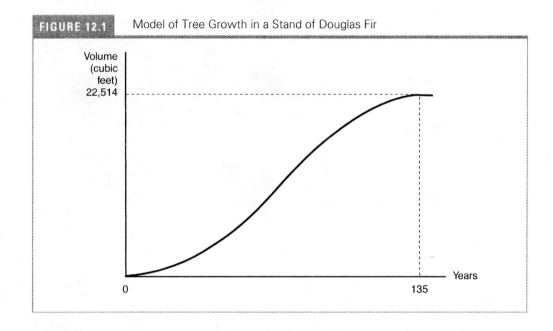

---

[2]The numerical model in the text is based loosely on the data presented in (Clawson, 1977). The mathematical function relating volume to age of the stand in Figure 12.1 is a third-degree polynomial of the form $v = a + bt + ct^2 + dt^3$, where v = volume in cubic feet, t = age of the stand in years, and $a, b, c,$ and d are parameters that take on the values 0, 40, 3.1, and −0.016, respectively.

When should this stand be harvested? Foresters have come up with a calculation called the *mean annual increment (MAI)*, which provides the basis for a biological approach to answering this question. Developing this concept provides a useful contrast to the economic approach, which is represented in subsequent sections.

The MAI is calculated by dividing the cumulative volume of the stand at the end of each decade by the cumulative number of years the stand has been growing up to that decade. For growth patterns like the ones represented by Figure 12.1, the MAI rises during the early ages and then falls during the later ages (see Table 12.1).

According to the *biological decision rule*, the forest should be harvested at the age when the MAI is maximized. According to our Douglas Fir example, this occurs when the stand is 100 years old. Column 4 in Table 12.1 helps us to understand what is special about this age. Annual incremental growth rises until the trees are about 70 years old, declining thereafter. The MAI rises for the first 100 years because the annual incremental growth is above the MAI during that period; it falls in the following years because the annual incremental growth is below the MAI.

The Economics of Forest Harvesting

It is possible to use the basic biological model of growth portrayed in Figure 12.1 as the basis for an economic model of the harvesting decision.

TABLE 12.1 The Biological Harvesting Decision: Douglas Fir

Age (Years) (1)	Volume[a] (Cubic Feet) (2)	MAI[b] (Cubic Feet) (3)	Annual Incremental Growth[c] (Cubic Feet) (4)
10	694	69.4	69.4
20	1,912	95.6	121.8
30	3,558	118.6	164.6
40	5,536	138.4	197.8
50	7,750	155.0	221.4
60	10,104	168.0	235.4
70	12,502	178.6	239.8
80	14,848	185.6	234.6
90	17,046	189.4	219.8
100	19,000	190.0	195.4
110	20,614	187.4	161.4
120	21,792	184.6	117.8
130	22,438	172.6	64.4
135	22,514	166.8	11.6

[a] Calculated from the formula used to produce Figure 12.1 (see footnote 2)
[b] Column 2 divided by column 1
[c] Change over intervening period in column 1 divided by change in number of years in column 1

From the definition of *profit maximization*, the optimal time to harvest this stand would be the particular age that maximizes the present value of the net private benefits from the wood. The size of the net benefits from the wood depends on whether the land will be perpetually committed to forestry or left to natural processes after harvest. We will assume that the stand will be harvested once and the land will be left as is following the harvest.

Two costs are presumed to be important in this decision: (1) *planting costs* and (2) *harvesting costs*. Apart from their magnitudes, these costs differ in one significant characteristic—the time at which they are borne. Planting costs are borne immediately, whereas harvesting costs are borne at the time of harvest. In a present-value calculation, harvesting costs are discounted (as is the value of the wood), because they are paid (received) in the future; however, planting costs are not discounted, because they are paid immediately. For the sake of our example, let's assume that planting this stand costs $1,000 and harvesting costs $0.30 per cubic foot of wood harvested.

With these additions to the model, it is now possible to calculate the present value of private net benefits that would be derived from harvesting this stand at various ages (Table 12.2). The net benefits are calculated by subtracting the present value of costs from the present value of the timber at that age. Different *discount rates* are used to illustrate the influence of discounting on the harvesting decision. The undiscounted calculations ($r = 0.0$) simply indicate the actual values that would prevail at each age; the positive discount rates take the time value of money into account.

An interesting conclusion can be gleaned from Table 12.2. Discounting shortens the profit-maximizing age when the stand is harvested. Whereas the maximum undiscounted net benefits occur at 135 years, when a discount rate of only 0.02 is used, the maximum occurs at 68 years— roughly half the time of the undiscounted case. A higher discount rate yields an even shorter harvesting time, as shown in the table.

Higher discount rates imply shorter harvesting periods because they are less tolerant of the slow timber growth that occurs as the stand reaches maturity. The use of a positive discount rate implies a direct comparison between the increase in the value of the timber that occurs without harvesting and the increase in value that would occur if the forest were harvested and the money from the sale invested at rate r. In the undiscounted case, the opportunity cost of capital is zero; therefore, it pays to leave the money invested in trees as long as some growth is occurring. As long as r is positive, however, the trees will be harvested as soon as the growth rate declines sufficiently that more will be earned from financial investments. Notice, however, that high discount rates may destroy the incentive to replant. (This is the case when $r = 0.04$ as shown in Table 12.2.)

Sources of Inefficiency

The previous section demonstrates how profit-maximizing decisions can lead to deforestation by promoting high rates of harvest, coupled with low rates of replanting. Chapter 10 demonstrated how perverse incentives can lead to an inefficiently high conversion of forest land to other uses. In this section we will discover *sources of inefficiency* in harvesting decisions. These inefficiencies have the effect of biasing profit-maximizing decisions toward excess rates of deforestation.

Perverse Incentives for the Landowner

Profit maximization does not produce efficient outcomes when the pattern of incentives facing decision makers is perverse. Forestry provides an unfortunately large number of situations where perverse incentives have produced very inefficient and unsustainable outcomes.

TABLE 12.2 The Economic Harvesting Decision: Douglas Fir

Age (years)	10	20	30	40	50	60	68	70
Volume (cu. ft.)	694	1,192	3,558	5,536	7,750	10,104	12,023	12,502
Undiscounted ($r = 0.0$)								
Value of timber ($)	694	1,192	3,558	5,536	7,750	10,104	12,023	12,502
Cost ($)	1,208	1,574	2,067	2,661	3,325	4,031	4,607	4,751
Net benefits ($)	−514	338	1,491	2,875	4,425	6,073	7,416	7,751
Discounted ($r = 0.01$)								
Value of timber ($)	628	1,567	2,640	3,718	4,712	5,562	6,112	6,230
Cost ($)	1,188	1,470	1,792	2,115	2,414	2,669	2,833	2,869
Net benefits ($)	−560	97	848	1,603	2,299	2,893	3,278	3,361
Discounted ($r = 0.02$)								
Value of timber ($)	567	1,288	1,964	2,507	2,879	3,080	3,128	3,126
Cost ($)	1,170	1,386	1,589	1,752	1,864	1,924	1,938	1,938
Net benefits ($)	−603	−98	375	755	1,015	1,156	**1,190**	1,188
Discounted ($r = 0.04$)								
Value of timber ($)	469	873	1,097	1,153	1,091	960	835	803
Cost ($)	1,141	1,262	1,329	1,346	1,327	1,288	1,251	1,241
Net benefits ($)	−672	−389	−232	**−193**	−237	−328	−415	−438

Age (years)	80	90	100	110	120	130	135
Volume (cu. ft.)	14,848	17,046	19,000	20,614	21,792	22,438	22,514
Undiscounted ($r = 0.0$)							
Value of timber ($)	14,848	17,046	19,000	20,614	21,792	22,438	22,514
Cost ($)	5,454	6,114	6,700	7,084	7,538	7,731	7,754
Net benefits ($)	9,394	10,932	12,300	13,430	14,254	14,707	**14,760**
Discounted ($r = 0.01$)							
Value of timber ($)	6,698	6,961	7,025	6,899	6,603	6,155	5,876
Cost ($)	3,009	3,088	3,107	3,070	2,981	2,846	2,763
Net benefits ($)	3,689	3,873	**3,917**	3,830	3,622	3,308	3,113
Discounted ($r = 0.02$)							
Value of timber ($)	3,046	2,868	2,623	2,334	2,024	1,710	1,449
Cost ($)	1,914	1,860	1,787	1,700	1,607	1,513	1,435
Net benefits ($)	1,132	1,008	836	634	417	197	14
Discounted ($r = 0.04$)							
Value of timber ($)	644	500	376	276	197	137	113
Cost ($)	1,193	1,150	1,113	1,083	1,059	1,041	1,034
Net benefits ($)	−549	−650	−737	−807	−862	−904	−921

Notes:
Volume of timber, from Table 12.1
Value of timber = price × volume/$(1 + r)^t$
Cost = $1,000 + ($0.30 × volume)/$(1 + r)^t$
Net benefits = value of timber − cost

Privately owned forests are a significant force all over the world, but in some countries, such as the United States, they are the dominant force. Private forest decisions are plagued by externally generated costs of various types. Yields are adversely affected by externally imposed costs, such as air pollution. When heavy investments in forested lands can be wiped out by factors totally out of the control of the owners, the incentive to invest is undermined.

Providing a sustainable flow of timber is not the sole purpose of the forest, however. When the act of harvesting timber imposes costs on other valued aspects of the forest (e.g., watershed maintenance, prevention of soil erosion, and protection of biodiversity), these costs may not (and normally will not) be adequately considered in the decision.

The value of the standing forest as wildlife habitat or as a key element in the local ecosystem is one external cost that can lead to several inefficient decisions. Undervaluing the standing forest provides an incentive to harvest an inefficiently large amount of timber and an incentive to harvest timber even when preservation is the preserved alternative. It also provides an incentive to convert forest to other uses even when social net benefits are maximized by retaining the land as forest. The controversy that erupted in the Pacific Northwest of the United States between environmentalists concerned with the northern spotted owl and loggers can, in part, be explained by the different values these two groups put on habitat destruction. This region contains a number of old-growth Douglas Firs, which can reach a height of 30 stories. These 200-year-old trees would be very valuable sources of timber, but they are also important components of the local ecosystem. (Among other ecosystem contributions, these trees provide a home for the endangered northern spotted owl.)

Perverse incentives can be created by governments as well. The historically high rate of deforestation in Brazil was in no small part due to perverse incentives created by the Brazilian government (Binswanger, 1989; Mahar, 1989).

For example, the Brazilian government reduced taxes on income derived from agriculture by as much as 90 percent. This tax discrimination overvalued agriculture and made it profitable to cut down forests and convert the land to agriculture even when, in the absence of discriminatory tax relief, agriculture in these regions would not be profitable.

The system of property rights over land also is at fault. How do individuals establish a solid claim to unclaimed land in Brazil? Acquiring land by squatting has been formally recognized since 1850. A squatter acquires a usufructory right (the right to continue using the land) by (1) living on a plot of unclaimed public land and (2) using it "effectively" for at least a year and a day. If these two conditions are met for five years, the squatter acquires ownership of the land, including the right to transfer it to others. A claimant gets title for an amount of land up to three times the amount cleared of forest; hence, the more deforestation the squatter engages in, the larger the amount of land he or she acquires! In effect, deforestation was a necessary step in order for landless peasants to acquire land.

In the Far East and in the United States, perverse incentives take another form. Logging is the major source of deforestation in both regions. Why don't loggers act efficiently? The sources of inefficiency can be found in the concession agreements, which define the terms under which public forests can be harvested.

To loggers, existing forests have a substantial advantage over new forests: They can be harvested immediately. This advantage is reflected in the *economic rent* (called *stumpage value* in the industry) associated with a standing forest. In principle, governments have a variety of policy instruments at their disposal to extract this rent from the concessionaires, but they have typically given out the concessions to harvest this timber without capturing anywhere near all of the rent.[3] The result is that the cost of harvesting is artificially reduced and loggers can afford to harvest much more forest than is efficient. The failure of government to capture this rent also means that the wealth tied up in these forests has typically been captured by a few, now wealthy, individuals and corporations rather than the government to be used for the alleviation of poverty or other worthy social objectives.

Because forest concessions are typically awarded for limited terms, the concession holders have little incentive to replant, to exercise care in their logging procedures, or even to conserve younger trees until they reach the efficient harvest age. The future value of the forest will not be theirs to capture. The resulting logging practices destroy a multiple of the number of trees represented by the high-value species because of the destruction caused by the construction of access roads, the felling and dragging of the trees, and the elimination of the protective canopy. Although sustainable forestry would be possible for many of these nations, concession agreements such as these make it unlikely.[4]

The list of losers from inefficient forestry practices frequently includes indigenous peoples who have lived in and derived their livelihood from these forests for a very long time. As the loggers and squatters push deeper and deeper into forests, the indigenous people, who lack the power to stem the tide, are forced to relocate farther and farther away from their traditional lands.

Perverse Incentives for Nations

Another source of deforestation involves external costs that transcend national borders. Because the costs transcend national borders, it is unrealistic to expect national policy to solve the problem. Some international action would normally be necessary.

Biodiversity. Because of species extinction, the diversity of the forms of life that inhabit the planet is diminishing at an unprecedented rate. The extinction of species is an irreversible process. Deforestation, particularly the destruction of the tropical rain forests, is a major source of species extinction because it destroys the most biologically active habitats. In particular, Amazonia has been characterized by Norman Myers (1984) as the "single richest region of the tropical biome." The quantity of bird, fish, plant, and insect life that is unique to that region is unmatched anywhere else on the planet.

One of the tragic ironies of the situation is that these extinctions are occurring at precisely the moment in history when we would be most able to take advantage of the gene pool this biodiversity represents. Modern techniques now make it possible to transplant desirable genes from one species into another, creating species with new characteristics such as enhanced resistance to disease or pests. But the gene pool must be diverse if it is to serve as a useful source of donor

---

[3]One way for the government to capture this rent would be to put timber concessions up for bid. Bidders would have an incentive to pay up to the stumpage value for these concessions. The more competitive the bidding was, the higher the likelihood that the government would capture all of the rent. In practice, many of the concessions have been given to those with influence in the government—at far below market rates (Vincent, 1990).

[4]Currently, foresters believe that the sustainable yield for closed tropical rain forests is zero, because they have not yet learned how to regenerate the species in a harvested area. Destroying the thick canopy, thereby allowing the light to penetrate, so changes the growing conditions and the nutrient levels of the soil that even replanting is unlikely to regenerate the types of trees included in the harvest.

genes. Tropical forests have already contributed genetic material to increase disease resistance of cash crops such as coffee and cocoa, and they have been the source of some entirely new foods. Approximately one-quarter of all prescription drugs have been derived from substances found in tropical plants. Future discoveries, however, are threatened by deforestation's deleterious effect on habitats.

Global Warming. Deforestation also contributes to global warming. Because trees absorb carbon dioxide, a major greenhouse gas, deforestation eliminates a potentially significant means of ameliorating the rise in CO_2 emissions. Furthermore, burning trees, an activity commonly associated with agricultural land clearing, adds CO_2 to the air by liberating the carbon sequestered within the trees.

Why is deforestation occurring so rapidly when the benefits conferred by a standing forest are so significant by virtually anyone's reckoning? The concept of externalities provides the key to resolving this paradox. Both the global warming and biodiversity benefits are largely external to the nation containing the forest, whereas the costs of preventing deforestation are largely internal. The loss of biodiversity precipitated by deforestation is perhaps most deeply felt by the industrialized world, not the countries hosting the tropical forests. Currently, the technologies to exploit the gene pool this diversity represents are in widest use in the industrialized countries. Similarly, most of the damage from global warming would be felt outside the borders of the country being deforested, yet stopping deforestation means giving up the jobs and income derived from harvesting the wood or harvesting the land made available by clearing the forests. It is therefore not surprising that the most vociferous opposition to the loss of biodiversity is mounted in the industrialized nations, not the tropical forest nations. Global externalities provide not only a clear rationale for market failure, but also a clear reason why the governments involved cannot be expected to solve the problem by themselves.

Poverty and Debt

Poverty and debt are also major sources of pressure on the forests. Peasants see unclaimed forest-land as an opportunity to own land. Nations confronted with masses of peasants see unowned or publicly owned forests as a politically more viable means of providing land for the landless than taking it forcibly from the rich. Without land, larger numbers of peasants descend upon the urban areas in search of jobs than can be accommodated by urban labor markets. Politically explosive tensions, created and nourished by the resulting atmosphere of frustration and hopelessness, force governments to open up forested lands to the peasants, or at least to look the other way as peasants stake their claims.

In eastern and southern Africa, positive feedback loops have created a downward cycle in which *debt and deforestation* reinforce each other. Most natural forests have long since been cut down for timber, fuelwood, and cleared land for agricultural purposes. As forests disappear, the rural poor divert more time toward locating fuelwood. When fuelwood is no longer available, dried animal waste is burned, thereby eliminating it as a source of fertilizer to nourish depleted soils. Fewer trees lead to more soil erosion and soil depletion leads to diminished nutrition. Diminished nutrition reinforces the threats to human health posed by an inability to find or afford fuelwood or animal waste for cooking and for boiling unclean water. Degraded health saps energy, increases susceptibility to disease, and reduces productivity. Survival strategies may necessarily sacrifice long-term goals simply to ward off starvation or death; the forests are typically an early casualty.

At the national level, poverty takes the form of staggering levels of debt to service in comparison to the capacity to generate foreign exchange earnings. In periods of high real interest rates, servicing these debts commands most if not all foreign exchange earnings. Using these foreign exchange earnings to service the debt eliminates the possibility of using them to finance imports for sustainable activities to alleviate poverty.

The large debts owned by many developing countries may also encourage these countries to overexploit their resource endowments in order to raise the necessary foreign exchange. Timber exports represent a case in point.

Sustainable Forestry

We have examined two types of decisions by landowners—the harvesting decision and the conversion decision—that affect the rate of deforestation. The first type of decision involves how much timber to harvest, how often to harvest it, and whether to replant after a harvest. The second type of decision concerns whether and when to convert a forest to a different land use.

In both cases profit-maximizing decisions may not be efficient and these inefficiencies tend to create a bias toward higher rates of deforestation. In these cases correcting these inefficiencies can promote both efficiency and sustainability.

Does the restoration of efficiency guarantee sustainable outcomes? The answer depends on what is meant by *sustainable forestry*. If the possibility of compensation is entertained along with the "nondeclining welfare among generations" definition, then efficiency can be fully compatible with sustainability as long as the economic gains from harvest are invested and shared with future generations. In this case, even when efficiency results in some deforestation, future generations will not suffer.

Let's suppose, however, that we apply the environmental sustainability definition to forestry. Under this definition sustainable forestry can be realized only when the forests are sufficiently protected that harvests can be maintained perpetually. Under this definition, sustainable forestry would require harvests to be limited to the growth of the forest, leaving the volume of wood unaffected over some specified period of time.

Efficiency is not necessarily compatible with this definition of sustainable forestry. Maximizing the present value involves an implicit comparison between the increase in value from delaying harvest (largely because of the growth in volume) and the increase in value from harvesting the timber and investing the earnings (largely a function of r, the interest rate earned on invested savings). With slow-growing species, the growth rate in volume is small; maximizing the present value may well involve harvest volumes higher than the net growth of the forest.

The search for sustainable forestry practices that are also economically sustainable has led to the development of rapidly growing tree species and plantation forestry. Rapidly growing species raise the attractiveness of replanting, because the invested funds are tied up for a shorter period of time. These species are raised in plantations, where they can be harvested and replanted at a low cost. Forest plantations have been established for such varied purposes as supplying fuelwood in developing countries to supplying pulp for paper mills in both the industrialized and developing countries.

Plantation forestry is controversial. Not only do plantation forests typically involve a single species of tree, which results in a poor wildlife habitat, they also require large inputs of fertilizer and pesticides.

In some parts of the world the natural resilience of the forest ecosystem is sufficiently high that sustainability is ultimately achieved, despite decades of unsustainable levels of harvest. In the United States, for example, sometime during the 1940s the net growth of the nation's timberlands exceeded timber removals. The surveys conducted since that time confirm that net growth has continued to exceed harvests, in spite of a rather large and growing demand for timber. The harvests during that period have been sustainable in terms of total forest volume, although the harvests of specific species in specific locations may not have been.

Public Policy

Does public ownership of the forests provide an answer? With the large amount of resources at its disposal, plus the ability to acquire land through eminent domain proceedings, the government can achieve the efficient scale rather easily. Furthermore, because it is not obligated to maximize profits, it can more easily take external effects on wildlife or recreation into account. Unfortunately, if the U.S. experience is typical, the potential to solve these problems by public ownership is more illusory than real.

Public ownership of lands in the United States started even before the fledgling nation had a constitution. The first public land, much of it forestland, was accepted as a donation by the Confederation of Congress on October 29, 1782. Though these lands were owned by the government, they were not managed by the government until more than a century later. The forest was treated as common property.

By the second half of the nineteenth century, a number of voices began to decry the apparent wanton destruction of the forests and to call for more enlightened use of the resource. The first piece of legislation designed to respond to this outcry was the *Forest Reserve Act of 1891*, which authorized the first permanent system of forest reserves. No provision for private harvesting of trees on the forest reserves was included. It was not until 1897, with the passage of a general administration bill, that Congress provided the funds and a process to manage this system. This Act authorized private harvesting on forest reserves under other restrictive conditions.

The management for these reserves was transferred in 1905 to the U.S. Department of Agriculture's Forest Service. The ambitious chief of the USDA Forest Service at that time, Gifford Pinchot, was to have an enormous influence over Forest Service management for several decades. Unlike other contemporaries—such as John Muir, who wanted to withdraw these lands from use—Pinchot vigorously pursued a philosophy that they should be used. Focusing first on timber production, his goal was the promotion of a sustainable level of harvest from the national forests. Concern over wildlife and recreation would come much later.

The desire to maintain a sustained level of harvest gave rise to the acceptance of a number of operational procedures by the Forest Service that were explicitly biologically based. Chief among these were the maximum average annual increment described earlier and the requirement to keep the allowable cut on the national forests steady through time to reduce the potential instability that would be faced by private forest owners if the market were flooded with timber from the public lands.

Although the Forest Service had, to some extent, followed a multiple-use philosophy since its inception, in the period following World War II public interest in nontimber uses grew sufficiently that the rather ad hoc methods of the Forest Service for achieving a balance were no longer deemed sufficient.

In 1960 the Multiple Use–Sustained Yield Act mandated a *multiple use philosophy*, without giving any guidance on how to implement that philosophy. In part, this Act had been sought by the Forest Service to protect its multiple use philosophy from attack by those seeking congressional or judicial support for single interests. However, subsequent legislation would force the Forest Service to be much more systematic in how it sought to define and implement a multiple use philosophy.

The Wilderness Act of 1964 set aside specific forest areas to be preserved in their pristine state. No roads were permitted, and timber harvests were prohibited in wilderness areas. Although initially limited to designating specific areas that had traditionally not been harvested, the Act has in fact been the basis of a significant amount of judicial and agency interpretation, with the ultimate effect that it has ushered in much more wilderness land than was envisioned by those discussing it in Congress at the time the bill was passed.

Although the management of public forests in the United States has been evolving since 1782, it has not yet produced efficient outcomes. Harvests from the public forests are subsidized by taxpayers.[5] The benefits of the forests to wildlife and recreation are inadequately protected. Too many political pressures influence the process. Other policy approaches offer the prospect of an alternative transition to efficiency.

Changing Incentives

One such approach involves restoring efficient incentives. Concessionaires should pay the full cost for their rights to harvest publicly controlled lands, including compensating for damage to the forests surrounding the trees of interest. The magnitude of land transferred to squatters should not be a multiple of the amount of cleared forest. The rights of indigenous peoples should be respected.

Another approach involves enlisting the power of consumers in the cause of sustainable forestry. The process typically involves the establishment of standards for sustainable forestry, employing independent certifiers to verify compliance with these standards, and allowing certified suppliers to display a label designating compliance (see Example 12.1). For this system to work well several preconditions need to be met. Consumers must trust the *forest certification* process and it must address issues they care about. Additionally, consumers must be sufficiently concerned about sustainable forestry to pay a price premium (over prices for otherwise comparable, but uncertified, products) that is large enough to make certification an attractive option for forestry companies. This means that the revenue should be at least sufficient to cover the higher costs associated with producing certified wood. Nothing guarantees that these conditions would be met in general.

---

[5]A review of several studies estimating the size of these subsidies can be found in (Repetto, 1988).

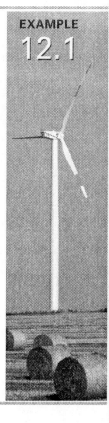

Producing Sustainable Forestry Through Certification

EXAMPLE
12.1

The Forest Stewardship Council (FSC) is an international, not-for-profit organization headquartered in Oaxaca, Mexico. The FSC was conceived in large part by environmental groups, most notably the World Wide Fund for Nature (WWF). The goal of the FSC is to foster "environmentally appropriate, socially beneficial, and economically viable management of the world's forests." It pursues this goal through independent third-party certification of well-managed forests.

The FSC has developed standards to assess the performance of forestry operations. These standards address environmental, social, and economic issues. Forest assessments require one or more field visits by a team of specialists representing a variety of disciplines typically including forestry, ecology/wildlife, management/biology, and sociology/anthropology. Additionally, the FSC requires that forest assessment reports be subject to independent peer review. Any FSC assessment may be challenged through a formal complaints procedure. FSC certified products are identified by an on-product label and/or off-product publicity materials.

Although the FSC is supported by a broad coalition of industry representatives, social justice organizations and environmental organizations, it is opposed by some mainstream industry groups, particularly in North America, and by some landowners associations in Europe. One unresolved issue is how to certify small- and medium-size landholdings since conventional certification is expensive.

Source: The Forest Stewardship Council Web site: http://www.fsc.org/en (accessed 4/3/09).

Most of these changes could be implemented by individual nations to protect their own forests, and to do so would be in their interests. By definition, inefficient practices cost more than the benefits received. The move to a more efficient set of policies would necessarily generate more net benefits, which could be shared in ways that build political support for the change. But what about the global inefficiencies? How can those be resolved?

Several economic strategies exist. They share the characteristic of compensating the nations that confer external benefits so as to encourage conservation actions consistent with global efficiency.

Debt-Nature Swaps

One strategy involves reducing the pressure on the forests caused by the international debt owed by many developing countries. Private banks hold most of the debt, and they are not typically motivated by a desire to protect biodiversity. Nonetheless, it is possible to find some common ground for negotiating strategies to reduce the debt. Banks realize that complete repayment of the loans is probably not possible. Rather than completely writing off the loans, an action that not only causes harm to the income statement but also creates adverse incentives for repayment of future loans, they are willing to consider alternative strategies.

One of the most innovative policies that explores common ground in international arrangements has become known as the *debt-nature swap*. It is innovative in two senses: (1) the uniqueness of the policy instrument and (2) the direct involvement of nongovernmental organizations in implementing the policy. A debt-nature swap involves the purchase (at a discounted value in the secondary debt market) of a developing-country debt, usually by a non-governmental environmental organization (NGO). The new holder of the debt, the NGO, offers to cancel the debt in return for an environmentally related action on the part of the debtor nation. The first debt-nature swap took place in Bolivia in 1987. Since then, debt-for-nature swaps have been arranged or explored in many developing countries including Ecuador, the Philippines, Zambia, Jamaica, Madagascar, Guatemala, Venezuela, Argentina, Honduras, and Brazil.

A brief examination of the Madagascar case can illustrate how these swaps work. Recognized as a prime source of biodiversity, the overwhelming majority of Madagascar's land mammals, reptiles, and plants are found nowhere else on Earth. Madagascar is also one of the poorest countries in the world. Burdened with high levels of external debt, Madagascar had limited domestic financial resources to counter the serious environmental degradation it was experiencing. From 1989–1996, Conservation International, the Missouri Botanical Garden, and the World Wildlife Fund negotiated nine commercial debt-for-nature swaps in Madagascar. These generated $12.7 million in conservation funds. Agreements signed by the government and the participating conservation organizations identified the programs to be funded. One such program trained more than 320 nature protection agents, foresters who focused on involving local communities in forest management.

The main advantage of these arrangements to the debtor nation is that a significant foreign exchange obligation can be paid off with domestic currency. Debt-nature swaps offer a realistic possibility of turning what has been a major force for unsustainable economic activity (the debt crisis) into a force for resource conservation.

Extractive Reserves

One strategy designed to protect the indigenous people of the forest as well as to prevent deforestation involves the establishment of *extractive reserves*. These areas would be reserved for the indigenous people to engage in their traditional hunting and gathering activities.

Extractive reserves have already been established in the Acre region of Brazil. Acre's main activity comes from the thousands of indigenous men who tap the rubber trees scattered throughout the forest, a practice dating back 100 years. Because of the activities of Chico Mendes, a leader of the tappers who was subsequently assassinated, the Brazilian government established four extractive reserves in June 1988 to protect the rubber tappers from encroaching development.

The World Heritage Convention

The *World Heritage Convention* came into being in 1972 with the primary mission of identifying and preserving the cultural and natural heritage of outstanding sites throughout the world, and ensuring their protection through international cooperation. Currently, 178 countries have ratified the convention.

Ratifying nations have the opportunity to add their natural properties of outstanding universal value to the World Heritage List. The motivation for taking this step is to gain international recognition for the properties, using the prestige that comes from this designation to raise awareness for heritage preservation and increase the likelihood that the site can be preserved. A ratifying nation may receive both financial assistance and expert advice from the World Heritage Committee as support for promotional activities related to the preservation of its properties as well as for the development of educational materials.

Responsibility for providing adequate protection and management of these sites falls on the host nations, but a key benefit of ratification, particularly for developing countries, is access to the World Heritage Fund. This fund is supported by mandatory contributions from ratifying nations, calculated at one percent of each country's contribution to UNESCO, the administering agency. Annually, about $3 million are made available, mainly to low-income countries. These funds finance technical assistance and training projects as well as support preparation of nomination proposals for the development of conservation projects. Emergency assistance may also be made available for urgent action to repair damage caused by human-made or natural disasters.

Royalty Payments

One potential source of revenue for biodiversity preservation involves taking advantage of the extremely high degree of interest the pharmaceutical industry has indicated in searching for new drugs derived from these biologically diverse pools of flora and fauna. Establishing the principles that nations containing these biologically rich resources within their borders would be entitled to a stipulated *royalty payment* on any and all products developed from the genes obtained from these preserves would provide both an incentive to preserve the resources and some revenue to accomplish the preservation.

Nations harboring rich biological preserves have begun to realize their value and to extract some of that value from the pharmaceutical industry. The revenue so derived is in part placed back into inventorying and learning more about the resource.

In 1996 Medichem Research, an Illinois pharmaceutical company, entered into a joint venture with the Sarawak government. The organization created by this joint venture has the right to file exclusive patents on two compounds that offer some promise as cancer treatments. Currently, the agreement specifies a 50:50 split from royalties once the drug is marketed. The Sarawak government has been given the exclusive right to supply the latex raw material from which the compounds are derived. Sarawak scientists are involved in screening and isolating the compounds and Sarawak physicians are involved in the clinical trials. This agreement not only provides a strong rationale for protecting the biological source, but also it enables the host country to build its capacity for capturing the value of its biodiversity in the future (Laird and ten Kate, 2002). These arrangements are particularly significant because they facilitate transboundary sharing of the costs of preservation. It is unrealistic to expect that countries harboring these preserves should be expected to shoulder the entire cost of preservation when the richer countries of the world are the major beneficiaries. It may also be unrealistic to assume that pharmaceutical demand is always sufficient for preservation (see Example 12.2).

Recognizing the limited availability of international aid for the preservation of biodiversity habitat, nations have begun to tap other revenue sources. Tourist revenues have become an increasingly popular source, particularly where the tourism is specifically linked to the resources that are targeted for preservation. Rather than mixing these revenues with other public funds, nations are earmarking them for preservation (see Example 12.3).

Does Pharmaceutical Demand Offer Sufficient Protection to Biodiversity?

The theory is clear—incentives to protect plants are stronger when the plants are valuable to humans. Is the practice equally clear?

The case of taxol is instructive. Derived from the slow-growing Pacific yew, taxol has been proven effective in treating advanced forms of breast and ovarian cancers. As of 1998 it was the best-selling anticancer drug.

Since the major sites for this tree were in the old-growth forests of the Pacific Northwest, the hope of environmental groups was that the rise in the importance of taxol might provide sustainable employment and some protection for old-growth forests.

In fact, that is not how it worked out. The taxol for the chemical trials was derived from the bark of the tree. Stripping the tree of its bark killed it. And supplying enough bark for the chemical trials put a tremendous strain on the resource.

Ultimately, the private company that marketed taxol, Bristol-Squibb, developed a semisynthetic substance that could be made from imported renewable tree parts.

The Pacific yew, the original source for one of the most important medical discoveries in the twentieth century, was left completely unprotected. And the industry that had grown up to supply the bark collapsed. In the end its value proved transitory and its ability to support a sustainable livelihood in the Pacific Northwest was illusory.

Source: Goodman, Jordan and Vivian Walsh. *The Story of Taxol: Nature and Politics in the Pursuit of an Anti-Cancer Drug* (New York: Cambridge University Press, 2001).

Summary

Tree stands typically go through three distinct growth phases—slow growth in volume in the early stage, followed by rapid growth in the middle years, and slower growth as the stand reaches full maturity. The owner who harvests the timber receives the income from its sale, but the owner who delays harvest will receive additional growth. The amount of growth depends on the part of the growth cycle the stand is in.

From an economic point of view, the efficient time to harvest a stand of timber is when the social net benefits are maximized. The net benefits are maximized when the marginal gain from delaying harvest one more year is equal to the marginal cost of the delay. For longer-than-efficient delays, the additional costs outweigh the increased benefits, whereas for earlier-than-efficient harvests, more benefits (in terms of the increased value of the timber) are given up than costs are saved. Typically, the efficient harvest age is 25 years or older.

The harvest age depends on the circumstances. In general, the larger the discount rate the earlier the harvest. If standing timber provides amenity services (such as recreation or wildlife management) in proportion to the volume of the standing timber, the efficient rotation will be longer than it would be in the absence of any amenity services.

Trust Funds for Conservation

EXAMPLE

12.3

How can local governments finance biodiversity preservation when faced with limited availability of both international and domestic funds? One option, which is being aggressively pursued by the World Wildlife Fund, involves trust funds. *Trust funds* are moneys whose use is legally restricted to a specific purpose (as opposed to being placed in the general government treasury). They are administered by a trustee or board of trustees who is responsible for assuring compliance with the terms of the trust. Most, but not all, trust funds are *endowments*, meaning that the trustees can spend the interest and dividends from the funds, but not the principal. This assures the continuity of funds for an indefinite period.

Where does the money come from? Many nations that harbor biodiversity preserves can ill afford to spend the resources necessary to protect them. One possibility is to tap into foreign demands for preservation. In Belize the revenue comes from a "conservation fee" charged to all arriving foreign visitors. The initial fee, $3.75, was passed by Belize's parliament in January 1996. It is expected to raise $500,000 in revenues each year for the trust fund. Similar fees are being designed in Namibia and Papua, New Guinea.

Income from the trust funds can be used for many purposes, including training park rangers, developing biological information, paying the salaries of key personnel, and conducting environmental education programs, depending on the terms of the trust agreement.

Biodiversity preservation that depends on funds from the general treasury becomes subject to the vagaries of budgetary pressures. When the competition for funds intensifies, the funds may disappear or be severely diminished. The virtue of a trust fund is that it provides long-term sustained funding for the protection of biodiversity.

Source: Spergel, Barry. "Trust Funds for Conservation," *FEEM Newsletter* 1 (April 1996): 13–16.

Profit maximization can be compatible with both efficient and sustainable forest management under the right circumstances, but not always. In particular, when amenity services are small, profit-maximizing private owners have an incentive to adopt the efficient rotation and to undertake investments that increase the yield of the forest. Efficient harvest behavior is consistent with sustainability of a particular forest when the growth rate of the forest is larger than the discount rate.

In reality, not all private firms will follow efficient forest management practices because externalities may create inefficient incentives. When amenity values are large and not captured by the forest owner, the private rotation period may fail to consider these values, leading to an inefficiently short rotation period. Furthermore, these undervalued forests may be inefficiently converted to other land uses.

Inefficient deforestation has been encouraged by a failure to incorporate global benefits from standing forests; by concession agreements that provide incentives to harvest too much too soon, and fail to provide adequate incentives to protect the interests of future generations; by land property-right systems that make the amount of land acquired by squatters a multiple of cleared forestland; and by tax systems that discriminate against standing forests.

Substantial strides toward restoring efficiency as well as sustainability can be achieved simply by recognizing and correcting the perverse incentives. Some corrective actions can be and should be taken by the tropical forest nations themselves as they are in their own interests. But these domestic actions will not, by themselves, provide adequate protection for the global interests in the tropical forests. Schemes designed to internalize some of these benefits—debt-nature swaps, extractive reserves, and royalty payments—have already begun to be implemented.

Key Concepts

biological decision rule, *p.* 256

debt and deforestation, *p.* 261

debt-nature swap, *p.* 266

discount rates (and harvest age), *p.* 257

economic rent, *p.* 259

endowments, *p.* 269

extractive reserves, *p.* xx

forest certification, *p.* 264

mean annual increment (MAI), *p.* 256

multiple use philosophy, *p.* 264

planting cost (effect of on harvest age), *p.* 257

profit maximization, *p.* 257

royalty payment, *p.* 267

sources of inefficiency, *p.* 257

    perverse incentives (of landowners), *p.* 257

    perverse incentives (of nations), *p.* 260

stumpage value, *p.* 259

sustainable forestry, *p.* 262

trust funds, *p.* 269

World Heritage Convention, *p.* 266

Further Reading

Bowes, Michael D. and John V. Krutilla. "Multiple Use Management of Public Forestlands," *Handbook of Natural Resource and Energy Economics,* Vol. II, Kneese, Allen V. and James L. Sweeney, eds. (Amsterdam: North-Holland, 1985). Excellent analytical treatment of the multiple-use strategy as it applies to U.S. forest policy. Somewhat mathematical.

Deacon, R. T. "The Simple Analytics of Forest Economics," *Forestlands: Public and Private,* Deacon, R. T. and M. B. Johnson, eds. (San Francisco: Pacific Institute for Public Policy Research, 1985). An especially accessible treatment of forestry economics.

Gregory, G. Robinson. *Resource Economics for Foresters* (New York: Wiley, 1987). An undergraduate text in forest economics that could be used to go beyond the material in this chapter.

Pagiola, Stefano, Joshua Bishop, and Natasha Landell-Mills. *Selling Forest Environmental Services: Market-Based Mechanisms for Conservation and Development* (London: Earthscan Publications, 2002). Market-based approaches are thought to offer considerable promise as a means to promote forest conservation and as a new source of income for rural communities. Based on extensive research and case studies, this book demonstrates the feasibility and effectiveness of payment systems and their implications for the poor.

Price, Colin. *The Theory and Application of Forest Economics* (Oxford: Basil Blackwell, 1989). A text aimed at "students of forestry and of natural resource management at both undergraduate and graduate levels."

Van Kooten, C., R. A. Sedjo, et al. "Tropical Deforestation: Issues and Policies," *The International Yearbook of Environmental and Resource Economics 1999/2000.* T. Tietenberg and H. Folmer, eds. (Cheltenham, UK: Edward Elgar, 1999): 198–249. A review of the economic research on tropical deforestation.

Wibe, Sören and Tom Jones, eds. *Forests: Market and Intervention Failures* (London: Earthscan Publications, 1992). Case studies of forest policy in the United Kingdom, Sweden, Italy, Germany, and Spain.

Additional References

Berck, P. "Optimal Management of Renewable Resources with Growing Demand and Stock Externalities," *Journal of Environmental Economics and Management* 8 (1981): 105–117.

Binswanger, Hans P. "Brazilian Policies that Encourage Deforestation in the Amazon," Working Paper No. 16 (Washington, DC: World Bank, 1989).

Caviglia-Harris, Jill. L. "Household Production and Forest Clearing: The Role of Farming in the Development of the Amazon," *Environment and Development Economics* 9 (2004): 181–202.

Chomitz, K. M. and T. S. Thomas. "Determinants of Land Use in Amazonia: A Fine-Scale Spatial Analysis," *American Journal of Agricultural Economics* 85 (2003) (4): 1016–1028.

Clawson, Marion. "Decision Making in Timber Production, Harvest, and Marketing," Research Paper R-4 (Washington, DC: Resources for the Future, 1977), Table 1, p. 13.

Deininger, K. and B. Minten. "Determinants of Deforestation and the Economics of Protection: An Application to Mexico," *American Journal of Agricultural Economics* 84 (2002) (4): 943–960.

Johansson, Per-Olov. *Economics of Forestry and Natural Resources* (New York: Basil Blackwell, 1985).

Laird, S. A. and K. ten Kate. "Linking Biodiversity Prospecting and Forest Conservation," *Selling Forest Services: Market-based Mechanisms for Conservation and Development,* Pagiola, S., J. Bishop, and N. Landell-Mills, eds. (London: Earthscan Publications Limited 2002).

Mahar, Dennis J. *Government Policies and Deforestation on Brazil's Amazon Region* (Washington, DC: World Bank, 1989).

Merrifield, David E. and Richard W. Hayes. "The Adjustment of Product and Factor Markets: An Application to the Pacific Northwest Forest Products Industry," *American Journal of Agricultural Economics* 66 (February 1984): 79–87.

Myers, Norman. *The Primary Source: Tropical Forests and Our Future* (New York: W. W. Norton, 1984): 50.

Neumayer, E. "Does High Indebtedness Increase Natural Resource Exploitation?" *Environment and Development Economics* 10 (2005) (Part 2): 127–142.

OECD. *OECD Environmental Data: Compendium 1997* (Paris: Organization for European Co-operation and Development, 1997): 111.

Repetto, Robert. *The Forest for the Trees? Government Policies and the Misuse of Forest Resources* (Washington, DC: World Resources Institute, 1988).

Repetto, R. and M. Gillis, eds. *Public Policy and the Misuse of Forest Resources* (Cambridge, UK: Cambridge University Press, 1988).

Sedjo, R. A. and S. K. Swallow. "Voluntary Eco-Labeling and the Price Premium," *Land Economics* 78 (2002) (2): 272–284.

Vincent, Jeffrey R. "Rent Capture and the Feasibility of Tropical Forest Management," *Land Economics* 66 (May 1990) (2): 212–223.

Discussion Questions

1. Should the U.S. national forests become "privatized" (i.e., sold to private owners)? Why or why not?

2. In his book *The Federal Lands Revisited*, Marion Clawson proposed what he called the "pullback concept":

Under the pullback concept any person or group could apply, under applicable law, for a tract of federal land, for any use they chose; but any other person or group would have a limited time between the filing of the initial application and granting of the lease or the making of the sale in which to "pull back" a part of the area applied for. ... The user of the pullback provision would become the applicant for the area pulled back, required to meet the same terms applicable to the original application, ... but the use could be what the applicant chose, not necessarily the use proposed by the original applicant [p. 216].

Evaluate the pullback concept as a means for conservationists to prevent some mineral extraction or timber harvesting on federal lands.

Common-Pool Resources: Fisheries and Other Commercially Valuable Species

In an overpopulated (or overexploited) world, a system of the commons leads to ruin ... Even if an individual fully perceives the ultimate consequences of his actions he is most unlikely to act in any other way, for he cannot count on the restraint his conscience might dictate being matched by a similar restraint on the part of all others.

—GARRETT HARDIN, *Carrying Capacity As an Ethical Concept* (1967)

● Introduction

Humans share the planet with many other living species. How those biological resources are treated depends on whether they are commercially valuable and the incentives of those who are best positioned to protect those species.

As discussed in Chapter 12, a major threat to wildlife is the destruction of its habitat. It follows that one important means of protecting wildlife is to protect the habitat in which it lives. In previous chapters we have seen how agricultural subsidies can cause excessive conversion of productive habitat to agriculture and how perverse incentives cause the destruction of forested ecosystems. Changing these perverse incentives can serve as a means of protecting wildlife habitat.

Protecting habitat is not enough, however, when the species becomes commercially valuable. A commercially valuable species is like a double-edged sword. On the one hand, the value of the species to humans provides a reason for human concern about its future. On the other hand, the level of exploitation may be excessive—even leading to extinction if the population is drawn down beyond a critical threshold.

Extinction, though important, is not the only critical renewable-resource-management issue. If it were, public policy could concentrate exclusively on avoiding extinction, a luxury actual fisheries managers can ill-afford.

Biological populations belong to a class of renewable resources we will call *interactive resources*, wherein the size of the resource stock (population) is determined jointly by biological considerations and by actions taken by society. The size of the population, in turn, determines the availability of resources for the future. Thus, humanity's actions determine the flow of these resources over time. Because this flow is not purely a natural phenomenon, a second crucial dimension is the optimum rate of use across time and across generations. What is the efficient rate of use of interactive renewable resources? In the absence of outside influences, can the market be relied upon to achieve and sustain this rate?

Using the fishery as a case study, we begin by defining what is meant by the *efficient level of harvest* from a fishery; next, we examine how well our economic and political institutions meet the efficiency test. We then consider how economic incentive systems can be used to assure sustainable harvests. Finally, we examine how another type of commercial opportunity, that associated with ecotourism, can be used to protect certain specific types of wildlife.

Efficient Harvests

The Biological Dimension

Like many other studies, our characterization of the fishery rests on a biological model originally proposed by Schaefer (1957). The Schaefer model posits a particular average relationship between the growth of the fish population and the size of the fish population. This is an average relationship in the sense that it abstracts from such influences as water temperature and the age structure of the population. The model, therefore, does not attempt to characterize the fishery on a day-to-day basis, but rather in terms of some long-term average in which these various random influences tend to counterbalance each other (see Figure 13.1).

The size of the population is represented on the horizontal axis and the growth of the population on the vertical axis. The graph suggests that there is a range of population sizes ($\underline{S}$ to S^*) where population growth increases as the population increases and a range (S^* to $\overline{S}$) where initial increases in population lead to eventual declines in growth.

We can shed further light on this relationship by examining more closely the two points $\underline{S}$ and $\overline{S}$ where the function intersects the horizontal axis and, therefore, growth in the stock is zero. $\overline{S}$ is known as the *natural equilibrium* because it is the population size that would persist in the absence of outside influences. Reductions in the stock because of mortality or out-migration would be exactly offset by increases in the stock because of births, growth of the fish in the remaining stock, and in-migration.

This natural equilibrium would persist because it is stable. A *stable equilibrium* is one in which movements away from this population level set forces in motion to restore it. If, for example, the stock temporarily exceeded $\overline{S}$, it would be exceeding the capacity of its habitat (called the *carrying capacity*). As a result, mortality rates or out-migration would increase until the stock was once again within the confines of the carrying capacity of its habitat at $\overline{S}$.

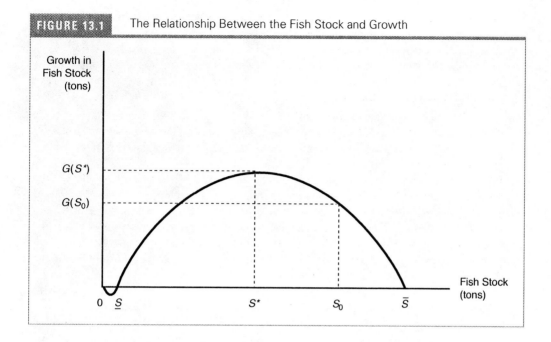

FIGURE 13.1 The Relationship Between the Fish Stock and Growth

This tendency for the population size to return to $\overline{S}$ works in the other direction as well. Suppose the population is temporarily reduced below $\overline{S}$. Because the stock is now smaller, growth would be positive and the size of the stock would increase. Over time, the fishery population would move along the curve to the right until $\overline{S}$ were reached again.

What about the other points on the curve? $\underline{S}$, known as the *minimum viable population*, represents the level of population below which growth in population is negative (i.e., deaths and out-migration exceed births and in-migration). In contrast to $\overline{S}$, this equilibrium is unstable. Population sizes to the right of $\underline{S}$ lead to positive growth and a movement along the curve to $\overline{S}$ and away from $\underline{S}$. When the population moves to the left of $\underline{S}$, the population declines until it eventually becomes extinct. In this region no forces act to return the population to a viable level.

A catch level is said to represent a *sustainable yield* whenever it equals the growth rate of the population, because it can then be maintained forever. As long as the population size remains constant, the growth rate (and, hence, the catch) will remain constant as well.

S^* is what is known in biology as the *maximum sustainable yield* population, defined as the population size that yields the maximum growth; hence, the maximum sustainable yield is equal to this maximum growth, and it represents the largest catch that can be perpetually sustained. If the catch is equal to the growth, the sustainable yield for any population size between $\underline{S}$ and $\overline{S}$ can be determined by drawing a vertical line from the stock size of interest on the horizontal axis to the point where it intersects the function and then drawing a horizontal line over to the vertical axis. The sustainable yield is the growth in the biomass defined by the intersection of this line with the vertical axis. Thus, in terms of Figure 13.1, $G(S_0)$ is the sustainable yield for population size S_0. Because the catch is equal to the growth, population size (and next year's growth) remains the same.

It should now be clear why $G(S^*)$ is the maximum sustainable yield. Larger catches would be possible in the short run, but these could not be sustained; they would lead to reduced population sizes and, eventually, if the population were drawn down to a level smaller than $\underline{S}$, to the extinction of the species.

Efficient Sustained Yield

Is the concept of maximum sustainable yield synonymous with that of efficiency? The answer is no. Efficiency, it may be remembered, is associated with maximizing the net benefit from the use of the resource. If we are to define the efficient allocation, we must include the costs of harvesting, as well as the benefits.

Let's begin by defining the *efficient sustainable yield*. The efficient sustainable yield is the catch level that, if maintained perpetually, would produce the largest annual net benefit. We will condition our analysis on three assumptions that simplify the analysis without sacrificing too much realism: (1) the price of fish is constant and does not depend on the amount sold; (2) the marginal cost of a unit of fishing effort is constant; and (3) the amount of fish caught per unit of effort expended is proportional to the size of fish population (i.e., the smaller the population, the fewer fish caught per unit of effort).

In any sustainable yield, catches, population, effort levels, and net benefits remain constant over time. The *efficient sustainable yield* allocation maximizes the constant net benefit.

In Figure 13.2 the benefits (revenues) and costs are portrayed as a function of fishing effort and can be measured in vessel-years, hours of fishing, or some other convenient metric. The shape of the revenue function is dictated by the shape of the function in Figure 13.1, because the price of fish is assumed to be constant. To avoid confusion, notice that increasing fishing effort in Figure 13.1 would result in smaller population sizes and would be recorded as a movement from right to left. Because the variable on the horizontal axis in Figure 13.2 is effort, not population, an increase in fishing effort is recorded as a movement from left to right.

As sustained levels of effort are increased, eventually a point is reached (E^m) where further effort reduces the sustainable catch and revenue for all years. That point, of course, corresponds to the maximum sustainable yield in Figure 13.2, which involves identical population and growth levels. Every effort level portrayed in Figure 13.2 corresponds to a population level in Figure 13.1.

The net benefit is presented in Figure 13.2 as the difference (vertical distance) between benefits (prices times the quantity caught) and costs (the constant marginal cost of effort times the units of effort expended). The efficient level of effort is E^e, the point in the diagram where the vertical distance between benefits and costs is maximized.

E^e is the efficient level of effort, because it is where marginal benefit (that graphically is the slope of the total-benefit curve) is equal to marginal cost (the *constant* slope of the total-cost curve). Levels of effort higher than E^e are inefficient, because the additional cost associated with them exceeds the value of the fish obtained. Can you see why lower levels of effort are inefficient?

Now we are armed with sufficient information to determine whether or not the maximum sustainable yield is efficient. The answer is clearly no. The maximum sustainable yield is efficient only if the marginal cost of additional effort is zero. Can you see why? (*Hint*: What is the marginal benefit at the maximum sustainable yield?) Because this is not the case, the efficient level of effort is *less* than that necessary to harvest the maximum sustainable yield. Thus, the static efficient level of effort leads to a *larger* fish population than does the maximum sustainable yield level of effort.

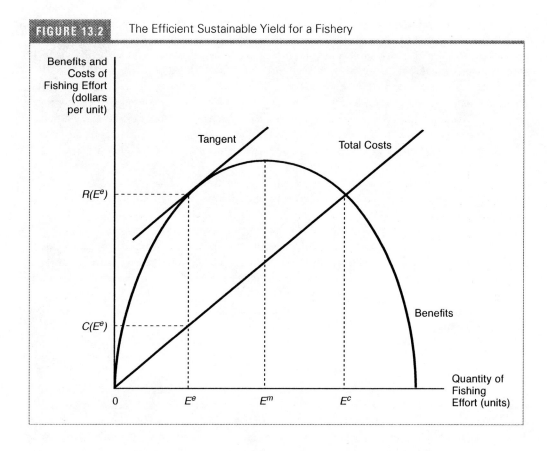

FIGURE 13.2   The Efficient Sustainable Yield for a Fishery

To fix these concepts firmly in mind, consider what would happen to the static efficient sustainable yield if a technological change (e.g., the use of sonar detection) were to occur, lowering the marginal cost of fishing. The lower marginal cost would result in a rotation of the total-cost curve to the right. With this new structure, the old level of effort is no longer efficient. The marginal cost of fishing (slope of the total-cost curve) is now lower than the marginal benefit (slope of the total-benefit curve). Because the marginal cost is constant, the equality of marginal cost and marginal benefit can only result from a decline in marginal benefits. This implies an increase in effort. The new efficient sustainable yield equilibrium implies more effort, a lower population level, a larger catch, and a higher net benefit for the fishery.

Appropriability and Market Solutions

We have now defined an efficient allocation of the fishery. The next step is to characterize the normal market allocation and to contrast these two allocations. Where they differ, we can entertain the possibility of various public-policy corrective means.

Let's first consider the allocation resulting from a fishery managed by a competitive individual or sole owner. A sole owner would have a well-defined property right to the fish.

A sole owner would want to maximize his or her profits. Ignoring discounting for the moment, the owner can increase profits by increasing fishing effort until marginal revenue equals marginal cost. Clearly, this is effort level E^e, the efficient sustainable yield. This will yield positive profits equal to the difference between $R(E^e)$ and $C(E^e)$ in Figure 13.2.

In ocean fisheries, however, sole owners are not normal. Ocean fisheries are typically open-access resources—no one exercises control over them. Because the property rights to the fishery are not conveyed to any single owner, no single fisherman can keep others from exploiting the fishery.

What problems arise when access to the fishery is completely unrestricted? Open-access resources create two kinds of external costs: (1) a *contemporaneous external cost* and (2) an *intergenerational external cost*. The contemporaneous external cost, which is borne by the current generation, involves the overcommitment of resources to fishing—too many boats, too many fishermen, too much effort. As a result, current fishermen earn a substantially lower rate of return on their efforts. The intergenerational external cost, borne by the future generations, occurs because overfishing reduces the stock, which in turn lowers future profits from fishing.[1]

Once too many fishermen have unlimited access to the same common-pool fishery, the property rights to the fish are no longer efficient. Since each boat would receive a profit equal to its share of the scarcity rent, this rent serves as a stimulus for new fishermen to enter, drawing up costs and ultimately eliminating the rent. Hence, open access results in overexploitation.

In contrast a sole owner chooses not to expend more effort than E^e, because to do so would reduce the profits of the fishery, resulting in a personal loss. In this case societal losses and personal losses coincide. When access to the fishery is unrestricted, a decision to expend effort beyond E^e reduces profits to the fishery as a whole—but not to that individual fisherman. Most of the decline in profits falls on the other fishermen.

At what point does the individual fisherman in an open-access fishery have an incentive to stop further harvests? The individual fisherman has an incentive to expend further effort, until all fishery scarcity rent has been exhausted. In Figure 13.2 that point is at effort level E^c, where net benefits are zero. It is now easy to see the contemporaneous external cost—too much effort is being expended to catch too few fish, and the cost is substantially higher than it would be in an efficient allocation.

If this point seems abstract, it shouldn't. Many fisheries are currently plagued by precisely these problems. In a productive fishery in the Bering Sea and Aleutian Islands, for example, one study by Huppert (1990) found significant overcapitalization. Although the efficient number of "motherships" (used to take on and process the catch at sea so that the catch boats do not have to return to port as often) was estimated to be 9, the actual level was 140. As a result, a significant amount of net benefits ($124 million a year) were lost. Had the fishery been harvested more slowly, the same catch could have been achieved with fewer boats used closer to their capacity.

An intergenerational externality occurs because the size of the population is reduced, causing future profits to be lower than would otherwise be the case. As the existing population is overexploited, the open-access catch initially is higher, but as population growth rates are affected, the steady-state profit level, once attained, becomes lower.

---

[1]This will result in fewer fish for future generations as well as smaller profits if the resulting effort level exceeds that associated with the maximum sustainable yield. If the open-access common-property effort level is lower than the maximum-sustainable-yield effort level (when extraction costs are very high), then reductions in stock would increase the growth in this stock, thus supplying more fish (albeit lower net benefits) to future generations.

When the resource owner has exclusive property rights, the use value of the resource is balanced against the asset value. When access to the resource is unrestricted, exclusivity is lost. As a result, it is rational for the individual fisherman to ignore the asset value, because he or she can never appropriate it, and simply maximize the use value. In the process, all the scarcity rent is dissipated.

Open-access resources do not automatically lead to a stock lower than that maximizing the sustained yield. We can draw a cost function with a slope sufficiently steep that it intersects the benefit curve at a point to the left of E^m. Nonetheless, mature open-access common-pool fisheries are commonly exploited well beyond the point of maximum sustainable yield.

Open-access fishing may or may not pose the threat of species extinction. It depends on the nature of the species and the benefits and costs of harvesting below the minimum viable population. Because the threat of extinction can only be determined in the context of empirical studies, it must be determined on a case-by-case basis (see Example 13.1).

Open-Access Harvesting of the Minke Whale

EXAMPLE
13.1

Amundsen, Bjørndal, and Conrad examined the effects of open-access fishing on the minke whale using an economic model that is very similar to the model developed in this chapter. Their model was designed to capture harvesting behavior, stock dynamics, and the response of the size of the fishing fleet relative to profitability. Their model was able to simulate both efficient and open-access equilibria.

Although the minke whale is found in the northern and southern hemispheres, this study examined the North Atlantic stock that can be found in the areas around Spitsbergen (Norway), in the Barents Sea, along the Norwegian coast, and in the area around the British Isles.

The study results suggest that the efficient stock size is in the range of 52,000 to 82,000 adult males, whereas the open-access stock level is in the 10,000–41,000 range. According to these results, open-access does cause substantial depletion of the stock, but it does not cause extinction. The benefits of further harvesting are lower than the costs.

Because the minke whale hunt was unregulated until 1973 (and was only loosely regulated for a while after that), it is possible for results from this simulation to be compared to the pre-regulation (open-access) historical experience with the fishery. In fact, the results of the model seem to conform rather well to that experience. Although it experienced a substantial increase after World War II, the harvest declined to a relatively stable level of 1,700 to 1,800 whales by 1973 and continued at approximately that level for some time, until effective regulation ultimately restricted fishing effort.

The regulation apparently worked. The Scientific Committee of the North Atlantic Marine Mammal Commission (NAMMCO) estimates the current stock of minke whales at 72,130, which is at the high end of the efficient stock size. Amidst intense international controversy, Japan targeted 935 Minke whales in its 2007–2008 annual hunt in Antarctic waters.

Source: Amundsen, E. S., T. Bjørndal, and J. M. Conrad, "Open Access Harvesting of the Northeast Atlantic Minke Whale," *Environmental and Resource Economics* 6(2), September 1995: 167–185.

Are open-access resources and common-property resources synonymous concepts? They are not. On the one hand, governments can restrict entry, a topic we will address in the next section. On the other hand, informal arrangements among those harvesting the common-property resource can also serve to limit access[2] (see Example 13.2).

Open access resources generally violate both the efficiency and sustainability criteria. If these criteria are to be fulfilled, some restructuring of the decision-making environment is necessary. How that could be done is the subject of the next section.

EXAMPLE 13.2

Historical Example: Harbor Gangs of Maine

Unlimited access to common-pool resources reduces net benefits drastically, and this loss encourages those harvesting the resource to restrict access, if possible. The Maine fishery is one setting where informal arrangements have served to limit access.

Key among these arrangements is a system of territories that rely on informally established boundaries between fishing areas. These territories, particularly those near the offshore islands, tend to be exclusively harvested by close-knit, disciplined "gangs." Some gangs restrict access to their territory by various covert means, such as cutting the lines to lobster traps owned by new entrants, rendering them unretrievable. The income and catch levels achieved by the members of these gangs exceed those for comparable gangs lobstering less exclusive territories. Wilson (1977), for example, found that fishermen in the most restricted areas had 39 percent higher incomes and a 69 percent higher catch per trap haul.

Although it would be a mistake to assume that all common-property resources are characterized by open access, it would also be a mistake to assume that these informal arrangements automatically provide sufficient social means for producing efficient harvests, thereby eliminating any need for public policy. The Maine lobster stock is also protected by regulations limiting the size of lobsters that can be taken and prohibiting the harvest of bearing females. Because estimates suggest that over 95 percent of legally harvestable lobsters are harvested, these regulations apparently afford significant protection to the stock. The main role of the informal arrangements has been to prevent the overcapitalization problem. When fewer fishermen harvest the available yield, income levels for those fishermen are higher.

Sources: Acheson, James M., *The Lobster Gangs of Maine* (Hanover, NH: University Press of New England, 1988); and Wilson, J. A., "A Test of the Tragedy of the Commons," *Managing the Commons*, Hardin, G. and J. Braden, eds. (San Francisco: Freeman, 1977): 96–111.

---

[2]For other examples of these arrangements, see Berkes, Feeny, and Acheson (1989).

Public Policy Toward Fisheries

What can be done? A variety of public policy responses are possible. Perhaps it is appropriate to start with the approach of simply allowing the market to work.

Aquaculture

Having demonstrated that inefficient management of a fishery results from treating it as open-access, rather than exclusive, property, we have one obvious solution—allowing some fisheries to be privately, rather than commonly, held. This approach can work when the fish are not very mobile (e.g., as lobsters), when they can be confined by artificial barriers, or when they instinctively return to their place of birth to spawn.

The advantages of such a move go well beyond the ability to preclude overfishing. The owners are encouraged to invest in the resource and undertake measures that will increase the productivity (yield) of the fishery.[3] This movement toward controlled raising and harvesting of fish is called *aquaculture*. Probably the highest yields ever attained through aquaculture resulted from using rafts to raise mussels. Some 300,000 kg/hectare (ha) of mussels, for example, have been raised in this manner in the Galician bays of Spain.[4] This productivity level approximates those achieved in poultry farming, widely regarded as one of the most successful attempts to increase the productivity of farm-produced animal protein.

Japan became an early leader in aquaculture, undertaking some of the most advanced aquaculture ventures in the world. The government has been supportive of these efforts, mainly by creating private-property rights for waters formerly held commonly. Prefectures, which are comparable to states in the United States, initiate the process by designating the areas to be used for aquaculture. The local fishermen's cooperative associations then partition these areas and allocate the subareas to individual fishermen for exclusive use. This exclusive control allows the individual owner to invest in the resource and to manage it effectively and efficiently.

Another market approach to aquaculture involves *fish ranching* rather than *fish farming*. Whereas fish farming involves cultivating fish over their lifetime in a controlled environment, fish ranching involves holding them in captivity only for the first few years of their lives. Fish ranching relies on the strong homing instincts in certain fish, such as Pacific salmon or ocean trout, which permits their ultimate capture. The young salmon or ocean trout are hatched and confined in a convenient catch area for approximately two years. When released, they migrate to the ocean. Upon reaching maturity, they return by instinct to the place of their births, where they are harvested.

Fish farming and fish ranching have certainly made an impact on the total supply of harvested fish. Aquaculture is currently the fastest growing animal food production sector with an average annual growth rate of 8.8 percent worldwide since the 1970s. In 1970 it was estimated that 3.9 percent of fish consumed globally were raised on farms. By 2006 this proportion had

---

[3]For example, adding certain nutrients to the water or controlling the temperature can markedly increase the yields of some species.

[4]A *hectare* is a measure of surface area equal to 10,000 square meters, or 2.471 acres.

risen to 36 percent! Currently, more than one-third of the world's total fish supply comes from aquaculture (see Figure 13.3). In China growth rates in aquaculture have been even higher and aquaculture represents more than two-thirds of fisheries production (see Figure 13.4). While the top five producers (in volume) of fish from aquaculture in 2006 were China, India, Vietnam, Thailand, and Indonesia, growth rates in aquaculture production were highest in Uganda, Guatamal, Mozambique, Malawi, and Togo.[5]

Aquaculture is certainly not the answer for all fish. Today it works well for certain species, but other species will probably never be harvested domestically. Furthermore, fish farming can create environmental problems, ranging from the pollution caused by the fish wastes, to the destruction of ecologically valuable sites as fish farms are developed. Debate 13.1 explores these issues. Nonetheless, it is comforting to know that aquaculture can provide a safety valve in some regions and for some fish and in the process take some of the pressure off the overstressed natural fisheries.

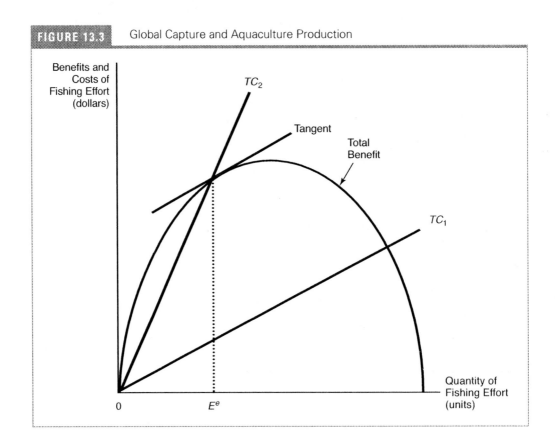

FIGURE 13.3   Global Capture and Aquaculture Production

---

[5]Food and Agriculture Organization of the United Nations. *State of the World's Fisheries and Aquaculture* (2008) ftp://ftp.fao.org/docrep/fao/011/i0250e/i0250e.pdf.

FIGURE 13.4 Chinese Capture and Aquaculture Production

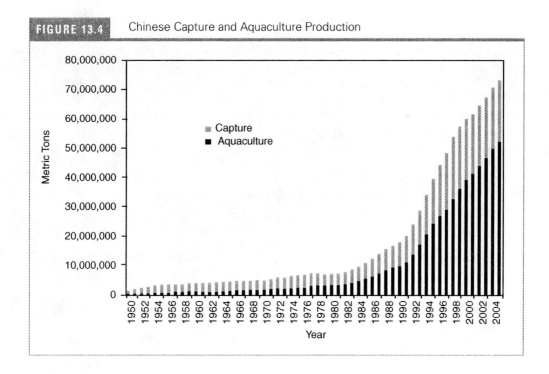

DEBATE 13.1

Aquaculture: Does Privatization Cause More Problems Than It Solves?

Privatization of commercial fisheries, namely through fish-farming, has been touted as a solution to the overfishing problem. For certain species, it has been a great success. For example, shellfish are easily managed and farmed through commercial aquaculture. For other species, however, the answer is not so clear cut.

Atlantic salmon is a struggling species in the northeastern United States and is listed as endangered in several rivers. Salmon farming takes the pressure off of the wild stocks. Atlantic salmon are intensively farmed off the coast of Maine, in northeastern Canada, in Norway, and in Chile. While farmed salmon offer a good alternative to wild salmon and aquaculture has helped meet the demand for salmon from consumers, it is not problem free. Escapees from the pens threaten native species, pollution that leaks from the pens creates a large externality, and pens that are visible from the coastline degrade the view for coastal residents. The crowded pens also facilitate the prevalence and diffusion of several diseases and illnesses such as sea lice and salmon anemia. Antibiotics used to keep the fish healthy are considered dangerous for humans. Diseases in the pens can also be transferred to wild stocks. In 2007 the Atlantic Salmon Federation and 33 other conservation groups called on salmon farms to move their pens farther away from sensitive wild stocks.

Aquaculture can also provide a sustainable food source in developing countries. With a rapidly growing aquaculture industry, China has become the largest producer of seafood in the world (see Figure 13.5). China produces 70 percent of the global supply of farmed fish. Shrimp, eel, and tilapia are all intensively farmed. In 2005 China exported $8.95 billion in seafood, making it the largest exporter of seafood.

However, along with the increased production, pollution externalities include contaminated water supplies for the fish ponds and heavily polluted wastewater. Farmers raising their fish in contaminated water have managed by adding illegal veterinary drugs and pesticides to the fish feed, creating food safety concerns. Tested fish flesh has contained heavy metals, mercury, and flame retardants. In 2007 the United States refused 310 import shipments of seafood, 210 of those were drug-chemical refusals. Consequently, eel shipments to Japan have declined 50 percent.

While solving some problems, intensive aquaculture has created others. Potential solutions include open ocean aquaculture—moving pens out to sea, closing pens, monitoring water quality, and improving enforcement. Clearly, well-defined property rights to the fishery aren't the only solution when externalities are prevalent.

FIGURE 13.5 China's Rising Share of Global Aquaculture

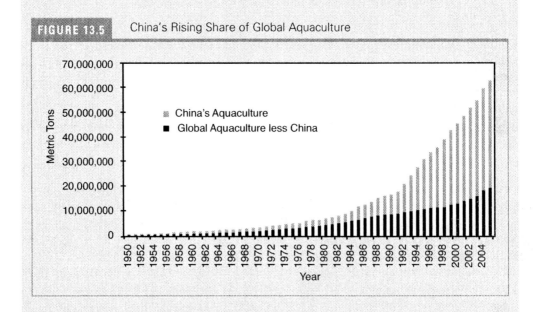

Sources: Atlantic Salmon Federation, Fishstat FAO 2007, and David Barboza. "China's Seafood Industry: Dirty Water, Dangerous Fish," *The New York Times*, December 15, 2007.

Raising the Real Cost of Fishing

Perhaps one of the best ways to illustrate the virtues of using economic analysis to help design policies is to show the harsh effects of policy approaches that ignore it. Because the earliest approaches to fishery management had a single-minded focus on attaining the maximum sustainable yield with little or no thought given to maximizing the net benefit, they provide a useful contrast.

Perhaps the best concrete example is the set of policies originally designed to deal with over-exploitation of the Pacific salmon fishery in the United States. The Pacific salmon is particularly vulnerable to overexploitation, and even extinction, because of its migration patterns. Pacific salmon are spawned in the gravel beds of rivers. As juvenile fish they migrate to the ocean, only to return as adults to spawn in the rivers of their birth. After spawning, they die. When the adults swim upstream with an instinctual need to return to their native streams, they can easily be captured by traps, nets, or other catching devices.

Recognizing the urgency of the problem, the U.S. government took action. To reduce the catch, it raised the cost of fishing. Initially, this was accomplished by preventing the use of any barricades on the rivers and by prohibiting the use of traps (the most efficient catching devices) in the most productive areas. These measures proved insufficient, because mobile techniques (e.g., trolling and nets) proved quite capable, by themselves, of overexploiting the resource. Officials then began to close designated fishing areas and suspend fishing in other areas for certain periods of time. In Figure 13.3 these measures would be reflected as a rotation of the cost curve to the left until it intersected the benefits curve at a level of effort equal to E^e. The aggregate of all these regulations had the desired effect of curtailing the yield of salmon.

Were these policies efficient? They were not and would not have been even if they had resulted in the efficient catch! This statement may seem inconsistent, but it is not. Efficiency implies both that the catch must be at the efficient level and that it must also be extracted at the lowest possible cost. This latter condition was violated by these policies (see Figure 13.3).

Figure 13.3 shows the total cost in an efficient allocation (TC_1) and the total cost after these policies were imposed (TC_2). The net benefit received from an efficient policy is shown graphically as the vertical distance between total cost and total benefit. After the policy, however, the net benefit was reduced to zero; the net benefit (represented by vertical distance) was lost to society. Why?

The net benefit was wasted because of the use of excessively expensive means to catch the desired yield of fish. Traps would reduce the cost of catching the desired number of fish, but traps were prohibited, so that larger expenditures on capital and labor were required to catch the same number of fish. This additional capital and labor represents one source of the waste.

The limitations on fishing times had a similar effect on cost. Rather than allowing fishermen to spread their effort out over time so that the boats and equipment could be more productively utilized, fishermen were forced to buy larger boats that would allow them to take as much fish as possible during the shorter seasons.[6] Significant overcapitalization resulted.

Regulation imposed other costs as well. It was soon discovered that, although the preceding regulations were adequate to protect the depletion of the fish population, they had no effect on the

---

[6]In one extreme example, the 1982 herring season in Prince William Sound lasted only four hours, and the catch still exceeded the area quota. This case is described in Tillions (1985).

incentive for individual fishermen to increase their share of the take. Even though the profits would be small because of high costs, new technological changes would allow those who adopted them to increase their share of the market and put others out of business. To protect themselves, the fishermen were successful in introducing bans on new technology. These restrictions took various forms, but two are particularly noteworthy. The first was the banning of the use of thin-stranded monofilament net. The coarse-stranded net it would have replaced was visible to the salmon in the daytime and therefore could be avoided by them. As a result, it was useful only at night. By contrast, the thinner monofilament nets could be successfully used even during the daylight hours. The monofilament nets were banned in both Canada and the United States soon after they appeared.

The most flagrantly inefficient regulation was one in Alaska that barred gill-netters in Bristol Bay from using engines to propel their boats. This regulation lasted until the 1950s and heightened the public's awareness of the anachronistic nature of this regulatory approach. The world's most technologically advanced nation was reaping its harvest from the Bering Sea in sailboats while the rest of the world—particularly Japan and the Soviet Union—was swiftly modernizing its fishing fleets!

Time-restriction regulations had a similar effect. Limiting fishing time provides an incentive to use that time as intensively as possible. Huge boats facilitate large harvests within the period and therefore are attractive, but they are very inefficient: The same harvest could have been achieved with fewer, smaller boats used to their optimum capacity.

Guided by a narrow focus on the maximum sustainable yield that ignored costs, these policies led to a substantial loss in the net benefit received from the fishery. Costs are an important dimension of the problem; when they are ignored, the incomes of fishermen suffer. When incomes suffer, further conservation measures become more difficult to implement, and incentives to violate the regulations are intensified.

Technical change presents a further problem with attempts to use cost-increasing regulations to reduce fishing effort. Technical innovations can lower the cost of fishing, thereby offsetting the increases imposed by the regulations. In the New England fishery, for example, Jin et al. (2002) report that the introduction of new technologies such as fishfinders and electronic navigation aids in the 1970s and 1980s led to higher catches and declines in the abundance of the stock despite the extensive controls in place at the time.

Taxes

Is it possible to provide incentives for cost reduction while assuring that the yield is reduced to the efficient level? Can a more efficient policy be devised? Economists who have studied the question believe that more efficient policies are possible.

Consider a tax on effort. In Figure 13.3 taxes on effort would be represented as a rotation of the TC line, and the after-tax cost to the fishermen would be adequately represented by line TC_2. Because the after-tax curve coincides with TC_2, the cost curve for all those inefficient regulations, doesn't this imply that the tax system is just as inefficient? No! The key to understanding the difference is the distinction between *transfer costs* and *real-resource costs*.

Under a regulation system of the type described earlier in this chapter, all of the costs included in TC_2 are real-resource costs, which involve utilization of resources. Transfer costs, by contrast, involve transfers of resources (from one part of society to another) rather than their use. Transfer costs apply to that part of society bearing them but are exactly offset by the gain received by the recipients. Resources are not used up; they are merely transferred. Thus, the calculation of the size of the net benefit should subtract real-resource costs, but not transfer costs, from benefits. For society as a whole, transfer costs are retained as part of the net benefit.

In Figure 13.3 the net benefit under a tax system is identical to that under an efficient allocation. The net benefit represents a transfer cost to the fisherman that is exactly offset by the revenues, received by the tax collector. This discussion should not obscure the fact that, as far as the individual fisherman is concerned, these are very real costs. Rent normally received by a sole owner is now received by the government. Because the tax revenues involved can be substantial, fishermen wishing to have the fishery efficiently managed may object to this particular way of doing it. They would prefer a policy that restricts catches while allowing them to keep the rents. Is that possible?

Individual Transferable Quotas (ITQs)

One policy making it possible to obtain an efficient allocation is a properly designed quota on the number or volume of fish that can be taken from the fishery. These are also called "catch-shares." The "properly designed" caveat is important because there are many different types of quota schemes, and not all are of equal merit. An efficient quota system has three identifiable characteristics:

1. The quotas entitle the holder to catch a specified share of the total authorized catch of a specified type of fish.
2. The total catch authorized by the quotas held by all fishermen should be equal to the efficient catch for the fishery.
3. The quotas should be freely transferable among fishermen and quota markets should send appropriate price signals about the value of the fishery.

Each of these three characteristics plays an important role in obtaining an efficient allocation. Let's suppose, for example, the quota were defined in terms of the right to own and use a fishing boat rather than in terms of catch—not an uncommon type of quota. Such a quota is not efficient, because an inefficient incentive still remains for each boat owner to build larger boats, to place extra equipment on them, and to spend more time fishing. These actions would expand the capacity of each boat and cause the actual catch to exceed the target (efficient) catch. In a nutshell, the boat quota limits the number of boats fishing but does not limit the amount of fish caught by each boat. If we are to reach and sustain an efficient allocation, it is the catch that ultimately must be limited.

Although the purpose of the second condition is obvious, the role of the third, transferability, deserves more consideration. With transferability, the entitlement to fish flows naturally to those gaining the most benefit from it because their costs are lower. Because it is valuable, the transferable quota commands a positive price. Those who have quotas but also have high costs find they make more money by selling the quotas than by using them. Meanwhile, those who have lower costs find they can purchase more quotas and still make money.

Transferable quotas also encourage technological progress. Adopters of new cost-reducing technologies can make more money on their existing quotas and profit from purchasing new quotas from others who have not adopted the technologies.

Therefore, in marked contrast to the earlier regulatory methods used to raise costs, both the tax system and the transferable quota system encourage low extraction rates.

How about the distribution of the rent? In a quota system the distribution of the rent depends crucially on how the quotas are initially allocated. There are many possibilities, each with different outcomes. The first possibility is for the government to auction off these quotas. But the government would then appropriate all the rent, and the outcome would be very similar to the outcome of the tax system. If the fishermen do not like the tax system, they would not like the auction system either.

In an alternative approach, the government could give the quotas to the fishermen—say, in proportion to their historical catch. The fishermen could then trade among themselves until a market equilibrium is reached. All the rent would be retained only by the *current* generation of fishermen. Fishermen who might want to enter the market would have to purchase the quotas from existing fishermen. Competition among the potential purchases would drive up the price of the transferable quotas until it reflected the market value of future rents, appropriately discounted.[7]

Thus, this type of quota system allows the rent to remain with the fishermen, but only with the current generation. Future generations see little difference between this quota system and a tax system; in either case, they have to pay to enter the industry, whether it is through the tax system or by purchasing the quotas.

In 1986 a limited individual transferable quota system was established in New Zealand to protect its deepwater trawl fishery (Newell et al., 2005). Although this was far from being the only, or even the earliest, application of ITQs (see Table 13.1), it is the world's largest and provides an unusually rich opportunity to study how this approach works in practice. The Fisheries Amendment Act of 1986 that set up the program covered 17 inshore species and 9 offshore species. By 2004 it had expanded to cover 70 species. Newell et al. found that the export value of these species ranged from NZ \$700/metric ton for jack mackerel to NZ \$40,000/metric ton for rock lobster.

Because this fishery was newly developed, allocating the quotas proved relatively easy. The New Zealand Economic Exclusion Zone (EEZ) was divided geographically into quota management regions. The total allowable catches for the seven basic species were divided into individual transferable quota by quota management regions. By 2000 275 quota markets were in operation.

TABLE 13.1   Countries with Individual Transferable Quota Systems

Countries	Number of Species Covered
Australia	4
Canada	14
Chile	3
Iceland	16
Netherlands	4
New Zealand	33
United States	4

Sources: Information compiled from OECD, *Implementing Domestic Tradable Permits for Environmental Protection* (Paris: Organization for Economic Co-operation and Development, 1999): 19; and Bernal, P. and B. Aliaga, "ITQs in Chilean Fisheries," *The Definition and Allocation of Use Rights in European Fisheries, Proceedings of the Second Concerted Workshop on Economics and the Common Fisheries Policy*, Hatcher, A. and K. Robinson, eds. (Brest, France, May 5–7, 1999), (published by the Center for the Economics and Management of Aquatic Resources, University of Portsmouth, UK): 117–130.

---

[7]This occurs because the maximum bid any potential entrant would make is the value to be derived from owning that permit. This value is equal to the present value of future rents (the difference between price and marginal cost for each unit of fish sold). Competition will force the purchaser to bid near that maximum value, lest he or she lose the quota.

Quotas were initially allocated to existing harvesters based on average catch during 1982–1984. The rights to harvest were denominated in terms of a specific amount of fish, but were granted only for a 10-year period.

At the same time that the deep-sea fishery policy was being considered, the inshore fisheries began to fall on hard times. Too many participants were chasing too many fish. Some particularly desirable fish species were being seriously overfished. Although the need to reduce the amount of pressure being put on the population was rather obvious, how to accomplish that reduction was not at all obvious. It was relatively easy to prevent new fishermen from entering the fisheries, but it was harder to figure out how to reduce the pressure from those who had been fishing in the areas for years and decades. Because fishing is characterized by economies of scale, simply reducing everyone's catch proportionately wouldn't make much sense. That would simply place higher costs on everyone and waste a great deal of fishing capacity as all boats sat around idle for a significant proportion of time. A better solution would clearly be to have fewer boats harvesting the stock. That way, each boat could be used closer to its full capacity, without depleting the population. Which fishermen should be asked to give up their livelihood and leave the industry?

The economic incentive approach addressed this problem by having the government buy back catch quotas from those willing to sell them. Although initially this was financed out of general revenues, subsequently it was financed by a fee on catch quotas. Essentially, each fisherman stated the lowest price that he or she would accept for leaving the industry; the regulators selected those who could be induced to leave at the lowest price, paid the stipulated amount from the fee revenues, and retired their licenses to fish for this species. It wasn't long before a sufficient number of licenses had been retired, and the population was protected. Because the program was voluntary, those who left the industry only did so when they felt they had been adequately compensated.

Meanwhile, those who paid the fee realized that this small investment would benefit them greatly in the future as the population recovered. A difficult and potentially dangerous pressure on a valuable natural resource had been alleviated by the creative use of an approach that changed the economic incentives.

Toward the end of 1987, however, a new problem emerged. The original stock of one species (orange roughy) turned out to have been seriously overestimated by biologists. Since the total allocation of quotas was derived from this estimate, the practical implication was that an unsustainably high level of quotas had been issued; the stock was inadvertently placed in jeopardy.

The New Zealand government began buying some quotas back from fishermen, but this turned out to be quite expensive with NZ$45 million spent on 15,000 tons of quotas from inshore fisheries. Faced with the unacceptably large budget implications of buying back a significant amount of quota, the government ultimately shifted to a percentage-share allocation of quota. Under this system, instead of owning quota defined in terms of a specific quantity of fish, fishermen own percentage shares of a total allowable catch (TAC). The *total allowable catch* is determined annually by the government. In this way the government can annually adjust the total allowable catch, based on the latest stock assessment estimates, without having to buy back (or sell) large amounts of quota. This approach affords greater protection to the stock, but increases the financial risk to the fishermen.

The quota markets in New Zealand have been quite active. By 2000 140,000 leases and 23,000 sales of quotas had occurred. Newell et al. (2005) found that 22 percent of quota owners participated in a market transaction in the first year of the program. By 2000 this number had risen to 70 percent.

Despite this activity, some other implementation problems have emerged. Fishing effort is frequently not very well targeted. Species other than those sought (known as *by-catch*) may well end up as part of the catch. If those species are also regulated by quotas and the fishermen do not have sufficient ITQs to cover the by-catch, they are faced with the possibility of being fined when they land the unauthorized fish. Dumping the by-catch overboard allows them to avoid the fines. However, because the jettisoned fish frequently do not survive, this represents a double waste—not only is the stock reduced, but also the harvested fish are wasted.

High-grading is another problem fisheries managers have had to deal with. High-grading can occur when quotas specify the catch in terms of weight of a certain species, but the value of the catch is affected greatly by the size of the individual fish. To maximize the value of the quota, fishermen have an incentive to throw back the less valuable (typically, smaller) fish, keeping only the most valuable individuals. As with by-catch, when release mortality is high, high-grading results in both smaller stocks and wasted harvests.

Some fisheries managers have successfully solved both problems by allowing fishermen to cover temporary overages with allowances subsequently purchased or leased from others. As long as the market value of the "extra" fish exceeds the cost of leasing the quota, the fishermen will have an incentive to land and market the fish, and the stock will not be placed in jeopardy. Although ITQ systems are far from perfect, frequently they offer the opportunity to improve on traditional fisheries management (see Example 13.3). Worldwide, ITQs are used to manage approximately 80 different species. The fact that they are spreading to new fisheries so rapidly suggests that their potential is being increasingly recognized.

This does not imply the absence of concerns. Issues about the duration of shares, whether shareholders are active in the fishery, and the distributional implications all remain contentious. In 1997 the United States, in response to these conflicts, issued a six-year moratorium on the implementation of new ITQ programs. Although the moratorium expired in 2002, new programs are still being debated.

Does the regulation of catch protect the biological integrity of the fishery? Costello, Gaines, and Lynham (2008) compiled a global database of fisheries catch statistics in more than 11,000 fisheries from 1950–2003. Fisheries with catch share rules including ITQs showed *much much* less frequent collapse than fisheries without ITQs. In fact, they found that by 2003 the fraction of fisheries with ITQs that had collapsed was only half that of non-ITQ fisheries. They suggest that this might be an underestimate since many fisheries with ITQs have not had them for very long. This large study suggests that well-designed property rights regimes (ITQs) may help prevent fisheries collapse and/or help stocks of some species recover, but it also sugests they provide no guarantees.

Subsidies and Buybacks

As illustrated in Figure 13.3 excess fleet capacity or overcapitalization is prevalent in many commercial fisheries. Overcapacity encourages overfishing. If vessel owners do not have alternative uses for their vessels, they may resist catch restrictions or other measures meant to help depleted stocks. Management options have included the buyback or decommissioning subsidies to reduce fishing capacity. In 2004 the U.S. government spent $100 million to buy out 28 of the 260 Alaskan snow crab fishery vessels and the EU has proposed spending an additional €272 million on

The Relative Effectiveness of Transferable Quotas and Traditional Size and Effort Restrictions in the Atlantic Sea Scallop Fishery

EXAMPLE

13.3

Theory suggests that transferable quotas will produce more cost-effective outcomes in fisheries than traditional restrictions, such as minimum harvest size and maximum effort controls. Is this theoretical expectation compatible with the actual experience in implemented systems?

In a fascinating study, economist Robert Repetto (2001) examines this question by comparing Canadian and American approaches to controlling the sea scallop fishery off the Atlantic coast. While Canada adopted a transferable quota system, the United States adopted a mix of size, effort, and area controls. The comparison provides a rare opportunity to exploit a natural experiment since scallops are not migratory and the two countries used similar fishing technologies. Hence, it is reasonable to presume that the differences in experience are largely due to the difference in management approaches.

What were the biological consequences of these management strategies for the two fisheries?

* The Canadian fishery was not only able to maintain the stock at a higher level of abundance, but also it was able to deter the harvesting of undersized scallops.
* In the United States, stock abundance levels declined and undersized scallops were harvested at high levels.

What were the economic consequences?

* Revenue per sea-day increased significantly in the Canadian fishery, due largely to the seven-fold increase in catch per sea-day made possible by the larger stock abundance.
* In the U.S. fishery, revenue per sea-day fell, due not only to the fall in the catch per day that resulted from the decline in stock abundance, but also to the harvesting of undersized scallops.
* Although the number of Canadian quota holders was reduced from nine to seven over a fourteen-year period, 65 percent of the quota remained in its original hands. The evidence suggests that smaller players were apparently not at a competitive disadvantage.

What were the equity implications?

* Both the U.S. and Canadian fisheries have traditionally operated on the "lay" system, which divides the revenue among crew, captain, and owner according to preset percentages, after subtracting certain operating expenditures. This means that all parties remaining in the fishery after regulation shared in the increasing rents.

In this fishery at least, it seems that the theory was supported by experience.

Source: Repetto, Robert, "A Natural Experiment in Fisheries Management," *Marine Policy* 25 (2001): 252–264.

decommissioning (Clark et al., 2005). Payments used to buy out excess fishing capacity are useful subsidies in that they reduce overcapacity, but if additional capacity seeps in over time, they are not as effective as other management measures. Clark et al. (2005), also note that if fishermen come to anticipate a buyback, they may acquire more vessels than they otherwise would have, which would lead to even greater levels of overcapacity.

Marine Protected Areas and Marine Reserves. Regulating only the amount of catch may prove insufficient; it does not control either the type of gear that is used or locations where the harvests take place. Failure to control these two elements can lead to environmental degradation of the habitat on which the fishery depends. Some gear may be particularly damaging, not only to the targeted species (e.g., by capturing juveniles that cannot be sold, but that don't survive capture) but also to nontargeted species (by-catch). Similarly harvesting in some geographic areas (such as those used for spawning) might have a disproportionately large detrimental effect on the sustainability of the fishery.

Conservation biologists have suggested complementing current policies with the establishment of a system of marine protected areas (MPAs), which are designated ocean areas involving restrictions on human activity. Restrictions range from minimal to full protection. A marine reserve, a marine protected area with full protection, is an area that prohibits harvesting and enjoys a very high level of protection from other threats such as pollution. The U.S. Federal Government defines MPAs as "any area of the marine environment that has been reserved by federal, state, tribal, territorial, or local laws or regulations to provide lasting protection for part or all of the natural and cultural resources therein"—Executive Order 13158 (May 2000).[8]

Biologists believe that marine protected areas can perform several maintenance and restorative functions. First, they protect *individual species* by preventing harvest within the reserve boundaries. Second, they reduce *habitat damage* caused by fishing gear or practices that alter biological structures. Third, in contrast to quotas on single species, reserves promote *ecosystem balance* by protecting against the removal of ecologically pivotal species (whether targeted species or by-catch) that could throw an ecosystem out of balance by altering its diversity and productivity (Palumbi, 2002).

Reducing harvesting in these areas protects the stock, the habitat, and the ecosystem on which it depends. This protection results in a larger population and, ultimately, since the species swim beyond the boundaries of the reserve, larger catches in the remaining harvest areas.

Since reserves allow the population to recover, it is clear how they promote sustainability. Their relationship to the welfare of current users, however, is less clear. Proponents of MPAs suggest that they can promote sustainability in a win-win fashion (meaning current users benefit as well). This is an important point since users who would not benefit might oppose marine reserve proposals, thereby making their establishment very difficult.

Would the establishment of a marine protected area maximize the present value of net benefits for fishermen? If MPAs work as planned, they reduce harvest in the short run (by declaring areas previously available for harvest off-limits), but they increase it in the long run (as the population recovers). However, the delay would impose costs (remember the discount rate?). To take one concrete example of the costs of delay, harvesters may have to pay off a mortgage on their boat. Even if the bank grants them a delay in making payments, total payments will rise. So,

---

[8]For information and maps of marine protected areas of the United States see www.mpa.gov.

by itself, a future rise in harvests does not guarantee that establishing the reserve maximizes present value unless the rise in catch is large enough and soon enough to compensate for the costs imposed by the delay.

Since the present value of this policy depends on the specifics of the individual cases, a case study can be revealing. In their interesting case study of the California sea urchin industry, Smith and Wilen (2003) state the following:

> Our overall assessment of reserves as a fisheries policy tool is more ambivalent than the received wisdom in the biological literature. … We find … that reserves can produce harvest gains in an age-structured model, but only when the biomass is severely overexploited. We also find … that even when steady state harvests are increased with a spatial closure, the discounted returns are often negative, reflecting slow biological recovery relative to the discount rate.

Does this mean that marine protected areas or marine reserves are a bad idea? Certainly not! In some areas they may be a necessary step for achieving sustainability; in others they may represent the most efficient means of achieving sustainability. It does mean, however, that we should be wary of the notion that they always create win-win situations; sacrifices by local harvesters might be required. Marine protected area policies must recognize the possibility of this burden and deal with it directly, not just assume it doesn't exist.

The 200-Mile Limit

The final policy dimension concerns the international aspects of the fishery problem. Obviously, the various policy approaches to effective management of fisheries require that some governing body have jurisdiction over a fishery so that it can enforce the regulations.

This is not currently the case for many of the ocean fisheries. Much of the open water of the ocean is an open-access resource to governments as well as to individual fishermen. Therefore, no single body can exercise control over it. As long as that continues to be the case, the corrective action will be difficult to implement. In recognition of this fact, there is an evolving law of the sea, defined by international treaties. One of the concrete results of this law has been some limited restrictions on whaling. Whether or not this process ultimately yields a consistent and comprehensive system of management remains to be seen.

Countries bordering the sea have declared that their ownership rights extend some 200 miles out to sea. Within these areas, the countries have exclusive jurisdiction and can proceed to implement effective management policies. These *200-mile limits* have been upheld and are now firmly entrenched in international law. Thus, very rich fisheries in coastal waters can be protected, whereas those in the open waters await the outcome of an international negotiations process.

The Economics of Enforcement

Enforcement is an area of fisheries management that traditionally has not received much analytical treatment but is gradually becoming recognized as a key aspect. Policies can be designed to be perfectly efficient as long as everyone follows them voluntarily, but these same policies may turn out to be quite ineffective in the harsh realities of costly and imperfect enforcement.

Fisheries policies are especially difficult to enforce. Coastlines are typically long and rugged; it is not difficult for fishermen to avoid detection if they are exceeding their limits or catching species illegally.

Recognizing these realities immediately suggests two implications: (1) policy design should take enforcement into consideration and (2) what is efficient when enforcement is ignored may not be efficient once enforcement is considered.

Policies should be designed to make compliance as inexpensive as possible. Regulations that impose very high costs are more likely to be disobeyed than regulations that impose costs in proportion to the purpose. Regulations should also contain provisions for dealing with noncompliance. A common approach is to levy monetary sanctions against those failing to comply. The sanctions should be set at a high enough level to bring the costs of noncompliance (including the sanction) into balance with the costs of compliance.

The enforcement issue points out another advantage of private-property approaches to fisheries management—they are self-enforcing. Fish farmers or fish ranchers have no incentive to deviate from the efficient scheme because they would only be hurting themselves. No enforcement activity is necessary.

On the other hand, in common-pool resources noncompliance with some kind of regulatory constraint could, in the absence of effective enforcement, increase profits for the noncomplying fisherman. Mounting this enforcement effort is yet another cost associated with the public management of fisheries.

Since enforcement activity is costly, it follows that it should be figured into our definition of efficiency. How would our analysis be changed by incorporating enforcement costs? One study (Sutinen and Anderson, 1985) suggests that the incorporation of realistic enforcement cost considerations tends to reduce the efficient population below the level declared efficient in the presence of perfect, costless enforcement.

Their rationale is not difficult to follow. Assume that some kind of quota system is in effect to ration access. Enforcement activity would involve monitoring compliance with these quotas and assigning penalties on those found in noncompliance.[9] If the quotas are so large as to be consistent with the free-access equilibrium, enforcement cost would be zero; no enforcement would be necessary to ensure compliance. Moving the fishery away from the free-access equilibrium increases both net benefits and enforcement costs. For this model, as the steady-state population size is increased, marginal enforcement costs increase and marginal net benefits decrease. At the efficient population size (considering enforcement cost), the marginal net benefit equals the marginal enforcement cost. This necessarily involves a smaller population size than the efficient population size ignoring enforcement costs, because the latter occurs when the marginal net benefit is zero.

Policy design can actually affect enforcement costs by increasing the likelihood that compliance will be the norm. For example, in their study of Malaysian fishermen Kuperan and Sutinen (1998) find that perceived legitimacy of the laws and the moral obligation to comply with legitimate laws do influence compliance behavior.

---

[9]In theory it would be possible to set the penalty so high that only a limited amount of enforcement activity would be necessary. Since large penalties are rarely imposed in practice and are typically not large relative to the illegal gains, the model rules these out and assumes that increasing enforcement expenditures are necessary to enforce increasingly stringent quotas.

Preventing Poaching

A second type of threat to commercially valuable species comes from poaching. *Poaching* is the illegal harvest of a species. Poaching can introduce the possibility of unsustainability even when a legal structure to protect the population has been enacted. For example, in 1986 the International Whaling Commission set a ban on commercial whaling, but because of a loophole in the law, Japan has continued to kill hundreds of whales each year. In November 2007 a fleet embarked on a five-month hunt in the Antarctic despite numerous international protests. While originally intending to target humpback whales, in response to the protests Japan eventually dropped humpbacks from the list of target whale species. Since humpback whales are considered "vulnerable," commercial hunts have been banned since 1966, but Japan had claimed that harvests for research were not covered by this ban.

From an economic point of view poaching can be discouraged if it is possible to raise the relative cost of illegal activity. In principle, that can be accomplished by increasing the sanctions levied against poachers, but it is effective only if monitoring can detect the illegal activity and apply the sanctions to those who engage in it. In many places that is a tall order, given the large size of the habitat to be monitored and the limited budgets for funding enforcement. Example 13.4 shows, however, how economic incentives can be enlisted to promote more monitoring by local inhabitants as well as to provide more revenue for enforcement activity.

Example 13.4 also points out that many species are commercially valuable even in the absence of any harvest. Fish have benefitted from the rise of marine *ecotourism* since large numbers of people will pay considerable sums of money simply to witness these magnificent creatures in their native habitat. This revenue, when shared with local people, can provide an incentive to protect the species and decrease the incentive to participate in illegal poaching activity that would threaten the source of the ecotourism revenue.

Other incentives have also proved successful. In Kenya, for example, Massai tribesmen have transitioned from hunting lions to protecting them because they have been given an economic incentive. Massai from the Mbirikani ranch, are now compensated for livestock killed by predators. They receive $80 for each donkey and $200 for each cow killed. The Mbirikani Predator Fund has compensated herders for the loss of 750 head of livestock each year since the program began in 2003. As an additional collective incentive, if any one herder kills a lion, no one gets paid.[10]

Rearranging the economic incentives so that local groups have an economic interest in their preservation can provide a powerful means of protecting some biological populations. Open access undermines those incentives.

Although it is important to recognize that much of what we have covered in this chapter carries over from marine-based wildlife to land-based wildlife, it is equally important to recognize a significant difference. Land-based wildlife is threatened not only by the open-access problem we have been discussing, but also by competition for the land that provides their habitat (a subject covered in Chapters 10 and 12).

Hence, for land-based wildlife, preventing open-access overexploitation may be a necessary, but not sufficient, strategy. It is also necessary to complement strategies that limit access with strategies that prevent excessive conversion of habitat.[11]

---

[10]Conservation International June 21, 2007.

[11]For an excellent treatment of this aspect of protecting wildlife, see Swanson (1994).

EXAMPLE

13.4

Local Approaches to Wildlife Protection: Zimbabwe

In 1989 an innovative program was initiated in Zimbabwe. It stands out as a success among other African wildlife protection schemes. The program transformed the role of wildlife from a state-owned treasure to be preserved into an active resource—one that is controlled and used by both commercial farmers and smallholders in communal lands. The transformation has been good for the economy and the wildlife.

The initiative is called the Communal Areas Management Program for Indigenous Resources (CAMPFIRE). It was originally sponsored by several different agencies—including the University of Zimbabwe's Center for Applied Study, the Zimbabwe Trust, and the Worldwide Fund for Nature (WWF)—in cooperation with the Zimbabwean government.

Under the *CAMPFIRE program*, villagers collectively utilize local wildlife resources on a sustainable basis. Trophy hunting by foreigners is perhaps the most important source of revenue, because hunters require few facilities and are willing to pay substantial fees to kill a limited number of large animals. The government sets the prices of hunting permits, as well as quotas for the number of animals that can be taken per year in each locality. Individual communities sell the permits and contract with safari operators, who conduct photographic and hunting expeditions on the community lands.

The associated economic gains accrue to the villages, which then decide how the revenues should be used. The money may be paid out in one of two ways—(1) payments to households in the form of cash dividends, which may amount to 20 percent or more of an average family's income or (2) payments to be used for capital investments in the community (e.g., schools, clinics, or labor saving machines)—or some combination of the two methods. In at least one area, revenues compensate citizens who have suffered property loss because of wild animals. Households may also receive nonmonetary benefits, such as meat from problem animals or culled herds. By consistently meeting their needs from their own resources on a sustainable basis, local communities become self-reliant. For the 1989-2001 period Frost and Bond (2008) found that, although CAMPFIRE generated over US$20 million of transfers to the participating communities (89% of which came from sport hunting), the scale of benefits varied greatly across districts, wards, and households. Twelve of the 37 districts with authority to market wildlife produced 97% of all CAMPFIRE revenues, reflecting both the variability in wildlife resources and local institutional arrangements.

Sources: Frost, Peter G. H. and Ivan Bond, "The CAMPFIRE Programme in Zimbabwe: Payments for Wildlife Services" *Ecological Economics* 65(2008): 776–787; Barbier, Edward, "Community-Based Development in Africa" in Timothy Swanson, Edward Barbier, eds. *Economics for the Wilds: Wildlife, Diversity, and Development* (Washington, DC: Island Press, 1992): 107–118; and the Web site: http://www.colby.edu/personal/thtieten/end-zim.html.

Summary

Unrestricted access to commercially valuable species will generally result in overexploitation. This overexploitation, in turn, results in overcapitalization, depressed incomes for harvesters, and depleted biological populations. Even extinction is possible, especially for species characterized by particularly low extraction costs (e.g., the Pacific salmon). Where extraction costs are higher, extinction is unlikely, even with unrestricted access.

Both the private and public sectors have moved to ameliorate the problems associated with past mismanagement of wildlife populations. For marine-based wildlife, Japan and other countries have stimulated the development of aquaculture by reasserting private-property rights. Governments in Canada and the United States have moved to limit overexploitation of the Pacific salmon. International agreements have been reached that place limits on whaling.

For land-based wildlife, countries such as Zimbabwe have initiated strategies to prevent excessive conversion of land currently used for habitat to uses such as agriculture, mining, and urbanization. In part, these strategies protect habitat by recognizing and capturing the value of that particular use of the land.

Creative strategies for sharing the gains from moving to an efficient level of use could prove to be a significant technique in the arsenal of weapons designed to protect a broad class of biological resources from overexploitation. An increasing reliance on individual transferable quotas (ITQs) offers the possibility to preserve stocks without jeopardizing the incomes of those whose livelihoods depend on harvesting them. Furthermore, giving local communities a stake in preserving wildlife has provided a vehicle for building political coalitions to prevent overexploitation of this resource.

It would be folly to ignore barriers to further action, such as the reluctance of individual harvesters to submit to many forms of regulation, the lack of a firm policy governing open ocean waters, and the difficulties of enforcing various approaches. Whether these barriers will fall before the pressing need for effective management remains to be seen.

Key Concepts

Further Reading

Acheson, James M. *Capturing the Commons: Devising Institutions to Manage the Maine Lobster Industry* (Hanover, NH: University Press of New England, 2003). An impressive synthesis of theory and empirical work, combined with an insider's knowledge of the institutions and the people who run them makes this a compelling examination of the history of one of America's most important fisheries.

Bjørndal, T. and G. R. Munro. "The Economics of Fisheries Management: A Survey," *The International Yearbook of Environmental and Resource Economics 1998/1999,* Tietenberg, T. and H. Folmer, eds. (Cheltenham, UK: Edward Elgar, 1998): 153–188. A review of current economic research on fisheries management.

Clark, Colin W. *Mathematical Bioeconomics: The Optimal Management of Renewable Resources,* 2nd ed. (New York: Wiley Interscience, 1990). A careful development of the mathematical models that underlie current understanding of the exploitation of renewable resources under a variety of property-rights regimes.

National Research Council Committee to Review Individual Fishing Quotas. *Sharing the Fish: Toward a National Policy on Fishing Quotas* (Washington: National Academy Press, 1999). A detailed look at the experience with ITQs around the world.

Schlager, Edella and Elinor Ostrom. "Property-Right Regimes and Natural Resources: A Conceptual Analysis," *Land Economics* 68 (1992): 249–262. A conceptual framework for analyzing a number of property-rights regimes and use this framework to interpret findings from a number of empirical studies.

Townsend, Ralph E. "Entry Restrictions in the Fishery: A Survey of the Evidence," *Land Economics* 66 (1990): 361–378. Reviews the relevant experience with about 30 limited-entry programs around the world. Identifies those features of limited-entry programs that seem to contribute to success or failure.

Additional References

Arnason, R. "The Icelandic Individual Transferable Quota System: A Descriptive Account," *Marine Resource Economics* 8 (1993): 201–218.

Barbier, Edward B. "Community-Based Developments in Africa," *Economics for the Wilds: Wildlife, Diversity and Development,* Swanson, Timothy and Edward Barbier, eds. (Washington, DC: Island Press, 1992).

Berkes, F., D. Feeny, B. J. McCay, and J. M. Acheson. "The Benefits of the Commons," *Nature* 340 (1989): 91–93.

Boyce, John R. "Individual Transferable Quotas and Production Externalities in a Fishery," *Natural Resource Modeling* 8 (1992): 385–408.

Boyce, John R. "Instrument Choice in a Fishery," *Journal of Environmental Economics and Management* 47 (2004) (1): 183–206.

Brown, Gardner, Jr. and Wes Henry. "The Economic Value of Elephants," *London Environmental Economics Centre Working Paper,* November 1989.

Brown, Lester R. "Maintaining World Fisheries," *State of the World: 1985,* Lester Brown et al., eds. (New York: W. W. Norton, 1985): 90.

Burton, P. S. "Community Enforcement of Fisheries Effort Restrictions," *Journal of Environmental Economics & Management* 45 (2003) (2): 474–491.

Campbell, H. F. and R. K. Lindner. "The Production of Fishing Effort and the Economic Performance of License Limitation Programs," *Land Economics* 66 (1990): 56–66.

Cheng, Juo-Shung, et al. "Analysis of Modified Model for Commercial Fishing with Possible Extinctive Fishery Resources," *Journal of Environmental Economics and Management* 8 (1981): 151–155.

Clark, Colin W., Gordon R. Munro, and Ussif Rashid Sumaila, "Subsidies, Buybacks, and Sustainable Fisheries," *Journal of Environmental Economics and Management* 50 (2005) (1): 47–58.

Costello, Christopher, Steven D. Gaines, and John Lynham, "Can Catch Shares Prevent Fisheries Collapse?" Science, 321: 1678–1680.

Dupont, Diane P. "Rent Dissipation in Restricted Access Fisheries," *Journal of Environmental Economics and Management* 19 (1990): 26–44.

Food and Agriculture Organization of the United Nations. *State of the World's Fisheries and Aquaculture* (2008) ftp://ftp.fao.org/docrep/fao/011/i0250e/i0250e.pdf. Accessed 3/14/2009.

Geen, Gerry and Mark Nayar. "Individual Transferable Quotas in the Southern Bluefin Tuna Fishery: An Economic Appraisal," *Marine Resource Economics* 5 (1988): 365–388.

Huppert, Daniel D. "Managing Alaska's Groundfish Fisheries: History and Prospects," *University of Washington Institute for Marine Resources Working Paper,* May 1990.

Iudicello, S., R. M. Weber, and R. Wieland. *Fish, Markets, and Fishermen: The Economics of Overfishing* (Washington, DC: Island Press, 1999).

Jin, D., E. Thunberg, H. Kite-Powell, and K. Blake. "Total Factor Productivity Change in the New England Groundfish Fishery: 1964–1993," *Journal of Environmental Economics & Management* 44 (2002) (3): 540–556.

Kuperan, K. and Jon G. Sutinen, "Blue Water Crime: Deterrence, Legitimacy, and Compliance in Fisheries," *Law and Society Review* 32 (1998) (2): 309–338.

Merrifield, J. "Implementation Issues: The Political Economy of Efficient Fishing," *Ecological Economics* 30 (1999) (1): 5–12.

Munro, G. R. "Fisheries, Extended Jurisdiction, and the Economics of Common Property Resources," *Canadian Journal of Economics* 15 (1982): 405–425.

Muse, Ben. "Survey of Individual Quota Programs," *Alaska Commercial Fisheries Entry Commission Paper* CFEC 91-7, July 1991.

Muse, Ben and Kurt Schelle. "Individual Fisherman's Quotas: A Preliminary Review of Some Recent Programs," *Alaska Commercial Fisheries Entry Commission Paper* CFEC 89-1, February 1989.

Newell, R. G., J. N. Sanchirico, et al. "Fishing Quota Markets," *Journal of Environmental Economics and Management* 49 (2005) (3): 437–462.

Palumbi, Stephen R. *Marine Reserves: A Tool for Ecosystem Management and Conservation.* (Arlington: Pew Oceans Commission, 2002).

Simmons, Randy T. and Urs P. Keuter. "Herd Mentality: Banning Ivory Sales Is No Way to Save the Elephant," *Policy Review* 50 (1989): 46–49.

Smith, M. D. and J. E. Wilen. "Economic Impacts of Marine Reserves: The Importance of Spatial Behavior," *Journal of Environmental Economics and Management* 46 (2003) (2): 183–206.

Stokes, R. L. "The Economics of Salmon Ranching," *Land Economics* 58 (1982): 464–477.

Sutinen, Jon G. and Peder Anderson. "The Economics of Fisheries Law Enforcement," *Land Economics* 61 (1985): 387–397.

Swanson, Timothy M. "International Regulation of the Ivory Trade," *London Environmental Economics Centre Working Paper* 89-04, May 1989.

Swanson Timothy. "The Economics of Extinction Revisited and Revised: A Generalized Framework for the Analysis of the Problems of Endangered Species and Biodiversity Losses," *Oxford Economic Papers* 46 Supplement (1994): 822–840.

Tillion, C. V. "Fisheries Management in Alaska," *Fisheries Report 298: Papers Presented at the Expert Consultation on the Reduction of Fishing Effort (Fishing Mortality)* (Rome: Food and Agriculture Organization of the United Nations, 1985): 291–297.

Historically Significant References

Clark, C. W. "Profit Maximization and the Extinction of Animal Species," *Journal of Political Economy* 81 (1973): 950–960.

Crutchfield, J. A. and G. Pontecovo. *The Pacific Salmon Fisheries: A Study of Irrational Conservation* (Baltimore: Johns Hopkins University Press, 1969).

Gordon, H. Scott. "The Economic Theory of a Common-Property Resource: The Fishery," *Journal of Political Economy* 62 (1954): 124–142.

Schaefer, M. D. "Some Considerations of Population Dynamics and Economics in Relation to the Management of Marine Fisheries," *Journal of the Fisheries Research Board of Canada* 14 (1957): 669–681.

Discussion Questions

1. Is the establishment of the 200-mile limit a sufficient form of government intervention to ensure that the "tragedy of the commons" does not occur for fisheries within the 200-mile limit? Why or why not?

2. With discounting, it is possible for the efficient fish population to fall below the level required to produce the maximum sustained yield. Does this violate the sustainability criterion? Why or why not?

Environmental Economics: An Overview

14

Democracy is not a matter of sentiment, but of foresight. Any system that doesn't take the long run into account will burn itself out in the short run.

—CHARLES YOST, *The Age of Triumph and Frustration: Modern Dialogues* (1964)

Introduction

In the last few chapters we have dealt extensively with achieving a balanced set of mass and energy flows; now we examine how a balance can be achieved in the reverse flow of waste products back to the environment. Because the waste flows are inexorably intertwined with the flow of mass and energy into the economy, establishing a balance for waste flows will have feedback effects on the input flows as well.

Two questions must be addressed: (1) What is the appropriate level of waste flow? (2) How should the responsibility for achieving this flow level be allocated among the various sources of the pollutant when reductions are needed?

In this chapter we shall lay the foundation for understanding the policy approach to controlling pollution. We define efficient and cost-effective levels of control for a variety of pollutant types, compare these control levels with those achieved by market forces, and demonstrate how these insights can be used to design desirable policy responses. This overview is then followed by a series of chapters that show how these principles have been applied to the design of pollution control policies in various countries around the world.

A Pollutant Taxonomy

The amount of waste products emitted determines the load upon the environment. The damage done by this load depends on the capacity of the environment to assimilate the waste products (see Figure 14.1). We will refer to this ability of the environment to absorb pollutants as its *absorptive capacity*. If the emissions load exceeds the absorptive capacity, then the pollutant accumulates in the environment.

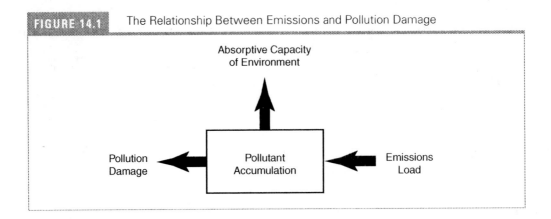

FIGURE 14.1   The Relationship Between Emissions and Pollution Damage

Pollutants for which the environment has little or no absorptive capacity are called *stock pollutants*. Stock pollutants accumulate over time as emissions enter the environment. Examples of stock pollutants include nonbiodegradable bottles tossed by the roadside; heavy metals, such as lead, that accumulate in the soils near the emission source; and persistent synthetic chemicals, such as dioxin and PCBs (polychlorinated biphenyls).

Pollutants for which the environment has some absorptive capacity are called *fund pollutants*. As long as the emission rate does not exceed the absorptive capacity of the environment, these pollutants do not accumulate. Examples of fund pollutants are easy to find. Many organic pollutants injected into an oxygen-rich stream will be transformed by the resident bacteria into less harmful inorganic matter. Carbon dioxide is absorbed by plant life and the oceans. The point is *not* that the mass is destroyed; the law of conservation of mass suggests this cannot be the case. Rather, when fund pollutants are injected into the air or water, they may be transformed into substances that are not considered harmful to people or to the ecological system, or they may be so diluted or dispersed that the resulting concentrations are not harmful.

Pollutants can also be classified by their zone of influence, defined both horizontally and vertically. The horizontal dimension deals with the domain over which damage from an emitted pollutant is experienced. The damage caused by *local* pollutants is experienced near the source of emission, while the damage from *regional* pollutants is experienced at greater distances from the source of emission. The limiting case is a *global pollutant*, where the damage affects the entire planet. The categories are not mutually exclusive; it is possible for a pollutant to be more than one. Sulfur oxides and nitrogen oxides, for example, are both local and regional pollutants.

The vertical zone of influence describes whether the damage is caused mainly by ground-level concentrations of an air pollutant or by concentrations in the upper atmosphere. For some pollutants such as lead or particulates, the damage caused by a pollutant is determined mainly by concentrations of the pollutant near the earth's surface. For others, such as ozone-depleting substances or greenhouse gases the damage is related more to its concentration in the upper atmosphere. This taxonomy will prove useful in designing policy responses to these various types of pollution problems, since each type of pollutant requires a unique policy response. The failure to recognize these distinctions leads to counterproductive policy.

Defining the Efficient Allocation of Pollution

Pollutants are the residuals of production and consumption. These residuals must eventually be returned to the environment in one form or another. Because their presence in the environment may depreciate the service flows received, an efficient allocation of resources must take this cost into account. What, precisely, constitutes the *efficient allocation of pollution* depends on the nature of the pollutant.

Fund Pollutants

To the extent that the emission of fund pollutants exceeds the assimilative capacity of the environment, such pollutants accumulate. When the emission rate is low enough, however, the discharges can be assimilated by the environment, with the result that the link between present emissions and future damage may be broken.

When this happens, current emissions cause current damage and future emissions cause future damage, but the level of future damage is independent of current emissions. This independence of allocations among time periods allows us to explore the efficient allocation of fund pollutants using the concept of static, rather than dynamic, efficiency. Because the static concept is simpler, this affords us the opportunity to incorporate more dimensions of the problem without unnecessarily complicating the analysis.

The normal starting point for the analysis would be to maximize the net benefit from the waste flows. However, pollution is more easily understood if we deal with an equivalent formulation involving the minimization of two rather different types of costs: (1) damage costs and (2) control or avoidance costs.

In order to examine the efficient allocation graphically, we need to know something about how control costs vary with the degree of control and how the damages vary with the amount of pollution emitted. Although our knowledge in these areas is far from complete, economists generally agree on the shapes of these relationships.

Usually, the marginal damage caused by a unit of pollution increases with the amount emitted. When small amounts of the pollutant are emitted, the incremental damage is quite small. However, when large amounts are emitted, the marginal unit can cause significantly more damage. It is not hard to understand why. Small amounts of pollution are easily diluted in the environment, and the body can tolerate small quantities of substances. However, as the amount in the atmosphere increases, dilution is less effective and the body is less tolerant.

Marginal control costs commonly increase with the amount controlled. For example, suppose a source of pollution tries to cut down on its particulate emissions by purchasing an electrostatic precipitator that captures 80 percent of the particulates as they flow past in the stack. If the source wants further control, it can purchase another precipitator and place it in the stack above the first one. This second precipitator captures 80 percent of the remaining 20 percent, or 16 percent, of the uncontrolled emissions. Thus, the first precipitator would achieve an 80 percent reduction from uncontrolled emissions, whereas the second precipitator, which costs the same as the first, would achieve only a further 16 percent reduction. Obviously, each unit of emission reduction costs more for the second precipitator than for the first.

In Figure 14.2 we use these two pieces of information on the shapes of the relevant curves to derive the efficient allocation. A movement from right to left refers to greater control and less

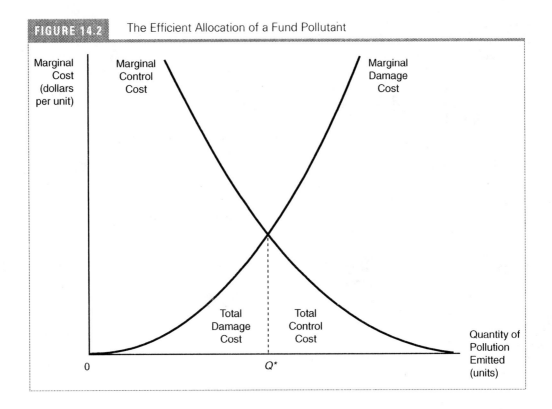

FIGURE 14.2 The Efficient Allocation of a Fund Pollutant

pollution emitted. The efficient allocation is represented by Q^*, the point at which the damage caused by the marginal unit of pollution is exactly equal to the marginal cost of avoiding it.[1]

Greater degrees of control (points to the left of Q^*) are inefficient, because the further increase in avoidance costs would exceed the reduction in damages. Hence, total costs would rise. Similarly, levels of control lower than Q^* would result in a lower cost of control, but the increase in damage costs would be even larger, yielding an increase in total cost. Either increasing or decreasing the amount controlled causes an increase in total costs. Hence, Q^* must be efficient.

The diagram suggests that, under the conditions presented, the optimal level of pollution is not zero. If you find this disturbing, remember that we confront this principle every day. Take the damage caused by automobile accidents, for example. Obviously, a considerable amount of damage is caused by automobile accidents. Yet we do not reduce that damage to zero, because the cost of doing so would be too high.

The point is *not* that we do not know how to stop automobile accidents. All we would have to do is eliminate automobiles! Rather, the point is because we value the benefits of automobiles,

---

[1]At this point, we can see why this formulation is equivalent to the net-benefit formulation. Because the benefit is damage reduction, another way of stating this proposition is to state that marginal benefit must equal marginal cost. That is, of course, the familiar proposition derived by maximizing net benefits.

we take steps to reduce accidents (using speed limits) only to the extent that the costs of accident reduction are commensurate with the damage reduction achieved; that is, the efficient level of automobile accidents is not zero.

The second point to be made is that in some circumstances the optimal level of pollution *may* be zero, or close to it. This situation occurs when the damage caused by even the first unit of pollution is so severe that it is higher than the marginal cost of controlling it. This would be reflected in Figure 14.2 as a leftward shift of the damage-cost curve of sufficient magnitude that its intersection with the vertical axis would lie above the point where the marginal-cost curve intersects the vertical axis. This circumstance would characterize the treatment of highly danger- ous radioactive pollutants such as plutonium.

Additional insights are easily derived from our characterization of the efficient allocation. For example, it should be clear from Figure 14.2 that the optimal level of pollution generally is not the same for all parts of the country. Areas that have higher population levels or are particu- larly sensitive to pollution would have a marginal damage cost curve that intersected the mar- ginal control cost curve closer to the vertical axis. This would imply lower levels of pollution. Areas that have lower population levels or are less sensitive would have higher levels.

Examples of ecological sensitivity are not hard to find. For instance, some natural settings are less sensitive to acid rain than others because the local geological strata neutralize moderate amounts of the acid. Thus, the marginal damage caused by a unit of acid rain is lower in those fortunate regions than in others less tolerant. It can also be argued that pollutants affecting visi- bility are more damaging in national parks and other areas where visibility is an important part of the aesthetic experience than in other, more industrial, areas.

Market Allocation of Pollution

Because air and water are treated in our legal system as open-access resources, it should surprise no one at this point that the market misallocates them. Our previously derived general conclusion that open-access resources are overexploited certainly also applies here. Air and water resources have been overexploited as waste repositories. However, this conclusion only scratches the surface of the issue; much more can be learned about the *market allocation of pollution*.

When firms create products, rarely does the process of converting raw material into outputs use 100 percent of the mass. Some of the mass, called a *residual*, is left over. If the residual is valu- able, it is simply reused. However, if it is not valuable, the firm has an incentive to deal with it in the cheapest manner possible.

The typical firm has several alternatives. It can control the amount of the residual by using inputs more completely so that less of the residual is created. It can also produce less output, so that smaller amounts of the residual are generated. Recycling the residual is sometimes a viable option, as is removing the most damaging components of the waste stream and disposing of the rest.

Pollutant damages are commonly externalities.[2] When pollutants are injected into water- courses or the atmosphere, they cause damages to those firms and consumers downstream or downwind of the source, not to the source itself. These costs are *not* borne by the emitting source

---

[2]Note that pollution damage is not inevitably an externality. For any car rigged to send all exhaust gases into its interior, those exhaust gases would not be an externality to the driver.

and, therefore, not considered by it, although they certainly are borne by society at large.[3] As with other services that are systematically undervalued, the disposal of wastes into the air or water becomes inefficiently attractive. In this case the firm minimizes its costs when it chooses not to abate anything, since the only costs it bears are the control costs. What is cheapest for the firm is not cheapest for society.

In the case of stock pollutants, the problem is particularly severe. Uncontrolled markets would lead to an excessive production of output, too few resources committed to pollution control, and an inefficiently large amount of the stock pollutant in the environment. Thus, the burden on future generations caused by the presence of this pollutant would be inefficiently large.

The inefficiencies associated with the extraction or production of minerals, energy, and food exhibit some rather important differences. For private-property resources, the market forces provide automatic signals of impending scarcity. These forces may be understated, but they operate in the correct direction. Even when some resources are treated as open-access resources (e.g., fisheries), the possibility for a private-property alternative (e.g., fish farming) is enhanced. When private-property and open-access resources sell in the same market, the private-property owners tend to ameliorate the excesses of those who exploit open-access properties. Efficient firms are rewarded with higher profits.

No comparable automatic amelioration mechanism is evident with pollution.[4] Because this cost is borne partially by consumers, rather than solely by producers, it does not find its way into product prices. Firms that attempt to control their pollution unilaterally can be placed at a competitive disadvantage; because of the added expense, their costs of production are higher than those of their less conscientious competitors. Not only does the unimpeded market fail to generate the efficient level of pollution control, it penalizes those firms that might attempt to control an efficient amount. Hence, the case for some sort of government intervention is particularly strong for pollution control.

● Efficient Policy Responses

Our use of the efficiency criterion has helped to demonstrate why markets fail to produce an efficient level of pollution control and to trace the effects of this less-than-optimal degree of control on the markets for related commodities. It can also be used to define efficient policy responses.

In Figure 14.2 we demonstrated that for a market as a whole, efficiency is achieved when the marginal cost of control is equal to the marginal damage caused by the pollution. This same principle applies to each emitter. Each emitter should control its pollution until the marginal cost of controlling the last unit is equal to the marginal damage it causes. One way to achieve this outcome would be to impose a legal limit on the amount of pollution allowed by each emitter. If the limit were chosen precisely at the level of emission where marginal control cost equaled the marginal damage, efficiency would have been achieved for that emitter.

---

[3] Actually, the source certainly considers some of the costs—if only to avoid adverse public relations. The point, however, is that this consideration is likely to be incomplete; the source is unlikely to internalize all of the damage.

[4] Affected parties do have an incentive to negotiate among themselves, a topic covered in Chapter 3. As pointed out in that chapter, however, that approach only works well in cases where the number of affected parties is small.

An alternative approach would be to internalize the marginal damage caused by each unit of emissions by means of a tax or charge on each unit of emissions (see Example 14.1). This per unit charge could either increase with the level of pollution (following the marginal-damage curve for each succeeding unit of emission) or be constant, as long as the rate is equal to the marginal social damage at the point where the marginal-social-damage and marginal-control costs cross (see Figure 14.2). Because the emitter is paying the marginal social damage when confronted by these fees, pollution costs would be internalized. The efficient choice would also be the cost-minimizing choice for the emitter.[5]

While the efficient levels of these policy instruments can be easily defined in principle, they are very difficult to implement in practice. To implement either of these policy instruments, it is necessary to know the level of emissions at which the two marginal-cost curves cross for every

Environmental Taxation in China

EXAMPLE
14.1

China's high pollution levels are causing considerable damage to human health. Traditional means of control have not been particularly effective. To combat this pollution China has instituted a wide-ranging system of environmental taxation with tax rates that are quite high by historical standards.

Phased in over a three-year period, this program involves a two-rate tax system. Lower rates are imposed on emissions below an official standard and higher rates are charged on all emissions over that standard. The tax is expected not only to reduce pollution and the damage it causes, but also to provide needed revenue to local Environmental Protection Bureaus.

According to the World Bank (1997) this strategy makes good economic sense. Conducting detailed analysis of air pollution in two Chinese cities (Beijing and Zhengzhou) and relying on "back of the envelope" measurements of benefits, they found that the marginal cost of further abatement was significantly less than the marginal benefit for any reasonable value of human life. Indeed in Zhengzhou they found that achieving an efficient outcome (based upon an assumed value of a "statistical Life" of $8,000 per person) would require reducing current emissions by some 79 percent. According to their results, the current low abatement level makes sense only if China's policymakers value the life of an average urban resident at approximately $270. It is hard to imagine that such a low value could be justified.

Source: Bohm, Robert et al., "Environmental Taxes: China's Bold Initiative," *Environment* 40(7): September 1998, 10–13, 33–38; and Dasgupta, Susmita, Hua Wang, and David Wheeler, "Surviving Success: Policy Reform and the Future of Industrial Pollution in China" (Washington, DC: The World Bank, 1997), available at http://www.worldbank.org/NIPR/work_paper/survive/china-htmp6.htm (August 1998).

---

[5]Another policy choice is to remove the people from the polluted area. The U.S. government has used this strategy for heavily contaminated toxic waste sites such as Times Beach, Missouri, and Love Canal, New York.

emitter. That is a tall order, one that imposes an unrealistically high information burden on control authorities. Control authorities typically have very poor information on control costs and little reliable information on marginal-damage functions.

How can environmental authorities allocate pollution control responsibility in a reasonable manner when the information burdens are apparently so unrealistically large? One approach, the approach now chosen by a number of countries (including the United States) is to select specific legal levels of pollution based upon some other criterion, such as providing adequate margins of safety for human or ecological health. Once these thresholds have been established, by whatever means, half of the problem has been resolved. The other half deals with deciding how to allocate the responsibility for meeting predetermined pollution levels among the large numbers of emitters.

This is precisely where the cost-effectiveness criterion comes in. Once the objective is stated in terms of meeting the predetermined pollution level at minimum cost, it is possible to derive the conditions that any cost-effective allocation of the responsibility must satisfy. These conditions can then be used as a basis for choosing among various kinds of policy instruments that impose more reasonable information burdens on control authorities.

Cost-Effective Policies for Emission Reduction

Defining a Cost-Effective Allocation

Let's suppose that the regulatory authorities are interested in controlling the total weight of emissions in a manner that minimizes the cost of control. What can we say about the cost-effective allocation of control responsibility for reducing emissions by a predetermined amount?

Let's consider a simple example. Assume that two emission sources are currently emitting 15 units each for a total of 30 units. Assume further that the control authority determines that the environment can assimilate 15 units in total, so that a reduction of 15 units is necessary. How should this 15-unit reduction be allocated between the two sources in order to minimize the total cost of the reduction?

Figure 14.3 demonstrates the answer. The figure is drawn by measuring the marginal cost of control for the first source from the left-hand axis (MC_1) and the marginal cost of control for the second source from the right-hand axis (MC_2). Notice that a total of 15 units of reduction is achieved for every point on this graph; each point represents some different combination of reduction by the two sources. Drawn in this manner, the diagram represents all possible allocations of the 15-unit reduction between the two sources. The left-hand axis, for example, represents an allocation of the entire reduction to the second source; the right-hand axis represents a situation in which the first source bears the entire responsibility. All points in between represent different degrees of shared responsibility. What allocation minimizes the cost of control?

In the cost-effective allocation, the first source cleans up 10 units; the second source cleans up 5 units. The total variable cost of control of this particular assignment of the responsibility for the reduction is represented by area A plus area B. Area A is the cost of control for the first source, area B the cost of control for the second. Any other allocation would result in a higher total control cost (convince yourself that this is true).

Figure 14.3 also demonstrates one of the most important propositions in the economics of pollution control. *The cost of achieving a given reduction in emissions will be minimized if and only*

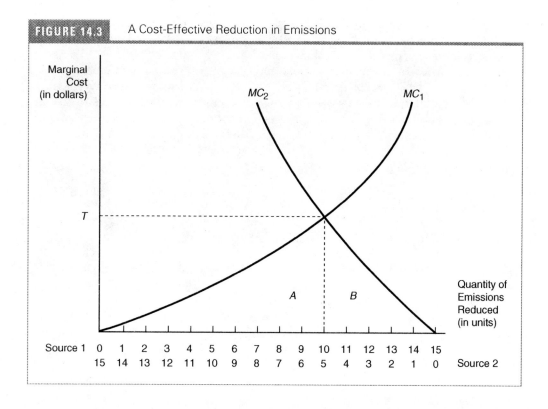

FIGURE 14.3   A Cost-Effective Reduction in Emissions

if the marginal costs of control are equalized for all emitters.[6] This is demonstrated by the fact that the marginal-cost curves cross at the cost-effective allocation.

Cost-Effective Pollution Control Policies

This proposition can be used as a basis for choosing among the various policy instruments that the control authority might use to achieve this allocation. Sources have a large menu of options for controlling the amount of pollution they inject into the environment. For example, they can change input mixes (low-sulfur versus high-sulfur coal), output mixes, or the type of pollution (air, water, or solid waste); they can move the plant to a less vulnerable area; or they can isolate the population at risk by relocating it. The cheapest method of control will differ widely, not only among industries, but also among plants in the same industry. Selecting the cheapest method requires detailed information on the possible control techniques and their associated costs.

Plant managers are generally able to acquire this information for their plants when it is in their interest to do so. However, the government authorities responsible for meeting pollution targets are not likely to have this information. Because the degree to which these plants would be

[6]This statement is true when marginal cost increases with the amount of emissions reduced (see Figure 14.3). Suppose that, for some pollutants, the marginal cost were to decrease with the amount of emissions reduced. What would be the cost-effective allocation in this admittedly unusual situation?

regulated depends on cost information, it is unrealistic to expect the plant managers to transfer unbiased information to the government. Plant managers have a strong incentive to overstate control costs in hopes of reducing their ultimate burden.

This situation poses a difficult dilemma for control authorities. The cost of incorrectly assigning the control responsibility among various polluters is likely to be large, yet the control authorities do not have the information at their disposal to make a correct allocation. Those who have the information—the plant managers—are not inclined to share it. Can the cost-effective allocation be found? The answer depends on the particular approach taken by the control authority.

Emission Standards

We start our investigation of this question by supposing that the control authority pursues a traditional legal approach by imposing a separate emission standard on each source. In the economics literature, this approach is referred to as the *command-and-control (CAC)* approach. An *emission standard* is a legal limit on the amount of the pollutant an individual source is allowed to emit. In our example, it is clear that the two standards should add up to the allowable 15 units. However, it is not clear how, in the absence of information on control costs, these 15 units are to be allocated between the two sources. The easiest method of resolving this dilemma—and the one chosen in the earliest days of pollution control—would be to allocate each source an equal reduction. As is clear from Figure 14.3, this strategy would not be cost effective. Although the first source would have lower costs, this cost reduction would be substantially smaller than the increase faced by the second source; compared to a cost-effective allocation, total costs would increase if both sources were forced to clean up the same amount.

When emission standards are the policy of choice, there is no reason to believe that the authority will assign the responsibility for emission reduction in a cost-minimizing way. This is probably not surprising. Who would have believed otherwise?

Nonetheless, some policy instruments do allow the authority to allocate the emission reduction in a cost-effective manner even when it has no information on the magnitude of control costs. These policy approaches rely on economic incentives to produce the desired outcome. The two most common approaches are known as *emission charges* and *emissions trading* (or one variant of emissions trading known popularly as cap-and-trade).

Emission Charges

An emission charge is a fee, collected by the government, levied on each unit of pollutant emitted into the air or water. The total payment any source would make to the government could be found by multiplying the fee times the amount of pollution emitted. The emission-charge approach reduces pollution because, under it, pollution costs the firm money. To reduce its outlay on fees, the source seeks ways to reduce its pollution.

How much pollution control would the firm choose to purchase? A profit-maximizing firm would control, rather than emit, pollution whenever it proved cheaper to do so. We can illustrate the firm's decision with Figure 14.4. The level of uncontrolled emission is 15 units, and the emission charge is T. Thus, if the firm were to decide against controlling any emissions, it would have to pay T times 15, represented by area $0TBC$.

Is this the best the firm can do? Obviously not, because it can control some pollution at a lower cost than paying the emission charge. It would pay the firm to reduce emissions until the

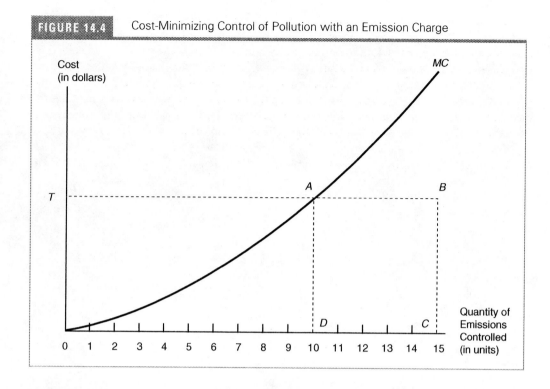

FIGURE 14.4   Cost-Minimizing Control of Pollution with an Emission Charge

marginal cost of reduction is equal to the emission charge. The firm would minimize its cost by choosing to clean up 10 units of pollution and emitting 5 units. At this allocation the firm would pay control costs equal to area 0*AD* and total emission charge payments equal to area *ABCD*, for a total cost of 0*ABC*. This is clearly less than 0*TBC*, the amount the firm would pay if it chose not to clean up any pollution.

Let's carry this one step further. Suppose that we levied the same emission charge on both sources shown in Figure 14.3. Each source would then control its emissions until its marginal-control cost equaled the emission charge. (Faced with an emission charge *T*, the second source would clean up 5 units.) Because they both are facing the same emission charge, they will *independently* choose levels of control consistent with equal marginal-control costs. This is precisely the condition that yields a cost-minimizing allocation.

This is a rather remarkable finding. We have shown that as long as the control authority imposes the same emission charge on all sources, the resulting incentives are *automatically* compatible with minimizing the costs of achieving that level of control. This is true in spite of the fact that the control authority may have no knowledge of control costs.

However, we have not yet dealt with the issue of how the appropriate level of the emission charge is determined. Each level of a charge will result in *some* level of emission reduction. Furthermore, as long as each firm minimizes its own costs the responsibility for meeting that reduction will be allocated in a manner that minimizes control costs for all firms.

How high should the charge be set in order to ensure that the resulting emission reduction is the *desired* level of emission reduction? Without having information on control costs, the control authority cannot establish the correct tax rate on the first try. It is possible, however, to develop an iterative trial-and-error process to find the appropriate charge rate. This process is initiated by choosing an arbitrary charge rate and observing the amount of reduction that occurs when that charge is imposed. If the observed reduction is larger than desired, the charge should be lowered; if the reduction is smaller, the charge should be raised. The new reduction that results from the adjusted charge can then be observed and compared with the desired reduction. Further adjustments in the charge can be made as needed. This process can be repeated until the actual and desired reductions are equal. At that point, the correct emission charge would have been found.

The charge system not only causes cost-minimizing sources to choose a *cost-effective allocation* on the control responsibility, but also it stimulates the development of newer, cheaper means of controlling emissions, as well as promoting technological progress. This is illustrated in Figure 14.5.

The reason for this is rather straightforward. Control authorities base the emission standards on specific technologies. As new technologies are discovered by the control authority, the standards are tightened. These stricter standards force firms to bear higher costs. Therefore, with emissions standards, firms have an incentive to hide technological changes from the control authority.

With an emissions-charge system the firm saves money by adopting cheaper new technologies. As long as the firm can reduce its pollution at a marginal cost lower than T, it pays to adopt the new technology. In Figure 14.5 the firm saves A and B by adopting the new technology and voluntarily reduces its emissions from Q_0 to Q_1.

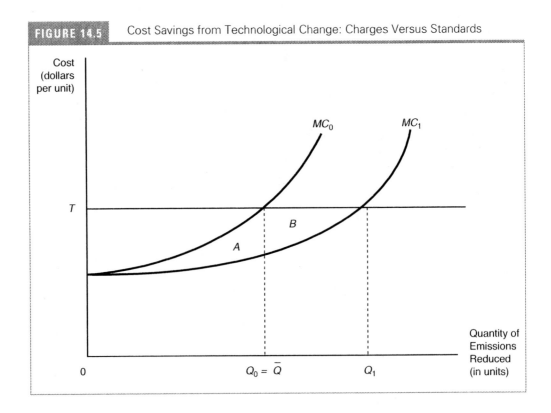

FIGURE 14.5   Cost Savings from Technological Change: Charges Versus Standards

With an emissions charge, the minimum cost allocation of meeting a predetermined emission reduction can be found by a control authority even when it has no information on control costs. An emission charge also stimulates technological advances in emission reduction. Unfortunately, the process for finding the appropriate rate would take some experimentation. During the trial-and-error period of finding the appropriate rate, sources would be faced with a volatile emission charge. Changing emission charges would make planning for the future difficult. Investments that would make sense under a high emission charge might not make sense when it falls. From either a policymaker's or business manager's perspective, this process leaves much to be desired.

Cap-and-Trade

Is it possible for the control authority to find the cost-minimizing allocation without going through a trial-and-error process? It is possible if *cap-and-trade* is the chosen policy. Under this system, all sources face a limit on their emissions and they are allocated allowances to emit. Each allowance authorizes a specific amount of emissions (commonly one ton). The control authority issues exactly the number of allowances needed to produce the desired emission level. These can be distributed among the firms either by auctioning them off to the highest bidder or by granting them directly to firms free-of-charge (an allocation referred to as "*gifting*"). However they are acquired the allowances are freely transferable; they can be bought and sold. Firms emitting more than their holdings would buy additional allowances from firms that are emitting less than authorized. Any emissions by a source in excess of those allowed by its allowance holdings at the end of the year would cause the source to face severe monetary sanctions.

Why this system automatically leads to a cost-effective allocation can be seen in Figure 14.6, which treats the same set of circumstances as in Figure 14.3. Consider first the gifting alternative. Suppose that the first source was allocated 7 allowances (each allowance corresponds to 1 emission unit). Because it has 15 units of uncontrolled emissions, this would mean it must control 8 units. Similarly, suppose that the second source was granted the remaining 8 allowances, meaning that it would have to clean up 7 units. Notice that both firms have an incentive to trade. The marginal cost of control for the second source (C) is substantially higher than that for the first (A). The second source could lower its cost if it could buy an allowance from the first source at a price lower than C. Meanwhile, the first source would be better off if it could sell an allowance for a price higher than A. Because C is greater than A, grounds for trade certainly exist.

A transfer of allowances would take place until the first source had only 5 allowances left (and controlled 10 units), while the second source had 10 allowances (and controlled 5 units). At this point, the allowance price would equal B, because that is the marginal value of that allowance to both sources, and neither source would have any incentive to trade further. The allowance market would be in equilibrium.

Notice that the market equilibrium for an emission-allowance system is the cost-effective allocation! Simply by issuing the appropriate number of allowances (15) and letting the market do the rest, the control authority can achieve a cost-effective allocation without having even the slightest knowledge about control costs. This system allows the government to meet its policy objective while allowing greater flexibility in how that objective is met.

How would this equilibrium change if the allowances were auctioned off? Interestingly, it wouldn't; both allocation methods lead to the same result. With *auctioned allowances* the

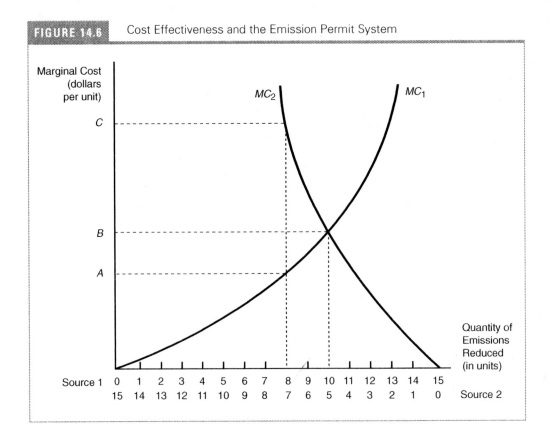

FIGURE 14.6 Cost Effectiveness and the Emission Permit System

allowance price that clears demand and supply is *B* and we have already demonstrated that *B* supports a cost-effective equilibrium.

The incentives created by this system ensure that sources use this flexibility to achieve the objective at the lowest possible cost. As we shall see in the next two chapters, this remarkable property has been responsible for the prominence of this type of approach in current attempts to reform the regulatory process. How far can the reforms go? Can developing countries use the experience of the industrialized countries to move directly into using these market-based instruments to control pollution?

As Debate 14.1 points out, that may be easier said than done.

◉ Other Policy Dimensions

Two main pollution-control policy instruments rely on economic incentives—charges and cap-and-trade. Both of these allow the control authority to distribute the responsibility for control in a cost-effective manner. The major difference between them that we have discussed so far is that, for the charge approach, the appropriate charge can be determined only by an iterative

Should Developing Countries Rely on Market-Based Instruments to Control Pollution?

Since the case for using market-based instruments seems so strong in principle, some observers, most prominently the World Bank (2000, pp. 40 and 43), have suggested that developing countries should capitalize on the experience of the industrialized countries to move directly to market-based instruments to control pollution. The desirability of this strategy is seen as flowing from the level of poverty in developing countries; abating pollution in the least expensive manner would seem especially important to poorer nations. Furthermore, since developing countries are frequently also starved for revenue, revenue-generating instruments (such as emissions charges or auctioned allowances) would seem to serve two significant social purposes at once. Proponents also point out that a number of developing countries already use market-based instruments.

Another school of thought (e.g., Russell and Vaughan, 2003) suggests that the differences in infrastructure between the developing and industrialized countries make the transfer of lessons from one context to another fraught with peril. They note that the effectiveness of market-based instruments presumes an effective monitoring and enforcement system, something that is frequently not present in developing countries. In their absence the superiority of market-based instruments is much less obvious.

Some middle ground is clearly emerging. Russell and Vaughan do not argue that market-based instruments should never be used in developing countries, but rather they argue that they may not be as universally appropriate as the most enthusiastic proponents suggest. They see themselves as telling a cautionary tale. And proponents are certainly beginning to see the crucial importance of infrastructure. Recognizing that some developing countries may be much better suited (by virtue of their infrastructure) to implement market-based systems than others, proponents are beginning to see capacity building as a logically prior step for those countries that need it.

As with other aspects of life, for market-based instruments, if it looks too good to be true, it probably is.

Sources: World Bank, *Greening Industry: New Roles for Communities, Markets and Governments* (Washington, DC: World Bank and Oxford University Press, 2000); and Russell, C. S. and W. J. Vaughan, "The Choice of Pollution Control Policy Instruments in Developing Countries: Arguments, Evidence and Suggestions," *The International Yearbook of Environmental and Resource Economics 2003/2004,* Folmer, H. and T. Tietenberg, eds. (Cheltenham, UK: Edward Elgar, 2003): 331–371.

trial-and-error process over time, whereas, for the cap-and-trade approach, the allowance price can be determined immediately by the market. Can other differences be identified?

The Revenue Effect

One of the differentiating characteristics of these instruments is their ability to raise revenue. Environmental taxes and *auctioned allowances* raise revenue, but cap-and-trade programs that gift the allowances do not. Does this difference matter?

It does for at least two reasons.[7] First, a number of authors (Parry, 1995; Bovenberg and Goulder, 1996; and Goulder, 1997) have noted that the revenue from environmental taxes or transferable allowances could be substituted for the revenue from distortionary taxes, thereby reducing those taxes and their associated distortions. When this substitution is made, the calculations indicate that it allows an increase in the present value of net benefits from the application of this instrument, an effect that has been called the *double dividend*. This effect creates a preference for instruments that can raise revenue as long as both the implementation of a revenue-raising instrument and the use of this revenue to reduce distortionary taxes are politically feasible.

The second important consideration is that the revenue from taxes or auctions could be used to reduce the burden on low-income households. The empirical evidence suggests that gifting allowances produces a regressive distribution of the control burden. (A *regressive distribution* is one that places a higher relative cost burden on low-income households or individuals as a percentage of their income than middle- or high-income households or individuals.) That same evidence has also demonstrated that the revenue from auctions or taxes can eliminate the regressiveness of the policy with proper targeting.

A final consequence of raising revenues involves their political feasibility. It seems quite clear that until 2008 using a gifting approach for the initial allocation of allowances has been a necessary ingredient to build the necessary political support for cap-and-trade legislation to be implemented (Raymond 2003). Existing users frequently have the power to block implementation while potential future users do not. This has made it politically expedient to allocate a substantial part of the economic rent from these resources to existing users as the price of securing their support, sometimes in creative ways (see Example 14.2).

On January 1, 2009, this historic tendency to gift allowances changed with the implementation of the Regional Greenhouse Gas Initiative (RGGI) in 10 northeastern states, from Maryland to Maine. This cap-and-trade program covers CO_2 emissions from large fossil-fuel fired electricity-generating plants.

A number of RGGI states have chosen to auction 100% of these allowances, using a sealed-bid system, with the revenue returned to the states. Most states have chosen to use the revenue to promote energy efficiency (see Example 14.3).

This particular approach not only caps carbon emissions, but also it simultaneously raises the level of investment in energy efficiency. These investments in energy efficiency reduce the cost of meeting the carbon targets. Costs are reduced not only because less energy is used, but also because the lower demand for energy lowers the demand (and hence the price) of the allowances.

It would be hard to overemphasize what a departure from the previous norm this venture into auctioning represented at the time. Allowing emitters to pollute up to the emissions standard without paying for the right to pollute (the traditional approach) implies that emitters have an implicit property right to pollute already; they don't have to buy it.

A cap-and-trade program with allowance auctions implies, in contrast, that the atmosphere is held in trust for the community and institutions that use the atmosphere for emission must

---

[7]The literature contains a fourth reason. It suggests that unless emitters cover all external costs via a revenue-raising instrument, the cost of production will be artificially low, production will be artificially high, and the industry will contain too many firms.

The Swedish Nitrogen Charge

EXAMPLE
14.2

One of the dilemmas facing those who wish to use charges to control pollution is that the amounts of revenue extracted from those subject to the tax can be considerable; this additional expense can produce significant political resistance to the policy. This resistance can be lowered if the revenue is rebated to those who pay it. But if all firms know they will receive their money back, the economic incentive to limit emissions is lost. Is it possible to design a system of rebates that will promote political feasibility without undermining abatement incentives?

The *Swedish nitrogen charge* was designed specifically to resolve this dilemma. Sweden's nitrogen oxide emission charge was first imposed in 1992 on large energy sources. Some 120 heating plants and industrial facilities with about 180 boilers were subject to the tax.

The plan was intended from the beginning to have a significant incentive effect, not to raise revenue. Although the charge rate is high by international standards (thereby producing an effective economic incentive), the revenue from this tax is not retained by the government, but rather is rebated to the emitting sources (thereby promoting acceptance of the policy of the regulated sources). It is the form of this rebate that makes this an interesting scheme. While the tax is collected on the basis of *emissions,* it is rebated on the basis of *energy production.* In effect, this system rewards plants that emit little per unit of energy and penalizes plants that emit more per unit of energy, thereby providing incentives to reduce emissions per unit of energy produced.

As expected, emissions per unit of energy produced fell rather dramatically. The Swedish Ministry of the Environment and Natural Resources has estimated that the benefits exceeded the costs by a factor of more than 3 to 1. Notice, however, that rebating the revenue means that this tax cannot produce a double dividend and it provides no incentives to reduce energy consumption.

Sources: Anderson, R. and A. Lohof, "Foreign Experience with Incentive Systems," *The United States Experience with Economic Incentives in Environmental Pollution Control Policy,* Section 11 (Washington, DC: Environmental Law Institute, 1997); and Sterner, T., *Policy Instruments for Environmental and Natural Resource Management.* (Washington, DC: Resources for the Future, 2003): 286–288.

pay to acquire that scarce right. Notice that this understanding of who actually holds the property right to the atmosphere completely changes the lens through which this regulation is viewed.

Economic analysis reminds us that putting a price on carbon (as a cap-and-trade policy does) is a necessary, but not sufficient, component of the efficient path to stabilizing the climate. Pricing carbon is necessary to correct the externality associated with the damages from climate change, but it is not sufficient to promote the efficient level of investment in energy efficiency (remember the discussion in Chapter 8?). While the cap-and-trade program corrects the climate externality whether or not the allowances are auctioned, auctioning the allowances and using the revenue to promote energy efficiency provides a faster, more efficient transition.

EXAMPLE

14.3

Maine's Energy and Carbon Savings Trust

The revenue received by Maine from the quarterly RGGI auctions is deposited into the Energy and Carbon Savings Trust, a specially created, quasi-independent organization. The enabling statute requires the Trustees to spend 85 percent of the efficiency funds on measures that reduce electricity use (remember the funds are raised from electricity generators) through the year 2011. The remaining 15 percent may be used for measures that directly reduce the consumption of fossil fuels.

The statute further stipulates that the money is to be allocated on a competitive bid basis, where the bids are compared on the basis of the amount of kilowatt-hours reduced (for electricity) or tons of CO_2 reduced (for fossil fuels) *per trust dollar expended*. (Notice how focusing on public dollars, as opposed to the sum of public and private dollars, provides an incentive for cost-sharing on the part of bidders—putting more of their own money and less public money into the project raises the ratio of the savings per trust dollar and, hence, increases the competitiveness of their bid.)

The first three allowance auctions raised approximately $8.9 million for this Trust. Facing a heating cost emergency soon after its formation, the Trust initially focused on allocating money as soon as possible to weatherize low-income households, but subsequent allocations were targeted at other residential customers, commercial and industrial enterprises as well as municipalities.

It is too early to judge the overall effectiveness of this program, but the evidence from other programs involving investment in energy efficiency is promising. Numerous studies indicate that government energy efficiency investments have a high rate of return.

Responses to Changes in the Regulatory Environment

One major additional difference concerns the manner in which these two systems react to changes in external circumstances in the absence of further decisions by the control authority. This is an important consideration, because bureaucratic procedures are notoriously sluggish and changes in policies are usually rendered rather slowly.[8] We will consider three such circumstances: (1) growth in the number of sources, (2) inflation, and (3) technological progress.

In a graphical representation, if the number of sources were to increase in a permit market, the demand for allowances would shift to the right. Given a fixed supply of allowances, the price would rise, as would the control costs, but the amount of emissions would remain the same. If charges were being used, in the absence of additional action by the control authority, the charge level would remain the same. This implies that the existing sources would control only what they would control in the absence of growth. Therefore, the arrival of new sources would cause a deterioration of air or water quality in the region. The costs of abatement would rise, because the costs

---

[8]This is probably particularly true when the modification involves a change in the rate at which firms are charged for their emissions.

of control paid by the new sources must be considered; however, they would rise by a lesser amount than in a permit market because of the lower amount of pollution being controlled. If the choice is between a fixed fee and a fixed number of allowances in a growing economy, the dominance of the permit system over the fixed-fee system increases over time (Butler and Maher, 1982).

With a permit system, inflation in the cost of control would automatically result in higher permit prices, but with a charge system it would result in lower control. Essentially, the real charge (i.e., the nominal charge adjusted for inflation) declines with inflation if the nominal charge remains the same.

However, we should not conclude that, over time, charges always result in less control than allowances do. Suppose, for example, that technological progress in designing pollution control equipment were to cause the marginal cost of abatement to fall. In an allowance system, this would result in lower prices and lower abatement costs but the same aggregate degree of control. With a charge system, the amount controlled would actually increase (remember Figure 14.5) and would therefore result in more control than an allowance system that, prior to the fall in costs, controlled the same amount.

If the control authority were to adjust the charge in each of these cases appropriately, the outcome would be identical to that achieved by an allowance market. The allowance market reacts automatically to these changes in circumstances, whereas the charge system requires a conscious administrative act to achieve the same result.

Instrument Choice Under Uncertainty

Another major difference between allowances and charges involves the cost of being wrong. Suppose that we have very imprecise information on damages caused and avoidance costs incurred by various levels of pollution, yet we have to choose either a charge level or a cap and live with it. What can be said about the relative merits of allowances versus charges in the face of this uncertainty?

The answer depends upon the circumstances. Allowances offer a great deal of certainty about the quantity of emissions; charges confer more certainty about the marginal cost of control. Therefore, an approach using allowances is the only system that allows an aggregate emission standard to be met with certainty. In other cases, however, when the objective is to minimize total costs (the sum of damage cost and control costs), allowances would be preferred when the costs of being wrong are more sensitive to changes in the quantity of emission than to changes in the marginal cost of control. Charges would be preferred when control costs were more important. When would that be the case?

When the marginal-damage curve is steeply sloped and the marginal-cost curve is rather flat, certainty about emissions is more important than certainty about control costs. Smaller deviations of actual emissions from expected emissions can cause a rather large deviation in damage costs, whereas control costs would be relatively insensitive to the degree of control. Allowances would prevent large fluctuations in these damage costs and would therefore yield a lower cost of being wrong than would charges (Weitzman, 1974).

Now suppose that the marginal-control-cost curve was steeply sloped, but the marginal-damage curve was flat. Small changes in the degree of control would have a large effect on abatement costs but would not affect damages very much. In this case, it makes sense to rely on charges to exercise more precise control over control costs, and to accept the less dire consequences of possible fluctuations in damage costs.

These cases suggest that a preference either for allowances or for charges in the face of uncertainty is not to be predetermined—it depends on the circumstances. Theory is not strong enough to dictate a choice. Empirical studies are necessary in order to establish a preference in a particular situation.

One interesting case involves the control of the greenhouse gases that intensify climate change. Though both the costs and benefits of control are subject to uncertainty, the long atmospheric lives of most greenhouse gases almost certainly make the marginal benefit cost curve (in present value terms) much flatter than the marginal control cost curve (Pizer, 2002). Therefore, following Weitzman, it would be better to use a tax-based instrument to control the price of greenhouse gas emissions, than to use allowances to control the quantity of emissions. As we will see, the Kyoto Protocol, the international agreement to control greenhouse gases, does not follow this prescription.

Product Charges: Another Form of Environmental Taxation

The use of emission charges presumes that it is possible to monitor and track the level of emissions in order to levy the appropriate tax. Sometimes it is either impossible or impractical.

One strategy that has been employed in this circumstance is to tax the commodity most directly responsible for the emissions, rather than the emissions themselves. For example, one might tax gasoline rather than attempt to measure (and tax) the emissions from every gasoline-powered vehicle. And several countries tax fertilizer rather than attempt to measure the amount of contamination of groundwater sources from each bag sold. The Irish have even taxed plastic bags to prevent littering (see Example 14.4).

While frequently product charges are simpler to administer, it is important to keep in mind that they are not equivalent to emissions charges. Not every unit of the taxed product may have the same impact on the environment. For example, some purchased fertilizer may be used in sensitive areas (and therefore should be heavily taxed for efficiency), while others may be used in areas with lots of natural buffering (and therefore should not be taxed as heavily). Since the product charge would be the same per bag of fertilizer, it would not be able to make these kinds of distinctions. Product charges are most efficient when all purchased units of that product cause exactly the same marginal damage. Although full efficiency is probably rarely achieved by product charges, they may be better (even much better) than doing nothing.

Summary

In this chapter we developed the conceptual framework needed to evaluate current approaches to pollution control policy. The efficient amount of a fund pollutant was defined as the amount that minimizes the sum of damage and control costs. Using this definition, we were able to derive two propositions of interest: (1) The efficient level of pollution would vary from region to region and (2) the efficient level of pollution would not generally be zero, though in some particular circumstances it might.

The Irish Bag Levy

EXAMPLE
14.4

Rapid economic growth in Ireland in the 1990s was marked by a significant increase in the amount of solid waste per capita. The lack of adequate landfill sites resulted in escalating costs of waste disposal, which in turn led to illegal dumping and littering. It was feared that tourism, one of Ireland's largest industries, would be negatively affected as a consequence of environmental degradation. The food industry, which had based a significant amount of its marketing strategies on a healthy, wholesome reputation, also suffered as a result of the public's perception of the industry's role in the increased litter.

Plastic bags were the most visible element of litter, so in 2002, the government introduced the Plastic Bag Environmental Levy on all plastic shopping bags, with a few exceptions that were sanctioned for health and safety reasons. Retailers were charged a fee of 15c per plastic bag, which they were obliged, by the government, to pass on to the consumer. This levy was designed to alter consumer behavior by creating financial incentives for consumers to choose more environmentally friendly alternatives to plastic, such as bags-for-life (heavy-duty, re-usable cloth or woven bags, which are available in all supermarkets, at an average cost of €1.27).

The government's expectation that this levy would bring about a 50 percent reduction in the number of plastic bags used was exceeded when the estimated actual reduction turned out to be 95 percent! In a single year, Irish consumers reduced their consumption of plastic bags from 1.26 billion to 120,000, while concurrently raising approximately €10 million in revenue for the government. The revenue was placed in the Environmental Fund, which finances environmental initiatives such as recycling, waste management, and most importantly, anti-litter campaigns.

This levy has been viewed as a major success by the government and environmental groups alike. It has also been enthusiastically embraced by Irish consumers, thanks to an intensive environmental awareness campaign that was launched in conjunction with the levy. Irish retailers, although skeptical in the beginning, have also recognized the huge benefits of the levy. Estimates suggest that their costs are offset by the savings from no longer having to provide free disposable bags to customers, as well as the profit margin earned on the sale of bags-for-life whose sales have increased by 600 percent to 700 percent since the introduction of the levy. The amount of plastic being sent to Irish landfills has been dramatically reduced, bringing about a clear, visual improvement.

Source: Dungan, Linda, "What Were the Effects of the Plastic Bag Environmental Levy on the Litter Problem in Ireland?" available at http://www.colby.edu/~thtieten/litter.htm.

Because pollution is a classic externality, markets will generally produce more than the efficient amount of both fund pollutants and stock pollutants. For both types of pollutants, this will imply higher-than-efficient damages and lower-than-efficient control costs. For stock pollutants, an excessive amount of pollution would build up in the environment, imposing a detrimental externality on future generations as well as on current generations.

The market would not provide any automatic ameliorating response to the accumulation of pollution as it would in the case of natural-resource scarcity. Firms unilaterally attempting to control their pollution can be placed at a competitive disadvantage. Hence, the case for some sort of government intervention is particularly strong for pollution control.

Although policy instruments could, in principle, be defined in such a way as to achieve an efficient level of pollution for every emitter, in practice, it is very difficult because the amount of information required by the control authorities is unrealistically high.

Cost-effectiveness analysis provides a way out of this dilemma. When the objective is defined in terms of reducing emissions by a predetermined amount, uniform emission charges or a cap-and-trade system could be used to attain the cost-effective allocation even when the control authority has no information whatsoever on either control costs or damage costs. Uniform emission standards would not, except by coincidence, be cost effective. In addition, reliance on either allowances or charges would stimulate more technological progress in pollution control than would reliance on emission standards.

An important characteristic of auctioned allowances and taxes is that they can raise revenue. If the revenue from pollution charges or auctioned allowances can be used to reduce revenue from other, more distortionary taxes (such as labor or income taxes), greater welfare gains can be achieved from revenue-raising instruments than instruments that raise no revenue. While a cap-and-trade approach that relies on gifting is regressive in the distribution of its burden, targeting some of the revenue from auctions at lower income individuals or households can produce a *progressive distribution of the cost burden*. Politically, however, until RGGI transferring some or all of that revenue back to the sources either by gifting the allowances or including some sort of tax rebate has been an important aspect of securing political support for implementing the system. Whether the historical model of gifting to the emitters or the RGGI model of auctioned allowances with revenue used to reduce the burden of all ultimately prevails remains to be seen.

Finally note that a cap-and-trade approach and the charge approach respond differently to growth in the number of sources, to inflation, to technological change, and to uncertainty.

We can now use this framework to evaluate the rather different policy approaches that have been taken toward the major sources of pollution.

Key Concepts

absorptive capacity, *p.* 301

auctioned allowances, *p.* 315

cap-and-trade, *p.* 313

command-and-control (CAC), *p.* 310

cost-effective allocation (of uniformly mixed pollutants), *p.* 312

double dividend, *p.* 316

efficient allocation of pollution, *p.* 303

emission charges, *p.* 310

emission standard, *p.* 310

emissions trading, *p.* 310

energy production, *p.* 317

fund pollutants, *p.* 302

gifting, *p.* 313

global pollutant, *p.* 302

market allocation of pollution, *p.* 305

progressive distribution of the cost burden, *p.* 322

regressive distribution of the cost burden, *p.* 316

residual, *p.* 305

stock pollutants, *p.* 302

Swedish nitrogen charge, *p.* 317

Further Reading

Baumol, W. J. and W. E. Oates. *The Theory of Environmental Policy,* 2nd ed. (Cambridge, UK: Cambridge University Press, 1988). A classic on the economic analysis of externalities. Accessible only to those with a thorough familiarity with multivariate calculus.

Harrington, W., R. D. Morgenstern, and T. Sterner. *Choosing Environmental Policy: Comparing Instruments and Outcomes in the United States and Europe* (Washington, DC: Resources for the Future, 2004). Uses paired case studies from the United States and Europe to contrast the costs and outcomes of direct regulation on one side of the Atlantic with an incentive-based policy on the other.

OECD. *Economic Instruments for Environmental Protection* (Paris: Organization for Economic Co-operation and Development, 1989). A survey of how economic incentive approaches to pollution control have been used in the industrialized nations that belong to the OECD.

OECD. *Environment and Taxation: The Cases of the Netherlands, Sweden and the United States* (Paris: Organization for Economic Co-operation and Development, 1994). Background case studies for a larger research project seeking to discover the extent to which fiscal and environmental policies could be made not only compatible, but mutually reinforcing.

Rock, M. *Pollution Control in East Asia: Lessons from Newly Industrializing Countries* (Washington, DC: Resources for the Future, Inc., 2002). These studies of pollution management in East Asia's newly industrialized economies (NIEs) include successful government responses in Singapore and Taiwan, qualified results in China and Indonesia, and much more limited success in Thailand and Malaysia.

Stavins, R. N. "Experience with Market Based Environmental Policy Instruments," *Handbook of Environmental Economics, Volume 1: Environmental Degradation and Institutional Responses,* Maler, K. G. and J. R. Vincent, eds. (Amsterdam: Elsevier, 2003): 355–435. A review of what we have learned from our experience with market-based instruments.

Sterner, T. *Policy Instruments for Environmental and Natural Resource Management.* (Washington, DC: Resources for the Future, Inc., 2003). Intended primarily for audiences in developing and transitional countries, the book compares the accumulated experiences of the use of economic policy instruments in the United States and Europe, as well as in select rich and poor countries in Asia, Africa, and Latin America.

Tietenberg, T., ed. Emissions Trading Programs, *Volume 1: Implementation and Evolution and Volume II Theory and Design,* International Library of Environmental Economics and Policy (Aldershot, UK: Ashgate, 2001). A two-volume collection of the leading published articles on emissions trading, coupled with an editor's introduction that traces the history of our state of knowledge about this policy instrument.

Additional References

Bovenberg, A. L. and L. H. Goulder. "Optimal Environmental Taxation in the Presence of Other Taxes: General-Equilibrium Analyses," *American Economic Review* 86 (1996) (4): 985–1000.

Bovenberg, A. Lans and Lawrence H. Goulder. "Neutralizing the Adverse Industry Impacts of CO_2 Abatement Policies: What Does It Cost?" *Behavioural and Distributional Effects of*

Environmental Policies: Evidence and Controversies, Carraro, C. and G. Metcalf, eds., (Chicago: University of Chicago Press, 2001).

Boyd, J. "Water Pollution Taxes: A Good Idea Doomed to Failure?" *Public Finance and Management* 3 (2003) (1): 34–66.

Bressers, H.T.A. and K.R.D. Lulofs. "Industrial Water Pollution in the Netherlands: A Fee-Base Approach," *Choosing Environmental Policy: Comparing Instruments and Outcomes in the United States and Europe,* Harrington, W.R.D. Morgenstern, and T. Sterner, eds. (Washington, DC: Resources for the Future Inc., 2004): 91–116.

Butler, Richard V. and Michael D. Maher. "The Control of Externalities in a Growing Economy," *Economic Inquiry* 20 (January 1982) (1): 155–163.

Collinge, R. A. and W. E. Oates. "Efficiency in Pollution Control in the Short and Long Runs: A System of Rental Emission Permits," *Canadian Journal of Economics* 15 (May 1982): 347–354.

Goulder, L. H. "Environmental Taxation in a Second-Best World," *The International Yearbook of Environmental and Resource Economics 1997/1998,* Tietenberg, T. and H. Folmer, eds. (Cheltenham, UK: Edward Elgar, 1997): 28–54.

Harrington, W. "Industrial Water Pollution in the United States; Direct Regulation or Market Incentive," *Choosing Environmental Policy: Comparing Instruments and Outcomes in the United States and Europe,* Harrington, W., R. D. Morgenstern, and T. Sterner, eds. (Washington, DC: Resources for the Future, 2004): 67–90.

Jurado, J. and D. Southgate. "Dealing with Air Pollution in Latin America: The Case of Quito, Ecuador," *Environment and Development Economics* 4 (1999) (3): 375–387.

Kelman, Steven. *What Price Incentives? Economists and the Environment* (Westport, CT: Greenwood Publishing Group, 1981).

Kraemer, A. and K. M. Banholzer. "Tradable Permits in Water Resource Management and Water Pollution Control," *Implementing Domestic Tradable Permits for Environmental Protection,* OECD, Organization for Economic Co-operation and Development (1999): 75–107.

Levinson, A. "Grandfather Regulations, New Source Bias, and State Air Toxics Regulations," *Ecological Economics* 28 (1999) (2): 299–311.

Milliman, Scott R. and Raymond Prince. "Firm Incentives to Promote Technological Change in Pollution Control," *Journal of Environmental Economics and Management* 17 (November 1989): 247–265.

Montgomery, David W. "Markets in Licenses and Efficient Pollution Control Programs," *Journal of Economic Theory* 5 (December 1982): 395–418.

Parry, I.W.H. "Pollution Taxes and Revenue Recycling," *Journal of Environmental Economics and Management* 29 (1995) (3 Suppl. Part 2): S64–S77.

Pezzey, J.C.V. "Emission Taxes and Tradeable Permits—A Comparison of Views on Long-run Efficiency," *Environmental & Resource Economics* 26 (2003) (2): 329–342.

Pizer, William A. "Combining Price and Quantity Controls to Mitigate Global Climate Change," *Journal of Public Economics* 85 (2002): 409–434.

Raymond, L. *Private Rights in Public Resources: Equity and Property Allocation in Market-Based Environmental Policy* (Washington, DC: Resources for the Future, 2003).

Sipes, K. N. and R. Mendelsohn. "The Effectiveness of Gasoline Taxation to Manage Air Pollution," *Ecological Economics* 36 (2001) (2): 299–309.

Soderholm, P. "Pollution Charges in a Transition Economy: The Case of Russia," *Journal of Economic Issues* 33(1999) (2): 403–410.

Stavins, Robert N. "Harnessing Market Forces to Protect the Environment," *Environment* 31 (January/February 1989): 4–7, 28–35.

Tietenberg, T. "Lessons from Using Transferable Permits to Control Air Pollution in the United States," *Handbook of Environmental and Resource Economics,* VandenBergh, J.C.J., ed. (Cheltenham, UK: Edward Elgar, 1999): 275–292.

Tietenberg, T. H. "Tradable Permits for Pollution Control When Emission Location Matters: What Have We Learned?" *Environmental and Resource Economics* 5 (1995) (2): 95–113.

Tisato, Peter. "Pollution Standards vs. Charges Under Uncertainty," *Environmental and Resource Economics* 4 (1994): 295–304.

Woodward, R. T., R. A. Kaiser, et al. "The Structure and Practice of Water Quality Trading Markets," *Journal of the American Water Resources Association* 38 (2002) (4): 967–979.

Historically Significant References

Dales, J. H. *Pollution, Property and Prices* (Toronto: Toronto University Press, 1968).

Weitzman, M. L. (1974). "Prices vs. Quantities." *Review of Economic Studies* 41: 477–491.

Discussion Questions

1. In his book (*What Price Incentives?*) Steven Kelman suggests that from an ethical point of view, the use of economic incentives (e.g., emission charges or emission permits) in environmental policy is undesirable. He argues that transforming our mental image of the environment from a sanctified preserve to a marketable commodity has detrimental effects not only on our use of the environment but also on our attitude toward it. His point is that applying economic incentives to environmental policy weakens and cheapens our traditional values with regard to the environment.

   a. Consider the effects of economic-incentive systems on prices paid by the poor, on employment, and on the speed of compliance with pollution control laws—as well as the Kelman arguments. Are economic-incentive systems more or less ethically justifiable than the traditional regulatory approach?

   b. Kelman seems to feel that because emission permits automatically prevent environmental degradation, they are more ethically desirable than emission charges. Do you agree? Why or why not?

15 Stationary-Source Local and Regional Air Pollution

When choosing between two evils, I always like to try the one I've never tried before.

—MAE WEST, Actress

Introduction

Attaining and maintaining clear air is an exceedingly difficult policy task. In the United States, for example, an estimated 27,000 major stationary sources of air pollution, as well as hundreds of thousands of more minor sources, are subject to control. Many distinct production processes emit many different types of pollutants. The resulting damages range from minimal effects on plants and vegetation to the possible modification of the earth's climate.

The policy response to this problem has been continually evolving. The *Clean Air Act Amendments of 1970* set a bold new direction, which has been retained and refined by subsequent acts. By virtue of that Act, the federal government assumed a much larger and much more vigorous direct role. The U.S. Environmental Protection Agency (EPA) was created to implement and oversee this massive attempt to control the injection of substances into our air. Individually tailored strategies were created to deal with mobile and stationary sources.

Conventional Pollutants

Conventional pollutants are relatively common substances, found in almost all parts of the country, and are presumed to be dangerous only in high concentrations. In the United States these pollutants are called *criteria pollutants* because the Clean Air Act Amendments require that the EPA produce "criteria documents" to be used in setting acceptable standards for these pollutants. These documents summarize and evaluate all of the existing research on the various health and environmental effects associated with these pollutants. The central focus of air pollution control during the 1970s was on criteria pollutants.

The Command-and-Control Policy Framework

In Chapter 14 several possible approaches to controlling pollution were described and analyzed in theoretical terms. The historical approach to air pollution control has been based primarily on emission standards, a traditional command-and-control (CAC) approach. In this section we will outline the specific nature of this approach, analyze it from both an efficiency and a cost-effectiveness perspective, and examine how a series of rather recent reforms based on economic incentives has worked to rectify some of these deficiencies.

For each of the conventional pollutants, the typical first step is to establish *ambient air quality standards*. These standards set legal ceilings on the allowable concentration of the pollutant in the outdoor air averaged over a specified time period. For many pollutants the standard is defined in terms of a long-term average (normally, as an annual average) and a short-term average (e.g., a three-hour average). These short-term averages can usually be exceeded no more than once a year. These standards have to be met everywhere, although as a practical matter they are monitored at a large number of specific locations. Control costs can be quite sensitive to the level of these short-term averages.

In the United States two ambient standards have been defined.[1] The *primary standard*, which is designed to protect human health, was the first standard to have been determined, and it had the earliest deadlines for compliance. All pollutants have a primary standard. The primary ambient standards are required by statute to be set at a level sufficient to protect even the most sensitive members of the population without any consideration given to the costs of meeting them.

The *secondary standard* has been designed to protect other aspects of human welfare from those pollutants having separate effects. Protection is afforded by the secondary standard for aesthetics (particularly visibility), physical objects (houses, monuments, and so on), and vegetation. When a separate secondary standard exists, both it and the primary standard must be met. The existing primary and secondary standards are given in Table 15.1.

Although the EPA is responsible for defining the ambient standards, the primary responsibility for ensuring that the ambient air quality standards are met falls on the state control agencies. They exercise this responsibility by developing and executing an acceptable *state implementation plan (SIP)*, which must be approved by the EPA. This plan divides the state up into separate air quality control regions. There are special procedures for handling regions that cross state borders, such as the metropolitan New York area.

The SIP spells out for each control region the procedures and timetables for meeting local ambient standards and for abatement of the effects of locally emitted pollutants on other states. The degree of control required depends on the severity of the pollution problem in each of the control regions. All areas not meeting the original deadlines are designated as *nonattainment regions*.

The areas receiving this designation are subjected to particularly stringent controls. Nonattainment areas are placed within one of seven categories (basic, marginal, moderate, serious, two

---

[1] We will discuss the U.S. approach in some detail. Many industrialized countries have rather similar policies.

TABLE 15.1 National Ambient Air Quality Standards

Pollutant	Standard Value	Standard Type
Carbon Monoxide (CO)		
8-hour average[a]	9 ppm (10 mg/m^3)	Primary
1-hour average[a]	35 ppm (40 mg/m^3)	Primary
Nitrogen Dioxide (NO$_2$)		
Annual arithmetic mean	0.053 ppm (100 µg/m^3)	Primary and secondary
Ozone (O$_3$)		
1-hour average[f]	0.12 ppm (235 µg/m^3)	Primary and secondary
8-hour average[e]	0.08 ppm (157 µg/m^3)	Primary and secondary
Lead (Pb)		
Quarterly average	1.5 µg/m^3	Primary and secondary
Particulate (PM 10) *Particles with diameters of 10 micrometers or less*		
Annual arithmetic mean[b]	50 µg/m^3	Primary and secondary
24-hour average[a]	150 µg/m^3	Primary and secondary
Particulate (PM 2.5) *Particles with diameters of 2.5 micrometers or less*		
Annual arithmetic mean[c]	15 µg/m^3	Primary and secondary
24-hour average[d]	65 µg/m^3	Primary and secondary
Sulfur Dioxide (SO$_2$)		
Annual arithmetic mean	0.03 ppm (80 µg/m^3)	Primary
24-hour average[a]	0.14 ppm (365 µg/m^3)	Primary
3-hour average[a]	0.50 ppm (1,300 µg/m^3)	Secondary

[a]The standard may not be exceeded more than once per year.

[b]To attain this standard, the expected annual arithmetic mean PM10 concentration at each monitor within an area must not exceed 50 µg/m^3.

[c]To attain this standard, the 3-year average of the annual arithmetic mean PM2.5 concentrations from single or multiple community-oriented monitors must not exceed 15.0 µg/m^3.

[d]To attain this standard, the 3-year average of the 98th percentile of 24-hour concentrations at each population-oriented monitor within an area must not exceed 65 µg/m^3.

[e]To attain this standard, the 3-year average of the fourth-highest daily maximum 8-hour average ozone concentrations measured at each monitor within an area over each year must not exceed 0.08 ppm.

[f](a) The standard is attained when the expected number of days per calendar year with maximum hourly average concentrations above 0.12 ppm is ≤1.

(b) The 1-hour NAAQS will no longer apply to an area one year after the effective date of the designation of that area for the 8-hour ozone NAAQS. The effective designation date for most areas is June 15, 2004 (40 CFR 50.9; see Federal Register of April 30, 2004 (69 FR 23996)).

Source: USEPA http://www.epa.gov/airtrends/sixpoll.html.

categories of severe, and extreme). Each category has its own criteria for compliance with the standard. Generally, the more severe the degree of nonattainment in an area, the more stringent the requirements imposed on it. To prod the states into action, Congress gave the EPA the power to halt the construction of major new or modified pollution sources and to deny federal sewage and transportation grants for any state not submitting a plan showing precisely how and when attainment would be reached.

Recognizing that it is typically much easier and cheaper to control new sources rather than existing ones, the Clean Air Act established the *New Source Review (NSR) Program*. This program requires all new major stationary sources (as well as those undergoing major modifications) in both attainment and nonattainment areas to seek a permit for operation. This permit requires compliance with the lowest achievable emission rate standard (LAER) in nonattainment areas and the best available control technology (BACT) in attainment areas. The theory is that as old, dirtier plants become obsolete, the NSR program will assure that replacements will be significantly less polluting. As Debate 15.1 points out, the specific approach embodied in the New Source Review Program is controversial.

DEBATE 15.1

Does Sound Policy Require Targeting New Sources via the New Source Review?

One of the characteristics of the New Source Review program is that it requires major stationary sources that are undergoing major modifications (not just routine maintenance) to meet the same stringent standards as new sources, while allowing old sources to avoid installing the more stringent control technology. Due to the routine maintenance exemption, a number of older plants have never triggered the major modification threshold and therefore have never been upgraded. As a result, these older plants have become responsible for a larger share of the total emissions.

One approach, taken by the Clinton Administration, was to take enforcement actions against individual companies, including numerous electric utilities that own and operate coal-fired power plants in the Southeast and Midwest. The lawsuits alleged that plants that should have been retired years earlier were being modified and retained past their normal life under the cover of "routine maintenance." Using this exemption to prop up the plants was seen as an evasion of the need to retire older plants and replace them with modern plants meeting the more stringent (and costly) new source control requirements.

Opponents of the New Source Review process argue that it has been counter productive, resulting in worse air quality, not better, and it should be replaced, not merely better enforced. According to this view not only has New Source Review deterred investment in newer, cleaner technologies, but it has also discouraged companies from keeping power plants maintained. The solution, they argue, is to use cap-and-trade to create a level playing field, where all electricity generators would have the same environmental requirements, whether plants are old or new. Under this new approach policy plant owners would pursue the investment and/or retirement strategies that secured emissions reductions at minimum cost. Since an artificial delay in replacing plants would no longer make any economic sense with the new incentives created by cap-and-trade, private, and social goals would be harmonized.

Source: Stavins, Robert, "Vintage-Differentiated Environmental Regulation," Stanford Environmental Law Journal, 25(1), 2006: 29-63.

One final characteristic of the Clean Air Act is that it rules out tailoring the degree of control to the prevailing meteorological conditions. All strategies must achieve better air quality through emission reductions stringent enough to ensure compliance in quite adverse conditions.

The Efficiency of the Command-and-Control Approach

Efficiency presumes that the ambient standards are set where the marginal benefit equals the marginal cost. To ascertain whether or not the current standards are efficient, it is necessary to inquire into five aspects of the standard-setting process: (1) the threshold concept on which the standards are based, (2) the level of the standard, (3) the choice of uniform standards over standards more tailored to the regions involved, (4) the timing of emission flows, and (5) the failure to incorporate the degree of human exposure in the standard-setting process.

The Threshold Concept. Some basis is needed for setting the ambient standard. Because the Clean Air Act prohibits the balancing of costs and benefits, some alternative criterion must be used. For the primary (health-related) standard, this criterion is known as the *health threshold*. The standard is to be defined with a margin of safety sufficiently high that no adverse health effects would be suffered by any member of the population as long as the air quality is at least as good as that specified by the standards. This approach presumes the existence of a threshold such that concentrations above that level produce adverse health effects, but concentrations below it produce none.

If the threshold concept were valid, the marginal-damage function would be zero until the threshold were reached and would be positive at higher concentrations. The belief that the actual damage function has this shape is not consistent with the latest evidence. Adverse health effects can occur at pollution levels lower than the ambient standards. The standard that produces no adverse health effects among the general population (which, of course, includes especially susceptible groups) is probably zero or close to it. It is certainly lower than the established ambient standards. What the standards purport to accomplish and what they actually accomplish are rather different.

The Level of the Ambient Standard. The absence of a defensible threshold complicates the analysis (see Debate 15.2). Some other basis must be used for determining the level at which the standard should be established. Efficiency would dictate setting the standard in order to maximize the net benefit, which includes a consideration of costs as well as benefits.

The current policy explicitly excludes costs from consideration in setting the ambient standards. Costs are allowed to enter the process only when the policy instruments used to meet ambient standards are being defined. It is difficult to imagine that the process of setting the ambient standards would yield an efficient outcome when it is prohibited from considering one of the key elements of that outcome!

Unfortunately, for reasons that were discussed in some detail in Chapter 3, our current benefit measurements are not sufficiently reliable as to permit the identification of the efficient level with any confidence. The EPA study of the Clean Air Act, summarized earlier in Chapter 2, found that the total monetized benefits of the Clean Air Act realized during the period from

DEBATE 15.2

The Particulate and Smog Ambient Standards Controversy

In proposing more stringent ambient standards for ozone and particulates, the USEPA concluded that 125 million Americans, including 35 million children, were not adequately protected by the existing standards. The new standards were estimated to prevent one million additional serious respiratory illnesses each year, and 15,000 additional premature deaths.

The proposed revisions were controversial because the cost of compliance would be very high. No health threshold existed at the chosen level (some health effects would be noticed at even more stringent levels than those proposed) and the EPA was, by law, prohibited from using a benefit/cost justification. In the face of legal challenge the EPA found it very difficult to defend the superiority of the chosen standards from slightly more stringent or slightly less stringent standards.

In a decision issued May 14, 1999, the United States Court of Appeals for the District of Columbia Circuit overturned the proposed revisions. In a 2:1 ruling, the three-judge panel rejected the EPA's approach to setting the level of those standards:

> ...the construction of the Clean Air Act on which EPA relied in promulgating the NAAQS at issue here effects an unconstitutional delegation of legislative power. Although the factors EPA uses in determining the degree of public health concern associated with different levels of ozone and PM are reasonable, EPA appears to have articulated no 'intelligible principle' to channel its application of these factors ... EPA's formulation of its policy judgment leaves it free to pick any point between zero and a hair below the concentrations yielding London's Killer Fog.

Though the threat to the EPA's authority posed by this decision was ultimately overturned by the Supreme Court, the dilemma posed by the absence of a compelling health threshold remains.

1970 to 1990 range from $5.6 trillion to $49.4 trillion, with a central estimate of $22.2 trillion (USEPA, Office of Air and Radiation, 1997). That is a very large band of uncertainty.

The study further noted:

> The central estimate of 22.2 trillion dollars in benefits may be a significant underestimate due to the exclusion of large numbers of benefits from the monetized benefit estimate (e.g., all air toxics effects; ecosystem effects; numerous health effects. (p. ES-8)

These figures suggest that a high degree of confidence can be attached to the belief that government intervention to control air pollution in the United States was justified, but they provide no evidence whatsoever on whether current policy was, or is, efficient.

Uniformity. The same primary and secondary standards apply to all parts of the country. No account is taken of the number of people exposed, the sensitivity of the local ecology, or the costs of compliance in various areas. All of these would have some effect on the efficient standard, and efficiency would therefore dictate different standards for different regions. In general, the evidence suggests that the inefficiencies associated with uniformity are greatest in rural areas.

Timing of Emission Flows. Because concentrations are important for criteria pollutants, the timing of emissions is an important policy concern. Emissions clustered in time are as troublesome as emissions clustered in space. How do we handle those relatively rare but devastating occasions when thermal inversions prevent the normal dispersion and dilution of the pollutants?

From an economic efficiency point of view, the most obvious approach is to tailor the degree of control to the circumstances. Stringent control would be exercised when meteorological conditions were relatively stagnant; less stringent control would be applied under normal circumstances. A reliance on a constant degree of control, rather than allowing intermittent controls, raises compliance costs substantially, particularly when the required degree of control is high. The strong stand against intermittent controls in the Clean Air Act, however, rules out this approach.

Concentration Versus Exposure. Present ambient standards are defined in terms of pollutant concentrations in the outdoor air, yet health effects are more closely related to human exposure to pollutants. (Exposure is determined both by the concentrations of air pollutants in each of the places in which people spend time and by the amount of time spent in each place.) Because in the United States only about 10 percent of the population's person-hours are spent outdoors, indoor air becomes very important in designing strategies to improve the health risk of pollutants. Some studies have suggested that exposure to pollutants is several times higher indoors than it is outdoors (Smith, 1988). To date, despite its apparent importance, very little attention has been focused on controlling indoor air pollution.[2]

Cost-Effectiveness of the Command-and-Control Approach

The ambient standards are not efficient, but determining the magnitude of the inefficiency is plagued by uncertainties. It is not possible to state definitively just how inefficient they are.

Cost-effectiveness is based on somewhat more solid evidence. Although it does not allow us to shed any light on whether a particular ambient standard is efficient or not, cost-effectiveness studies do allow us to see whether the command-and-control policy described earlier has resulted in the ambient standards being met in the least costly manner possible.

As we have seen, the CAC strategy will normally not be cost effective, but general principles are not enough to establish the degree to which this strategy diverges from the least-cost ideal. If the divergence is small, the proponents of reform would not likely be able to overcome the inertia of the status quo. If the divergence is large, the case for reform is stronger.

The cost-effectiveness of the CAC approach depends on local circumstances. Several simulation models capable of dealing with these complexities have been constructed for a number of different pollutants for a variety of metropolitan areas (see Table 15.2).

---

[2]The one major policy response to indoor air pollution has been the large number of states that have passed legislation requiring "smoke-free" areas in public places to protect nonsmokers.

For a number of reasons, the estimated costs cannot be directly compared across studies; therefore, it is appropriate to develop a means of comparing them that minimizes the comparability problems. One such technique, the one we have chosen, involves calculating the ratio of

TABLE 15.2 Empirical Studies of Air Pollution Control

Study and Year	Pollutants Covered	Geographic Area	CAC Benchmark	Assumed Pollutant Type	Ratio of CAC Cost to Least Cost
Atkinson and Lewis (1974)	Particulates	St. Louis metropolitan area	SIP regulations	Nonuniformly mixed	6.00
Roach et al. (1981)	Sulfur dioxide	Four Corners in Utah, Colorado, Arizona, and New Mexico	SIP regulations	Nonuniformly mixed	4.25
Hahn and Noll (1982)	Sulfates	Los Angeles standards	California emission	Nonuniformly mixed	1.07
Krupnick (1983)	Nitrogen dioxide	Baltimore regulations	Proposed RACT	Nonuniformly mixed	5.96
Seskin, Anderson, and Reid (1983)	Nitrogen dioxide	Chicago	Proposed RACT regulations	Nonuniformly mixed	14.40
McGartland (1984)	Particulates	Baltimore	SIP regulations	Nonuniformly mixed	4.18
Spofford (1984)	Sulfur dioxide	Lower Delaware Valley	Uniform percentage reduction	Nonuniformly mixed	1.78
	Particulates	Lower Delaware Valley	Uniform percentage reduction	Nonuniformly mixed	22.00
Maloney and Yandle (1984)	Hydrocarbons	All domestic DuPont plants	Uniform percentage reduction	Uniformly mixed	4.15
O'Ryan (1995)	Particulates	Santiago, Chile	PER/APS	Nonuniformly mixed	1.31

Definitions:
APS = Ambient permit system
CAC = Command-and-control, the traditional regulatory approach
PER = Percentage emisson reduction
SIP = State implementation plan
RACT = Reasonably available control technologies, a set of standards imposed on existing sources in nonattainment areas

the CAC allocation costs to the lowest cost of meeting the same objective for each study. A ratio equal to 1.0 implies that the CAC allocation is cost effective. By subtracting 1.0 from the ratio in the table, it is possible to interpret the remainder as the percentage increase in cost from the least-cost ideal that results from relying on the CAC system.

Of the 10 reported comparisons, 8 find that the CAC policy costs at least 78 percent more than the least-cost allocation. If we omit the 1982 study by Hahn and Noll (1982) (for reasons discussed in the next two paragraphs), the study involving the *smallest* cost savings (particulates in Santiago) finds that the CAC allocation results in abatement costs that are 31 percent higher than is necessary to meet the standards. In the Chicago study the CAC costs are estimated to be 14 times as expensive as necessary, and, for particulates in the Lower Delaware Valley they are estimated to be 22 times more expensive than necessary.

The Hahn and Noll finding that the CAC strategy was close to being cost effective was unique in a couple of respects. Because we can learn something from this study about the conditions under which CAC policies may not be far off the mark, it is worth subjecting it to close scrutiny.

Los Angeles, the city studied by Hahn and Noll, had a large sulfate problem, necessitating a very high degree of control. In effect, virtually every source was forced to control as much as is economically feasible. All policies must ultimately arrive at this allocation. As Example 15.1 points out, the program to control SO_2 emissions in Germany had a similar outcome (quite cost effective) for similar reasons (stringent controls resulting in similar marginal costs). In that case, most of the excessive cost resulted mainly from the policy's lack of temporal flexibility.

Air Quality

Each year, the USEPA derives air quality trends using measurements from monitors located across the country. Table 15.3 shows the national improvement in air quality (the pollutant concentrations in the ambient air) as well as the reduction in emissions from the criteria pollutants that have occurred over the 20 years from 1983 to 2002.

Though improvements have occurred for all six pollutants over that twenty-year period, notice that reductions in air quality concentrations do not always match reductions in nationwide emissions. The EPA identifies several reasons for this:

❋ Most monitors are located in urban areas so air quality is most likely to track changes in *urban* air emissions rather than in the *total* emissions measured in the table.

❋ Ozone is formed after directly emitted gases (NO_2 and VOCs) react chemically so its concentration depends on the chemical reactions as well as emissions. And those chemical reactions depend on the weather. For example, peak ozone concentrations typically occur during hot, dry, stagnant summertime conditions.

❋ In these data some portion of emissions is estimated rather than measured, while the air quality is directly measured.

How typical has the U.S. experience been? Is global pollution declining? The Global Environmental Monitoring System (GEMS), operating under the auspices of the United Nations Environment Program and the World Health Organization, monitors air quality around the globe. Scrutiny of its reports reveals that the U.S. experience is rather typical for the industrialized

Controlling SO$_2$ Emissions by Command-and-Control in Germany

EXAMPLE

15.1

Germany and the United States took quite different approaches to controlling SO$_2$ emissions. Whereas the United States used a version of emissions trading, Germany used traditional command-and-control regulation. Theory would lead us to believe that that U.S. approach, due to its flexibility, would achieve its goals at a considerably lower expense. The evidence suggests that it did, but the reasons are a bit more complicated than one might suppose.

Due to the large amount of forest death (Waldsterben) in Germany in which SO$_2$ emissions were implicated, the public put pressure on the government to reduce SO$_2$ emission dramatically from large combustion sources in a relatively short period of time. Both the degree of control and the mandated deadlines for compliance were quite stringent.

The stringency of the targets meant that sources had very little control flexibility; only one main technology could meet the requirements, so every covered combustion source had to install that equipment. Even if firms would have been allowed to engage in emissions trading once the equipment was installed, the pre-trade marginal costs would have been very similar. Since the purpose of trading is to equalize marginal costs, the fact that they were very similar before trading left little room for cost savings from trade.

The main cost disadvantage to the German system turned out not to be due to unequal marginal costs but rather to the temporal inflexibility of the command-and-control regulations. As Wätzold (2004) notes:

> The nearly simultaneous installation of desulfurization equipment in LCPs [Large Combustion Plants] all over Germany led to a surge in demand for this equipment with a resulting increase in prices. Furthermore, because Germany had little experience with the necessary technology, no learning effects were achieved; ... shortcomings that should have come to light before the systems were introduced in the entire fleet of power stations. ... had to be remedied in all power stations. (p. 35)

This was quite different from the U.S. experience. In the U.S. program (described in detail in Chapter 16) the ability to bank permits, which provided an incentive for some firms to comply early, and the phased deadline allowed much more flexibility in the timing of the installation of abatement controls; not all firms had to comply at the same time.

Source: Wätzold, Frank F., "SO$_2$ Emissions in Germany: Regulations to Fight Waldsterben," *Choosing Environmental Policy: Comparing Instruments and Outcomes in the United States and Europe*, Harrington, W., R. D. Morgenstern, and T. Sterner, eds. (Washington, DC: Resources for the Future 2004): 23–40.

nations, which have generally reduced pollution (both in terms of emissions and ambient outdoor air quality). Some of the reductions achieved in countries such as Japan and Norway have been spectacular. However, the air quality in most developing nations has steadily deteriorated, and the number of people exposed to unhealthy levels of pollution in those countries is frequently

TABLE 15.3   Trends in U.S. Emissions and Air Quality

	Percent Change in Air Quality	
	1983–2002	1993–2002
NO_2	−21	−11
O_3 1-h	−22	−2[a]
8-h	−14	+4[a]
SO_2	−54	−39
PM_{10}	—	−13
$PM_{2.5}$	—	−8[b]
CO	−65	−42
Pb	−94	−57
	Percent Change in Emissions	
	1983–2002	1993–2002
NO_x	−15	−12
VOC	−40	−25
SO_2	−33	−31
PM_{10}[c]	−34[d]	−22
$PM_{2.5}$[c]	—	−17
CO	−41	−21
Pb[e]	−93	−5

—Trend data not available.
[a]Not statistically significant.
[b]Based on percentage change from 1999.
[c]Includes only directly emitted particles.
[d]Based on percentage change from 1985. Emission estimates prior to 1985 are uncertain.
[e]Lead emissions are included in the toxic air pollutant emissions inventory and are presented for 1982–2001.
Negative numbers indicate improvements in air quality or reductions in emissions. Positive numbers show where emissions have increased or air quality has gotten worse.

Source: USEPA http://www.epa.gov/airtrends/sixpoll.html.

very high.[3] Because these countries typically are struggling merely to provide adequate employment and income to their citizens, they cannot afford to waste large sums of money on inefficient environmental policies, especially if the inefficiencies tend to subsidize the rich at the expense of the poor. Some cost-effective but fair means of improving air quality must be found.

---

[3]For sulfur oxides, for example, the GEMS study estimates that only 30 to 35 percent of the world's population lives in areas where air is at least as clean as recommended by the World Health Organization guidelines.

Innovative Approaches

Fortunately, some innovative approaches are available. Because various versions of these approaches have now been implemented around the world, we can learn from the experience gained from their implementation.

Smog Trading (RECLAIM)

Although the U.S. emissions trading program was initiated and promoted by the federal government, subsequent programs arose from state initiatives. Faced with the need to reduce ozone concentrations considerably in order to come into compliance with the ozone ambient standard, states have chosen to use trading programs as a means of facilitating rather drastic reductions in precursor pollutants (those involved in the chemical reactions that result in ozone).

One of the most ambitious of these programs is California's Regional Clean Air Incentives Market (*RECLAIM*) established by the South Coast Air Quality Management District, the district authority responsible for the greater Los Angeles area. Under RECLAIM, each of the almost 400 participating industrial polluters is allocated an annual pollution limit for nitrogen oxides and sulfur, which will decrease by 5 percent to 8 percent each year for a decade. Polluters are allowed great flexibility in how they meet these limits, including approaches such as purchasing credits from other firms that have controlled more than their legal requirements.

As a result of this flexibility, many new control strategies are emerging. Instead of the traditional focus on "end-of-pipe" control technologies, this program gives pollution prevention an economic underpinning. All possible pollution-reduction strategies can, for the first time, compete on a level playing field.

The RECLAIM program also illustrates a couple of potential problems with allowance markets. Compromises of the system designed to gain political feasibility may affect the level of the cap, at least initially. This was certainly the case with RECLAIM as initial allocations were inflated (Harrison, 2004). An early evaluation of the program by the EPA concluded that due to these inflated initial allocations in the earlier years of the program, fewer emissions had been reduced by RECLAIM than would have been reduced by more traditional regulation. The effects over the longer term remain to be seen.

The second problem for RECLAIM arose from a confluence of forces, including electricity deregulation. During the summer of 2001, in-state power plants generated an abnormally large amount of emissions. Since the supply of allowances that determined the level of authorized emissions was fixed by the cap, the price of these allowances shot up to politically unsupportable levels.

The very large price increases triggered a "safety valve" mechanism. RECLAIM procedures specified that if allowance prices went over some threshold (as they did in this case), the program would be temporarily suspended and an alternative fee per ton would be imposed until the normal operation of the program could resume. This alternative fee, of course, in essence replaced the unacceptably high market price with a somewhat lower administratively determined price that was politically acceptable. This fee was designed to retain some financial pressure on the plants to reduce emissions without straining the system beyond its tolerance limits and the revenue was used to secure emission reductions from other sources.

This experience provides some insights about the nature of the problem and a potential solution. When prices rise to levels that jeopardize the integrity of the program, a possibility whenever the fixed supply of permits meets a large, temporary increase in emissions, it is possible to switch to a fee-based system until more normal conditions once again prevail.

Emission Charges

Air pollution emission charges have been implemented by a number of countries, including France and Japan. The French air pollution charge was designed to encourage the early adoption of pollution control equipment, with the revenues returned to those paying the charge as a subsidy for installing the equipment. In Japan the emission charge is designed to raise revenue to compensate victims of air pollution.

The French charge system has been in effect since 1985. Originally designed to operate only until 1990, it was renewed and expanded in that year. The charge is levied on all industrial firms having a power-generating capacity of 20 megawatts or more, or industrial firms discharging over 150 metric tons of taxable pollutants per year. Some 1,400 plants are affected. The charge is levied on the actual amount of sulfur oxides emitted. Some 90 percent of the charge revenue is recovered by charge payers as a subsidy for pollution control equipment; the remaining 10 percent is used for new technological developments.

Although data are limited, a few areas can be highlighted. The charge level is too low to have any incentive impact. Total revenues are estimated to be about one-tenth of the revenue that would result from a charge sufficient to bring French industries in line with the air pollution control directions of the European Union (Opschoor and Vos 1989).

Economists typically envision two types of effluent or emissions charges. The first, an efficiency charge, is designed to produce an efficient outcome by forcing the polluter to compensate completely for all damage caused. The second, a cost-effective charge, is designed to achieve a predefined ambient standard at the lowest possible control cost. In practice, the French approach fits neither of these designs.

In Japan the charge takes on a rather different function. As a result of four important legal cases where Japanese industries were forced to compensate victims for pollution damages caused, in 1973 Japan passed the Law for the Compensation of Pollution-Related Health Injury. According to this law, upon certification by a council of medical, legal, and other experts, victims of designated diseases are eligible for medical expenses, lost earnings, and other expenses; they are not eligible for other losses, such as pain and suffering. Two classes of diseases are funded: (1) specific diseases, where the specific source is relatively clear and (2) nonspecific respiratory diseases, where all polluters are presumed to have some responsibility.

This program is funded by an emissions charge on sulfur dioxides and from an automobile weight tax. The level of the tax is determined by the revenue needs of the compensation fund.

In contrast to emissions trading, where ERC prices respond automatically to changing market conditions, emission charges have to be determined by an administrative process. When the function of the charge is to raise revenue for a particular purpose, charge rates will be determined by the costs of achieving that purpose; when the costs of achieving that purpose rise, the level of the charge must rise in order to secure the additional revenue.[4]

---

[4]Although it is theoretically possible (depending on the elasticity of demand for pollution abatement) for a rise in the tax to produce less revenue, this has typically not been the case.

Sometimes, that process produces an unintended dynamic. In Japan, for example, the charge is calculated on the basis of the amount of compensation paid to victims of air pollution in the previous year. Although the amount of compensation has been increasing, the amount of emissions (the base to which the charge is applied) has been decreasing. As a result, unexpectedly high charge rates are necessary in order to raise sufficient revenue for the compensation system.

What about the impact of environmental regulation on the diffusion of more environmentally benign technologies? Does the evidence suggest that new technologies with reduced environmental impact are being developed and adopted? As Example 15.2 points out, for chlorine manufacturing the answer is a definite "yes," but not quite in the manner expected.

Regional Pollutants

The primary difference between regional pollutants and local pollutants is the distance they are transported in the air. Although the damage caused by local pollutants occurs in the vicinity of emission, for regional pollutants the damage can occur at significant distances from the emission point.

The same substances can be both local pollutants and regional pollutants. Sulfur oxides, nitrogen oxides, and ozone, for example, have already been discussed as local pollutants, but they are regional pollutants as well. For example, sulfur emissions, the focal point for most acid rain legislation, have been known to travel some 200 to 600 miles from the point of emission before returning to the earth. As the substances are being transported by the winds, they undergo

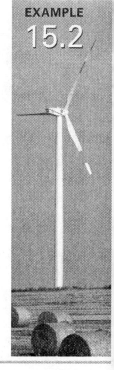

EXAMPLE

15.2

Technology Diffusion in the Chlorine Manufacturing Sector

Most of the world's chlorine is produced using one of three types of cells: the mercury cell, the diaphragm cell, and the membrane cell. Generally, the mercury-cell technology is considered to pose the highest environmental risk with the diaphragm-cell technology posing the next highest risk.

Over the last 25 years the mercury-cell share of total production has fallen from 22 percent to 10 percent, the diaphragm-cell's share has fallen from 73 percent to 67 percent, while the membrane-cell's share has risen from less than 1 percent of the total to 20 percent.

What role did regulation play? One might normally expect that, prodded by regulation, chlorine manufacturers would have increasingly adopted the more environmentally benign production technique. But that is not what happened. Rather, other regulations made it beneficial for users of chlorine to switch to non-chlorine bleaches, thereby reducing the demand for chlorine. In response to this reduction in demand, a number of producers shut down and a disproportionate share of the remaining plants were those using the cleaner, membrane-cell production.

Source: Snyder, L. D., N. H. Miller, and R. N. Stavins, "The Effects of Environmental Regulation on Technology Diffusion: The Case of Chlorine Manufacturing," *American Economic Review* 93(2), 2003: 431–435.

a complex series of chemical reactions. Under the right conditions, both sulfur and nitrogen oxides are transformed into sulfuric and nitric acids. Nitrogen oxides and hydrocarbons can combine in the presence of sunlight to produce ozone.

Acid Rain

What Is It? *Acid rain*, the popular term for atmospheric deposition of acidic substances, is actually a misnomer. Acidic substances are not only deposited by rain and other forms of moist air, they are also deposited as dry particles. In some parts of the world, such as the southwestern United States, dry deposition is a more important source of acidity than is wet deposition. Though natural sources of acid deposition do exist, the evidence is quite clear that anthropogenic (human-made) sources have dominated in recent years.

Precipitation is normally mildly acidic, with a global background pH of 5.0 (pH is the common measurement for acidity; the lower the number, the more acidic the substance, with 7.0 being the border between acidity and alkalinity). Industrialized areas commonly receive precipitation well in excess of the global background level. Rainfall in eastern North America, for example, has a typical pH of 4.4. Wheeling, West Virginia, once experienced a rainstorm with a pH of 1.5. The fact that battery acid has a pH of 1.0 may help put this event into perspective.

The Effects. In 1980 the U.S. Congress funded a 10-year study (called the National Acid Rain Precipitation Assessment Program) to determine the causes and effects of acid rain and to make recommendations concerning its control. The study concluded that damage from current and historic levels of acid rain ranged from negligible (on crops) to modest (on aquatic life in some lakes and streams).

The findings from this study were significantly less dire than expected and provided a rather sharp contrast with findings of higher levels of damage in Europe. Studies have documented that Sweden has some 4,000 highly acidified lakes; in southern Norway, lakes with a total surface area of 13,000 square kilometers support no fish at all; similar reports have been received from Germany, Scotland, and Canada.

Acid rain has also been implicated in the slower growth, injury, or death not only of European forests, particularly German forests, but also of forests in the United States (see Example 15.3). Acid rain has now been shown to result in forest and soil degradation in many areas of the eastern United States. The high elevation forests of the Appalachian Mountains from Maine to Georgia, including such high visibility areas as the Shenandoah and Great Smoky Mountain National Parks are particularly susceptible.

According to this research, acid rain rarely kills trees directly. Instead, it is more likely to weaken trees by damaging their leaves, limiting the available nutrients, or exposing the trees to toxic substances slowly released from the soil by the acidic deposition. Quite often, injury or death of trees is a result of the combined effects of acid rain and one or more additional threats such as drought, disease, or exposure to other pollutants.

In many countries with a federal form of government, such as the United States, the policy focus in the past has been on treating all pollutants as if they were local pollutants, overlooking the adverse regional consequences in the process. By giving local jurisdictions a large amount of responsibility for achieving the desired air quality and by measuring progress at local monitors, the stage was set for making regional pollution worse rather than better.

Adirondack Acidification

EXAMPLE

15.3

About 180 lakes in the Adirondack Mountains of New York State, mostly at higher altitudes, which had supported natural or stocked brook trout populations in the 1930s, no longer supported these populations by the 1970s. In some cases entire communities of six or more fish species had disappeared.

The location of these lakes, some distance east of any local emission sources, makes it quite clear that most of the acid deposition is coming from outside of the region. These lakes have relatively little capacity to neutralize deposited acid because they are in areas with little or no limestone or other forms of basic rock that might serve to buffer the acid.

This is a prime recreational area, particularly for fishing. Most of the sites are within the boundary of the 6-million acre Adirondack Park, the last substantially undeveloped area of its size in the northeastern United States. Its remoteness, mountainous terrain, and multitude of lakes provide an accessible outdoor recreation experience for the 55 million people who live within a day's traveling distance.

Although the 1990 amendments to the Clean Air Act (described below) resulted in substantial reductions in acid deposition, subsequent legislative proposals encouraged policymakers to determine if further reduction efforts would be justified in terms of net benefits. Using a contingent valuation method that includes both use and nonuse values, Banzhaf, Burtraw, Evans, and Krupnick (2004) estimated the benefits from further reductions in SO_2 and NO_x and compared them with the costs of achieving those reductions.

Their preferred estimates of the mean willingness to pay (WTP) for ecological improvements ranged from $48 to $107 per year per household in New York state. Multiplying these population-weighted estimates by the approximate number of households in the state yielded benefits ranging from about $336 million to $1.1 billion per year.

Their estimate of the costs of those reductions attributable to Adirondack improvements range from $86 million in 2010 to $126 million in 2020. Since these cost estimates are significantly less than the benefit estimates, further reductions would be economically justified despite the large reductions already achieved.

Source: Banzhaf, Spencer, Dallas Burtraw, David Evans, and Alan Krupnick, "Valuation of Natural Resource Improvements in the Adirondacks," *A Report to the Environmental Protection Agency* (Resources for the Future, Inc., September 2004).

In the early days of pollution control, local areas adopted the motto "Dilution is the solution." As implemented, this approach suggested that the way to control local pollutants was to emit them from tall stacks. By the time the pollutants hit the ground, according to this theory, the concentrations would be diluted, making it easier to meet the ambient standards at nearby monitors.

This approach had several consequences. First, it lowered the amount of emission reduction necessary to achieve ambient standards; with tall stacks, any given amount of emission would produce lower nearby ground-level concentrations than an equivalent level of emission from a shorter-stack source. Second, the ambient standards could be met at a lower cost. Using Cleveland as a case study, Scott Atkinson (1983) has shown that control costs would be approximately 30 percent lower but emissions would be 2.5 times higher if a local, rather than a regional, strategy were followed in a cap-and-trade system. In essence, local areas would be able to lower their own cost by exporting emissions to other areas. By focusing its attention exclusively on local pollution, the Clean Air Act actually made the regional pollution problem worse.

Crafting a Policy. By the end of the 1980s, it had become painfully clear in the United States that the Clean Air Act was ill-suited to solve regional pollution problems. Revamping the legislation to do a better job of dealing with regional pollutants, such as acid rain, became a high priority.

Politically, that was a tall order. By virtue of the fact that these pollutants are transported long distances, the set of geographic areas receiving the damage is typically not the same as the set of geographic areas responsible for most of the emission causing the damage. In some cases the recipients and the emitters are even in different countries! In this political milieu it should not be surprising that those bearing the costs of damages should call for a large, rapid reduction in emissions, whereas those responsible for bearing the costs of that cleanup should want to proceed more slowly and with greater caution.

Economic analysis was helpful in finding a feasible path through this political thicket. In particular, a Congressional Budget Office (CBO) study helped to set the parameters of the debate by quantifying the consequences of various courses of action. To analyze the economic and political consequences of various strategies designed to achieve reductions of SO_2 emissions from utilities anywhere from 8 to 12 million tons below the emission levels from those plants in 1980, the CBO used a computer-based simulation model that relates utility emissions, utility costs, and coal-market supply and demand levels to the strategies under consideration.

The results of this modeling exercise will be presented in two segments. In the first segment we will examine the basic available strategies, including both a traditional command-and-control strategy that simply allocates reductions on the basis of a specific formula and an emission charge strategy. This analysis demonstrates how sensitive costs were to various levels of emission reduction and to highlight some of the political consequences of implementing these strategies. The second segment of analysis then considers various strategies designed to mitigate the adverse political effects of the basic strategies as a means of ascertaining what is gained and lost by adopting these compromises.

The first implication of the analysis is that the marginal cost of additional control would rise rapidly, particularly after 10 million tons have been reduced (see Table 15.4). The cost of reducing a ton of SO_2 would rise from $270 for an 8-million-ton reduction to $360 for a 10-million-ton reduction, and it would rise to a rather dramatic $779 per ton for a 12-million-ton reduction. Costs would rise much more steeply as the amount of required reduction was increased, because reliance on the more expensive *scrubbers* would become necessary. (Scrubbers involve a chemical process to extract, or "scrub," sulfur gases before they escape into the atmosphere.)

The second insight, one that should be no surprise to readers of this book, is that the emission charge would be more cost effective than the comparable CAC strategy. Whereas the CAC strategy could secure a 10-million-ton reduction at about $360 a ton, the emission charge could

TABLE 15.4   Costs Associated with Basic Strategies to Reduce Sulfur Emissions

Strategy	Total Program Cost[a] (billions of $)	Annual Cost to Utilities[b] (billions of $)	Cost-Effectiveness[c] ($ per ton)
8-million-ton rollback	$20.4	$1.9	$270
10-million-ton rollback	$34.5	$3.2	$360
12-million-ton rollback	$93.6	$8.8	$779
Emission charge	$37.5	$7.7	$327

[a] The present value (in 1985 dollars) of additional discounted utility costs incurred (over a current policy benchmark) from 1986 to 2015, using a real discount rate of 0.03. Any emission charges paid are not included.
[b] The additional cost to utilities of this strategy over the current policy benchmark in 1995 expressed in 1985 dollars. This value includes any emission charges paid.
[c] The discounted program cost divided by the annual discounted SO_2 reduction measured over the 1986–2015 period.

Source: U.S. Congress. Congressional Budget Office. *Curbing Acid Rain: Cost, Budget, and Coal-Market Effects* (Washington, DC: Government Printing Office, 1986): xx, xxii, 23, and 80.

do it for $327 a ton. The superiority of the emissions charge is due to the fact that it results in equalized marginal costs, a required condition for cost-effectiveness.

Although the emission charge approach may be the most cost-effective policy, it was not the most popular, particularly in states with a lot of old, heavily polluting power plants. With an emission charge approach, utilities not only have to pay the higher equipment and operating costs associated with the reductions, but also they have to pay a charge on all uncontrolled emissions. The additional financial burden associated with controlling acid rain by means of an emission charge would have been significant. Instead of paying the $3.2 billion for reducing 10 million tons under a CAC approach, utilities would be saddled with a $7.7 billion financial burden with an emission charge. The savings from lower equipment and operating costs achieved because the emission charge approach is more cost effective would have been more than outweighed by the additional expense of paying the emission charges. What is least cost to society is not, in this case, least cost for the utilities.

The Sulfur Allowance Program. The political dilemma posed by this additional financial burden was resolved by adopting an emissions trading system known as the *Sulfur Allowance Program* (see Example 15.4). Adopted as part of the Clean Air Act Amendment of 1990, this approach would complement, not replace, the traditional approach, which was geared to the attainment of local ambient air quality standards.

The sulfur allowance program is a cap-and-trade program. It sets an aggregate cap (limit) on emissions from the covered emitters and allocates allowances (emission authorizations) that sum to this cap. Under the traditional system, where emissions from each unit were directly regulated, but aggregate emissions were not, as the number of emitters grew, so did aggregate emissions. This cannot happen with a cap; new emitters must be accommodated within the cap (since total emissions cannot increase). This will only happen if existing emitters reduce emissions sufficiently to accommodate the increases from the new emitter. The allowance program not only

EXAMPLE
15.4

The Sulfur Allowance Program

Under the Sulfur Allowance Program, allowances to emit sulfur oxides have been allocated to older sulfur-emitting electricity-generating plants. The number of allowances has been restricted in order to assure a reduction of 10 million tons in emissions from 1980 levels by the year 2010.

These allowances, which provide a limited authorization to emit 1 ton of sulfur, are defined for a specific calendar year, but unused allowances can be carried forward into the next year. They are transferable among the affected sources. Any plants reducing emissions more than required by the allowances could transfer the unused allowances to other plants. Emissions in any plant may not legally exceed the levels permitted by the allowances (allocated plus acquired) held by the managers of that plant. An annual year-end audit balances emissions with allowances. Utilities that emit more than they are authorized to do by their holdings of allowances must pay a $2,000 a ton penalty and are required to forfeit an equivalent number of tons of emissions in the following year.

An important innovation in this program is that the availability of allowances is assured by the institution of an auction market. Each year the EPA withholds 2.24 percent of the allocated allowances; these go into the auction. These withheld allowances are allocated to the highest bidders, with successful buyers paying their bid price. The proceeds are refunded to the utilities from whom the allowances were withheld, on a proportional basis. One main advantage of this auction is that it made allowance prices publicly transparent. By providing more information to investors, business investment strategies were facilitated.

Private allowance holders may also offer allowances for sale at these auctions. Potential sellers specify minimum acceptable prices. Once the withheld allowances have been disbursed, the EPA then matches the highest remaining bids with the lowest minimum acceptable prices on the private offerings and matches buyers and sellers until the sum of all remaining bids is less than that of the remaining minimum acceptable prices. Unfortunately, this specific auction design is not particularly efficient, because it provides incentives for inefficient strategic behavior, but the inefficiences are apparently small.

Sources: Burtraw, Dallas, "The SO$_2$ Emissions Trading Program: Cost Savings without Allowance Trades," *Contemporary Economic Policy* XIV (2), 1996: 79–94; Kete, Nancy, "The U.S. Acid Rain Control Allowance Trading System," *Climate Change: Designing a Tradeable Permit System*, Jones, T. and J. Corfee-Morlot, eds. (Paris: Organization for Economic Co-operation and Development, 1992): 69–93; and Rico, Renee, "The U.S. Allowance Trading System for Sulfur Dioxide: An Update on Market Experience," *Environmental and Resource Economics* 5(2), 1995: 115–129.

limits aggregate emissions to the level specified by the cap, but also it provides an economic incentive (due to the right to sell excess reductions) for those additional reductions to occur.

Under the sulfur allowance program, anyone can purchase allowances. This option is increasingly being chosen by environmental groups as a means of producing fewer sulfur emissions than allowed by law (see Example 15.5).

Results of the Program. According to official EPA reports in 2007, for the first time, SO_2 emissions were below the program's long-term emission cap of 8.95 million tons—three years before the 2010 statutory deadline. Significantly, the electric power industry achieved nearly 100 percent compliance with program requirements—only 1 unit had emissions exceeding the SO_2 allowances that it held.

According to Burtraw and Mansur (1999), national health benefits were estimated to be $125 million higher in 2005 than they would have been had the same reduction in emissions been achieved without trading.

Why and How Do Environmentalists Buy Pollution?

EXAMPLE

15.5

Among the rather unique features of the Sulfur Allowance Program, two have found particular favor with environmentalists. Not only does the program put a fixed upper limit on total annual sulfur emissions from the utilities sector, but also it allows environmental groups to lower that limit by acquiring allowances.

In the auctions run by the Chicago Board of Trade, anyone (including environmental groups) can place a bid. Environmental group bids are typically financed by donations from individuals who want to reduce pollution. Successful bidders acquire allowances for whatever purpose they see fit—including "retiring" them so that they cannot be used to legitimize emissions. Every 1-ton sulfur oxide allowance that is retired represents an authorized ton of pollution that will not be emitted.

In the 1996 auction, one nonprofit organization known by the acronym *INHALE* purchased 454 allowances. The Maryland Environmental Law Society (MELS) bought and retired an allowance in the 1994 auction—the first student group to do so. Since then, a number of other schools, including Bates College, have purchased and retired allowances.

Another organization that has raised funds to retire allowances is the Working Assets Funding Source. This nonprofit public-interest company regularly contributes 1 percent of its revenues to public-service organizations and uses its monthly bills to solicit charitable donations from customers for various featured causes. A summer 1993 campaign asked the 80,000 customers of its long-distance telephone service to add a small donation when paying their bills in order to support "our goal to reduce SO_2 emissions by 300 tons ... and spark a movement to do much more." The result was $55,000 in donations, which enabled the group to purchase 289 allowances.

Allowances have also been retired through charitable donations. An agreement between Arizona Public Service Company and Niagara Mohawk Power Corporation, for example, resulted in the donation of 25,000 allowances to the Environmental Defense Fund. In another transaction, Northeast Utilities of Connecticut donated 10,000 allowances to the American Lung Association. The Lung Association has since contacted other utilities through its local chapters in an effort to receive further donations to be used to reduce pollution.

Source: http://www.epa.gov/acidrain/auctions/00index.html.

Has the program resulted in cost savings? According to Ellerman et al. (2000) it has. They find Phase I cost savings of 33 to 67 percent over the nontrading alternative. The cost savings apparently resulted from switching to low-sulfur coal, falling prices of low-sulfur coal (due primarily to falling rail rates for transporting that coal), and technical change that reduced the cost of scrubbers. A subsequent study by Ellerman (2003) makes it clear that Phase II costs are estimated to be considerably lower as well. In addition to the above-mentioned factors responsible for lowering costs, additional savings resulted from the banking provisions, which provided plants with great flexibility in timing their reduction investments.

Summary

Although air quality has improved in industrialized nations, it has deteriorated in developing nations. Because the historical approach to air pollution control has been a traditional command-and-control approach, it has been neither efficient nor cost effective.

The CAC policy has not been efficient, in part, because it has been based on a legal fiction, a threshold below which no health damages are inflicted on any member of the population. In fact, damages occur at levels lower than the ambient standards to especially sensitive members of the population, such as those with respiratory problems. This attempt to formulate standards without reference to control costs has been thwarted by the absence of a scientifically defensible health-based threshold. Additionally, the policy fails to adequately consider the timing of emission flows. By failing to target the greatest amount of control on those periods when the greatest damage is inflicted, the current policy encourages too little control in high-damage periods and excessive control during low-damage periods. Current policy has also failed to pay sufficient attention to indoor air pollution, which may now well pose larger health risks than are posed by outdoor pollution. Unfortunately, because the existing benefit estimates have large confidence intervals, the size of the inefficiency associated with these aspects of the policy has not been measured with any precision.

The policy is not cost-effective either. The allocation of responsibility among emitters for reducing pollution has resulted in control costs that are typically several times higher than necessary to achieve the air quality objective. This has been shown to be true for a variety of pollutants in a variety of geographic settings.

The recent move toward cap-and trade polices is based on the cost-effective economic incentives they provide. Providing more flexibility in meeting the air quality goals has reduced both the cost and the conflict between economic growth and the preservation of air quality.

France and Japan have introduced emission charges as part of their approaches to pollution control, but neither application fits the textbook model very well. In France the charge level is too low to have the appropriate incentive effects. In Japan the charge is designed mainly to raise revenue with which to compensate victims of respiratory damage caused by pollution.

Regional pollutants differ from local pollutants chiefly in the distance they are transported in the air. Whereas local pollutants damage the environment near the emission site, regional pollutants can cause damage some distance away. Some substances, such as sulfur oxides, nitrogen oxides, and ozone, are both local and regional pollutants.

As the zone of influence of pollutants extends beyond local boundaries, the political difficulties of implementing comprehensive, cost-effective control measures increase. Pollutants crossing political boundaries impose external costs; neither the emitters nor the nations within which they emit have the proper incentives to institute efficient control measures.

Acid rain is a case in point. Sulfate and nitrate deposition has caused problems both among regions within countries and among countries. In the United States, the Clean Air Act had had a distinctly local focus until 1990. To control local pollution problems, state governments encouraged the installation of tall stacks to dilute the pollution before it hit the ground level. In the process, a high proportion of the emissions were exported to other areas, reaching the ground hundreds of miles from the point of injection. A focus on local control made the regional problem worse.

Finding solutions to the acid rain problem has been very difficult because those bearing the costs of further control are not those who will benefit from the control. In the United States, for example, opposition from the midwestern and Appalachian states delayed action on acid rain legislation. Stumbling blocks included the higher electricity prices that would result from the control and the employment impacts on those states that would suffer losses of jobs in the high-sulfur coal-mining industry.

These barriers were overcome by the 1990 Clean Air Act Amendments, which instituted the sulfur allowance program. This program placed a cap on total emissions from the utility sector for the first time and implemented a cost-effective way of reducing emissions to the level specified by the cap.

Key Concepts

acid rain, *p.* 340
ambient air quality standards, *p.* 327
   primary standard, *p.* 327
   secondary standard, *p.* 327
Clean Air Act Amendments of 1990, *p.* 326
conventional pollutants, *p.* 326
criteria pollutants, *p.* 326

health threshold, *p.* 330
New Source Review Program (NSR), *p.* 329
nonattainment regions, *p.* 327
RECLAIM, *p.* 337
scrubbers, *p.* 342
state implementation plan (SIP), *p.* 327
Sulfur Allowance Program, *p.* 343

Further Reading

Kosobud, Richard F., William A. Testa, and Donald A. Hanson, eds. *Cost Effective Control of Urban Smog* (Chicago: Federal Reserve Bank of Chicago, 1993). The proceedings of a conference providing background information for the Illinois smog-trading program.

Lave, Lester B. and Eugene P. Seskin. *Air Pollution and Human Health* (Baltimore, MD: Johns Hopkins University Press, 1977). The work describes a positive association between pollution and mortality even in those cities meeting the primary standards.

National Center for Environmental Economics. *The United States Experience with Economic Incentives in Environmental Pollution Control Policy* (Washington, DC: U.S. Environmental Protection Agency, 2001). A survey of what has been tried in the United States and how it has worked. Available on the Web through the portal at: http://yosemite.epa.gov/ee/epa/eed.nsf/webpages/homepage.

Nichols, Albert L. *Targeting Economic Incentives for Environmental Protection* (Cambridge, MA: MIT Press, 1984). An excellent review of the use of economic incentives to control pollution, with a detailed treatment of the use of exposure charges to control airborne carcinogens.

Additional References

Anderson, Robert and Andrew Lohof. *The United States Experience with Economic Incentives in Environmental Pollution Control Policy* (Washington, DC: Environmental Law Institute, 1997).

Blackman, A. "Informal Sector Pollution Control: What Policy Options Do We Have?" *World Development* 28 (2000) (12): 2067–2082.

Burtraw, D. and E. Mansur (1999). "Environmental Effects of SO2 Trading and Banking," *Environmental Science and Technology* 33(20): 3489-3494.

Ellerman, A. D. "The U. S. SO2 Cap-and-Trade Program," Proceedings of the OECD Workshop on Ex Post Evaluation of Tradable Permits: Policy Evaluation, Design and Reform (Paris: Organization for Economic Co-operation and Development, 2003).

Ellerman, A. D., P. L. Joskow, et al. *Markets for Clean Air: The U. S. Acid Rain Program* (Cambridge, UK: Cambridge University Press, 2000).

Hahn, Robert W. "Market Power and Transferable Property Rights," *Quarterly Journal of Economics* 99 (November 1984) (4): 753–765.

Hahn, Robert W. and Roger G. Noll. "Designing a Market for Tradeable Emissions Permits," *Reform of Environmental Regulation*, Magat, Wesley A., ed. (Cambridge, MA: Ballinger, 1982).

Haigh, John A., David Harrison, Jr., and Albert L. Nichols. "Benefits Assessment and Environmental Regulation: Case Studies of Hazardous Air Pollutants," Discussion Paper E-83-07, John F. Kennedy School of Government Energy and Environment Policy Center, Cambridge, MA, August 1983.

Harrison, David, Jr. "*Ex Post* Evaluation of the RECLAIM Emissions Trading Program for the Los Angeles Air Basin" in OECD, *Tradable Permits: Policy Evaluation, Design and Reform* (Paris: Organization for Economic Co-operation and Development, 2004): 45–69.

Henderson, J. V. "Effects of Air Quality Regulation," *American Economic Review* 86 (1996) (4): 789–813.

Krupnick, Alan J. "Costs of Alternative Policies for the Control of NO_2 in the Baltimore Region," *Journal of Environmental Economics and Management* 13 (June 1986): 189–197.

Levinson, A. "Grandfather Regulations, New Source Bias, and State Air Toxics Regulations," *Ecological Economics* 28 (1999) (2): 299–311.

List, J. A. and W. W. McHone. "Measuring the Effects of Air Quality Regulations on 'Dirty' Firm Births: Evidence from the Neo and Mature Regulatory Periods," *Papers in Regional Science* 79 (2000) (2): 177–190.

McGartland, Albert M. "Marketable Permit Systems for Air Pollution Control: An Empirical Study," Ph.D. dissertation, University of Maryland, 1984.

Oates, Wallace E., Paul R. Portney, and Albert M. McGartland. "The Net Benefits of Incentive-Based Regulation: A Case Study of Environmental Standard-Setting," *American Economic Review* 79 (December 1989): 1233–1242.

OECD. *Tradable Permits: Policy Evaluation, Design and Reform* (Paris: Organization for Economic Co-operation and Development, 2004).

Opschoor, J. B. and Hans B. Vos. *Economic Instruments for Environmental Protection* (Paris: Organization for Economic Co-operation and Development, 1989): 34–35.

Popp, D. "Pollution Control Innovations and the Clean Air Act of 1990," *Journal of Policy Analysis and Management* 22 (2003) (4): 641–660.

Roach, Fred, Charles Kolstad, Allen V. Kneese, Richard Tobin, and Michael Williams. "Alternative Air Quality Policy Options in the Four Corners Region," *Southwest Review* 1 (Summer 1981): 29–58.

Roumasset, James A. and Kirk R. Smith. "Exposure Trading: An Approach to More Efficient Air Pollution Control," *Journal of Environmental Economics and Management* 18 (May 1990): 276–291.

Seskin, Eugene P., Robert J. Anderson, and Robert O. Reid. "An Empirical Analysis of Economic Strategies for Controlling Air Pollution," *Journal of Environmental Economics and Management* 10 (June 1983): 112–124.

Smith, Kirk R. "Air Pollution: Assessing Total Exposure in the United States," *Environment* 30 (October 1988) (8): 10–15, 33–38.

Soderholm, P. "Pollution Charges in a Transition Economy: The Case of Russia," *Journal of Economic Issues* 33 (1999) (2): 403–410.

Sorrell, S. and J. Skea, eds. *Pollution for Sale: Emissions Trading and Joint Implementation* (Cheltenham, UK: Edward Elgar, 1999).

United Nations Environment Program and the World Health Organization. "Monitoring the Global Environment: An Assessment of Urban Air Quality," *Environment* 31 (October 1989) (8): 6–13, 26–37.

U.S. Environmental Protection Agency, Office of Air and Radiation. *The Benefits and Cost of the Clean Air Act, 1970 to 1990* (October 1997).

U.S. General Accounting Office. "Electric Supply Older Plants' Impact on Reliability and Air Quality" (GAO/RCED-90-200, 1990).

Discussion Questions

1. Efficiency analysis suggests that the regulation of hazardous pollutants should take exposure into account—the more persons exposed to a given pollutant concentration, the larger is the damage caused by it and therefore the smaller is the efficient concentration level, all other things being equal. An alternative point of view would simply ensure that concentrations be held below a uniform threshold, regardless of the number of people exposed. From this latter point of view, the public policy goal is to expose any and all people to the same concentration level—exposure is not used to establish different concentrations for different settings. What are the advantages and disadvantages of each approach? Which do you think represents the best approach? Why?

2. European countries have relied to a much greater extent on emission charges than has the United States, which seems to be moving toward a greater reliance on transferable emission permits. From an efficiency point of view, should the United States follow Europe's lead and shift the emphasis toward emission charges? Why or why not?

16 Climate Change

Everything should be made as simple as possible, but not simpler.

—ALBERT EINSTEIN

Introduction

As the zone of influence of pollutants extends beyond local boundaries, the political difficulties of implementing comprehensive, cost-effective control measures are compounded. Pollutants crossing boundaries impose external costs; neither the emitters nor the nations within which they emit have the proper incentives for controlling them.

Compounding the problem of improper incentives is the scientific uncertainty that limits our understanding of most of these problems. Our knowledge about various relationships that form the basis for our understanding of the magnitude of the problems and the effectiveness of various strategies to control them is far from complete. Unfortunately, the problems are so important and the potential consequences of inaction so drastic that procrastination is not usually an optimal strategy. To avoid having to act in the future under emergency conditions when the remaining choices are few in number, strategies that have desirable properties must be formulated now on the basis of the available information, as limited as it may be. As many future options as possible must be preserved.

In this chapter we will survey the scientific evidence on climate change and the potential effectiveness of policy strategies designed to alleviate the problems associated with it. We will also consider difficulties confronted by the government in implementing solutions and the role of economic analysis in understanding how to circumvent these difficulties.

The Science of Climate Change

Greenhouse gases, one class of global pollutants, absorb the long-wavelength (infrared) radiation from the Earth's surface and atmosphere, trapping heat that would otherwise radiate into space. The mix and distribution of these gases within the atmosphere is in no small part responsible for both the hospitable climate on the Earth and the rather inhospitable climate on other planets. Changing the mix of these gases can modify the climate.

Though carbon dioxide is the most abundant and the most studied of these greenhouse gases, many others have similar thermal radiation properties. These include, but are not limited to, the chlorofluorocarbons, nitrous oxide, and methane.

The current concern over the effect of this class of pollutants on *climate change* arises because emissions of these gases are increasing over time, changing their mix in the atmosphere. Evidence is mounting that by burning fossil fuels, leveling tropical forests, and injecting more of the other greenhouse gases into the atmosphere, humans are creating a thermal blanket capable of trapping enough heat to raise the temperature of the Earth's surface.

The Intergovernmental Panel on Climate Change, the body charged with compiling and assessing the scientific information on climate change, reported its findings in 2007 on both the sources and likely outcomes of climate change. With respect to the role of humans, they found that most of the warming observed over the last 250 years can with a very high level of confidence be attributed to human activity. With respect to projected climatic changes they found the following:

* The global increases in carbon dioxide concentration are due primarily to fossil fuel use and land use change, while those of methane and nitrous oxide are due primarily to agriculture.

* Warming of the climate system is unequivocal, as is now evident from observations of increases in global average air and ocean temperatures, widespread melting of snow and ice, and rising global average sea level.

* Human induced warming and sea level rise would continue for centuries due to the time scales associated with the climate processes and feedbacks, even if greenhouse gases were stabilized.

* Projected impacts of the warming include contracting snow cover, shrinking sea ice in the Arctic and Antarctic regions, and increasing weather events such as extreme heat, heavy precipitation, and intense storms.

Interestingly, since that report was finalized, new evidence suggests that the warming process may be moving faster than was anticipated in the IPCC report, thereby raising the expected economic damages (Stern, 2008).

Scientists have also recently uncovered evidence to suggest that climate change may occur rather more abruptly than previously thought. Since the rate of temperature increase is a significant determinant of how well ecosystems can adapt to temperature change, the projected rate has become a matter of some concern. Two examples that raise this concern are the methane trapped in the frozen tundra of the North and the ocean's thermohaline circulation system.

Large quantities of methane gas lie trapped in the frozen tundra. As temperatures warm, this tundra can thaw, releasing the trapped methane. Since methane is a powerful greenhouse gas, this release could accelerate the rate of warming.

Thermohaline circulation, known popularly as the ocean conveyer belt, involves flows of warm water near the surface from the Southern Hemisphere to the Norwegian Sea and deep-water return flows of cold water. The process that powers this circulation, the sinking of the colder water, is affected by the salinity of the surrounding ocean water in the Norwegian Sea. As climate change results in the melting of ice caps and glaciers, adding considerable amounts of fresh water to that part of the ocean, scientists believe that the resulting salinity changes could shut down the thermohaline circulation system, potentially resulting in a prolonged period of intense cold for Northern Europe.

What are the likely impacts of this combination of rapidly rising temperatures, rising sea levels, and the potential for more frequent and more intense storms? Another working group of the panel, tasked with the responsibility to find out, reached the following conclusions:

◈ Recent regional climate changes, particularly temperature increases, have already affected many physical and biological systems.

◈ Natural systems (including coral reefs, mangroves, and tropical forests) are vulnerable to climate change and some will be irreversibly damaged.

◈ Developing countries, especially in Africa, are expected to feel the most severe effects of climate change since they will experience multiple stresses and have the fewest resources to commit to adaptation.

◈ Adaptation will be necessary to address impacts resulting from the warming that is already unavoidable due to past emissions.

These threats pose a significant challenge to our economic and political institutions. Are they up to the challenge? The answer is unclear because this particular challenge has some unique features that present significant barriers to attempts at moving toward a solution. Concepts developed earlier in the text can help us understand the nature of these barriers.

Any action taken to moderate climate change provides a global public good, implying the strong possibility of free-rider actions. (Those who do not control greenhouse gases cannot be prevented from reaping the benefits of the actions of those who do.) Free-rider effects not only cause emissions to be abnormally high, but also they inhibit investment in research and development, a key ingredient in promoting innovative, low-carbon technologies. Free-rider effects also inhibit the participation of nations in the climate change agreements that are designed to correct these market failures.

To further complicate matters, the damage caused by greenhouse pollutants is an externality in both space and time. Spatially, the largest emitters (historically the industrialized nations) have the greatest capacity to reduce emissions, but they are not expected to experience as much damage from insufficient actions as the developing countries. Temporally, the costs of controlling greenhouse gases fall on current generations, while the benefits from controlling greenhouse gases occur well in the future, making it more difficult to convince members of the current generation to join the mitigation effort. The implication of these insights is that decentralized actions by markets and governments are likely to violate both the efficiency and sustainability criteria. International collective action is both necessary and terribly difficult.

◈ Negotiations over Climate Change Policy

Characterizing the Broad Strategies

What can be done? Three strategies have been identified: (1) climate engineering, (2) adaptation, and (3) mitigation. *Climate engineering* envisions taking actions such as shooting particulate matter into the atmosphere in order to provide compensating cooling or seeding the ocean to increase its ability to absorb carbon dioxide. *Adaptation* strategies would allow us to function more effectively in warmer temperatures and reduce the damages from associated impacts such as sea-level rise. *Mitigation* would attempt to moderate the temperature rise by using strategies designed to reduce emissions or increase the planetary capacity to absorb greenhouse gases. In this chapter we shall focus mainly on mitigation.

The most significant mitigation strategy deals with our use of fossil fuel energy. Combustion of fossil fuel energy results in the creation of carbon dioxide. Carbon dioxide emissions can be reduced either by using less energy or by using alternative energy sources (e.g., wind, photovoltaics, or hydro) that produce no CO_2. Because any serious reduction in CO_2 emissions would involve rather dramatic changes in our energy-consumption patterns and an uncertain economic cost, how vigorously this strategy is to be followed is a controversial public policy issue.

Another possible strategy involves encouraging activities that allow additional carbon to be absorbed by trees or soils. As Debate 16.1 points out, however, the desirability of this approach is controversial in current climate change negotiations.

DEBATE 16.1

Should Carbon Sequestration in the Terrestrial Biosphere Be Credited?

Both forests and soils sequester (store) a significant amount of carbon. Research suggests that with appropriate changes in practices, they could store much more. Increased *carbon sequestration* in turn would mean less carbon in the atmosphere. Recognition of this potential has created a strong push in the climate change negotiations to give credit for actions that result in more carbon uptake by soils and forests. Whether this should be allowed, and, if so, how it would be done are currently heavily debated.

Proponents argue that this form of carbon sequestration is typically quite cost-effective. Cost-effectiveness not only implies that the given goal can be achieved at lower cost, but also it may increase the willingness to accept more stringent goals with closer deadlines. Allowing credit for carbon absorption may also add economic value to sustainable practices (such as limiting deforestation or preventing soil erosion), thereby providing additional incentives for those practices. Proponents further point out that many of the prime beneficiaries of this increase in value would be the poorest people in the poorest countries.

Opponents say that our knowledge of the science of carbon sequestration in the terrestrial biosphere is in its infancy, so the amount of credit that should be granted is not at all clear. Obtaining estimates of the amount of carbon sequestered could be both expensive (if done right) and subject to considerable uncertainty. Because carbon absorption could be easily reversed at any time (by cutting down trees or changing agricultural practices) continual monitoring and enforcement would be required, adding even more cost. Even in carefully enforced systems, the sequestration is likely to be temporary (the carbon in completely preserved forests, for example, may ultimately be released to the atmosphere by decay). And finally, the practices that may be encouraged by crediting sequestration will not necessarily be desirable, as when slow-growing old-growth forests are cut down and replaced with fast-growing plantation forests in order to increase the amount of carbon uptake.

Finding a global solution to climate change is certainly one of the most challenging and pressing problems of our time, but it is not the first global pollutant to be the subject of international negotiations. The negotiations aimed at reducing ozone-depleting gases broke the ice.

The Precedent: Reducing Ozone Depleting Gases

In the stratosphere, the portion of the atmosphere lying just above the troposphere, rather small amounts of ozone present have a crucial positive role to pay in determining the quality of life on the planet. In particular, by absorbing the ultraviolet wavelengths, the stratospheric ozone shields people, plants, and animals from harmful radiation, and by absorbing infrared radiation, it is a factor in determining the Earth's climate.

Chlorofluorocarbons (CFCs), which are greenhouse gases, have been implicated in depleting this stratospheric ozone shield as a result of a complicated series of chemical reactions. These highly stable chemical compounds have been used as aerosol propellants and in cushioning foams, packaging and insulating foams, industrial cleaning of metals and electronics components, food freezing, medical instrument sterilization, refrigeration for homes and food stores, and air conditioning of automobiles and commercial buildings.

The major known effect of the increased ultraviolet radiation resulting from *tropospheric ozone depletion* is an increase in nonmelanoma skin cancer. Other potential effects, such as an increase in the more serious melanoma form of skin cancer, suppression of human immunological systems, damage to plants, eye cancer in cattle, and an acceleration of degradation in certain polymer materials, are suspected but not as well established.

Responding to the ozone depletion threat, an initial group of 24 nations signed the *Montreal Protocol* in September 1988. A series of new agreements followed that generally broadened the number of covered substances and established specific schedules for phasing out their production and use. Currently, some 96 chemicals are controlled to some degree by these agreements.

The protocol is generally considered to have been a noteworthy success. As of 2008 more than 95 percent of ozone-depleting substances have been phased out and the ozone layer is expected to return to its pre-1980 levels by mid-century.

Part of the reason for the success of this approach was an early recognition of the importance of the need to solicit the active participation of developing countries. Part of the success in eliciting that participation was achieved by offering later phase-out deadlines for developing countries, but another important aspect involved providing some financial help for the phase-out.

In 1990 the parties agreed to establish a *Multilateral Fund*, which was designed to cover the incremental costs that developing countries incur as a result of taking action to eliminate the production and use of ozone-depleting chemicals. Contributions to the Multilateral Fund come from the industrialized countries. The fund has been replenished seven times. As of July 2008 the contributions made to the Multilateral Fund by some 49 industrialized countries, including Countries with Economies in Transition (CEIT), totaled more than $2.4 billion.

The fund promotes technical change and facilitates the transfer of more environmentally safe products, materials, and equipment to developing countries. It offers developing countries that have ratified the agreement access to technical expertise, information on new replacement technologies, training and demonstration projects, and financial assistance for projects to eliminate the use of ozone-depleting substances.

The existence of the Multilateral Fund, however, does not deserve all the credit for the success of the Montreal Protocol. The success of ozone protection has been possible in no small measure because producers were able to develop and commercialize alternatives to ozone-depleting chemicals. Countries and producers ended the use of CFCs faster and cheaper than was originally anticipated due to the availability of these substitutes.

Although the agreements specify national phase-down targets, it is up to the countries to design policy measures to reach those targets. The United States chose a unique combination of product charges and tradable permits to control the production and consumption of ozone-depleting substances (see Example 16.1).

Most observers believe this combination was highly effective in encouraging the transition away from ozone-depleting substances, but full resolution will take time. Scientists predict that ozone depletion will reach its worst point during the next few years and then gradually decline until the ozone layer returns to normal around 2050, assuming that the Montreal Protocol and subsequent agreements are fully implemented.

The Policy Focus of the Climate Change Negotiations

Early in climate change negotiations it became clear that cost-effective strategies were a priority. For reasons explained in Chapter 13, the policy choices were quickly narrowed to a carbon tax and cap-and-trade. In general, Europe tended to favor a carbon tax, while the United States preferred cap-and-trade.

The form of a carbon tax is remarkably simple in the climate change case. Because greenhouse gases are uniformly mixed pollutants, a uniform per unit charge imposed on all emission sources would be cost-effective. And emissions charges could be expected not only to encourage new, more environmentally benign technologies, but also to raise significant revenue. In addition, the use of taxes could more easily hold costs in check and assure more stable carbon prices.

Concerns about emissions charges also rose, however, particularly when it became clear that the amount of revenue collected from these taxes would be significant. The concept of taxes imposed by some international authority (that would then have control over the revenue) was soon replaced by a concept relying on harmonized national taxes where the revenue would stay in the nation that collected it. Nations were not the only ones concerned about the magnitude of tax revenues, however; firms that would pay taxes were also concerned about the financial burden imposed. Simply knowing that the revenue would be kept by their national governments was generally not enough to overcome these concerns.

Initial concerns over the magnitude and distribution of the revenue were soon expanded by concerns over the consequences of participating in a system that taxed only some of the parties. The United States was reluctant to go along with emission charges. And developing countries would likely not be asked to bear charges, at least in the early years of control. A system of partial taxation could lead to *leakage* (offsetting greenhouse gas emissions from non-participating countries) and to significant competitiveness issues.

Leakage can occur when taxed producers try to pass on their additional costs to consumers. If consumers have the choice of importing products from producers in nations with no emissions charges, they are inclined to favor those imports over domestic (taxed) products because they are likely to cost less. Meanwhile, producers in the taxed nations, noticing their market share being eroded by competitors in the untaxed nations, have an incentive to shift their production facilities to the untaxed nations to take advantage of the lower costs. Ultimately, not only could

EXAMPLE
16.1

Tradable Permits for Ozone-Depleting Chemicals

On August 12, 1988, the U.S. Environmental Protection Agency issued its first regulations implementing a tradable permit system to achieve the targeted reductions in ozone-depleting substances. According to these regulations, all major U.S. producers and consumers of the controlled substances were allocated baseline production or consumption allowances using 1986 levels as the basis for the proration. Each producer and consumer was allowed 100 percent of this baseline allowance initially, with smaller allowances granted after predefined deadlines. Following the London conference, these percent-of-baseline allocations were reduced in order to reflect the new, earlier deadlines and lower limits.

These allowances are transferable within producer and consumer categories, and allowances can be transferred across international borders to producers in other signatory nations if the transaction is approved by the EPA and results in the appropriate adjustments in the buyer or seller allowances in their respective countries. Production allowances can be augmented by demonstrating the safe destruction of an equivalent amount of controlled substances by an approved means. Some interpollutant trading is even possible within categories of pollutants. (The categories are defined so as to group pollutants with similar environmental effects.) All information on trades is confidential (known only to the traders and the regulators), which makes it difficult to know how effective this program has been.

Since the demand for these allowances is quite inelastic, supply restrictions increase revenue. Because of the gifting of allowances to the seven major domestic producers of CFCs and halons, the EPA was concerned that its regulation would result in sizable wind-fall profits (estimated to be in the billions of dollars) for those producers. The EPA handled this problem by imposing a tax on production in order to "soak up" the rents created by the regulation-induced scarcity.

This application was unique in two ways. It not only allowed international trading of allowances, but also it involved the simultaneous application of allowance and tax systems. Taxes on production, when coupled with allowances, have the effect of lowering allowance prices. The combined policy, however, is no less cost effective than allowances would be by themselves, and it does allow the government to acquire some of the rent that would otherwise go to allowance holders.

Source: Tietenberg, Tom, "Design Lessons from Existing Air Pollution Control Systems: The United States," *Property Rights in a Social and Ecological Context: Case Studies and Design Applications*, Hanna, S. and M. Munasinghe, eds. (Washington, DC: World Bank, 1995): 15–32.

the taxed nations lose production and jobs, but also total greenhouse gases could even increase if the reduction in the taxed nations is more than offset by increases in the untaxed nations.

So the emphasis of negotiations began to shift toward emissions trading. In one of the interesting ironies of climate change policy, the *Kyoto Protocol*, which is the main international agreement controlling greenhouse gases, specifically incorporates emissions trading, but its prime proponent, the United States, did not ratify the agreement.

The Evolution of International Agreements on Climate Change

The 1992 United Nations Framework Convention on Climate Change (UNFCCC) recognized the principle of global cost-effectiveness of emission reduction and opened the way for flexibility. Because this early agreement did not fix a binding emission target for any country, however, the need to invest in emission reduction either at home or abroad was not pressing.

In December 1997, however, industrial countries and countries with economies in transition (primarily the former Soviet Republics) agreed to legally binding emission targets at the Kyoto Conference and negotiated a legal framework as a protocol to the UNFCCC—the Kyoto Protocol. This Protocol became effective in February 2005 once at least 55 parties, representing at least 55 percent of the total carbon dioxide (CO_2) emissions, had ratified. Russia's ratification put the protocol over the 55 percent total; the 55-country total had been reached much earlier.

The Kyoto Protocol defines a five-year commitment period (2008–2012) for meeting the individual country emission targets, called "assigned amount obligations," set out in Annex B of the protocol. Quantified country targets are defined by multiplying the country's 1990 emission level by a reduction factor and multiplying that number by five (to cover the five-year commitment period). Collectively, if fulfilled, these targets would represent a 5 percent reduction in annual average emissions below 1990 levels. The actual compliance target is defined as a weighted average of six greenhouse gases: carbon dioxide, methane, nitrous oxide, HFCs, PFCs, and sulfur hexafluoride. Defining the target in terms of this multigas index, rather than only CO_2, has been estimated to reduce compliance costs by some 22 percent (Reilly et al., 2002).

The Intergovernmental Panel on Climate Change reviewed a host of studies to find out what difference emissions trading would make on costs and concluded that it would typically cut the costs in half.

How large are the resulting costs? These studies predict that the effect of controlling climate change is to slow growth, but not to stop or reverse it. As Azar and Schneider (2002) point out, one way to contextualize the cost of stabilizing emissions in the 350–550 ppm range is to recognize that the cost involves a one- to three-year delay in reaching the new higher wealth level.

The Kyoto Protocol authorizes three cooperative implementation mechanisms that involve *tradable* permits: Emission Trading, Joint Implementation, and the Clean Development Mechanism.

* *Emissions Trading (ET)*, a cap-and-trade policy, allows trading of "assigned amounts" (the national quotas established by the Kyoto Protocol) among countries listed in Annex B of the Kyoto Protocol, primarily the industrialized nations and the economics in transition.

* Under *Joint Implementation (JI)* Annex B parties can receive emissions reduction credit when they help to finance specific projects that reduce net emissions in another Annex B party country. This "project-based" program is designed to exploit opportunities in Annex B countries that have not yet become fully eligible to engage in the ET program described above.

* The *Clean Development Mechanism (CDM)* enables Annex B parties to finance emission-reduction projects in non-Annex B parties (primarily developing countries) and to receive certified emission reductions (CERs) for doing so. These CERs can be used to fulfill "assigned amount" obligations.

These programs have, in turn, spawned others. Despite the fact that the United States has not signed the Kyoto Protocol, as discussed in Chapter 14 some American states have accepted mandatory caps on CO_2 and are using trading to facilitate meeting those goals.

The largest and most important of the existing programs is the cap-and-trade system developed by the European Union to facilitate implementation of the Kyoto Protocol (see Example 16.2).

While the Emissions Trading mechanism is the driving force behind the suite of cooperative mechanisms, the Clean Development Mechanism (CDM) provides a means for motivating industrialized countries (or individual companies) to invest in projects within developing countries that result in reductions of greenhouse gases. The incentive to invest is provided by credits that investors can earn for reductions that are above and beyond those that would have been achieved otherwise. Once verified and certified, these credits can be used as one means of meeting the investor's assigned amount obligations. The incentive for participation by the host developing countries comes from the increased productivity that frequently accompanies emission

---

EXAMPLE

16.2

The European Emissions Trading Scheme (EU ETS)

The *European Emissions Trading Scheme (EU ETS)* applies to 25 countries, including the 10 "accession" countries, most of which are former members of the Soviet bloc. The first phase, from 2005 through 2007, was considered to be a trial phase. The second phase coincides with the first Kyoto commitment period, which began in 2008 and continues through 2012. Subsequent negotiations will specify the details of future phases.

Initially, the program will cover only carbon dioxide (CO_2) emissions from four broad sectors: iron and steel, minerals, energy, and pulp and paper. All installations in these sectors larger than established thresholds are included in the program. More than 12,000 installations are covered by the program, making it the largest emissions trading program ever established.

The allocation scheme provides installations with gifted allowances. Gifting the allowances turned out in the light of experience to result in inflated profits in the utility sectors, a fact that has helped propel the movement toward auction in more recent programs such as the Regional Greenhouse Gas Initiative in the Northeastern U.S. (see Example 14.3).

Countries can use emission reductions acquired from outside the European Union (via the JI or CDM mechanisms) to meet their obligations under the EU ETS. Estimates by Criqui and Kitous (2003) indicate that allowing unrestricted trades among all these options should reduce compliance cost by about 24 percent.

Sources: Kruger, J. A. and William A. Pizer, "Greenhouse Gas Trading in Europe: The New Grand Policy Experiment," *Environment* 46(8), 2004: 8–23; and Criqui, P. and A. Kitous, *Kyoto Protocol Implementation: (KPI) Technical Report: Impacts of Linking JI and CDM Credits to the European Emissions Allowance Trading Scheme*, CNRS-IEPE and ENERDATA S.A. for Directorate General Environment, Service Contract No. B4-3040/2001/330760/MAR/E1 (2003) as cited in Kruger and Pizer (2004, Table 2).

reductions. Projects that replace old coal-burning power plants with facilities based on photo-voltaics or natural gas illustrate the point.

Complementary Strategies

Given the problems associated with identifying promising projects, quantifying the magnitude of the reductions, and monitoring the results, some means to reduce those barriers was clearly called for. In response, in 1999 the *Prototype Carbon Fund (PCF)* was established by the World Bank to serve as an intermediary for encouraging CDM reductions in greenhouse gases. The PCF, which acts as a kind of greenhouse gas mutual fund, invests company and government contributions in projects designed to produce emission reductions consistent with the Kyoto Protocol. Investors in the PCF receive a pro rata share of the emission reduction credits. These credits are verified and certified in accordance with agreements reached with the respective countries hosting the projects.

Another complementary agency, the *Global Environmental Facility (GEF)*, has begun to play an important role in funding deserving projects. Drawing from a Global Environmental Trust Fund, which is funded by direct contributions from some 26 countries, the GEF provides loans and grants to projects that have a global impact, including projects that reduce climate change. The GEF uses a *marginal external cost rule* to determine the suitability of projects and the amount of funding provided.

Recognizing that many projects have benefits that flow beyond national borders, and that individual nations are unlikely to consider those global benefits, the GEF picks up costs (called the marginal external costs) that cannot be justified domestically but can be justified internationally. For example, suppose building a coal-fired power plant is the cheapest way for China to provide electricity to its people, but a slightly more expensive wind power plant would result in substantially lower carbon dioxide emissions. Since the benefits from lower CO_2 emissions are largely global, not national, China has little incentive to consider them in its decision and the coal-fired plant would likely be chosen. By picking up the extra cost for the wind facility, the GEF can increase the attractiveness of the alternative facility and thereby assure that China's decision makes sense globally as well as nationally.

Controversies

Emission trading is not without its problems, however. In Debate 16.1 we explored the issues associated with allowing carbon sequestration credits to be certified as tradable allowances. Other controversies range from such fundamental issues as the morality of global emissions trading (see Debate 16.2) to concerns about weaknesses in the implementation details.

Perceived implementation deficiencies contribute to the sense of unease about this approach. Greenhouse gas emissions trading will only achieve the goals of the protocol with adequate monitoring and enforcement. This is much more difficult for international agreements than the enforcement of domestic laws and regulations. Effective monitoring and enforcement in this international context is far from a forgone conclusion.

Policy Timing

What is the necessary level of current investment in greenhouse gas reduction? In order to answer this question, first we must discover just how serious the problem is and then ascertain

Is Global Greenhouse Gas Trading Immoral?

In a December 1997 editorial in *The New York Times,* Michael Sandel, a Harvard professor, suggested that greenhouse gas trading is immoral. He argues that treating pollution as a commodity that can be bought and sold not only removes the moral stigma that is appropriately associated with it, but also trading reductions undermines the important sense of shared responsibility required by global cooperation. Sandel illustrated the point by suggesting that legitimizing further domestic emission by offsetting it with a credit acquired from a project in a poorer nation would be very different from penalizing the firm for emitting, even if the cost of the credit were equal to the penalty. Not only would the now-authorized emission become inappropriately "socially acceptable," but also the wealthier nation would have met its moral obligation by paying a poorer nation to fulfill a responsibility that should have been fulfilled by a domestic emission reduction.

Published responses to this editorial countered with several points. First, it was pointed out that since it is voluntary, international emissions trading typically benefits both nations; one nation does not impose its will on the other. Second, historical use of these programs has resulted in much cleaner air at a much lower cost than would otherwise have been possible, so the ends would seem to justify the means. Third, with few exceptions, virtually all pollution control regulations allow some emission that is not penalized; this is simply a recognition that zero pollution is rarely efficient or politically feasible.

Source: Sandel, Michael J., "It's Immoral to Buy the Right to Pollute," with replies by Shavell, Steven, Robert Stavins, Sanford Gaines, and Eric Maskin from *The New York Times*, December 17, 1997. Excerpts reprinted in Stavins, Robert N., ed. *Economics of the Environment: Selected Readings*, 4th ed. (New York: W. W. Norton & Company, 2000): 449–452.

the costs of being wrong, either by acting too hastily or by procrastinating. Because rampant uncertainties attend virtually every link in the logical chain from human activities to subsequent consequences, we cannot at this juncture, state unequivocally how serious the damage will be. We can, however, begin to elaborate the range of possibilities and see how sensitive the outcomes are to the choices before us.

With regard to options for controlling climate change, benefit/cost studies that ignore uncertainties in the state of our knowledge typically suggest a "go slow" or "wait and see" policy. The reasons for these results are instructive. First, the benefits from current control are experienced well into the future, while the costs occur now. The present-value criterion in benefit-cost analysis discounts future values more than current values. Second, both energy-using and energy-producing capital are long-lived. Replacing the entire capital stock at an accelerated pace now would be more expensive than replacing individual components over time closer to the end of their useful life. Third, the models anticipate that the number of new emissions-reducing technologies would be larger in the future and, due to this larger menu of options, the costs of reduction would be lower with delay.

The first reason is controversial because the use of benefit/cost analysis based upon the present-value criterion in climate change discussions is itself controversial. Although this approach is not inherently biased against future generations, their interests will only be adequately protected if they are adequately compensated for the damage inflicted on them. Because it is not obvious that any material compensation supplied by growth would be adequate, the long lead times associated with this particular problem place the interests of future generations in maintaining a stable climate in jeopardy, raising an important ethical concern (Portney and Weyant, 1999).

The other reasons have economic merit, but they do not imply a "wait-and-see" policy. Spreading the capital investment decisions over time assumes that some of them take place now as current capital is replaced. Furthermore, the expectation that future technical change can reduce costs will only be fulfilled if the incentives for producing the technical change are in place now. In both cases waiting simply postpones their start.

Another powerful consideration in the debate over the timing of control investments involves uncertainty about both the costs and benefits of climate change. Governments must act without complete knowledge. How can they respond reasonably to this uncertainty?

The risks of being wrong are clearly asymmetric. If it turns out that if we controlled more than we needed, current generations would bear a larger than necessary cost. On the other hand, if the problem turns out to be as serious as the worst predictions indicate, catastrophic and largely irreversible damage to the planet could be inflicted on future generations.

Yohe, Andronova, and Schlesinger (2004) investigate both consequences of being wrong using a standard, well-respected global climate model. Their model assumes that decision makers choose global mitigation policies that will be in effect for 30 years, but at the end of those 30 years policymakers would be able to modify the policies to take into account the better understanding of climate change consequences that would have arisen during the intervening years. The specific source of uncertainty in their model results from our imperfect knowledge about the relationship between the atmospheric greenhouse gas concentrations and the resulting increase in temperature. The specific question they examine is "What is the best strategy now?"

They find that a hedging strategy that involves modest reductions now dominates a "wait-and-see" strategy. Not only does current action initiate the capital turnover process and provide incentives for technical change, but also it allows the avoidance of costly and potentially irreversible mistakes later. Since emissions from the wait-and-see strategy would be much higher after 30 years, the reductions necessary to meet a given concentration target would have to be larger and concentrated within a smaller period of time. If, for example, scientists subsequently discover the need to stabilize the greenhouse gas concentration target at a specific level to avoid exceeding important thresholds (such as the thermohaline circulation or methane examples discussed above), that may not only be much more difficult and more expensive to do later, but also it may be impossible.

Creating Incentives for Participation
in Climate Change Agreements

Since ratifying any climate change agreement is a voluntary act, the branch of economics known as game theory has been used to study what mechanisms can be used to encourage participation in light of the serious free-rider problems any coalition-formation process will face (Barrett, 1990). This has been a productive analytical undertaking because it demonstrates that the free-rider problem is not necessarily a fatal flaw in the search for solutions to the climate change problem (Carraro, 2002).

One strategy, which we have already discussed, relies upon the use of cost-effective policies. Since cost-effective policies reduce the cost, but not the benefits, of participation, those policies should make participation more likely by increasing its net benefits.

Another strategy involves "issue linkage" in which countries simultaneously negotiate a climate change agreement and a linked economic agreement. Typical candidates for linkage are agreements on trade liberalization, cooperation on research and development (R&D), or international debt. The intuition behind this approach is that some countries gain from resolving the first issue, while others gain from the second. Linking the two issues increases the chances that cooperation may result in profitable participation in both agreements and, hence, increases the incentives to join the coalition of those ratifying the climate change agreement.

To illustrate how this works, consider a research and development example from Cararro (1999). To counteract the incentive to free ride on the benefits from climate change, suppose that only ratifiers of both agreements share in the insights gained from research and development in the ratifying countries. The fact that this benefit can only be obtained by ratifying the climate change agreement as well as the R&D agreement provides an incentive to ratify both. Since those nations choosing not to ratify can be excluded from the valuable research and development benefits, they would have to join the agreement to obtain those benefits.

Another strategy for encouraging participation involves transfers from the gainers to the losers. Some countries have more to gain from an effective agreement than others. If the gainers were willing to share some of those gains with reluctant nations with more to lose, the reluctant nations could be encouraged to join. Some interesting work (Chandler and Tulkens, 1997) has shown that it is possible to define a specific set of transfers such that each country is better off participating than not participating. That is a powerful, comforting result.

In terms of operationalizing this concept, the Bali climate change conference in 2007 established a funding mechanism for adaptation, which could generate up to $300 million over 2008–2012. It was established to finance concrete adaptation projects and programs in developing countries that are Parties to the Kyoto Protocol. The fund, which will fall under the auspices of the Global Environmental Facility, is to be financed primarily from a 2 percent levy on proceeds from Clean Development Mechanism (CDM) projects. Note that while this fund is directed toward adaptation, rather than mitigation, the fact that it is available only to parties to the agreement provides an incentive for nonsignatories to participate.

Summary

The first global pollutant problem confronted by the international community arose when ozone-depleting gases were implicated in the destruction of the stratospheric ozone shield that protects the Earth's surface from harmful ultraviolet radiation. Because these are accumulating pollutants, an efficient response to this problem would involve reducing use over time.

To restrict their accumulation in the atmosphere, the international agreements on ozone-depleting substances created a system of limits on production and consumption. As part of its obligation under the agreements, the United States adopted a transferable allowance system, coupled with a tax on the additional profits generated by restricting the supply of allowances. Internationally this agreement is considered a success in no small part because the Multilateral Fund and other incentives, such as delayed compliance deadlines, facilitated the participation of developing countries.

Climate change is appropriately considered a more difficult problem to solve. In addition to the features it shares with ozone-depletion, such as the free-rider problem and the fact that the current generation bears the costs, while the benefits accrue in the future, climate change presents some unique challenges. Some countries, for example, may be benefited, not harmed, by climate change, diminishing even further their incentive to control. And in contrast to ozone-depleting substances, which had readily available substitutes, controlling greenhouse gases means controlling energy use from fossil fuels, the linchpin of modern society.

Fortunately, economic analysis of the climate change problem not only defines the need for action, but also sheds light on effective forms that action might take. Empirical studies suggest that it makes sense to take action now to reduce emissions of greenhouse gases in order to provide insurance against adverse, possibly irreversible consequences if the damage tends to be higher than anticipated. Although polices in the Kyoto Protocol, such as the emissions trading program, joint implementation, and the clean development mechanism use basic economic concepts to forge practical, cost-effective means of controlling climate change, we have also seen that the implementation details matter.

Economics sheds light on both the barriers to effective participation in climate change agreements, and some potential solutions as well. The free-rider effect is a significant barrier to participation, but strategies that flow from game theory (such as international transfers and issue linkage) can be used to build incentives for participation. Some international cost sharing is likely to be a necessary ingredient in a successful attack on the climate problem as it was in the ozone depletion case.

During the next few decades, options must not only be preserved, they must be enhanced. Responding to the threat of climate change in a timely and effective fashion will not be easy. Our political institutions are not configured in such a way to simplify decision making on a global scale. International organizations exist at the pleasure of the nations they serve. Only time will tell if the mechanisms of international agreements described in this chapter will prove equal to the task.

Key Concepts

adaptation, *p.* 353
carbon sequestration, *p.* 353
climate change, *p.* 351
climate engineering, *p.* 352
European Emissions Trading Scheme
  (EU ETS), *p.* 358
Global Environmental Facility (GEF), *p.* 359
Kyoto Protocol, *p.* 356
  Clean Development Mechanism (CDM),
  p. 357

Emissions Trading (ET), *p.* 357
  Joint Implementation (JI), *p.* 357
leakage, *p.* 351
marginal external cost rule, *p.* 359
mitigation, *p.* 353
Montreal Protocol, *p.* 354
Multilateral Fund, *p.* 354
Prototype Carbon Fund (PCF), *p.* 359
tropospheric ozone depletion, *p.* 354

Further Reading

Intergovernmental Panel on Climate Change (2007). *Climate Change 2007—Mitigation of Climate Change: Working Group III Contribution to the Fourth Assessment Report of the IPCC,* Cambridge, Cambridge University Press. The official international peer-reviewed survey of the evidence and its implications.

Mendelsohn, R., A. Dinar, et al. (2006). "The Distributional Impacts of Climate Change on Rich and Poor Countries," *Environment and Development Economics* 11: 159–178. This economic analysis concludes that poor countries will suffer the bulk of the damages from climate change, due primarily to their location.

Metcalf, Gilbert E. (2009). "Designing a Carbon Tax to Reduce U.S. Greenhouse Gas Emissions," *Review of Environmental Economics and Policy* 3(1): 63–83. Describes considerations for designing a carbon tax to control greenhouse gas emissions in the United States.

Stavins, Robert N. (2008). "Addressing Climate Change with a Comprehensive US Cap-and-Trade System," *Oxford Review of Economic Policy,* 24(2): 298–321. Describes considerations for designing a cap-and-trade policy to control greenhouse gas emissions in the United States.

Stern, N. 2008. "The Economics of Climate Change," *American Economic Review* 98(2): 1–37. A recent assessment by the former chief economist of the World Bank.

Additional References

Adams, D. M., R. J. Alig, et al. "Minimum Cost Strategies for Sequestering Carbon in Forests," *Land Economics* 75 (1999) (3): 360–374.

Antle, J. M. and B. A. McCarl. "The Economics of Carbon Sequestration in Agricultural Soils," *The International Yearbook of Environmental and Resource Economics 2002/2003,* Tietenberg, Tom and H. Folmer, eds. (Cheltenham, UK: Edward Elgar, 2002): 278–310.

Azar, C. and S. H. Schneider. "Are the Economic Costs of Stabilizing the Atmosphere Prohibitive?" *Ecological Economics* 42 (2002) (1–2): 73–80.

Barrett, S. "The Problem of Global Environmental Protection," *Oxford Review of Economic Policy* 6 (Spring 1990) (1): 68–79.

Bernard, A. L. and M. Vielle. "Measuring the Welfare Cost of Climate Change Policies: A Comparative Assessment Based on the Computable General Equilibrium Model GEMINI-E3," *Environmental Modeling & Assessment* 8 (2003) (3): 199–217.

Boyd, R. and M. E. Ibarraran. "Costs of Compliance with the Kyoto Protocol: a Developing Country Perspective," *Energy Economics* 24 (2002) (1): 21–39.

Buonanno, P., C. Carraro, et al. "Endogenous Induced Technical Change and the Costs of Kyoto," *Resource and Energy Economics* 25 (2003) (1): 11–34.

Carraro, C. E. "Climate Change Policy: Models, Controversies and Strategies," *The International Yearbook of Environmental and Resource Economics 2002/2003,* Tietenberg, T. and H. Folmer, eds. (Cheltenham, UK: Edward Elgar, 2002): 1–65.

Chandler, P. and H. Tulkens. "The Core of an Economy with Multilateral Environmental Externalities," *International Journal of Game Theory* 26 (1997): 279–295.

Newell, R. G. and R. N. Stavins. "Climate Change and Forest Sinks: Factors Affecting the Costs of Carbon Sequestration," *Journal of Environmental Economics & Management* 40 (2000) (3): 211–235.

Parry, I.W.H., R. C. Williams, et al. "When Can Carbon Abatement Policies Increase Welfare? The Fundamental Role of Distorted Factor Markets," *Journal of Environmental Economics and Management* 37 (1999) (1): 52–84.

Portney, P. R. and J. P. Weyant *Discounting and Intergenerational Equity* (Washington, DC: Resources for the Future, Inc., 1999).

Reilly, J., M. Mayer, and J. Harnisch. "Multiple Gas Control under the Kyoto Agreement," *Second International Symposium on Non-CO$_2$ Greenhouse Gases*, van Ham, J. A., P. M. Baede, L. A. Mayer, and R. Ybema, eds. (The Netherlands: Kluwer Academic Publishers, Dordrecht, 2002).

Yohe, G., N. Andronova, and M. Schlesinger. "To Hedge or Not to Hedge Against an Uncertain Climate Future?" *Science* 306 (October 15, 2004): 416–417.

Discussion Questions

1. Most experts agree that international agreements to control ozone-depleting gases have been successful in the sense that global emissions for those gases have clearly been substantially reduced. Despite the fact that climate change also involves a global public good, almost no one would claim that the international agreements on climate change, at least in the early stages, have had anywhere near the same degree of success. Why not? Are there differences between the two problems that could explain the different response?

2. Is a cap-and-trade policy or a carbon tax a better strategy for controlling climate change. Why?

17 Transportation

There are two things you shouldn't watch being made, sausage and law.

—Anonymous

Introduction

Although they emit many of the same pollutants as stationary sources, mobile sources require a different policy approach. These differences arise from the mobility of the source, the number of vehicles involved, and the role of the automobile in the modern lifestyle.

Mobility has two major impacts on policy. On the one hand, pollution is partly caused by the temporary location of the source—a case of being in the wrong place at the wrong time. This occurs, for example, during rush hour in metropolitan areas. Because the cars have to be where the people are, relocating them—as might be done with electric power plants—is not a viable strategy. On the other hand, it is more difficult to tailor vehicle emission rates to local pollution patterns because any particular vehicle may end up in many different urban and rural areas during the course of its useful life.

Mobile sources are also more numerous than stationary sources. In the United States, for example, while there are only approximately 27,000 major stationary sources, well over 200 million vehicles travel on U.S. roadways. Enforcement is obviously more difficult the larger the number of sources being controlled. Additionally, in the United States alone, 20 percent of carbon emissions from anthropogenic sources come from the combustion of gasoline. As discussed in Chapter 15, creating incentives to reduce human-induced sources of carbon emissions is a large focus for environmental policymakers. When the sources are mobile, the problem of creating appropriate incentives is even more complex.

Whereas stationary sources generally are large and run by professional managers, automobiles are small and run by amateurs. Their small size makes it more difficult to control emissions without affecting performance, and amateur ownership makes it more likely that emission control will deteriorate over time because of a lack of dependable maintenance and care.

These complications might lead us to conclude that perhaps we should ignore mobile sources and concentrate our control efforts solely on stationary sources. Unfortunately, that is not possible. Although each individual vehicle represents a minuscule part of the problem, mobile sources collectively represent a significant proportion of three criteria pollutants—ozone, carbon monoxide, and nitrogen dioxide—as well as a significant source of greenhouse gases.

For two of these pollutants—ozone and nitrogen dioxide—the process of reaching attainment has been particularly slow. With the increased use of diesel engines, mobile sources are becoming responsible for a rising proportion of particulate emissions, and vehicles that burn leaded gasoline were (until legislation changed the situation) a major source of airborne lead.

Because it is necessary to control mobile sources, what policy options exist? What points of control are possible, and what are the advantages and disadvantages of each? In exercising control over these sources, the government must first specify the agent charged with the responsibility for the reduction. The obvious candidates are the manufacturer and the owner-driver. The balancing of this responsibility should depend on a comparative analysis of costs and benefits, with particular reference to such factors as (1) the number of agents to be regulated, (2) the rate of the sources' emission deterioration over time, (3) the life expectancy of automobiles, and (4) the availability, effectiveness, and cost of programs to reduce emissions at the point of production and at the point of use.

Although automobiles are numerous and ubiquitous, they are manufactured by a small number of firms. It is easier and less expensive to administer a system that controls relatively few sources; therefore, regulation at the point of production has considerable appeal.

Some problems are associated with limiting controls solely to the point of production, however. If the factory-controlled emission rate deteriorates during normal vehicle usage, control at the point of production may buy only temporary emission reduction. Although the deterioration of emission control can be combatted with warranty and recall provisions, the costs of these supporting programs have to be balanced against the costs of local control.

Automobiles are durable, so *new* vehicles make up only a relatively small percentage of the total fleet of vehicles. Therefore, control at the point of production, which affects only new equipment, takes longer to produce a given reduction in aggregate emissions. Newer, controlled cars replace old vehicles very slowly. Thus, a program of control at the point of production would produce emission reductions more slowly than would a program securing emission reductions from used as well as new vehicles.

Some possible means of reducing mobile-source pollution cannot be accomplished by regulating emissions at the point of production because they involve choices made by the owner-driver. The point-of-production strategy is oriented toward reducing the amount of emissions *per mile driven* in a particular type of car, but only the owner can decide what kind of car to drive, as well as when and where to drive it.

These are not trivial concerns. Diesel and hybrid automobiles, buses, trucks, and motorcycles emit different amounts of pollutants than do standard gasoline-powered automobiles. By changing the mix of vehicles on the road, the amount and type of emissions can be affected, even if passenger miles are not changed.

Where and when the car (or other vehicle) is driven is also important. Clustered emissions cause higher concentration levels than do dispersed emissions; therefore driving in urban areas causes more environmental damage than driving in rural areas does. Local control strategies could internalize these location costs; a uniform national strategy focusing solely on the point of production could not.

Timing of emissions is particularly important because conventional commuting patterns lead to a clustering of emissions during the morning and evening rush hours. Indeed, plots of pollutant concentrations in urban areas during an average day typically produce a graph with two peaks, corresponding to the two rush hours.[1] Because high concentrations are more dangerous than low ones, some spreading over the 24-hour period could also prove beneficial.

The Economics of Mobile-Source Pollution

Vehicles emit an inefficiently high level of pollution because their owner-drivers do not bear the full cost of that pollution. This inefficiently low cost, in turn, has two sources: (1) implicit subsidies for road transport and (2) a failure to internalize external costs.

Implicit Subsidies

Several categories of the social costs associated with transporting goods and people over roads are related to mileage driven, but the private costs do not reflect that relationship. For example:

* Road construction and maintenance costs, which are largely determined by vehicle-miles, are mostly funded from tax dollars. The marginal private cost of an extra mile driven in terms of road construction and maintenance is zero, but the social cost is not.

* Despite the fact that building and maintaining parking space is expensive, parking is frequently supplied by employers at no marginal cost to the employee. The ability to park a car for free creates a bias toward private auto travel, because other modes receive no comparable subsidy.

Other *transport subsidies* create a bias toward gas-guzzling vehicles that produce inefficiently high levels of emissions. Until recently, in the United States, business owners who purchase large, gas-guzzling sport utility vehicles (SUVs) get a substantial tax break worth tens of thousands of dollars, while purchasers of small energy efficient cars get none (Ball and Lundegaard, 2002). (Only vehicles weighing over 6,000 pounds qualify.)

This tax break was established 20 years ago for "light trucks," primarily to benefit small farmers who depended upon the trucks for chores around the farms. Today, most purchasers of SUVs, considered "light trucks" for tax purposes, have nothing to do with farming.

Externalities

Road users also fail to bear the full cost of their choices, because many of the costs associated with those choices are actually borne by others. For example:

* The social costs associated with accidents are a function of vehicle-miles. The number of accidents rises as the number of miles driven rises. Generally, the costs associated with these accidents are paid for by insurance, but the premiums for these insurance policies

---

[1]The exception is ozone formed by a chemical reaction involving hydrocarbons and nitrogen oxides in the presence of sunlight. For the evening rush-hour emissions, too few hours of sunlight remain for the chemical reactions to be completed, so graphs of daily ozone concentrations frequently exhibit a single peak.

rarely reflect the mileage-accident relationship. As a result, the additional private cost of insurance for additional miles driven is typically zero, although the social cost is certainly not zero.

- Road congestion creates externalities by increasing the amount of time required to travel a given distance. Increased travel times also increase the amount of fuel used.
- (Recent studies have indicated high levels of pollution inside vehicles, caused mainly by the exhaust of cars in front.)

To elaborate on the *congestion inefficiency* point, let's consider Figure 17.1. As traffic volumes get closer to the design capacity of the roadway, traffic flow decreases; it takes more time to travel between two points. At this point the marginal social costs and marginal private costs begin to diverge. The driver entering a congested roadway will certainly consider the extra time it will take him or her to travel that route, but he or she will not consider the extra time that his or her presence imposes on everyone else; it is an externality.

The efficient ratio of traffic volume to road capacity (V_e) occurs where the marginal benefits (as revealed by the demand curve) equal the marginal social cost. Because individual drivers do

FIGURE 17.1   Congestion Inefficiency

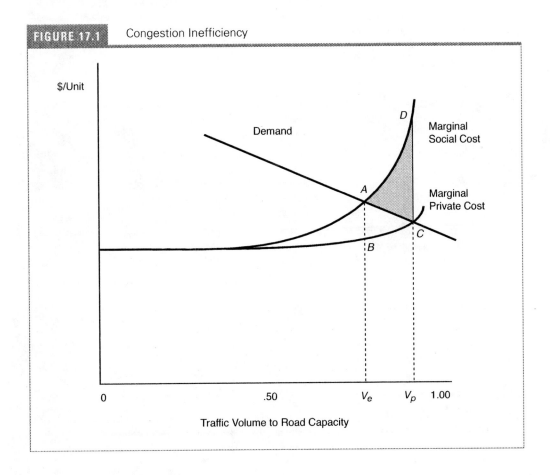

not internalize the external costs of their presence on this roadway, too many drivers will use the roadway, and traffic volume will be too high (V_p). The resulting efficiency losses would be represented by area ACD (the shaded area).

One recent study estimates that highway congestion in 2005 caused 4.2 billion hours of delay and 2.9 billion gallons of additional fuel to be used, resulting in a cost of $78 billion to highway users.[2]

The Consequences

Understated road transport cost creates a number of perverse incentives. Too many roads are crowded. Too many miles are driven. Too many trips are taken. Transport energy use is too high. Pollution from transportation is excessive. Competitive modes of transportation—including mass transit, bicycles, and walking—all suffer from an inefficiently low demand.

Perhaps the most pernicious effect of understated transport costs, however, is its effect on land use. Low transport cost encourages dispersed settlement patterns. Residences can be located far from work and shopping because the costs of travel are so low. Unfortunately, this pattern of dispersal creates a tendency toward dependence that is hard to reverse. Once settlement patterns are dispersed, it is difficult to justify high-volume transportation alternatives (e.g., trains or buses). For example, both trains and buses need high-density travel corridors in order to generate the ridership necessary to pay the high fixed costs associated with building and running these systems. With dispersed settlement patterns, sufficiently high travel densities are difficult, if not impossible, to generate.

◉ Policy Toward Mobile Sources

Some History

Concern about mobile-source pollution originated in southern California in the early 1950s following a path-breaking study by Dr. A. J. Haagen-Smit of the California Institute of Technology. The study by Dr. Haagen-Smit identified motor vehicle emissions as a key culprit in forming the photochemical smog for which southern California was becoming infamous.

In the United States, the Clean Air Act Amendments of 1965 set national standards for hydrocarbon and carbon monoxide emissions from automobiles, which were to take effect during 1968. It is interesting to note that the impetus for the Act came not only from the scientific data on the effects of automobile pollution, but also from the automobile industry itself. The industry saw uniform federal standards as a way to avoid a situation in which every state passed its own unique set of emission standards, something the auto industry wanted to avoid. This pressure was successful in that the law prohibits all states except California from setting their own standards.

By 1970 there was general dissatisfaction with the slow progress being made on air pollution control in general and automobile pollution in particular. In a "get tough" mood as it developed the Clean Air Act amendments of 1970, Congress required new emissions standards that would reduce emissions by 90 percent below their uncontrolled levels. This reduction was to have been

---

[2]2007 Annual Urban Mobility Report, Texas Transportation Institute. http://mobility.tamu.edu/ums/ as cited in "Using Pricing to Reduce Congestion" (2009), Congressional Budget Office.

achieved by 1975 for hydrocarbon and carbon monoxide emissions and by 1976 for nitrogen dioxide. It was generally agreed at the time the Act was passed that the technology to meet the standards did not exist. By passing this tough law, Congress hoped to force the development of an appropriate technology.

It did not work out that way. The following years ushered in a series of deadline extensions. In 1972 the automobile manufacturers requested a one-year delay in the implementation of the standards. The administrator of the EPA denied the request and was taken to court. At the conclusion of the litigation in April 1973, the administrator granted a one-year delay in the 1975 deadline for the hydrocarbon and carbon monoxide standards. Subsequently, in July 1973, a one-year delay was granted for nitrogen oxides as well.[3] It was the first of many delayed deadlines.

Structure of the U.S. Approach

The current U.S. approach to mobile-source air pollution has served as a model for mobile-source control in many other countries (particularly in Europe). Therefore, we will examine this approach in some detail.

The U.S. approach represents a blend of controlling emissions at the point of manufacture with controlling emissions from vehicles in use. New-car emission standards are administered through a certification program and an associated enforcement program.

Certification Program. The certification program tests prototypes of car models for conformity to federal standards. During the test, a prototype vehicle from each engine family is driven 50,000 miles on a test track or a dynamometer. The vehicle follows a mandated strict pattern of fast and slow driving, idling, and hot-and-cold starts. The manufacturers run the tests and record emission levels at 5,000-mile intervals. If the vehicle satisfies the standards over the entire 50,000 miles, it passes the deterioration portion of the certification test.

The second step in the certification process is to apply less demanding (and less expensive) tests to three additional prototypes in the same engine family. Emission readings are taken at the 0- and 4,000-mile points and then, using the deterioration rate established in the first portion of the test, are projected to the 50,000-mile point. If those projected emission levels meet the standards, then that engine family is given a certificate of conformity. Only engine families with a certificate of conformity may be sold.

Associated Enforcement Programs. The certification program is complemented by an associated enforcement program, which contains assembly-line testing, as well as recall and antitampering procedures and warranty provisions. To ensure that the prototype vehicles are representative, the EPA tests a statistically representative sample of assembly-line vehicles. If these tests reveal that more than 40 percent of the cars do not conform with federal standards, the certificate may be suspended or revoked.

The EPA has also been given the power to require manufacturers to recall and remedy manufacturing defects that cause emissions to exceed federal standards. If the EPA uncovers a defect, it usually requests the manufacturer to recall vehicles for corrective action. If the manufacturer refuses, the EPA can order a recall.

---

[3]The only legal basis for granting an extension was technological infeasibility. Only shortly before the extension was granted, the Japanese Honda CVCC engine was certified as meeting the original standards. It is interesting to speculate on what the outcome would have been if the company meeting the standards had been American rather than Japanese.

The Clean Air Act also requires two separate types of warranty provisions. These warranty provisions are designed to ensure that a manufacturer will have an incentive to produce a vehicle that, properly maintained, will meet emission standards over its useful life. The first of these provisions requires the vehicle to be free of defects that could cause it to fail to meet the standards. Under this provision, any defects discovered by consumers would be fixed at the manufacturer's expense.

The second warranty provision requires the manufacturer to bring any car that fails an inspection and maintenance test (described below) during its first 24 months or 24,000 miles (whichever occurs first) into conformance with the standards. After the 24 months, or 24,000 miles, the warranty is limited solely to the replacement of devices specifically designed for emission control, such as catalytic converters. This further protection lasts 60 months.

The earliest control devices used to control pollution had two characteristics that rendered them susceptible to tampering: (1) they adversely affected vehicle performance and (2) they were relatively easy to circumvent. As a result, the Clean Air Act Amendments of 1970 prohibited anyone from tampering with an emission control system prior to the sale of an automobile, but, curiously, prohibited only dealers and manufacturers from tampering after the sale. The 1977 amendments extended the coverage of the postsale-tampering prohibition to motor-vehicle repair facilities and fleet operators.

Lead. Section 211 of the Clean Air Act provides the EPA with the authority to regulate lead and any other fuel additives used in gasoline. Under this provision, gasoline suppliers are required to make unleaded gasoline available. By ensuring the availability of unleaded gasoline, this regulation sought to reduce the amount of airborne lead and to protect the effectiveness of the catalytic converter, which was poisoned by lead.[4]

On March 7, 1985, the EPA issued regulations imposing strict new standards on the allowable lead content in refined gasoline. The primary phaseout of lead was completed by 1986.[5] These actions followed a highly publicized series of medical research findings on the rather severe health and developmental consequences, particularly to small children, of even rather low levels of atmospheric lead. The actions worked. A 1994 study showed that U.S. blood-lead levels declined 78 percent from 1978–1991.

CAFE Standards. The *Corporate Average Fuel Economy (CAFE)* program, established in 1975, was designed to reduce American dependence on foreign oil by producing more fuel-efficient vehicles. Although it is not an emission control program, fuel efficiency does affect emissions.

The program requires each automaker to meet government-set miles-per-gallon targets (CAFE standards) for all its car and light truck fleets sold in the United States each year. The unique feature is that the standard is a *fleet average,* not a standard for each vehicle. As a result, automakers can sell some low-mileage vehicles as long as they sell enough high-mileage vehicles to raise the average to the standard. The CAFE standards took effect in 1978, mandating a fleet average of 18 miles per gallon (mpg) for automobiles. The standard increased each year until 1985 when it reached 27.5 mpg. The standards have been controversial. Most observers believe

---

[4]Three tanks of leaded gasoline used in a car equipped with a catalytic converter would produce a 50 percent reduction in the effectiveness of the catalytic converter.

[5]These can be found in 40 *Code of Federal Regulations* 80 (1990).

that the CAFE standards did in fact reduce imports. During 1977–1986, oil imports fell from 47 to 27 percent of total oil consumption.

CAFE standards, however, have had their share of problems. When Congress instituted the CAFE standards, light trucks were allowed to meet a lower fuel-economy standard because they constituted only 20 percent of the vehicle market and were used primarily as work vehicles. Light truck standards were set at 17.2 mpg for the 1979 model year and went up to 20.7 mpg in 1996 (combined two-wheel and four-wheel drive). With the burgeoning popularity of SUVs, which are counted as light trucks, trucks now comprise nearly half of the market. In addition, intense lobbying by the auto industry resulted in an inability of Congress to raise the standards from 1985 until 2004. As a result of the lower standards for trucks and SUVs and the increasing importance of trucks and SUVs in the fleet of on-road vehicles, the average miles per gallon for all vehicles declined, rather than improved. In 2005 the standard for light trucks saw its first increase since 1996 to 21 mpg. Recently the standards for all types of vehicles have been raised again to 27.5 mpg for passenger cars and 22.5 mpg for light trucks.

Local Responsibilities. The U.S. Clean Air Act Amendments of 1977 recognized the existence of nonattainment areas. Special requirements were placed on control authorities to bring nonattainment areas into attainment. Many of the nonattainment areas received that designation because of the presence of pollutants generated by mobile sources, so local authorities in those areas were required to take further actions to reduce emissions from mobile sources.

Measures that local authorities are authorized to use include requiring new cars registered in that area to satisfy the more stringent California standard (with EPA approval) and the development of comprehensive transportation plans. These plans could include measures such as on-street parking controls, road charges, and measures to reduce the number of vehicle-miles traveled.

In nonattainment regions that could not meet the primary standard for photochemical oxidants, carbon monoxide, or both by December 31, 1982, control authorities could delay attainments until December 31, 1987, provided they agreed to a number of additional restrictions. For the purposes of this chapter, the most important of these is the requirement that each region gaining this extension must establish a vehicle *inspection and maintenance (I&M) program* for emissions.

The objective of the I&M program is to identify vehicles that are violating the standards and bring them into compliance, to deter tampering, and to encourage regular routine maintenance. Because the federal test procedure used in the certification process is much too expensive to use on a large number of vehicles, shorter, less expensive tests were developed specially for the I&M programs. Because of the expense and questionable effectiveness of these programs, they are one of the most controversial components of the policy package used to control mobile-source emissions.

Alternative Fuels and Vehicles. In an attempt to foster the development of alternative vehicles and *alternative fuels* that would be less damaging to the environment, Congress and some states have passed legislation requiring their increased use. Title II of the Clean Air Act Amendments of 1990 mandates the sale of cleaner-burning reformulated gasoline in certain carbon monoxide (CO) and severe ozone nonattainment regions. In the Energy Policy Act, passed in 1992, Congress required the federal government (and some private fleet owners) to purchase alternative-fueled vehicles. The government also attempted to induce some regulatory flexibility designed to provide incentives for further adoptions (see Example 17.1). California pushed the envelope even further. In September 1990, the California Air Resources Board (CARB) passed its low-emission vehicle (LEV) and zero-emission vehicle (ZEV) regulations. The former requires increasingly stringent emissions standards over time for conventionally fueled vehicles. The latter mandated that a certain percent of new cars and light trucks sold in the state must be zero emission vehicles (defined as vehicles that directly emit no VOCs, NO_x, or CO; any indirect emissions from producing the electricity are not counted).

When these ZEV regulations were written, the focus was on electric vehicles, but over time the emphasis has come to include hybrids (vehicles powered by a combination of gasoline and electric power) and fuel-cell vehicles. In response to this trend the California regulations were modified in 2004. Under the new regulations auto manufacturers can meet their ZEV obligations in one of two ways:

> To fulfill the first option manufacturers must sell a vehicle mix of 2 percent pure ZEVs, 2 percent AT-PZEVs (vehicles earning advanced technology partial ZEV credits) and 6 percent PZEVs (extremely clean conventional vehicles). The ZEV obligation is based on the number of passenger cars and small trucks a manufacturer sells in California.

EXAMPLE 17.1

Project XL—The Quest for Effective, Flexible Regulation

Project XL is a U.S. pilot program that allows state and local governments, businesses, and federal facilities to develop with USEPA innovative strategies to test better or more cost-effective ways of achieving environmental and public health protection. In exchange, the EPA authorizes sufficient regulatory flexibility to conduct the experiment. The objective is to produce both better environmental quality and lower compliance cost than would otherwise be possible with traditional "one-size-fits-all" regulation.

One example of a project involves the United States Postal Service (USPS), the state of Colorado, and the USEPA. The USPS wanted to replace some of its aging, high polluting vehicles in the Denver area. Denver is a nonattainment area for carbon monoxide. Colorado rules required that in the Denver area 50 percent of all new fleet vehicles purchased must be certified as low emitting vehicles (LEVs). Due to the special requirements for USPS vehicles the only bid that met the other USPS specifications was for Transitional Low-Emitting Vehicles (TLEVs), which could not meet the LEV requirement.

Rather than continue operating its aging fleet, the USPS applied for, and received, permission from both Colorado and USEPA to replace 512 aging postal vehicles in Denver with TLEVs. The new vehicles are able use up to 85 percent ethanol fuel. In addition, the USPS would relocate 282 1987–1991 vintage vehicles to areas with less need to reduce emissions.

The USPS proposal will result in lower emissions of carbon monoxide than would have been achieved even if compliance with the original Colorado rules were possible and will become part of Denver's state implementation plan to reach attainment.

Source: http://www.epa.gov/projectxl/usps/index.htm.

Or, manufacturers may choose a new alternative ZEV compliance strategy. Part of their ZEV requirement may be met by producing their sales-weighted market share of approximately 250 fuel cell vehicles by 2008. The remainder of their ZEV requirements could be achieved by producing 4 percent AT-PZEVs and 6 percent PZEVs. The required number of fuel cell vehicles (to which the market share is applied) will increase to 2,500 from 2009–2011, 25,000 from 2012–2014, and 50,000 from 2015–2017. Automakers are allowed to substitute battery electric vehicles for up to 50 percent of their fuel cell vehicle requirements.

Clearly this is an attempt to force automotive technology using a rather innovative method—mandated sales quotas for clean vehicles. Notice that selling this number of clean vehicles depends not only on how many are manufactured, but also on whether demand for those vehicles is sufficient. Without sufficient demand, manufacturers will have to rely on factory rebates or other strategies to promote sales. Since inadequate demand is not a legal defense for failing to meet the deadlines, manufacturers also have a strong incentive to hold down costs.

How well this strategy works in forcing the development and market penetration of new automotive technologies remains to be seen. Other U.S. states, particularly in the Northeast, have followed suit so the size of the potential market is growing.

European Approaches

By the late 1980s, emission standards patterned after the 1983 U.S. standards were introduced for all new cars in Austria, Sweden, Switzerland, Norway, and Finland. West Germany, Denmark, and the Netherlands have introduced tax incentives and lower registration fees for cleaner cars.

On October 1, 1989, the European Community's 12-member nations imposed U.S.-style emission standards on all new cars, starting with cars equipped with engines over two liters. Similar emission controls were extended to all engine sizes by 1993. The European Union banned leaded gasoline in 2000. The EU implemented stricter emission standards for light duty vehicles in 2005.

Russia has, in principle, agreed to follow the example of Western Europe in introducing more stringent emission controls, but phaseout of lead has been much slower. By 1995 only eight of Russia's 25 oil refineries manufactured unleaded gasoline. This made up 40 percent of the gasoline produced in Russia. Many former Soviet Union transition economies have permitted lead content in gasoline that is twice the level allowed by the EU. A few, however, have launched initiatives to phase out lead completely. Slovakia phased out leaded gasoline in 1995, going from a market share of unleaded gasoline of 6 percent in 1992 to 100 percent in 1995 (World Bank, 2001). A 2001 World Bank study found that it would cost between $0.005 and $0.02 per liter of gasoline to phase out lead at a less modern refinery in Russia. These costs could be cut in half, however, if the refinery's production was modified to meet market demand.[6]

The Netherlands, Norway, and Sweden are using differential tax rates to encourage consumers to purchase (and manufacturers to produce) low-emitting cars before regulations take effect requiring all cars to be low-emitting.[7] Tax differentiation confers a tax advantage (and,

---

[6]Lovei, Magdolna. *Toward an Unleaded Environment: World Bank Support to Transition Economies*, 2001 http://www .worldbank.org/html/prddr/trans/m&j96/art5.htm.

[7]For the details on these approaches see Opschoor and Vos (1989).

hence, an after-tax price advantage) on cleaner cars. The amount of the tax usually depends on (1) the emission characteristics of the car (heavier taxes being levied on heavily polluting cars); (2) the size of the car (e.g., in Germany, heavier cars qualify for larger tax advantages to offset the relatively high control requirements placed upon them); and (3) the year of purchase (the tax differential is declining because all cars will eventually have to meet the standards). Apparently it works. In Sweden, 87 percent of the new cars sold have qualified for the tax advantage, and in Germany the comparable percentage has been more than 90 percent.

Europe not only has much higher gasoline prices, but also it has developed strategies to make better use of transportation capital. Its intercity rail system is better developed than in the United States and public transit ridership is typically higher within cities. Europe has also been a pioneer in the use of car sharing arrangements (see Example 17.2).

EXAMPLE 17.2

Car Sharing: Better Use of Automotive Capital?

One of the threats to sustainable development is the growing number of vehicles on the road. Though great progress has been made since the 1970s in limiting the pollution each vehicle emits per mile of travel, as the number of vehicles and the number of miles increase, the resulting increases in pollution offset much of the gains from the cleaner vehicles.

How to limit the number of vehicles? One strategy that has become rather widespread in Europe and is just beginning to make a dent in America is car sharing. Car sharing recognizes that the typical automobile sits idle most of the time, a classic case of excess capacity. (Studies in Germany suggest the average vehicle use per day is one hour.) Therefore, the car sharing strategy tries to spread ownership of a vehicle over several owners who share both the cost and the use.

The charges imposed by car-sharing clubs typically involve an upfront access fee plus fees based both on time of actual use and mileage. (Use during the peak periods usually costs more.) Some car-sharing clubs offer touch-tone automated booking, 24-hour dispatchers, and such amenities as child-safety seats, bike racks, and roof carriers.

Swiss and German clubs started in the late 1980s. As of 1998 an estimated 25,000 Germans and 20,000 Swiss belonged to car-sharing groups.

What could the contribution of car-sharing be to air pollution control in those areas where it catches on? It probably does lower the number of vehicles and the resulting congestion. In addition, peak-hour pricing probably encourages use at the less-polluted periods. On the other hand, it does not necessarily lower the number of miles driven, which is one of the keys to lowering pollution. The contribution of this particular innovation remains to be clarified by some solid empirical research.

Source: Walsh, Mary Williams. "Car-Sharing Holds the Road in German," *Los Angeles Times* (July 23, 1998): A1.

An Economic and Political Assessment

Perhaps the most glaring deficiency in the 1970 amendments occurred when an infeasible compliance schedule for meeting the ambient standards was established for mobile-source pollutants. The chief instruments to be used by local areas in meeting these standards were the new-car emission standards. Because these applied only to new cars, and because new cars make up such a small proportion of the total fleet, significant emission reductions were not experienced until well after the deadline for meeting the ambient standards. This created a very difficult situation for local areas, because they were forced to meet the ambient standards prior to the time that the emission standards (the chief sources of reduction) would have much of an impact.

All they could do was to develop local strategies to make up the difference. Recognizing the difficulties the states faced, the EPA granted an extension of the deadline for submitting the transportation plans that would spell out the manner in which the standards would be met. This extension was challenged in court by the Natural Resource Defense Council,[8] which successfully argued that the EPA did not have the authority to grant the extension. Faced with the court's decision, the EPA was forced to reject the implementation plans submitted by most states as inadequate because those plans could not ensure attainment by the deadlines. Because the law clearly states that the EPA must substitute its own plan for an inadequate plan, the EPA found itself thrust into the unfamiliar and unpleasant role of defining transportation control plans for states with rejected SIPs.

Two main problems with this development surfaced: (1) The EPA was not administratively equipped in terms of staff or resources to design and implement these plans and (2) because of the severity of the mismatch between deadline and implementation, the EPA could have done very little, even if the staff and resources had been available.

The EPA made a valiant but futile attempt to meet its statutory responsibilities. It concluded that the best way to resolve its dilemma was to work backward from the needs to the transportation plans and, once the plans were defined, to require states to implement and enforce them. To ensure state cooperation, it set up a system of civil penalties to be applied against states that failed to cooperate.

The resulting plans were virtually unenforceable because they were so severe. For example, in order to meet the ambient standard in Los Angeles by the deadline, the plan designed by the EPA called for an 82 percent reduction in gasoline consumption in the Los Angeles basin. The reduction was to be achieved through gasoline rationing during the six months of the year when the smog problem is most severe. In publishing the plan, EPA Administrator William Ruckelshaus acknowledged that it was infeasible and would effectively destroy the economy of the state if implemented, but argued that he had no other choice under the law.

The states raised a number of legal challenges to this approach, which were never really resolved in the courts by the time Congress revised the Act in 1977. The Clean Air Act Amendments of 1977 remedied the situation by extending the deadlines.

---

[8] 475 F. 2d 968 (1973).

The lesson from this episode seems to be that tougher laws do not necessarily result in more rapid compliance. In this case, because the statutory requirement could not be met, virtually nothing was accomplished as the various parties attempted to fashion a resolution through the courts.

Technology Forcing and Sanctions

The lesson described above was underscored by the EPA's experience in gaining compliance with the national emission standards by the automobile manufacturers. The industry was able to obtain a number of delays in meeting those standards. The law was so tough that it was difficult to enforce within the time schedule envisioned by Congress.

This problem was intensified by the sanctions established by the Act to ensure compliance. They were so brutal that the EPA was unwilling to use them; therefore, they did not represent a credible threat. For example, when an engine family failed the certification test, the law is quite specific in stating that vehicle classes not certified as conforming to the standards cannot be sold! Given the importance of the automobile industry in the U.S. economy, this sanction was not likely to be applied. As a result, there were considerable pressures on the EPA to avoid the sanctions by defining more easily satisfied procedures for certification and by setting sufficiently flexible deadlines that no manufacturer would fail to meet them.

Differentiated Regulation

In controlling the emissions of both mobile and stationary sources, the brunt of the reduction effort is borne by new sources. This raises the cost of the new sources and, from the purchaser's point of view, increases the attractiveness of used cars relative to new ones. The benefit from increased control is a public good and therefore cannot be appropriated exclusively by the new-car purchasers. One result of a strategy focusing on new sources would be to depress the demand for new cars while enhancing that for used cars.

Apparently, this is precisely what happened in the United States. In response to the higher cost of new cars, people hold on to old automobiles longer. This has produced several unfortunate side effects. Because new cars are substantially cleaner than old cars, emission reductions have been delayed. In effect, this shift in fleet composition was equivalent to a setback of three to four years in the timetable for reducing emissions. Also, because older cars get worse gas mileage, gasoline consumption was higher than it would otherwise be. The focus on new sources is to some extent inevitable; the lesson to be drawn is that by ignoring these behavioral responses to *differentiated regulation*, the policymaker is likely to expect results to occur sooner than they are likely to.

Uniformity of Control

With the exception of the California standards, which are more stringent, the Clean Air Act requires the same emission standards on all cars. The calculations were designed to assure that required levels of control would be sufficient to meet the ambient standards in large cities such as Los Angeles or in high-altitude cities such as Denver. As a result, many of the costs borne by people in other parts of the country—particularly rural areas—do not yield much in the way of benefits.

This sounds like an inefficient policy, because the severity of control is not tailored to the geographic need. Indeed most of the studies that have been accomplished indicate that this is so.

The conclusion that the costs of control exceed the benefits for automobile pollution control seems to be generally shared. Large uncertainties in the benefit estimations, a theme we have explored in several previous chapters, and the failure of any of these studies to consider the role of auto emissions of carbon in global warming force us to take these results with a grain of salt. Nonetheless it is interesting that because the current policy forces manufacturers to operate on a very steep portion of the marginal-control-cost function, benefit uncertainty does not seem to affect the conclusion that the current standards are inefficiently strict with current technologies. New technologies may change that conclusion.

The Deterioration of New-Car Emission Rates

As part of its investigation of the Clean Air Act, the National Commission on Air Quality investigated the emissions of vehicles in use and compared these emission levels to the standards. Its estimates were a blend of actual measured emissions for model years already in the fleet and forecasts for future model years based on knowledge of the technologies to be used. Particularly for hydrocarbons and carbon monoxide, the deterioration of emission rates in use was pronounced.

The Commission also investigated the factors contributing to poor in-use emission performance. It found that the principal reason for the poor performance was improper maintenance. Carburetor and ignition-timing misadjustment were key factors. Component failure and tampering were also found to affect emission levels, but to a lesser degree.

Inspection and Maintenance (I&M) Programs. One policy response to emission rate deterioration (along with requiring manufacturers to grant extended warranties for emission control systems) was to require I&M programs in nonattainment areas. How successful was this approach?

Over the past decade these programs have met with mixed success at best. Motorists have little incentive to comply with the requirements unless forced to do so, since repair costs can be high and the benefits of repair are mostly externalities. This means that enforcement is key, but due to the sheer number of vehicles involved, it is also very difficult.

What is the evidence? One study (Harrington et al., 2000) found I&M programs to be relatively cost effective, although significant opportunities for targeting the programs remain unexploited. In addition to targeting programs at areas where vehicle air pollution problems are most severe, programs could also improve targeting of the problem vehicles. A relatively few vehicles are typically responsible for a disproportionate share of the mobile source pollution. This implies that for most vehicles the test is expensive, but it produces little private or social benefit. To the extent that these programs could identify the few high-emitting vehicles (through remote sensing, for example) and bring them into conformance at a reasonable cost, these programs could be much more cost-effective.

A few states have adopted I&M programs that assign a supplementary role to on-road emissions testing by using remote-sensing technology (National Research Council, 2004) In some states (Texas, for example), roadside enforcement officers use remote sensors to identify vehicles with malfunctioning emission-control systems (similar to the way radar is used to identify speeders). Using the recorded license numbers, officers can contact the owners of the vehicles who are then required to take appropriate corrective action. Other states, such as Colorado and Missouri, use a "clean screening" program, in which roadside remote sensing is used to exempt vehicles from central testing requirements.

Challenges remain for expanded use of remote sensing, however. Further controlled testing of remote sensing devices is necessary to improve quality control, and the technology must be further developed to be able to measure the full range of automotive pollutants (especially particulate matter).

Alternative Fuels. In addition to controlling in-use emissions by means of I&M programs, the Clean Air Act Amendments of 1990 required nonattainment areas to use cleaner-burning automotive fuels (oxygenated fuels) during the winter months in some cases and reformulated gasoline year-round in the worst cases. Ethanol and MTBE were the two additives most widely used to meet the oxygen content standard.

Largely due to cost, most non-midwestern states opted for gasoline with the additive MTBE rather than ethanol. MTBE (methyl tertiary butyl ether) is designed to make gasoline burn cleaner and more efficiently. Unfortunately, once it entered into widespread use, it was discovered that it spreads rapidly following gasoline leaks from underground storage tanks, thereby contaminating sources of groundwater and drinking water. Once in soil or water, it turns out that MTBE breaks down very slowly while it can accelerate the spread of other contaminants in gasoline, such as benzene, a known carcinogen. Once these properties became known, several states passed measures to ban or significantly limit the use of MTBE in gasoline.

The MTBE story provides an interesting case study of the problems that can occur with a strategy that relies on a "technical fix" to solve air pollution problems. Sometimes the effects of the "solution" can, in retrospect, turn out to be worse than the original problem.

Even before the MTBE water contamination issue surfaced, questions were raised about the cost-effectiveness of using oxygenated fuels. For example, when Rask (2004) compared the oxy-fuel smog test results to emissions improvements resulting from emissions system repairs, he found increased maintenance and repairs to be a much more cost-effective strategy for lowering CO and HC emissions than oxyfuels.

Lead Phaseout Program

Following the path established by the Emissions Trading Program, the government began applying the transferable-permit approach more widely. In the mid-1980s, prior to the issuance of new, more stringent regulations on lead in gasoline, the EPA announced the results of a benefit/cost analysis of their expected impact. The analysis concluded that the proposed 0.01 gplg standard would result in $36 billion (in 1983 dollars) in benefits (from reduced adverse health effects), at an estimated cost to the refining industry of $2.6 billion.

Although the regulation was unquestionably justified on efficiency grounds, the EPA wanted to allow flexibility in how the deadlines were met, without increasing the amount of lead used. Although some refiners could meet early deadlines with ease, others could do so only with a significant increase in cost. Recognizing that meeting the goal did not require that every refiner meet every deadline, the EPA initiated an innovative program to provide additional flexibility in meeting the regulations (see Example 17.3).

The program was very successful in reducing both lead emissions and the concentration of lead in the ambient air. From 1982–2001, emissions of lead decreased by 93 percent and the concentrations in the ambient air fell by 94 percent.

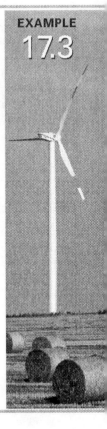

Getting the Lead Out: The Lead Phaseout Program

EXAMPLE 17.3

Under the *Lead Phaseout Program* a fixed number of "lead rights" (authorizing the use of a fixed amount of lead in gasoline produced during the period) were allocated to the 195 or so refineries. (Because of a loophole in the regulations, some new "alcohol-blender" refineries were created in order to take advantage of the program, but their impact was very small.) The number of issued rights declined over time. Refiners who did not need their full share of authorized rights could sell their rights to other refiners.

Initially, no banking of rights was allowed (i.e., rights had to be created and used in the same quarter), but the EPA subsequently allowed banking. Once banking was initiated, created rights could be used in that period or any subsequent period up to the end of the program in 1987. Prices of rights, which were initially about 0.75 cents per gram of lead, rose to 4 cents after banking was allowed.

Refiners had an incentive to eliminate the lead quickly, because early reductions freed up rights for sale. Acquiring these credits made it possible for other refiners to comply with the deadlines, even in the face of equipment failures or "Acts of God"; furthermore, fighting the deadlines in court, the traditional response, became unnecessary. Designed purely as a means of facilitating the transition to this new regime, the lead-banking program ended as scheduled on December 31, 1987.

Sources: Nussbaum, Barry D., "Phasing Down Lead in Gasoline in the U.S.: Mandates, Incentives, Trading and Banking," *Climate Change: Designing a Tradeable Permit System,* Jones, T. and J. Corfee-Morlot, eds. (Paris: Organization for Economic Co-operation and Development, 1992): 21–34; and Hahn, Robert W. and Gordon L. Hester, "Marketable Permits: Lessons from Theory and Practice," *Ecology Law Quarterly* 16, 1989: 361–406.

Possible Reforms

We have seen that the current U.S. approaches have some salient weaknesses. Reliance on controlling emissions at the point of production has produced major improvements in cars leaving the assembly line, but emission rates deteriorate with use. The use of uniform standards has resulted in more control than necessary in rural areas and perhaps less than necessary in the most heavily polluted areas. Manufacturers have been able to delay implementation deadlines because the sanctions for noncompliance are so severe that the EPA has often been reluctant to deny a certificate of conformity.

Fuel Taxes

As controls on manufacturers have become more common and vehicles have become cleaner, attention is increasingly turning to the user. Drivers have little incentive to drive or maintain their cars in a manner that minimizes emissions, because the full social costs of road transport have not been internalized by current policy. How far from a full internalization of cost are we? Parry et al. (2007) compile estimates from the literature and find the sum of mileage-related external marginal costs to be approximately $2.10 per gallon. Mileage-related externalities include local pollution, congestion, and accidents. Fuel external costs such as oil dependency and climate change are another $0.18 per gallon. Figure 17.2 illustrates current *fuel taxes* by country. These data suggest current fuel taxes would have to be much higher in most countries in order to internalize the full social cost of road transport. Debate 17.1 explores the debate about the use of fuel taxes versus CAFE standards. As Debate 17.1 points out, the theoretical case for fuel taxes is clear, but when political feasibility enters the picture, identifying the best option is more difficult.

But fuel taxes are not the only way to begin to internalize costs and, by themselves, they would be only a blunt instrument, because they would typically not take into account when and where the emissions occurred. One way to focus on these temporal and spatial concerns is through *congestion pricing*, charging higher prices for access to congested roadways.

Congestion Pricing

Congestion is influenced by vehicle miles traveled, but also by time and place. Congestion pricing addresses this externality by charging for driving on congested roads or at congested times. There are four different types of congestion pricing mechanisms: cordon pricing, priced facilities, priced lanes, and high occupancy toll lanes (HOT) lanes.[9] Peak-period pricing of roads or zones has recently been gaining considerable attention as a remedy for dealing with these time and space specific pollutant concentrations.

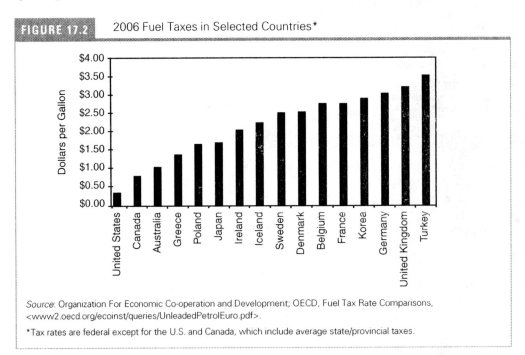

FIGURE 17.2   2006 Fuel Taxes in Selected Countries*

Source: Organization For Economic Co-operation and Development; OECD, Fuel Tax Rate Comparisons, <www2.oecd.org/ecoinst/queries/UnleadedPetrolEuro.pdf>.

*Tax rates are federal except for the U.S. and Canada, which include average state/provincial taxes.

---

[9]Congressional Budget Office (2009). "Using Pricing to Reduce Traffic Congestion," A CBO Study.

DEBATE 17.1

CAFE Standards or Fuel Taxes?

Increasing the fuel efficiency of oil consumption could in principle be accomplished by increasing either fuel taxes or fuel-efficiency standards. By raising the cost of driving, the former would encourage auto purchasers to seek more fuel-efficient vehicles, while the latter would ensure that the average new vehicle sold was fuel efficient. Does it make a difference which strategy is followed?

It turns out that it does, and economics can help explain why. Think about what each strategy does to the marginal cost of driving an extra mile. Increased fuel taxes raise the marginal cost per mile driven, but fuel-economy standards lower it. In the first case, each mile consumes more fuel and that fuel costs more. In the second case, the more fuel-efficient car uses less fuel per mile so the cost has gone down.

Following economic logic leads immediately to the conclusion that even if both strategies resulted in the same fuel economy, the tax would reduce oil consumption by more because it would promote fewer miles driven. On these grounds, a tax is better than a fuel-economy standard.

Austin and Dinan (2005) test these ideas with a simulation model in which they compare an increase in the CAFE standards to a gasoline tax designed to save the same amount of gasoline. Using a highly stylized representation of the U.S. automobile market, they examine a policy that would reduce gasoline consumption by 10 percent after the retirement of all existing vehicles (assumed to be 14 years). They estimate that an increase in the CAFE standards by 3.8 miles per gallon would achieve this result. They compare this to a gasoline tax designed to save 10 percent over the same 14-year period. They also estimate the cost savings from allowing fuel-economy credits to be bought and sold by manufacturers. They find that, even with tradable fuel-economy credits that reduce the cost of increasing the fuel-economy standards, a tax is still advantageous. With a tax, the savings occur much earlier than with the standards (while the costs rise gradually), supporting the arguments above. Using a 12 percent discount rate, they estimate that a tax of $0.30 per gallon would save the same amount of gasoline and do so at a cost that is 71 percent lower than the comparable change in fuel-economy standards!

Supporters of fuel-economy standards, however, counter with a political feasibility argument. They point out that in the United States, sufficiently high gasoline taxes to produce that level of reduction could never have passed Congress, so the fuel-economy standards were better, much better, than no policy at all. Indeed, the $0.30 increase estimated by Austin and Dinan represents a 73 percent increase in the tax on gasoline in the United States. Additionally, some argue that as fuel efficiency standards go up, the gas tax offers less of an incentive to drive less. Would a mileage tax work better?

Source: David Austin and Terry Dinan, "Clearing the Air: The Costs and Consequences of Higher CAFE Standards and Increased Gasoline Taxes," *Journal of Environmental Economics and Management,* 50, 2005: 562–582.

Toll rings have existed for some time in Oslo, Norway, and Milan, Italy. In the United States, electronic toll collection systems are currently in place in many states. Express lanes for cars with electronic meters reduce congestion at toll booths. Reserved express bus lanes are also common in the United States. (Reserved lanes for express buses lower the relative travel time for bus commuters, thereby providing an incentive for passengers to switch from cars to buses.) High occupancy vehicle (HOV) lanes have also been established for some highways. During certain hours, vehicles traveling in the HOV lanes must have at least one passenger. EZ Pass lanes frequently offer toll discounts. Honolulu, Hawaii, has a high occupancy "zipper lane." The zipper lane is in the middle of the highway and in the morning commute hours the traffic travels toward Honolulu and by mid-afternoon, the lane is literally zipped up on one side and unzipped on the other, creating an additional lane for the outgoing evening commute. In Central London, a cordon pricing system is in place for approximately 15-square miles of the city. Drivers pay a charge to drive or park within the zone Monday through Friday from 7:00 a.m. to 6:00 p.m.[10]

Several Asian cities have undertaken some innovative approaches. Perhaps the most innovative can be found in Singapore, where the price system is used to reduce congestion (see Example 17.4). Bangkok bars vehicles from transporting goods from certain parts of the metropolitan area during various peak hours, leaving the roads available to buses, cars, and motorized tricycles.

Safirova et al. (2007) compare six different road pricing instruments all aimed at internalizing the congestion externality. These include three types of cordon pricing schemes (area-based congestion taxes): a distance-based toll on highways, a distance-based toll on metro roads only, and a gas tax. Examining the effectiveness of these instruments for the Washington, DC metropolitan area in 2000, their model allows drivers to choose a zone of residence and hence travel time. The question they ask is, "But how do policies designed to address congestion alone fare, once the many other consequences associated with driving—traffic accidents, air pollution, oil dependency, urban sprawl, and noise, to name a few—are taken into account?"[11] They find that using "social-cost pricing" (incorporating the social costs of driving) instead of simple congestion pricing changes the outcome of instrument choice. Specifically, when the policy goal is solely to reduce congestion, variable time-of-day pricing on the entire road network is the most effective and efficient policy. However, when additional social costs are factored in, the vehicle miles traveled (VMT) tax is almost as efficient.

Private Toll Roads

New policies are also beginning to consider how to assure that road users pay all the costs of maintaining the highways, rather than transferring that burden to taxpayers generally. One strategy, which has been implemented in Mexico and in Orange County, California, is to allow construction of new private toll roads. The tolls are set high enough to recover all consumption and maintenance costs and, in some cases, may include congestion pricing.

---

[10]www.tfl.gov/uk/roadusers/congestioncharging.

[11]http://www.rff.org/rff/News/Releases/2008Releases/MarginalSocialCostTrafficCongestion.cfm.

Innovative Mobile-Source Pollution Control Strategies: Singapore	**EXAMPLE** **17.4**

Singapore has one of the most comprehensive strategies to control vehicle pollution in the world. In addition to imposing very high vehicle registration fees, this approach also includes the following:

- Central Business District parking fees that are higher during normal business hours than during the evenings and weekends.
- An area-licensing scheme that requires the display of a specific purchased vehicle license in order to gain entry to restricted downtown zones during restricted hours. These licenses are very expensive and penalties for not having them displayed when required are very steep.
- Electronic peak-hour pricing on roadways. These charges, which are deducted automatically using a "smart card" technology, vary by roadway and by time of day. Conditions are reviewed and charges are adjusted every three months.
- An option for people to purchase an "off-peak" car. Identified by a distinctive red license plate that is welded to the vehicle, these vehicles can only be used during off-peak periods. Owners of these vehicles pay much lower registration fees and road taxes.
- Limiting the number of new vehicles that can be registered each year. In order to assure that they can register a new car, potential buyers must first secure one of the fixed number of licenses by submitting a winning financial bid.
- An excellent mass transit system that provides a viable alternative to automobile travel.

Has the program been effective? Apparently, it has been effective in two rather different ways. First, it has provided a significant amount of revenue for the government, which the government can use to reduce more burdensome taxes. (The revenues go into the General Treasury; they are not earmarked for the transport sector.) Second, it has caused a large reduction in traffic-related pollution in the affected areas. The overall levels of carbon monoxide, lead, sulfur dioxide, and nitrogen dioxide are now all within the human health guidelines established by both the World Health Organization and the United States Environmental Protection Agency.

Source: China, N.–C. and S.–Y. Phang, "Motor Vehicle Taxes as an Environmental Management Instrument: The Case of Singapore," *Environmental Economics and Policy Studies* 4(1), 2004: 67–93.

Parking Cash Outs

Providing parking spaces for employees costs employers money, yet many of them provide this benefit free of charge. This employer-financed *parking cash out* reduces one significant cost of driving to work. Since this subsidy only benefits those who drive to work, it lowers the relative cost of driving vis-à-vis all other transport choices, such as walking, biking, public transport, and so on. Since most of those alternatives create much less air pollution, the resulting bias toward driving creates an inefficiently high level of pollution.

One way to rectify this bias is for employers to compensate employees who do not use a parking space with an equivalent increase in income. This would transfer the employer's savings in not having to provide a parking spot to the employee and remove the bias toward driving to work.

Feebates

Some research has found that consumers may undervalue fuel economy. One study found that consumers only consider the first three years of fuel savings when choosing a more fuel efficient vehicle. This understates the value of fuel savings by up to 60 percent. (NRC 2002) Thus, another policy strategy is targeted at consumers purchasing new vehicles. *Feebates* combine taxes on purchases of new high-emitting (or high fuel consumption) vehicles with subsidies for purchases of new low-emitting/low fuel consumption vehicles. By raising the relative cost of high-emitting vehicles, it encourages consumers to take the environmental effects of those vehicles into account. Feebate system structures are based on a pivot point that separates vehicles charged a tax from those entitled to rebates. The simplest feebate structure uses a constant dollar rate per gallon of fuel consumed (Greene et al., 2005). The revenue from the taxes can serve as the financing for the subsidies, but previous experience indicates that policies such as this are rarely revenue-neutral. Feebates are not yet widely used, but Ontario, Canada, and Austria have implemented feebates. Greene et al. (2005) find that feebates achieve fuel economy increases that are two times higher than those achieved by either rebates or gas guzzler taxes.

Pay-As-You-Drive (PAYD) Insurance

Changing the way car insurance is financed is another possibility for internalizing an environmental externality associated with automobile travel, thereby reducing both accidents and pollution. As Example 17.5 points out, small changes in the manner premiums are calculated could potentially make a big difference.

Accelerated Retirement Strategies

A final reform possibility involves the implementation of strategies to accelerate the retirement of older, more heavily polluting vehicles. This could be accomplished either by raising the cost of holding on to older vehicles (e.g., with higher registration fees for vehicles that pollute more) or by providing a bounty of some sort to those retiring heavily polluting vehicles early.

One version of the bounty program has become known as *cash for clunkers*. Under this program, stationary sources are allowed to claim emission reduction credits (ERCs) for heavily polluting vehicles that are removed from service. In one version of the program, heavily polluting vehicles are identified either by inspection and maintenance programs or remote sensing. A vehicle owner can bring his or her vehicle up to code, usually an expensive proposition, or can sell it to the company running the cash for clunkers program. Purchased vehicles are usually disassembled for parts and the remainder of the hulk is recycled. The number of ERCs earned by the company running the program depends on such factors as the remaining useful life of the car and the estimated number of miles it would be driven, and this number is generally controlled so that the transaction results in a net increase in air quality.

Modifying Car Insurance as an Environmental Strategy

EXAMPLE

17.5

Although improvements in technology (such as airbags, antilock brakes, and so on) have made driving much safer than in the past, the number of road deaths and injuries is still inefficiently high. Since people do not consider the full societal cost of accident risk when deciding how much and how often to drive, the number of vehicle miles traveled is inefficiently excessive. Although drivers may take into account the risks of injury to themselves and other family members, other risks are likely to be externalized. These include the risk of injury to other drivers and pedestrians, the costs of vehicular damage that is covered through insurance claims, and the costs to other motorists held up in traffic congestion caused by accidents. Externalizing these costs artificially lowers the marginal cost of driving, thereby inefficiently increasing the pollution from the resulting high number of vehicle miles.

Implementing *Pay-As-You Drive (PAYD)* insurance could reduce those inefficiencies. With PAYD insurance, existing rating factors (such as age, gender, previous driving experience, and so on) would be used by insurance companies to determine a driver's per-mile rate, and this rate would be multiplied by annual miles driven to calculate the annual insurance premium. This approach has the effect of drastically increasing the marginal cost of driving an extra mile without raising the amount people spend annually on insurance. Estimates by Harrington and Parry (2004) suggest that calculating these insurance costs on a per-mile basis would have the same effect as raising the federal gasoline tax from $0.184 to $1.50 per gallon for a vehicle that gets 20 miles per gallon. This is a substantial increase and could likely have a dramatic effect on people's transport choices (and, therefore, the pollution they emit) despite the fact that it imposes no additional financial burden on them.

Source: Harrington, Winston and Ian Parry, "Pay-As-You-Drive for Car Insurance," *New Approaches on Energy and the Environment: Policy Advice for the President,* Morgenstern, R. and P. Portney, eds. (Washington, DC: Resources of the Future, 2004): 53–56.

Another version, introduced by the South Coast Air Quality Management Board (serving the greater Los Angeles area), involves public funding rather than privately purchased emission reduction credits and tries to influence the choice of a replacement vehicle. Using the remote sensing data, the operator of the program contacts owners of the dirtiest 1 percent to 2 percent of vehicles tested and offers them the opportunity to receive either up to $500 for repairs so their vehicle meets Smog Check requirements or $1,000 to scrap the vehicle.

Residents who meet state low-income guidelines are eligible to qualify for additional funding of up to $3,000, if they choose to scrap their vehicle and replace it with a model meeting the state's certification criteria for a Low Emission Vehicle (LEV). Residents would receive either a voucher or reimbursement upon proof of purchase of a LEV or cleaner vehicle.

Retirement strategies would tend to counteract the tendency for vehicles to be used longer as a result of the new-source focus of current automotive regulations. By eliminating these heavily polluting vehicles from the fleet earlier than would otherwise be the case, greater emission reductions could be achieved at an earlier date. This approach could be applied selectively in those local areas for which it could make a significant difference.

We also have learned some things about what doesn't work very well. One increasingly common strategy involves limiting the days any particular vehicle can be used in order to limit miles traveled. As Example 17.6 indicates, this strategy can backfire!

Summary

The current policy toward motor vehicle emissions blends point-of-production control with point-of-use control. Point of production control began with uniform emissions standards.

Grams-per-mile emissions standards, the core of the current approach in both the United States and Europe, have had, in practice, many deficiencies. While standards have promoted lower emissions per mile, they have been less effective in lowering aggregate emissions and in assuring cost-effective reductions.

Aggregate mobile source emissions have been reduced by less than expected because of the very large offsetting increase in the number of miles traveled. Unlike sulfur emissions from power plants, aggregate mobile source emissions are not capped, so as miles increase, emissions increase.

EXAMPLE 17.6

Counterproductive Policy Design

As one response to unacceptably high levels of traffic congestion and air pollution, the Mexico City administration imposed a regulation that banned each car from driving on a specific day of the week. The specific day when a given car could not be driven was determined by the last digit of the license plate.

This approach appeared to offer the opportunity for considerable reductions in congestion and air pollution, at a relatively low cost. In this case, however, the appearance was deceptive, because of the way in which the population reacted to the ban.

An evaluation of the program by the World Bank found that, in the short run, the regulation was effective. Both pollution and congestion were reduced. However, in the long run, the regulation was not only ineffective, it was counterproductive (paradoxically, it *increased* the level of congestion and pollution). The paradox resulted because a large number of residents reacted by buying an additional car (which would have a different license plate number and, therefore, be banned on a different day). Once the additional cars became available, total driving increased. Policies that are overly quick to anticipate and incorporate behavioral reactions run the risk that actual and expected outcomes may diverge considerably.

Source: Eskeland, Gunnar S. and Tarhan Feyzioglu, "Rationing Can Backfire: The 'Day Without a Car Program' in Mexico City," World Bank Policy Research Working Paper 1554 (December 1995).

The efficiency of the emissions standards has been diminished by their geographic uniformity. Too little control has been exercised in highly polluted areas and too much control in areas with air quality that exceeds the ambient standards.

Local point-of-use approaches, such as targeted inspection and maintenance strategies and accelerated retirement strategies, have had mixed success in redressing this imbalance. Since a relatively small number of vehicles typically contribute a disproportionately large share of the emissions, reliance on remote sensing to identify the most polluting vehicles has been growing. This strategy allows the policy to target control resources where they will produce the largest net benefit.

The historic low cost of auto travel has led to a dispersed pattern of development. Since dispersed travel patterns make mass transit a less viable alternative, a downward spiral of population dispersal and low mass transit ridership occur. In the long run, part of the strategy for meeting ambient standards will necessarily involve changing land use patterns to create the kind of high-density travel corridors that are compatible with effective mass transit use. Though these conditions already exist in much of Europe, it is likely to evolve in the United States only over a long period of time. The process can begin moving in the right direction by ensuring that the true social costs of transportation are borne by those making residential and mode-of-travel choices.

Several important insights about the conventional environmental policy wisdom can be derived from the history of mobile source control. Contrary to the traditional belief that tougher laws produce more environmental results, the sanctions associated with meeting the grams-per-mile emissions standards were so severe that, when push came to shove, authorities were unwilling to impose them. Threatened sanctions will only promote the desired outcome if the threat is credible. The largest "club" is not necessarily the best "club."

The second insight confronts the traditional belief that simply applying the right technical fix can solve environmental problems. The gasoline additive MTBE was advanced as a way to improve the nation's air. With the advantage of hindsight we now know that its contaminating effects on groundwater have dwarfed its positive effects on air quality. Though technical fixes can and do have a role to play in environmental policy, they also can have large adverse unintended consequences.

Two new emphases are emerging for the future of mobile source air pollution control. The first involves encouraging the development and commercialization of new, cleaner automotive technologies ranging from gas-electric hybrids to fuel-cell vehicles powered by hydrogen. Policies such as fuel economy standards, gasoline taxes, feebates, and sales quotas imposed on auto manufacturers for low emitting vehicles are designed to accelerate the entry of cleaner automotive technologies into the vehicle fleet.

The second new emphasis focuses on influencing driver choices. The range of available policies is impressive. One set of strategies focuses on bringing the private marginal cost of driving closer to the social marginal cost through such measures as congestion pricing and pay-as-you-drive auto insurance. Another, parking cash outs, attempts to create a more level playing field for choices involving the mode of travel for the journey to work.

Complicating all of these strategies is the increased demand for cars in developing countries. In 2007 Tata Motors, the Indian automaker, introduced "the world's cheapest car"—the Tata

Nano. The Nano will sell for 100,000 rupees ($2,500). Tata Motors expects to sell millions of these affordable, stripped down vehicles. Fuel efficiency of these cars is quite good (over 50 mpg), but the sheer number of vehicles implies sizable increases in the demand for fuel, congestion, and pollution emissions.

Appropriate regulation of emissions from mobile sources requires a great deal more than simply controlling the emissions from vehicles as they leave the factory. Vehicle purchases, driving behavior, fuel choice, and even residential and employment choices must eventually be affected by the need to reduce mobile source emissions. Affecting the choices facing automobile owners can transpire only if the economic incentives associated with those choices are structured correctly.

Key Concepts

alternative fuels, *p.* 373

cash for clunkers, *p.* 386

congestion inefficiency, *p.* 369

congestion pricing, *p.* 382

Corporate Average Fuel Economy (CAFE), *p.* 372

differentiated regulation, *p.* 378

feebates, *p.* 386

fuel taxes, *p.* 382

inspection and maintenance (I&M) program, *p.* 373

Lead Phaseout Program, *p.* 381

parking cash outs, *p.* 385

Pay-As-You-Drive (PAYD) insurance, *p.* 387

transport subsidies, *p.* 368

Further Reading

Button, Kenneth J. *Market and Government Failures in Environmental Management: The Case of Transport* (Paris: Organization for Economic Co-operation and Development, 1992). Analyzes and documents the types of government interventions—such as pricing, taxation, and regulations—that often result in environmental degradation.

Harrington, W. and V. McConnell. "Motor Vehicles and the Environment," *International Yearbook of Environmental and Resource Economics 2003/2004*, Folmer, H. and T. Tietenberg, eds. (Cheltenham, UK: Edward Elgar, 2003): 190–268. A comprehensive survey of what we have learned from economic analysis about cost-effective ways to control pollution from motor vehicles.

MacKenzie, James J., Roger C. Dower, and Donald D. T. Chen. *The Going Rate: What It Really Costs to Drive* (Washington, DC: World Resources Institute, 1992). Explores the full cost of a transportation system dominated by the automobile.

MacKenzie, James J. *The Keys to the Car: Electric and Hydrogen Vehicles for the Twenty-First Century* (Washington, DC: World Resources Institute, 1994). Surveys the environmental and economic costs and benefits of alternative fuels and alternative vehicles.

OECD. *Cars and Climate Change* (Paris: Organization for Economic Co-operation and Development and the International Energy Agency, 1993). Examines the possibilities, principally from enhanced energy efficiency and alternative fuels, for reducing greenhouse emissions from the transport sector.

Additional References

Aasness, J. and E. R. Larsen. "Distributional Effects of Environmental Taxes on Transportation," *Journal of Consumer Policy* 26 (2003) (3): 279–300.

Austin, D. and T. Dinan. "Clearing the Air: The Costs and Consequences of Higher CAFE Standards and Increased Gasoline Taxes," *Journal of Environmental Economics and Management* 50 (2005) (3): 562–582.

Ball, Jeffrey and Karen Lundegaard. "SUVs Get Big Tax Break—As Drivers Seize Loophole," *The Wall Street Journal* (December 19, 2002).

Dobes, L. "Kyoto: Tradeable Greenhouse Emission Permits in the Transport Sector," *Transport Reviews* 19 (1999) (1): 81–97.

Espey, M. and S. Nair. "Automobile Fuel Economy: What Is It Worth?" *Contemporary Economic Policy* 23 (2005) (3): 1–7.

Forkenbrock, D. J. and L. A. Schweitzer. "Environmental Justice in Transportation Planning," *Journal of the American Planning Association* 65 (1999) (1): 96–111.

Green, David, Philip D. Patterson, Margaret Singh, and Jia Le. "Feebates, Rebates, and Gas-Guzzler Taxes: A Study of Incentives for Increased Fuel Economy," *Energy Policy* 33 (April 2005) (6).

Haagen-Smit, A. J. "Chemistry and Physiology of Los Angeles Smog," *Industrial and Engineering Chemistry* 44(6): 1342–1346.

Hahn, Robert W. and Gordon L. Hester. "Marketable Permits: Lessons for Theory and Practice," *Ecology Law Quarterly* 16 (1989): 380–391.

Harrington, W. and V. McConnell. "A Lighter Tread? Policy and Technology Options for Motor Vehicles," *Environment* 45 (2003) (9): 22+.

Harrington, W., V. McConnell, A. Ando. "Are Vehicle Inspection Programs Living Up to Expectations?," *Transportation Research Part D* 5 (2000) (3): 153–172.

Krunpnick, A., W. Harrington, et al. "Public Support for Pollution Fee Policies for Motor Vehicles with Revenue Recycling: Survey Results," *Regional Science and Urban Economics* 31 (2001) (4): 505–522.

Lofgren, A. and H. Hammar. "The Phase-Out of Leaded Gasoline in the EU: A Successful Failure?" *Transportation Research: Part D. Transport and the Environment* 5 (2000) (6): 419–431.

McConnell, Virginia D. "A Social Cost-Benefit Study of the Maryland Vehicle Emissions Inspection Program," Maryland Institute for Policy Analysis and Research (1986).

Nash, C., T. Sansom, et al. "Modifying Transport Prices to Internalize Externalities: Evidence from European Case Studies," *Regional Science and Urban Economics* 31 (2001) (4): 413–431.

National Commission on Air Quality. *To Breathe Clean Air* (Washington, DC: Government Printing Office, 1981)

National Research Council. *Air Quality Management in the United States* (Washington, DC: The National Academies Press, 2004).

Ogden, J. M., R. H. Williams, et al. "Societal Lifecycle Costs of Cars with Alternative Fuels/Engines," *Energy Policy* 32 (2004) (1): 7–27.

Opschoor J. B. and Hans B. Vos. *Economic Instruments for Environmental Protection* (Paris: Organization for Economic Co-operation and Development, 1989): 69–71.

Rask, K. "Clean Air Policy and Oxygenated Fuels: Do We Get What We Pay for?" *Energy Economics* 26 (2004) (1): 161–177.

Safirova, Elena, Sébastien Houde, and Winston Harrington. "Marginal Social Cost Pricing on a Transportation Network: A Comparison of 2nd Best Policies," *Resources for the Future*, December 2007.

Southworth, F. "On the Potential Impacts of Land Use Change Policies on Automobile Vehicle Miles of Travel," *Energy Policy* 29 (2001) (14): 1271–1283.

Tanguay, G. A. and N. Marceau. "Centralized versus Decentralized Taxation of Mobile Polluting Firms," *Resource and Energy Economics* 23 (2001) (4): 327–341.

Van Wee, B., H. C. Moll, and J. Dirks. "Environmental Impact of Scrapping Old Cars," *Transportation. Research: Part D: Transport and the Environment* 5 (2000) (2): 137–143.

Walls, M. and J. Hanson. "Distributional Aspects of an Environmental Tax Shift: The Case of Motor Vehicle Emission Taxes," *National Tax Journal* 52 (1999) (1): 53–65.

Discussion Questions

1. "While gasoline taxes and fuel economy standards can both be effective in increasing the number of miles per gallon in new vehicles, gasoline taxes are a superior means of reducing emissions from the vehicle fleet." Discuss.

2. When a threshold concentration is used as the basis for pollution control as it is for air pollution, one possibility for meeting the threshold at minimum cost is to spread the emissions out over time. One way to accomplish this is to establish a peak-hour pricing system in which the charges for emissions during peak periods are higher.

   a. Would this represent a move toward efficiency or not? Why?

   b. What effects should this policy have on mass-transit usage, gasoline sales, downtown shopping, and travel patterns?

3. What are the advantages and disadvantages of using an increase in the gasoline tax to move transport decisions toward both efficiency and sustainability?

Water Pollution

18

It was the best of times, it was the worst of times, it was the age of
wisdom, it was the age of foolishness, it was the epoch of belief, it was
the epoch of incredulity. ...

—CHARLES DICKENS, *A Tale of Two Cities* (1859)

Introduction

Although various types of pollution have common attributes, important differences are apparent
as well. These differences form the basis for the elements of policy unique to each pollutant. We
have seen, for example, that although the types of pollutants emitted by mobile and stationary
sources are often identical, the policy approaches differ considerably.

Water pollution control has its own unique characteristics as well. The following stand out
as having particular relevance for policy:

1. Recreation benefits are much more important for water pollution control than for air
   pollution control.

2. Large economies of scale in treating sewage and other wastes create the possibility for
   large, centralized treatment plants as one control strategy, whereas for air pollution, on-
   site control is the standard approach.

3. Many causes of water pollution are difficult to trace to a particular source as in smoke-
   stacks or cars for air pollution. Examples of major nonpoint sources of water pollution
   include runoff from streets and agriculture as well as atmospheric deposition of pollutants. Control of these sources adds additional complexities for water pollution control.

These characteristics create a need for yet another policy approach. In this chapter we will
explore the problems and prospects for controlling this unique and important form of pollution.

The Nature of Water Pollution Problems

Types of Waste-Receiving Water

Two primary types of water are susceptible to contamination. The first, surface water, consists of the rivers, lakes, and oceans covering most of the earth's surface. In the past, policymakers have focused almost exclusively on preventing and cleaning up lake and river water pollution. Only recently has ocean pollution received the attention it deserves.

Groundwater, once considered a pristine resource, has been shown to be subject to considerable contamination from toxic chemicals. Groundwater is subsurface water that occurs beneath a water table in soils or rocks, or in geological formations that are fully saturated.

Groundwater is a vast natural resource. It has been estimated that the volume of groundwater is approximately 50 times the annual flow of surface water. Though groundwater currently supplies only 25 percent of the fresh water used for all purposes in the United States, its use is increasing more rapidly than the use of surface water. Groundwater is used primarily for irrigation and as a source of drinking water.

Surface water also serves as a significant source of drinking water, but it has many other uses as well. Recreational benefits such as swimming, fishing, and boating are important determinants of surface water policy in areas where the water is not used for drinking.

Sources of Contamination

Although some contamination has been accidental—the product of unintended and unexpected waste migration to water supplies—a portion of contamination has been deliberate. Watercourses were simply a convenient place to dump municipal or private sewage and industrial wastes. Along the shoreline of many lakes or rivers, pipes dumping human or industrial wastes directly into the water were a common occurrence before laws limiting this activity were enacted and enforced.

Contamination of groundwater occurs when polluting substances leach into a water-saturated region. Many potential contaminants are removed by filtration and adsorption as the water moves slowly through the layers of rock and soil. Toxic organic chemicals are one major example of a type of pollutant that may not be filtered out during migration. Once these substances enter groundwater, very little, if any, further cleansing takes place. Moreover, because the rate of replenishment for many groundwater sources is small relative to the stock, very little mixing and dilution of the contaminants occurs.

For lake and river pollution policy purposes it is useful to distinguish between two sources of contamination—point and nonpoint sources—even though the distinction is not always crystal clear. *Point sources of water pollution* generally discharge into surface waters at a specific location through a pipe, an outfall, or a ditch, whereas nonpoint sources usually affect the water in a more indirect and diffuse way. Examples include agricultural and urban runoff. From the policy point of view, *nonpoint sources of water pollution* are more difficult to control because both the source and timing are hard to predict and as such, they have received little legislative attention until recently. As a result of the gains made in controlling point sources, however, nonpoint sources now compose over half of the waste load borne by the nation's waters.

Rivers and Lakes. The primary point sources are industries and municipalities. The most important nonpoint sources of pollution for rivers and lakes are agricultural activity, urban storm-water runoff, silviculture, and individual disposal systems. Contamination from agriculture has been attributed to eroded topsoil, pesticides, and fertilizer. Urban storm-water runoff contains a number of pollutants, including, typically, high quantities of lead. Forestry, if not carefully done, can contribute to soil erosion and, by removing shade cover, could have a large impact on the temperature of normally shaded streams. In the developing countries, more than 95 percent of urban sewage is discharged into surface waters without treatment.

The contamination of groundwater supplies usually results from the migration of harmful substances from sites where high concentrations of chemicals can be found. These include industrial waste storage sites, landfills, and farms.

Ocean Pollution. The two primary sources of ocean pollution that we will discuss are oil spills and ocean dumping. Oil spills have become less frequent and have decreased in magnitude since 1970 (see Figure 18.1), but spills are still not uncommon, as shown in Table 18.1, which lists the largest ones. Various unwanted by-products of modern life have also been dumped in ocean waters based upon the mistaken belief that the vastness of the oceans allowed them to absorb large quantities of waste without suffering noticeable damage. Dumped materials have included sewage and sewage sludge, unwanted chemicals, trace metals, and even radioactive materials.

FIGURE 18.1   The Decreasing Frequency of Oil Spills

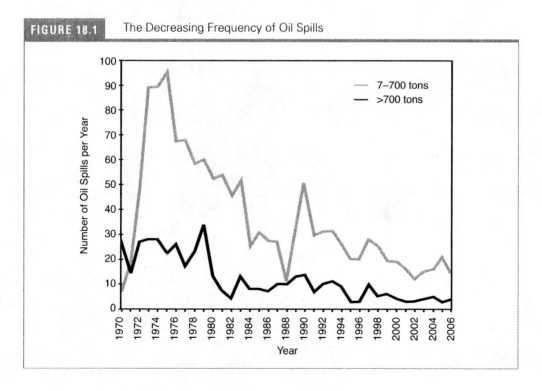

TABLE 18.1   Notable Oil Spills

Rank	Spill Size (metric tons)	Ship Name	Year	Location
1	287,000	Atlantic Empress	1979	Off Tobago, West Indies
2	260,000	ABT Summer	1991	700 nautical miles off Angola
3	252,000	Castillo de Bellver	1983	Off Saldanha Bay, South Africa
4	223,000	Amoco Cadiz	1978	Off Brittany, France
5	144,000	Haven	1991	Genoa, Italy
6	132,000	Odyssey	1988	700 nautical miles off Nova Scotia, Canada
7	119,000	Torrey Canyon	1967	Scilly Isles, UK
8	115,000	Sea Star	1972	Gulf of Oman
9	100,000	Irenes Serenade	1980	Navarino Bay, Greece
10	100,000	Urquiola	1976	La Coruna, Spain
11	95,000	Hawaiian Patriot	1977	300 nautical miles off Honolulu
12	95,000	Independenta	1979	Bosphorus, Turkey
13	88,000	Jakob Maersk	1975	Oporto, Portugal
14	85,000	Braer	1993	Shetland Islands, UK
15	80,000	Khark 5	1989	120 nautical miles off Atlantic coast of Morocco
16	74,000	Aegean Sea	1992	La Coruna, Spain
17	72,000	Sea Empress	1996	Milford Haven, UK
18	72,000	Katina P	1992	Off Maputo, Mozambique
19	70,000	Nova	1985	Off Kharg Island, Gulf of Iran
20	63,000	Prestige	2002	Off Galicia, Spain
35	37,000	Exxon Valdez	1989	Prince William Sound, Alaska, U.S.

Source: International Tanker Owners Pollution Federation Limited Web site: http://www.itopf.com/information-services/data-and-statistics/statistics/ (accessed 3/23/09).

Types of Pollutants

For our purposes, the large number of water pollutants can be usefully classified by means of the taxonomy we developed earlier and review below.

Fund Pollutants. *Fund pollutants* are those for which the environment has some assimilative capacity. If the absorptive capacity is high enough relative to the rate of injection, such pollutants may not accumulate at all. One type of fund water pollutants is called *degradable* because it degrades, or breaks into its component parts, within the water. Degradable wastes are normally organic residuals that are attacked and broken down by bacteria in the stream.

The process by which organic wastes are broken down into component parts consumes oxygen. The amount of oxygen consumed depends upon the magnitude of the waste load. All of the higher life forms in watercourses are aerobic; that is, they require oxygen for survival. As a stream's oxygen level falls, fish mortality increases, with the less tolerant fish becoming the first to succumb. The oxygen level can become low enough that even the aerobic bacteria die. When this happens, the stream becomes anaerobic, and the ecology changes drastically. This is an extremely unpleasant circumstance because the stream takes on a dark hue and the stream water stinks!

To control these waste loads, two different types of monitoring are needed: (1) monitoring the ambient conditions in the watercourse and (2) monitoring the magnitude of emissions. The measure commonly used to keep track of ambient conditions for these conventional fund pollutants is *dissolved oxygen (DO)*. The amount of dissolved oxygen in a body of water is a function of ambient conditions, such as temperature, stream flow, and the waste load.[1] The measure of the oxygen demand placed on a stream by any particular volume of effluent is called the *biochemical oxygen demand (BOD)*.

Using modeling techniques, emissions (measured as BOD) at a certain point can be translated into DO measures at various receptor locations along a stream. This step is necessary in order to tailor the degree of control to the amount of damage caused by the emissions.

If we were to develop a profile of DO readings in a stream where organic effluent is being injected, that profile would typically exhibit one or more minimum points called *oxygen sags*. These oxygen sags represent locations along the stream where the DO content is lower than at other points. An ambient permit or ambient charge system would be designed to reach a desired DO level at those sag points, whereas an emission permit or emission charge system would simply try to hit a particular BOD reduction target. The former would take the location of the emitter into account; the latter would not. Later in this chapter we will examine studies that model these systems on particular watercourses.

A second type of fund pollutant, *thermal pollution*, is caused by the injection of heat into a watercourse. Typically, thermal pollution is caused when an industrial plant or electric utility uses surface water as a coolant, returning the heated water to the watercourse. This heat is dissipated in the receiving waters by evaporation. By raising the temperature of the water near the outfall, thermal pollution lowers the DO content and can result in dramatic ecological changes in that area.

Yet another example is provided by a class of pollutants, such as nitrogen and phosphorus, which are plant nutrients. These pollutants stimulate the growth of aquatic plant life, such as algae and water weeds. In excess, these plants can produce odor, taste, and aesthetic problems. A lake with an excessive supply of nutrients is called *eutrophic*.

The various types of fund pollutants could be ordered on a spectrum. On one end of the spectrum would be pollutants for which the environment has a very large absorptive capacity, on the other end pollutants for which the absorptive capacity is virtually nil. The limiting case—those for which the environment has no absorptive capacity—are stock pollutants.

Near the end of that spectrum is a class of inorganic synthetic chemicals called *persistent pollutants*. These substances are so-named because their complex molecular structures are not effectively broken down in the stream. Some degradation takes place, but so slowly that these pollutants can travel long distances in water in a virtually unchanged form.

These persistent pollutants accumulate, not only in the watercourses, but in the food chain as well. The concentration levels in the tissues of living organisms rise with the order of the species. Concentrations in lower life forms such as plankton may be relatively small, but, because small fish eat a lot of plankton and do not excrete the inorganic synthetic chemicals, the concentrations

---

[1]The danger of anaerobic conditions is highest in the late summer and early fall, when temperatures are high and the stream flow is low.

in small fish would be higher. The magnification continues as large fish consume small fish; concentration levels in the larger fish would be even higher.

Because they accumulate in the food chain, persistent pollutants present an interesting monitoring challenge. The traditional approach involves measurements of pollutant concentration in the water, but that is not the only variable of interest. The damage is related not only to its concentration in the water, but also in its concentration in the food chain as well. Although monitoring the environmental effects of these pollutants may be more compelling than monitoring other pollutants, it is also more difficult.

A final type of fund pollutant, comprising infectious organisms such as bacteria and viruses, is carried into surface and groundwater by domestic and animal wastes and by wastes from such industries as tanning and meat packing. These live organisms may thrive and multiply in water, or their population may decline over time, depending upon how hospitable or hostile the watercourse is for continued growth.

Accumulating Pollutants. The most troublesome cases result when pollutants accumulate in the environment. No natural process removes or transforms stock pollutants; the watercourse cannot cleanse itself of them.

Inorganic chemicals and minerals comprise the main examples of stock pollutants. Perhaps the most notorious members of this group are the heavy metals, such as lead, cadmium, and mercury. Extreme examples of poisoning by these metals have occurred in Japan. One ocean-dumping case was responsible for *Minamata disease,* named for the location where it occurred. Some 52 people died and 150 others suffered serious brain and nerve damage. Scientists puzzled for years over the source of the ailments, until it was traced to an organic form of mercury that had accumulated in the tissues of fish eaten three times a day by local residents.

In the United States, mercury contamination of fish has led to consumption advisories for many fresh water and migratory fish. Women of childbearing age and children are cautioned against eating large amounts of certain species. Debate 18.1 examines the effects of fish consumption advisories on consumer behavior.

DEBATE 18.1

Toxics in Fish Tissue: Do Fish Consumption Advisories Change Behavior?

In January 2001 the Food and Drug Administration (FDA) released an advisory on methyl mercury in fish. An updated advisory was issued in 2004 and again in 2006. Part of that advisory reads as follows:

> However, nearly all fish and shellfish contain traces of mercury. For most people, the risk from mercury by eating fish and shellfish is not a health concern. Yet, some fish and shellfish contain higher levels of mercury that may harm an unborn baby or young child's developing nervous system. The risks from mercury in fish and shellfish depend on the amount of fish and shellfish eaten and the levels of mercury in the fish and shellfish. Therefore, the Food and Drug Administration (FDA) and the Environmental Protec-

tion Agency (EPA) are advising women who may become pregnant, pregnant women, nursing mothers, and young children to avoid some types of fish and eat fish and shellfish that are lower in mercury.[2]

The FDA targeted women planning on becoming pregnant within six months, pregnant women, and nursing women to receive information about the new advisory on methyl mercury.

Since mercury persists and bioaccumulates, the concentrations of mercury rise as you move up the food chain.

Consumers of fish ingest the mercury, which has been linked to neurological disorders in infants and children.

Using the Bureau of Labor Statistics' Consumer Expenditure Survey, Shimshack, Ward, and Beatty (2007) examine consumer responses to this advisory. In particular, they look at the effects of the advisory on the consumption of canned fish during 1999–2002, a time period that includes two years before and two years after the advisory. They examine whether the groups targeted reduced their consumption of canned fish and what determined the responses.

Comparing target households (those with young children) to nontarget households, they find that targeted consumers significantly reduced their canned fish consumption as a result of the warning. College educated consumers responded quite strongly. Additionally, they found that newspaper and magazine readership were significant in influencing the post advisory reduction in fish consumption, but health consciousness was not. Interestingly, they also found evidence of spillover effects; nontargeted consumers also reduced their consumption of canned fish.

Access to information is clearly important to the success of a health advisory. At-risk consumers who are less educated and nonreaders did not significantly reduce consumption. The authors suggest that this particular group is also less likely to be able to withstand negative health shocks.

What is the best way to get information to different population groups? Unequal access to information creates unevenly distributed health risks and might be labeled an environmental justice issue.

Sources: Jay P. Shimshack, Michael B. Ward, and Timothy K. M. Beatty, "Mercury Advisories: Information, Education and Fish Consumption," *Journal of Environmental Economics and Management*, 53(2), 2007, 158–179; www.fda.gov.

In another case in Japan, involving the Itai Itai (literally, "ouch-ouch") disease, scientists traced the source of a previously undiagnosed, extremely painful bone disease to the ingestion of cadmium. Nearby mines were the source of the cadmium, which apparently was ingested by eating contaminated rice and soybeans.

Most recently, medicinal waste has been found in watercourses and in fish tissue. In 2002 the USGS tested 139 rivers in 30 states and found that 80 percent of the sampled streams resulted in evidence of residuals from drugs such as birth control pills and antidepressants. Residuals

---

[2]http://www.cfsan.fda.gov/~dms/admehg3.html.

from soaps and perfumes were also found. While the damage that will ultimately be caused by these substances is not yet clear, it is certainly a new twist in water pollution control policy.

As is typical with persistent pollutants, some of the stock pollutants are difficult to monitor. Those accumulated in the food chains give rise to the same problem as is presented by persistent pollutants. Ambient sampling must be supplemented by sampling tissues from members of the food chain. To further complicate matters, the heavy metals may sink rapidly to the bottom of the water body, remaining in the sediment. Although they could be detected in sediment samples, merely drawing samples from the water itself would allow these pollutants to escape detection.

Water Pollution Control Policy

Traditional Water Pollution Control Policy

Water pollution control policies vary around the world. In this section we begin with a somewhat detailed discussion of U.S. policy that provides a rather rich example of a typical legal approach to regulation. This is followed by a discussion of the European approach, which depends more heavily on economic incentives.

U.S. policy for water pollution control predates federal air pollution control. We might suppose that the policy for water pollution control would, therefore, be superior, because authorities have had more time to profit from earlier mistakes. Unfortunately, that is not the case.

Early Legislation

The first federal legislation dealing with discharge into the nation's waterways occurred when Congress passed the 1899 Refuse Act. Designed primarily to protect navigation, this Act focused on preventing any discharge that would interfere with using rivers as transport links. All discharges into a river were prohibited unless approved by a permit from the Chief of the U.S. Engineers. Most permits were issued to contractors dredging the rivers, and they dealt mainly with the disposal of the removed material. This Act was virtually unenforced for other pollutants until 1970, when the permit program was "rediscovered" and used briefly (with little success) as the basis for federal enforcement actions.

The Water Pollution Control Act of 1948 represented the first attempt by the federal government to exercise some direct influence over what previously had been a state and local function. A hesitant move, because it reaffirmed that the primary responsibility for water pollution control rested with the states, it did initiate the authority of the federal government to conduct investigations, research, and surveys.

Early hints of the current approach are found in the Amendments to the Water Pollution Control Act, which was passed in 1956. Two provisions of this Act were especially important: (1) federal financial support for the construction of waste treatment plants and (2) direct federal regulation of waste discharges via a mechanism known as the *enforcement conference*.

The first of these provisions envisioned a control strategy based on subsidizing the construction of a particular control activity—waste treatment plants. Municipalities could receive federal grants to cover up to 55 percent of the construction of municipal sewage treatment plants. This approach not only lowered the cost to the local government of constructing these facilities, but also it lowered the cost to users. Because the federal government contribution was a grant, rather than a loan, the fees charged to users did not reflect the federally subsidized construction portion of the cost. The user fees were set at a lower rate, one that was only high enough to cover the unsubsidized portion of the construction cost as well as the operating and maintenance costs.

The 1956 amendments envisioned a relatively narrow federal role in the regulation of discharges. Initially, only polluters contributing to interstate pollution were included, but subsequent laws have broadened the coverage. By 1961 discharges into all navigable water were covered.

The mechanism created by the Amendments of 1956 to enforce the regulation of discharges was the enforcement conference. Under this approach, the designated federal control authority could call for a conference to deal with any interstate water pollution problem or could be requested to do so by the governor of an affected state. Because this authority was discretionary (not mandatory) and the control authority had very few means of enforcing any decisions reached, the conferences did not achieve the intended results.

The Water Quality Act of 1965 attempted to improve the process by establishing ambient water quality standards for interstate watercourses and by requiring states to file implementation plans. This sounds like the approach currently being used in air pollution control, but there are important differences. The plans forthcoming from states in response to the 1965 Act were vague and did not attempt to link specific effluent standards on discharge to the ambient standards. They generally took the easy way out and called for secondary treatment, which removes 80 to 90 percent of BOD and 85 percent of suspended solids. The fact that these standards bore no particular relationship to ambient quality made them difficult to enforce in the courts, because the legal authority for them was based on this relationship.

Subsequent Legislation

Point Sources. As discussed in the preceding chapters, an air of frustration regarding pollution control pervaded Washington in the 1970s. In terms of water pollution legislation, as with air pollution legislation, this frustration led to the enactment of a very tough Clean Water Act. The tone of the Act is established immediately in the preamble, which calls for the achievement of two goals: (1) "that the discharge of pollutants into the navigable waters be eliminated by 1985" and (2) "that wherever attainable, an interim goal of water quality which provides for the protection and propagation of fish, shellfish, and wildlife and provides for recreation in and on the water be achieved by June 1, 1983." The stringency of these goals represented a major departure from past policy.

This Act also introduced new procedures for implementing the law. Permits were required of all dischargers (replacing the 1899 Refuse Act, which, because of its navigation focus, was difficult to enforce). The permits would be granted only when the dischargers met certain technology-based *effluent standards*. The ambient standards were completely bypassed, as these effluent standards were uniformly imposed and so could not depend upon local water conditions.[3]

According to the 1972 amendments, the effluent standards were to be implemented in two stages. By 1977 industrial dischargers, as a condition of their permits, were required to meet effluent limitations based on the "best practicable control technology currently available" (BPT). In setting these national standards, the EPA was required to consider the total costs of these technologies and their relation to the benefits received, but not to consider the conditions of the

---

[3]Actually the ambient standards were not completely bypassed. If the uniform controls were not sufficient to meet the desired standard, the effluent limitation would have to be tightened accordingly.

individual source or the particular waters into which it was discharged. In addition, all publicly owned treatment plants were to have achieved secondary treatment by 1977. By 1983 industrial discharges were required to meet effluent limitations based on the presumably more stringent "best available technology economically achievable" (BAT) and publicly owned treatment plants were required to meet effluent limitations that depended upon the "best practicable waste treatment technology."

The program of subsidizing municipal water treatment plants, begun in 1956, was continued in a slightly modified form by the 1972 Act. Whereas the 1965 Act allowed the federal government to subsidize up to 55 percent of the cost of construction of waste treatment plants, the 1972 Act raised the ceiling to 75 percent. The 1972 Act also increased the funds available for this program. In 1981 the federal share was reduced to 55 percent.

The 1977 amendments continued this regulatory approach, but with some major modifications. This legislation drew a more careful distinction between the conventional and toxic pollutants, with more stringent requirements placed on the latter, and it extended virtually all of the deadlines in the 1972 Act.

For conventional pollutants a new treatment standard was created to replace the BAT standards. The effluent limitations for these pollutants were to be based on the "best conventional technology" and the deadline for these standards was set at July 1, 1984. In setting these standards, the EPA was required to consider whether the costs of adding the pollution control equipment were reasonable when compared with the improvement in water quality. For unconventional pollutants and toxics (i.e., any pollutant not specifically included on the list of conventional pollutants), the BAT requirement was retained, but the deadline was shifted to 1984.

Other deadlines were also extended. The year by which municipalities had to meet the secondary treatment deadline was moved from 1977 to 1983. Industrial compliance with the BPT standards was delayed until 1983, or whenever the contemplated system had the potential for application throughout the industry.

The final modification made by the 1977 amendments involved the introduction of pretreatment standards for waste being sent to a publicly owned treatment system. These standards were designed to prevent the discharges that could inhibit the treatment process and to prevent the introduction of toxic pollutants that would not be removed by the waste treatment facility. Existing facilities were required to meet the standards three years after their date of publication, and facilities constructed later would be required to meet the pretreatment regulations upon commencement of operations.

Nonpoint Sources. In contrast to the control of point sources, the EPA was given no specific authority to regulate nonpoint sources. This type of pollution was seen by Congress as a state responsibility.

Section 208 of the Act authorized federal grants for state-initiated planning that would provide implementable plans for areawide waste treatment management. Section 208 further specified that this area-wide plan must identify significant nonpoint sources of pollution, as well as procedures and methods for controlling them. The reauthorization of the Clean Water Act, passed over President Reagan's veto during February 1987, authorized an additional $400 million for a new program to help states control runoff, but it still left the chief responsibility for controlling nonpoint sources to the states.

One federal role for controlling nonpoint sources has been the Conservation Reserve Program. Designed to remove some 40 to 45 million acres of highly erodible land from cultivation, this Act provides subsidies to farmers for planting grass or trees. The subsidies are designed to produce a nationwide reduction of total erosion and a reduction in nitrogen, phosphorus, and total suspended solid loadings.

Another recent role for municipalities has been the separation of storm water and sewer drains so that sewage treatment plants do not overflow during rain storms. Federal subsidies have also assisted with these projects.

The TMDL Program

In 1999, recognizing the problems with both the technology-based national effluent standards and the growing importance of nonpoint pollution control, the USEPA proposed new rules designed to breathe fresh life into the previously unenforced *Total Maximum Daily Load (TMDL) program* of the Clean Water Act. A TMDL is a calculation of the maximum amount of a pollutant that a water body can receive and still meet water quality standards as well as an allocation of that amount to the pollutant's sources. The calculation must include a margin of safety to ensure that the water body can be used for its designated purpose. The calculation must also account for seasonal variation in water quality.

The TMDL program moves water pollution control toward the ambient standard approach long used to control air pollution. Under this program water quality standards are promulgated by states, territories, and/or tribes. The promulgated standards are tailored to the designated uses for each water body (such as drinking water supply or recreation [swimming and/or fishing]). The states must then undertake strategies for achieving the standards, including bringing nonpoint source pollutants under control.

Since the late 1980s efforts focused on nonpoint sources have increased dramatically. Voluntary programs and cost-sharing programs with landowners have been the most common tools. Regulatory approaches for storm sewers are also used. Section 319 of the Clean Water Act specifies guidelines for state implementation of nonpoint source management plans. In 2003, the EPA devoted a large portion of its Section 319 funds ($100 million) to address areas in which nonpoint source pollution has significantly impaired water quality.[4]

The Safe Drinking Water Act

The 1972 policy focused on achieving water quality sufficiently high for fishing and swimming. Because that quality is not high enough for drinking water, the Safe Drinking Water Act of 1974 issued more stringent standards for community water systems. The primary drinking water regulations set maximum allowable concentration levels for bacteria, turbidity (muddiness), and chemical or radiological contaminants. National secondary drinking water regulations were also established to protect "public welfare" from odor and aesthetic problems that might cause a substantial number of people to stop using the affected water system. The secondary standards are advisory for the states; they cannot be enforced by the EPA.

---

[4]U.S. Federal Register Vol. 68, No. 205 (October 2003).

The 1986 amendments required the EPA to (1) issue primary standards within three years for 83 contaminants and by 1991 for at least 25 more, (2) set standards based on the BAT, and (3) monitor public water systems for both regulated and unregulated chemical contaminants. Approximately 60,000 public water systems are subject to these regulations. Civil and criminal penalties for any violations of the standards were also increased by the amendments.

More recent drinking water rules and standards cover MTBE, arsenic, radon, lead, microbials, and disinfection byproducts. In 2007, the EPA issued a final ruling on lead and copper in drinking water—two contaminants that enter through plumbing materials. Many older homes have faucets or fittings of brass (which contains some lead), lead pipes, or copper pipes with solder.

Ocean Pollution

Oil Spills. The Clean Water Act prohibits discharges of "harmful quantities" of oil into navigable waters. Because the EPA regulations define harmful to include all discharges that "violate applicable water quality standards or cause a film or sheen upon the surface of the water," virtually all discharges are prohibited.

Industry responsibilities include complying with Coast Guard regulations (which deal with contingency planning in case of a spill and various accident avoidance requirements) and assuming the financial liability for any accident. If a spill does occur, it must be immediately reported to the Coast Guard or the EPA. Failure to report a spill can result in a fine of up to $10,000, imprisonment for not more than one year, or both.

In addition to giving notice, the discharger must either contain the spill or pay the cost of cleanup by a responsible government agency. The discharger's liability for the government's actual removal cost is limited to $50 million, unless willful negligence or willful misconduct can be proved. Successful proof of willful negligence or willful misconduct eliminates the liability limit. In addition to cleanup costs, removal costs also include compensation for damages to the natural resources. (*Natural resource damages* are defined as "any costs or expenses incurred by the federal government or any state government in the restoration or replacement of natural resources damaged or destroyed as a result of a discharge of oil.")

Ocean Dumping. Except for oil spills, which are covered by the Clean Water Act, discharges to the ocean are covered by the Marine Protection Research and Sanctuaries Act of 1972. This Act governs all discharges of wastes to ocean waters within U.S. territorial limits and discharges of wastes in ocean waters by U.S. vessels or persons, no matter where the dumping occurs. With only a few exceptions, no ocean dumping of industrial wastes or sewer sludge is now permitted. Radiological, chemical, and biological warfare agents and high-level radioactive wastes are specifically prohibited by the statute. Under the amended statute, the only ocean-dumping activities permitted are the disposal of dredged soil, fish wastes, human remains, and scuttled vessels. This dumping is subject to specific regulations and is approved on a case-by-case basis.

Private Enforcement

The degree to which environmental quality is improved by public policy depends not only on the types of policies, but also on how well those policies are enforced. Policies that seem to offer promise may prove unsuitable if enforcement is difficult or lax.

The enforcement of the environmental statutes has long been the responsibility of state and federal environmental agencies. Enforcement at the state and federal level occurs through administrative proceedings or through civil and criminal judicial action. Because limited staff and resources do not enable these government agencies to fully enforce all of the environmental statutes, these methods alone do not provide the necessary level of enforcement.

During the early 1970s a pervasive recognition that the federal government had neither the time nor resources to provide sufficient enforcement led Congress to create a private alternative—*citizen suits*. Though citizen suits are now authorized by a number of different environmental statutes, the program has been particularly successful in enforcing the Clean Water Act.

Empowered as private attorneys general, citizens are authorized to exercise oversight over government actions and to initiate civil proceedings against any private or public polluter violating the terms of its effluent standard. Environmental groups such as the Natural Resources Defense Council and the Sierra Club have become active participants in the process. Citizens may sue for an injunction (a court order requiring the illegal discharge to cease); they are also given the power to "apply any appropriate civil penalties." The amount of penalty can vary between $10,000 and $25,000 per day, per violation.

Efficiency and Cost-Effectiveness

Ambient Standards and the Zero Discharge Goal

The 1956 amendments to the Water Pollution Control Act defined ambient standards as a means of quantifying the objective being sought. A system of ambient standards allows the control authority to tailor the quality of a particular body of water to its use. Water used for drinking would be subject to the highest standards, for swimming, the next highest, and so on. Once the ambient standards are defined, the control responsibility can be allocated among sources. Greater efforts to control pollution would be expended where the gap between desired and actual water quality was the largest.

Unfortunately, the early experience with ambient standards for water was not reassuring. Rather than strengthening the legal basis for the effluent standards while retaining their connection to the ambient standards, Congress chose to downgrade the importance of ambient standards by specifying a zero discharge goal. Additionally, the effluent standards were given their own legal status apart from any connection with ambient standards. The wrong inference was drawn from the early lack of legislative success. In his own inimitable style, Mark Twain (1897) put the essential point rather well:

> We should be careful to get out of an experience only the wisdom that is in it—and stop there; lest we be like the cat that sits down on a hot stove lid. She will never sit down on a hot stove lid again—and that is well; but also she will never sit down on a cold one anymore.

The most fundamental problem with the current approach is that it rests on the faulty assumption that the tougher the law, the more that is accomplished. The zero discharge goal provides one example of a case in which passing a tough standard, in the hopes of actually achieving a weaker one, can backfire. In the late 1960s the French experimented with a law that required zero discharge and imposed severe penalties for violations. The result was that the law was never enforced because it was universally viewed as unreasonable. Less control was accomplished under this law than would have been accomplished with a less stringent law that could have been enforced.

Is the U.S. case comparable? It appears to be. In 1972 the EPA published an estimate of the costs of meeting a zero discharge goal, assuming that it is feasible. They concluded that over the decade from 1971 to 1981, removing 85 to 90 percent of the pollutants from all industrial and municipal effluents would cost $62 billion. Removing all of the pollutants would cost $317 billion, more than five times as much, and this figure probably understates the true cost (Kneese and Schultze, 1975).

Is this cost justified? Probably not for *all* pollutants, but for some it may be. Unfortunately, the zero discharge goal makes no distinction among pollutant types. For some fund pollutants it seems extreme. Perhaps the legislators realized this, because when the legislation was drafted, no specific timetables or procedures were established to ensure that the zero discharge goal would be met by 1985 or, for that matter, anytime.

National Effluent Standards

The first prong in the two-pronged congressional attack on water pollution was the national effluent standards (the other being subsidies for the construction of publicly owned waste treatment facilities). Deciding on the appropriate levels for these standards for each of the estimated 60,000 sources is not a trivial task. It is not surprising that difficulties arose.

Enforcement Problems. Soon after passage of the 1972 amendments, the EPA geared up to assume its awesome responsibility. Relying on a battery of consultants, it began to study the technologies of pollution control available to each industry in order to establish reasonable effluent limits. In establishing the guidelines, the EPA is required to take into account

> the age of the equipment and facilities involved, the process employed, the engineering aspects of the application of various types of control techniques, process changes, nonwater quality environmental impact (including energy requirements) and such factors as the Administrator deems appropriate.

It is not clear whether this provision means that individual standards should be specified for each source, or general standards for broad categories of sources. Cost-effectiveness would require the former, but in a system relying on effluent standards (however, not one relying on emission charges or permits), the transaction costs associated with that approach would be prohibitively high and the delay unacceptably long. Therefore, the EPA chose the only feasible interpretation available and established general standards for broad categories of sources. Although the standards could differ among categories, they were uniformly applied to the large number of sources within each category.

The EPA inevitably fell behind the congressional deadlines. In fact, not one effluent standard was published within the one-year deadline. As the standards were published, they were immediately challenged in the courts. By 1977 some 250 cases challenging the published standards were already pending. Some of the challenges were successful, requiring the EPA to revise the standards. All of this took time.

By 1977 the EPA was having so much trouble defining the BPT standards that it became evident that the deadlines for the BAT standards were completely unreasonable. Furthermore, for conventional pollutants, not only the deadlines but also the standards themselves were irrational. Many bodies of water would have met the ambient standards without the BAT standard, whereas for others the effluent standards were not sufficient, particularly in areas with large nonpoint pollution problems. Additionally, in some cases the technologies required by BPT would not be compatible (or even necessary) once the BAT standards were in effect. The situation was in a shambles.

The 1977 amendments changed both the timing of the BAT standards (delaying the deadlines) and their focus (toward toxic pollutants and away from conventional pollutants). As a result of these amendments, the EPA was required to develop industry effluent standards based on the BAT guidelines for control of 65 classes of toxic priority pollutants. In a 1979 survey, the EPA discovered that all primary industries regularly discharge one or more of these toxic pollutants. As of 1980 the EPA had proposed BAT effluent limitations for control of toxic priority pollutants for nine primary industries.

The 1977 amendments certainly improved the situation. Because toxics represent a more serious problem, it makes sense to set stricter standards for those pollutants. Extension of the deadlines was absolutely necessary; there was no alternative. However, these amendments have not resulted in a cost-effective strategy. In particular, they tend to retard technological progress and to assign the responsibility for control in an unnecessarily expensive manner.

Allocating Control Responsibility. Because the effluent standards established by the EPA are based upon specific technologies, these technologies are known to the industries. Therefore, in spite of the fact that the industry can choose any technology that keeps emissions under the limitation stated in the standard, in practice, industries tend to choose the specific equipment cited by the EPA when it established the standard. This, they reason, minimizes their risk. If anything goes wrong and they are hauled into court, they can simply argue they did precisely what the EPA had in mind when it set the standard.

The problem with this reaction is that it focuses too narrowly on a particular technology rather than on the real objective, emission reduction. The focus should be less on the purchase of a specific technology and more on doing what is necessary to hold emissions down, such as maintenance, process changes, and so on. In a field undergoing rapid technological change, tying all control efforts to a particular technology (which may become obsolete well before the standards are revised) is a poor strategy. Unfortunately, and to the detriment of securing clean water, technological stagnation has become a routine side effect of the current policy.

In allocating the control responsibility among various sources, the EPA was constrained by the inherent difficulty of making unique determinations for each source and by limitations of the Act itself, such as the need to apply relatively uniform standards. We know that uniform effluent standards are not cost effective, but it remains an open question whether or not the resulting increases in cost are sufficiently large to recommend an alternative approach, such as effluent charges or permits. The fact that the cost increases are large in the control of stationary-source air pollution does not automatically imply that they are large for water pollution control as well.

A number of empirical studies have investigated how closely the national effluent standards approximate the least-cost allocation. These studies support the contention that the EPA standards are not cost effective, although the degree of cost-ineffectiveness is typically smaller than that associated with the standards used to control air pollution.

Perhaps the most famous study examining the cost-effectiveness of uniform standards was conducted on the Delaware Estuary.[5] This river basin, though small by the standards of the Mis-

---

[5]This study is described in some detail in Kneese and Bower (1968) and Kneese (1977).

sissippi or other major basins, drains an area serving a population in excess of 6 million people. It is a highly industrial, densely populated area.

In the study a simulation model was constructed to capture the effect on ambient DO content of a variety of pollutants discharged by a large number of polluters into the river at numerous locations. Additionally, this model was capable of simulating the cost consequences of various methods used to allocate the responsibility for controlling effluent to meet DO standards.

The traditional approach was compared with the least-cost (LC) approach. Under the *uniform treatment (UT) strategy*, all discharges were faced with an effluent standard requiring them to remove a given percentage of their waste before discharging the remainder into the river. This method mirrors, in a crude way, the current EPA strategy. The LC strategy simply allocated the responsibility cost effectively.

For control of water pollution, this evidence suggests that the UT strategy does increase the cost substantially. For either DO objective, the costs are roughly three times higher.

Despite this evidence, the regulatory reform movement that played such an important role in air pollution control has been much slower to emerge for water pollution control. An early attempt at trading was implemented for the Fox River in Wisconsin, but only one trade was made in the first 10 years after implementation.

In an early study focusing on the steel, paper, and petroleum-refining industries in the 11-county Delaware Estuary Region, Russell (1981) estimated the change in permit use for three water pollutants (BOD, total suspended solids, and ammonia) that would have resulted if a marketable-permit system were in place over the 1940–1978 period. The calculations assume that the plants existing in 1940 would have been allocated permits in order to legitimize their emissions at that time, that new sources would have had to purchase permits, and that plant shutdowns or contractions would free up permits for others to purchase.

This study found that, for almost every decade and pollutant, a substantial number of permits would have been made available by plant closings, capacity contractions, product-mix changes, and the availability of new technologies. In the absence of a marketable-permit program, a control authority would not only have to keep abreast of all technological developments so that emission standards could be adjusted accordingly, but it would also have to assure an overall balance between effluent increases and decreases so as to preserve water quality. This tough assignment is handled completely by the market in a marketable-permit system, thereby facilitating the evolution of the economy by responding flexibly and predictably to change. Marketable permits encourage, as well as facilitate, this evolution.

More recently, *watershed-based trading programs* are gaining attention. In 1996 the EPA issued a "Draft Framework for Watershed Based Trading" and began exploring trading programs for the Tar-Pamlico River in North Carolina, Long Island Sound, Chesapeake Bay, and the Snake and Lower Boise Rivers in Idaho. Dozens of small trading programs are now in existence. Trading for water pollution control typically involves point source polluters meeting water quality standards by purchasing reductions from other sources (point or nonpoint sources) that have lower marginal costs of abatement.

Most of the markets currently in place focus on either nitrogen or phosphorous trading and are too new to evaluate, but at least 23 U.S. water trading programs have carried out at least one trade (see Table 18.2). Ex-ante studies, however, suggest that the economic benefits can be large as illustrated in Example 18.1. Tradable permit cost savings were explored for treating hypoxic conditions in Long Island Sound. Allowing firms the flexibility to exploit economies of scale in

TABLE 18.2   Summary of NPDES Trading Programs That Have Traded at Least Once
as of June 2007

Point-point Trades	Pollutant(s) Traded	Point-nonpoint Trades	Pollutant(s) Traded
Long Island Sound, CT	Total Nitrogen	Wayland Center, MA	Total Phosphorus
Bear Creek, CO	Total Phosphorus	Croton Watershed, NY	Total Phosphorus
Neuse River, NC	Total Nitrogen	Pinnacle, DE	Total Nitrogen, Total Phosphorus
Charlotte-Mecklenburg, NC	Total Phosphorus	Rahr Malting, MN	Offset Biological Oxygen Demand with Total Phosphorus
Cobb County, GA	Total Phosphorus	Southern MN Beetsugar Cooperative, MN	Total Phosphorus
City of Newnan, GA	Total Phosphorus	Red Cedar River, WI	Total Phosphorus
MN General Permit	Total Phosphorus	Great Miami River, OH	Total Nitrogen, Total Phosphorus
Las Vegas Wash, NV	Total Ammonia, Total Phosphorus	Taos Ski Valley, NM	Total Nitrogen
		Carlota Copper, AZ	Copper
		Clean Water Services, OR	Temperature
		Cherry Creek, CO	Total Phosphorus
		Chatfield Res, CO	Total Phosphorus
		Lake Dillon, CO	Total Phosphorus

Source: Kibler, Virginia, and Kavya Kasturi. "Status of Water Quality Trading Programs Today," 2007.
http://ecosystemmarketplace.com/pages/article.news.php?component_id=5335&component_version_id=7748&language
_id=12. www.epa.gov/owow/watershed/trading//tradingmap.htm, accessed March 2009.

pollution control technology can provide for large savings. This point-point trading program has resulted in cheaper *and* faster cleanup.

In 2007 the EPA issued a "Water Quality Trading Toolkit." The EPA supports market-based programs for certain pollutants if they can help meet Clean Water Act Goals (USEPA, 2004).[6]

Municipal Waste Treatment Subsidies

The second phase of the two-pronged water pollution control program involves *waste treatment plant subsidies*. This program has run into problems as well, ranging from deficiencies in the allocation of the subsidies to the incentives created by the program.

The Allocation of Funds.   Because the available funds were initially allocated on a first-come, first-served basis, it is not surprising that the funds were not spent in areas having the greatest impact. It was not uncommon, for example, for completed treatment plants to dump effluent that was significantly cleaner than the receiving water. Also, federal funds have traditionally been concentrated on smaller, largely suburban communities rather than the larger cities with the most serious pollution problems.

[6]For a map of current U.S. water quality trading programs, see www.epa.gov/owow/watershed/trading/tradingmap.html.

EXAMPLE
18.1

Effluent Trading and the Cost of Reducing Waste Treatment Discharges into Long Island Sound

Long Island Sound experiences severe hypoxia (low levels of dissolved oxygen) during the summer months. This eutrophication is caused primarily by excess nitrogen discharges from municipal sewage treatment plants. As discussed previously, most past policies for water pollution control focused on technology standards to control discharges. Economic theory suggests that lower costs can be achieved by providing flexibility to the plants via a permit trading program. In the late 1990s Connecticut, New York, and the USEPA began exploring this possibility for sewage treatment plants with discharges reaching Long Island Sound. The plan targeted trading to certain management zones. The plan was aimed at meeting the management goals of Phase III of the 1994 Management Plan to control hypoxia. The overall goal of this management plan was a 58.5 percent reduction in nitrogen over 15 years, beginning in 1999.

Bennett et al. (2000) estimate the costs associated with the proposed scheme whereby trading is restricted to the 11 management zones designated by the Long Island Sound Study. Then they estimate the cost savings of alternative programs that expand the zone of trading to (1) trading among sources and across zones, but within state boundaries and (2) trading across all sources. For each trading scenario, polluting sources are grouped into trading bubbles based on geographic location. Trading is allowed to take place within each bubble, but not among bubbles. The first scenario consists of 11 bubbles (the management zones). The second scenario has two bubbles, one for Connecticut and one for New York. The third scenario consists of one large bubble.

Bennett et al. find what economic theory would predict, that costs savings rise (and rise substantially) as the scope of trading expands (meaning fewer bubbles). Expanding trading across the two state bubbles could save up to 20 percent or $156 million dollars based on their estimates. The following table is reproduced from their results.

The Effects of Zone Size on the Magnitude of Control Costs

Number of Trading Bubbles	Present Value of Total Costs ($ mil)	Cost Savings Relative to 11 Bubbles ($ mil)	Percentage Savings
11	781.44	—	—
2	740.55	40.89	5.23
1	625.14	156.30	20.00

Not all discharges have the same impact on the problem. It turns out that discharges from zones in the eastern portion of Long Island Sound and the northern parts of Connecticut have fewer detrimental effects than those closer to New York City.

Despite differences in abatement cost, the proposed management plan recommends that each management zone be responsible for an equal percentage of nitrogen reduction.

While marginal abatement costs vary widely across management zones (suggesting that trades could reduce costs), the marginal contributions to damages also vary widely, thus ruling out a simple system of ton-for-ton effluent trades. Currently, in recognition of this complexity, trading is not being considered across the boundaries of the 11 management zones despite the apparent potential cost savings.

Between 2002 and 2004 the Long Island Sound program in Connecticut has reduced more total nitrogen via trading than was needed to meet the TMDL requirement.

Source: Bennett, Lynne Lewis, Steven G. Thorpe, and A. Joseph Guse, "Cost-Effective Control of Nitrogen Loadings in Long Island Sound," *Water Resources Research* Vol. 36, No. 12 (December 2000): 3711–3720; Kibler, Virginia, and Kavya Kasturi, "Status of Water Quality Trading Programs Today," Katoomba Group's Ecosystem Marketplace http://www.ecosystemmarketplace.com, 2007.

The 1977 amendments attempted to deal with this problem by requiring states to set priorities for funding treatment works while giving the EPA the right, after holding public hearings, not only to veto a state's priority list but also to request a revised list. This tendency to ensure that the funds are allocated to projects having the highest priority was reinforced with the passage of the Municipal Wastewater Treatment Construction Grant Amendments of 1981. Under this Act, states are required to establish project priorities that target funds to projects with the most significant water quality and public health consequences.

Operation and Maintenance. The current approach subsidizes the construction of treatment facilities but provides no incentive for operating them effectively. The existence of a municipal waste treatment plant does not, by itself, guarantee cleaner water. The EPA's annual inspection surveys of operating plants in 1976 and 1977 found only about half of the plants performing satisfactorily. More recent surveys have found that the general levels of waste treatment performance have remained substantially unchanged from previous years.

When sewage treatment plants chronically or critically malfunction, the EPA may take a city to court in order to force compliance with a direct order or a fine. Because of various constitutional legal barriers, it is very difficult to force a city to pay a fine to the federal treasury. Without an effective and credible sanction, the EPA is in a difficult position when dealing with municipalities. Therefore, the resolution of the treatment plant malfunction problem cannot yet be pronounced with any assurance.

Capital Costs. Because of the federal subsidies, local areas ended up paying only a fraction of the true cost of constructing these facilities. Because much of the money came from federal taxpayers, local communities had less incentive to hold construction costs down. One Congressional Budget Office study estimated that substantially increasing the local share could reduce capital costs by as much as 30 percent. Local areas are more careful with their own money.

Pretreatment Standards

To deal with hazardous wastes entering municipal waste treatment plants that cannot be treated or removed by those plants, the EPA has defined *pretreatment standards* regulating the quality of the wastewater flowing into the plants. These standards suffer the same deficiencies as other effluent standards; they are not cost effective (see Example 18.2). The control over wastewater flows

EXAMPLE

18.2

Cost-Effective Pretreatment Standards

The electroplating operations of the Rhode Island jewelry industry produce high concentrations of cyanide, copper, nickel, and zinc, which are routinely discharged into municipal sewer systems. Because the treatment plants are not designed to remove these hazardous substances, the EPA has defined pretreatment standards to prohibit excessive concentrations of these metals from entering the plants. These standards are financially burdensome, with some estimates suggesting that some 30 to 60 percent of the small firms could go out of business if the standards were imposed.

An economic analysis by Opaluch and Kashmanian (1985) of the alternative for meeting the EPA concentration objectives concludes that the EPA pretreatment standards achieve the objective at a cost almost 50 percent greater than the least-cost means of achieving the same concentration objectives. An emission permit system with a permit price of $40 per pound would, after trading, achieve the target at a cost of $12.5 million. Compared to the $19.3 million the EPA proposal would cost, this represents a considerable savings.

If the permits were auctioned off, the government would collect some $5 million from the sale. Although the financial burden of this auction system for allocating permits would be lower on the jewelry industry as a whole than complying with the EPA proposal, even considering this $5 million transfer, not every segment of the industry would be better off with this auction. In particular, the permit fees paid by large firms would be sufficiently high that they would bear more financial burden under the auction scheme than with the EPA proposal. If the permits were "grandfathered" (allocated free of charge) rather than auctioned off, however, all existing firms would be better off under the permit system than under the EPA proposal.

Source: Opaluch, J. James and Richard M. Kashmanian, "Assessing the Viability of Marketable Permit Systems: An Application in Hazardous Waste Management," *Land Economics* 61(August 1985) (3): 263–271.

into treatment plants provides one more example of an environmental policy area where economic-incentive approaches offer an opportunity to achieve equivalent results at a lower cost.

Nonpoint Pollution

Nonpoint source pollution has become, in many areas, a significant part of the total problem. In some ways, the government has tried to compensate for this uneven coverage by placing more intensive controls on point sources. Is this emphasis efficient?

It could conceivably be justified on two grounds. If the marginal damages caused by nonpoint sources are significantly smaller than those of point sources, then a lower level of control could well be justified. Since in many cases nonpoint source pollutants are not the same as point source pollutants, this is a logical possibility.

Or, if the costs of controlling nonpoint sources even to a small degree are very high, this could justify benign neglect as well. Are either of these conditions met in practice?

Costs. Research on economic incentives for nonpoint source pollution control is relatively new as cost information is relatively scarce. Some of the case-specific studies available, however, can give us a sense of the economic analysis. Most of the available studies focus on nonpoint source pollution from agriculture.

McCann and Easter (1999) measured the size of transaction costs associated with various agricultural nonpoint source pollution control policies. Transaction costs (the administrative costs associated with implementing a policy) are an important consideration for nonpoint source pollution control, because monitoring costs tend to be much higher than for point sources. The net gain from implementing a policy is the abatement cost savings minus the transaction costs; if the transaction costs are too high, they can offset all or a major part of the abatement cost gains from implementing the policy.

McCann and Easter looked specifically at the Minnesota River, where severe water-quality problems made the river "unswimmable, unfishable and uncanoeable" near the Twin Cities. Four policies aimed at reducing agricultural sources of phosphorous were considered: education about best management practices, a conservation tillage requirement, expansion of a program that obtained permanent development rights, and a tax on phosphorous fertilizers. They found that a tax on phosphorous fertilizers had the lowest transaction costs ($0.94 million). Educational programs had the second lowest transaction costs at $3.11 million. Conservation tillage and expansion of the conservation easement program had the highest transaction costs at $7.85 million and $9.37 million, respectively. In terms of transaction costs, their results suggest a comparative advantage for input taxes relative to the other approaches. However, since the price elasticity of demand for phosphorous fertilizers has been estimated at between −0.25 and −0.29, a considerable tax increase would be needed to guarantee the desired level of water-quality improvements.

Schwabe (2001) examines various policy options for nonpoint source pollution control for the Neuse River in North Carolina. He compares cost-effectiveness of both the initial and final proposed rules considered by the state of North Carolina. In 1998 nutrient loads in the Neuse River basin were so high that the basin received a *Nutrient Sensitive Waters* classification.[7] In the two years prior to his study, two large swine waste spills caused major algal blooms and 11 million fish kills. The state of North Carolina initially proposed a rule requiring all farms with land adjacent to a stream to install vegetative filter strips. This was compared to a uniform rollback that measured loadings by county with the objective of a 30 percent reduction in total nitrogen loadings. Using a least-cost mathematical programming model, Schwabe finds that the uniform rollback is the more cost-effective strategy, especially since the 30 percent reduction target would be unlikely to be met using the initial rule. However, the author notes that the dominance of the uniform strategy is specific to this particular setting and should not be taken as a general proposition.

The fact that point and nonpoint sources have received such different treatment from the EPA suggests the possibility that costs could be lowered by a more careful balancing of these con-

---

[7]Nutrient Sensitive Waters are defined as waters subject to excessive plant growth and requiring limitations on nutrient inputs.

trol options. One study of phosphorous control in the Dillon reservoir in Colorado by Industrial Economics, Inc. (1984) supports the validity of this suspicion.

In this reservoir, four municipalities constitute the only point sources of phosphorous, while there are numerous uncontrolled nonpoint sources in the area. The combined phosphorous load on the reservoir from point and nonpoint sources was projected to exceed its assimilative capacity.

The traditional way to rescue the projected phosphorous load would be to impose even more stringent controls on the point sources. The study found, however, that by following a balanced program controlling both point and nonpoint sources, the desired phosphorous target could be achieved at a cost of approximately $1 million a year less than would be spent if only point sources were controlled more stringently. The more general point to be carried away from this study is that as point sources are controlled to higher and higher degrees, rising marginal control costs will begin to make controlling nonpoint sources increasingly attractive.

Table 18.2, presented earlier, also shows thirteen point-nonpoint source programs that have traded at least once. Economic theory predicts that if the marginal cost of additional point source reductions is high (since point sources have already been forced to cleanup), then it will suddenly be most cost-effective to trade with nonpoint sources whose marginal cost of cleanup is lower for the early trades. Can you see why this is the case?

Kibler and Kasturi (2007) describe a case for which reductions have been much greater than anticipated. When the Southern Minnesota Sugar Beet Industry needed to offset 6,500 pounds of total phosphorous per year, they actually achieved 15,767 pounds per year reductions, by trading. Does your state have a water pollutant trading program?

Atmospheric Deposition of Pollution

An additional complexity comes in the form of the nonpoint source pollution from the atmosphere that ends up in water bodies. Airborne pollutants such as sulfur dioxide, mercury, and nitrogen eventually find their way to rivers and lakes via atmospheric deposition. *Wet deposition* refers to pollutants that travel to the ground with rainfall. *Dry deposition* occurs when pollutants become too heavy and fall to the ground.

Debate 18.1 highlighted fish consumption advisories due to mercury levels found in many fish. The complication for water pollution control stems from air quality regulations and market mechanisms that may or may not take into consideration the impacts on the ground (or in the water). The external benefits from air quality improvements are likely to be quite large. What does this suggest about the optimal level of air quality and the fact that air and water quality are controlled by separate offices within EPA?

The European Experience

Economic incentives have been important in water pollution control in Europe, where effluent charges play a prominent role in a number of countries. These charge systems take a number of forms. One common approach is illustrated by Czechoslovakia, which uses charges to achieve predetermined ambient standards. Others, such as the former West Germany, use charges mainly to encourage firms to control more than their legal requirements. A third group, illustrated by Hungary and the former East Germany, shows how charge systems have been combined with effluent standards.

Czechoslovakia has used effluent charges to maintain water quality at predetermined levels for several decades. A basic charge is placed on BOD and suspended solids and complemented by a surcharge ranging from 10 to 100 percent, depending upon the contribution of the individual discharge to ambient pollutant concentrations. The basic rates can be adjusted to reflect the quality of the receiving water. This system is conceptually very close to the ambient emission charge system known to be cost-effective.

The charge system in the former West Germany was announced in 1976 and implemented in 1981. The level of charge is related to the degree of compliance with the standards. Firms failing to meet their required standards pay a charge on all actual emissions. If, according to the issued permit, federal emission standards (which are separately defined for each industrial sector) are met, the charge is lowered to 50 percent of the base rate and is applied to the level of discharge implied by the minimum standard. If the firm can prove the discharge to be lower than 75 percent of minimum standards, one-half of the base rate is applied to the (lower) actual discharge level. The charge is waived for three years prior to the installation of new pollution control equipment promising further reductions of at least 20 percent. Revenues from the charges can be used by the administering authorities for administrative costs and financial assistance to public and private pollution abatement activities.

The final approach, used in Hungary and the former East Germany, combines effluent charges with effluent standards. The charge is levied on discharges in excess of fixed effluent limits. In the Hungarian system, the level of the charge is based on the condition of the receiving waters, among other factors. Initially the Hungarian charges had little effect, but when the charge levels were raised, a flurry of waste treatment activity resulted.

Although these European approaches differ from one another and are not all cost-effective, their existence suggests that effluent charge systems are possible and practical. The German Council of Experts on Environmental Questions estimated the German effluent charge policy to be about one-third cheaper for the polluters as a group than an otherwise comparable uniform treatment policy. Furthermore, it encouraged firms to go beyond the uniform standards when such effort was cost-justified.

In a very different approach, Bystrom (1998) examines reducing nonpoint source nitrogen pollution by constructing wetlands in Sweden, where reducing nitrogen loads to the Baltic Sea is an important policy goal. Although it is well known that wetlands can help reduce nitrogen concentrations through the uptake of biomass, how cost-effective is this approach when it is compared to alternative, more traditional methods of control?

To answer this question, Bystrom estimates nonpoint source abatement costs for constructed wetlands and compares them to the costs of reducing nitrogen by means of land-use changes such as the planting of fuel woods. This study finds that marginal abatement costs for wetlands are lower than transitioning to different crops, but still higher than the marginal costs of simply reducing the use of nitrogen fertilizer.

Developing Country Experience

The move from command and control regulations to economic incentives for water pollution control has not seen as rapid a transition in developing countries. Several attempts to use discharge fees and marketable permits have failed. Some argue this is due to lack of regulatory capacity, for example, lack of technical, political, and financial means to set up and monitor a fee or permit program effectively. Noncompliance and lack of infrastructure has hampered many programs. Example 18.3 explores Colombia's experience with a discharge fee program—one case deemed successful.

For developing countries, water pollution control is further complicated by poverty, lack of enforcement, and lack of technology. Deaths from waterborne diseases are much more frequent

---

EXAMPLE 18.3

Economic Incentives for Water Pollution Control: The Case of Colombia

In 1997 Colombia experimented with a new nation-wide program of pollution discharge fees. Polluters would be charged per unit of pollution emitted. Colombia has 33 regional environmental authorities (CARs) some of whom had discharge fees in place for 30 years. This was the first nation-wide program.

This new program mandated that CARs would first collect and map out data on all discharging facilities that generated biological oxygen demand (BOD) and total suspended solids (TSS). They were then to set five-year reduction goals for aggregate discharge in each basin and charge a fee per unit of BOD and TSS. The ministry set a minimum fee, but CARs could adjust this fee upward every six months if reduction targets were not being met.

The program ran into several problems including uneven levels of implementation across CARs, incomplete coverage of dischargers and widespread noncompliance by municipal sewage authorities. Between the start of the program in 1997 and 2003, municipal sewage authorities were assessed over 30 percent of all discharge fees, but only paid 40 percent of what they were charged. Given that some CARs were raising fees based on meeting reduction targets, noncompliance by one group of dischargers was responsible for large rate hikes for others.

Was the Colombia program thus unsuccessful? Surprisingly, evidence actually suggests no! In a number of basins, discharges dropped significantly between 1997 and 2003. BOD discharge from point sources in the program dropped by 27 percent and TSS discharges fell by 45 percent.

One suggested reason for the apparent success of the program is that previously lacking enforcement had to be improved simply to set up a discharge program. Collecting information on discharge amounts and locations also is a necessary component for successful implementation. Increased transparency over command and control programs contributed to the program's success.

The author of this study suggests that one of the most important components of a successful program is adequate infrastructure.

Source: Allen Blackman, "Economic Incentives to Control Water Pollution in Developing Countries: How Well Has Colombia's Wastewater Discharge Fee Program Worked and Why?" *Resources*, (2006) Spring: 20–23.

in developing countries. Of the 1.6 million deaths in 2003 attributed to water and sanitation, 90 percent were children under five and most were from developing countries. In 2004 there were 2,331 deaths from cholera in Africa. There were no deaths from cholera in the Americas. According to the World Health Organization, improved water supply reduces diarrhea morbidity by 6 to 25 percent, and improved sanitation reduces diarrhea morbidity by 32 percent.

A study on the costs and benefits of meeting the United Nations Millennium Development Goal of halving the proportion of people without sustainable access to improved water supply and sanitation determined it would "definitely bring economic benefits, ranging from US$3 to US$34 per US$ invested, depending on the region. Additional improvement of drinking-water quality, such as point-of-use disinfection, in addition to access to improved water and sanitation would lead to benefits ranging from US$5 to US$60 per US$ invested."(Hutton and Haller, 2004)

Oil Spills

One of the chief characteristics of the current approach to oil spills is that it depends heavily on the ability of the legal system to internalize the costs of a spill through liability law. In principle, the approach is straightforward. By forcing the owner of a vessel to pay for the costs of cleaning up the spill, including compensating for natural resource damages, a powerful incentive to exercise care is created. But is the outcome likely to be efficient in practice?

One problem with legal remedies is their high administrative cost. As Example 18.4 points out, assigning the appropriate penalties is no trivial matter. Even if the court were able to act expeditiously, the doctrines it imposes are not necessarily efficient, because the financial liability for cleaning up spills is limited by statute. The owner will minimize costs by choosing the level of precaution that equates the marginal cost of additional precaution with the resulting reduction in the marginal expected penalty. The marginal reduction in expected penalty is a function of two factors—the likelihood of a spill and the magnitude of the financial obligation it would trigger.

As long as the imposed penalty equaled the actual damage and the probability of having to pay the damage, once an accident occurred, was 1.0, this outcome would normally be efficient. The external costs would be internalized. The owner's private costs would be minimized by taking all possible cost-justified precaution measures to reduce both the likelihood and the seriousness of any resulting spill; taking precaution would simply be cheaper than paying for the cleanup.

Limited liability produces a different outcome, however. Lower levels of precaution imply damages that exceed the limit, but the vessel owner would not have to pay anything above the limit. (The only benefit to the vessel owner faced with limited liability that is offered by increasing precaution at lower levels of precaution is the reduction in the likelihood of a spill; in this range, increasing precaution does not reduce the magnitude of the financial payment should a spill occur.)

What is the effect of limited liability on the vessel owner's choice of precaution levels? As long as the *oil spill liability* limit is binding (which appears routinely to be the case with recent spills), the owner will choose too little precaution. Therefore, both the number and magnitude of resulting spills will be inefficiently large.

Anatomy of an Oil Spill Suit: The *Amoco Cadiz*

On March 17, 1978, the *Amoco Cadiz,* an oil transport ship traveling in a bad storm, lost steering control and, after unsuccessful towing attempts, drifted onto the rocks off the shore of Portsall, France, on the Brittany coast. Ultimately, the ship broke in two and discharged 220,000 tons of crude oil and 4,000 tons of bunker fuels along the coast of a resort area, two months prior to the opening of the tourist season.

Before the end of the year of the grounding, a mountain of claims had been filed involving France, a consortium of resort owners, and fishermen, Amoco (the owner of the vessel), Bugsier (the owner of the tug), Shell Oil (the owner of the oil being carried at the time), and Astilleros Españoles (the Spanish company that built the *Amoco Cadiz*). After extensive and expensive preparations by all parties, the trial began in May 1982.

During March 1984 a preliminary opinion was issued finding Amoco and the shipbuilder jointly liable. The process then turned to the separate issue of the magnitude of the damages to be awarded. On February 21, 1989, a judgment of 670 million francs (approximately $120 million) was levied against Amoco and Astilleros. The verdict was immediately appealed.

The trial judge, now retired from the bench, summed up the situation:

So here we are, twelve years after the accident, eleven years after the suit was filed, with the plaintiffs in possession of an enormous judgment and subject to enormous legal fees without one cent having changed hands. The case marches onward to the Court of Appeals with each principal party expected to appeal those aspects of the final judgment with which they disagree. This raises the possibility, almost unimaginable, but very real, that the whole case could have to be tried again.

Source: McGarr, Frank J., "Inadequacy of Federal Forum for Resolution of Oil Spill Damages," a talk given at a conference on oil spills at Newport, Rhode Island, on May 16, 1990. Judge McGarr was the trial judge for the *Amoco Cadiz* case.

● Citizen Suits

As noted earlier, citizen suits add a private enforcement alternative to public enforcement in correcting environmental market failures. Public and private enforcement are partial substitutes. If government enforcement were complete, all polluters would be in compliance, and citizen suits would have no role to play. Noncompliance is a necessary condition for a successful suit. In the early 1980s when public enforcement decreased, private enforcement—citizen suits—increased to take up the slack. Lax public enforcement appears to have played a significant role in the increase of citizen suits.

All attorneys' fees incurred by the citizen group in any successful action under the Clean Water Act must be reimbursed by the defendants. Reimbursement of attorneys' fees has affected both the level and focus of litigation activity. By lowering the costs of bringing citizen suits, attorney fee reimbursement has allowed citizen groups to participate far more often in the enforcement process than otherwise would have been possible. Because courts only reimburse for appropriate claims (noncompliance claims that are upheld by the court), citizen groups are encouraged to litigate appropriate cases only.

The existence of citizen suits should affect the decision-making process of the polluting firm. Adding citizen suits to the enforcement arena increases the expected penalty to the non-complying firm by increasing the likelihood that the firm will face an enforcement action. This can be expected to increase the amount of precaution taken by the firm, but the unavailability of compliance data makes it impossible to confirm this expectation, though participants believe compliance has increased.

Although citizen suits probably do lead to greater compliance, greater compliance is not necessarily efficient. Complete compliance is not necessarily efficient if the defendant polluters face inefficiently harsh standards. If the standards are excessively high, citizen suits have the potential to promote inefficiency by forcing firms to meet standards where the marginal benefits are significantly lower than the marginal costs. However, if the effluent standards are either inefficiently low or efficient, the existence of citizen suits will necessarily create a more efficient outcome. In these cases, increasing compliance is perfectly compatible with efficiency.

Water Quality, Watershed Based Trading, and GIS[8]

Land use change (see Chapter 10) significantly affects watershed health. Agricultural and urban runoff into rivers, streams, and estuaries is the largest contributor to water pollution. Hascic and Wu (2006) use digital land use maps and examine the relationship between land use and water quality. They find that the levels of nutrient and conventional water pollutants are significantly affected by the amount of land in agriculture and urban development while the level of toxic pollution is dependent on land in transportation or mining. Their results suggest that water quality trading programs should take into account land uses within the watershed as well as overall watershed health.

Summary

Historically, policies for controlling water pollution have been concerned with conventional pollutants discharged into surface waters. More recently, concerns have shifted toward toxic pollutants, which apparently are more prevalent than previously believed; toward groundwater, which traditionally was thought to be an invulnerable pristine resource, and toward the oceans, which were mistakenly considered immune from most pollution problems, because of their vast size.

Early attempts at controlling water pollution followed a path similar to that of air pollution control. Legislation prior to the 1970s had little impact on the problem. Frustration then led to the enactment of a tough federal law that was so ambitious and unrealistic that little progress resulted.

---

[8]The U.S. EPA maintains digital data by watershed with indicators of both conventional ambient water quality and toxic ambient water quality as well as other water quality indicators. See http://www.epa.gov/surf.

There the similarity ends. Whereas in air pollution a wave of recent reforms has improved the process by making it more cost effective, no parallel exists for control of water pollution. Historic policy toward cleaning up rivers and lakes was based upon two approaches: (1) the subsidization of municipal waste treatment facilities and (2) the imposition of national effluent standards on industrial sources. Recently this has been complemented by the introduction of the Total Maximum Daily Load Program. This moves water pollution control away from national effluent standards and toward ambient standards tailored to the desired use of the water body.

The historic approach has been hampered by delays, by problems in allocating funds, and by the fact that about half of the constructed plants are not performing satisfactorily. Additionally, effluent standards have assigned the control responsibility among point sources in a way that excessively raises cost. Nonpoint pollution sources have, until recently, been virtually ignored. Technological progress is inhibited rather than stimulated by the current approach. Benefit/cost analyses show the net benefit from the current approach was positive up to 1990, but may become negative as more expensive controls are imposed.

This lack of progress could have been avoided. It did not result from a lack of toughness, but from a reliance on direct regulation rather than on emission charges or emission permits, which are more flexible and cost effective in both the dynamic and static sense. In this respect, the United States can perhaps take some lessons from the European experience.

The court system has assumed most of the responsibility for controlling oil spills. Those responsible for the spills are assessed the financial liability for cleaning up the site and compensating for any resulting damages to natural resources. Although, in principle, this approach can be efficient, in practice, it has been hampered by liability limitations and the huge administrative burden an oil spill trial entails.

Enforcement is always a key to successful environmental and natural resource policy. One rather recent innovation in enforcement involves giving private citizen groups the power to bring noncomplying firms into court. By raising the likelihood that noncomplying firms would be brought before the court and assessed penalties for noncompliance, this new system can be expected to increase compliance.

Key Concepts

biochemical oxygen demand (BOD), *p.* 397

citizen suits, *p.* 405

degradable, *p.* 396

dissolved oxygen (DO), *p.* 397

dry deposition, *p.* 414

effluent standards, *p.* 401

enforcement conference, *p.* 400

eutrophic, *p.* 397

fund pollutants, *p.* 396

Minamata disease, *p.* 398

natural resource damages, *p.* 404

nonpoint sources of water pollution, *p.* 394

oil spill liability, *p.* 418

oxygen sags, *p.* 397

persistent pollutants, *p.* 397

point sources of water pollution, *p.* 394

pretreatment standards, *p.* 411

thermal pollution, *p.* 397

Total Maximum Daily Load (TMDL) program, *p.* 403

uniform treatment (UT) strategy, *p.* 408

waste treatment plant subsidies, *p.* 408

watershed-based trading programs, *p.* 408

wet deposition, *p.* 414

Further Reading

Brouwer, Roy and David Pearce, ed. *Cost Benefit Analysis and Water Resources Management*. Edward Elgar, (2005). A collection of benefit/cost analyses case studies for water pollution control projects, flood control, and water allocation. Most of the cases occurred in Europe.

Letson, D. "Point/Nonpoint Source Pollution Reduction Trading: An Interpretive Survey," *Natural Resources Journal* 32 (1992): 219–232. Considers a host of implementation details that must be resolved if point-nonpoint source trading is to live up to its potential.

Russell, Clifford and Jason Shogren, eds. *Theory, Modeling and Experience in the Management of Nonpoint-Source Pollution* (Hingham, MA: Kluwer Academic Publishers, 1993). A collection of 12 essays providing a state-of-the-art review of the economic perspective on nonpoint source pollution.

Yoshida, F. *The Economics of Waste and Pollution Management in Japan* (Tokyo, Springer-Verlag, 2002).

Additional References

Andreasson, I. M. "A Cost-Efficient Reduction of the Nitrogen Load to Laholm Bay," *Economic Aspects of Environmental Regulations in Agriculture*, Bubgard, A. and A. Nielson, eds. (Kiel, Germany: Wissenschaftsverlag Vauk, 1989).

Bennett, Lynne Lewis. "The Integration of Water Quality into Transboundary Allocation Agreements: Lessons from the Southwestern United States," *Agricultural Economics* 24 (2000): 113–125.

Bennett, Lynne Lewis, Steven G. Thorpe, and A. Joseph Guse. "Cost-Effective Control of Nitrogen Loadings in Long Island Sound," *Water Resources Research* 36 (2000): 3711–3720.

Bockstael, N. E. et al. "Measuring the Benefits of Improvements in Water Quality: The Chesapeake Bay," *Marine Resources Economics* 6 (1989): 1–18.

Boyd, J. "Water Pollution Taxes: A Good Idea Doomed to Failure?" *Public Finance and Management* 3 (2003) (1): 34–66.

Bressers, H. "A Comparison of the Effectiveness of Incentives and Directives: The Case of Dutch Water Quality Policy," *Policy Studies Review* 7 (1988): 500–518.

Bressers, H.T.A. and K.R.D. "Lulofs Industrial Water Pollution in the Netherlands: A Fee-Base Approach," *Choosing Environmental Policy: Comparing Instruments and Outcomes in the United States and Europe*. Harrington, W., R. D. Morgenstern, and T. Sterner, eds. (Washington, DC: Resources for the Future, 2004): 91–116.

Brown, G. M., Jr. and R. W. Johnson. "Pollution Control by Effluent Charges: It Works in the Federal Republic of Germany, Why Not in the U.S.?" *Natural Resources Journal* 24 (1984): 929–966.

Bystrom, Olof. "The Nitrogen Abatement Cost in Wetlands," *Ecological Economics* 26 (1998): 321–331.

Driscoll, C., D. Whitall, et al. "Nitrogen Pollution: Sources and Consequences in the U.S. Northeast," *Environment* 45 (2003) (7): 8.

Griffin, Ronald C. "Environmental Policy for Spatial and Persistent Pollutants," *Journal of Environmental Economics and Management* 14 (March 1987): 41–53.

Hanley, N. and D. Oglethorpe. "Emerging Policies on Externalities from Agriculture: An Analysis for the European Union," *American Journal of Agricultural Economics* 81 (1984) (5): 1222–1227.

Harrington, W. "Industrial Water Pollution in the United States; Direct Regulation or Market Incentive," *Choosing Environmental Policy: Comparing Instruments and Outcomes in the United States and Europe,* Harrington, W., R. D. Morgenstern, and T. Sterner, eds. (Washington, DC: Resources for the Future, 2004): 67–90.

Hascic, Ivan and JunJie Wu. "Land Use and Watershed Health in the United States," *Land Economics* 82 (2006) (2): 214–239.

Hutton, Guy and Lawrence Haller. "Evaluation of the Costs and Benefits of Water and Sanitation Improvements at the Global Level," Water, Sanitation and Health Protection of the Human Environment, World Health Organization (2004), accessed at http://www.who.int/water_sanitation_health/wsh0404/en/index.html.

Industrial Economics Inc. *Case Studies on the Trading of Effluent Loads: Dillon Reservoir Final Report* (Cambridge, MA: Industrial Economics, 1984).

Johnsen, F. H. "Economic Analyses of Measures to Control Phosphorous Run-Off from Nonpoint Agricultural Sources," *European Review of Agricultural Economics* 20 (1993): 399–418.

Johnson, Edwin L. "A Study in the Economics of Water Quality Management," *Water Resources Research* 3 (second quarter 1967): 291–305.

Kibler, Virginia and Kavya Katsuri. "Status of Water Quality Trading Programs Today," (2007), accessed at http://ecosystemmarketplace.com/pages/article.news.php?component_id=5335&component_version_id=7748&language_id=12

Kneese, Allen V. *Economics and the Environment* (New York: Penguin Books, 1977).

Kneese, Allen V. and Blair T. Bower, *Managing Water Quality: Economics, Technology, Institutions* (Baltimore, MD: Johns Hopkins University Press, 1968): Chapter 11.

Kneese, Allen V. and Charles L. Schultze. *Pollution, Prices, and Public Policy* (Washington, DC: Brookings Institution, 1975): 78.

Kraemer, A. and K. M. Banholzer. "Tradable Permits in Water Resource Management and Water Pollution Control," *Implementing Domestic Tradable Permits for Environmental Protection* (Washington, DC: OECD, Organization for Economic Co-operation and Development, 1999): 75–107.

McCann, Laura and William K. Easter. "Transaction Costs of Policies to Reduce Agricultural Phosphorous Pollution in the Minnesota River," *Land Economics* 75 (1999) (3): 402–415.

McConnell, Virginia D., John H. Cumberland, and Patrice L. Gordon. "Regional Marginal Costs and Cost Savings from Economies of Scale in Municipal Waste Treatment: An Application to the Chesapeake Bay," *Growth and Change* 19 (Fall 1988): 1–13.

Naysnerski, Wendy and Tom Tietenberg. "Private Enforcement of Environmental Law," *Land Economics* 68 (1992): 28–48.

Opaluch, James J. and Thomas A. Grigalunas. "Controlling Stochastic Pollution Events with Liability Rules: Some Evidence from OCS Leasing," *Rand Journal of Economics* 15 (1984): 142–151.

Peskin, Henry M. and Eugene P. Seskin. *Cost-Benefit Analysis and Water Pollution Control Policy* (Washington, DC: Urban Institute, 1975).

Raucher, Robert L. "The Benefits and Costs of Policies Related to Groundwater Contamination," *Land Economics* 62 (February 1986): 33–45.

Ribaudo, Marc. "Targeting the Conservation Reserve Program to Maximize Water Quality Benefits," *Land Economics* 65 (November 1989): 320–332.

Russell, Clifford O. "Controlled Trading of Pollution Permits," *Environmental Science and Technology* 15 (January 1981) (1): 1–5.

Schwabe, Kurt A. "Nonpoint Source Pollution, Uniform Control Strategies and the Neuse River Basin," *Review of Agricultural Economics* 23 (2001) (2): 352–369.

Twain, Mark. *Pudd'nhead Wilson* (New York: Harper, 1897): 125.

U.S. Environmental Protection Agency, *Water Quality Trading Assessment Handbook,* EPA 841-B-040-001, November 2004.

Wetzstein, M. E. and T. J. Centner. "Regulating Agricultural Contamination of Groundwater through Strict Liability and Negligence Legislation," *Journal of Environmental Economics and Management* 22 (1992): 1–11.

Woodward, R. T., R. A. Kaiser, et al. "The Structure and Practice of Water Quality Trading Markets," *Journal of the American Water Resources Association* 38 (2002) (4): 967–979.

Discussion Questions

1. "The only permanent solution to water pollution control will occur when all production by-products are routinely recycled. The zero discharge goal recognizes this reality and forces all dischargers to work steadily toward this solution. Less stringent policies are, at best, temporary palliatives." Discuss.

2. "In exercising its responsibility to protect the nation's drinking water, the government needs to intervene only in the case of public water supplies. Private water suppliers will be adequately protected without any government intervention." Discuss.

19 Managing Waste

Man is endowed with reason and creative powers to increase and multiply his inheritance; yet up to now he has created nothing, only destroyed. The forests grow ever fewer; the rivers parch; the wildlife is gone; the climate is ruined; and with every passing day the earth becomes uglier and poorer.

—ANTON CHEKHOV, *Uncle Vanya, Act I* (1896)

Introduction

As the level of waste rises and the amount of space available to store it safely without contaminating groundwater declines, what can be done? The traditional answer involves the three R's: reduce, reuse, recycle.

How can economics help to assure that the three R's play an appropriate role in managing waste? What measures can be taken to reduce the level of waste? What is an efficient amount of recycling? Will the market automatically generate this amount in the absence of government intervention? How does the efficient allocation over time differ between recyclable and nonrecyclable resources?

Our investigation begins by describing how an efficient market in recyclable, depletable resources would work. This benchmark is then used to examine recycling in some detail. We conclude by introducing the special complications that arise when the waste is hazardous or toxic and discuss the policy approaches that are targeted specifically at that category of waste.

Efficient Recycling

Extraction and Disposal Costs

What determines the recycling rate? Historically, reliance has generally been on the natural inputs, because they have been cheaper. As the natural inputs have become scarce relative to the demand for them, industry has begun to search for other sources.

At the same time, the costs of disposing the products have risen as the world has experienced a large increase in the geographic concentration of people. The attraction of cities and the

424

exodus from rural areas led an increasingly large number of people to live in urban or near-urban environments.

This concentration creates waste-disposal problems. When land was plentiful and the waste stream was less hazardous, waste could be buried in landfills. But as land has become scarce, burial has become increasingly expensive. In addition, concerns over environmental effects on water supplies and economic effects on the value of surrounding land have made buried waste less acceptable.

The rising costs of virgin materials and of waste disposal have increased the attractiveness of recycling. By recovering and reintroducing materials into the system, recycling provides an alternative to virgin ores and also reduces the waste-disposal load (see Example 19.1).

EXAMPLE 19.1

Population Density and Recycling: The Japanese Experience

Since Japan has a much greater population density than any of the other industrialized nations, it has been forced by necessity to come to terms with its solid waste problems somewhat earlier than countries with more land area available for disposal. Japan has accomplished this with a combination of technological solutions, reduction strategies, and recycling.

Currently, Japan recycles about 50 percent of its paper, 80 percent of its steel cans, and 75 percent of its glass bottles. For the sake of comparison, comparable numbers for the United States are 45 percent, 59 percent, and 21 percent.

Since the early 1970s Japanese citizens have been forced to separate combustible from noncombustible trash. Combustible waste, which is some 72 percent of the total, is burned in some 1,850 incinerators. (This compares to about 140 large incinerators in the United States.) About 80 percent of the volume of incinerated waste in Japan is used to generate power. What's left, about 9 percent of the total waste generated, ends up in landfills. (In the United States about 56 percent of the generated waste ends up in landfills.)

Additionally, Japan has been a leader in mandating the return of appliances (washing machines, refrigerators, televisions, and air conditioners) for recycling. In April 2001 the Home Appliances Recycling Law was enacted. While it places most of the responsibility on manufacturers, it requires consumers to deliver the appliances to the appropriate collection sites and to provide the financing. When consumers trade in an old appliance for a new one or they deliver their used appliances to a collection site, they must pay a fee to cover the cost of recycling. Manufacturers are responsible for recycling the appliances. They are also responsible for ensuring that future products incorporate materials supplied by the recycling program and are easier to recycle.

Sources: Japanese Recycling Statistics, http://web-japan.org/stat/stats/19ENV51.html; U.S. Statistics http://www.epa.gov/epaoswer/non-hw/muncpl/facts.htm.

Consumers and manufacturers play a role on both the demand and supply side of the market. On the demand side, consumers would find that products depending exclusively on virgin raw materials are subject to higher prices than those relying on recycled materials. Consequently, consumers would have a tendency to switch to products made with the cheaper, recycled raw materials, as long as quality is not adversely affected. This powerful incentive is called the *composition-of-demand effect*.

As long as consumers bear the cost of disposal, they have the additional incentive to return their used recyclable products to collection centers. By doing so, they avoid disposal costs while reaping financial rewards for supplying a product someone wants.

For the cycle to be complete, the demand for the recycled products must be sufficiently high to justify making them available. New markets may ultimately emerge, but the transition has proved to be somewhat turbulent. Simply returning recycled products to the collection centers accomplishes little if they are simply dumped into a nearby landfill or if the supply is increased so much by mandatory recycling laws that prices for recycled materials fall through the floor. The purity of the recycled products also plays a key role in explaining the strength of demand for them. One of the reasons for the high rate of aluminum recycling and much lower rate of plastics recycling is the differential difficulty of producing a high-quality product from scrap. Whereas bundles of aluminum cans have a relatively uniform quality, waste plastics tend to be highly contaminated with nonplastic substances, and the plastics manufacturing process has little tolerance for impurities. Remaining contaminants in metals can frequently be eliminated by high-temperature combustion, but plastics are destroyed by high temperatures.

Recycling: A Closer Look

The model in the preceding section would lead us to expect that recycling would increase over time as virgin ore and disposal costs rose. This seems to be the case. Take copper, for example. In 1910 recycled copper accounted for about 18 percent of the total production of refined copper in the United States. By 2001 this figure had risen to 70 percent.

Recycling Faces Many Barriers. The expectation that virgin prices are steadily increasing is not always valid (see Example 19.2). Coupled with artificially low disposal costs, these depressed prices contribute to depressed markets for recycled materials.

In most cases recycling is not cheap. Several types of costs are involved. Transport and processing costs are usually significant. The sources of scrap may be concentrated around cities where most of the products are used, while for historical reasons the processing facilities are near the sources of the virgin ore. The scrap must be transported to the processing facility and the processed scrap to the market.

Labor costs are also important. Collecting, sorting, and processing the scrap are typically very labor intensive. Higher labor costs can make the recycled scrap less competitive in the input market. Recognizing the importance of labor costs raises the possibility that recycling rates would be higher in areas where labor costs are lower and that does seem to be the case. Porter (1997), for example, shows how vibrant markets for scrap have emerged in Africa.

And, finally, since the processing of scrap of input into the production process can produce its own environmental consequences, complying with environmental regulations on processing facilities can add to the cost of recycled input. In the United States, for example, relatively low

EXAMPLE

19.2

The Bet

In 1980 each of two distinguished protagonists in the scarcity debate "put his money where his mouth was." Paul Ehrlich, an ecologist with a strong belief in impending scarcity, answered a challenge from Julian Simon, an economist known for his equally strong belief that concerns about impending scarcity were groundless.

According to the terms of the bet, Ehrlich would hypothetically invest $200 in each of any five commodities he selected. (He picked copper, chrome, nickel, tin, and tungsten.) Ten years later, the aggregate value of the same amounts of those five commodities would be calculated in real terms (after accounting for normal inflation). If the value increased, Simon would send Ehrlich a check for the difference. If it decreased, Ehrlich would send Simon a check for the difference.

In 1990 Ehrlich performed the calculations and sent Simon a check for $576.07. Not only were real prices lower for each of the five commodities, but also some were at less than half their former levels. New sources of the minerals had been discovered, substitutions of these minerals had occurred in many of their uses (particularly computers), and the tin cartel, which had been holding up tin prices, collapsed.

Would the outcome of the Simon-Ehrlich wager have been the same if the bet had covered the entire twentieth century? According to analysis of the data on these same minerals by McClintock and Emmett (2005), despite ups and downs in prices over the course of the past century, Simon would also have won the century-long wager.

Finally, how would Simon have fared in the other decades? Was he just lucky to have picked the 1980s? It turns out that to some extent he was lucky. Of the ten decades in that century he would have won in five (the 1900s, 1910s, 1940s, 1980s, and 1990s). He would have lost by a few dollars in the 1950s and by more significant amounts in the other four decades.

Does this evidence provide a lesson for the future? You be the judge.

Sources: Tierney, John, "Betting the Planet," _The New York Times Magazine_ (December 2, 1990): 52–53, 74, 76, 78, and 80–81 and McClintick, D. and Ross B. Emmett, "The Simon-Ehrlich Debate," _PERC Reports_ 23(3), 2005: 16–17.

world copper prices, coupled with high environmental compliance costs created a cost squeeze that contributed to the closure of all U.S. secondary smelters and associated electrolytic refineries by 2001.

When recycling markets operate smoothly, however, and scrap becomes a cost-competitive input, rather dramatic changes occur in the manufacturing process. Not only do manufacturers rely more heavily on recycled inputs, they also begin to design their products in order to facilitate recycling. Facilitating recycling through product design is already important in industries where the connection between the manufacturer and disposal agent is particularly close. Aircraft manufacturers, who are often asked to scrap old aircraft, may stamp the alloy composition on parts during manufacturing to facilitate recycling. The idea is beginning to spread to other industries. For example, ski boot manufacturers in Switzerland have begun to stamp all component parts with a code to identify their composition.

An efficient economic system will orchestrate *optimal recycling*—a balance between the consumption of depletable and recycled materials, between disposing of used products and recycling, and between imports and domestic production. Example 19.3 shows the market at work.

How close are we to efficiency? Have we achieved an efficient balance between imports and domestic production? Is the common pejorative notion that we are a "throwaway society" an accurate one? If so, is the market behaving efficiently—in the sense that the time for recycling has not yet come—or are there clearly identified sources of market failure, implying that the wrong price signals are being sent? The next few sections investigate these issues.

**EXAMPLE
19.3**

Lead Recycling

The domestic demand for lead has changed significantly over the last 35 years. In 1972 dissipative, non-recyclable uses of lead (primarily gasoline additives, pigments in paint, and ammunition) accounted for about 30 percent of reported consumption. Only about 30 percent of all produced lead came from recycled material.

Over the last two and a half decades, however, congressional recognition of lead's negative health effects on children has led to a series of laws limiting the amount of allowable lead in gasoline and paints. Not only has this resulted in a decline in the total amount of lead used, but also the decline has been most dramatic for the dissipative uses (which, by 1997 had fallen to only 13 percent of total demand). A declining role for dissipative uses implies an increasing proportion of the production is available to be recycled. And, in fact, more was. By 2007 76 percent of the domestic lead consumption came from recycled scrap.

Post-consumer scrap accounts for nearly all of the total lead scrap recovered with used batteries supplying about 90 percent. Battery manufacturers have begun entering buyback arrangements with retail outlets, both as a marketing tool for new batteries and as a means of ensuring a supply of inputs to their downstream manufacturing operations.

Source U.S. Department of the Interior. *Minerals Yearbook,* available on the Web at: http://minerals.usgs.gov/minerals/pubs/commodity/lead/.

● Waste Disposal and Pollution Damage

The treatment of waste by producers and consumers can lead to biases in the market balance between recycling and the use of virgin materials. Because disposal cost is a key ingredient in determining the efficient amount of recycling, the failure of an economic agent to bear the full cost of disposal implies a bias toward virgin materials and away from recycling. We begin by considering how the method of financing the disposal of potentially recyclable waste affects the level of recycling.

Disposal Costs and Efficiency

First, let us examine the relationship of the *marginal disposal cost* to the efficient level of recycling. Suppose, for example, it costs a community $20/ton to recycle a particular waste product that can ultimately be sold to a local manufacturer for $10/ton. Can we conclude that this is an inefficient recycling venture because it is losing money?

No, we can't! In addition to earning the $10/ton from selling the recycled product, the town is avoiding the cost of disposing the product. This avoided marginal cost is appropriately considered a marginal benefit from recycling. Suppose the marginal avoided disposal cost were $20/ton. In this case, the benefits to the town from recycling would be $30/ton ($20/ton avoided cost plus $10/ton resale value) and the cost would be $20/ton; the benefits from recycling would exceed the costs. Both marginal disposal costs and the prices of recycled materials directly affect the efficient level of recycling.

The Disposal Decision

Potentially recyclable waste can be divided into two types of scrap: (1) new scrap and (2) old scrap. *New scrap* is composed of the residual materials generated during production. For example, as steel beams are formed, the small remnants of steel left over are new scrap. *Old scrap* is recovered from products used by consumers.

To illustrate the relative importance of new scrap and old scrap, consider the U.S. aluminum industry. About 40 percent of the recovered aluminum scrap in the United States comes from old scrap. Recycling new scrap is significantly less difficult than recycling old scrap. New scrap is already at the place of production, and with most processes it can simply be reentered into the input stream without transportation costs. Transport costs tend to be an important part of the cost of using old scrap. Equally important are the incentives involved. Because new scrap never leaves the factory, it remains under the complete control of the manufacturer. Having the joint responsibility of creating a product and dealing with the scrap, the manufacturer now has an incentive to design the product with the use of the scrap in mind. It would, therefore, be advantageous to establish procedures guaranteeing the homogeneity of the scrap and minimizing the amount of processing necessary to recycle it. For all these reasons, it is likely that the market for new scrap will work efficiently and effectively.

Unfortunately, the same is not true for old scrap. The market works inefficiently because the product users do not bear the full marginal social costs of disposing their product. As a result, the market is biased away from recycling old scrap and toward the use of virgin materials.

The key to understanding why these costs are not internalized lies in the incentives facing individual product users. Suppose you had some small aluminum products that were no longer useful to you. You could either recycle them, which usually means driving to a recycling center, or you could toss them into your trash. In comparing these alternatives, notice that recycling imposes one cost on you (transport cost) whereas the second imposes another (disposal cost).

It is difficult for consumers to make this comparison accurately because of the way trash collection has traditionally been financed (see Table 19.1). Urban areas have generally financed trash collection with taxes, if publicly provided, or user fees, if privately provided. Since neither of these approaches directly relates the size of an individual's payment to the amount of waste,

TABLE 19.1 Description of User Charges on Municipal Waste, Selected Countries

Country	Charge Calculation	Target
Australia	Flat rate	Households, firms
Belgium	Flat rate or volume	Households
Canada	Flat rate	Households
	Flat rate + volume over threshold	Firms
Denmark	Flat rate	Households
	Waste volume	Firms
Finland	Waste volume	Households
	Volume + type + transport distance	Firms
France	Dwelling size (80% of population) *or*	Households, firms
	Waste volume (4% of population) *or*	Households, firms
	(None: Waste collection paid for from public budget)	
Italy	Dwelling size	Households, firms
The Netherlands	Flat rate	Households, firms
Norway	Flat rate	Households, firms
Sweden	Flat rate (53% of municipalities)	Households, firms
	Collection structure (45% of municipalities)	Households, firms
United Kingdom	Flat rate	Households, firms
	Waste volume	Firms

Source: Adapted from Opschoor, J. B. and Dr. Hans B. Vos. *Economic Instruments for Environmental Protection* (Paris: Organization for Economic Co-operation and Development, 1989): 53.

the marginal disposal cost to the homeowner of throwing out one more unit of trash is negligible, even when the cost to society is not.

This point can be reinforced by a numerical example. Suppose your city provides trash pickup for which you pay $150 a year in taxes. Your cost will be $150 regardless (within reasonable limits) of how much you throw out. In a given year your additional (marginal) cost from throwing out these items is *zero*. Certainly, the marginal cost to society is *not* zero, so that the balance between these alternatives as seen by the individual homeowner is biased in favor of throwing things out.[1]

Littering is an extreme example of what we have been discussing. In the absence of some kind of government intervention, the cost to society of littering is the aesthetic loss plus the risk of damage caused by sharp edges of discarded cans or glass. Tossing used containers out of a car window is relatively costless for the individual but costly for society.[2]

---

[1] The problem is not that $150 is too low; indeed, it may be too high! The point is that the cost of waste disposal does not increase with the amount of waste disposed of.

[2] Using economic analysis, would you expect transients or residents to have a higher propensity to litter? Why?

Disposal Costs and the Scrap Market

How would the market respond to a policy forcing product users to bear the true marginal disposal cost? The major effect would be on the supply of materials to be recycled. Consumers would now be able to avoid disposal costs and might even be paid for discarded products. This would cause the diversion of some materials to recycling centers, where they could be reintegrated into the materials process. If this expanded supply allows dealers to take advantage of previously unexploited economies of scale, it could well result in a lower average cost of processing, as well as more recycled materials.

The effect on the market is now clear. The total consumption of recycled inputs increases because the expanded supply causes the price to fall.

Subsidies on Raw Materials

Disposal costs are only part of the story. Inputs derived from recycling can only compete with raw materials if the playing field is level. Subsidies on raw materials are another troubling source of inefficiencies that create a bias away from recycled inputs.

Raw material subsidies can take many forms. One form is illustrated by the Mining Law of 1872. This law, which was originally passed well over a century ago to promote mining on public lands, is still on the books. Under this law, miners can stake lode claims (for subsurface materials) and placer claims (for surface materials) for mineral prospecting on public lands. A claim can be maintained for a payment of only $100 a year. If minerals are discovered in a claim area and at least $500 has been invested in development or extraction, the land could actually be bought for $5 an acre on lode claims or $2.50 an acre on placer claims. In 1999 the U.S. Congress enacted a moratorium on land acquisition, but not on staking claims.

These prices for access to public lands are so low relative to market prices that they constitute a considerable subsidy. As a result of this subsidy, not only are taxpayers not receiving the true value of the mining services provided by public lands, but also the subsidy is lowering the cost of extracting these raw minerals. As a result, raw materials are artificially cheap and can inefficiently undermine the market for recycled inputs.

Pollution Damage

Another situation influences the use of recycled and virgin ores. When environmental damage results from extracting and using virgin materials and not from the use of recycled materials, the market allocation will be biased away from recycling. The damage might be experienced at the mine, such as the erosion and aesthetic costs of strip mining, or at the point of processing, where the ore is processed into a usable resource.

Suppose that the mining industry was forced to bear the cost of this environmental damage. What difference would the inclusion of this cost have on the scrap market? The internalizing of this cost results in a leftward shift in the supply curve for the virgin ore. The market would be using less of the virgin resource—due to higher price—while recycling more. Thus, correctly treating both environmental costs and disposal would tend to increase the role for recycling.

Disposal also imposes external environmental costs in the form of odors, pests, and contaminants leaching into water supplies; obstruction of visual landscapes; and so on. Kinnaman and

Fullerton (2000) note that while the number of landfills in the United States has been decreasing, the aggregate capacity of these landfills has been increasing as small-town facilities are replaced by large regional sanitary landfills. Since local opposition from potential host communities is likely to rise with landfill size, locating these facilities can be extremely contentious.

Toxic and Hazardous Waste

Suppose the waste is hazardous. In one of the interesting ironies of history, the place that focused public attention in the United States on hazardous waste is called the Love Canal. *Love* is not a word any impartial observer would choose to describe the relationships among the parties to that incident.

In many ways the Love Canal typifies the dilemma posed by the creation and disposal of toxic substances. Until 1953 Hooker Electrochemical (subsequently Hooker Chemical, a subsidiary of Occidental Petroleum Corporation) dumped waste chemicals into an old abandoned waterway known as the Love Canal, near Niagara Falls, New York. At the time it seemed a reasonable solution, because the chemicals were buried in what was then considered to be impermeable clay.

In 1953 Hooker deeded the Love Canal property for $1 to the Niagara Falls Board of Education, which then built an elementary school on the site. The deed specifically excused Hooker from any damages that might be caused by the chemicals. Residential development of the area around the school soon followed.

The site became the center of controversy when, in 1978, residents complained of chemicals leaking to the surface. News reports emanating from the area included stories of spontaneous fires and noxious vapors in basements. Medical reports suggested that the residents had experienced abnormally high rates of miscarriage, birth defects, and liver disease.

Similar experiences plagued sites in Europe and Asia. In 1976 an accident at an F. Hoffman–La Roche & Co. plant in Sevesco spewed dioxin over the Italian countryside. Subsequently, explosions in a Union Carbide plant in Bhopal, India, spread deadly gases over nearby residential neighborhoods with significant loss of life. Water used to quell a warehouse fire at a Sandoz warehouse near Basel, Switzerland, carried an estimated 30 tons of toxic chemicals into the Rhine River, a source of drinking water for a number of towns in the former Federal Republic of Germany.

One large and growing type of hazardous waste, known as e-waste, involves electronic equipment. The EPA reports that in 2005 2 million tons of TVs, computers, computer accessories, and cell phones were discarded; 80 to 85 percent (1.5 to 1.9 million tons) was discarded in landfills. Although this represented less than 2 percent of the municipal solid waste stream, electronics waste is a fast growing segment of the waste stream, bringing with it rising concerns about the environmental and health effects of some of this waste. Lead, mercury, cadmium, and brominated flame retardants are all widely used in electronics. All of these substances considered hazardous waste and have been linked to health risks, especially for children.

According to the USGS some 1 billion cell phones were in use worldwide in 2002. In the United States alone, the number of cell phone subscribers increased from 340,000 in 1985 to 180 million in 2004. 130 million cell phones were retired in 2005. The U.S. EPA reports that currently less than 1 percent of cell phones discarded are recycled. Are the minerals used to make cell phones (primarily copper, iron, nickel, silver, and zinc with smaller amounts of aluminum, gold, lead, palladium, and tin) valuable? Apparently they are quite valuable! Table 19.2 shows the estimated value of the metals in cell phones in the United States. Did you upgrade your cell phone this year? Do you know what happened to the old one?

Policies Targeted at Conventional Waste

Why are recycling rates for conventional waste so low? As we have noted some of the responsibility for low recycling rates lies in improper incentives created by inappropriate pricing. Can this misallocation be corrected?

One approach, volume pricing, would impose disposal charges reflecting the true social cost of disposal (see Example 19.4).

One preimplementation concern about the volume pricing was that it might impose a hardship on the poor residents of the area. Strategies based on higher prices always raise the specter that they will end up placing an intolerable burden on the poor.

That concern apparently was misplaced at least in this case. Under the old system of financing trash collection, every household pays the same fee—regardless of how much trash is pro-

TABLE 19.2 Weight and Gross Value of Selected Metals in Cell Phones in the United States

Metal	Metal Content and Value Estimated for a Typical Cell Phone		Metal Content and Value for 180 Million Cell Phones in Use in 2004[2]		Metal Content and Value for 130 Million Cell Phones Retired in 2005[2]		Metal Content and Value for 500 Million Obsolete Cell Phones in Storage in 2005[2]	
	Wt[1] (g)	Value	Wt[3] (t)	Value	Wt[3] (t)	Value	Wt[3] (t)	Value
Copper	16	$0.03	2,900	$6.2 million	2,100	$4.6 million	7,900	$17 million
Silver	0.35	$0.06	64.1	$11 million	46	$7.9 million	178	$31 million
Gold	0.034	$0.40	6.2	$72 million	3.9	$52 million	17	$199 million
Palladium	0.015	$0.13	2.7	$22.7 million	2.0	$16 million	7.4	$63 million
Platinum	0.00034	$0.01	0.06	$1.4 million	0.04	$1 million	0.18	$3.9 million
Total	2,973			$113 million	2,152	$82 million	8,102	$314 million

[1]Metal content (wt) calculated from weight of a typical cell phone (Nokia, 2005) and data from Rob Bouma, Falconbridge Ltd., written and oral communications, 2005.

[2]Number of cell phones in use in 2004 from Charny (2005). Number of cell phones retired in 2005 from U.S. Environmental Protection Agency, 2005. Number of obsolete cell phones projected to be in storage in 2005 from Most (2003).

[3]Metal content (wt) calculated from data from Rob Bouma, Falconbridge Ltd., written and oral communications, 2005.

Note: The average weight (wt) of a cell phone is estimated to be 113 grams (g), exclusive of batteries and charger (Nokia, 2005). Metal contents are weights in metric tons (t), unless otherwise noted. Values in U.S. dollars are calculated by using the average of prices for 2002–2004 from USGS Mineral Commodity Summaries 2005 (Amey, 2005; Edelstein, 2005; Hilliard, 2005a,b). The gross values do not include costs of recycling. Data may not add to totals shown because of independent rounding.

Source: Sullivan, Daniel, "Recycled Cell Phones—A Treasure Trove of Valuable Materials," USGS (2007), http://pubs.usgs.gov/fs/2006/3097/fs2006-3097.pdf.

EXAMPLE

19.4

Pricing Trash in Marietta, Georgia

In 1994 the people of Marietta, Georgia, participated in a demonstration project that changed the way in which waste was priced. The traditional $15 monthly fee for trash pickup was cut to $8 per month. In addition, half of the residents faced a per-bag price on waste ($0.75 per bag), while the rest faced a monthly fee for pickup that depended on the maximum of cans per month that the customer wished to have picked up. This number was contracted in advance by the customer and did not vary from month to month. The fee was $3 or $4 per can (depending upon the number).

Economic theory suggests that while both plans should reduce waste and increase recycling, the per-bag fee should promote more. (Can you see why?)

And indeed that is what happened. The can program reduced nonrecycled waste by about 20 percent, whereas the bag program reduced it by as much as 51 percent. Both programs had an equally strong effect on encouraging households to recycle. The combined weights of waste and recyclables were reduced 36 percent under the bag program and 14 percent under the can program. Both programs not only diverted waste into recycling, they also reduced the amount of waste generated.

Could the costs associated with the program be justified in benefit/cost terms? According to the economists who conducted the study, they were. The net benefits for the city were estimated to be $586 per day for the bag program and $234 per day for the can program.

Source: Van Houtven, G. L. and G. E. Morris. "Household Behavior Under Alternative Pay-as-You-Throw Systems for Solid Waste Disposal," *Land Economics* 75(4), November 1999: 515–537.

duced. Because elderly (and other low-income) households produce less trash, they are, in effect, subsidizing wealthier households under the old system.

Another suggestion now being applied for promoting recycling in many areas is the refundable deposit. Already widely accepted for beverage containers, such deposits could become a remedy for many other products.

A *refundable deposit system* is designed to accomplish two purposes: (1) the initial charge reflects the cost of disposal and produces the desired composition-of-demand effect and (2) the refund, attainable upon turning the product in for recycling, helps conserve virgin materials. Refundable deposits have a much wider applicability than normally realized. In Sweden and Norway, for example, they are used to counter the problem of abandoned automobiles.

The recycling of aluminum beverage cans has been one clear beneficiary of deposit refund schemes.[3] Several countries, including Germany, Finland, Norway, Denmark, Sweden, the state of South Australia, and 11 U.S. states have container deposit refund programs in place. Although not all states have passed bottle bills, over 50 percent of aluminum beverage cans are

---

[3]A very strong demand for aluminum scrap was also influential. In fact, the price for aluminum scrap went so high in 1988 that pilferers were stealing highway signs and guardrails for their aluminum content.

now recycled in the United States. As a result, aluminum old scrap has become an increasingly significant component of total aluminum supplies. Recycling aluminum saves about 95 percent of the energy that is needed to make new aluminum from ore. The magnitude of these energy savings has had a significant influence on the demand for recycled aluminum as cost-conscious producers search for new ways to reduce energy costs. Debate 19.1 explores why some states have chosen not to implement refundable bottle deposits.

Beverage can recycling also reduces littering because an incentive is created to bring the bottle to a recycling center. In some cities, scavenging and returning these bottles has provided a significant source of income to the homeless. One Canadian study found that recycling creates six times as many jobs as landfilling.

Deposit-refund systems are also being used for batteries and tires. New Hampshire and Maine, for example, place a surcharge on new car batteries. Consumers in these states receive a rebate if they trade in their used battery for a new one. Oklahoma places a $1 fee on each new tire sold and then returns $0.50 to certified processing facilities for each tire handled.

Some states in the United States, as well as some developing countries, also use deposit-refund systems to assure that pesticide containers are returned after use. Since remaining toxic residues can contaminate water and soil, collecting the containers and either reusing them or properly decontaminating them can eliminate this contamination threat.

Some areas attempt to enlist economic incentives by imposing a disposal or recycling surcharge on the product. Paid at the time of purchase of a new product, this surcharge would normally be designed to recover the costs of recycling the product at the end of its useful life; more-difficult-to-recycle products would have larger fees. These fees would normally be coupled with a requirement that the revenue be used by sellers to set up recycling systems. Assuming these fees correctly internalize the costs of recycling, they will provide consumers with incentives to take the recycling and disposal costs into account, since easier-to-recycle products would have a lower price (including the fee). Note, however, that these purchase surcharges do not provide any incentive against illegal disposal (littering) since the consumer gets no rebate for dropping the product off at a collection center. On the other hand, unlike a trash collection charge it provides no specific incentive for illegal disposal either. Since the fee is paid up-front, it cannot be avoided by illegal disposal. In this sense the deposit-refund system is clearly superior to either purchase surcharges or volume pricing of trash.

The tax system can also be used to promote recycling by taxing virgin materials and by subsidizing recycling activities. The European approach to waste oil recycling, reinforced by the high cost of imported crude oil, was to require both residential and commercial users to recycle all waste oil they generate. Virgin lubricating oils are taxed, and the resulting income is used to subsidize the recycling industry. As a result, many countries collect up to 65 percent of the available waste oil.

In the United States, which does not subsidize waste oil recycling, the waste oil market has been less successful. Currently, only about 15 percent of waste oil is recovered. For most of the period following World War II the waste oil industry was in relative decline with the exception of the period immediately following the oil crisis during the 1970s, when oil prices rose dramatically.

Many areas are now using tax policy to subsidize the acquisition of recycling equipment in both the public and private sectors. Frequently taking the form of sales-tax exemptions or investment tax credits to private industries or loans or grants to local communities, these approaches are designed to get recycling programs off the ground with the expectation that they will ultimately be self-sustaining. The pioneers are being subsidized.

DEBATE 19.1

"Bottle Bills." Economic Incentives at Work?

Eleven states: California, Connecticut, Delaware, Hawaii, Iowa, Maine, Massachusetts, Michigan, New York, Oregon, and Vermont have passed "bottle bill" legislation. Six other states have proposed new legislation. Bottle deposits range from $0.05 to $0.15 and laws vary on which containers are redeemable for deposits. One city, Columbia, Missouri, also passed legislation, but it was repealed in 2002.

A bottle bill, or container deposit law, sets a refundable deposit on certain beverage containers with the goal of high rates of recycling or reuse. The retailer of the beverages initially pays the distributor a deposit and then collects this deposit from the consumer who buys the beverage. The consumer has the choice of receiving the refund by returning the bottle or either legally or illegally disposing of the container. In the case of nonreturned bottles, the distributors and bottlers typically realize the profits from these unreturned cans and bottles.

While on average, U.S. container recycling rates have been below 40 percent, recycling rates in bottle deposit states are much higher, averaging around 80 percent. In Michigan, with a $0.10 beverage can deposit, recycling rates are close to 100 percent. Statistics on litter show the largest reductions in bottle deposit states. Clearly this economic incentive is working. Why then, don't all states have deposits? Socioeconomic and geographic characteristics and population density all factor into the answer.

Economic studies on bottle deposits are limited. Porter (1983) estimated the costs and benefits of the then newly passed Michigan bottle bill. He calculated the litter and solid waste disposal cost savings, the amenity benefits of litter reduction, consumer surplus losses due to price increases, increase in beverage delivery costs, and consumer inconvenience costs (of having to return the bottles). He found that for most estimates of costs and benefits, the bill passed a cost-benefit test.

Can economic analysis tell us anything about the appropriate disposition of the revenue from unclaimed deposits? It can. Calcott and Walls (2005) show that contrary to conventional policy, in order for optimality to be achieved, manufacturers should forfeit all unclaimed deposits. Preserving the correct incentives requires manufacturers to be penalized, not rewarded with the unclaimed deposits, for producing products that end up in the landfill.

Although bottle deposit states have recycling rates double those of states without deposits, it does not automatically follow that all states should have bottle bills. Costs matter and key determinants of the relative costs vary from state to state. Disposal costs depend on landfill availability, while return rates depend on population densities and distances to redemption centers. Enforcement across state lines is costly and imperfect. States with large bottlers like Coca-Cola find it politically difficult to establish bottle deposits. Does your state have a bottle deposit? Does that seem the right choice? Why?

Sources: http://globalwarming.house.gov/mediacenter/pressreleases?id=0126; www.containerrecylinginstitute.org; Richard C. Porter, "Michigan's Experience with Mandatory Deposits on Beverage Containers," *Land Economics* 59 (1983); P. Calcott and M. Walls, "Waste, Recycling and Design for Environment: Roles for Markets and Policy Instruments" Resource and Energy Economics 27(4): 287–305.

Oregon's program illustrates how a tax approach works. From 1981 to 1987, to reduce energy consumption as well as to promote recycling, the Oregon Department of Energy granted tax credits to 163 projects. Being granted this credit allowed companies a five-year period in which to deduct from their taxes an amount equal to 35 percent of the cost of any equipment used solely for recycling. Oregon also offered a broader tax credit that covered equipment, land, and building purchases. Paper companies, the major recipients of both types of credits, have used them to increase the capacity for using recycled newsprint and cardboard in the papermaking process. According to Shea (1988), these incentives helped to raise Oregon's newspaper recycling rate (65 percent) to twice the national average.

Any long-run solution to the solid waste problem must not only influence consumer choices about purchasing, packaging, and disposal, it must also influence producer choices about product design (to increase recyclability), product packaging, and the use of recycled (as opposed to virgin materials) in the production process. One general approach is called expanded producer responsibility, and it involves requiring producers to take back packaging, and even their products, at the end of their useful lives (see Example 19.5).

Implementing the Take-Back Principle

EXAMPLE
19.5

According to the *take-back principle*, all producers should be required to accept responsibility for their products—including packaging—from cradle to grave by taking them back once they have outlived their useful lives. In principle, this requirement was designed to encourage the elimination of inessential packaging, to stimulate the search for products and packaging that are easier to recycle, and to support the substitution of recycled inputs for virgin inputs in the production process.

Germany has required producers (and retailers as intermediaries) to accept all packaging associated with products, including such different types of packaging as the cardboard boxes used for shipping hundreds of toothbrushes to retailers, to the tube in which that toothpaste is contained. Consumers are encouraged to return the packaging by means of a combination of convenient drop-off centers, refundable deposits on some packages, and high disposal costs for packaging that is thrown away.

Producers responded by setting up a new, private, nonprofit corporation, the Duales System Deutschland (DSD), to collect the packaging and to recycle the collected materials. This corporation is funded by fees levied on producers. The fees are based on the number of kilograms of packaging the producers use. The DSD accepts only packaging that it has certified as recyclable. Once certification is received, producers are allowed to display a green dot on their product, signaling consumers that this product is accepted by the DSD system. Other packaging must be returned directly to the producer or to the retailer, who returns it to the producer.

The law has apparently reduced the amount of packaging produced and has diverted a significant amount of packaging away from incineration and landfills. A most noteworthy failure, however, was the inability of the DSD system to find markets for the recycled materials it collected. Some German packaging even ended up in neighboring countries, causing some international backlash. The circumstance where the supply of recycled

materials far exceeds the demand is so common—not only in Germany but in the rest of the world as well—that further efforts to increase the degree of recycling will likely founder unless new markets for recycled materials are forthcoming.

Despite the initial difficulties with implementing the "take-back" principle, the idea that manufacturers should have ultimate responsibility for their products has a sufficiently powerful appeal that it has moved beyond an exclusive focus on packaging and is now expanding to include the products themselves. In 2002 the European Union passed a law that makes manufacturers financially responsible for recycling the appliances they produce. In 2004 The European Union's waste and electronic equipment (WEEE) directive came into effect, making it the responsibility of the manufacturers and importers in EU states to take back their products and to properly dispose of them.

Sources: A. S. Rousso and S. P. Shah, "Packaging Taxes and Recycling Incentives: The German Green Dot Program," *National Tax Journal* Vol. 47, No. 3 (September 1994): 689–701; Meagan Ryan. "Packaging a Revolution," *World Watch* (September–October 1993): 28–34; and Christopher Boerner and Kenneth Chilton, "False Economy: The Folly of Demand-Side Recycling," *Environment* Vol. 36, No. 1 (January/February 1994): 6–15; R. Widmer, H. Oswald-Krapf, D. Sinha-Khetriwal, M. Schnellmann, H. Boni, "Global Perspectives on E-waste," *Environmental Impact Assessment*, 25 (2005): 436–458.

While governments now regulate landfills to protect public safety, these regulations rarely eliminate all unpleasant aspects of these landfills for the host communities. As a result, many communities are all for the existence of these facilities as long as they are not located in their community. If every community feels this way, locating new facilities can be difficult, if not impossible.

One technique for resolving this problem relies on the imposition of host fees. *Host fees* compensate the local community (and sometimes surrounding communities) for accepting the location of a waste facility within their community. This approach not only gives local communities veto power over the location, but it also attempts to share the benefits of the regional facility in such a way that makes the net benefits sufficiently positive for them that the communities will accept the facility.

In one example Porter (2002) reports that a host fee agreement between Browning Ferris Industries and the township of Salem, Michigan, involves sharing with the town 2.5 percent of all landfill revenues and 4 percent of all compost revenues. The town also shares in the revenues derived from the sale of landfill gases (used for energy) and it can use the site free of charge for all town refuse, without limit on volume. These benefits are estimated to be worth about $400 per person per year, apparently enough to overcome local opposition.

Host fees are not a perfect resolution of the siting problem. Note, for example, that the fact that Salem can dispose of its waste free of charge provides no incentive for source reduction. In addition, it is important to ensure that the location of these facilities does not raise environmental justice concerns. At a minimum, the local community has to be fully informed of the risks it will face from a regional sanitary landfill and must be fully empowered to accept or reject the proposed compensation package. These preconditions frequently did not exist in the past.

Special Policies Targeted at Hazardous Waste

Because hazardous wastes are more dangerous to handle and to dispose of, special policies have been designed to keep those dangers efficiently low. The statutes have evolved over time in response to particular toxic substance problems. Each time a new problem surfaced and people were able to get legislators aroused, a new law was passed to deal with it. The result is a collage of laws on the books, each with its unique focus. We cover only the main ones here.

Resource Conservation and Recovery Act. To counteract the unsafe dumping of toxic wastes, Congress passed Subtitle C of the Resource Conservation and Recovery Act. This Act imposes standards for handling, shipping, and disposing of toxic wastes.

The regulations implementing this Act define hazardous waste and establish a cradle-to-grave management system, including standards for generators of hazardous wastes, standards for transporters, and standards and permit requirements for owners and operators of facilities that treat, store, or dispose of hazardous wastes.

The centerpiece of this rather large regulatory system is a manifest system for keeping track of the fate of the substances from their creation to their disposal. Waste generators are required to prepare a manifest for all controlled substances. If the substance is on the EPA list, it must be properly packaged and labeled, and must be delivered only to a permitted waste disposal site. Through this recording system, the EPA hopes to monitor all hazardous substances and detect any surreptitious dumping. Failure to comply with the Act is punishable by civil penalties and, in certain cases, by fines and imprisonment.

This Act was amended by the Hazardous and Solid Waste Amendments of 1984. The 1984 amendments contain three major categories of changes: (1) they expanded the amount of waste covered by the regulations; (2) they limited or, in some cases, banned the use of land disposal for certain kinds of waste; and (3) they regulated some activities not previously controlled, such as underground storage tanks for certain chemicals.

Toxic Substances Control Act. The Toxic Substances Control Act was passed as a complement to the Resource Conservation and Recovery Act. Whereas the Resource Conservation and Recovery Act was designed to ensure safe handling and disposal of existing substances, the Toxic Substances Control Act was designed to provide a firmer basis for deciding which of the chemical substances not controlled by the existing acts should be allowed to be commercially produced.

This Act requires the EPA to inventory the approximately 55,000 chemical substances in commerce, to require premanufacture notice to the EPA of all new chemical substances, and to enforce record-keeping, testing, and reporting requirements so that the EPA can assess and regulate the relative risks of chemicals. At least 90 days before manufacturing or importing a new chemical, a firm must submit test results or other information to the EPA showing that the chemical will not present "an unreasonable risk" to human health or the environment.

On the basis of the information in the premanufacture notification, the EPA can limit the manufacture, use, or disposal of the substance. The Act is significant in that it represents one of the few instances where the burden of proof is on the manufacturer who must prove that the product should be marketed, rather than forcing the EPA to show why it should not be marketed.

Comprehensive Environmental Response, Compensation, and Liability Act. Known popularly as the *Superfund Act,* the Comprehensive Environmental Response, Compensation, and Liability Act created a fund to be used to clean up existing toxic waste sites.

As amended, this Act authorized federal and state government to respond quickly to incidents such as occurred in Times Beach, Missouri. Times Beach, a town of 2,800 residents located about 30 miles southwest of St. Louis, had been contaminated by dioxin, a waste by-product created during the production of certain chemicals. One such chemical is Agent Orange, the defoliant used during the Vietnam War. The contamination occurred when a state oil hauler bought about 55 pounds of dioxin in 1971 from a now defunct manufacturer, mixed it with oil, and, under contract with the local government, spread it on unpaved roads as a dust control measure. On December 23, 1982, after soil tests revealed dangerous levels of dioxin, the Centers for Disease Control recommended total evacuation of the town.

By February 22, 1983, the federal government had authorized a transfer of some $33 million from the Superfund to cover the cost of buying out all businesses and residents and relocating them. For its part, the state of Missouri agreed to pay 10 percent of the cost—$3.3 million—into the Superfund, and fund representatives could attempt to recover damages from the responsible parties. Federal and state agencies then burned more than 265,000 tons of contaminated soil. In 1999 the state of Missouri opened Route 66 State Park on the site and it has been removed from the Superfund list.

The existence of the Superfund allows the governments involved to move rapidly. They are not forced to wait until the outcome of court suits against those responsible in order to raise the money nor are they forced to face the uncertainty associated with suits' ultimate success or failure.

In addition to programs that focus on setting standards, another set of policies emphasizes the strategic use of information to inform and motivate change.

The Toxic Release Inventory Program. The *Toxic Release Inventory (TRI)* was enacted by the U.S. Congress in January 1986 as a part of the Environmental Protection and Community Right to Know Act (EPCRA). It is designed to inform the public about releases of toxic substances into the environment. Most of the substances involved are not subject to release standards.

TRI states that firms with 10 or more full-time employees that use 10,000 pounds or more of a listed chemical in a given calendar year, or firms that import, process, or manufacture 25,000 pounds or more of a listed chemical must file a report on each of the chemicals in existence within the plant.

Public reporting of emissions or use of listed chemicals is accomplished annually. (For the data see http://www.epa.gov/tri/.) The reports include such information as the name of the company, name of the parent company if it exists, toxic release and frequency of release, as well as the medium in which the chemical is released. Firms must also report emissions to their state and local authorities as well as fire and emergency officials.

Has TRI reduced toxic emissions into the environment? The EPA's annual reports reveal that substantial reductions have occurred. Although careful examination of the filings (e.g., Natan and Miller, 1998) have found that some of these reductions merely reflect a change in definition, other reductions have been found to be genuine. Apparently the reported magnitude of the reductions is overstated, but real reductions have occurred.

The 33/50 Program. To complement and reinforce the TRI Program, the EPA initiated the *33/50 Program* in February 1991. This program set national goals of 33 percent reduction in 17 priority toxic chemicals by 1992, and 50 percent reduction by 1995. The reductions were to be achieved voluntarily by program participants; compliance with the guidelines was measured using the TRI reports.

The 33/50 Program emphasized pollution prevention rather than end-of-pipe control. The initial invitation list, which contained the names of 555 companies with substantial chemical releases, was subsequently expanded to 5,000. Some 1,300 corporations ultimately registered to participate. Participants collectively reduced their emissions by more than 50 percent, a total of 757 million pounds of pollutants, by 1994—a year ahead of schedule.

Can we learn anything about the kinds of firms that joined this voluntary program and what motivated them to do so? Arora and Cason (1996) attempted to isolate the factors that influenced a firm's decision to participate. The study found the following: (1) the largest firms with the greatest toxic releases were the most likely to participate, (2) firms apparently do not free ride on emission reductions prior to the program's initiation or participate to divert attention from poor compliance with other regulations, and (3) firms in industries with more contact with final consumers were more likely to participate in the program than firms that sell to other firms only.

Proposition 65. California's *Proposition 65*, an initiative overwhelmingly approved by voters in 1986, uses a different mandatory information approach as a regulatory strategy. Specifically, for any chemical that appears on a list of known carcinogens or reproductive toxicants, business must provide a "clear and reasonable" warning prior to "knowingly and intentionally" exposing any individual to a listed chemical. Exposures to products are covered as well as occupational and general environmental exposures. Proposition 65 only exempts exposures or discharges below a specified level (known as a "safe harbor" standard) defined by the statutes as exposures or discharges that "pose no significant risk" of cancer or that are below 1/1000 of the "no observable effect" level for reproductive toxicants.

Under the proposition, private citizens, other industry members, and environmental groups can sue companies that fail to notify people of exposure appropriately. Plaintiffs who make a successful legal claim can keep a substantial portion of the settlement; this encourages private enforcement of the law and reduces government monitoring. Industry members also have a strong incentive to monitor each other, so that one company does not cheat and look greener than its rivals.

Did this program change behavior? At least in controlling exposure to lead, it clearly did (see Example 19.6).

E-waste. States have begun to take some initiative. California passed a bill in 2003 that charges consumers a fee for buying computer monitors or televisions and pays recyclers to dispose of the displays safely when users no longer want them. In 2004 California passed a bill that makes it unlawful for retailers to sell mobile phones without the establishment of a collection, reuse, and recycling system for proper disposal of used cell phones This bill places the responsibility for recycling squarely upon the industry, but leaves the implementation details up to them. While this approach allows the industry to minimize recycling costs, it remains to be seen whether the resulting policy promotes reuse of the materials in a manner that is safe for human health and the environment. At least a dozen other states have passed e-waste laws since 2006. The California Advance Recycling Fee is one of the few that incorporates an economic incentive.[4]

---

[4]Current electronics recycling laws can be accessed at www.epa.gov and www.electronicsrecycling.com.

EXAMPLE
19.6

Regulating Through Mandatory Disclosure:
The Case of Lead

Rechtschaffen (1999) describes a particularly interesting case study involving how Proposition 65 produced a rather major reduction in the amount of lead exposure due to its success in promoting a considerable number of new technologies, production process change, and pollution prevention measures. He even goes so far as to suggest that Proposition 65 was apparently even more effective than federal law in addressing certain lead hazards from drinking water, consumer products, and other sources.

Rechtschaffen identifies several characteristics about Proposition 65 that explain its relative success. We mention two here.

First, despite periodic calls for such an integrated strategy, no coordinated federal approach to controlling lead hazards had emerged. Rather, lead exposures were regulated by an array of agencies acting under a multitude of regulatory authorities. In contrast, the Proposition 65 warning requirement applies without limitation to *any* exposure to a listed chemical unless the exposure falls under the safe harbor standard regardless of its source. Thus, the coverage of circumstances leading to lead exposure is very high and the standards requiring disclosure are universally applied.

Second, unlike federal law, Proposition 65 is self-executing. Once a chemical is listed by the state as causing cancer or reproductive harm, Proposition 65 applies. This contrasts with federal statutes, where private activity causing lead exposures is permitted until and unless the government sets a restrictive standard. Whereas under the federal approach, fighting the establishment of a restrictive standard made economic sense (by delaying the date when the provisions would apply) under Proposition 65 exactly the opposite incentives prevail. In the latter case, since the provisions took effect soon after enactment, the only refuge from the statute rested on the existence of a safe harbor standard that could insulate small exposures from the statute's warning requirements. For Proposition 65, at least some subset of firms had an incentive to make sure the safe harbor standard was in place; delay in implementing the standard was costly, not beneficial.

Source: Rechtschaffen, C. "How to Reduce Lead Exposure with One Simple Statute: The Experience with Proposition 65," *Environmental Law Reporter* 29, 1999: 10581–10591.

International Agreements

One of the toxic substances issues that erupted during the 1980s concerns the efficiency and morality of exporting hazardous waste to areas that are willing to accept it in return for suitably large compensation. A number of areas, particularly in poor countries, appeared ready to accept hazardous waste under the "right conditions." The right conditions usually involved alleviating safety concerns and providing adequate compensation (e.g., in employment opportunities, money, and public services) so as to make acceptance of the wastes desirable from the receiving community's point of view. Generally, the compensation required is less than the costs of dealing in other ways with the hazardous waste, so that the exporting nations find these agreements attractive as well.

A strong backlash against these arrangements arose when opponents argued that communities receiving hazardous waste were poorly informed about the risks they faced and were not equipped to handle safely the volumes of material that could be expected to cross international boundaries. In extreme cases, the communities were completely uninformed, as sites were secretly located by individuals with no public participation in the process at all.

The *Basel Convention* on the Control of Transboundary Movements of Hazardous Wastes and Their Disposal was developed in 1989 in order to provide a satisfactory response to these concerns. Under the Basel Convention, the 24 nations that belong to the Organization for Economic Co-operation and Development (OECD) were required to obtain written permission from the government of any developing country before sending toxic waste there for disposal or recycling. This was followed in 1994 by an additional agreement that completely prohibited the export of toxic wastes from any OECD country to any non-OECD country.

The Basel Convention regulates the international movement of electronic waste although not all countries have ratified this treaty. One component of the convention would prohibit the export of e-waste from developed to industrializing countries since, in addition to valuable materials, the waste contains hazardous materials such as lead and mercury.

In their analysis of trends of e-waste Widner et al. (2005) find that for countries such as China and India, e-waste is rapidly growing from both domestic sources and illegal imports. They also estimate that 50 to 80 percent of collected domestic e-waste from nonratifying Basel Convention countries, such as the United States, is shipped to China and other Asian countries. These countries are just beginning to impose laws to fight e-waste imports, but enforcement is lacking and the valuable materials create a business opportunity (recall Table 19.1).

Summary

Market mechanisms typically create pressures for recycling and reuse that are generally in the right direction, although rarely of the correct intensity. Higher disposal costs and increasing scarcity of virgin materials create a larger demand for recycling. For some products, such as copper and aluminum, this process is already in full swing.

However, a number of imperfections in the market suggest that the degree of recycling we are currently experiencing is less than the efficient amount. Changing incentives can improve the situation.

Efficient disposal pricing must reflect the true marginal costs of disposal. As such efficient prices are set on a per unit volume basis and must reflect all the costs of environmental damage that results from disposal. Volume-based pricing and refundable deposit systems are two examples of strategies that move the balance between recycling and disposal in a more efficient direction.

In principle, these strategies could also provide incentives for manufacturers to design products that are easy to recycle. In practice, if that link does not work as well as expected, stronger strategies, such as the "take back" principle can be invoked.

Pricing strategies are also beginning to play a role in locating waste facilities. The "not in my back yard" effect can effectively limit the ability to place waste facilities anywhere. One key to resolving this conflict is to make it worthwhile for the local community to host such a facility.

One increasingly common way of getting closer to that goal is through the use of "host fees," which compensate towns for hosting the facilities. In this way the disposers pay the higher costs associated with finding an acceptable site and the host can receive sufficient benefits from hosting the site to make its location there politically feasible.

The efficient role of government in controlling hazardous substances ranges from providing proper incentives for reducing the amount of toxic substances in use, for recycling those that remain in use, and for informing those exposed to the remaining risks about the magnitude of those risks. It also has a responsibility for establishing safe processes for creating, handling, shipping, and disposing of hazardous substances and monitoring compliance with the established standards.

The weakness to date of these waste strategies, as evidenced by the limited use of recycled materials in making new products, is that they have not yet set the stage for what has been called the "cradle to cradle" ultimate vision for managing waste (McDonough & Braungart, 2002). According to this vision, to the extent possible waste, especially toxic waste, should be eliminated. Any residual that cannot be eliminated should either become an input to some process (treated as a raw material) or be biodegradable such that when it is returned to the earth it will simply become part of the soil.

Key Concepts

33/50 Program, *p.* 440
Basel Convention, *p.* 443
composition-of-demand effect, *p.* 426
host fees, *p.* 438
marginal disposal cost, *p.* 429
new scrap, *p.* 429
old scrap, *p.* 429

optimal recycling, *p.* 428
Proposition 65, *p.* 441
raw material subsidies, *p.* 431
refundable deposit system, *p.* 434
Superfund Act, *p.* 440
take-back principle, *p.* 437
Toxic Release Inventory (TRI), *p.* 440

Further Reading

Dinan, Terry. "Economic Efficiency Aspects of Alternative Policies for Reducing Waste Disposal," *Journal of Environmental Economics and Management* 25 (1993): 242–256. Argues that a tax on virgin materials is not enough to produce efficiency; a subsidy on reuse is also required.

Graham, John D., Laura C. Green, and Marc J. Roberts. *In Search of Safety: Chemicals and Cancer Risk* (Cambridge, MA: Harvard University Press, 1988). A detailed examination of the attempts to regulate two suspected carcinogens: benzene and formaldehyde.

Jenkins, Robin R. *The Economics of Solid Waste Reduction: The Impact of User Fees* (Cheltenham, UK: Edward Elgar, 1993). An analysis that examines whether user fees do, in fact, encourage people to recycle waste. Using evidence derived from nine U.S. communities, the author concludes that they do.

Kinnaman, T. C. and D. Fullerton. "The Economics of Residential Solid Waste Management," in *The International Yearbook of Environmental and Resource Economics 2000/2001.* T. Tietenberg and H. Folmer, eds. (Cheltenham, UK: Edward Elgar, 2000): 100–147. A survey of the economics literature that reviews trends in residential solid waste collection and disposal and the effectiveness of policies designed to combat inefficiencies.

McDonough, William and Michael Braungart. *Cradle to Cradle: Remaking the Way We Make Things* (New York: North Point Press, 2002. The authors envision a world where industrial processes are redesigned so they mimic natural processes—all waste becomes raw material for another process, be it part of nature or human.

Porter, Richard C. *The Economics of Waste* (Washington, DC: Resources for the Future, Inc., 2002). A highly readable, thorough treatment of how economic principles and policy instruments can be used to improve the management of a diverse range of both business and household waste.

Reschovsky, J. D. and S. E. Stone. "Market Incentives to Encourage Household Waste Recycling: Paying for What You Throw Away," *Journal of Policy Analysis and Management* 13 (1994): 120–139. An examination of ways to change the zero-marginal-cost-of-disposal characteristic of many current disposal programs.

Shapiro, Michael. "Toxic Substances Policy," in Paul R. Portney, ed., *Public Policies for Environmental Protection* (Washington, DC: Resources for the Future, 1990): 195–242. A comprehensive analysis of the U.S. statutes and implementation procedures used to combat environmental risks posed by toxic substances.

Additional References

Alberini, A. and D. Austin. "Accidents Waiting to Happen: Liability Policy and Toxic Pollution Releases," *Review of Economics and Statistics* 84 (2002) (4): 729–741.

Allen, J. et al. "Using Coupon Incentives in Recycling Aluminum: A Market Approach to Energy Conservation Policy," *Journal of Consumer Affairs* 27 (1993): 300–318.

Arora, S. and T. N. Cason. "Why Do Firms Volunteer to Exceed Environmental Regulations? Understanding Participation in EPA's 33/50 Program," *Land Economics* 72 (1996) (4): 413–432.

Conrad, K. "Resource and Waste Taxation in the Theory of the Firm with Recycling Activities," *Environmental and Resource Economics* 14 (1999) (2): 217–242.

Davis, Dechert W. and James L. Smith. "Environmental Liability and Economic Incentives for Hazardous Waste Management," *Houston Law Review* 25 (1988): 935–942.

Graham, M. and C. Miller. "Disclosure of Toxic Releases in the United States," *Environment* 43 (2001) (8): 8–20.

Grant, D. and A. W. Jones. "Are Subsidiaries More Prone to Pollute? New Evidence from the EPA's Toxic Release Inventory," *Social Science Quarterly* 84 (2003) (1): 162–173.

Hanley, Robert. "Pay-by-Bag Trash Disposal Really Pays, Town Learns," *The New York Times* (November 24, 1988): B1, B7.

Hong, S. and R. M. Adams. "Household Responses to Price Incentives for Recycling: Some Further Evidence," *Land Economics* 75 (1999) (4): 505–514.

Khanna, M. and L. A. Damon. "EPA's Voluntary 33/50 Program: Impact on Toxic Releases and Economic Performance of Firms," *Journal of Environmental Economics and Management* 37 (1999) (1): 1–25.

Khanna, M., W.R.H. Quimio, and D. Bojilova. "Toxics Release Information: A Policy Tool for Environmental Protection," *Journal of Environmental Economics and Management* 36 (1998) (3): 243–266.

Levinson, A. "Grandfather Regulations, New Source Bias, and State Air Toxics Regulations," *Ecological Economics* 28 (1999) (2): 299–311.

Marakovits D. M. and T. J. Considine. "An Empirical Analysis of Exposure-Based Regulation to Abate Toxic Air Pollution," *Journal of Environmental Economics and Management* 31 (1996) (3): 337–351.

Natan, T. and C. Miller. "Are Toxic Release Inventory Reductions Real?" *Environmental Science & Technology* 35 (1998) (5): 368–374.

Porter, Richard C. *The Economics of Water and Waste in Three African Capitals* (Aldershot: Ashgate Press, 1997).

Rechtschaffen, C., "How to Reduce Lead Exposure with One Simple Statute: The Experience with Proposition 65," *Environmental Law Reporter* 29 (1999): 10581–10591.

Shea, Cynthia Pollock. "Building a Market for Recyclables," *World Watch* (May–June 1988): 12–18.

Tietenberg, T. and D. Wheeler. "Empowering the Community: Information Strategies for Pollution Control," *Frontiers of Environmental Economics,* Folmer H., H. L. Gabel, S. Gerking, and A. Rose, eds. (Cheltenham, UK: Edward Elgar, 2001): 85–120.

U.S. Environmental Protection Agency. *Cleaning Up the Nation's Waste Sites: Markets and Technology Trends, 2004 Edition* (Washington, DC: USEPA, 2004) Report #68-W-03-038.

VanHoutven, G. L. and G. E. Morris. "Household Behavior under Alternative Pay-as-You-Throw Systems for Solid Waste Disposal," *Land Economics* 75 (1999) (4): 515–537.

Viscusi, W. Kip and Joseph E. Aldy. "The Value of a Statistical Life: A Critical Review of Market Estimates throughout the World," *Journal of Risk and Uncertainty* 27 (August 2003) (1): 5–76.

Discussion Questions

1. Glass bottles can be either recycled (crushed and melted) or reused. The market will tend to choose the cheapest path. What factors will tend to affect the relative cost of these options? Is the market likely to make the efficient choice?

2. In Europe conventional waste is primarily controlled by the centralized implementation of the "take back" principle whereas in the United States conventional waste management is primarily handled locally by means of disposal fees or deposit refund systems. Is one approach better than the other or is this a case where both have chosen the best policies for their unique circumstances?

3. Many areas have attempted to increase the amount of recycled waste lubricating oil by requiring service stations to serve as collection centers or by instituting deposit-refund systems. On what grounds, if any, is government intervention called for? In terms of the effects on the waste-lubrication-oil market, what differences should be noticed among those states that do nothing, those that require all service stations to serve as collection centers, and those implementing deposit-refund systems? Why?

4. "As society's cost of disposing of trash increases over time, recycling rates should automatically increase as well." Discuss.

5. Over the last several decades in product liability law, the court system has moved from a *caveat emptor* ("buyer beware") to *caveat venditor* ("seller beware") doctrine. In other words, the liability for using and consuming risky products has been shifted from buyers to sellers. Does this shift represent a movement toward or away from an efficient allocation of risk? Why?

6. Should it be illegal for the industrialized countries to ship their hazardous waste to the developing countries for disposal? Why or why not?

7. How should the public sector handle a toxic gas such as radon that occurs naturally and seeps into some houses through the basement or the water supply? Is this a case of an externality or not? Does the homeowner have the appropriate incentives to take an efficient level of precaution?

20

Development, Poverty, and the Environment

If there is any period one would desire to be born in, is it not the age of revolution when the old and the new stand side by side and admit of being compared? When the energies of all men are searched by fear, and by hope? When the historic glories of the old can be compensated by the rich possibilities of the new era? This time, like all times, is a very good one, if we but know what to do with it.

—RALPH WALDO EMERSON, *The American Scholar* (1873)

Introduction

In previous chapters we invested a considerable amount of time and effort investigating individual environmental and natural resource problems and the policy responses that have been, and could have been, taken to solve them. In general, solutions are possible, and our economic and political institutions, with some exceptions, seem to be muddling through.

Our next step must be a consideration of the global economic system and the scale of the challenges it will face in this. Perhaps the major challenge is finding a way to deal effectively with global poverty without jeopardizing the environment or degrading the resource base passed on to future generations.

Poverty has emerged as one significant cause of environmental problems. The worst recorded air pollution is not found, as might be expected, in the highly industrialized cities of the high-income countries, but rather in the major cities of lower-income or rapidly developing countries. Deforestation is caused, in part, by the migration of landless peasants into the forests, seeking a plot of land to work. Soil erosion is caused, in part, when the poor are driven to farm highly erodible land to try to survive. Dealing effectively with these environmental problems and the human suffering that lies behind them will require raising living standards.

Traditionally, this has been accomplished through economic development.[1] One model for the development of the less industrialized countries is the path for rapid economic growth followed by the industrialized countries. This seems, at least initially, to be the model being followed by China and India as both experience very high rates of economic growth. How appropriate a model is this?

Examining the appropriateness of the traditional economic growth approach to development should start by understanding that approach and its success or lack of success as a means of eliminating poverty. We will begin by defining how economic growth takes place and how the growth process is affected by increasing resource scarcity and rising environmental costs. This understanding will then be used to characterize what changes in the growth process in the industrialized nations can be expected in the future.

The relationship between growth and development in the industrialized countries is then explored. Has growth increased the well-being of the average citizen in the developed countries? Or has the evident elevated consumption of material goods made possible by economic growth merely masked large offsetting problems that would cause an appropriately measured standard of living to go down, not up?

The fate of the average citizen, of course, does not always shed light on the fate of the poor. How have the poor fared in periods of rapid economic growth? Is John Kennedy's metaphor "A rising tide lifts all ships" apt, or does a rising tide leave more people treading water?

Although the historical experience in the industrialized countries is revealing, the transferability of this experience into a third-world context is by no means obvious. To what extent can economic growth provide an answer to the crushing problems of poverty that infect the third world? What are the barriers to achieving increased standards of living for the poor in third-world countries in a finite world?

● The Growth Process

The Nature of the Process

How does economic growth occur? It occurs in two main ways: (1) through increases in inputs (e.g., capital, labor, energy, and other resources) and (2) through increases in the productivity of those inputs (or resources) as a result of technological progress. The former source of growth involves increasingly greater outputs, given the state of the art in production, whereas the latter source involves improvements in the state of the art.

Increases in Inputs. The amount of growth occurring from increases in inputs is governed by two important economic concepts: (1) economies of scale and (2) the law of diminishing returns. The term *economies of scale* refers to the amount of increase in output obtained when all inputs

---

[1]Herman Daly's useful distinction between growth and development is employed here. *Development* refers to a qualitative increase in well-being, whereas *growth* refers to a physical expansion in physical output of goods and services. They are related, but by no means synonymous, concepts. It is conceptually possible to have growth without development and development without growth, but historically the two have been inextricably entwined (see Daly and Cobb [1989]).

are increased in the same proportion. The *law of diminishing returns* governs the relationship between inputs and outputs when some inputs are increased and others are held fixed.

The law of diminishing returns governs what happens when some, but not all, of the inputs are increased. Suppose, for example, that all the inputs are held fixed except for capital, which increases. As constant and successive increments of capital are added to the other fixed resources, the law of diminishing returns implies that eventually a point will be reached where each increment of input will produce smaller and smaller increments of output.

Technological Progress. The other major source of growth, technological progress, involves the implementation of better, less wasteful ways of doing things. With technological progress, growth can occur even in the absence of increases in inputs simply because the inputs available are used more effectively. For example, with a new production technique, less energy might be wasted or fewer resources used to make a particular product.

Potential Sources of Reduced Growth

Historically, increases in factor inputs and technological progress were both important sources of growth. This does not automatically mean that they will continue to provide growth at historic levels in the future, however. A number of reasons suggest caution in extrapolating historically valid arguments into the future.

Reduced Input Flows. Not all input flows are continuing at historic levels. Population growth has slowed considerably in most countries, which causes the growth in the labor force to slow and possibly stop. The growth fed by increasing labor is diminishing and will continue to diminish in the future.

The cost of energy and of raw materials seems to be rising, even in real terms. Producers respond to higher relative prices by cutting back on the use of these inputs, which diminishes their contribution to the growth process.

Capital formation has played a pivotal role in the past and is likely to continue doing so.[2] As workers were given more sophisticated capital equipment to work with, their productivity increased.

Capital has broken down the barriers imposed by human limitations. With the advent of bulldozers, earth moving, once limited by the strength and endurance of workers, is no longer limited. The size of the market, once limited by the time and effort required to transport commodities in a horse and buggy, expanded with the advent of the railroad, the truck, and the airplane. Limits on corporate controllability imposed by the size and competence of record-keeping staffs—as they attempted to stay on top of the information and paper flows—have expanded in the face of computers that can provide instant access to important information compiled in the most useful format.

Although capital is a reproducible asset, some indirect limits may diminish its role in the future. These include limitations on capital's substitutability for other factors, on the productivity of future investment, and on the incentive to invest.

---

[2]One of the most sophisticated studies to date on the determinants of U.S. economic growth during 1948–1979 finds capital formation to be the dominant force (Jorgenson et al., 1988).

The ability of capital to promote historical growth rates lies, in part, in its ability to substitute for those factor inputs that are experiencing limits. When substitution is easy, scarcity of particular inputs should not inhibit growth, but when substitution is difficult, scarcity imposes a drag on growth.

The first substitution possibility to be considered is between capital and labor. As population growth dwindles, the growth rate in the supply of labor diminishes as well. Historically, the economic growth rate has exceeded the growth rate of labor supply, as capital was continually substituted for labor. Most studies of production have found the *capital-labor relationship* to be quite strong; they are substitutes for one another. When we think about the modern manufacturing sector, this seems quite reasonable. Therefore, dwindling population, by itself, doesn't seem a particularly large barrier.

Describing the substitution possibilities for other resources, however, becomes more complex. Studies of the *capital-energy relationship* over time in the United States have found that capital and energy are complements, rather than substitutes. Complementarity also seems to characterize the rapid industrialization in China. Thus, in both cases capital and energy have together substituted for labor and other resources—but not for each other. If one thinks of the tractor, the bulldozer, and the airplane, this seems like a natural finding.

The question of interest is whether capital and energy will remain complements in the future or whether substitution of capital for energy might be possible. This is an especially important question in light of the links between fossil fuel energy use and global warming. If the attack on global warming includes a reduction in the use of fossil fuel energy and capital is a complement of energy, global-warming strategies would have the side effect of reducing the rate of capital formation.

In some energy uses, substitution of capital for energy is clearly feasible, because energy-saving equipment, such as computer-controlled heating and cooling, already exists. Furthermore, some capital investments will clearly hasten the transition to passive solar energy, which conserves energy by making better use of what is available.

In other sectors, such as transportation, the substitution possibilities are not quite as obvious, but that does not mean they do not exist. One obvious substitute for personal transportation is the bicycle (heavily used in many European countries), as are cars powered by solar energy. To some extent, communication can even substitute for transportation, as more people use home-based computers and phones to do their jobs without leaving home. Although our historical experience would suggest limited substitution possibilities, it is not at all clear that this experience is relevant for the future. Some drag on economic growth from higher energy prices appears likely.

The second possible source of growth drag relates to the future productivity of capital. As pollution concentrations rise, the amount of resources committed to combating pollution also rise. A substantial proportion of new plant and new equipment expenditures is being allocated to pollution control. Unlike conventional investments, however, these investments do not cause more goods to be produced; they produce a cleaner environment. Because the value of this cleaner environment is not usually recorded in the conventional measures of economic output, conventionally measured output should rise more slowly as a large proportion of inputs is diverted from productivity enhancement to environment enhancement.

The final source of drag concerns the incentive to invest. The amount of capital investment should depend upon the rate of return on that investment. The more profitable the investment, the larger the amount undertaken. Yet we have already identified two related factors that reduce the rate of return on investments—the regulatory bias against new sources and the composition of investment. By focusing on new sources, the regulatory system diminishes the relative profitability of new investment while enhancing the profitability of existing capital stock. This new source bias diminishes the incentive to invest in new capital. Meanwhile, the large proportion of new plant and new equipment expenditures going for pollution control tends to diminish the profitability of those expenditures being made, because improvements in the environment do not, in general, add to profits.

In sum, it appears that expecting increases in capital to completely compensate for reduced flows of other inputs would be risky. Some important transitions are occurring. Although they do not imply a cessation of growth catastrophically or otherwise in the near future, these transitions certainly suggest some diminution in the rate of economic growth resulting from reduced factor-input flows.

Limits on Technological Progress. Can technological progress take up the slack? If technological progress is to compensate for declining input flows, an increase in the rate of technological progress must occur. Is that likely?

Some observers are beginning to suggest that the degree to which technological progress can continue to play its historic role as a growth stimulant may be limited. Some of these limits are perceived as institutional and a matter of choice; others are perceived as natural and inexorable.

The new-source regulatory bias in pollution control policy provides an example of an institutional limit. Because most technological progress bears fruit when it is embodied in new or modified production facilities, this new source bias inhibits technological progress by reducing the number of these facilities.

Another institutional barrier is the decreasing commitment of resources to basic research, particularly by the public sector. Because basic research is frequently a precursor for technological progress, this trend could also diminish the rate of technological progress.

The Natural Resource Curse

A final, especially intriguing, possible source of growth drag might pose special problems for resource abundant nations. Common sense suggests that those countries blessed with abundant resource endowments would be more likely to prosper. In fact, the evidence suggests the opposite—resource abundant countries suffer the *natural resource curse* and are less likely to experience rapid development (see Example 20.1).

Energy

A second possible source of growth drag is energy. Because large price increases occurred during 1973–1974, this period provides a unique opportunity to study the magnitude of the growth-inhibiting effects of energy.

What should we expect to find? Because energy and capital historically have been complements, we should find that price increases would slow down capital formation. At the same time, the fact that energy and labor are substitutes would suggest that the use of labor should be rising, which, in turn, would cause the average productivity of labor to fall.

On a general level, the evidence is consistent with this set of expectations. Investment was lower, and the average productivity of labor fell. Work by Jorgenson (1981) and others, such as Uri and Hassanein (1982), confirms this impression.

The "Natural Resource Curse" Hypothesis

EXAMPLE
20.1

Perhaps surprisingly, the evidence that countries endowed with an abundance of natural resources as likely to develop less rapidly is quite robust. And it is not merely because resource-rich countries are subject to volatile commodity prices.

Why might a large resource endowment exert a drag on growth? Several possibilities have been suggested. Most share the characteristic that resource-rich sectors are thought to "crowd out" investment in other sectors that might be more likely to support development.

- One explanation, known popularly as the "Dutch Disease," is usually triggered by a significant increase in revenues from raw material exports. The resulting boom draws both labor and capital out of traditional manufacturing and causes it to decline.
- Another explanation focuses on how the increase in domestic prices that typically accompanies the resource boom impedes the international competitiveness of manufactured exports and therefore export-led development.
- A third explanation suggests that the large rents to be gained from the resource sectors in resource-abundant countries would cause entrepreneurial talent and innovation to be siphoned away from other sectors. Thus, resource-rich countries could be expected to have lower rates of innovation, which, in turn, results in lower rates of development.

While countries with large resource endowments may not have the significant opportunities for development that might have been expected, it is encouraging to note that lots of countries without large resource endowments have not been precluded from achieving significant levels of development.

Source: Sachs, J. D. and A. M. Warner, "The Curse of Natural Resources," *European Economic Review* 45(4–6), 2001: 827–838; Auty, R. M., *Sustaining Development in Mineral Economies: The Resource Curse Thesis* (London, UK: Routledge, Inc., 1993); and Kronenberg, T., "The Curse of Natural Resources in the Transition Economies," *Economics of Transition* 12(3), 2004: 399–426.

Focusing on the period 1973–1976, a time characterized by rapidly increasing energy prices, Jorgenson first examined the question of whether the decline in growth was due to declines in input growth or to declines in productivity. He found that input declines were much less significant than declines in productivity. He then attempted to discover the sources of this productivity decline by looking at the specific experience of 35 different industries.

Though a decline in economywide productivity could conceivably be caused either by a shift in resources from high-productivity industries to low-productivity industries or by a decline in productivity within each industry, Jorgenson found the latter to be far more important than the former. His analysis of the causes of these declines revealed that in 29 of the 35 sectors examined, technological change was biased toward the use of energy. This result suggests that from 1973 to 1976, productivity growth resulting from technological progress declined as energy prices rose.

One puzzle to be explained by those who believe energy prices have already played a significant role in productivity declines is how that could be so when the energy cost share is so small. Factors with small cost shares should, in general, have rather small effects on output.

One resolution to this puzzle seems consistent with the evidence. Berndt and Wood (1987) suggest that in the short run, the capital services provided by the capital stock are largely fixed, as are its operating characteristics. Once the capital stock is in place, the ratio of energy to capital services actually utilized is fixed. Dramatic changes in energy prices therefore affect the degree to which this capital is used, with the most energy-inefficient vintages being used least. By lowering the utilization of the existing capital stock, higher energy prices reduce total factor productivity.

In this story, the lower productivity does not necessarily persist. As long as new capital that uses less energy can be purchased, utilization rates rise, and productivity is restored as these new machines are installed. Once the stock of capital adjusts to the new regime of higher energy prices, productivity growth rebounds.

The key to thinking about the long run is to keep straight the differences between *ex ante* and *ex post substitution possibilities*. *Ex ante* refers to the time period prior to investment, whereas *ex post* refers to the time period after the equipment is installed. Limited *ex post* substitution possibilities, which seem to have played a significant role in the slowdown of productivity growth after the major energy price increases in the 1970s and in the early 1980s, do not automatically indicate that *ex ante* substitution possibilities will be small. It is the *ex ante* substitution possibilities that will determine the future of economic growth over the long run.

During the relatively robust U.S. economy of the 1990s, the surge of technical change in the form of the digital revolution was apparently very important in increasing labor productivity (Jorgenson et al., 2002). Was this surge in technical change promoted by the relatively low energy prices at the time, or independent of them? The energy price spikes in the first decade of the twenty-first century will provide a new source of variation to be analyzed once sufficient time has elapsed to assess their impact. Stay tuned!

Most visions of sustainable development suggest the need for increasing the efficiency with which energy is used. In practice, this means investing in energy conservation in order to make better use of a smaller fossil fuel energy flow. What employment and income effects can be expected from investments in energy conservation?

Geller et al. (1992) have investigated this question by constructing two quantitative scenarios: (1) a business-as-usual scenario and (2) a high-energy-efficiency scenario. The high-energy-efficiency scenario involves an additional annual investment of about \$49 billion in energy efficiency. They conclude that in addition to producing some rather dramatic reductions in pollutants (e.g., a 24 percent reduction in carbon dioxide), the high-energy-efficiency scenario results in both a rise in personal income (0.5 percent by 2010) and a net increase in jobs (an additional 1.1 million by 2010). The largest increases in jobs were estimated to occur in the construction, retail trade, and service industries, whereas the largest decreases were in the traditional energy-supply sectors. Other studies have found that transitioning from depletable to renewable energy sources is also likely to increase, rather than decrease, employment.

Environmental Policy

We have seen that pollution control laws impose large compliance costs on industry. These costs should have some effect on inflation (by boosting output prices) and employment, as well as on growth. The questions of interest are (1) how large those impacts have been and (2) how large they could be expected to be in the future.

Generally, studies suggest that the impact of environmental policy on the rate of inflation (measured by using the urban consumer price index) is very small, less than one-half of a percentage point. This should not be surprising, since pollution control expenditures make up only a small proportion of costs.

The effect on employment is particularly interesting because it requires balancing the losses experienced by firms that have become technologically obsolete with the gains to firms that are now producing for new markets (e.g., the market for pollution control equipment). The evidence suggests that the gains to those producing the equipment more than offset the losses to those installing the equipment, resulting in more, not less, employment in the economy as a whole (Goodstein, 1996).

The employment impacts of environmental policy are complex. Some evidence suggests that environmental spending costs jobs, while other analysis suggests that environmental spending may actually promote job growth. As Debate 20.1 points out, both may be right depending on how the employment effects of environmental policy are measured.

However, positive prognoses for the impact of environmental policy on employment should not obscure the problems. Gains in employment generally benefit a different set of workers than do losses. New jobs are rarely in the same location as those lost and, rarely involve the same skill levels. Even when overall employment effects are positive, the rising costs of environmental control could cause severe localized problems.

How much responsibility for the slowdown in productivity in the 1970s can be attributed to environmental policy? Using comparative data from the United States, Canada, and the former West Germany, Conrad and Morrison (1989) found that only a small part was the result of diverting investments toward environmental control. In fact, some government requirements to install cleaner equipment may have raised productivity by forcing firms to invest in newer and more efficient equipment. For industries in the United States, a common finding seems to be that somewhere in the neighborhood of 12 percent of the responsibility of the productivity slowdown can be attributed to environmental regulations. If these conclusions are at all accurate, environmental policy does not bear responsibility for much of the decline in the economic growth rate in the late 1970s.

Outlook for the Near Future

Some of what the future holds for the United States and other developed countries is becoming clear. Because we are in a period of transition, some striking differences between our experiences in the recent past and what we will encounter in the near future are emerging. Though a detailed examination would be beyond the scope of this study, the following discussion will highlight some of the emerging changes.

DEBATE 20.1

Jobs Versus the Environment: Which Side Is Right?

The employment effects of environmental regulation are a hot political topic. Public opinion surveys show strong support for measures intended to produce a cleaner environment, but workers often feel that these measures threaten their jobs.

Is their anxiety justified? Theory tells us that regulation can reduce employment by raising marginal costs and decreasing sales; it also tells us that environmental regulation can increase employment by creating a demand for workers to monitor and maintain pollution control equipment. How important are these conflicting tendencies?

Debates over environmental regulations frequently boil down to whether or not companies having to install abatement technologies will have to cut jobs in order to pay for the cleanup. Anticipated job losses can sway voters and legislators toward imposing more lenient standards.

Morgenstern et al. (2002) examine the jobs-versus-the-environment argument for four industries: pulp and paper mills, plastic manufacturers, petroleum refiners, and iron and steel mills. They find that increased stringency of environmental policies does not cause significant job loss.

Key to this study is the measurement of job loss. Environmental regulations can cause displacement of workers from their current jobs, but they also can create jobs in pollution abatement. Some industries may lose while others gain. Thus, gross job loss figures for the nation as a whole, which net out the gains and losses across industries, may camouflage the fact that some industries have been hit particularly hard. Gross job changes for the nation as a whole and net job loss within the industry are both relevant, but they have different social implications.

Using the Longitudinal Research Database collected by the U.S. Census Bureau, the Pollution Abatement Cost and Expenditure Survey, and the Manufacturing Energy Consumption Survey, Morgenstern et al. (2002) estimate the net job effect from regulation as between 2.8 jobs lost and 5.9 jobs gained per $1 million of regulatory expense. Nationally, the average gross job effect is a net gain of 1.5 jobs per $1 million in additional abatement spending (across the four industries).

Assessing the results, the authors suggest that, however measured, only a small portion (2 percent) of job decreases in manufacturing can be attributed to environmental regulation (14,000 of the 632,000 jobs lost between 1984 and 1994). Additionally, environmental spending may have created 29,000 jobs during the same time period.

While this study does not solve the entire debate, it certainly sheds some light on the issue. Policymakers should not only examine potential job losses, but also potential job shifts and gains from environmental spending.

Source: Richard D. Morgenstern, William Pizer, and Jhih-Shyang Shih. "Jobs Versus the Environment: An Industry-Level Perspective," *Journal of Environmental Economics and Management* 43, 2002: 412–436.

Population Impacts

The dramatic fall in fertility rates experienced by most countries of the world will have a profound impact on productivity and well-being. Inevitably, the average age of the population will rise, putting pressure on social security systems. Because the United States relies on an unfunded social security system, current payments to retirees are financed out of current payments by workers. As long as the population is growing, the ratio of workers to retirees remains high enough to provide adequate benefit levels for retirees without putting excessive strain on current workers. When population growth declines, however, as is now happening, the ratio of workers to retirees declines as well. To keep the system solvent, benefit growth has to decline and/or worker payments have to increase.

Studies by economists and demographers suggest that labor-market implications of declining population growth will be significant. One very positive effect will be a reduction in the unemployment rates of young adults. As fewer young, inexperienced workers enter the labor market, it will be easier to absorb those who do.

As a result of declines in population growth, the labor force will not grow as much as it has historically; this will create some upward pressure on wages. These higher wages should reinforce and support the rising participation rates for women and should entice older workers to stay in the workforce longer. In turn, these enhanced job opportunities for women should keep the fertility low, reinforcing the tendency for low rates of population growth.

Periods of tight labor markets should also have an equalizing effect on the income distribution.

The Information Economy

The importance of capital and resources in the U.S. economy is a product of the industrial revolution, which ushered in an era of mass production where manufacturing replaced agriculture as the dominant source of employment and earnings. This transformation depended upon massive amounts of capital investment, and the scale of operations it brought about consumed large amounts of resources.

It now seems clear that the economy is in the midst of an equally important transformation from an industrial society to an economy based on information. The key elements of this transformation are a change from a goods-producing to a service economy, a rise in the importance of theoretical knowledge as a source of growth, and an increasing reliance on information processing.

Until 1905 agricultural workers outnumbered industrial, service, and information workers. Industrial workers became the dominant force for the next 50 years. By 1955 information workers already made up the largest category.

This transformation has profound implications for our society. Computer-controlled technology has stepped in to fill the slots vacated by lower population growth in a direct substitution of capital for labor. Working at home has become possible for larger numbers of people as computer communication provides a substitute for transportation. Such changes can boost productivity while reducing pollution and our dependence on raw materials and energy. Can intelligence eventually replace oil as the prime mover of the system?

Other effects of the information economy will directly affect environmental policy. The lower cost of gathering, storing, and structuring information as well as the lower cost of providing more universal access to it will enable a host of new disclosure strategies. These can serve to promote both efficient policy and environmental justice. New possibilities for quick and effective information sharing will streamline cooperation among governments and nongovernmental organizations as they jointly seek sustainable outcomes. Technology has facilitated information on the effects of pollution as well as facilitated incentives to reduce it. Imagine trading carbon allowances without computer technology! Better information technology also enhances monitoring and enforcement of environmental policies, historically one of the weak links. The new analytical techniques that are part and parcel of the information economy (such as geographic information systems) will be able to provide a better foundation for policy.

This vision suggests that in the future the demand for skilled labor will rise more rapidly than the demand for unskilled labor. Education will therefore grow in importance, not only as the means of providing that skilled labor, but also as the wellspring of ideas that fuel the new growth.

Better information technology is, however, a two-edged sword. Following the events of 9/11, it has become clear that better information technology has also made coordination easier for those seeking to destroy, rather than to build. In response to that threat, governments have allowed measures that significantly change the privacy border, a different, but nonetheless troubling threat. Information technology, it seems, is a mixed bag.

The Growth-Development Relationship

Has economic growth historically served as a vehicle for development? Has growth really made the average person better off? Would the lowest-income members of the United States and the world fare better with economic growth or without it?

These are difficult questions to answer in a way that satisfies everyone, but we must start somewhere. One appropriate point of departure is clarifying what we mean by *growth*. Some of the disenchantment with growth can be traced to how growth is measured. It is not so much that all growth is bad, but rather that increases in conventional indicators of growth are not always good. Some of the enthusiasm for zero economic growth stems from the fact that economic growth, as currently measured, can be shown to have several undesirable characteristics.

Conventional Measures

A true measure of development would increase whenever we, as a nation or as a world, were better off and decrease whenever we were worse off. Such a measure is called a *welfare measure*, and no existing *conventional measure* is designed to be a welfare measure.

What we currently have are *output measures*, which attempt to indicate how many goods and services have been produced, not how well-off we are. Measuring output sounds fairly simple, but in fact it is not. The measure of economic growth with which most are familiar is based upon the GDP, or gross domestic product. This number represents the sum of the outputs of goods and services in any year produced by the economy. Prices are used to weigh the importance of these goods and services in GDP. Conceptually, this is accomplished by totaling the value added by each sector of the production process until the product is sold.

Why weight by prices? Some means of comparing the value of extremely dissimilar commodities is needed. Prices provide a readily available system of weights that takes into account the value of those commodities to consumers. From earlier chapters, we know that prices should reflect both the marginal benefit to the consumer and the marginal cost to the producer.

GDP is not a measure of welfare and was never meant to be one. One limitation of this indicator as a measure of welfare is that it includes the value of new machines that are replacing worn out ones rather than increasing the size of the capital stock. To compensate for the fact that some investment merely replaces old machines and does not add to the size of capital stock, a new concept known as *net domestic product (NDP)* was introduced. NDP is defined as the gross domestic product minus depreciation.

NDP and GDP share a deficiency in that they are both influenced by inflation. If the flow of all goods and services were to remain the same while prices doubled, both NDP and GDP would also double. Because neither welfare nor output would have increased, an accurate indicator should reflect that fact.

To resolve this problem, national income accountants present data on *constant-dollar GDP* and *constant-dollar NDP*. These numbers are derived by "cleansing" the actual GDP and NDP data to take out the effects of price rises. Conceptually, this is accomplished by defining a market basket of goods that stays the same over time. Each year, this same basket is repriced. If the cost of the goods in the basket went up by 10 percent, then, because the quantities are held constant, we know that prices went up by 10 percent. This information is used to remove the effects of prices on the indicators; remaining increases should be due to an increased production of goods and services.

However, this correction does not solve all problems. For one thing, not all components of GDP contribute equally to welfare. Probably the closest component we could use in the existing system of accounts would be *consumption*, the amount of goods and services consumed by households. It leaves out government expenditures, investments, exports, and imports.

The final correction that could easily be made to the existing accounts would involve dividing real consumption by the population in order to get *real consumption per capita*. This correction allows us to differentiate between rises in output needed to maintain the standard of living for an increasing population and rises indicating that more goods and services were consumed by the average member of that population.

Real consumption per capita is about as close as we can get to a welfare-oriented output measure using readily available data, but it is a far cry from being an ideal welfare indicator.

In particular, changes in real consumption per capita fail to distinguish between economic growth resulting from a true increase in income and economic growth resulting from a depreciation in what economists have come to call "natural capital"—that is, the stock of environmentally provided assets such as the soil, the atmosphere, the forests, wildlife, and water.

The traditional definition of *income* was articulated by Sir John Hicks (1947):

> *The purpose of income calculations in practical affairs is to give people an indication of the amount they can consume without impoverishing themselves. Following out this idea, it would seem that we ought to define a man's income as the maximum value which he can consume during a week, and still expect to be as well off at the end of the week as he was at the beginning.*

Although human-created capital (e.g., buildings and bridges) is treated in a manner consistent with this definition, natural capital is not. As human-created capital wears out, the accounts set aside an amount, called *depreciation*, to compensate for the decline in value. No increase in economic activity is recorded as an increase in income until depreciation has been subtracted from gross returns. That portion of the gains that merely serves to replace worn-out capital is not appropriately considered income.

No such adjustment is made for natural capital in the standard national income accounting system. Depreciation of the stock of natural capital is incorrectly counted as income. Development strategies that "cash in" the endowment of natural resources are, in these accounts, indistinguishable from development strategies that do not depreciate the natural capital stock; the returns from both are treated as income.

Consider an analogy. Many high-quality private educational institutions in the United States have large financial endowments. In considering their budgets for the year, these institutions take the revenue from tuition and other fees and add in some proportion of the interest and capital gains earned from the endowment. Except in extraordinary circumstances, however, standard financial practice does not allow the institution to attack the principal. Drawing down the endowment and treating this increase in financial resources as income is not allowed.

However, that is precisely what the traditional national accounts allow us to do in terms of natural resources. We can deplete our soils, cut down our forests, and douse ocean coves with oil, and the resulting economic activity is treated as income, not as a decline in the endowment of natural capital.

Because the Hicksian definition is violated for natural capital, policymakers are misled. By relying upon misleading information, policymakers are more likely to undertake unsustainable development strategies.

Adjusting the national income accounts to apply the Hicksian definition uniformly to human-made and natural capital could make quite a difference in resource-dependent countries. For example, Robert Repetto (1989) and colleagues of the World Resources Institute studied the growth rates of gross domestic product in Indonesia using both conventional unadjusted figures and figures adjusted to account for the depreciation of natural capital. Their study found that, whereas the unadjusted GDP increased at an average annual rate of 7.1 percent from 1971 to 1984, the adjusted estimates rose by only 4 percent per year.

Motivated by a recognition of these serious flaws in the current system of accounts, a number of industrialized countries have now proposed (or, in a few cases, have already set up) systems of adjusted accounts. Included among these countries are Norway, France, Canada, Japan, the Netherlands, Germany, and the United States. Significant differences of opinion on such issues as whether the changes should be incorporated in a complementary system of accounts or in a complete revision of the standard accounts remain to be resolved.

In the United States the Bureau of Economic Analysis has published its initial estimates of the value of the U.S. stock of minerals—oil, gas, and coal, as well as nonfuel minerals—and how the value of that stock (in constant dollars) has changed over time. The objective was to determine whether current use patterns are consistent with the constant-value version of the sustainability criterion. Declining values would indicate a violation of the criterion, whereas constant or increasing values would be compatible with it. In general, it found that the value of additions just about offsets the value of the depletion; for the period 1958–1991, its estimates suggest that the criterion was not violated. It is not possible to examine what has happened over time since these estimates fell victim to budget cutting and were discontinued.

Alternative Measures

Are we fulfilling the sustainability criterion or not? Although this turns out to be a difficult question to answer, a number of indicators have been designed to allow us to make some headway. These indicators differ in both their construction and the insights that can be derived from them.

Adjusted Net Savings. We begin with an indicator that attempts to provide an empirical method for judging whether or not we are fulfilling the weak sustainability criterion. Recall from Chapter 5 that a decline in total capital indicates unsustainability. This implies that net savings, which is the addition to the value of total capital, must be positive. Negative net savings implies the total capital stock has gone down, violating the weak sustainability criterion.

Adjusted net savings (formerly called "genuine savings") is the sustainability indicator that examines a net savings concept explicitly considering natural capital. Constructed by the Environmental Economics group of the World Bank, adjusted net savings estimates are derived by making four types of adjustments to standard national accounting measures of gross national savings:

1. Estimates of capital consumption of produced assets are deducted to obtain net national savings.

2. Current expenditures on education are added to net domestic savings as an appropriate value of investments in human capital (in standard national accounting these expenditures are treated as consumption).

3. Estimates of the depletion of a variety of natural resources are subtracted to reflect the decline in asset values associated with their extraction and harvest. Estimates of resource depletion are based on the calculation of resource rents. Rents are derived by taking the difference between world prices and the average unit extraction or harvest costs (including a 'normal' return on capital).

4. Pollution damages are deducted. Because many pollution damages are local in their effects, and therefore difficult to estimate without location-specific data, the estimates include only global climate change damages from carbon dioxide emissions.

What do these estimates show? Generally, adjusted savings indicate that some of the former Soviet Republics and countries in Sub-Saharan Africa and the Middle East are violating the weak sustainability criterion.[3] Higher income countries are generally estimated to be weakly sustainable because their savings and expenditures on education are large enough to offset declines in the value of natural capital.

Wealth Estimates. The World Bank has also begun collecting wealth estimates for a large group of countries. The wealth estimates include produced capital, natural capital, and intangible capital. This latter category includes human capital, institutions, and governance. For all countries, intangible capital makes up the largest component of wealth, but for the poorest developing countries, natural capital is also a significant component and is larger than produced capital.[4] Traditional measures of wealth may underestimate the significance of this fact, if sale of natural resources shows up as income.

---

[3]Up-to-date data can be found on the World Bank's Environmental Economics and Indicators Web site at: http://lnweb18.worldbank.org/ESSD/envext.nsf/44ByDocName/GreenAccountingAdjustedNetSavings.

[4]Details on this measure can be found at http://web.worldbank.org/WBSITE/EXTERNAL/TOPICS/ENVIRONMENT/ EXTEEI/0,,contentMDK:20487828~menuPK:1187788~pagePK:148956~piPK:216618~theSitePK:408050,00.html.

Genuine Progress Indicator. The *genuine progress indicator (GPI)*, developed and maintained by an organization called Redefining Progress in San Francisco, differs from adjusted savings in two main ways: (1) it focuses on an adjusted measure of consumption, rather than savings and (2) it includes many more categories of adjustments.[5]

The GPI adjusts national personal consumption expenditures in several ways. The most unique (and the most controversial) adjusts personal consumption expenditures for income distribution; more equal income distributions increase the GPI while less equal income distributions reduce it.[6] Using personal consumption expenditures adjusted for income inequality as its base, the GPI then adds or subtracts categories of spending based on whether they enhance or detract from national well-being. Examples of additions include the value of time spent on household work, parenting, and volunteer work and the value of services of consumer durables (such as cars and refrigerators) and services of highways and streets. Examples of subtractions include defensive expenditures (defined as money spent to maintain the household's level of comfort), security or satisfaction (such as personal water filters, locks, or security systems, hospital bills from auto accidents, or the cost of repainting houses damaged by air pollution), social costs (such as the cost of divorce, crime, or loss of leisure time), and the depreciation of environmental assets and natural resources (due to the loss of farmland, wetlands, and old-growth forests, the reduction of stocks of energy and other natural resources, and the damaging effects of wastes and pollution). In 2004 for example, $1.8 trillion is subtracted for cumulative carbon dioxide emissions. Per capita GDP in the United States was $36,595 while the per capita GPI was estimated to be $15,036 (2000$). While the GDP rose at approximately 3.8 percent per year between 1950 and 2004, the GPI rose at only 1.8 percent per year during this same time period.[7]

According to this indicator not only do traditional accounting measures such as the GDP considerably overstate the health of the economy, but also they camouflage the fact that per capita well-being has actually declined in several years since the 1970s. In those years, declines in income inequality and leisure time, coupled with increases in the costs of crime, pollution, and other social ills have more than offset the increases from larger levels of economic activity and increases in socially productive activities such as volunteerism.

Ecological Footprint. Another example of an indicator, the ecological footprint, differs considerably from the previous two in that it is based upon a physical measure rather than an economic measure. The *ecological footprint indicator* attempts to measure the amount of renewable and nonrenewable ecologically productive land area that is required to support the resource demands and absorb the wastes of a given population or specific activities.[8] The

---

[5]Details about this indicator, including the data and its calculation can be found on the Redefining Progress Web site at: http://www.redefiningprogress.org/.

[6]This step relies on the measure of inequality known as the *Gini coefficient*.

[7]Talberth, John, Clifford Cobb, and Noah Slattery (2006). "The Genuine Progress Indicator 2006. A Tool for Sustainable Development," http://www.rprogress.org/publications/2007/GPI%202006.pdf, redefining progress, accessed March 2009.

[8]The details about this indicator can also be found on the Redefining Progress Web site at: http://www.redefiningprogress.org/footprint/. Anyone can have his/her own ecological footprint calculated by answering a few questions at http://www.myfootprint.org/.

footprint is expressed in "global acres." Each unit corresponds to one acre of biologically productive space with "world average productivity." Each year has a specific set of equivalence factors since land-use productivities change over time. Deficits or surpluses can be uncovered by comparing this footprint to the amount of ecologically available land.

This indicator, like the others, departs from a calculation of national consumption, which is calculated by adding imports to, and subtracting exports from, domestic production. This footprint balance is computed for 72 categories including, for example, cereals, timber, fishmeal, coal, and cotton. The footprint (in terms of acres) for each category of resource use is calculated by dividing the total amount consumed in each category by its ecological productivity (or yield per unit area). In the case of carbon dioxide (CO_2) emissions, the footprint is calculated by dividing the emissions by the average assimilative capacity of forests to find the number of acres necessary to absorb the pollutants.

According to the ecological footprint indicator, the industrialized nations have the most unsustainable consumption levels (meaning that their consumption requires more ecologically productive land than is domestically available). This analysis also suggests that current global consumption levels cannot be sustained indefinitely by the current amount of ecologically productive land—the earth is estimated to be in a deficit situation.

The Human Development Index. One reason for dissatisfaction with all of these measures of well-being is the focus on an average citizen. To the extent that the most serious problems of deprivation are not experienced by the average member of society, this focus may leave a highly misleading impression about well-being. To rectify this problem, the United Nations Development Program (UNDP) constructed an alternative measure, the *human development index (HDI)*. This index has three major components: (1) longevity, (2) knowledge, and (3) income. Though highly controversial (because both the measures to be included in this index and the weights assigned to each component are rather arbitrary), the UNDP has drawn some interesting conclusions from the results of comparing HDIs among countries.

- The link between per capita national income and human development is not automatic; it depends on how the income is spent. Some relatively high-income countries (e.g., South Africa and the Persian Gulf states) do not fare as well as expected in human development terms, whereas some low-income countries (e.g., Sri Lanka and Cuba) were able to achieve a higher level of human development than would be expected, given their income level.

- Nonetheless, income is a major determinant of the capacity to improve human development. It is not a coincidence that the top five countries in terms of HDI (Canada, Norway, Sweden, Australia and the Netherlands) are all very-high-income countries.

A Summary of Alternative Measures. All of the alternative measures described above acknowledge and attempt to address flaws in the traditional measures of wealth. Each offers a potential contribution. However, some of the characteristics of the alternative measures rely on prices to weight their importance, but in many nonmarket circumstances those prices are difficult, but not impossible, to measure (see Chapter 3).

The estimation difficulties become most problematic in developing countries where nonmarket valuation methods have been utilized the least. Whittington (2002) offers some reasons why the contingent valuation studies that have been implemented in developing countries are unreliable. Suggesting that typical surveys are poorly administered and poorly crafted for the target audience, he goes on to recommend more research since the questions being addressed tend to be extremely important for policy and the cost of policy mistakes can be tragic in poor countries.

The preceding measures all suggest that intrinsic values are important. The ability to measure these values with some confidence is vital, but difficult.

Growth and Poverty: The Industrialized Nations

Conceiving of the growth-development relationship only in terms of the effects on the average citizen obscures a great deal of what may be happening in a society. Two societies may have the same per capita growth in average well-being, but if the fruits of this growth are shared uniformly in one and unequally in the second, it seems overly simplistic to argue that the increase in welfare levels would be the same in the two countries.

Although the evidence suggests that economic growth has improved the lot of the average citizen in the developed world, it tells us little about how the poorest members of society fare. To determine whether the poorest citizens also benefit from growth, we must dig deeper into the nature of the growth process.

One source of information about this relationship is history. To exploit that source, we will examine the data for a period of particularly high economic growth in the United States. Did it benefit the poor, or were they left behind?

The Effects on Income Inequality

Growth can help the poor in two main ways. First, it can provide more opportunity to earn income either by increasing the number of available jobs, by increasing the wages paid, or some combination of the two. Second, it is generally believed that income transfers are easier when the amount to be shared is growing. The donors can give up some of their gains and still be better off, whereas in a no-growth situation, any sharing must come from a reduction in the real income of the donors.

The experience from the United States suggests that periods of economic growth have reduced the degree of poverty. Although growth itself has been a factor, government transfers have made the most difference. Economic growth, in the absence of transfers, would not have lifted many persons from below to above the poverty threshold. The linkage between growth and the poor depends more upon its effect on the willingness to transfer than on direct market effects. Although growth cannot be seen as a vehicle that inevitably creates equality of income among the rich and poor, the evidence shows that, in the United States at least, the quality of life experienced by the poor has been improved by it. This improvement has come both from a general rising standard of living and a rise in transfers from the rich to the poor.

Poverty in the Developing Countries

Economic growth can be a vehicle for development, and this form of development can benefit the poor as well as the rich, according to the historical experience in the industrialized nations. Though the relationship between economic growth and poverty is neither inevitable nor universally effective, it does provide one possible path for dealing with poverty.

How relevant is this experience for developing countries? Is economic development solving the poverty problem?

In September 2000 the United Nations unanimously adopted the *Millennium Declaration,* which set a number of specific Millennium Development Goals. Among others, these goals call for the following:

* Reducing the proportion of people living on less than $1 a day to half the 1990 level by 2015; that is, reducing the number from 27.9 percent of all people in low- and middle-income economies to 14 percent

* Halving, between 1990 and 2015, the proportion of people who suffer from hunger

* Ensuring that by 2015 children everywhere (boys and girls alike) will be able to complete primary schooling

* Reducing by two-thirds the under-five mortality rate between 1990 and 2015

* Halting and reversing by 2015 the spread of HIV/AIDS

* Halving, by 2015, the proportion of people without sustainable access to safe drinking water and basic sanitation

* Achieving, by 2020, a significant improvement in the lives of at least 100 million slum dwellers

These goals serve as useful benchmarks for judging progress. What is the evidence?

According to the World Bank (2004) the proportion of people surviving on less than $1 a day dropped by almost half between 1981 and 2001, from 40 percent to 21 percent of the global population, but that is not near the goal of 14 percent. Furthermore, the progress that has been achieved has been uneven. While rapid economic growth in East and South Asia pulled over 500 million people out of poverty in those two regions alone, the proportion of poor grew or fell only slightly, in many countries in Africa, Latin America, Eastern Europe, and Central Asia. Only China seems to have made some progress toward meeting these goals.

Uneven regional progress is accompanied by uneven progress across the various hazards poor people face. Worldwide, for example, an estimated 840 million people, most of them in low-income countries, are chronically undernourished; economic growth, by itself, does not seem to resolve this problem. Despite impressive economic growth in South Asia, for example, that region still registers malnutrition among children that reaches almost 50 percent, along with chronically low school enrollment and completion rates. The World Bank reports that if current trends persist, by 2015 children in more than half of the developing countries will still not be on track to complete their primary education.

Public services in health, nutrition, and education often fail poor people. For example, in 20 developing countries where sufficient data for analysis is available, child mortality rates fell only half as fast for the poorest 20 percent of the population as for the population as a whole. In addition, HIV/AIDS has infected more than 60 million people worldwide. More than 95 percent of them are in developing countries, and 70 percent are in Sub-Saharan Africa.

The United Nations Millennium Development Goals Monitor contains interactive maps to track the progress of these goals.[9] Maps and data are available on poverty, education, child mor-

---

[9]http://www.mdgmonitor.org/map.cfm?goal=&indicator=&cd=.

tality, maternal health, disease, CO_2 emissions, land use, and development. Also found on this site are numerous success stories such as the introduction of NERICA or New Rice for Africa. NERICA is a hybrid between Asian and African rice that is high-yielding, drought resistant, and protein-rich. NERICA has contributed to food security and improved nutrition in several African countries.

While success stories are common, others are more pessimistic. Volatile food prices and rising energy costs will make meeting these goals by 2015 all the more difficult. For example, recall the discussion on ethanol production and food prices in Chapter 11. Developing countries are most sensitive to rising food prices and to volatility in prices. Elobeid and Hart (2007) examine the impact of ethanol expansion in the United States on agricultural prices and the resulting impacts on the global market for food. They find that for countries where corn is the major food grain, food basket costs rise the most. Countries in which rice is the major food grain have the lowest price increases and countries with wheat and/or sorghum as the major food grains fall in the middle. Recent dramatic fluctuations in food prices affect the rural poor disproportionately harder and create hardships in developing countries.

The Appropriateness of the Traditional Model

How appropriate is the traditional economic growth model for these countries? Does it point the way out of poverty?

Scale. One of the first indicators that traditional models may be inappropriate derives from the ecological effects of the proposed global scale of economic activity necessary to eradicate poverty if the model of development followed by the industrialized nations of Asia, Europe, and Africa were adopted by the rest of the world. As Jim MacNeill, the former director of the World Commission on Environment and Development, has stated,

> If current forms of development were employed, a five- to ten-fold increase in economic activity would be required over the next fifty years to meet the needs and aspirations of a population twice the size of today's … as well as to begin to reduce mass poverty.

Whether increases of this magnitude could be accomplished while still respecting the atmospheric and ecological systems on which all economic activity ultimately depends is not at all obvious.

Increased energy consumption to support new industry would add greenhouse gases. Increased refrigeration would add more of the gases depleting the stratospheric ozone level. The industrialized nations have freely used the very large capacity of the atmosphere to absorb these gases. Little absorptive capacity is left. Most observers seem to believe that in order to meet the challenge, we need to take an activist stance by controlling population, severely reducing emissions of these gases in the industrialized world, and discovering new forms of development that are sustainable.

Forms of Development. Economics can assist in the process of characterizing how the forms should differ. Appropriate development should capitalize on local strengths and stay away from weaknesses; it should be sensitive to factor prices.

Many, if not most, of the developing nations, are labor-surplus economies. It follows that their strategy for development, at least in the beginning stages, should be labor-intensive. Labor-

---

[10]Contrast this with capital-intensive processes, which use much less labor and distribute more of the returns to the owners of capital, who are typically well-off.

intensive processes serve the twin purposes of capitalizing on an abundant resource and providing a source of income to large numbers of people.[10]

Although the forms of development in the industrialized nations are increasingly going to rely on a highly skilled labor force, it is inappropriate for countries where the educational systems may not currently be able to supply sufficient numbers of skilled workers to fill the need. By effectively utilizing the low-skilled workforce, developing countries can increase their incomes, decrease population growth, and ultimately create the wealth needed to support strong education systems.

Development in the industrialized countries has also been very fossil-fuel-dependent. Although this may be appropriate when supplies of fossil fuels are plentiful and the remaining capacity of the environment to accept the by-product gases is unlimited, it is certainly less appropriate for a future plagued by diminishing supplies and global warming.

Barriers to Development

What are the barriers to raising standards of living in the third world? Rising populations face increasingly limited access to land, health services, education, and financial resources. Many of these problems are intensified by the current international economy. Heavy debt burdens, falling prices for exports, and the flight of capital that could be used to create jobs and income are all significant *barriers to sustainable development.*

Population Growth. Poverty begets poverty. The positive feedback loop between population growth and poverty is one powerful example. Population growth rates are typically higher— substantially higher—in low-income populations. High infant mortality causes parents to compensate with large numbers of births. Children provide one of the few available means of old-age security. Knowledge about birth control techniques is sparse, and the availability of contraceptives is limited. Women frequently have low levels of education, and in some cultures large families are the only possible way for women to achieve status. Larger populations, in turn, tend to increase the degree of poverty by lowering wages and by spreading the resources allocated to children over a larger number.

Population growth also puts increased pressure on the natural resource base. Pushing larger numbers of people onto marginal land increases soil erosion and deforestation. Increasing population density can cause the carrying capacity of the land to be exceeded. In parts of Africa where nomadic tribes have coexisted for centuries with a fragile ecosystem, larger populations and reduced mobility have resulted in such a serious deterioration of the ecosystem that it is no longer able to satisfy basic human needs.

Land Ownership Patterns. Pressures on the land arising from population growth are exacerbated by patterns of land ownership in many of the lower-income countries. In agricultural economies, access to land is a key ingredient in any attempt to eradicate poverty, but land ownership is frequently highly concentrated among a few extremely wealthy owners. Much of the undeveloped land that exists is ecologically valuable in its preserved state. Improvements in agricultural techniques can do little to raise living standards if peasants do not have access to their own land.

One common measure of the degree of inequality in land ownership is the Gini coefficient. The Gini coefficient can take on values of 0.0 (which would indicate perfect equality) to 1.0 (which would indicate perfect inequality). *Perfect equality* would occur if every farmer owned exactly the same amount of land. *Perfect inequality* would imply that all land was owned by a single farmer.

In Latin America, Gini coefficients in excess of 0.75 are common. This region has the most skewed land-ownership patterns on the globe, a legacy of colonial times when colonial rulers accumulated vast amounts of land. Asian nations are somewhat better, with Gini coefficients ranging from 0.47 to 0.64 and in Africa, where collective tribal land ownership is common, the coefficients fall between 0.36 and 0.55.

Lack of well-defined property rights for land and lack of good enforcement mechanisms are additional barriers that many developing countries face. Example 20.2 looks at a unique solution for the Los Negros Valley in Bolivia.

Trade Policies. Some of the barriers faced by developing countries as they attempt to raise living standards have been erected by the industrialized nations. Trade policies are one example. The terms of trade for many developing countries have deteriorated in the recent past.

EXAMPLE 20.2

Trading Water for Beehives and Barbed Wire in Bolivia

Amboro National Park in Bolivia is one of the most biologically diverse places on the world. The Park and surrounding areas are under intense pressure from illegal land incursions. Migrants from the surrounding highlands, with encouragement from local political leaders, extract timber from the park and clear areas for agriculture. Lack of well-defined property rights for local communities leaves few alternative options. Due to increased timber harvesting and increased agriculture, the Los Neros River dries up earlier than it did in the past, causing suffering among the local communities that depend on the river for irrigation.

Asquit (2006) describes a unique solution to this property rights problem involving payments for environmental services. Natura Bolivia, an environmental group, helped negotiate an agreement through which downstream water users would pay for the protection of native vegetation in the watershed. Instead of money as compensation though, payment would be in the form of one beehive and training in honey production per ten hectares of cloud forest protected. In 2003 60 beehives were provided to farmers in exchange for 600 hectares of cloud forest conservation. In 2004 the municipal government provided another 11 hives to farmers. By 2006 2,100 hectares had been protected.

The Los Negros scheme is slowly building a market for environmental services and helping to define property rights in the region. In 2006, when contracts were renewed, some farmers requested barbed wire instead of beehives in order to help them strengthen their land claims. Combining a market mechanism (payment for environmental services) with developing a local enforcement mechanism and strengthening local property rights has proven to be a successful scheme so far.

Source: Nigel Asquith, "Bees and Barbed Wire for Water on the Bolivian Frontier," PERC 24 (2006), December.

Some of the reasons for this deterioration are natural effects of markets rather than when the terms of trade deteriorate, exports from developing countries can purchase fewer imports misguided policies. Included in this category are the import substitutions in the industrialized world (e.g., when optical fibers are substituted for copper in phone lines) and lower demand for developing country exports triggered by lower economic growth in the industrialized countries.

Political factors are also important. When political forces in the developed countries conspire to eliminate or substantially reduce natural markets for the developing countries, these policies not only exacerbate the poverty in the developing nations, they have a direct degrading effect on the environment.

The Multi-Fiber Arrangement, originally implemented in 1974, is a case in point. Its effect has been to severely reduce developing-country exports of textiles and other products made from fibers. In developing countries, fiber products are produced by labor-intensive techniques, causing the employment impact to be high. For local sustainable agriculture, the opportunity to provide the fiber raw materials is another source of employment. By artificially reducing the markets for these products and the fibers from which these products are manufactured, the agreement has forced some nations to substitute resource-intensive economic activities, such as timber exports, for the more environmentally congenial fiber-based manufacturing in order to earn foreign exchange.

Agricultural trade flows not only demonstrate how price distortions can be translated into unsustainable development but also show how they can exacerbate poverty. In general, price distortions and artificially supported exchange rates have resulted in a pattern of trade that involves excessive agricultural production in the developed world and too little in the developing world. Agriculture in the developed world is supported by a number of different subsidies. In the developing world, the bias operates to promote underproduction rather than overproduction. Overvalued exchange rates increase the attractiveness of importing food and decrease the attractiveness of exporting food.

By discouraging small-scale agriculture in developing countries, an activity that would provide income to a segment of the population faced with the most severe forms of poverty, biased trade flows exacerbate the poverty problem. Furthermore, because income increases targeted on this particular group typically lead to slower population growth, even some of the population pressures on the environment could ultimately be related to biases in current trade patterns.

One common stereotype of the difference between developed and less-developed countries involves their respective supplies of minerals. According to this stereotype, less-developed countries control most of the world's mineral resources, and the developed world creates the demand for them. If accurate, this view would suggest that rising mineral prices would eventually create favorable terms of trade for most developing countries.

Unfortunately, upon closer inspection this stereotype represents, at best, an oversimplification. Although exports of minerals have increased from less-developed to developed countries, not all less-developed countries share these higher export levels. A few have large reserves of petroleum or nonfuel minerals, but most do not. The benefits from increasing mineral prices tend to bypass most less-developed countries.

Debt. Many third-world countries have staggering levels of debt to service.

Unfortunately, even private capital is flowing out of the capital-poor countries, where it is desperately needed, and into the capital-rich countries. The World Bank estimates that the stock of "flight" capital held abroad by citizens of severely indebted countries equals a significant fraction of those countries' external debt.

In periods of high real interest rates, servicing these debts puts a significant drain on foreign exchange of earnings. Using these foreign exchange earnings to service the debt eliminates the possibility of using them to finance imports for sustainable activities to alleviate poverty. One study found that, in all but one of the most indebted countries, the ratio of investment to GDP was substantially lower in the 1982–1988 period (when the debt burden was heaviest) than in the previous six years.[11] In Argentina the ratio fell from 25 percent to 15 percent, whereas comparable figures for Venezuela indicate a fall from 33 percent to 18 percent. This fall in investment has, in turn, reduced the growth of output and exports in debtor nations and, thereby, further undermined their ability to repay their debts.

With the notable exception of a relatively few oil-rich nations, most developing countries import a great deal of energy. Because this demand is relatively price inelastic, their expenditures on imports have risen tremendously, without similar compensating increases in receipts from the sale of exports.

The situation is reversed in many of the oil-exporting countries, which are commanding abnormally high prices for their oil. Their favorable terms of trade, however, have not always insulated them from development difficulties. Nigeria is a classic example. Buoyed by oil exports, the local wage structure and exchange rates ended up severely harming agricultural production. Resources flowed out of agricultural production and into oil production. Even the income distribution was adversely affected, becoming much more unequal. In recognition of the threat to development posed by debt the "Heavily Indebted Poor Countries (HIPC) Initiative" was established in 1996 as a joint collaboration between the World Bank and the International Monetary Fund. Its stated aim is to reduce the excessive debt burdens faced by the world's poorest nations.

As of September 2004, 27 countries were receiving debt relief under the initiative. HIPC relief, together with other debt-relief initiatives, represents a two-thirds reduction in the overall debt stock of these countries. Debt service-to-exports ratios have also been substantially reduced to an average of 10 percent, allowing more resources to be committed to public expenditures. As a result, poverty-reducing government spending is projected to rise from less than twice that of debt-service payments to almost four times. Poverty-reducing expenditures in the 27 countries currently receiving HIPC assistance increased from 6.4 percent of GDP in 1999 to 7.9 percent of GDP in 2003.[12]

The HIPC Initiative is not a panacea. Even if all of the external debts of these countries were forgiven, most would still depend on significant levels of external assistance. As a group their receipts from external assistance have exceeded their debt-service payment for many years. Example 20.3 revisits the Debt-for-Nature discussion from Chapter 12 to extract the effects of a large swap in Costa Rica.

The evidence suggests that, although growth is no panacea for the problems of the developing world, it is probably better than no growth. However, the traditional form of growth experi-

---

[11]"Debtors' Hangover," *The Economist* (May 20, 1989): 73.

[12]Up to-date information on this program is available at http://www.imf.org/external/np/exr/facts/hipc.htm.

Debt-for-Nature Revisited: The Nature Conservancy, the Tropical Forest Conservation Act, and Costa Rica

EXAMPLE

20.3

Debt-for-nature swaps were introduced in Chapter 13 as an innovative approach to conserving biodiversity by reducing the pressure on the forests caused by the international debt owed by many developing countries. The Nature Conservancy recently brokered a deal to protect six biodiversity rich regions of Costa Rica. Under the terms of this agreement, signed in October 2007, the United States will forgive $26 million in debt owed by Costa Rica. The money will be used to help finance forest conservation over the next 16 years.[13]

Costa Rica's tropical forests are rich in biodiversity and home to several endangered species including tree frogs, howler monkeys, jaguars, and scarlet macaws. These important habitats are under intense pressure from human activities including agricultural expansion, logging, mining development, and tourism. Local communities will be able to use funding from this swap to pursue sustainable and economically viable alternative livelihoods. This is the largest debt-for-nature swap to date under the U.S. Tropical Forest Conservation Act.

The Tropical Forest Conservation Act (TFCA) was "enacted in 1998 to offer eligible developing countries options to relieve certain official debt owed the U.S. government while at the same time generating funds in local currency to support tropical forest conservation activities. In addition to forest conservation and debt relief, TFCA is intended to strengthen civil society by creating local foundations to support small grants to NGOs and local communities. As of October 2006 12 TFCA agreements have been signed, which are expected to generate more than $135 million over the life of the agreements, for tropical forest conservation in 11 countries."[14]

Source: The Nature Conservancy, http://www.nature.org/wherewework/centralamerica/costarica/misc/art22576 .html; and USAID, http://www.usaid.gov/our_work/environment/forestry/tfca.html; both accessed March 2009.

enced in the industrialized countries is not likely to be the most appropriate form for the less-developed countries in the future. Circumstances have changed since the industrial revolution. Furthermore, the factor endowments in third-world countries are not the same as those in the industrialized countries. Changing circumstances call for changing approaches.

Natural Disasters. As the Asian tsunami in December 2004 demonstrated, natural disasters can deal a devastating blow to development. Not only were hundreds of thousands of people killed, but also the economic infrastructure (tourism, fishing, agriculture, and so on) on which the livelihoods of survivors depend was badly damaged or destroyed. While natural disasters cannot be controlled in the same way pollution is controlled, we are not powerless. For a given risk,

---

[13]Costa Rica owes approximately $90 million to the United States.

[14]http://www.usaid.gov/our_work/environment/forestry/tfca.html.

warning systems and disaster planning can help reduce the damage. The magnitude of the risk may also be lessened by reducing the vulnerability of populations. As the amount of available land decreases and the number of people to be accommodated grows, the tendency to exploit land with a higher vulnerability to natural disaster increases. Whether this is manifested as building on highly erodible hillsides that are susceptible to wild fires in California or farming the deltas that are vulnerable to storm surge in Bangladesh, human choices affect the magnitude of the risk. Population pressure makes risky choices more likely.

Summary

Historically, increases in inputs and technological progress were important sources of economic growth in the industrialized nations. In the future, some factors of production, such as labor, will not increase as rapidly as they have in the past. The effect of this decline on growth depends on the interplay among the law of diminishing marginal productivity, substitution possibilities, and technological progress. The law of diminishing marginal productivity suggests slower growth rates, but technological progress and the availability of substitution possibilities counteract this drag.

Our examination of empirical evidence suggests that currently increased environmental control has not had a large impact on the economy as a whole, although certain industries have been hit quite hard. Environmental policy has triggered only a small rise in the rate of inflation and a mild reduction in growth. Environmental policy has apparently contributed more jobs than it has cost.

The situation is similar for energy. Rather large increases in energy prices have occurred, but the portion of the slowdown in economic growth during the 1970s attributed to these increases is not large. Some diminution of growth has certainly occurred, but it seems premature to suggest that rising energy prices have already forced a transition to a period of substantially lower growth rates.

This is not to say, however, that the economy is not being transformed. It is. Two particularly important aspects of this transformation are (1) the decline in population growth and (2) the rise in the importance of information as a driving economic force. Both aspects tend to reduce the degree to which physical limits constrain economic growth and increase the degree to which current welfare levels are sustainable.

We have examined a series of indicators that attempt to shed light on the degree to which current national practices are sustainable. Although each of these indicators is incomplete and flawed to some degree, they all convey some important insights.

Because it is based on the weak sustainability criterion, which is limited in scope, the adjusted net savings indicator is not particularly helpful in validating a country's practices as sustainable. Yet this indicator can be helpful in identifying countries that are not sustainable (as well as the sources of their unsustainability), since failure of this weak test sends a powerful signal of serious problems. The fact that many of the countries failing this test are low-income countries reminds us that poverty can be both a cause and an effect of unsustainability.

The genuine progress indicator provides a helpful reminder that increases in traditional accounting measures, which are uniformly trumpeted in the press as evidence of "progress," may not represent an increase in well-being at all. Traditional accounting techniques measure economic activity, not well-being.

The ecological footprint provides a helpful reminder that scale does matter and the earth on which we all depend is ultimately limited in its ability to fulfill our unlimited wants. Though the Ecological Footprint calculation does not provide definitive proof that we have already exceeded the earth's carrying capacity, the calculation does lay to rest the naïve view that our ability to consume is limitless. It serves as a useful reminder that thinking about how to stay within those limits is crucial. The ecological footprint also points out that affluence is fully as big a challenge to sustainability as poverty is.

The human development index reminds us that the relationship between income growth and the well-being of the poorest citizens of the world is far from a certainty, in contrast to conventional wisdom. While income growth can provide the means for empowerment of the poor, it can only do so when accompanied by appropriate policy measures such as universal health care and education and limits on the perverse effects of corruption. The index also identifies a number of low-income countries that have made great strides in ensuring that the fruits of development do reach the poor—countries that can serve as examples for the future.

The outlook for the less industrialized nations is, at best, mixed. Solving many of their future environmental problems will require raising the standards of living. However, it is probably not possible for them to follow the path of development pioneered by the industrialized nations without triggering severe global environmental problems; the solution would become the problem. New forms of development will be necessary.

The less industrialized countries must overcome a number of significant barriers if development is to become a reality. At the local level, rising populations face increasingly limited access to land or productive assets. At the national level, corruption and development policies discriminate against the poor. Globally, their situation is worsened by rising debt burdens, falling export prices for the products they sell, and the flight of capital that could be used to create jobs and income.

How can the barriers be overcome? What new forms of development can be introduced? By what means can they be introduced? We will deal with these questions in Chapter 21.

Key Concepts

adjusted net savings, *p.* 461

barriers to sustainable development, *p.* 467

capital-energy relationship, *p.* 451

capital-labor relationship, *p.* 451

constant-dollar GDP, *p.* 459

constant-dollar NDP, *p.* 459

consumption, *p.* 459

conventional measure, *p.* 458

depreciation, *p.* 459

ecological footprint indicator, *p.* 462

ex post and *ex ante* substitution possibilities,
  p. 456

Genuine Progress Indicator (GPI), *p.* 461

Gini coefficient, *p.* 462

human development index (HDI), *p.* 463

natural resource curse, *p.* 452

net domestic product (NDP), *p.* 458

output measures, *p.* 458

perfect equality, *p.* 467

perfect inequality, *p.* 467

real consumption per capita, *p.* 459

welfare measure, *p.* 458

Further Reading

Dasgupta, Partha. *An Inquiry into Well-Being and Destitution* (Oxford: Oxford University Press, 1993). A seminal work that deals comprehensively with the forces that create and accentuate poverty and their interaction with economic growth.

Neumayer, E. "Indicators of Sustainability," *The International Yearbook of Environmental and Resource Economics: 2004/2005*, Tietenberg, T. and H. Folmer, eds. (Cheltenham, UK: Edward Elgar, 2004): 139–188. This survey essay reviews empirical methods for judging sustainability and provides solid critiques of their strengths and weaknesses.

Additional References

Ahlburg, Dennis A., ed. *The Impact of Population Growth on Well-Being in Developing Countries* (Berlin: Springer, 1996).

Akerman, M. "What Does 'Natural Capital' Do? The Role of Metaphor in Economic Understanding of the Environment," *Environmental Values* 12 (2003) (4): 431–448.

Bartelmus, P. "Green Accounting for a Sustainable Economy—Policy Use and Analysis of Environmental Accounts in the Philippines," *Ecological Economics* 29 (1999) (1): 155–170.

Bartelmus, P. "Dematerialization and Capital Maintenance: Two Sides of the Sustainability Coin," *Ecological Economics* 46 (2003) (1): 61–81.

Beckerman, W. *A Poverty of Reason: Sustainable Development and Economic Growth* (Oakland, CA: The Independent Institute, 2002).

Berndt, Ernst R. and David O. Wood, "Energy Price Shocks and Productivity Growth: A Survey," *Energy: Markets and Regulation*, Gordon, Richard L., Henry D. Jacoby, and Martin B. Zimmerman, eds. (Cambridge, MA: MIT Press, 1987): 305–342.

Carraro, C., M. Galeotti, et al. "Environmental Taxation and Unemployment: Some Evidence on the 'Double Dividend Hypothesis' in Europe," *Journal of Public Economics* 62 (1996) (1–2): 141–181.

Choi, J. S. and B. C. Patten. "Sustainable Development: Lessons from the Paradox of Enrichment," *Ecosystem Health* 7 (2001) (3): 163–177.

Cobb, Clifford W. and John B. Cobb Jr., eds. *The Green National Product: A Proposed Index of Sustainable Economic Welfare* (Lanham, MD: University Press of America, 1994).

Conrad, Klause and Catherine Morrison. "The Impact of Pollution Abatement Investment on Productivity Change: An Empirical Comparison of the United States, Germany and Canada," *Southern Economic Journal* 55 (January 1989): 684–698.

Dinda, S. "Environmental Kuznets Curve Hypothesis: A Survey," *Ecological Economics* 49 (2004) (4): 431–455.

Ebert, U. and H. Welsch. "Meaningful Environmental Indices: A Social Choice Approach," *Journal of Environmental Economics and Management* 47 (2004) (2): 270–283.

Elobeid, A. and C. Hart. "Ethanol Expansion in the Food versus Fuel Debate: How Will Developing Countries Fare?" *Journal of Agricultural and Food Industrial Organization* 5 (2007) (2): Article 6.

Geller, Howard, John De Cicco, and Skip Laitner, *Energy Efficiency and Job Creation: The Employment and Income Benefits from Investing in Energy-Conserving Technologies* (Washington, DC: American Council for an Energy-Efficient Economy, 1992).

Goldemberg, J. (2002). "How Significant Is Sustainable Investment?" *Environment* 44 (2002) (3): 7.

Goodstein, E. "Jobs and the Environment—an Overview," *Environmental Management* 20 (1996) (3): 313–321.

Hall, C.S.S., C. I. Perez, et al., eds. *Quantifying Sustainable Development: The Future of Tropical Economies* (Orlando, FL: Academic Press, 2000).

Hamilton, K. and J. A. Dixon. "Measuring the Wealth of Nations," *Environmental Monitoring and Assessment* 86 (2003) (1–2): 75–89.

Hanley, N. "Macroeconomic Measures of "Sustainability," *Journal of Economic Surveys* 14 (2000) (1): 1–30.

Hecht, J. E. "Sustainability Indicators on the Web," *Environment* 45 (2003) (1): 3–4.

Hicks, J. R. *Value and Capital,* 2nd ed. (Oxford, UK: Oxford University Press, 1947): 172.

Hogendorn, J. S. *Economic Development*, 2nd ed. (Reading, MA: Addison-Wesley, 1997).

Jorgenson, Dale W. "Energy Prices and Productivity Growth," *Scandinavian Journal of Economics* 83 (1981): 165–179.

Jorgenson, D. W., F. M. Gollop, and B. Fraumeni. *Productivity and U.S. Economic Growth* (Cambridge, MA: Harvard University Press, 1988).

Lintott, J. "Environmental Accounting: Useful to Whom and for What?" *Ecological Economics* 16 (1996) (3): 179–190.

Markandya, A. "Employment and Environmental Protection—The Trade-offs in an Economy in Transition," *Environmental—Resource Economics* 15 (2000) (4): 297–322.

Massey, R. "Just Sustainabilities: Development in an Unequal World," *Ecological Economics* 49 (2004) (4): 486–487.

Moffatt, I. "Ecological Footprints and Sustainable Development," *Ecological Economics* 32 (2000) (3): 359–362.

Neumayer, E. "The Human Development Index and Sustainability—A Constructive Proposal," *Ecological Economics* 39 (2001) (1): 101–114.

Nijkamp, P., E. Rossi, et al. "Ecological Footprints in Plural: A Meta-Analytic Comparison of Empirical Results," *Regional Studies* 38 (2004) (7): 747–765.

Rees, W. E. "An Ecological Economics Perspective on Sustainability and Prospects for Ending Poverty," *Population and Environment* 24 (2002) (1): 15–46.

Repetto, Robert "Nature's Resources as Productive Assets," *Challenge* 32 (September/October 1989) (5): 16–20.

United Nations Development Program. *Human Development Report: 2004* (New York: UNDP, 2004).

Uri, Noel D. and Saad A. Hassanein. "Energy Prices, Labour Productivity, and Causality: An Empirical Examination," *Energy Economics* 4 (April 1982): 98–104.

Van Dieren, Wouter, ed. *Taking Nature Into Account: A Report to the Club of Rome* (New York: Springer-Verlag, 1995).

vanVuuren, D. P. and E.M.W. Smeets. "Ecological Footprints of Benin, Bhutan, Costa Rica, and the Netherlands," *Ecological Economics* 34 (2000) (1): 115–130.

Vargas, C. M. "Women in Sustainable Development: Empowerment through Partnerships for Healthy Living," *World Development* 30 (2002) (9): 1539–1560.

Veron, R. "The New Kerala Model: Lessons for Sustainable Development," *World Development* 29 (2001) (4): 601–617.

Walz, R. "Development of Environmental Indicator Systems: Experiences from Germany," *Environmental Management* 25 (2000) (6): 613–623.

Whittington, Dale. "Improving the Performance of Contingent Valuation Studies in Developing Countries," *Environmental and Resource Economics* 22(2002): 323–367..

World Bank. *World Development Report 2004: Making Services Work for Poor People* (Washington, DC: World Bank and Oxford University Press, 2004).

Zoeteman, K. "Sustainability of Nations—Tracing Stages of Sustainable Development of Nations with Integrated Indicators," *International Journal of Sustainable Development and World Ecology* 8 (2001) (2): 93–109.

Discussion Questions

1. "Economic growth has historically provided a valuable vehicle for raising the standard of living. Now that the standard of living is so high, however, further economic growth is unnecessary. When the undesirable side effects are considered, it is probably counterproductive. Economic growth is a process that has outlived its usefulness." Discuss.

2. Is affluence part of the problem or part of the solution when it comes to environmental problems? Why?

3. Consider the "happy planet index" at http://www.happyplanetindex.org/calculated.htm. In what ways is this index more revealing or less revealing than the others presented in this chapter? Do you think it has some unique advantages or disadvantages relative to the others? If so, what are they?

The Quest for Sustainable Development

21

The challenge of finding sustainable development paths ought to provide the impetus—indeed the imperative—for a renewed search for multilateral solutions and a restructured international economic system of co-operation. These challenges cut across the divides of national sovereignty, of limited strategies for economic gain, and of separated disciplines of science.

—GRO HARLEM BRUNDTLAND, **Former Prime Minister of Norway,**
Our Common Future (1987)

Introduction

Delegations from 178 countries met in Rio de Janeiro during the first two weeks of June 1992 to begin the process of charting a sustainable development course for the future global economy. Billed by its organizers as the largest summit ever held, the United Nations Conference on Environment and Development (known popularly as the "Earth Summit") sought to lay the groundwork for solving global environmental problems. The central focus for this meeting was *sustainable development*.

What is sustainable development? According to the "Brundtland report," which is widely credited with raising the concept to its current level of importance, "Sustainable development is development that meets the needs of the present without compromising the ability of future generations to meet their own needs" (World Commission on Environment and Development, 1987). However, that is far from the only possible definition; sustainable development is still in the process of being refined and clarified.

Part of the widespread appeal of the concept, according to critics, is due to its vagueness. Being all things to all people can build a large following, but it also has a rather substantial disadvantage: Close inspection may reveal that the concept is vacuous. As the emperor discovered about his new clothes, things are not always what they seem.

477

In this chapter we will take a hard look at the concept of sustainable development and whether or not it is useful as a guide to the future. What are the basic principles of sustainable development? What does sustainable development imply about changes in the way our system operates? How could the transition to sustainable development be managed? Will the global economic system automatically produce sustainable development, or will policy changes be needed? What policy changes?

Sustainability and Development

Suppose we were to map out possible future trends in the long-term welfare of the average citizen. Using a time scale measured in centuries on the horizontal axis (see Figure 21.1), four basic culture trends (labeled A, B, C, and D) emerge, with t_0 representing the present. Scenario D portrays continued exponential growth in which the future becomes a simple repetition of the past. Although this scenario is generally considered to be infeasible, we pose it here for the sake of comparison. In this scenario, not only would current welfare levels be sustainable, but also growth in welfare would be sustainable. Our concern for intergenerational justice would lead us to favor current generations because they would be the poorest. Worrying about future generations would be unnecessary if unlimited growth were possible.

Scenario C envisions slowly diminished growth culminating in a steady state where growth diminishes to zero. Each future generation is at least as well off as all previous generations.

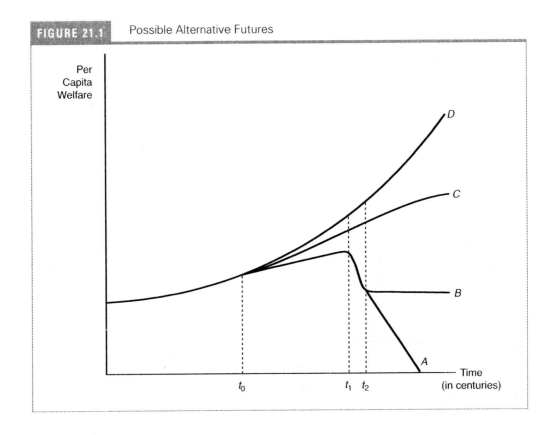

FIGURE 21.1 Possible Alternative Futures

Current welfare levels are sustainable, though current levels of welfare growth would not be. Because the level of welfare of each generation is sustainable, artificial constraints on the process would be unnecessary. To constrain growth would injure all subsequent generations.

Scenario (B) is similar in that it envisions initial growth followed by a steady state, but with an important difference—those generations between time t_1 and time t_2 are worse off than the generations preceding them. Neither growth nor welfare levels are sustainable at current levels, and the sustainability criterion would call for an immediate transition to sustainable welfare levels.

The final scenario (A) denies the existence of sustainable per capita welfare levels, suggesting that the only possible sustainable level is zero. All consumption by the current generation serves simply to hasten the end of civilization.

These scenarios suggest that three dimensions of the sustainability issue are important: (1) the existence of a positive sustainable level of welfare, (2) the magnitude of the ultimate sustainable level of welfare vis-à-vis current welfare levels, and (3) the sensitivity of the future level of welfare to actions by previous generations. The first dimension is important because, if positive sustainable levels of welfare are possible, scenario A, which in some ways is the most philosophically difficult, is ruled out. The second dimension is important because, if the ultimately sustainable welfare level is higher than the current level, radical surgery to cut current living standards is not necessary. The final dimension raises the issue of whether the ultimate sustainable level of welfare would be increased or reduced by the actions of current generations. If it can be affected, the sustainability criterion would suggest taking these impacts into account, lest future generations be unnecessarily impoverished by involuntary wealth transfers to previous generations.

The first dimension is relatively easy to dispense with. The existence of positive sustainable welfare levels is guaranteed by the existence of renewable resources, particularly solar energy, as well as by nature's ability to assimilate a certain amount of waste.[1] Therefore, we can rule out scenario A.

Both scenarios B and C require current actions to assure the maintenance of a sustainable level of welfare. They differ in terms of how radical the actions must be. Although no one knows exactly what level of economic activity can ultimately be sustained, the ecological footprint measurements discussed in Chapter 20 suggest that current welfare levels are not sustainable. If that assessment is valid, rather radical measures would be called for. If scenario C is more likely the actions could be more measured, but still necessary.

Current generations can affect the sustainable welfare levels of future generations both positively and negatively. We could use our resources to accumulate a capital stock, providing future generations with shelter, productivity, and transportation, but our decaying inner cities illustrate that machines and buildings do not last forever. Even capital that physically stands the test of time may become economically obsolete by being ill-suited to the needs of subsequent generations.

Our most lasting contribution to future generations would probably come from what economists call human capital—investments in people. Though the people who receive education and training are mortal, the ideas they bring forth are not. Knowledge endures.[2]

---

[1]One study has estimated that humans are currently using approximately 19 to 25 percent of the renewable energy available from photosynthesis. On land the estimate is more like 40 percent (Vitousek et al., 1986).

[2]Although it is true that ideas can last forever, the value of those ideas may decline with time as they are supplanted by new ones. The person who conceived of horseshoes made an enormous contribution to society at the time, but the value of that insight to society has diminished, along with our reliance on horses for transportation.

Current actions could also reduce future welfare levels, however. Fossil fuel combustion is likely to alter the climate to the detriment of future agriculture in some regions. By depleting the atmosphere's ozone, current chlorofluorocarbon emissions are likely to raise the incidence of skin cancer. The storage of radioactive wastes could increase the likelihood of genetic damage in the future. The reduction of genetic diversity in the stock of plants and animals could well reduce the number of medical discoveries in the future.

Suppose that high levels of sustainable welfare are feasible. Would our economic system automatically choose a growth path that produces sustainable welfare levels, or could it choose one that enriches current generations at the expense of future generations?

Market Allocations

Market imperfections—including intertemporal externalities, open-access resources, and market power—create incentives that can interfere in important ways with the quest for sustainable development.

Allowing open access to resources promotes unsustainable allocations. In the extreme, it is even possible that some harvested species would become extinct. Even the continued availability of renewable resources cannot assure sustainability if diminished stocks are left for the future.

Intertemporal externalities also undermine the ability of the market to produce sustainable outcomes. Emissions of greenhouse gases impose a cost on future generations that is external to current generations. Current actions to reduce the gases will impose costs on this generation, but the benefits would not be felt until significantly later. Economic theory clearly forecasts that too many greenhouse gas emissions would be forthcoming for the sustainability criterion to be satisfied.

The general conclusion that *market imperfections* exacerbate the problem of unsustainability, however, would not be universally correct. For example, the existence of an oil cartel holding up prices serves to retard demand and conserve more for future generations than would otherwise be the case.

Markets can sometimes provide a safety valve to ensure sustainability when the supply of a renewable resource is threatened. Fish farming is one example where declining supplies of a renewable resource trigger the availability of an alternative, renewable substitute. Even when the government intervenes detrimentally in a way that benefits current generations at the expense of future generations, as it did with natural gas, the market can limit the damage by providing substitutes.

These ameliorating qualities of markets, however, should not be assumed to undergird the stronger conclusion that markets are sufficient. As demonstrated in the next section the notion that left to their own devices markets would automatically provide for the future is naive, despite some success in providing for generations in the past.

Efficiency and Sustainability

Suppose future governments were able to eliminate all market imperfections, restoring *efficiency* to the global economic system. In this idealized world, intertemporal and contemporaneous externalities would be reduced to efficient levels. Access to common resources would be restricted to efficient levels, and harvesting excess capacity would be eliminated. Competition would be restored to previously cartelized natural resource markets. Would this package of policies be sufficient to achieve sustainability, or is something more required?

One way to examine this question is to consider a number of different models that capture the essence of intertemporal resource allocation. For each model, the question becomes, "Will efficient markets automatically produce sustainable development?" The conclusion to be drawn from these models is very clear: Restoring efficiency is not sufficient to produce sustainability.

Take the allocation of depletable resources over time. Imagine a simple economy where the only activity is the extraction and consumption of a single, depletable resource. Even when the population is constant and the demand curves are temporally stable, the efficient-quantity profiles show declining consumption over time. In this hypothetical world, later generations would be unambiguously worse off unless current generations transferred some of the net benefits into the future. Even an efficient market allocation would not be sustainable in the absence of transfers.

The existence of an abundant, renewable resource to serve as a backstop (e.g., solar energy) would not solve the problem. Even in this more congenial set of circumstances, the quantity profile of the depletable resource would still involve declining consumption until the renewable backstop was reached. In the absence of compensating transfers, even efficient markets would use the depletable resources to support a higher current standard of living than could be supported indefinitely.

In a historically important article Dasgupta and Heal (1979) find a similar result for a slightly more realistic model. They examine an economy where a single consumption good is produced by combining capital with a depletable resource. The finite supply of the depletable resource can either be used to produce capital or it can be used in combination with capital to produce the consumption good. The more capital that is produced, the higher is the marginal product of the remaining depletable resource in making the consumption good.

They prove that a sustainable constant consumption level exists in this model. The rising capital stock (implying a rising marginal product for the depletable resource) would compensate for the declining availability of the depletable resource. They also prove, however, that the use of any positive discount rate would necessarily result in declining consumption levels, a violation of the sustainability criterion. Discounting, of course, is an inherent component of dynamically efficient allocations.

In this model, sustainable development is possible, but it is not the choice made by markets, even efficient markets. Why not? What would it take to assure sustainable allocations? Hartwick (1977) shows that the achievement of a constant per capita consumption path (which would satisfy our weak definition of sustainability) results when all scarcity rent is invested in capital. None of it should be consumed by current generations.

Would this be the normal outcome? No. With a positive discount rate, some of the scarcity rent is consumed by the current generation, violating the Hartwick rule. The point is profound. Restoring efficiency will typically represent a move toward sustainability, but it will not, by itself, always be sufficient. Further policies must be implemented in order to guarantee sustainable outcomes.

In Chapter 4 we pointed out that maintaining a nondeclining value of the capital stock (both physical and natural) provides an observable means of checking on the sustainability of current activity. If the value of the capital stock is declining, that is sufficient to determine that the activity is unsustainable (see Example 21.1). How about the converse case? Can we automatically conclude that a nondeclining value of the capital stock implies the sustainability of current consumption levels?

According to work undertaken by Asheim (1994) and elaborated on by Pezzey (1994), we cannot. Rising net wealth can coincide with unsustainability when the capital stock is being

EXAMPLE
21.1

Resource Depletion and Economic Sustainability: Malaysia

The historical record suggests, oddly enough, that countries with abundant natural resources tend to suffer a disadvantage in economic development. Why? One possible explanation for the apparent "natural resource curse" is that resource-rich countries have not invested enough of the scarcity rent in reproducible capital to offset resource depletion. Natural resources are a form of capital, which, if depleted, must be either replenished or substituted for if countries are to expand their asset base and sustain their consumption levels.

Malaysia is a particularly interesting country for examining this issue because on the surface it seems to have avoided the natural resource curse. Although it is one of the most resource-rich countries in the world, its per capita GDP growth rate during the 1970–1990 period was among the highest in the world. But the very extraordinariness of Malaysia's resource-richness raises a troubling question: Is the country indeed on a sustainable growth path, or has it managed to keep growing simply by developing new resources?

In the Vincent (1997) study net investment (gross investment minus depreciation of physical and natural capital) and net domestic product (NDP; GDP minus depreciation of the two types of capital) were estimated for Malaysia and its three constituent regions (Peninsular Malaysia, Sabah, and Sarawak) during 1970–1990. The estimates reflected depreciation of two categories of natural resources, mineral and timber, the two most important natural resources in the country.

At the national level, per capita net investment was found to be positive in all years but one. Hence, per capita total capital stocks increased in Malaysia during the 1970s and 1980s, despite the depletion of the country's mineral and timber resources. This was not the case in all three regions, however. Per capita net investment was positive in Peninsular Malaysia in all years, but it was negative in every year after 1975 in Sabah and in every year but one after 1983 in Sarawak.

The lesson for other resource-rich countries is to emulate Peninsular Malaysia's example, by adopting economic policies that result in the productive reinvestment of a substantial portion of resource rents. Sabah and Sarawak have instead grown by simply raising their natural resource output and consuming much of the rents thus generated. Although Malaysia's development appears to be sustainable at the national level, it is not sustainable in all subnational regions.

Source: Vincent, Jeffrey R., "Resource Depletion and Sustainability in Malaysia," *Environment and Development Economics* 2(1), February 1997: 19–37.

valued at the wrong (i.e., unsustainable) prices. When depletable resources are being used up too rapidly, this drives prices down. Using these prices can create the false impression that the value of the depletion is less than the value of the additional investment and, therefore, that the value of the capital stock is rising. In fact, at the correct prices, it may be falling.

How about renewable resources? At least in principle, renewable resource flows could endure forever. Are efficient market allocations of renewable resources compatible with sustainable development? John Pezzey (1992) has examined the sustainability of an allocation of a single renewable resource (e.g., corn) over time. Sustained growth of welfare can occur in this model, but only if two conditions both hold: (1) the resource growth rate exceeds the sum of both the discount rate and the population growth and (2) the initial food supply is sufficient for the existing population. The first condition is sometimes difficult to meet, particularly in countries with rapid population growth and slow-growing biological resources. Sustainable development based upon renewable resources is very much harder in the presence of rapid population growth rates because the pressure to exceed sustainable harvest rates becomes irresistible.

The second condition raises a more general—and a more difficult—concern. It implies the distinct possibility that, if the starting conditions are sufficiently far from a sustainable path, sustainable outcomes may not be achievable without outside intervention. The simplest way to see this point is to note that a country that is so poor that it is reduced to eating all of its seed corn sacrifices its future in order to survive in the present. The double message that can be derived from these results is that (1) it is important to assure that conditions do not deteriorate to this extent by acting quickly and (2) foreign aid is probably an essential part of sustainability policies for the poorest nations.

Global climate change presents a rather different example—one in which efficiency may not be sufficient for sustainability. Because the present-value component of dynamic efficiency emphasizes short-term over long-term consequences, the current costs of controlling emissions would be weighted more heavily than the distant future damages caused by global warming. Though this approach is not inherently biased against future generations, their interests would only be adequately protected (1) if they would be willing to accept monetary compensation for a modified climate and (2) if current generations would be willing to set aside sufficient proceeds to provide this compensation. Because it is not obvious that either condition would be satisfied in practice, the long lead times associated with this particular problem place in jeopardy the interests of future generations in maintaining a stable climate.

Efficient allocations can also violate the notion of sustainability in a deeper sense. Because the definition of weak sustainability that we have used in the immediately preceding analysis is based upon nondeclining average welfare levels, it does not require the preservation of individual resources. Harvesting fish stocks to extinction, for example, would be compatible with this concept of sustainability as long as future generations were sufficiently compensated for the missing fish stock.

However, we don't really know how much they would value the continued existence of those fish stocks. Not only is our knowledge about the ultimate ecosystem effects of the extinction of any species extremely limited, but also we have no idea how valuable those fish would be to future generations. It is possible that they would value the continued existence of the population substantially more than we. Not only would the appropriate amount of the compensation be difficult to determine (because we don't know their preferences), but making compensation would be silly if they were to value the continued existence of the population more than they would any compensation (including accrued interest) we would be willing to pay.

One rather straightforward way to deal with this uncertainty is to include in the definition of sustainability some protection of the resources themselves. According to this logic, because it is impossible to know the value future generations place on specific renewable resources, we can only preserve their options by guaranteeing access to the resources. Efficiency would certainly not guarantee this outcome, but preserving resources would.

We must be careful to distinguish between what has been said and what has not been said. Restoring efficiency may well result in an improvement in sustainability, but efficiency may not be either necessary or sufficient even for weak sustainability. Three different cases can emerge. In the first case, the private inefficient outcome is sustainable, and the efficient outcome is also sustainable. In this case, restoring efficiency will raise well-being, but it is not necessary for sustainability. This case might prevail when resources are extraordinarily abundant relative to their use. In the second case, the private inefficient equilibrium is unsustainable, but the efficient outcome is sustainable. In this case, restoring efficiency not only increases current well-being, but is sufficient to assure sustainability. In the final case, neither the private inefficient outcome nor the efficient outcome is sustainable. In this case, restoring efficiency will not be enough to produce a sustainable outcome. Some sacrifice by current generations would be necessary in order to assure adequate protection for the well-being of future generations.

Although efficient markets cannot always achieve sustainable development paths, this does not mean that such sustainability would not be the norm. Indeed, the historical record suggests that the incompatibility of the efficiency criterion and the sustainability criterion has been the exception, not the rule. Capital accumulation and technological progress have expanded the ways in which resources can be used and have increased subsequent welfare levels—in spite of a declining resource base. Nonetheless, the two criteria are not inevitably compatible. As resource bases diminish and global externalities increase, the conflict between these criteria can be expected to become more intense.

Trade and the Environment

One of the traditional paths to development involves opening the economy to trade. Freer international markets provide lower prices for consumer goods (due to the availability of and competition from imported products) and the opportunity for domestic producers to serve foreign markets. As we have seen, the law of comparative advantage suggests that trade can benefit both parties. One might suspect (correctly) that as one moves from theory to practice, the story would become a bit more complicated.

The Role of Property Rights. From our previous discussions it should be clear that trade can certainly inflict detrimental (and inefficient) effects on the environment when some nations (presumably the less-developed nations) have poorly defined property rights or have not internalized their externalities (such as pollution). Chichilnisky (1994) has shown that in this kind of situation the tragedy of the commons can become greatly intensified by freer trade. Poorly defined property rights in the exporting nations encourage the importing nations (by artificially lowering prices) to greatly expand their consumption of the under-priced resources. In this scenario, trade intensifies environmental problems by increasing the pressure on open-access resources and hastening their degradation.

Pollution Havens and the Race to the Bottom. The failure to control externalities such as pollution in developing countries provides another possible route, known as the *pollution havens* hypothesis, for trade to induce environmental degradation. According to this hypothesis, producers affected by stricter environmental regulations in one country will either move their dirtiest production facilities to countries with less stringent environmental regulations (presumed to be lower-income countries) or face a loss of market share. This movement is reinforced if consumers in the country with the strict regulation have an incentive to prefer cheaper goods (those produced in the pollution havens).

Pollution levels can change in the pollution havens for three reasons: (1) the composition effect, (2) the technique effect, or (3) the scale effect. According to the *composition effect,* emissions change as the mix of dirty and clean industries changes; as the ratio of dirty to clean industries increases, emissions increase, even if total output remains the same. (Notice that this is the expected outcome from the pollution havens hypothesis as the dirtiest industries have the greatest incentives to move to the pollution havens.) The *technique effect* involves the ratio of emissions per unit output in each industry. Emissions could increase in pollution havens if each firm in the pollution haven became dirtier as a result of openness to trade. And finally, the *scale effect* looks at the role of output level on emissions; even if the composition and technique effects were zero, emissions could increase in pollution havens simply because output levels increased.

In addition to suggesting a channel for degradation, this hypothesis, if correct, could provide a justification for developing countries to accept lower environmental standards. In this view lower environmental standards encourage an expansion in the availability of jobs.. In other words, it suggests a *race to the bottom* feedback mechanism where competitive incentives among nations force developing countries to keep environmental standards weak in order to attract jobs and jobs move to those locations in search of the lower costs resulting from lower standards.

What does the evidence suggest about the empirical validity of the pollution havens hypothesis and its race to the bottom implication? Earlier surveys of the empirical work found absolutely no support for the effect of environmental regulation on either trade or capital flows. Several recent studies, however, have begun to find that environmental regulation can influence trade flows and plant location, all other things being equal, although the effects are small.

Has there been a large exodus of dirty industries to developing countries? Apparently not, but some exodus has occurred.

Actually these results should not be surprising. Because pollution control costs comprise a relatively small part of the costs of production, it would be surprising if lowering environmental standards would become the major determinant of firm location or the direction of trade, although marginally it could play a role.

Go Further Online

For a closer look at the evidence of dirty industries moving to developing countries, see the pollution havens policy investigation discussion at www.pearsonhighered.com/tietenberg.

The Porter "Induced Innovation" Hypothesis. The story does not end there. Michael Porter (1991), a Harvard business school professor, has argued that more environmental protection can, under the right circumstances, promote jobs, not destroy them. Now known as the *Porter induced innovation hypothesis*, this view suggests that firms in nations with the most stringent regulations experience a competitive advantage rather than a competitive disadvantage. Under this nontraditional view, strict environmental regulations force firms to innovate, and innovative firms tend to be more competitive. This advantage is particularly pronounced for firms producing pollution control equipment (which can then be exported to firms in countries subsequently raising their environmental standards). It might also be present, however, for firms which, when forced to change their production processes for environmental reasons, find that their production costs are lower, not higher. Some instances of regulation-induced lower production costs have been recorded in the literature (Barbera and McConnell, 1990), but few studies have attempted to examine the economy-wide validity of the Porter hypothesis.

While it seems clear that innovation induced by environmental regulation could simultaneously increase productivity (lower costs) and lower emissions, it is less clear why this would necessarily always or even normally be the case. And if it were universally true, it is not clear why all firms would fail to adopt these techniques even in the absence of regulations.

The Porter hypothesis is valuable because it reminds us that a particularly ingrained piece of conventional wisdom ("environmental regulation reduces firm competitiveness") is frequently wrong. It would be a mistake, however, to use it as confirmation of the much stronger proposition that environmental regulation is universally good for competitiveness.

The Environmental Kuznets Curve. Although proponents of free trade have come to recognize the potential problems for the environment posed by free trade, particularly in the face of externalities or poor property right regimes in the exporting countries, they tend to suggest that these problems will be self-correcting. Specifically, they argue that as freer trade increases incomes, the higher incomes will promote more environmental protection.

The specific functional relationship underlying this view comes from some earlier work by Simon Kuznets, a former Harvard professor, and has become known as the *Environmental Kuznets Curve*. According to this relationship, environmental degradation increases with higher incomes up to some income level (the turning point). After the turning point, however, higher incomes result in reductions in environmental degradation. Some apparent confirmation of this view came from early studies that plotted variables such as SO_2 concentrations against per capita incomes using countries as the unit of observation (data points).

Since those early studies, the existence of this relationship and its use to suggest the self-correcting nature of trade-induced environment problems have little empirical support (Neumayer, 2001). The early studies used different nations as data points, but the interpretation that was put on the relationship was that an individual country would eventually increase environmental protection as its income increased. Subsequent studies that looked at how environmental protection varied over time within an individual country as income increased, frequently did not find the expected relationship (Vincent, 1997; Deacon and Norman, 2006). Other studies found that it seemed to apply to some pollutants (such as SO_2) but not others (such as CO_2) (World Bank, 1992; List and Gallet, 1999). And finally, as Example 21.2 illustrates, some case studies in countries that have experienced considerably freer trade regimes, have generally experienced intensified, not reduced, environmental degradation.

What are we to make of this evidence? Apparently environmental regulations are not a major determinant of either firm location decisions or the direction of trade. This implies that reasonable environmental regulations should not be held hostage to threats that polluters will leave the area, taking their jobs with them; with few exceptions, firms that are going to move will move anyway, while firms that are not going to move will tend to stay regardless of the regulatory environment.

When deterioration is caused by inadequate local property right regimes or inadequate internalization of externalities, it may not be necessary or desirable to prevent trade, but rather to correct these sources of market failure. These inefficiencies associated with trade could be solved with adequate property regimes and appropriate pollution control mechanisms. On the

Has NAFTA Improved the Environment in Mexico?

EXAMPLE
21.2

The North American Free Trade Agreement (NAFTA) took effect in 1994. By lowering tariff barriers and promoting the freer flow of goods and capital, NAFTA integrated the United States, Canada, and Mexico into a single, giant market. The agreement has apparently been successful in promoting trade and investment. Has it also been successful in promoting environmental protection in Mexico?

According to a study by Kevin Gallagher (2004) it has not, although not necessarily due to the forces identified by the pollution havens hypothesis. Some effects clearly resulted in less pollution and others more, although on balance air quality has deteriorated.

The pollution havens hypothesis might lead us to expect a relocation of heavily polluting firms from the United States to Mexico, but that apparently did not happen. None of the numerous statistical tests performed by the author supported the hypothesis.

In terms of positive effects on air quality from trade, Gallagher found significant shifts in Mexican industry away from pollution-intensive sectors; the post-trade Mexican industrial mix was less polluting than the pre-trade industrial mix (the opposite of what would be expected from the pollution havens hypothesis). He even found that some Mexican industries (specifically steel and cement) were cleaner than their counterparts in the United States, a fact he attributes to their success in securing new investment for more modern plants with cleaner technologies.

The largest trade-related source of air quality degradation was the scale effect. Though the post-trade industrial mix generally shifted away from the most polluting sectors (meaning fewer average emissions per unit output), the promotion of exports increased output levels considerably. Increased output meant more emissions (in this case almost a doubling).

One expectation emanating from the Environmental Kuznets Curve is that the increased incomes from trade would result in more environmental regulation, which in turn, would curb emissions. That expectation was not met either. Gallagher found that both real government spending on environmental policy and the number of Mexican plant-level environmental compliance inspections fell by 45 percent after NAFTA, despite the fact that income levels reached the turning point expected by the pre-trade studies.

Source: Gallagher, K. P., *Free Trade and the Environment: Mexico, NAFTA and Beyond* (Palo Alto, CA: Stanford University Press, 2004).

other hand, if establishing appropriate property regimes or pollution control mechanisms is not politically feasible, other means of protecting the resources must be found, including possibly restricting trade. Care must be exercised in using trade restrictions. However, caution must be used in imposing these trade restrictions, since they are second-best policy instruments in this case and they can even be counterproductive (Barbier and Schulz, 1997).[3]

[3]The work notes a case in which a trade restriction designed to protect against deforestation from excessive export logging sufficiently lowered the value of the forest that the land was deforested to facilitate its conversion to agriculture.

While the forgoing argument suggests that the starkest claims against the environmental effects of free trade do not hold up under close scrutiny, it would be equally wrong to suggest that opening borders to freer trade inevitably results in a gain in efficiency and/or sustainability. The truth, it seems, depends on the circumstances, so pure ideology does not get us very far. The context matters.

Since new trade institutions are now emerging, new issues with enormous implications for the environment are emerging with them. Among these issues are the environmental consequences of (1) protections for companies investing in foreign countries that are adversely affected by environmental regulations and (2) international trade rules under the General Agreement on Trade and Tariffs (GATT) and the World Trade Organization (WTO).

Investor Protections: NAFTA's Chapter 11. The North American Free Trade Agreement (NAFTA) includes an array of new corporate investment rights and protections that are unprecedented in scope and power. NAFTA allows corporations to sue the national government of a NAFTA country in secret arbitration tribunals if they feel that a regulation or government decision adversely affects their investment in a way that violates these new NAFTA rights. If the corporation wins, the taxpayers of the "losing" NAFTA nation must foot the bill.

The environmental concern raised by this provision is that it could be used to require governments to compensate companies that are financially damaged by legitimate environmental regulations, a consequence that has not been common. Requiring companies to be compensated could put a significant damper on efforts to enact environmental legislation if it became more common.

How strong this effect will be remains to be seen, but several cases involving environmental legislation have already arisen. For example, consider the effect of this rule on the movement away from the gasoline additive MTBE discussed in Chapter 18. In 1999 the state of California decided to phase out MTBE. Suspected by the World Health Organization of being carcinogenic, MTBE had been found to have contaminated at least 10,000 groundwater wells in the state. The MTBE ban went into effect January 1, 2004.

A Canadian company, Methanex Corporation, which has a subsidiary in the United States, filed a *NAFTA Chapter 11* claim against the United States. The company produces methanol, a component of MTBE, and alleged that California's ban of MTBE constitutes an expropriation of their investment, by interfering with their ability to do business. During 2005 the Methanex claims were found to be without merit and the corporation was ordered to reimburse the United States for all legal costs it incurred in defending itself against their claim.

Many observers, including many proponents of freer trade, believe that Chapter 11 has gone too far, although the concerns are based more on potential harms than actual settled cases. It is, however, hard to imagine how secret proceedings could be justified. They are an anachronism in a society that places so much emphasis on freedom of information. In addition, observers have called for a change in the burden of proof. A finding that a uniformly applied action had a differentially large impact on a company should not be sufficient to justify compensation. Plaintiffs in Chapter 11 actions should have to show that the government agency was discriminating against the foreign firm.

Trade Rules under GATT and the WTO. The General Agreement on Tariffs and Trade (GATT), the international agreement that laid the groundwork for the WTO, was first signed in 1947. That agreement provided an international forum for encouraging free trade between member states by regulating and reducing tariffs on traded goods and by providing a common mechanism for resolving trade disputes. Having now replaced the GATT forum, the WTO is the sole global international organization dealing with the rules of trade between nations.

As an organization devoted to freer trade, the WTO adjudicates disputes among trading nations through the lens of its effect on trade. Domestic restrictions on trade of any kind (including environment restrictions) are suspect unless they pass muster. To decide whether they pass muster or not, the WTO has evolved a set of rules to define the border between acceptable and unacceptable actions.

These rules examine, for example, such things as differential treatment. A disputed environmental action that discriminates against goods from another country (rather than holding imports and domestically produced goods to the same standard) is deemed differential treatment and is accordingly unacceptable. Disputed actions that are not the lowest cost (and least injurious to trade) action that could have been taken to address the particular environmental problem are also unacceptable.

One of the most controversial rules involves a distinction between "product" concerns and "process" concerns (see Debate 21.1). At the risk of oversimplification, regulations that address product concerns (such as mandating the highest acceptable residual pesticide levels in foods) are acceptable, but regulations addressing the process by which the product was made or harvested (such as banning steel imports from a particular country because it is made in coal-burning plants) is not acceptable. In the latter case the steel from coal-burning plants is considered to be indistinguishable from steel made by other processes so the product is considered to be homogeneous and treating it as different is unacceptable.

DEBATE 21.1

Should an Importing Country Be Able to Use Trade Restrictions to Influence Harmful Fishing Practices in an Exporting Nation?

Yellowfin tuna in the Eastern Tropical Pacific often travel in the company of dolphins. Recognizing that this connection could be exploited to more readily locate tuna, tuna fishermen used it to increase their catch with deadly effects for dolphins. Having located dolphins, tuna vessels would use giant purse seines to encircle and trap the tuna, capturing (and frequently killing) dolphins at the same time.

In response to public outrage at this technique, the United States enacted the Marine Mammal Protection Act (MMPA). This Act prohibited the importation of fish caught with commercial fishing technology that results in the incidental kill or serious injury of ocean mammals in excess of U.S. standards.

In 1991 a GATT panel ruled on an action brought by Mexico asserting that U.S. law violated GATT rules because it treated physically identical goods (tuna) differently. According to this ruling, countries could regulate products that were harmful (as long as they treated domestic and imported products the same), but not the processes by which the products were harvested or produced in foreign countries. Using domestic regulations to selectively ban products as a means of securing change in the production or harvesting decisions of other countries was ruled a violation of the international trade rules.

The United States responded by mandating an eco-labeling program. Under this law tuna caught in ways that killed dolphins could be imported, but they were not allowed to use the "dolphin safe" label. Tuna caught with purse seines could only use the "dolphin safe" label if special on-board observers witnessed no dolphin deaths. Mexico has since argued that this situation did not satisfy the GATT ruling of 1991 and continues to hold the threat of a WTO case over the United States' head.

Source: The official GATT history of the case can be found at http://www.wto.org/english/tratop_e/envir_e/envir_backgrnd_e/c8sl_e.htm#united_states_tuna_mexico and an environmental take on it can be found on the public citizen Web site at http://www.citizen.org/trade/wto/ENVIRONMENT/articles.cfm?ID=9298.

The inability of any country to address process concerns in its imports clearly limits its ability to internalize externalities. In light of this interpretation, one way to internalize externalities in other countries would be to use means other than trade (international agreements to limit carbon emissions, for example). Another, as Debate 21.1 points out, is to use eco-labeling as a means of putting as least some market pressure on the disputed practices. How far that labeling can go without triggering a negative WTO ruling remains to be seen.

A Menu of Opportunities

Is sustainable development just an unrealistic attempt to provide false hope in the face of a rather bleak future? Human nature being what it is, we must have hope. When the situation is hopeless, the natural human tendency is to imagine scenarios that offer the illusion of hope. Is sustainable development one of those scenarios? Or can reasonable, skeptical people find grounds for believing in the existence of new forms of development that can raise living standards while respecting both the environment and the rights of future generations?

Although it is not possible in the space we have to go into detail about the various techniques that fulfill this vision, it is possible to convey a flavor—with the hope that this flavor will be sufficient to demonstrate that sustainable development is a pragmatic possibility, not merely an illusion.

Agriculture

Most experts believe that food supply can be expanded to meet the forecasted increases in population, but sustainable development requires this expansion to take place in a way that does not destroy the natural environment. What are the prospects?

Multiple cropping—which includes crop rotations, intercropping (sometimes with trees and annual crops sharing the same fields), overseeding legumes into cereals, and double cropping—is one technique that offers the potential for reduced use of agricultural chemicals, increased productivity, less soil erosion, and more effective use of water. The concept is not new. A system employed in Central America since pre-Columbian times intermixes maize, beans, and squash. The maize provides a trellis for the beans; the beans enrich the soil with nitrogen; and the squash provides ground cover, reducing erosion, soil compaction, and weed growth.

Trees can be used in multiple cropping. In West Africa, leaf litter from the *Acacia alba* enriches the soil for the benefit of various grain and vegetable crops grown between them. In the

U.S. Midwest, farmers are experimenting with growing corn with other, low-growing plants. In one experiment in Nebraska, two-row corn windbreaks were spaced every 15 rows through a field of sugar beets. The wind shelter provided by the corn increased sugar production by 11 percent. The greater access to sunlight and carbon dioxide increased corn yields by 150 percent.

In Montana, tall wheatgrass, a perennial, has been used to protect winter wheat. In winter, wheatgrass barriers capture snow, forming a uniform layer that insulates dormant plants from the effects of extremely low temperatures. In spring, the snow melts, providing the moisture winter wheat needs for early growth. Once the winter wheat begins to grow, the wheatgrass serves as a wind barrier.

Multiple cropping can reduce the need for pesticides. In fields where crops are rotated regularly, pests (e.g., weeds, insects, and pathogens) cannot adapt themselves to a single set of environmental conditions and, therefore, do not increase as quickly.

Biotechnology and new irrigation techniques also offer prospects for reduced fertilizer and water use. Developing plants that "fix" nitrogen in the soil would lessen the demand for nitrogen fertilizer, and incorporating genes from pest-resistant plants into commercial crops could reduce the need for pesticides. Trickle (or drip) irrigation systems would reduce the amount of water needed by increasing the efficiency of the water used. Already widely used in Israel and parts of the United States, trickle irrigation can also reduce the problems associated with salt buildup.

Energy

Prior to the 1970s, increases in the gross domestic product (GDP) were always accompanied by proportionate increases in energy consumption. This relationship proved so stable that it was used for forecasting energy consumption. Some observers at the time took this relationship as evidence that proportionate increases in energy would be a necessary condition for growth.

Following the oil embargo and the accompanying increases in prices during the 1970s, it became clear that growth and energy consumption did not have to move in lockstep. The industrialized world's *energy intensity*—the amount of energy used to produce one unit of GDP—fell by 36 percent between 1973 and 1998. In the United States, the energy intensity fell by one-half between 1949 and 2004. The downward trend in energy intensity has continued to this day.[4]

Energy efficiency (getting the same energy services out of a smaller input of energy) and *energy conservation* (using fewer energy services) are the short-run keys to energy use because they make the depletable sources of energy last longer. We are already witnessing energy conservation as communication is substituted for transportation. Consider, for example, online shopping leading to fewer trips to the mall or working at home via computer leading to fewer commutes to the office. Examples of energy efficiency are easy to find as well. New light bulbs use much less electricity per lumen of output. Modern refrigerators and air conditioners provide a comfortable environment with much less electricity than historic models. The emerging field of green architecture is designing buildings that make a wide variety of much smaller demands on the environment. And studies of future possibilities suggest that we have only scratched the surface.

---

[4]Those interested in U.S. energy intensity trends can find the data at http://intensityindicators.pnl.gov/trend_data.stm.

In the long run we can turn to fuel substitution. A host of renewable fuel possibilities exist from passive and active solar, wind, photovoltaics, hydropower, hydrogen fuel cells, and tidal power from the ocean to mention some options currently receiving attention. Stimulated by diminishing fossil-fuel energy supplies, by national security concerns over energy imports and accumulating evidence of the energy sources of climate change, many more possibilities will presumably emerge as human ingenuity responds to the realization that our energy future must be quite different from our energy past.

Waste Reduction

Sustainable development is predicated upon a more integrated approach to production than has traditionally been practiced in order to reduce raw material demands and waste discharge. In such an integrated system (1) the consumption of energy and materials is optimized; (2) waste generation is minimized; and (3) the effluent of one process—whether they are spent catalysts from petroleum refining, fly and bottom ash from electric-power generators, or discarded plastic containers from consumer products—serve as raw materials for another process.

As the costs of waste disposal rise and the regulations dealing with hazardous waste disposal become stricter, examples of industries adopting this type of integrated approach become more prevalent. Meridian National, a midwestern steel-processing company, now reprocesses the sulfuric acid with which it removes scale from steel sheets and slabs, reuses the acid, and sells ferrous sulfate compounds to magnetic tape manufacturers.

At the Atlantic Richfield Company's Los Angeles refinery complex, a series of relatively low-cost changes reduced waste volumes from about 12,000 tons a year during the early 1980s to about 3,400 tons a year by the end of the decade. Because disposal costs were about $300 a ton, the company saved over $2 million a year in disposal costs alone.

Markets have been found for much of Atlantic Richfield's former waste, adding further revenue. The company sells its spent alumina catalysts to Allied Chemical and its spent silica catalysts to cement makers. Alkaline carbonate sludge from a water-softening operation at the refinery goes to a sulfuric acid manufacturer a few miles away, where it is used to neutralize acidic wastewater.

Sustainable development frequently requires changes in how economic activities are conducted. Some of those changes are already occurring, others await additional policy changes.

● Managing the Transition

If sustainable development is, in fact, possible and unfettered markets are not capable of managing the transition by themselves, what can be done? How can the transition to sustainable development be accomplished?

Our situation is similar to that of the thoroughly disoriented tourist, a central character in Maine folklore. Enticed by unusually brilliant fall foliage, a tourist forsook the security of the well-marked main highways for some less traveled country roads. After an hour of driving, he was no longer sure he was even headed in the right direction. Seeing a Maine native mending a fence, he pulled over to the side of the road to seek assistance. After hearing the tourist's destination, the native sadly shook his head and, in his best Maine accent, responded "If I was goin' they-uh, I sure wouldn't start from he-uh!"

Had we known long ago that human activities could seriously impact environmental life-support systems and could deny future generations the quality of life to which our generation has become accustomed, we might have chosen a different, more sustainable, path for improving human welfare. The fact that we did not have that knowledge and, therefore, did not make that choice years ago means that current generations are faced with making more difficult choices, with fewer options. These choices will test the creativity of our solutions and the resilience of our social institutions.

The task of managing the transition to sustainable development is made more difficult by the fact that some entrenched development paths are not only unsustainable themselves, they have so dominated sustainable strategies that switching from one to the other has become very difficult.

Southern California represents a case in point. In the Los Angeles air basin, the ambient air quality standards, designed to protect human health, are currently violated on the order of several times a year. Because of the way the city has developed, regulators in Los Angeles now face a very difficult problem. As a prime example of an automobile-centered city, population growth in Los Angeles has spawned land-use patterns that accommodate the automobile and are, in turn, accommodated by the automobile. Responding to a massive program of highway construction and low gasoline prices, the city has become very spread out, with highly dispersed residential and employment locations. Because the efficient use of mass transit requires the existence of high-density travel corridors, an effective public transit alternative is now difficult to implement, although it could have been quite possible before the highly dispersed land-use patterns became so firmly entrenched. The options left open to these regulators have steadily diminished over time. The entire fabric of life in the Los Angeles area is so interwoven with automobile access that the problem cannot be solved without envisioning fairly radical changes in lifestyle.

In addition to the problem of reversing historic land use patterns that seem inconsistent with the goal of sustainable development, we face the problem of how to prevent more inefficient development from occurring in the future. Coal, for example, is an attractive fuel for producing electricity because it has low out-of-pocket costs and it is plentiful. Yet as the fuel with the most carbon per BTU of heat output, it poses a significant threat to a stable climate. As long as the societal costs associated with carbon pollution remain external to both the consumer and producers of coal, coal use will be artificially high.

To meet the challenges of the next century, it will be necessary to foster and support institutional change by being somewhat more creative in how we deal with environmental policy. One key to exploiting these opportunities involves harnessing the power of the marketplace and focusing that power on the reduction, or even eradication, of poverty in an environmentally sound manner.

Prospects for International Cooperation

As the scale of economic activity has proceeded steadily upward, the scope of environmental problems triggered by that activity has transcended both geographic and generational boundaries. The nation-state used to be a sufficient form of political organization for resolving environmental problems, but that may no longer be the case. Whereas the earliest generations of humans had the luxury of being able to satisfy their own needs without worrying about the needs of generations to come, that is no longer the case, either. Solving problems such as poverty, global warming, ozone depletion, and the loss of biodiversity requires international cooperation. Ideally, the search for solutions would also involve intergenerational cooperation, but, of course, that is not possible. Future generations cannot speak for themselves; we must speak for them. Our policies must incorporate our obligation to future generations, however difficult or imperfect that incorporation might prove to be.

International cooperation is by no means a forgone conclusion. Global environmental problems can trigger very different effects on the countries that will sit around the negotiating table. Whereas low-lying countries could be completely submerged by the sea-level rise predicted by some climate change models or arid nations could see their marginal agricultural lands succumb to desertification, other nations may see agricultural productivity rise, as warmer climates support longer growing seasons in traditionally intemperate climates.

Countries that unilaterally set out to improve the global environmental situation run the risk of making their businesses vulnerable to competition from less conscientious nations. Industrialized countries that undertake stringent environmental policies may not suffer greatly at the national level (because of offsetting employment and income increases in the industries that produce pollution control equipment), but some individual industries confronting the stringent regulations will face higher costs than their competitors and can be expected to suffer accordingly. Declining market share and employment in industries confronted by especially stringent regulations are powerful political weapons that can be used to derail efforts to implement an aggressive environmental policy. The search for solutions must accommodate these concerns.

Forging new international agreements is not enough. To produce the desired effect, the agreements must be enforceable. Enforceability will be a difficult criterion to satisfy as long as the agreements infringe upon significant segments of society with legitimate claims to an alternative future. The most legitimate such claim is perhaps advanced by those currently in abject poverty.

Many individuals and institutions currently have a large stake in maintaining the status quo. Fishermen harvesting their catch from an overexploited fishery are loath to undertake any reduction in harvests, even if the reduction is necessary to conserve the stock and to return the population to a healthy level. Farmers who have come to depend on fertilizer and pesticide subsidies will be reluctant to give them up. The principle of inertia applies to political as fully as to physical bodies: A body at rest will tend to stay at rest unless a significant outside force is introduced. Changing economic incentives can provide that force.

Opportunities for Cooperation

This list of barriers to international cooperation is certainly imposing, but the new global environmental problems also offer new opportunities for cooperation, opportunities that in some ways are unprecedented. Although the degrees to which various nations are affected by these problems differ, a point made earlier, it is also true that some potential common ground exists.

One important foundation for this common ground is the inefficiency of many current economic activities. In many cases, these inefficiencies are very large indeed; resources are being wasted. Whenever resources are wasted, much more environmental improvement could be obtained for current expenditures, or the same improvement could be realized with a much smaller commitment of resources. By definition, moving from an inefficient policy to an efficient one creates gains to be shared. Agreements on how these gains should be shared among the cooperating parties can be used to build coalitions.

The natural reluctance of nations to impose increasingly stringent environmental policies within their borders can be diminished by assuring that the policies imposed are cost effective. We live in an age when the call for tighter environmental controls intensifies with each new discovery of yet another injury modern society is inflicting on the planet, but resistance to additional controls is growing with the recognition that the cost of compliance is also growing, as all the "easy" techniques become used up. Choosing cost-effective and flexible policy instruments can reduce the potential for backlash.

The choice of policy instruments can also affect enforceability. In developing countries local communities typically have the greatest accessibility to and knowledge about local biological resources. As these countries have undergone a centralization of political power, including the power to control these resources, some of the local commitment to preserve them has been lost. Policy instruments that reestablish this commitment by offering these local communities a stake in the preservation of the resources can enhance enforceability.

With creative design of policy instruments, the incentives of local and global communities can become compatible. In some cases, being creative requires the use of conventional economic instruments in unconventional ways; in others, it requires the use of unconventional instruments in unconventional ways.

Unconventional approaches are not pipe dreams. Most of them have been successfully employed in one form or another in local communities around the globe. The experience with these instruments in their current setting provides a model for their use on an international level. How well this model fits remains an open question, but it is better to sit down for a dinner with a full menu offering some novel, but interesting, choices than one offering only a limited selection of familiar, unappetizing fare.

Restructuring Incentives

How can economic incentives be used to provide the kinds of signals that will make sustainable development possible? Perhaps the best way to begin to answer this question is to recall a few examples of how this approach has worked in practice.

Consider a few specific examples drawn from earlier chapters:

- Establishing an individual transferable quota system for managing a fishery can raise incomes while protecting the fish stock. Changing the incentives for overfishing can lead to outcomes that are both ecologically and economically desirable.

- Introducing forest certification can enable conscientious buyers to purchase only sustainably harvested wood and provide price incentives to growers to become certified, while debt nature swaps can make debt work for preservation rather than against it.

- Removing the subsidies from water use and eliminating "use it or lose it" regulations can promote water conservation, making the available supplies last longer.

- Requiring new emitters entering a nonattainment area to purchase "offsets" at a 1.2:1 ratio makes economic growth a vehicle for improving air quality, not for degrading it.

- Using volume-based pricing for trash and imposing extended producer responsibility on manufacturers provides both consumers and producers with incentives to recycle more and dispose less.

❋ Imposing renewable portfolio standards provides incentives for utilities to increase their reliance on renewable sources of energy, while transferable renewable energy certificates lower the cost of the transition.

❋ Establishing mandatory caps on carbon emissions, coupled with emissions trading or carbon taxes, to level the playing field for energy choices, increasing the relative attractiveness of renewable, low carbon sources of energy.

❋ Using the revenue from auctioned carbon allowances or carbon taxes to lower the burden of the policy change on low-income households.

❋ Implementing microfinancing to simultaneously improve the economic well-being of women and lower population growth.

❋ Introducing conservation easements to provide a means for certain land amenities to be preserved with a smaller budget impact than buying the land.

❋ Requiring parking cash-outs to eliminate the inefficient bias created by employer-financed parking subsides on commuting choices.

❋ Mandating performance bonds to internalize the cost of reclaiming contaminated sites, thereby reducing the incidence of contamination as well as the budget-draining consequences of having the public sector assume the responsibility for clean up.

Now it remains to show how the entire menu of economic-incentive policies can be woven together in a manner that facilitates international cooperation in the resolution of international environmental problems. Economic analysis suggests five principles that can provide the foundation for this approach.

The Full-Cost Principle. According to the *full-cost principle*, all users of environmental resources should pay their full cost. Those using the environment as a waste repository, for example, would be presumed responsible not only for controlling pollution to the full extent required by the law, but also for restoring environmental resource damaged beyond some *de minimus* amount and for compensating those suffering damage.

This principle is based upon the presumption that humanity has a right to a reasonably safe and healthy environment. Because this right has been held in common for the stratosphere and the international sections of the oceans, no administrative body has either the responsibility or the authority to protect that right. As a result, it has been involuntarily surrendered on a first-come, first-served basis without compensation.

Although climate change imposes both an international and intergenerational environmental cost, currently, that cost is not being borne, or even recognized, by those who are not part of the Kyoto Protocol. Furthermore, those choosing unilaterally to reduce their emissions expose themselves to the higher costs associated with mitigating strategies. Applying the full-cost principle would send a strong signal to all users of the environment that the atmosphere is a scarce, precious resource and should be treated accordingly. Products produced by manufacturing processes that are environmentally destructive would become relatively more expensive; those produced by environmentally benign production processes would become relatively cheaper. Implementing the full-cost principle would end the implicit subsidy that all polluting activities have received since the beginning of time. When the level of economic activity was small, the corresponding subsidy was also small and therefore probably not worthy of political attention.

Because the scale of economic activity has grown, however, the subsidy has become very large indeed; ignoring it leads to significant resource distortion.

The transition to a more sustainable economic system will depend upon the development of new technologies and upon much greater levels of energy efficiency than are currently being achieved. Those transitions will not occur unless the prevailing economic incentives support and encourage them. Once the full-cost principle was in effect, the incentives would be changed; greater energy efficiency and the development of new technologies would become top-priority objectives.

Implications for the legal system would flow from the full-cost principle, as well. For example, international laws should permit full recovery for damage caused by oil spills or other environmental incidents. Not only should the contaminated sites be restored insofar as possible, but also those suffering demonstrable losses should be fully compensated.

Making explicit environmental costs that have heretofore been hidden is only one side of the coin; the other is eliminating inappropriate subsidies. Subsidies that are incompatible with the full-cost principle should be eliminated. Implicit subsidies should be targeted as well as explicit ones. For example, when the pricing of environmental resources is subject to government regulation (e.g., water in the U.S. Southwest), prices should not simply be determined by historic average cost, they should reflect the scarcity of the resource.

For one way to accomplish this, recall our discussion of incremental block pricing. Incremental block pricing provides a practical means of introducing the appropriate conservation incentives without jeopardizing the traditional legal constraint that water distribution utilities earn no more than a fair rate of return. With incremental block pricing, the price of additional water consumed rises with the amount consumed per unit of time. Although the first units consumed per month up to some predetermined threshold would be relatively cheap, units consumed beyond the threshold would face a much higher price that truly reflects the scarcity of the resource. By assuring that the marginal units consumed are priced at full cost, adequate incentives to conserve would be introduced.

The transition to the full-cost principle could proceed gradually, beginning in certain sectors and moving to others as greater familiarity with the approach was gained. A complete, immediate transition is not an essential ingredient of a rational approach.

The Cost-Effectiveness Principle. According to the *cost-effectiveness principle* all environmental policies should be cost-effective. A policy is cost-effective if it achieves the policy objective at the lowest possible cost. Cost-effectiveness is an important characteristic because it can diminish political backlash by limiting wasteful expenditures.

Appropriate implementation of the full-cost principle would automatically produce cost-effectiveness as a side benefit. Should acceptance of the full-cost principle falter, however, cost-effectiveness could be elevated to a primary policy goal, worthy in its own right. It provides a desirable, if less than perfect, fallback position.

Since political acceptance of the full-cost principle is by no means a foregone conclusion, emissions trading offers a practical way to implement the cost-effectiveness principle for pollution control and other policy venues. The case for emissions trading is based on the advantages that it would offer compared to other politically feasible alternatives.

Consider how the full-cost principle is playing out for climate change. In the short run the three Kyoto trading mechanisms (emissions trading, joint implementation, and the clean development mechanism) offer the possibility of reaching the stipulated goals at a lower cost than would be possible if each country were limited to reduction options within its own borders. Making it easier to reach the goals usually increases compliance and may provide the means for more countries to join the Protocol. That certainly seemed to be the case for convincing Russia to join.

Because these trading mechanisms separate the issue of who pays for control from who implements control, they facilitate transboundary cost sharing (an item of particular importance to both the developing countries and the transition economies of Eastern Europe). Emissions trading also facilitates the mobilization of private capital for controlling climate change, which is likely to be a critically important component of any effective strategy as long as public capital remains insufficient to do it alone.

Finally, and perhaps most importantly, emissions trading mechanisms facilitate the development and implementation of novel approaches to climate change control. By offering greater flexibility in how the emission reductions are achieved (as well as by providing economic incentives for the adoption and use of unconventional approaches), allowances can significantly lower the long-run cost. Lower long-run cost may be an important element in gaining greater international acceptance of the idea of tighter limits and reducing the difficulties associated with ensuring compliance.

And the tradable entitlement concept is increasingly being used in other environmental policy arenas such as managing fisheries and controlling water and land use.[5] In general this approach can be used any time a cap should be placed on resource use and it is appropriate to formalize the rights held by users. As scarcity deepens, caps may become a much more important part of the policy mix.

The Property Rights Principle. Part of the evident loss of efficiency in modern environmental problems involves perverse incentives resulting from misspecified property rights. According to the *property rights principle*, local communities should have a property right over flora and fauna within their borders. This property right would entitle the local community to share in any benefits created by preserving the species. Ensuring that local property rights over genetic resources are defined and respected would give local communities a much larger stake in some of the global benefits to be derived from the use of those resources and would enhance the prospects for effective enforcement.

For example, consider the problem of stemming the decline in the elephant population. Insofar as permitted by the migratory nature of the herd, the property rights principle would confer the right to harvest a fixed number of elephants to the indigenous peoples who live in the elephants' native habitat. Ownership of harvesting rights in addition to the possibility of continued employment as long as the herd was preserved would ensure an income to the local community, giving it a stake in preserving the herd. Preventing poaching would become easier because poachers would become a threat to the local community, not merely a threat to a distant national government that inspires little allegiance.

A somewhat related application of the property rights principle could provide an additional means of resolving the diminishing supply of biologically rich tropical rain forests. One of the arguments for preserving biodiversity is that it offers a valuable gene pool for the development of future products such as medicines and food crops. Typically, however, the nations that govern

---

[5]For a list of studies examining the range of uses of tradable entitlements in environmental policy see the extensive bibliography at: http://www.colby.edu/~thtieten/trade.html.

the forestland containing this biologically rich gene pool have not shared in the wealth created by the products derived from it.

One solution to this problem is universal acceptance of the principle that the nations that contain these biologically rich resources within their borders be entitled to a stipulated royalty on any and all products developed from the genes obtained from these preserves. In the absence of royalty arrangements, nations cutting down their tropical forests have little incentive to protect the gene pool harbored within those forests because they are unlikely to reap any of the rewards that will ultimately result.

Exploitation of the gene pool and the economic rewards that result from it typically accrue only to those nations and to those companies that can afford the extensive research. By establishing the principle that stipulated royalty payments would accrue to the nation from which the original genes were extracted, local incentives would become more compatible with global incentives.

Implementing this recommendation would not be trivial. Although it is not hard to envision licenses being required of all those conducting research or collecting specimens of local flora or fauna, it is more difficult to imagine a process that would guarantee royalty payments on every new derivative genetic discovery. For developing countries to be aware of new discoveries would be difficult enough, but the need to enforce the terms of the license on a company that is physically located in another country could prove inordinately time-consuming and expensive.

A frequently overlooked aspect of the property rights principle is the way in which it can promote human rights. Often the historic use of resources by indigenous peoples results in an informal set of access rights. Informal rights work fine as long as the pressure from competing rights is not too strong. However, when users with access to modern technology begin to expand their usage (think trawlers in fisheries or mining companies), informal rights can go by the boards. One way to protect indigenous rights is to formalize them, thereby increasing their security by making them enforceable.

The Sustainability Principle. According to the *sustainability principle*, all resources should be used in a manner that respects the needs of future generations. Adopting the foregoing three principles would go a long way toward restoring efficiency. And restoring efficiency would set in motion the transition toward producing sustainable outcomes. As we have seen, however, restoring efficiency would not be sufficient. Other policies would be needed in order to satisfy the sustainability principle.

Restoring intergenerational fairness in the use of depletable resources might be an appropriate place to start. As the economic models have made clear, current incentives for sharing the wealth from the use of depletable resources are biased toward the present, even in efficient markets. Clearly, this could be rectified by transferring some of the created wealth into the future, but how much wealth?

Salah El Serafy (1981) has developed an ingenious, practical way to answer this question. Calculate the present value of the net benefits received from the extraction of a depletable resource over its useful life. This becomes the wealth to be shared. Using standard annuity tables, calculate the constant annual payments that could be made from this fund forever. (In essence, these payments represent the dividends and interest derived from the wealth; the principle would be left intact.) This constant annual payment is what can be consumed from the wealth created from the depletable resources. Receipts in excess of this amount (in the years the resource is being extracted and sold) must be paid into the fund. All succeeding generations receive the same annual payment; the payments continue forever. (Recall the arrangements in the Alaska Permanent Fund discussed in Example 5.1).

The payments could be invested in research rather than in instruments producing a financial return. Such a strategy might envision, for example, setting aside through taxation a certain proportion of all proceeds from depletable resources for funding research on substitutes likely to be used by future generations. In the case of fossil fuels, for example, one might subsidize research into fuel cells or wind energy so that, as fossil fuels are depleted, future generations would have the ability to switch to alternative sources easily, without diminishing living standards in the process.

Another adjustment would confront the possibility of species extinction. Compensating future generations for extinct species (the implicit strategy in an efficient allocation) is not an adequate response. Not only do we not know the appropriate level of compensation, but also it is possible that the preferences of future generations would be such that the value of the preserved species would exceed any possible compensation our generation would be willing to offer. Given this uncertainty about the preferences of future generations, one strategy would be to incorporate species preservation into our concept of sustainability in order to preserve the option for future generations to make their own valuations. With this approach, strategies that lead to species extinction would simply be infeasible, regardless of the net-benefit calculations; they would never be chosen. The interests of future generations would be protected by preserving their options rather than by attempting to second-guess their preferences.

Adjusting the national income accounts would be another immediate implication of the sustainability principle. The income accounts must conform to the Hicksian definition of income. All of the costs, including the depreciation of natural capital, should be subtracted from the gross receipts in producing a national income figure. Failure to do this, as is the current practice, provides very misleading signals to the public sector. These misleading signals provide powerful incentives for public figures to engage in economic activities that violate the sustainability principle.

The Information Principle. Polls generally show that, regardless of their social circumstances, people care about the environment and are willing to commit resources to its preservation. To energize and focus that reservoir of goodwill, however, it is necessary to assure that the citizens are informed. Recognizing the wisdom of this simple observation has paved the way for a new set of strategies designed to improve citizen participation in environmental policy.

Implementing the *information principle* can take a number of forms. In some countries, it has meant increasing the freedom of the press to report on environmental matters. In others, it has meant providing better access to government records that reveal the quantities and types of pollutants being injected into the air and water. Placing computerized records on Web sites has certainly facilitated this access.

It can also mean labeling "green" products to allow environmentally conscious consumers to use that characteristic as one element of their choice. "Dolphin-safe tuna" provides a classic example of how this approach has been used quite successfully.

One of the appeals of information strategies is their ability to achieve results when more traditional approaches prove inadequate. In many developing countries, for example, human and financial resources are so scarce as to preclude traditional regulatory approaches to pollution control. Fortunately, that does not necessarily mean that pollution must necessarily go uncontrolled. Appropriately designed information strategies may result in significant pollution control, even in the absence of traditional monitoring and enforcement (see Example 21.3).

Disclosure Strategies for Pollution Control in Indonesia

EXAMPLE
21.3

Inhibited by a regulatory structure that was not able to produce widespread compliance with water pollution control laws because of a lack of resources, in 1993 the government of Indonesia instituted a unique complementary program to increase compliance. Known by its acronym, *PROPER* (Program for Pollution Control, Evaluation, and Rating), this system evaluated 187 factories. Depending upon their pollution output, these factories were assigned to one of five color-coded categories. The categories ranged from black (no effort to control pollution) to gold (polluter exceeds legal limits by at least 50 percent for air, water, and hazardous waste and makes extensive use of clean technology, pollution prevention, and so on).

The key to the *disclosure strategies* system was that the names of the factories and their ratings would be made public, and that the ratings would be conducted periodically, allowing factories to gain public acknowledgment for improving their ratings. The hope was that firms would be sufficiently motivated by possible damage to their reputations by adverse publicity that they would improve their environmental performance.

The early results were encouraging. In the first six months following the announcement of the ratings, the number of firms in the black ("no-effort") category fell by half (from 6 to 3), whereas the number of factories meeting or exceeding legal requirements went from 66 to 76.

Although the program was dropped in 1997, a victim of the Asian economic crisis, in recognition of its value it was reinstated in 2002 when economic conditions improved.

Sources: Afsah, S. and D. Wheeler, "Indonesia's New Pollution Control Program: Using Public Pressure to Get Compliance," *East Asian Executive Reports* 18(5), May 1996: 11–13; and Afsah, Shakeb et al., "What Is PROPER?: Reputational Incentives for Pollution Control in Indonesia," World Bank Working Paper (November 1995).

Forced Transition

Let's suppose that current levels of welfare were shown to be unsustainable and that an immediate transition to a new, lower standard of living was necessary to protect future generations. How could that more abrupt transition be negotiated?

The most concrete proposals for a forced transition to the steady state come from Herman Daly (1991), an economist with the University of Maryland. Daly is very sympathetic to the goal of a rapid transition to sustainable development and has spent a good deal of his professional life looking into the best way to achieve that objective. We will focus on his proposals in examining how an economy might be forced to this new sustainable path more rapidly than would normally be the case.

Defining the Target

Daly begins by attempting to define the steady state, the target of his approach, and to clarify how we know when it has been achieved. His definition is couched in physical, rather than value, terms. For Daly, the *steady-state economy* is characterized by constant stocks of people and physical wealth maintained at some chosen, desirable level by a low rate of throughput. This throughput—the flows of resources and energy—provides direct consumption benefits (e.g., food and shelter) and some investment, insofar as necessary to counteract depreciation of the capital stock.

Conceiving the steady state in physical rather than value terms is significant because it forms an important difference between Daly and others who see the steady state as simply the absence of any development. Daly recognizes that some development would and should occur even in the steady state in spite of a constant stock of people and physical wealth. For example, as society learns more efficient ways to use energy, the value derived from the flow of energy may increase, even when the flow itself does not. Because of technological progress, the value of the services received can grow, even if the physical stocks and flows are unchanging. *The steady state and zero economic growth are not necessarily the same thing.*

Institutional Structure

Daly sees three institutional modifications as necessary for the rapid attainment of the steady state:

1. An institution for stabilizing population
2. An institution for stabilizing the stock of physical wealth and throughput
3. An institution to ensure that the stocks and flows are distributed fairly among the population

Allocation among alternative uses is handled by the market. Collective decisions are made on scale and distribution, but allocation remains with the market. Daly argues that the questions of scale, distribution, and allocation involve three separate policy goals and cannot all be served by a single instrument (prices.) While market prices can achieve the goal of efficient allocation, other institutions are necessary to achieve an optimal (sustainable) scale and an optimal (fair) distribution.

Population Stabilization. According to the Daly proposals, population would be stabilized over the long run using an idea first put forth by Kenneth Boulding (1964). In this scheme, each individual would be given a transferable entitlement to produce one (and only one!) child. Because this scheme over a generation allows each member of the current population to replace himself or herself, births would necessarily equal deaths, and population stability would be achieved.

This scheme would award each person a certificate entitling the holder to have one child. Couples could pool their certificates to have two. Every time a child was born, a certificate would be surrendered. Failure to produce a certificate would cause the child to be put up for adoption.

Certificates would be fully transferable. Families who placed a particularly high value on children could purchase extra certificates, whereas those viewing parenting with less enthusiasm could sell certificates. As one of its virtues, this system would ensure that the overall objective of population stability would be achieved, but no family would be required to maintain a particular family size. Though every couple would be guaranteed the right to have two children, they could choose to have fewer or more than two.

Stock and Throughput Stabilization. Daly suggests that throughput (the flow of energy and resources) should be held at some minimum level using depletion quotas for all depletable resources. These quotas would define the amount of the resource that could be extracted and used. Any extraction and use in excess of this quota would be illegal.

The size of these quotas would be determined by bureaucrats, but according to Daly, these bureaucrats would follow a specific rule. The quotas would be set at a level sufficiently stringent that the price of the resource in question would equal the price of the closest renewable substitute. When no close renewable substitute was available, the bureaucrats would be empowered to decide the most ethical level. Because the quotas would be auctioned off by the government, the government would extract all of the scarcity rent associated with the depletable resources. The quota prices would equal the marginal scarcity rent of the covered resources.

Ensuring Distributional Fairness. Daly also sees a need to override the normal channels for distributing income in the steady-state economy. In a growth economy, tensions between the rich and poor can be ameliorated by the opportunities for social and economic mobility that a growth economy provides. In a steady-state economy, those opportunities are diminished, as the number of new jobs created is smaller.

To alleviate these tensions, Daly proposes establishing a maximum and minimum income level as well as a maximum limit on wealth. The minimum income level would be financed in part by progressive taxes, with 100 percent marginal rates above the maximum income and wealth limits. Because these 100 percent tax rates would presumably yield very little revenue (the incentive to earn more having been eliminated), most of the revenue would come from the sale of depletion quotas and from lower tax rates on income levels between the minimum and maximum.

Administration

Opponents point out that the Daly system would be expensive to implement. Large bureaucratic staffs would be needed to define the quotas, run the actions, and ensure compliance. In an age where public sentiment seems to be for decreasing rather than increasing bureaucracy, this proposal would buck the trend. A universal quota system for depletable and renewable resources, in addition to being bureaucratically cumbersome, holds the potential to disrupt a smoothly operating institutional structure. Historically, the only time a system such as this has been acceptable is during a war.[6]

Opposition to the child certificates is particularly strong, because they raise difficult moral questions. For example, this system has been seen by some as a means of preserving the existing racial and ethnic status quo. To minority groups with above-average birth rates and below-average incomes, this looks like a policy to limit their proportion in the population. Even though that is clearly not the intended result, the suspicions raised create tensions.

---

[6]In a personal communication honoring my request that he review this chapter and the one that precedes it, Herman Daly responded, "In my view the real threat to freedom and stimulus to bureaucratic control is *crisis,* and avoidance of crisis with a bit of collective action now seems a good strategy for maximizing freedom over the long run."

Summary

Sustainable development refers to a process for providing for the needs of the present generation (particularly those in poverty) without compromising the ability of future generations to meet their own needs.

Market imperfections frequently make sustainable development less likely. Intergenerational externalities such as climate modification impose excessive costs on future generations. Open access to biological common-property resources can lead to excessive exploitation and even extinction of the species.

Even efficient markets do not necessarily produce sustainable development. Restoring efficiency is a desirable and helpful, but insufficient, means for producing sustainable welfare levels. Although, in principle, dynamically efficient allocations produce extraction profiles for depletable resources that are compatible with the interests of future generations, in practice this is not necessarily the case. Guaranteeing sustainability frequently requires compensation from the present to future generations, but profit-maximizing behavior produces compensation levels that are too low. Furthermore, adequate compensation levels may be difficult to define, at best, and it is not clear that financial payments can adequately compensate future generations for all of the options they might be asked to forgo.

When trade is part of the development strategy, it must be used carefully. The effects of trade on the environment are neither universally benign nor universally detrimental. Context matters.

The empirical evidence on *trade and the environment* has two strong messages for developing countries: (1) lowering environmental standards to compete for jobs internationally is a self-defeating strategy and (2) waiting for higher incomes from development to solve environmental problems will substantially raise the cost of dealing with those problems.

New sustainable forms of development are possible, but they will not automatically be adopted. Economic incentive policies can facilitate the transition from unsustainable to sustainable activities. Five principles provide a framework for using economic incentives to manage this transition:

1. All users of environmental resources should pay their full cost to ensure a level playing field between those resources that damage the environment and those that don't (the "Full Cost" Principle).

2. All environmental policies should be implemented in a cost-effective manner to ensure that the maximum environmental quality is received for the expenditure (the "Cost-Effectiveness" Principle).

3. Rights over environmental resources should be designed in such a manner as to promote stewardship (the "Property Rights" Principle).

4. All current uses of resources should be compatible with the needs of future generations, and the present value criterion should be used only to choose among allocations that meet this sustainability test (the "Sustainability" Principle).

5. All citizens should be kept as informed as practical about the environmental consequences of current decisions to allow them to participate as fully as possible in the transition to sustainable development (the "Information" Principle).

If it turns out that universally higher standards of living are not possible without exceeding the carrying capacity of the planet, a rapid transition to a new, steady state involving levels of welfare lower than current levels would be needed. To examine how this might occur, we considered the proposals of economist Herman Daly. He sees three institutional modifications as necessary: (1) a plan to control population, (2) a system of annual quotas to govern the rate of consumption of both depletable and renewable resources, and (3) a new mechanism to control the distribution of income and wealth. The institutional modifications suggested by Daly would face considerable opposition.

The search for solutions must recognize that market forces are extremely powerful. Attempts to negotiate agreements that seek to block those forces or to meet them head-on are probably doomed to failure. Nonetheless, it is possible to negotiate agreements that harness those forces and channel them in directions that enhance the possibilities of international cooperation. To take these steps will require thinking and acting in somewhat unconventional ways. Whether the world community is equal to the task remains to be seen.

Key Concepts

cost-effectiveness principle, *p.* 497

disclosure strategy, *p.* 501

energy conservation, *p.* 491

energy efficiency, *p.* 491

energy intensity, *p.* 491

Environmental Kuznets Curve, *p.* 486

full-cost principle, *p.* 496

information principle, *p.* 500

market imperfections (and unsustainability), *p.* 480

multiple cropping, *p.* 490

NAFTA Chapter 11, *p.* 488

pollution havens, *p.* 484

    composition effect, *p.* 485

    scale effect, *p.* 485

    technique effect, *p.* 485

Porter induced innovation hypothesis, *p.* 485

property rights principle, *p.* 498

race to the bottom (hypothesis), *p.* 485

steady-state economy, *p.* 502

sustainability principle, *p.* 499

sustainable development, *p.* 477

trade and the environment, *p.* 504

Further Reading

Copeland, B. R. and M. S. Taylor. "Trade, Growth, and the Environment," *Journal of Economic Literature* 42 (March 2004): 7–71. An excellent survey of the lessons to be derived from the theory and empirical work focusing on the relationship between trade and the environment.

Deacon, R. and C. S. Norman (2006). "Does the Environmental Kuznets Curve Describe How Individual Countries Behave?," *Land Economics* 82(2): 291–315. Examining time series data within countries the authors find weak evidence of the existence of a Kuznets curve for SO_2 in wealthier countries, but no evidence for a Kuznets curve for other pollutants and for poorer countries.

De Soysa, Indra and Eric Neumayer (2005). "False Prophet, or Genuine Savior? Assessing the Effects of Economic Openness on Sustainable Development, 1980–1999" *International Organization* 59(3): 731–772. Estimates the effects of a dependence on trade, and foreign direct investment on sustainability as measured by the genuine saving rate. They find openness enhances sustainability.

Layard, R. (2005). *Happiness: Lessons from a New Science.* New York, Penguin Press. Using integrated insights from psychology, economics, neuroscience and sociology, a distinguished British economist explores the sources of human happiness.

OECD. *The Environmental Effects of Trade* (Paris: Organization for Economic Co-operation and Development, 1994). Contains background documents for OECD discussions on the environmental effects of trade, including sector studies on agriculture, forestry, fisheries, endangered species, and transport.

Pearce, David and Edward B. Barbier. *Blueprint for a Sustainable Economy* (London: Earthscan, 2000). Seeks to answer the question, "If we accept sustainable development as a working idea, what does it mean for the way we manage a modern economy?"

Pezzey, J.C.V. and M. A. Toman. "Progress and Problems in the Economics of Sustainability," *The International Yearbook of Environmental and Resource Economics: A Survey of Current Issues,* Tietenberg, T. and H. Folmer, eds. (Cheltenham, UK: Edward Elgar, 2002). A comprehensive review of what we have learned from economic analysis about the nature and consequences of sustainability by two major contributors to the literature.

Additional References

Alpay, S. "Does Trade Always Harm the Global Environment? A Case for Positive Interaction," *Oxford Economic Papers New Series* 52 (2000) (2): 272–288.

Antweiler, W., B. R. Copeland, et al. "Is Free Trade Good for the Environment?" *American Economic Review* 91 (2001) (4): 877–908.

Asheim, Geir B. "Net National Product as an Indicator of Sustainability," *Scandanavian Journal of Economics* 55 (1994): 257–265.

Barbera, Anthony J. and Virginia D. McConnell. "The Impact of Environmental Regulations on Industry Productivity: Direct and Indirect Effects," *Journal of Environmental Economics and Management* 18 (1990): 50–65.

Barbier, E. and C. Schulz. "Wildlife, Biodiversity and Trade," *Environment and Development Economics* 2 (1997) (2): 145–172.

Barrett, J. A. "The Global Environment and Free Trade: A Vexing Problem and a Taxing Solution," *Indiana Law Journal* 76 (2001) (4): 829–887.

Becker, R. and V. Henderson. "Effects of Air Quality Regulation on Polluting Industries," *Journal of Political Economy* 108 (2000) (2): 379–421.

Bhagwati, J. "On Thinking Clearly about the Linkage between Trade and the Environment," *Environment and Development Economics* 5 (2000) (4): 485–496.

Boulding, Kenneth E. *The Meaning of the Twentieth Century* (New York: Harper & Row, 1964).

Chichilnisky, Graciela. "North-South Trade and the Global Environment," *American Economic Review* 84 (1994): 851–874.

Cole, M. A. "Trade, the Pollution Haven Hypothesis and the Environmental Kuznets Curve: Examining the Linkages," *Ecological Economics* 8 (2004) (1): 71–81.

Daly, Herman E. "The Economic Growth Debate: What Some Economists Have Learned but Many Have Not," *Journal of Environmental Economics and Management* 14 (December 1987): 323–336.

Daly, Herman E. *Steady-State Economics* (San Francisco: W. H. Freeman, 1977). Expanded 2nd edition published by Island Press, 1991.

Dean, J. "Testing the Impact of Trade Liberalization on the Environment: Theory and Evidence," *Canadian Journal of Economics* 35 (2002) (4): 819–842.

Ekins, P. "International Trade and Sustainable Development," *Ecological Economics* 49 (2004) (3): 411–412.

Esty, D. C. "Bridging the Trade-Environment Divide," *Journal of Economic Perspectives* 15 (2001) (3): 113–130.

Gallagher, K. P. *Free Trade and the Environment: Mexico, NAFTA and Beyond* (Palo Alto, CA: Stanford University Press, 2004).

Greenstone, M. "The Impacts of Environmental Regulations on Industrial Activity: Evidence from the 1970 and the 1977 Clean Air Act Amendments and the Census of Manufacturers," *Journal of Political Economy* 110 (2002) (6): 1175–1219.

Hawken, P., A. Lovins, et al. *Natural Capitalism: Creating the Next Industrial Revolution* (Boston: Little, Brown and Company, 1999).

Hettige, H., M. Mani, and D. Wheeler. "Industrial Pollution in Economic Development: Kuznets Revisited," *Journal of Development Economics* 62 (2000) (2): 445–476.

Howarth, Richard B. and Richard B. Norgard. "Intergenerational Resource Rights," *Land Economics* 66 (February 1990): 1–11.

Hudson, D., D. Hite, et al. "Environmental Regulation through Trade: The Case of Shrimp," *Journal of Environmental Management* 68 (2003) (3): 231–238.

Kahn, M. "Particulate Pollution Trends in the United States," *Regional Science and Urban Economics* 27 (1997) (1): 87–107.

Lenhardt, W. C. "Green Trade on the Web," *Environment* 4 (2000) (9): 3–4.

Levinson, A. "The Missing Pollution Haven Effect," *Environmental and Resource Economics* 15 (2000) (4): 343–364.

List, J. A. and C. Gallet. "The Environmental Kuznets Curve: Does One Size Fit All?" *Ecological Economics* 31 (1999) (3): 409–423.

McNeeley, Jeffrey A. et al. "Strategies for Conserving Biodiversity," *Environment* 32 (April 1990): 16–20, 36–40.

Meyer, Stephen M. "Environmentalism and Economic Prosperity: Testing the Environmental Impact Hypothesis" (Cambridge, MA: M.I.T. Working Paper, 1993).

Muradian, R. and J. Martinez Alier. "Trade and the Environment: From a 'Southern' Perspective," *Ecological Economics* 36 (2001) (2): 281–297.

Neumayer, E. *Greening Trade and Investment* (London: Earthscan, 2001).

Parris, T. M. "Comparative International Indicators of Sustainable Development," *Environment* 38 (1996) (4): 3.

Pearce, David et al. "Measuring Sustainable Development: Progress on Indicators," *Environmental and Development Economics* 1 (1996) (1): 85–102.

Pezzey, J. (1992). *Sustainable Development Concepts: An Economic Analysis*, World Bank Environment Department.

Pezzey, J. "The Optimal Sustainable Depletion of Non-renewable Resources," presented at the Association of Environmental and Resource Economists Workshop at Boulder, Colorado, June 5–6, 1994.

Stavins, R. N. "Experience with Market-Based Environmental Policy Instruments," *Handbook of Environmental Economics,* Maler, K. G. and J. R. Vincent, eds. (Amsterdam: Elsevier, 2003): 355–435.

Van Beers, C. and J.C.J.M. van den Bergh. "Perseverance of Perverse Subsidies and their Impact on Trade and Environment," *Ecological Economics* 36 (2001) (3): 475–486.

Van den Bergh, J.C.J.M. and M. W. Hofkes. "Economic Models of Sustainable Development," *Handbook of Environmental and Resource Economics,* Van den Bergh, J.C.J.M., ed. (Cheltenham, UK: Edward Elgar, 1999): 1108–1122.

Vaughan, S. "How Green Is NAFTA? Measuring the Impacts of Agricultural Trade," *Environment* 46 (2004) (2): 26–42.

Vincent, J. R. "Testing for Environmental Kuznets Curves within a Developing Country," *Environment and Development Economics* 2 (1997) (4): 417–431.

Xu, X. P. "International Trade and Environmental Regulation: Time Series Evidence and Cross Section Test," *Environmental and Resource Economics* 17 (2000) (3): 233–257.

Historically Significant Articles

Dasgupta, P. S. and G. M. Heal. *Economic Theory and Exhaustible Resources* (Cambridge, UK: Cambridge University Press, 1979): 299.

Hartwick, J. M. "Intergenerational Equity and the Investing of Rents from Exhaustible Resources," *American Economic Review* 67 (December 1977): 972–974.

Pezzey, John. "Sustainable Development Concepts: An Economic Analysis," working paper (Washington, DC: World Bank Environment Department, 1992).

Porter, Michael E. "America's Green Strategy," *Scientific American* 264 (April 1991) (4): 168.

Serafy, Salah El. "Absorptive Capacity, the Demand for Revenue, and the Supply of Petroleum," *The Journal of Energy and Development* 7 (Autumn 1981) (1): Appendix A.

Vitousek, Peter M. et al. "Human Appropriation of the Products of Photosynthesis," *BioScience* 36 (June 1986) (6): 368–373.

World Commission on Environment and Development. *Our Common Future* (Oxford, UK: Oxford University Press, 1987).

Discussion Questions

1. Discuss the mechanism favored by Daly to control population growth. What are its advantages and disadvantages? Would it be appropriate to implement this policy now in the United States? For those who believe that it would be, what are the crucial reasons? For those who believe it is not appropriate, are there any circumstances in any countries where it might be appropriate? Why or why not?

2. "Every molecule of a nonrenewable resource used today precludes its use by future generations. Therefore, the only morally defensible policy for any generation is to use only renewable resources." Discuss.

3. "Future generations can cast neither votes in current elections nor dollars in current market decisions. Therefore, it should not come as a surprise to anyone that the interests of future generations are ignored in a market economy." Discuss.

4. "Trade simply represents economic imperialism where one country exploits another. The environment is the inevitable victim." Discuss.

Visions of the
Future Revisited

Mankind was destined to live on the edge of perpetual disaster. We are mankind because we survive. We do it in a half-assed way, but we do it.

—PAUL ADAMSON, a fictional character in James A. Michener's
Chesapeake

We have now come full circle. Having begun our study with two lofty visions of the future, we proceeded to dissect the details of the various components of these visions—population, the management of depletable and renewable resources, pollution, and the growth process itself. During these inquiries a number of useful insights were gained about individual environmental and natural resource problems. Now it is time to step back and coalesce those insights into a systematic assessment of the two visions.

Addressing the Issues

In Chapter 1 we posed a number of questions to serve as our focus for the overarching issue of growth in a finite environment. Those questions addressed three major issues: (1) How is the problem correctly conceptualized? (2) Can our economic and political institutions respond in a timely and democratic fashion to the challenges presented? (3) Can the needs of the present generation be met without compromising the ability of future generations to meet their own needs? Can short-term and long-term goals be harmonized? The next three segments of this section summarize and interpret the evidence.

Conceptualizing the Problem

At the beginning of this book we suggested that if the problem is characterized as an exponential growth in demand coupled with a finite supply of resources, the resources must eventually be exhausted. If those resources are essential, society will collapse when they are exhausted.

We have seen that this is an excessively harsh and somewhat misleading characterization. The growth in the demand for resources is not insensitive to their scarcity. Though the rise in energy prices in the 1970s was triggered more by cartel actions than by scarcity, it is possible to use higher energy prices as an example of how the economic system reacts.

The growth in demand following the increase in prices fell dramatically, with petroleum experiencing the largest reductions. In the United States, for example, total energy consumption in 1981 (73.8 quadrillion BTUs) was lower than it was in 1973 (74.6 quadrillion BTUs), despite increases in income and population. Petroleum consumption went from 34.8 quadrillion BTUs in 1973 to 32.0 quadrillion BTUs in 1981. Though some of this reduction was caused by sluggishness of the economy, price certainly played a major role.

Price is not the only factor that retards demand growth. Declines in population growth also play a significant role. Because the developed nations appropriate a disproportionate share of the world's resources, the dramatic decline in population growth in those countries has had a disproportionate effect on slowing the demand for resources.

Characterizing the resource base as finite—the second aspect of the model—is also excessively harsh: (1) This characterization ignores the existence of a substantial renewable resource base and (2) it focuses attention on the wrong issue.

In a very real sense, a significant proportion of the resource base is not finite. Plentiful supplies of renewable resources (including, significantly, energy) are available. The normal reaction to increasing scarcity of individual depletable resources, such as oil, is to switch to renewable resources. That is clearly happening. The most dramatic examples can be found in the transition to wind, solar, and hydrogen fuel cells.

For most resources labeling the resource base as finite is also misleading, because it suggests that our concern should be "running out." In fact, for most resources, we will never run out. Millions of years of finite resources are left at current consumption rates. The limits on our uses of these resources are not determined by their scarcity in the crust of the earth, but rather by the environmental consequences of their use. The implications of climate change, including rising sea level, heat extremes, droughts and storm surges, are potentially so severe as to force a major reevaluation of our carbon-based energy choices. Similarly the loss of biodiversity, which would be intensified by climate change, could irreversibly alter our ecosystems and reduce their resilience to future shocks.

Resource scarcity can be countered without violating sustainability by discovering new uses for unconventional materials, including what was previously considered waste. We can also stretch the useful life of these reserves by reducing the amount of materials needed to produce the products. Striking examples include the diminishing size of a typical computer system needed to process a given amount of information and the substantially diminished amount of energy needed to heat a well-designed home.

Paradoxically, some of the most obvious cases where limits are being approached and the carrying-capacity concept has the most validity involve renewable resources rather than depletable resources. Demand pressure, whether driven by population growth or rising incomes is a key contributor to this phenomenon. Expanding populations force the cultivation of marginal lands and the deforestation of large, biologically rich tracts. The erosion of overworked soils diminishes their fertility and, ultimately, their productivity. Demand pressure can also contribute to the overexploitation of biological resources such as fisheries, even to the point of extinction. Trade can intensify these pressures, especially when property regimes do not adequately protect the resources. The problem with these resources is not their finiteness, but the way in which they have been managed.

Correct conceptualization of the resource scarcity problem suggests that both extremely pessimistic and extremely optimistic views are wrong. Impenetrable proximate physical limits on resource availability are typically less of a problem than the adverse atmospheric and biological consequences of their use. Transitions to renewable resources, recycled resources, carbon-free fuels and less costly depletable resources have already begun.

Institutional Responses

One of the keys to understanding how society will cope with increasing resource scarcity and environmental damage lies in understanding how social institutions will react. Are market systems, with their emphasis on decentralized decision making, and democratic political systems, with their commitment to public participation and majority rule, equal to the challenge?

Our examination of the record seems to suggest that, although our economic and political systems are far from infallible and have some rather glaring deficiencies, no fatal flaws are apparent.

On the positive side, markets have responded swiftly and automatically to deal with those resources experiencing higher prices. Demand has been reduced and substitution encouraged. Markets for recycling are growing, and consumer habits are changing. Green buildings are proliferating. No one has had to oversee these responses to make sure they occur. As long as property rights are well-defined, the market system provides incentives for consumers and producers to respond to scarcity in a variety of useful ways (see Example 22.1).

Compelling as the evidence is for this point of view, it does not support the conclusion that left to itself, the market would automatically choose a dynamically efficient or a sustainable path for the future. Market imperfections frequently make sustainable development less likely. One serious limitation of the market arises from the way it treats common-pool resources, such as the fish we eat, the air we breathe, and the water we drink. Left to its own devices, a market faced with free-access will overexploit common-pool resources, substantially lowering the net benefits received by future generations. In the absence of sufficient compensating increases in net benefits elsewhere in the economy, such overexploitation could result in a violation of the sustainability criterion.

Even efficient markets do not necessarily produce sustainable development. Restoring efficiency is frequently a desirable, but insufficient, means for producing sustainable welfare levels. Although, in principle, dynamically efficient allocations can produce extraction profiles for depletable resources that are compatible with the interests of future generations, in practice, this is not necessarily or even normally the case.

The market has some capacity for self-correction. The decline of overexploited fish populations, for example, has led to the rise of private-property fish farming. The artificial scarcity created by imperfectly defined property rights gives rise to incentives for the development of a private-property substitute.

This capacity of the market for self-healing, although comforting, is not always adequate. In some cases, cheaper, more effective solutions (e.g., preventing the deterioration of the original natural resource base) are available. Preventive medicine is frequently superior to corrective surgery. In other cases, such as when our air is polluted, no good private substitutes are available. To provide an adequate response, it is sometimes necessary to complement market decisions with political ones.

The need for government intervention is especially necessary in controlling pollution. Uncontrolled markets not only produce too much pollution, they also tend to underprice com-

EXAMPLE
22.1

Private Incentives for Sustainable Development: Can Adopting Sustainable Practices Be Profitable?

Motivated by what it perceived to be great inefficiencies associated with its industry, the Interface Corporation, a carpet manufacturer, totally transformed the nature of its business.

First, the company recognized that unworn carpet, usually under furniture, did not need to be replaced. Thus, the traditional wall-to-wall carpet was superseded by a carpet tile system. Whereas in traditional practice wear in any part of the carpet meant that the entire carpet had to be replaced, with carpet tiles only those specific tiles showing wear are replaced. As an added benefit, the reduction in carpet replacement simultaneously reduces the amount of potentially harmful glue fumes being released into the indoor air.

Next, Interface totally changed its relationship to its customers. Rather than selling carpet, Interface leased it. In effect, it became a seller of carpet services rather than a seller of carpets. Carpet tiles can be easily replaced or cleaned overnight by Interface employees, eliminating the loss of productivity that could occur from halting company activities during the day. The cost to consumers is substantially lowered not only because less carpet is replaced, but also because leasing allows tax advantages. Leased carpet is treated by the tax code as an expense, not an asset.

The environment has also benefited. In traditional industry practice most used carpet was transported to a landfill. Much of the rest was remanufactured into much lower valued uses. Seeing that as a waste of resources, Interface created an entirely new product, Solarium, that, when recycled at the end of its useful life, could be remanufactured back into new Solarium. Not only is this production process reportedly 99.7 percent less wasteful in terms of its drain on energy and raw materials, apparently the product is highly stain-resistant, four times as durable as regular carpet material, and is easily cleaned with water.

These moves toward more sustainable manufacturing did not result from government mandates. Rather, an innovative company found that it could benefit itself and the environment at the same time.

Source: Hawken, Paul, Amory Lovins, and L. Hunter Lovins, *Natural Capitalism: Creating the Next Industrial Revolution* (Boston: Little, Brown and Company, 1999).

modities (coal, for example) that contribute to pollution either when produced or consumed. Firms that unilaterally attempt to control their pollution run the risk of pricing themselves out of the market. Government intervention is needed to ensure that firms that neglect environmental damage in their operating decisions do not thereby gain a competitive edge.

Significant progress has been made in reducing the amount of pollution, particularly conventional air pollution. Recent regulatory innovations, such as the sulfur allowance and RGGI programs and the Swedish NO_x charge, represent major steps toward the development of a flexible but potentially viable framework for controlling air pollutants. By making it less costly to achieve environmental goals, these reforms have limited the potential for a backlash against the policy. They have brought perceived costs more in line with perceived benefits.

It would be a great mistake, however, to assume that government intervention in resolving environmental problems has been uniformly benign. The acid rain problem, for example, was almost certainly initially made worse by a policy structure that focused on local rather than regional pollution problems. Using MTBE as a gasoline additive to reduce air pollution created new water pollution problems.

Another flagrant example of counterproductive government intervention is to be found in treatment of energy.[1] By imposing price ceilings on natural gas and oil, the government removed much of the normal resiliency of the economic system. With price controls, the incentives for expanding the supply are reduced and the time profile of consumption is tilted toward the present.

Resources that in a normal market would have been conserved for future generations are, with price controls, consumed by the current generation. When price controls are placed on normal market transactions, the smooth transition to renewable resources that characterizes the normal market allocation is eliminated; shortages can arise.

Price controls also play a key role in the world hunger problem. By controlling the price of food, many developing countries have undervalued domestic agriculture. The long-run effect of these controls has been to increase these countries' reliance on food imports at a time when foreign exchange to pay for those imports is becoming increasingly scarce. Whereas developed countries have gone substantially down the road to price decontrol, less-developed countries have not yet been able to extricate themselves to a similar degree.

One aspect of the policy process that does not seem to have been handled well is the speed with which improvement has been sought. Public opinion polls have unambiguously shown that the general public supports environmental protection, even when it raises costs and lowers employment. Historically, as shown by the regulation of automobile pollution, policymakers reacted to this resolve by writing very tough legislation designed to force rapid technological development.

Common sense suggests that tough legislation with early deadlines can achieve environmental goals more rapidly than weaker legislation with less tight deadlines. Common sense is frequently wrong. Writing tough legislation with early deadlines can have the opposite effect. Unreasonably tough regulations are virtually impossible to enforce. Recognizing this, polluters have repeatedly sought (and received) delays in compliance. It has frequently been better, from the polluter's point of view, to spend resources in order to challenge the regulations than to spend resources in order to comply with them. This would not have been the case with less stringent regulations, because the firms would have had no legally supportable grounds for delay.

In summary, the record compiled by our economic and political institutions has been mixed. It seems clear that simple prescriptions such as "leave it to the market" or "more government intervention" simply do not hold up under a close scrutiny of the record. The relationship between the economic and political sectors has to be one of selective engagement, complemented in some areas by selective disengagement. Each problem has to be treated on a case-by-case basis. As we have seen in our examination of a variety of environmental and natural

---

[1] A similar story can be told about water. By holding water prices below the marginal cost of supply, water authorities have subsidized excess use.

resource problems, the efficiency and sustainability criteria allow such distinctions to be drawn, and they can provide a powerful basis for policy reform.

Sustainable Development

Historically, increases in inputs and technological progress have been important sources of economic growth in the industrialized nations. In the future, some factors of production, such as labor, will not increase as rapidly as they have in the past. The effect of this decline on growth depends on the interplay among the law of diminishing marginal productivity, substitution possibilities, and technological progress. The law of diminishing marginal productivity suggests slower growth rates, whereas technological progress and the availability of substitutes counteract this drag.

Our examination of empirical evidence suggests that increased environmental control has not currently had a large impact on the economy as a whole, although certain industries have been hit quite hard. To date, environmental policy has triggered only a small rise in the rate of inflation and a mild reduction in growth, but the control of climate change may pose a more significant challenge to both. The notion that respecting the environment is incompatible with a healthy economy is demonstrably wrong.

The economy is being transformed, however. It is not business as usual. Two particularly important aspects of this transformation are the decline in population growth and the rise in the importance of information as a driving economic force. Both aspects tend to reduce the degree to which physical limits constrain economic growth and increase the degree to which current welfare levels would be sustainable.

Recognizing that conventional measures of economic growth shed little light on the question, some crude attempts have been made to estimate whether or not growth in the industrialized countries has made the citizens of those countries better off. Results of these studies suggest that, because growth has ultimately generated more leisure, longer life expectancy, and more goods and services, it has been beneficial. Yet other measures such as the ecological footprint convey a more cautionary message. They remind us that our inability to measure the earth's carrying capacity for humans precisely in no way diminishes the existence and importance of those limits.

Our examination of the evidence suggests that the notion that all of the world's people are automatically benefited by economic growth is naïve. Growth has demonstrably benefited the poor in the developed countries, but that is certainly not inevitable. The most successful countries use development to fund better access to education and health care.

The future outlook for the less-industrialized nations is, at best, mixed. Solving many of their future environmental problems will require higher standards of living. However, following the path of development pioneered by the industrialized nations is probably not possible without triggering severe global environmental problems; the solution would become the problem. New forms of development will be necessary.

The less-industrialized countries must overcome a number of significant barriers if development is to become a reality. At the local level, rising populations face increasingly limited access to land or productive assets. At the national level, corruption and development policies discriminate against the poor. Globally, their situation is worsened by rising debt burdens, falling prices for exports, and the flight of capital that could be used to create jobs and income.

New sustainable forms of development are possible and desirable, but they will not automatically be adopted in either the high-income or the low-income nations. Are cooperative solutions possible? Can any common ground be established?

The experience in the United States suggests that cooperative solutions may be possible, even among traditional adversaries. Environmental regulators and lobbying groups with a special interest in environment protection in the United States have traditionally looked upon the market system as a powerful and potentially dangerous adversary. That the market unleashed powerful forces was widely recognized and that those forces clearly acted to degrade the environment was widely lamented. Meanwhile, development proponents have traditionally seen environmental concerns as blocking projects that had the potential to raise living standards significantly. Conflict and confrontation became the *modus operandi* for dealing with this clash of objectives.

The climate for dealing effectively with both concerns has improved dramatically within the last few decades. Not only have development proponents learned that, in many cases, short-term wealth-enhancement projects that degrade the environment are ultimately counterproductive, but environmental groups have come to realize that poverty itself is a major threat to environmental protection. No longer are economic development and environmental protection seen as an "either-or" proposition. The focus has shifted toward the identification of policies or policy instruments that can promote the alleviation of poverty while protecting the environment.

The economic-incentive approach to environmental and natural resource regulation has become a significant component of environmental and natural resource policy. Instead of mandating prescribed actions, such as requiring the installation of a particular piece of pollution control equipment, this approach achieves environmental objectives by changing the economic incentives of those doing the polluting. Incentives can be changed by fees or charges, transferable entitlements, deposit-refund systems, or even liability law. When the incentives an individual agent faces are changed, that agent can use his or her typically superior information to select the best means of meeting his or her assigned responsibility. When it is in the interest of individuals to change to new forms of development, the transformation can be amazingly rapid.

Public policy and sustainable development must proceed in a mutually supportive relationship. In some cases that relationship takes the form of *public/private partnerships* that involve explicit agreements between government and the private sector regarding the provision of public services or infrastructure (see Example 22.2). In other cases it involves government regulatory action to ensure that the market is sending the right signals to all participants so that the sustainable outcome is compatible with other business objectives. Economic-incentive approaches are a means of establishing that kind of compatibility. The experience with the various versions of this approach used in the United States, Europe, and Asia suggests that allowing business great flexibility within a regulatory framework that harmonizes private and social costs in general is both feasible and effective.

How about global environmental problems? Economic-incentive approaches could be helpful here as well. Emissions trading facilitates cost-sharing among participants while assuring cost-effective responses to the need for additional control. By separating the question of what control is undertaken from the question of who ultimately pays for it, the government widens the control possibilities significantly. Conferring property rights for biological populations on local communities provides an incentive for those communities to protect the populations. Strategies for reducing debt can diminish the pressure on forests and other natural resources that may be "cashed in" to pay off the debt.

The courts are beginning to use economic incentives as well; judicial remedies for environmental problems are beginning to take their place alongside regulatory remedies. Take, for example, the problem of cleaning up already closed toxic waste sites. Allowing the government to sue

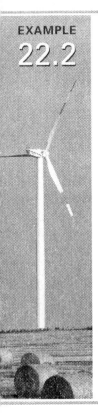

EXAMPLE
22.2

Public/Private Partnerships: The Kalundborg Experience

Located on an island 75 miles off the coast of Copenhagen, the city of Kalundborg has achieved a remarkable symbiosis among the various industries that provide the employment base for the city. The four main industries, along with small businesses and the municipal government, began developing cooperative relationships in the 1970s designed to lower disposal costs, attain less expensive input materials, and receive income from their waste products.

A coal-fired power plant (Asnaes) transports its residual steam to a refinery (Statoil). In exchange, Statoil gives Asnaes refinery gas that Asnaes burns to generate electricity. Asnaes sells excess steam to a local fish farm, to a heating system for the city, and to a pharmaceuticals and enzyme producer (Novo Nordisk). Continuing the cycle, the fish farm and Novo Nordisk send their sludge to farms to be used as fertilizer. Produced fly ash is sold to a cement plant and gypsum produced by its desulfurization process is sold to a wallboard manufacturer. Statoil, the refinery, sells the sulfur removed from its natural gas to a sulfuric acid manufacturer, Kemira.

This entire process resulted not from centralized planning, but simply because it was in the individual best interests of the public and private entities involved. Although the motives were purely financial, this synergetic situation has clear environmental benefits. It is therefore likely to be economically, as well as environmentally, sustainable.

Source: Desroches, Pierre, "Eco-Industrial Parks: The Case for Private Planning," Report #RS 00-1 Political Economy Research Center, Bozeman, MT 59718 (June 2000).

all potentially responsible parties accomplishes a double purpose: (1) Successful suits assure that the financial responsibility for contaminated sites is borne by those who directly caused the problem and (2) they encourage those who are currently using those sites to exercise great care, lest they be sued in the event of an incident. The alternative remedy of putting the burden on taxpayers would result in less revenue raised, fewer sites restored, and less adequate incentives for users to exercise care.

With the obvious exception of the EU ETS, Europe has tended to depend more on the effluent or emission charge. This approach places a per unit fee on each unit of pollution discharged. Faced with the responsibility for paying for the damage caused by their pollution, firms recognize it as a controllable cost of doing business. This recognition triggers a search for possible ways to reduce the damage, including changing inputs, changing the production process, transforming the residuals to less harmful substances, and recycling by-products. The experience in the Netherlands, a country where the fees are higher than in most other countries, suggests that the effects can be dramatic.

Fees also raise revenue. Successful development, particularly sustainable development, requires a symbiotic partnership between the public and private sectors. To function as an equal partner, the public sector must be adequately funded. If it fails to raise adequate revenue, the public sector becomes a drag on the transformation process, but if it raises revenue in ways that distort incentives, that, too, can act as a drag. Effluent or emission charges offer the realistic opportunity to raise revenue for the public sector while reducing the drag from more distortionary taxes. Whereas other types of taxation discourage growth by penalizing legitimate development incentives (such as taxes on labor), emission or effluent charges provide incentives for sustainable development.

Incentives for forward-looking public action are as important as those for private action. The current national income accounting system provides an example of a perverse economic signal. Although national income accounts were never intended to function as a device for measuring the welfare of a nation, in practice, that is how they are used. National income per capita is a common metric for evaluating how well off a nation's people are. Yet the current construction of those accounts conveys the wrong message.

Rather than recognizing oil spills for what they are—namely, a source of decline in the value of the endowment of natural resources in the area—spills actually boost GDP! All the cleanup expenditures serve to increase national income, but no account is taken of the consequent depreciation of the natural environment. Under the current system, the accounts make no distinction between growth that is occurring because a country is damaging its natural resource endowment, with a consequent irreversible decline in its value, and sustainable development, where the value of the endowment remains intact. Only when suitable corrections are made to these accounts will governments be judged by the appropriate standards.

The power of economic incentives is certainly not inevitably channeled toward the achievement of sustainable development. They can be misapplied, as well as appropriately applied. Tax subsidies to promote cattle ranching on the fragile soil in the Brazilian rain forest stimulated an unsustainable activity, which has done irreparable damage to an ecologically significant area. Incentives must be used with care.

A Concluding Comment

Our society is evolving. The emerging complementary relationship among the economic system, the court system, and the legislative and executive branches of government is promising. We are not yet out of the woods, however. We the public must learn that part of the responsibility is ours. The government cannot solve all problems without our significant participation.

Not all behavior can be regulated. It costs too much to catch every offender. Our law enforcement system works because most people obey the law, whether anyone is watching or not. A high degree of voluntary compliance is essential if the system is to work smoothly.

The best resolution of the toxic substance problem, for example, is undoubtedly for all makers of potentially toxic substances to be genuinely concerned about the safety of their products and to bite the bullet whenever their research raises questions. The ultimate responsibility for developing an acceptable level of risk must rest on the integrity of those who make, use, transport, and dispose of the substances. The government can assist by penalizing and controlling those few who fail to exhibit this integrity, but it can never substitute for integrity on a large scale. We cannot and should not depend purely upon altruism to solve these problems, but we should not underestimate its importance either.

We also need to recognize that markets serve our preferences as consumers. Making sure our purchases and investments reflect environmental values will help markets move in the right direction. Fuel-efficient automobiles will enter the market much faster if many consumers demand them. Builders will supply greener houses when home buyers prefer them.

The notion that we are at the end of an era may well be true, but we are also at the beginning of a new one. What the future holds is not the decline of civilization, but its transformation. As the opening quote to this chapter suggests, the road may be strewn with obstacles and our social institutions may deal with those obstacles with less grace and less finesse than we might hope for, but we are unquestionably making progress.

Key Concept

public/private partnerships, *p.* 515

Discussion Questions

1. One of the toughest problems in achieving sustainable development is ensuring that the environmental problems are not solved at the expense of the poor. Higher resource prices, for example, could simply make key resources available only to those who can afford them. Thinking back over the course, what specific approaches that we discussed allow sustainable development to be achieved in an equitable manner? Can you think of other approaches that meet the test of fairness?

2. In his book *Catastrophe*, Professor Jared Diamond argues that many societies throughout history, when confronted by resource scarcity problems, failed to respond appropriately and ultimately collapsed. Our society faces challenging problems such as the future energy choices, loss of biodiversity, and climate change. Do you think we will prove equal to the challenge or will our institutions fail to meet the test? Why? Is democracy part of the problem or part of the solution? Why?

Index